AMERICAN JUDICIAL PROCESS

This text is a general introduction to American judicial process. The authors cover the major institutions, actors, and processes that comprise the U.S. legal system, viewed from a social science perspective. Grounding their presentation in empirical social science terms, the authors identify popular myths about the structure and processes of American law and courts and then contrast those myths with what really takes place. Three unique elements of this "myth versus reality" framework are incorporated into each of the topical chapters:

1. "Myth versus Reality" boxes that lay out the topics each chapter covers, using the myths about each topic contrasted with the corresponding realities.
2. "Pop Culture" boxes that provide students with popular examples from film, television, and music that tie-in to chapter topics and engage student interest.
3. "How Do We Know?" boxes that discuss the methods of social scientific inquiry and debunk common myths about the judiciary and legal system.

Unlike other textbooks, *American Judicial Process* emphasizes how pop culture portrays—and often distorts—the judicial process and how social science research is brought to bear to provide an accurate picture of law and courts. In addition, a rich companion website will include PowerPoint lectures, suggested topics for papers and projects, a test bank of objective questions for use by instructors, and downloadable artwork from the book. Students will have access to annotated web links and videos, flashcards of key terms, and a glossary.

Pamela C. Corley is currently Associate Professor and Director of the Law and Legal Reasoning Minor in the Political Science Department at Southern Methodist University, where she teaches classes on judicial process, civil rights, First Amendment, criminal procedure, and jurisprudence. She received her J.D. and Ph.D. from Georgia State University.

Artemus Ward is currently Professor of Political Science at Northern Illinois University, where he teaches classes in public law and American politics. He received his Ph.D. from the Maxwell School of Citizenship and Public Affairs at Syracuse University and was formerly a staffer on the U.S. House Judiciary Committee.

Wendy L. Martinek is currently Associate Professor of Political Science at Binghamton University (SUNY), where she teaches classes in constitutional law, judicial politics, and political methodology. She received her M.A. from the University of Wisconsin-Milwaukee and her Ph.D. from Michigan State University, and was formerly a program officer for the Law and Social Sciences Program of the National Science Foundation.

4, 5, 11.

26, 40, 49

AMERICAN JUDICIAL PROCESS

Myth and Reality in Law and Courts

Pamela C. Corley
SOUTHERN METHODIST UNIVERSITY

Artemus Ward
NORTHERN ILLINOIS UNIVERSITY

Wendy L. Martinek
BINGHAMTON UNIVERSITY

Routledge
Taylor & Francis Group

NEW YORK AND LONDON

First published 2016
by Routledge
711 Third Avenue, New York, NY 10017

and by Routledge
2 Park Square, Milton Park, Abingdon, Oxon, OX14 4RN

Routledge is an imprint of the Taylor & Francis Group, an informa business

© 2016 Taylor & Francis

Library of Congress Cataloging-in-Publication Data
Corley, Pamela C., 1967–
   American judicial process : myth and reality in law and courts / Pamela C. Corley, Southern Methodist University; Artemus Ward, Northern Illinois University; Wendy L. Martinek, Binghamton University.
      pages cm
   1. Judicial process—United States.   2. Justice, Administration of—United States.   3. Courts—United States.   I. Ward, Artemus, 1971–   II. Martinek, Wendy L.   III. Title.
   KF8700.C67 2015
   347.73′5—dc23
   2015007296

ISBN: 978-0-415-53298-3 (pbk)
ISBN: 978-0-203-11336-3 (ebk)

Typeset in Warnock Pro
by Apex CoVantage, LLC

Brief Contents

Contents

Figures

Tables

Acknowledgments

Writing a textbook requires a lot of help from colleagues, family, and friends.

First, we are indebted to Michael Kerns, a former editor at Routledge, for his efforts in shepherding this text through the early stages of its development. His faith in the kind of textbook we wished to write and in our ability to execute it were absolutely essential. Thanks are also due to Darcy Bullock of Routledge for her extreme patience (and gentle prodding) as the project progressed. It is no exaggeration to say that if there were no Michael or no Darcy, there would be no book. We also thank Mary Altman, a former development editor at Routledge, for her help early in the process. We are also appreciative of the work of our production editors, Emily Davies and Elisabet Ainsworth, as well as that of Daniel Gaetán-Beltrán and Cinqué Hicks for their copyediting skills.

Our thinking about various aspects of the American judicial process has been shaped and informed (not to mention immeasurably improved) by a host of friends and colleagues in the discipline. The pages of this book are rife with evidence of their good influence. These include Lawrence Baum of Ohio State University, Sara C. Benesh of the University of Wisconsin-Milwaukee, Ryan Black of Michigan State University, Scott Boddery of Binghamton University, Raymond Carman, Jr. of SUNY Plattsburgh, Paul M. Collins, Jr. of the University of Massachusetts-Amherst, Jolly Emrey of the University of Wisconsin-Whitewater, Lee Epstein of Washington University in St. Louis, Rebecca Gill of the University of Nevada-Las Vegas, Susan Haire of the University of Georgia, Virginia Hettinger of the University of Connecticut, Lisa Holmes of the University of Vermont, Robert Howard of Georgia State University, Connie Lobur of Purchase College-SUNY, Stefanie A. Lindquist of the University of Georgia, Banks Miller of the University of Texas at Dallas, Harold Spaeth of Michigan State University, Amy Steigerwalt of Georgia State University, and Jeff Yates of Binghamton University. We also thank the anonymous reviewers who took the time to review early drafts of this book. We are grateful for their helpful feedback.

Trite as it may sound, we are also truly indebted to our students, both past and present, graduate and undergraduate, who have inspired us to be the best teachers we can be. They make class time fun time, especially Val Anias, Molly Ariotti, Gil Auslander, Elena Barberena, Elyce Bigford, Rob Burckhard, Emily Carapella, Martine Casey, Julie King Cersley, Jess Cherry, Jessica Cheuvront, Garrett Dorfman, Christina Dwyer, Eve Ellenbogen, Rachel Engle, Anna Fodor, Jay Fucilla, Kiranjit Gill, Chelsea Goodman, Jessica Gochman Goodstone, Gina Gregolunas, Abbey Hable, Natasha Jensen, Adam Kraut, Jessica Laredo, Amanda Levine, Steve Lickstein, Danielle Nunziato, Seth Peritz, Susan Richard, Sarah Skahill, A.J. Strollo, Meagan Szydlowski, Gary Timmins, Sean Warden, Emma Wright, Sophia Yanuzzi, and Julia Ziegler. A special thank you goes out to Sean Daly for his first-rate work on this project.

Last but not least, special thanks go to the family and friends who teach us every day. In this regard, Pam Corley thanks Greg Corley and Megan Corley. Artemus Ward thanks Annette Keca, Jim Josefson, and Scott Solomon. Wendy Martinek thanks Linda Lee Smith Clark, Sabrina Duckworth, Chris Martin, Judy Martinek, Lindsey Martinek, and Cameron Veal, in particular.

Preface

This textbook is a general introduction to the American judicial process. We cover the major institutions, actors, and processes that comprise the United States legal system, discussing each component of the judicial process in terms of myth and reality. We identify popular myths about the structure and processes of American law and courts and then contrast those myths with what really takes place—particularly through relevant discussion of social science research. Do the myths about law and courts harm the American judicial system? If so, could the system be better served by changes to existing practices?

Toward that end, we take an innovative approach to the topic. Specifically, we incorporate two unique elements into each of our topical chapters on the major structures of the American legal process: First, we provide a number of "Pop Culture" boxes that provide students with classic and contemporary examples from film and television that tie-in to chapter topics. For example, in Chapter One we discuss "The Perry Mason Syndrome" and provide examples from film and television that depict the Hollywood trope of courtroom attorneys inducing witness-stand confessions. Hollywood's depiction of oversimplified trials is not only inaccurate, its myth-making dramatizations can have real-life implications for jurors who have unrealistic expectations about the judicial process. While some of our pop culture examples are from recent films or televisions shows, many are from classics that are regularly shown on TV. For example, *A Few Good Men* (1992) is decades old but is widely known for its dramatic courtroom scene and Jack Nicholson's "You can't handle the truth" catchphrase. Still others may be lesser known classics but are instructive for thinking about the myths and realities of law and courts. Indeed, many of these pop culture classics would be excellent supplements to this textbook and in-class screenings (with popcorn provided!) are encouraged.

Second, we include "How Do We Know?" boxes that discuss one or more of the studies from which we draw in each chapter to support a particular point we make about the reality of the judicial process. At the same time, we take care to minimize jargon and sophisticated statistics so that undergraduates can fully understand how the research was conducted and what it found. So, for example, in Chapter Five we ask whether challengers can defeat incumbent judges by outspending them. We detail a recent empirical study on the question that finds, while increases in challenger spending increases their level of electoral support, increases in spending by incumbents does not. This means that campaign spending—at least by challengers—can lead to enhanced electoral competition, which in turn promotes electoral accountability. Hence, the myths and realities surrounding law and courts can be seen in how pop culture portrays—and often distorts—the judicial process and how social science research is brought to bear to provide an accurate picture.

There are a number of other features that we include to help students gain an understanding of the material. Illustrations including figures, tables, and images are provided throughout. Most of the figures and tables contain data while others contain graphic depictions of various aspects of the judicial process, such as how courts are hierarchically organized or the stages of a lawsuit. The images have been selected to not only provide a visual element to the concepts discussed in the text but also to stimulate students' critical thinking skills. Many of the images are historical—some from over a century ago. This is by design as we want students to consider how the judicial process has or has not changed over time and how historical change relates to the myths and realities we discuss. Students who desire to do further research on a particular topic—perhaps for a term paper or senior thesis—will find a list of suggested readings at the end of each chapter as well as detailed endnotes for the information presented in the text. Key terms are in bold throughout the text and a glossary of these terms is included on the book's companion website. The companion website for the book also includes annotated links to further resources and research, links to video and audio clips, and flashcards for students; and PowerPoint lecture slides, a test bank, suggested research paper topics and projects, and images and figures from the text for instructors.

In addition to these features, this textbook includes coverage of topics that are not generally discussed in other texts—namely legal education and law school as well as lawyers and law practice. We think that these topics are important not only for understanding why law and courts operate the way they do but also because they are of interest to undergraduates, many of who plan to enter careers in the legal profession. Chapter One sets the tone for the book by detailing how the judicial process is filled with myths and how social science can help us understand the reality. We define and discuss the concept of "law"—its sources, types, and purposes—and the functions of courts. We then provide a brief primer on social scientific inquiry so that students will be able to understand the research discussed in subsequent chapters.

Chapter Two covers the myths and realities of legal education and law school, such as the idea that law school teaches practical legal skills and virtually guarantees a career as an attorney. We detail why and how legal education changed from an apprentice model to formalized schooling. We detail the contemporary law school admissions process; the issue of campus diversity; the cost associated with law school; curriculum, teaching techniques, grading, and extracurricular activities; and passing the bar.

Chapter Three continues with a discussion of lawyers and law practice. We debunk a number of myths, including the notion that attorneys largely work in courtrooms, practice law broadly, and are unethical shysters. We discuss the job market for lawyers; lawyer demographics and rising diversity in the profession; attorney specialization and prestige; practice settings; whether lawyers are satisfied with their careers; issues involving access to lawyers, including low-cost legal help; and legal ethics.

Chapter Four is centered on the myth that courts are organized and structured in a logical, streamlined, and efficient way. The reality is that complex court systems and ambiguous jurisdictional rules allow attorneys to engage in forum shopping to advantage their clients and disadvantage opponents. We first address the federal court system including federal question and diversity jurisdiction as well as the different types of courts that have been created under Articles I–IV of the U.S. Constitution with particular attention to Article III courts: U.S. District Courts, U.S. Courts of Appeals, and the U.S. Supreme Court. In the latter half of the chapter, we discuss the organization of state courts, including the difference between trial courts of limited and general jurisdiction, intermediate appellate courts, and courts of last resort.

In Chapter Five we highlight myths surrounding choosing judges—particularly the mistaken notion that only the wisest, most qualified attorneys ascend to the bench. We begin with the selection of federal judges and detail both the nomination and confirmation processes before turning to the question of diversity and the federal bench. The second part of this chapter covers the various ways that state judges are chosen, including gubernatorial or legislative appointment, partisan and nonpartisan elections, merit-selection systems that attempt to fuse aspects of both appointment and election, and retention elections. We explore diversity on the state bench and examine the issues of judicial quality and the effects of money and constituency influence on judicial legitimacy.

Chapter Six dispels the myth that civil litigation in America is a growing trend driven by opportunism, manipulation, and greed. Americans cope with disputes by a process of naming, blaming, and claiming but not all disputes end up in court and many are instead resolved through negotiation, mediation, and arbitration. There are numerous obstacles to using courts and we discuss how and why individuals can overcome these to use courts. The processing of civil suits can be thought of as a method for promoting settlement and there is a major difference between the types of litigants—namely 'one-shotters' versus repeat players. We explore issues surrounding litigation rates and the question of tort reform.

Criminal law is detailed in Chapter Seven and we tackle the myth that substantive justice always results from the criminal process. There are problems with reporting and investigating crime, and police contact with the public is not always equal or fair. We detail the criminal justice process from the perspective of the process itself being the punishment. Because nearly every criminal case results in a plea bargain, we spend considerable time discussing how plea bargaining works and its implications—particularly for those who are innocent but who plead guilty.

Chapter Eight addresses the myths associated with trials, including the notion that everyone is entitled to a jury trial and that eyewitness testimony is reliable. We begin with a short history of juries and the circumstances that trigger a constitutional right to a jury trial. We discuss the implications of different jury sizes and differences between jury trials and bench trials where defendants waive their right to a jury. Each stage of a jury trial is detailed, including jury selection, opening statements, presentation of the evidence through witness testimony, closing arguments, jury instructions, jury deliberation, and verdicts.

The myths about the appellate process, including the idea that courts of appeals operate like trial courts and that everyone is entitled to take their case all the way to the Supreme Court, are discussed in Chapter Nine. We detail the process of appeal, including oral argument; obstacles to appeal, such as costs and low odds; appellate court workloads and outcomes; how appellate courts are forums for making public policy through judicial decisions; and various models of judicial behavior, such as the attitudinal model that suggests judges make decisions based on personal preferences, or ideology, as opposed to law.

Chapter Ten is an in-depth look at the U.S. Supreme Court. Myths about justices being driven solely by ideology or solely by law are belied by the reality that both operate, more or less, depending on the case and issue being considered. We detail a number of other myths and realities associated with the Court and its practices, including how law clerks do much of the Court's work—particularly at the agenda-setting stage. We explain the importance of oral argument—often thought to be little more than a dog and pony show—as well as voting and the conference procedure, how opinions are assigned and written, and the process of forming coalitions and achieving consensus—or dissensus as sometimes happens. We close the chapter with a number of Supreme Court issues, including allowing cameras in the Court, the interplay between controversial decisions and public opinion, and the implications for justices having life tenure.

The final chapter—Chapter Eleven—is about the implementation of judicial decisions and their impact. It is a myth that courts are powerful institutions in the sense that their decisions are always followed. Instead, the reality is that judicial pronouncements are part of an ongoing process of resolving conflict in society with executives, legislatures, other courts, and the people weighing in after a court decision is announced. We address the ongoing debate about whether courts are little more than a "hollow hope" for those seeking social change. Research suggests that while courts may not be able to directly implement decisions, they have impact by legitimizing issues and movements that seek change from the ground up.

About the Authors

Pamela C. Corley is currently Associate Professor and Director of the Law and Legal Reasoning Minor in the Political Science Department at Southern Methodist University, where she teaches classes on judicial process, civil rights, First Amendment, criminal procedure, and jurisprudence. She received her J.D. and Ph.D. from Georgia State University.

Her research focuses on three questions regarding judicial decision making. The first evaluates the content of court opinions, the second examines how consensus is formed on the United States Supreme Court, and the third analyzes how courts are constrained by Congress. Professor Corley is the author of *Concurring Opinion Writing on the U.S. Supreme Court* (SUNY Press, 2010), which is the first systematic examination of the content of Supreme Court concurrences. She is also the co-author of *The Puzzle of Unanimity: Consensus on the United States Supreme Court* (Stanford University Press, 2013), which provides the first comprehensive account of how the Court reaches consensus. She has published articles in *Journal of Politics, Law & Society Review, Political Research Quarterly, Judicature, Law & Policy, Journal of Legal Studies, Journal of Supreme Court History, Publius: The Journal of Federalism, Justice System Journal*, and *American Politics Research*.

Artemus Ward is currently Professor of Political Science at Northern Illinois University, where he teaches classes on constitutional law, civil rights, civil liberties, judicial process, law and film, American government, American presidential elections, media and politics, politics and popular music, politics and film, and politics and baseball. He periodically offers experiential learning/study abroad courses in Washington, D.C. and at Oriel College, Oxford University. He received his Ph.D. from the Maxwell School of Citizenship and Public Affairs at Syracuse University and worked as a staffer on the U.S. House Judiciary Committee.

He is a two-time winner of the Hughes-Gossett Prize for historical excellence from the Supreme Court Historical Society. His research focuses on judicial behavior and institutional development with an emphasis on the U.S. Supreme Court. Professor Ward's books include *Deciding to Leave: The Politics of Retirements on the U.S. Supreme Court* (SUNY Press, 2003), *Sorcerers' Apprentices: 100 Years of Law Clerks at the U.S. Supreme Court* (NYU Press, 2006), *In Chambers: Stories of Supreme Court Law Clerks and Their Justices* (University of Virginia Press, 2012), *The Puzzle of Unanimity: Consensus on the United States Supreme Court* (Stanford University Press, 2013), *Historical Dictionary of the U.S. Supreme Court* (Rowman & Littlefield, 2015), and *The Chief Justice: Appointment and Influence* (University of Michigan Press, 2015). He has published articles in *Political Analysis, Congress & the Presidency, White House Studies, Journal of Supreme Court History, Justice System Journal, Tulsa Law Review*, and *Marquette Law Review*.

Wendy L. Martinek is currently Associate Professor and Director of Graduate Studies in the Department of Political Science at Binghamton University (SUNY), where she teaches classes on constitutional law, judicial process and procedure, American political institutions, and research methods. She is the recipient of the Chancellor's Award for Excellence in Teaching from the State University of New York and the Teaching and Mentoring Award of the Law and Courts Section of the American Political Science Association. She received her M.A. from the University of Wisconsin-Milwaukee and her Ph.D. from Michigan State University.

Her research is centered on decision making on collegial courts, with a special interest in patterns of consensus and dissensus on state courts of last resort and the U.S. courts of appeals. Drawing on insights from social psychology and behavioral economics, her interest is in understanding how group dynamics (including the roles group members play and the identities they possess) and cognitive processes (such as motivated reasoning) structure judicial decision making. She has complementary interests in understanding how the political, economic, and social context in which courts are situated influence the choices judges make. She is the co-author of *Judging on a Collegial Court* (University of Virginia Press, 2007) and has published articles in numerous peer-reviewed outlets, including *American Journal of Political Science*, *Journal of Politics*, *Law & Society Review*, *Journal of Empirical Legal Studies*, *Political Research Quarterly*, *American Politics Research*, *Party Politics*, *Social Science Quarterly*, *Judicature*, and *Justice System Journal*.

MYTH AND REALITY IN THE JUDICIAL PROCESS

"The law will never make men free, it is men that have to make the law free."

—Henry David Thoreau, American Poet and Abolitionist[1]

"The legal system is often a mystery, and we, its priests, preside over rituals baffling to everyday citizens."

—Henry G. Miller, President New York State Bar Association[2]

American legal culture is filled with myths. One such myth is the "CSI Effect," which refers to the purported impact of the popular CBS forensic drama *CSI: Crime Scene Investigation*. Specifically, the theory is that shows such as *CSI* burden the prosecution because jurors now expect high-tech forensic science and they are disappointed when the prosecution fails to deliver, with the consequence that jurors acquit more defendants. Consider the following real-life examples: a jury in Maryland refused to convict a man who was accused of stabbing his girlfriend to death because a half-eaten hamburger—recovered from the crime scene and assumed to have been his—was not tested for DNA; a jury in the District of Columbia deadlocked in the case of a woman accused of stabbing another woman because fingerprints on the weapon did not belong to the suspect; a jury in Virginia acquitted a man charged with drug possession because a box containing 60 rocks of crack cocaine that he was accused of having thrown out of his car window during a traffic stop was not tested for fingerprints.[3] An alternative theory is that shows like *CSI* burden the defense because jurors have come to think that forensic science is a super science that can provide unequivocal answers. Jurors, therefore, believe whatever forensic science is presented, leading them to convict more defendants than they otherwise would. Although there is some anecdotal evidence to support each of these competing claims, how do we know whether the CSI Effect is a myth or reality?

We know the answer to this question because of social science research. In one recent study,[4] researchers posed the following questions: Do *CSI* viewers give forensic science evidence more weight than is warranted? Or, alternatively, are *CSI* viewers more skeptical of forensic science evidence because these types of shows raise their expectations for the evidence necessary to convict? In order to answer these questions, the researchers provided a hypothetical transcript of a criminal trial to 48 college students. In the transcript, the primary piece of evidence was hair recovered from a ski mask that had been left at the crime scene by the alleged perpetrator. During the trial, a forensic scientist testified that he had examined the crime scene hair and the defendant's hair under a microscope and that, in his opinion, the hair from the crime scene was the defendant's. After reading the transcript, the participants in the study completed a questionnaire that evaluated their perceptions of both the trial as a whole and the forensic science evidence specifically.

Image 1.1 Fingerprinting
*This 1917 photograph
shows a German being
fingerprinted by a New
York City police officer
during World War I.
Fingerprinting was an
early forensic science
technique first intro-
duced in American
police departments in
New York City in 1906.*
George Grantham Bain
Collection, Prints and
Photographs Division,
Library of Congress,
Washington, D.C.

The participants were also asked about how often they watched forensic science type programs (like *CSI*) and general crime shows (like *Law & Order*).

Participants who were forensic science program viewers (that is, those who reported watching one or more of these shows per month) were more critical of the forensic evidence presented in the hypothetical criminal trial than non-viewers. Specifically, those who were forensic science program viewers rated the forensic evidence as significantly less believable than non-viewers rated it. Despite this, there was no meaningful difference between forensic science show viewers and non-viewers when it came to votes to convict or acquit the defendant. Forensic science show viewers were, however, more confident in their verdicts than non-viewers were in theirs. When it came to general crime show viewers (that is, those who watched shows like *Law & Order*), they did not differ from the non-viewers in terms of voting to convict or acquit, the confidence they had in their verdicts, or in believing the forensic evidence. On the basis of this analysis, the researchers conducting the study concluded that there is some merit to the claims of those who argue that the CSI Effect increases the prosecution's burden. On the other hand, they did not find any impact on votes to convict or acquit, suggesting that "*CSI* does not alter verdicts as readily as some commentators have hypothesized."[5] Based on this research, the inference to be drawn is that the notion that the CSI Effect benefits the prosecution is more a myth than a reality.

In the following chapters, we discuss both the myths and the realities of the judicial process. Our goal is to provide a comprehensive portrait of law and courts in the American context. Along the way we will highlight how popular legal culture both reflects and distorts the judicial process. **Popular legal culture** means everything people know or think they know about law, lawyers, and the legal system.[6] For example, the Pop Culture Box on p. 3 describes the **Perry Mason Syndrome** regarding skillful attorneys obtaining courtroom confessions. Throughout the book we include a number of sidebars that illustrate how popular portrayals of law and courts often foster myths. We chose films and TV shows from different decades in order to show how they reflect and construct our evolving perceptions of the legal system. In the coming chapters we will highlight how popular, media-driven myths are often at odds with reality.

In addition, we include How Do We Know? boxes that illustrate how social science research is used to investigate the myths and uncover the realities of the judicial process. We discuss this in greater depth at the close of this chapter. But first, we consider two key concepts at the heart of the judicial process: <u>law and courts.</u>

POP CULTURE

The Perry Mason Syndrome

Hotshot military attorney Lt. Daniel Kaffee (played by Tom Cruise) has tough-as-nails Col. Nathan R. Jessup (played by Jack Nicholson) on the witness stand—right where he wants him. Kaffee knows Jessup wants to tell the truth because Jessup is proud of what he did, regardless of whether it was within the bounds of the law. Kaffee goads Jessup: "You had Markinson sign a phony transfer order. You doctored the logbooks. I'll ask for the fourth time. You ordered . . . " Jessup, visibly fuming, replies: "You want answers?" Kaffee: "I think I'm entitled to them." Jessup defiantly shouts: "You want answers?!" Kaffee shouts back: "I want the truth." Jessup: "You can't handle the truth!" Jessup lectures Kaffee about honor and duty but Kaffee persists: "Did you order the code red?!" Jessup: "You're goddamn right I did!"

Mythical courtroom attorneys regularly get witness-stand confessions. Real-life lawyers, however, seldom get witnesses to

Image 1.2 Perry Mason
This 1957 still from the long-running hit television show Perry Mason *shows the fictional attorney, played by actor Raymond Burr, questioning a witness in "The Case of the Runaway Corpse."* Photo by CBS via Getty Images.

confess in open court, the way Kaffee did with Jessup in *A Few Good Men*, Richard Gere's Martin Vail did with Edward Norton's Aaron Stampler in *Primal Fear*, Reese Witherspoon's Elle Woods did with Linda Cardellini's Chutney Windham in *Legally Blonde*, or Perry Mason did from 1957 to 1966 in hundreds of TV episodes. According to Fred Graham, Chief Anchor and Managing Editor of the American Trial Network:

A lawyer who specializes in defending white collar criminal defendants told me what happened when he unexpectedly lost a case and his client was convicted. He went up, just shattered, to a juror and asked,

"What happened?" The juror said, "When you cross-examined the prosecution's key witness, you did not get him to confess."[7]

The Perry Mason Syndrome refers to jurors having misconceptions about how the legal process works because the television show presented trial proceedings in an oversimplified manner. Indeed, the 2002 film *Catch Me If You Can* plays with this idea when Leonardo DiCaprio's character, Frank Abagnale, who is pretending to be an attorney, watches an episode of *Perry Mason* to prepare for his upcoming court appearance. The next day Abagnale replicates what he saw on television:

Now, look at this photograph, Mr. Stewart. It's a photograph of Prentice York where they found him, dead. Now, here is an enlargement of part of that photograph. This is a photograph of the defendant's signature on a canceled check. Now, here is an enlargement of that same signature which matches the signature on the letters that he wrote to Mrs. Simon which discuss the possibility of defrauding the great State of Louisiana. Your Honor, ladies and gentlemen of the jury, this is irrefutable evidence that the defendant is, in fact, lying. The judge responds: "This is a preliminary hearing. There is no defendant. There is no jury. It's just me. Son, what in the hell is wrong with you?!"

At the very least, the Perry Mason Syndrome gives the public an oversimplified and overly dramatized picture of what takes place in court. At its worst, however, the Perry Mason Syndrome may lead jurors to expect witnesses to confess. The reality of courtroom proceedings, effective client representation, and courtroom advocacy is much less dramatic and much more complex than Hollywood would have us believe.

WHAT IS LAW?

Law is a collection of principles and regulations established by judicial decision or by a designated authority in a community and applicable to the people of that community in the form of legislation. One of the first written sets of laws was the Code of Hammurabi, codified around the eighteenth century BC by the Babylonian King Hammurabi. Though there were other codes of law that preceded it, they exist only in fragments[8] while the Code of Hammurabi has survived virtually intact.[9] At its origination and throughout its history, the Code stood for the idea that people have an inherent right to justice.[10] Over time, official structures and procedures developed to ensure that the law was followed and that justice was administered. The American legal system is based on English law, which was itself a product of the Roman Empire.[11] There are many sources and types of law, including some not found in the U.S.

Sources and Hierarchy of Law

The very notion of "law" is often myth-based. School children in the United States are taught that, in a democracy, laws are made by and for "the people." They are further taught that the people elect legislators who pass the laws that govern the nation. But the reality is that "law" is much broader than this common oversimplification. Constitutions, statutes, regulations, executive orders, and court decisions are all examples of law. **Constitutions**, both state and federal, are considered the highest sources of law for their particular jurisdictions (see Table 1.1). They provide the fundamental laws and principles

Image 1.3 Hammurabi *1937 oil painting by Boardman Robinson of Hammurabi in the stairway of the Great Hall, United States Department of Justice, Washington, D.C.* Photographs in the Carol M. Highsmith Archive, Prints and Photographs Division, Library of Congress, Washington, D.C.

TABLE 1.1
Hierarchy of Legal Authority in Federal and State Systems

HIERARCHY IN THE FEDERAL SYSTEM	HIERARCHY IN THE STATE SYSTEM
United States Constitution ↓	United States Constitution ↓
Federal Statutes ↓	State Constitution ↓
Federal Regulations/Executive Order ↓	State Statutes ↓
Federal Case Law	State Regulations/Executive Order ↓
	State Case Law

that prescribe the nature, functions, and limits of the government. The U.S. Constitution governs the American people collectively, while various state constitutions govern those within their respective states.[12] **Statutes** are laws passed by legislative bodies and must comply with constitutional dictates. Statutes may originate at the national, state, or local level, with those originating at the local level (passed by municipal governments) most often referred to as ordinances.

An example of a federal statute is the Civil Rights Act of 1964. This act prohibits discrimination based on race, color, religion, sex, and national origin by federal and state governments as well as by some private actors. For example, it prohibits those serving the general public (e.g., hotels, restaurants) from discriminating. An example of a state statute is the Delaware Medical Marijuana Act of 2011. This Act permits an individual certified by his or her physician as having a debilitating medical condition that is likely to be alleviated with the therapeutic use of marijuana to possess a limited amount of this controlled substance. An example of a local ordinance is the Chicago curfew passed by the Chicago City Council, which requires children 12 years of age and younger to be in their homes by 8:30 p.m. on weekdays and by 9:00 p.m. on weekends, with those between the ages of 12 and 16 required to be indoors by 10:00 p.m. on weekdays and 11:00 p.m. on weekends.

After a statute is passed—either by Congress, a legislative body of a state, or a city council—many details of administering the law are left to an administrative agency. These administrative agencies are empowered to create and enforce rules—regulations—that carry the full force of a law. For example, Congress passed the Food, Drug, and Cosmetics Act and lodged the authority for putting the law into practice in the Food and Drug Administration (FDA).[13] The FDA is charged with creating rules and regulations to implement that Act, such as requiring firms selling food products to provide a label with specified nutritional information on its packaging. **Executive orders** are similar to administrative rules and are issued when an executive (e.g., the president, a governor) seeks to carry out the will of the legislature as specified in a statute. Sometimes, however, executives issue orders based solely on their executive authority. For example, during the Korean War, President Harry S. Truman issued an executive order directing Secretary of Commerce Charles Sawyer to seize the steel mills and keep them operating when an industry shutdown due to labor disputes seemed imminent.[14] President Truman argued that it would be a national catastrophe if steel production stopped. However, the U.S. Supreme Court declared this executive order unconstitutional and overturned it.[15] Thus, **case law**, which is law based on judicial decisions rather than statutes, is also a source of law.

Although the myth is that judges merely interpret the law, the reality is that judges also make law as they interpret it. As they override statutes, rules, regulations, and orders, judges invariably make law. If the decision is based on interpreting the Constitution, it can only be undone by another court decision or by an amendment to the Constitution; Congress or the President may not simply pass new legislation or issue a new executive order to reverse a **constitutional decision** of the Supreme Court.[16] In comparison, **statutory decisions** interpret legislation. A statute may have an unequivocal, straightforward meaning. But it may also be vague or ambiguous such that the meaning requires resolution by a judge. To resolve that kind of vagueness or ambiguity, judges may rely on different methods of statutory interpretation. For example, judges may evaluate the legislative history of the statute and consider its purpose and/or they may carefully deconstruct the plain meaning of the words used. When a decision is based on the interpretation of a statute rather than on the Constitution, then Congress can alter that decision simply with the passage of new legislation. Indeed, scholars have found that, on occasion, Court opinions virtually invite Congress to pass new legislation to change a judicial interpretation of a statute if that interpretation does not comport with congressional intention.[17]

Types of Law

In addition to categorizing law by source, law can also be usefully classified by its nature or type. Common distinctions regarding the nature or type of law are positive versus natural law, common versus civil law, and public versus private law. And, within each type, there can be further classification and nuance, reflecting the reality that law is far more complex than is ordinarily thought.

Positive law is man-made law that confers or denies privileges to individuals or groups. The American legal system's mass of constitutions, statutes, and judicial opinions are all examples of positive law. It is law conceived of, as well as enacted and implemented by, people. Positive law is generally traced back to the work of philosophers such as Thomas Hobbes, who argued that compliance with the laws of man was essential for civil peace and security.[18] By contrast, **natural law** is the idea that law reflects, or is based on, a built-in sense of right and wrong. It is described as "God's law," "divine law," or "moral law." Specifically, its proponents argue that there were natural rights that men possessed before the formation of political society. Furthermore, they argue that positive law derives its legitimacy from natural law. Accordingly, to the extent that natural law and positive law differ, natural law should prevail. Natural law is reflected in the Declaration of Independence, in which Thomas Jefferson described rights to "life, liberty, and the pursuit of happiness" as inalienable rights. Natural law ideas are also found in the U.S. Constitution. For example, the purposes of the Constitution are stated in the preamble as being "to establish Justice" and "secure the Blessings of Liberty," which reflect natural law ideas that "there were outside and absolute standards of justice and liberty to which governments and positive law must conform . . . "[19] Thus, the United States is a positive law system that is based on natural law concepts.

The **common law system** is a legal system based on precedent. This means that **common law** is "judge-made" law in the form of judicial decisions, or precedents, handed down over time. Specifically, **precedent** is a court decision that serves as authority for deciding similar issues in a later case. The principle that past decisions should be applied to resolve later decisions is referred to as *stare decisis*, translated from Latin as "let the decision stand." Accordingly, a decision on an issue of law made by a court should be followed by that same court or by a lower court within that jurisdiction in a subsequent case presenting substantially the same issue of law. English colonists transported common law principles to the United States, and these principles formed the foundation of the American legal system. As government developed on both the federal and state levels, much of the common law was codified and replaced with constitutions and statutes. However, since constitutions and statutes cannot address every potential issue in a given area of law, common law still serves an important function.

This differs from a **civil law system**, which is based on a fixed body of written rules usually made by legislators. Derived from the codes of the Roman Empire, civil law—sometimes called statutory or code law—systems are based on detailed statutes rather than on judicial decisions. As a result, civil law judges have little discretion in comparison to their common law counterparts. Civil law systems do include a version of reliance on precedent known as *jurisprudence constante*. But, while a single case can serve as precedent under the principle of *stare decisis, jurisprudence constante* requires a long line of consistent judicial decisions and is never considered definitively authoritative in the way

that precedent under *stare decisis* is. The United States is actually a mixed system of both common and civil law elements, with judges having more or less discretion depending on the type of issue before them. All but one of the fifty states also have common law legal systems at the state level. The exception, Louisiana, has a civil law system that is based largely on the Spanish and French legal codes of Louisiana's original colonizers.[20]

Private law governs the relationships between and among individuals. In particular, private law deals with how citizens or persons—such as landlords and tenants, employers and employees—are obligated to one another. For example, contracts, property, and family law are types of private law in which individuals use the legal process to address their grievances with one another. In contrast, **public law** deals with the relationship between individuals and the state. It includes criminal matters as well as compliance with government regulations. The public law that has developed around governmental regulations is known as **administrative law**. It consists of the rules and regulations issued by administrative agencies in areas such as taxes, anti-trust, health, and the environment.[21] Another type of public law is **constitutional law**. It details the political organization, powers, and limits of government as well as the rights and liberties of individuals. In the U.S., the Constitution is the highest law of the land and is interpreted by the U.S. Supreme Court through the decisions it renders. These decisions comprise the constitutional law of the nation. Each state also has its own body of state constitutional law, as enunciated by its respective court of last resort.

Another distinction in law is between criminal and civil matters. **Criminal law** is comprised of offenses against the state and is generally statutory in nature. Individuals accused of crimes by the state are said to have violated state statutes and are prosecuted by government officials on behalf of the people. They are subject to penalties, which are usually detailed in criminal statutes, if they are found guilty. Examples of major crimes— known as **felonies**—are murder, rape, armed robbery, and perjury. Minor crimes—called **misdemeanors**—include traffic violations and petty theft. **Civil law**—not to be confused with the statutory or codified legal system described previously—deals with disputes between private entities such as individuals or corporations, often over private property or monetary damages. Breach of contract, divorce, copyright, and insurance matters are examples of civil law.

Finally, law can be differentiated on the basis of whether it is substantive or procedural in nature. **Substantive law** is the written law that defines rights and duties. In the case of criminal law, substantive law identifies what is to be considered a crime and the associated penalties. In the case of civil law, substantive law identifies the civil rights and responsibilities individuals possess. **Procedural law**, on the other hand, details how those legal rights are enforced. Procedural law consists of the rules governing how a court hears a case and determines what happens in a criminal or civil lawsuit.

What Is the Purpose of Law?

What would happen if there were no law? Would society break down and anarchy prevail? Would society naturally move to erect laws to establish and maintain order? How would disputes be resolved? By brute force or more peaceful means? Each of these questions suggests that there are many purposes or functions of law. Perhaps most fundamentally, law promotes order. Individuals understand that if they disobey the rules there will be consequences and, though they may not agree with all of the rules, there is a general understanding that rules are necessary to keep people from harming one another.

Law helps individuals resolve disputes. Rather than simply have the strongest or smartest person win in a conflict, the law sets down rules to determine winners and losers and resolve disagreements. The law also protects persons and property from harm or damage. If individuals violate the law, the state will intervene on behalf of the individual who is harmed on the theory that a crime against one person is a crime against society. The law ensures individual freedoms such as speech and religion to guarantee that government majorities do not deny those freedoms to particular individuals or groups. Finally, law promotes the general welfare or overall happiness of society. Laws that provide for clean air and water, health care, public safety against terrorism, and the opportunity for equal education are examples of laws that promote the general welfare.

Image 1.5 Justice Out of a Job

This 1883 illustration "Justice Out of a Job" shows how the rule of law breaks down when people take the law into their own hands—in this case through lynchings in the South and West. Prints and Photographs Division, Library of Congress, Washington, D.C.

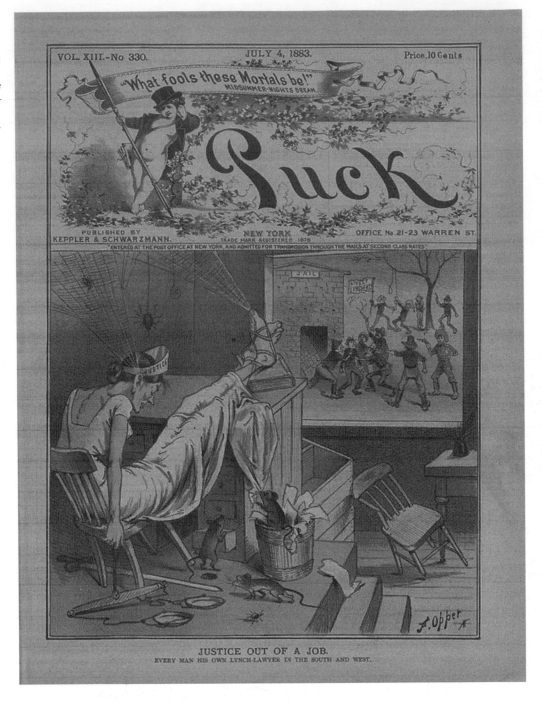

WHAT ARE THE FUNCTIONS OF COURTS?

Courts have several functions. First, courts provide a forum for people to settle their grievances. Individuals think of courts as available to them in order to resolve disputes that they may have with other individuals and groups. For example, in civil cases—such as those involving contracts or property disputes—plaintiffs may bring lawsuits against defendants for monetary damages, and in criminal matters—such as assaults or thefts— the state prosecutes defendants who allegedly violate the law. Second, courts promote accepted forms of behavior for individuals and groups in society by choosing winners and losers in individual cases. Successful lawsuits provide a deterrent for the losers, who might face similar suits if they do not change their ways. To illustrate, think of a company that is successfully sued for selling an unsafe product. That company will alter its product to make it safer, but similar companies may also do the same in order to head off potential litigation. Likewise, unsuccessful lawsuits signal future plaintiffs that their claims may be meritless. A third role that courts play is as a policymaker. Courts make policy by issuing rules and decisions that will govern future cases and influence societal behavior more generally. For example, the *Miranda* warnings issued by police officers ("You have the right to remain silent. Anything you say or do may be used against you in a court of law . . . ") not only modified the behavior of law enforcement but also provided a new policy for police to follow when questioning criminal suspects.[22]

Finally, another function of courts is the monitoring of government action through **judicial review**, meaning courts have the authority to examine the actions of the

Image 1.6 John Marshall
Painting of Chief Justice John Marshall who wrote the opinion in Marbury v. Madison *establishing judicial review—the power of courts to examine executive and legislative actions and invalidate if those actions are contrary to Constitutional principles.* Detroit Publishing Company Photograph Collection, Library of Congress Prints and Photographs Division Washington, D.C.

executive and legislative branches, and to invalidate those actions if they are contrary to constitutional principles. Though judicial review is usually associated with the U.S. Supreme Court, which has ultimate judicial authority, it is a power possessed by most federal and state courts of law in the United States. This is quite unlike the situation in the majority of other countries, where the power of judicial review is not a power belonging to all judges but only to judges on particular courts, usually referred to as constitutional courts.[23]

Judicial review was explicitly held to be a power of the U.S. Supreme Court in *Marbury v. Madison*.[24] In that case, William Marbury had been appointed by then-President John Adams as a justice of the peace in the District of Columbia,[25] but his commission was never delivered by then-Secretary of State John Marshall. The new administration under President Thomas Jefferson had no interest in having these commissions delivered because he preferred to have the opportunity to fill these positions himself. Accordingly, President Jefferson forbade his Secretary of State, James Madison, from delivering the commissions. Marbury brought his case directly to the U.S. Supreme Court under a provision of the Judiciary Act of 1789, and asked the Court to force Secretary Madison to deliver his commission by issuing a ***writ of mandamus***, an order of a court requiring an official under its jurisdiction to perform a particular act.

John Marshall, chief justice at the time the case came before the Court, wrote the opinion, which began by finding that Marbury did have a right to the commission and, further, that there should be a legal remedy. But, ultimately, the Court held that the provision of the Judiciary Act that enabled Marbury to bring his claim to the Supreme Court and seek a *writ of mandamus* was unconstitutional. The Court reasoned that a *writ of mandamus* was something that would come under a court's **original jurisdiction** (power of a court to hear a case for the first time) and that Congress had no authority to change the Court's original jurisdiction.[26] Thus, the Court was simultaneously power*less* to order Madison to deliver the commission and power*ful* in striking down an act of Congress. Although there were (and continue to be) debates regarding the Court's power of judicial review, *Marbury v. Madison* has become a cornerstone of the United State's constitutional system. Thus, courts review legislation passed by federal and state governments in order to determine if those acts comport with the Constitution.

MYTH VERSUS REALITY: HOW DO WE KNOW?

Does the death penalty deter people from committing murder? Do campaign contributions in judicial elections change how state court judges behave? Does precedent influence the votes of U.S. Supreme Court justices? Do the types of litigants bringing cases to court influence the outcomes in those cases? These are the kinds of questions that usually interest students taking classes on judicial process, procedure, and behavior. To be sure, there are a wide variety of opinions on these questions and a number of myths continue to endure. Is it possible to separate personal opinion or myth from reality?

Textbooks can certainly provide authoritative answers by making reference to a particular study (or set of studies) that speaks to the question at issue. What they do not often do is explain *how* the scholars who authored those studies actually conducted their research and the basis on which they reached their conclusions. While it is not necessary for students to be social scientists themselves to appreciate the answers to the kinds of questions addressed throughout this text, understanding generally how scholars go about finding the answers to those questions does give students unique insights about what we know regarding law and courts, and prepares them to evaluate the evidence that is brought to bear in public policy debates. With this in mind, here we provide a broad overview of the social scientific process.

Social science research begins with a **research question** about some behavior or phenomenon that the researcher finds of interest. There may be very little existing research regarding that question, or there may be a great deal of research already on point but the researcher is not convinced that the question has been adequately addressed. With the research question in hand, the social scientist next thinks about what the possible answers to that question might be. To do so, the researcher turns to identifying or developing a theory. A **theory** is a set of statements that provides a way to understand why actors behave the way they do. For example, when considering how judges make decisions, one prominent theory is the attitudinal model.[27] The attitudinal model posits that judges, at least the justices of the U.S. Supreme Court, base their decisions on their personal policy preferences. Specifically, "[Chief Justice William] Rehnquist vote[d] the way he [did] because he [was] extremely conservative; [Justice Thurgood] Marshall voted the way he did because he [was] extremely liberal."[28] An alternative theory is the legal model, which "centers around a rather simple assumption about judicial decision making, namely, that legal doctrine, generated by past cases, is the primary determinant of extant case outcomes."[29]

Of course, human behavior can be very complicated and these attitudinal and legal theories are simplified versions of reality. However, despite the complicated nature of human behavior, we can and do observe patterns of behavior. A theory is a careful articulation of those expected patterns of behavior. A theory cannot, by definition, predict exactly what will happen in each case. But it can tell us what we should expect to see on average.[30] More generally, a theory helps the researcher identify possible answers. That is the next step in the social science research process: to translate the theory into one or more empirical expectations. Specifically, the researcher must articulate her expectations (derived from the theory) as to how what we are trying to explain is related to what we think is doing the explaining. What we are trying to explain is conventionally referred to as the **dependent variable**. It is dependent in that it is caused, or depends on, what we think is doing the explaining. What we think is doing the explaining—that is, what we think is causing our dependent variable—is called the **independent variable**. It is independent in that it does not depend upon the dependent variable for explanation. Thus, for a scholar examining whether the ideology of the U.S. Supreme Court justices influences how they vote, ideology is the independent variable and how the justices vote is the dependent variable.

At this point, the researcher needs to determine how to **operationalize**, or define, the dependent and the independent variables. In terms of the dependent variable, the researcher might look at the ideological direction of the justices' vote choices. Did a justice vote liberally or conservatively? This requires the use of a **coding rule** that the researcher applies to each case to determine whether a given vote is liberal or conservative. For example, the U.S. Supreme Court Database contains more than 200 pieces of information on every decision issued by the Court since 1946, including whether the decision was decided in a liberal or conservative direction.[31] This data set is accompanied by a **codebook**, which explains the coding rules used for each variable. In the context of issues pertaining to criminal procedure, a decision is coded as liberal if it is in favor of a person accused or convicted of a crime, or denied a jury trial.

Continuing with this example, the researcher must also operationalize the independent variable: the ideology of the justice. One way that scholars have conventionally measured judicial ideology is by considering whether the justice was appointed by a Democratic or a Republican president.[32] On average, Democrats are more liberal and Republicans are more conservative and so, by extension, on average justices appointed by Democratic presidents are more liberal and justices appointed by Republican presidents are more conservative. For example, Democratic President Barack Obama appointed Elena Kagan to the Supreme Court in 2010. Thus, using this coding rule, Kagan would be considered liberal in terms of her judicial ideology.

Regardless of what is being measured, a good measure should be both **reliable** and **valid**. A reliable measure is one that "yields the same results on repeated trials."[33] In other words, a reliable measure is one for which the coding rule produces the same classification no matter who is applying that coding rule. If, in measuring the ideological direction of a justice's vote, one researcher classifies the vote as a liberal one and another researcher, looking at the same case, classifies the vote as conservative, then the measure is unreliable. For example, in cases dealing with economic regulation, one individual may conclude that an outcome is liberal because the outcome supported the ability of the government to regulate the economy whereas another individual may conclude that same outcome was conservative if the position being advanced by the government regulation was one that favored big business. Most issues involving reliability can be addressed with careful attention to coding rules.[34]

A **valid** measure, on the other hand, is one that measures what it is supposed to measure. It "refers to the degree of correspondence between the measure and the concept it is thought to measure."[35] If a measure of a concept (e.g., judicial ideology) is a valid one then it is an accurate operationalization of the concept. For example, the appointing president's party affiliation may not be a valid measure of a judge's ideology. To illustrate, a Republican president might appoint a justice who has a liberal background in terms of the occupations and associations the justice has had. For example, Republican President Dwight Eisenhower appointed liberal New Jersey Supreme Court Justice William Brennan to the U.S. Supreme Court. In that case, background may be a more valid measure of judicial ideology than the appointing president's party affiliation. Thus, researchers can, and sometimes do, disagree as to the best way to capture an important concept; there is no perfect measurement strategy. What is important is that scholars are clear in what measurement strategies they use and think carefully about which are appropriate and why.

Now, the researcher is ready to state her hypotheses. **Hypotheses** are explicit statements that indicate how a researcher thinks the phenomena of interest are related. In other words, they are educated guesses that represent a proposed explanation for how the independent variable is thought to affect the dependent variable. For example, if the researcher believes that the age of the Supreme Court case will affect whether lower courts follow that precedent when deciding cases, the researcher might hypothesize as follows: There is a relationship between the age of a Supreme Court precedent and the likelihood that a lower court will follow that precedent. This is a **correlative hypothesis**; the researcher believes there is a relationship between the independent variable and the dependent variable, but she does not know the nature of the relationship. In the above example, the researcher is unsure if lower courts will be more likely to follow older precedents or newer precedents. On the other hand, if the researcher does have an educated guess regarding the nature of the relationship, she might hypothesize as follows: The older the Supreme Court precedent, the greater the likelihood that a lower court will follow that precedent. When the direction of the relationship is specified, the hypothesis is said to be a **directional hypothesis**. Additionally, the relationship between concepts is a **positive relationship** if the concepts are predicted to increase

Image 1.7 William Brennan
Liberal Justice William Brennan, shown in this 1972 photograph, was appointed by Republican President Dwight Eisenhower. Why? Prints and Photographs Division, Library of Congress, Washington, D.C.

in size together while the relationship is a **negative relationship** if, as one concept increases in size or amount, the other will decrease. The preceding hypothesis predicts a positive relationship between the age of Supreme Court precedent and lower courts following the precedent while the following hypothesis is an example of a negative relationship: The older the Supreme Court precedent, the lower the likelihood that a lower court will follow that precedent.

The next task for the social scientist is to collect the appropriate data. **Data collection** can involve conducting interviews, surveys, or experiments and reviewing and analyzing documents, such as court opinions. In addition to engaging in original data collection, researchers may also rely on existing data sets that are publicly available and provide the scholar with many of the variables he is interested in investigating. One example is the State Supreme Court Data Project, a database containing information on state court of last resort decisions in all 50 states during their 1995 through 1998 sessions.[36] Which data collection strategy is appropriate is determined by the nature of the research question.

With the empirical hypotheses from the motivating theory and relevant data in hand, the researcher is now positioned to evaluate how well the empirical hypotheses (the expected relationships) fit with what is observed in the data. This may involve using a statistical procedure that allows the researcher to understand the relationship between the independent variable and the dependent variable. Analyzing two variables to determine the empirical relationship between them is known as **bivariate analysis**. As noted earlier, however, human behavior can be complicated. Accordingly, researchers usually take into account other independent variables that are thought to affect and influence the dependent variable. The use of data analysis techniques designed to test hypotheses involving more than two variables is known as **multivariate analysis**. More specifically, **multiple regression analysis** is a common technique for measuring the mathematical relationship between more than one independent variable and a dependent variable while controlling for all other independent variables in the equation.

Central to any of these analyses is the concept of probability. **Probability** simply means the likelihood of something occurring. Probability is about the likelihood that there is a relationship between the independent variable(s) and the dependent variable. **Statistical significance** tells the researcher how sure he is that the difference or relationship observed actually exists. And, social scientists want to have some precision about the likelihood of seeing the pattern between the independent and dependent variables that they observe. That is, they want to be confident about that relationship and not worry that what they observe is just a fluke. The general rule of thumb is that a researcher will feel confident if the level of statistical significance is at 0.05 or less. Roughly speaking, that means that there are only five chances (or less) out of 100 that the relationship between the independent variable and the dependent variable that the researcher observes in his data is simply by chance. In other words, there is a 95 percent probability or better that there is a relationship between the independent variable and the dependent variable that is not due to chance.

Throughout this text, we reference a variety of social science research that is relevant for many of the points we make. When we do so, we explain what researchers found in plain language. Further, we provide more detailed (though still easily accessible) explanations of some of the studies that are referenced in that chapter. Our purpose is not to convince students to go out and become social scientists themselves—though, as social scientists who love what we do, we certainly would not discourage them from doing so! Rather, our goal is to help students better understand how scholars carry out the work that is then later reflected in textbooks such as this. In short, we hope to help students understand how scholars know what it is that they claim to know.

In the following chapters we explore the American legal culture—the basic values about how the judicial process should function—and how legal culture is filled with myths at odds with reality. Specifically, we suggest that law and procedure do not provide the full picture of the judicial process. Instead, the reality is that the judicial process must be viewed as part of the larger political system. And, because the legal system is political, and because our popular political values shape law and courts, the judicial process can be studied in the same way that legislatures and executives are studied: through the tools of social science.

Suggested Readings

Michael Asimow and Shannon Mader. *Law and Popular Culture: A Course Book* (New York, NY: Peter Lang Publishing, 2013). This textbook is designed to be a reader for a course in law and popular culture. Each chapter is based on a particular movie or television show involving law and lawyers.

William D. Berry and Mitchell S. Sanders. *Understanding Multivariate Research: A Primer for Beginning Social Scientists* (New York, NY: Westview Press, 2000). Geared toward beginning graduate students and advanced undergraduates, this textbook provides an introduction to regression and other basic social science statistical techniques with examples drawn from political science, sociology, marketing, and higher education.

Janet Buttolph Johnson and H. T. Reynolds. *Political Science Research Methods*, Seventh Edition (Washington, DC: Congressional Quarterly Press, 2011). Intended for undergraduates, this textbook introduces students to the "how" and "why" of doing political science research with case studies of existing research and instruction on how to conduct research including sampling, content analysis, and basic statistical techniques.

Lee Epstein. "Studying Law and Courts," in *Contemplating Courts*, Lee Epstein, ed. (Washington, DC: Congressional Quarterly Press, 1995). This book chapter provides a brief and highly accessible overview of the process of conducting research on law and courts topics.

Connie Ireland, Bruce L. Berg, and Robert J. Mutchnick. *Research Methods for Criminal Justice and the Social Sciences* (Upper Saddle River, NJ: Prentice Hall, 2009). This textbook has a unique feature in that it combines brief readings with practice exercises that allow students to experience the research process directly.

Jeffrey A. Segal and Harold J. Spaeth. *The Supreme Court and the Attitudinal Model Revisited* (New York, NY: Cambridge University Press, 2002). Using a comprehensive database of Supreme Court decisions dating back to 1954, this book systematically presents statistical evidence to support the argument that judicial ideology (or attitudes) explains and predicts Supreme Court decision making.

Endnotes

1 Henry David Thoreau, "Slavery in Massachusetts," in *Citizen Thoreau* (Portland, OR: David Press, 2014).

2 Quoted in Ashton Applewhite and Tripp Evans, *And I Quote: The Definitive Collection of Quotes, Sayings, and Jokes for the Contemporary Speechmaker* (New York, NY: St. Martin's Press, 1992): 445.

3 Rick Weiss, "'CSI Effect' Vexes Real Sleuths," *Washington Post*, February 21, 2005.

4 N. J. Schweitzer and Michael J. Saks, "The *CSI* Effect: Popular Fiction About Forensic Science Affects the Public's Expectations About Real Forensic Science," *Jurimetrics*, vol. 47, no. 3 (Spring 2007): 357–364.

5 Ibid., 357–364, 364.

6 Michael Asimow and Shannon Mader, *Law and Popular Culture: A Course Book* (New York, NY: Peter Lang, 2013): 4.

7 Fred Graham, "Keynote Address: The Impact of Television on the Jury System: Ancient Myths and Modern Realism," *American University Law Review*, vol. 40, no. 2 (Winter 1991): 623–629, 628.

8 Edwin M. Good, "Capital Punishment and Its Alternatives in Ancient Near Eastern Law," *Stanford Law Review*, vol. 19, no. 5 (May 1967): 947–977, 947–948.

9 The Code was originally inscribed on clay tablets and stone slabs. The most complete copy of the Code is on display in the Louvre Museum in Paris. See H. Dieter Viel, *The New Complete Code of Hammurabi* (New York, NY: University Press of America, 2011).

10 The Code consists of over 280 laws, which include punishments that are scaled by both the severity of the infraction and the status of the perpetrator and victim. Much of the Code addresses issues related to contracts, with another substantial portion of it devoted to inheritance, marriage and divorce, adultery, and paternity.

11 Roman law began with the law of ancient Rome but developed in earnest starting with the Law of the Twelve Tables (circa the fifth century bc). The Justinian Code of the sixth century is often identified as the culmination of that development. Roman law, however, remained influential in Europe throughout the eighteenth century. See Andrew M. Riggsby, *Roman Law and the Legal World of the Romans* (New York, NY: Cambridge University Press, 2010).

12 State constitutions are generally longer than the federal Constitution and often include detailed provisions that, at the federal level, are more likely to be found in statutes than in the Constitution. State constitutions are also amended much more frequently. For example, while there has been only one U.S. Constitution with 27 amendments, there have been six Alabama constitutions with more than 800 amendments. See Council of State Governments, *Book of the States*, 2010 (Lexington, KY: Council of State Governments, 2010): Table 1.1.

13 The FDA is an agency within the Department of Health and Human Services (http://www.fda.gov/default.htm). It is responsible for, among other things, assuring the safety of human and animal drugs and vaccines and regulating tobacco.

14 Maeva Marcus, *Truman and the Steel Seizure Cases: The Limits of Presidential Power* (Durham, NC: Duke University Press, 1977).

15 The Court struck down the President's action in *Youngstown Sheet and Tube Co. v. Sawyer*, 343 U.S. 579 (1965).

16 This does not mean that there have not been attempts to overrule a constitutional decision of the Supreme Court by legislative enactment. For example, the Religious Freedom Restoration Act of 1993 was intended to overrule a Court decision that had eased the standards for evaluating whether a law impermissibly interfered with the free exercise of religion as protected under the First Amendment; *Employment Division v. Smith*, 494 U.S. 872 (1990). However, the Court rebuked Congress in *City of Boerne v. Flores*, 521 U.S. 507 (1997), reasserting the principle that the Court's interpretation of the Constitution is not subject to being overruled by statute.

17 In one study of statutory decisions in the 1986 through 1990 terms, researchers found that the pattern of Court opinions including language that could be considered an invitation to Congress (to pass new legislation to change the Court's interpretation of a statute) suggests that the Court feels constrained to follow the law as written but is sensitive to the fact that its interpretation may be at odds with the intended congressional policy. See Lori Hausegger and Lawrence Baum, "Inviting Congressional Action: A Study of Supreme Court Motivations in Statutory Interpretation," *American Journal of Political Science*, vol. 43, no. 1 (January 1999): 162–185.

18 James Bernard Murphy, *The Philosophy of Positive Law: Foundations of Jurisprudence* (New Haven, CT: Yale University Press, 2005): 117–168.

19 Charles S. Desmond, "Natural Law and the American Constitution," *Fordham Law Review*, vol. 22, no. 3 (December 1953): 235–245.

20 A. N. Yiannopoulos, "The Civil Codes of Louisiana," *Civil Law Commentaries*, vol. 1, no. 1 (Winter 2008): 1–23.

21 At the federal level, the Administrative Procedure Act governs how federal administrative agencies can go about establishing regulations. Though there is a model state administrative procedure act (drafted by the National Conference of Commissioners on Uniform State Laws), individual states are not required to adopt that model and there are considerable variations across the states as to how administrative agencies promulgate administrative regulations.

22 *Miranda v. Arizona*, 384 U.S. 436 (1966).

23 C. Neal Tate, "Comparative Judicial Review and Public Policy: Concepts and Overview," in *Comparative Judicial Review and Public Policy*, Donald W. Jackson and C. Neal Tate, eds (Westport, CT: Greenwood Press, 1992): 3–13.

24 5 U.S. 137 (1803). Interestingly, the case in which the Court first exercised judicial review was not *Marbury v. Madison* but, instead, was *Hylton v. United States*, 3 U.S. 171 (1796). In that case, the Court reviewed a federal carriage tax (thus exercising judicial review) but did not invalidate that tax.

25 A justice of the peace is a judicial officer with limited authority, typically over minor civil matters (e.g., marriage ceremonies) and minor criminal complaints (e.g., public drunkenness).

26 The language in Article III describes both the original (i.e., trial) and the appellate jurisdiction of the Supreme Court. While that language permits Congress to expand or contract the Court's appellate jurisdiction, the same is not true of the Court's original jurisdiction.

27 In general, an explanatory model is the same thing as a theory. Both focus on the causal process that accounts for what is observed. An explanatory (or causal) model should not be confused with a descriptive model. A descriptive model is one that merely describes a process or behavior. For example, a descriptive model of the indictment process would simply describe each step from the convention of a grand jury to the subpoena of witnesses to the deliberations of the jurors to the decision to issue an indictment or not. It would not, however, explain why some grand jury proceedings result in indictment and others do not.

28 Jeffrey A. Segal and Harold J. Spaeth, *The Supreme Court and the Attitudinal Model Revisited* (New York, NY: Cambridge University Press, 2002): 86.

29   Tracey E. George and Lee Epstein, "On the Nature of Supreme Court Decision Making," *American Political Science Review*, vol. 86, no. 3 (June 1992): 323–337, 324. For an overview of how social science research is brought to bear on law and courts questions, see Lee Epstein, "Studying Law and Courts," in *Contemplating Courts*, Lee Epstein, ed. (Washington, DC: Congressional Quarterly Press, 1995): 1–17.

30   To use an illustration that students should quickly understand, on average, the more students study for an exam, the higher those students' grades will be and, conversely, the less students study for an exam, the lower those students' grades will be. But, of course, as every student knows, even a student who studies a lot might perform poorly on any given exam and a student who barely cracks the text can perform quite well on occasion.

31   Harold J. Spaeth, *The United States Supreme Court Judicial Database, 1953–2006 Terms* (East Lansing, MI: Michigan State University, Department of Political Science, 2007) (scdb.wustl.edu).

32   See, for example, Daniel R. Pinello, "Linking Political Party to Judicial Ideology in American Courts: A Meta-Analysis." *Justice System Journal*, vol. 20, no. 3 (1999): 219–254.

33   Janet Buttolph Johnson and Richard Joslyn, *Political Science Research Methods*, Seventh Edition (Washington, DC: Congressional Quarterly Press, 2011): 133.

34   Though careful scholars are always concerned about the reliability of their measures, reliability is of particular concern when there is an element of subjectivity inherent in what is being measured. For example, a researcher who is examining the extent to which newspaper articles related to crime focus on the individual responsibility of the perpetrator versus the systemic causes of crime in society must develop very explicit rules about how any given article is determined to be focused on individual responsibility rather than on systemic causes of crime, or vice versa. Often in such cases the researcher will have two or more independent coders code the same subset of newspaper articles and assess the extent of inter-coder reliability to ensure the reliability of the measure.

35   Janet Buttolph Johnson and Richard Joslyn, *Political Science Research Methods*, Seventh Edition (Washington, DC: Congressional Quarterly Press, 2011): 136.

36   Paul Brace and Melinda Gann Hall, *State Supreme Court Data Project* (Houston, TX: Rice University, 2002) (http://www.ruf.rice.edu/~pbrace/statecourt).

2

THINKING LIKE A LAWYER
Legal Education and Law School

"Law school taught me one thing: how to take two situations that are exactly the same and show how they are different."

—Hart Pomerantz, Canadian Lawyer and Television Personality[1]

"Make crime pay. Become a lawyer."

—Will Rogers, Cowboy and Actor[2]

Meet Joan. She is a new lawyer at an 80-person law firm in Chicago. One day, about 2 months into her job, Joan is called into a meeting with her boss (a partner at the firm) and another lawyer.[3] They proceed to discuss how one of their clients—an international bank—has a customer that is considering acquiring a major company. Joan hears her boss explain a complex legal matter and that explanation includes the following phrases: "syndicated loan," "revolver," "three term facilities," "payment provisions," and "diligence." Specifically, Joan's boss tells her to "review the existing credit facility, understand the prepayment provisions, and arrange to terminate all of the company's existing liens and lien filings." In addition, Joan is told to "review the existing mortgage financing agreements among the customer's subsidiaries to determine whether there are any covenants that would prevent them from executing a guarantee and security agreement." The good news is that Joan spent 3 years in law school and took a first-year course on contracts—the setting for supposedly learning how to handle such an assignment. The bad news is that she learned nothing in that class or any other law school class about the practical issues in sophisticated commercial transactions: how to structure the transaction, advise the client on strategy, negotiate and draft the contracts, orchestrate the closing, and keep the transaction organized and moving forward. What will Joan (and nearly every other law firm associate) do? As a matter of course, Joan's firm will give her on-the-job training to develop the skills necessary to handle business transactions—skills not necessarily taught in law school.

The debate over how to bridge the gap between law school education and legal practice has been going on for some time.[4] Students may go to law school to learn how to be a lawyer, but law schools do not necessarily teach practical skills. Instead, the focus is on theory: teaching law students how to *think* like a lawyer rather than how to *be* a lawyer. For example, according to a 2011 survey, 40 percent of law school students felt that their legal education had contributed only some or very little to their acquisition of job-related knowledge and skills.[5] Others have also been less than enthusiastic about the practical skills new attorneys possess. For example, the general counsel of one large corporation recently said that law schools were producing a product (law school graduates who are not "practice ready") that no one wants. "And that's a real risk, I think, for law schools if they don't come into the modern world and realize that the luxury of people practicing law for three years to learn how to practice law . . . isn't there today."[6] The general consensus seems to be that many law school students graduate with a law degree without ever having seen a contract or a complaint and are simply not ready to actually practice law. In other words, the myth of law school education does not match the reality.

What is law school really like? What are law schools teaching their students? What does it take to become a practicing lawyer? In this chapter, we explain how the process of obtaining

MYTH AND REALITY IN LEGAL EDUCATION AND LAW SCHOOL

MYTH	REALITY
Law school teaches practical legal skills.	Lawyers learn practical legal skills on the job from their employer.
The formal legal education provided by law schools has always been the path to a career as a lawyer.	Formal legal education is a relatively new development that replaced practical apprenticeships as the path to a career in law.
All law students are created equal: they obtain the same law school educations and become lawyers.	Legal education is highly competitive and hierarchical: school, class rank, and activities determine job opportunities.
The LSAT tests students' knowledge of the law.	The LSAT contains no questions on law or any other substantive topic.
The LSAT provides an objective, neutral method for admitting law students.	Minority applicants have substantially lower LSAT scores than white applicants.
Most law students come from wealthy families who finance their legal educations.	Most law students pay for their legal education through student loans.
A typical law school course consists of students taking notes while the instructor lectures.	Typical law school courses are conducted via the Socratic method of students answering a series of questions posed by instructors.
The final grade in a typical law school course is comprised of multiple elements including participation, quizzes, research papers, and exams.	The final grade in a typical law school course is based on a single final exam.
Law students earn their final grades in typical law school courses regardless of what the other students earn.	Law students' final grades in typical law school courses (especially first-year courses) are based on mandatory curves.
Law students must take the bar exam and practice law in the state in which they attended law school.	Law students may sit for any state's bar exam and may practice in any state.
Law students should take many bar exam subject-matter courses to help them prepare for the bar exam.	Whether there is a relationship between taking these courses and passing the bar exam is still open for debate.

a legal education has changed over time from the early apprenticeship model to the formal education model that law schools provide today. We discuss common myths about legal education and reveal what students can expect from the process, from admissions and the law school experience to gaining admission to the bar. In short, the legal education process is not geared toward learning the law so much as it is a test of perseverance in the face of competition and hierarchy, with students learning to think, speak, and write like legal professionals.

EARLY LEGAL EDUCATION

The carefully structured legal education a law school student receives today—at least a stylized version of it—is familiar to fans of cinematic favorites like *Legally Blonde* and *The Paper Chase*. Though the former is a contemporary comedy while the latter is an older dramatic film, they portray the legal education process in similar ways. First-year law school students Elle Woods (played by Reese Witherspoon in *Legally Blonde*) and James Hart (played by Timothy Bottoms in *The Paper Chase*) are each subjected to a rigorous (and angst-inducing) set of courses taught in a conventional classroom setting (think of a podium at the front of the room with amphitheater-style seating for the students) by esteemed (often feared) law professors. Students subject themselves to the terrors of law

Image 2.1 Howard Law School Graduating Class *Graduating Class, Howard University School of Law, ca. 1900.* Prints and Photographs Division, Library of Congress, Washington, D.C.

school because it is a prerequisite to becoming a lawyer. Though that may be true today, it is a myth to believe that it has always been so. In fact, the reality is that formal legal education of the kind depicted in *Legally Blonde* and *The Paper Chase* is a relatively new development. The traditional English model of legal training required a general education followed by a lengthy period of time "reading the law" (learning the law) at one of the Inns of Court in London,[7] followed by an apprenticeship in the office of a barrister.[8] Early American legal training followed the English model with the exception of the Inns of Court.[9] In America, the **apprenticeship model** typically required an undergraduate education—although this was not a universal mandate—followed by a substantial period of time spent reading the standard legal treatises and commentaries as an apprentice to a practicing attorney.[10] Formalized apprenticeships varied from state to state, but Massachusetts was typical in requiring a 5-year apprenticeship period, with a 1-year reduction in the apprenticeship period if the apprentice possessed a college degree.[11]

The apprenticeship model worked well because an apprentice could perform a variety of functions, from secretarial work and other mundane office tasks to legal research and writing, providing hands-on experience to the apprentice while also providing useful service for the attorney to whom he was apprenticed. But this model of legal education was unstructured and uneven. Time was often devoted to menial tasks rather than studying the law[12] and even the best lawyers did not always have enough time to properly instruct their apprentices. Those that did have the requisite time, however, thrived. Indeed, the first law schools grew out of specialized law offices where popular practitioners employed and instructed several apprentices at the same time.[13] Judge Tapping Reeve founded the earliest school of this kind in 1784 in Litchfield, Connecticut.[14] Reeve's school was quite successful and it grew quickly in size, gaining a national reputation and attracting students from all over the country.[15] Originally, law schools were a supplement to the apprenticeship program and liberal arts colleges even offered the occasional course on law.

William & Mary Law School opened in 1779 and was the first university-affiliated law school. It closed, however, at the start of the Civil War and did not reopen until 1920. Harvard Law School began in 1817 and is the oldest continuously operating law school in the United States. Given that there had long been legal courses in which college undergraduates could enroll, the law degree was not initially a postgraduate degree. Further, it was not standard for law schools to require any prior college work. Like a bachelor's degree in philosophy, English, or mathematics, an LL.B. (bachelor of laws) was one of the many liberal arts degrees that undergraduates could pursue, and can still pursue in most common law countries.[16]

By 1860, 21 law schools had become popular alternatives to the apprenticeship model for prospective lawyers. Accordingly, state requirements regarding study as an apprentice eased, with only nine out of 39 jurisdictions requiring formal apprenticeships by this time.[17] **Proprietary law schools** (law schools not affiliated with a university) offered a structured and systematic approach to legal education but also offered students a more significant practice component than did university-based law schools. The universities distinguished themselves with a mission to teach theory, history, and philosophy of the law. Unlike proprietary schools, they assumed that skills training would take place in practice. In most schools, the instructors used the **lecture method**. In using the lecture method, the instructor stood before the class and presented information for the students to learn. There was usually very little exchange between the instructor and the students. Some law schools, such as Yale, used a method of instruction called **text-and-recitation**, where the students would read assigned treatises, such as Blackstone's *Commentaries on the Laws of England*, and in the classroom students were called on to recite what they had learned.[18]

Image 2.2 Harvard Law School
Langdell Hall, Harvard Law School, Cambridge, Massachusetts, ca. 1900. Prints and Photographs Division, Library of Congress, Washington, D.C.

Harvard and other law schools struggled to compete with the education provided to law students studying under a practitioner, which motivated Harvard to create a separate law school presidency along with a position for a dean. In 1870, **Christopher Columbus Langdell** became the first Dean of Law at Harvard. At the time that Langdell became dean, law school education lasted a mere 18 months or less and the curriculum consisted of ungraded, elementary courses. There were no exams or attendance requirements and the faculty was part time. Langdell elevated law to a postgraduate level of study and increased the length of study to 3 years. He introduced entrance exams, graduation exams, rigorous coursework, and the **casebook method**. Langdell also "believed that law should be taught, not as a skilled trade, but rather as a science."[19] Thus, Langdell thought that the best way to learn the law was to read the actual judicial opinions rather than study abstract summaries of legal rules. Langdell's casebook method was considered novel because it replaced textbooks with appellate cases arranged to illustrate the meaning and development of principles of law. In addition to the casebook method, Langdell incorporated the Socratic method into classroom discussion.[20] The **Socratic method** in the law school setting "involves a teacher asking a series of questions, ideally to a single student, in an attempt to lead the student down a chain of reasoning either forward, to its conclusions, or backward, to its assumptions."[21]

In using the Socratic method, the instructor initiates the questions, with the questions typically challenging assumptions anticipated or encountered in the students' answers and the professor frequently playing devil's advocate, forcing the student to defend his or her position. This question-and-answer dialogue is intended to hone students' critical thinking skills in addition to fostering their learning about the law. Specifically, the Socratic method involves "having a student analyze each of the cases and then asking a series of questions designed to draw out the legal content of the case. Langdell and the students would then work to synthesize and contrast the cases so that, ultimately, the entire area of the law would be made clear."[22]

Over time, the demand for lawyers increased and more and more law schools were established to supply that demand. At the same time, the apprenticeship model progressively waned. By 1890 the number of law schools had grown to 61 with over 7,000 students enrolled, and by 1900 there were 102 law schools.[23] Some schools—generally those affiliated with established colleges and universities—adopted the Harvard model of casebook instruction and the Socratic method. Other schools, however, were part time or night schools, emphasizing local practice and catering to poor, working class, and immigrant populations. At the turn of the century, the Association of American Law Schools (AALS)[24] and the American Bar Association (ABA) began accrediting law schools—establishing standards for schools to meet in order to gain the organizations' seals of approval.[25] Furthermore, states began requiring prospective attorneys to have formal law degrees in order to sit for the bar exam and be licensed to practice. The effect of these changes led to the exclusion of historically underrepresented groups that had been gaining entry into the legal profession. As a result, for most of the twentieth century, white males from the middle and upper classes dominated law schools, a reality at odds with the myth of the law as a field open to all.

Image 2.3 Law School the Modern Plague
This 1897 lithograph shows how the rapid growth of formal legal education through law schools was transforming society. Uncle Sam is sitting in a hammock, holding a fan, beset upon by swarms of locust-like pests streaming from a "Law School," "Medical College," and a "Theological Institute"—each carrying a diploma.
Prints and Photographs Division, Library of Congress, Washington, D.C.

CONTEMPORARY LEGAL EDUCATION

Most prospective law school students today understand that legal education is a highly competitive process and that the competition begins long before students step foot in a law school classroom. While schools consider a range of factors in the admissions process, grades and test scores carry the most weight. Once students have been admitted, instead of learning the actual practice of law in class, students face the Socratic method of instruction and mandatory grading curves, further reinforcing the fact that competition and hierarchy are the order of the day. At the same time, there is considerable variation in bar passage rates across schools, and jobs have become more difficult to come by for an increasing number of law school graduates. The result is that the reality of the legal education process students experience is often at odds with the myths they hold dear.

Reese Witherspoon as Elle Woods in the movie Legally Blonde *(2001). The Film depicts a Hollywood version of contemporary legal education.*

Photo by Buyenlarge/ Getty Images

Admissions

Law schools consider several factors in making admissions decisions, including an applicant's personal statement, letters of recommendation, personal achievements, and a host of criteria that schools consider in the hopes of fostering a diverse student body (such as undergraduate major, extracurricular activities, work experience, graduate study, and demographic characteristics like geographical background, gender, race, and class). But by far the two most important factors in gaining admission to law school are undergraduate grade point average (UGPA) and Law School Admission Test (LSAT) score.[26] Because UGPAs are not standard across all majors and all undergraduate institutions, many law schools give the most weight to the LSAT because it is a test that nearly all applicants take.

The LSAT itself is a half-day, timed test, administered four times a year. Prospective law school applicants first preparing to take the LSAT often mistakenly believe that the LSAT tests students' knowledge of the law. Hence, students assume that the substance of undergraduate courses related to constitutional law, criminal law, and judicial process will help to prepare them to do well on the LSAT. In truth, unlike the Medical College Admission Test (MCAT), which requires substantive knowledge of chemistry and biology, the LSAT requires no prior knowledge of law or any other substantive topic. It consists of five 35-minute sections of multiple-choice questions and one written essay.[27] It is intended to measure reading and verbal reasoning skills and contains a reading comprehension section (similar to what students have encountered on other standardized tests such as the SAT or ACT). It also includes two logical reasoning or "arguments" sections, in which test takers read short passages (perhaps a paragraph long) and answer a number of questions about them, and one analytical reasoning or "games" section, which requires test takers to draw diagrams and use deductive logic to determine the relationships between and among persons, things, or events. The exam itself is scored on a scale from 120 to 180, with the median score 150. Of the 101 multiple-choice questions, students need to get roughly 56 questions correct in order to earn the median score. Table 2.1 shows the number of errors those taking the test can make and their corresponding scores along with

TABLE 2.1
LSAT Scores: Highest Number of Errors and Percentile Rank

HIGHEST NUMBER OF ERRORS (OUT OF 101)	LSAT SCORE	PERCENTILE RANK
2	180	99.9
7	175	99.5
13	170	97.4
20	165	91.4
29	160	80.2
37	155	63.0
46	150	44.2
55	145	26.8
65	140	13.7

Source: LSAC, June 2014 test and http://www.cambridgelsat.com/resources/data/lsat-percentiles-table/

percentile rank. The curve is quite steep moving up from the median. Only 30 perce[r] all test takers score above a 155 and only 16 percent earn a 160 or better. It is also [i] esting to note that a student can miss numerous questions and still do relatively v the test. Accordingly, test-taking strategies center on identifying and correctly an[r] the easier questions while saving the more difficult ones until the end of each even guessing on the most difficult questions if necessary in order to ensure getting easier questions right.

There is a wealth of study guides, practice tests, and courses intended to aid students in mastering the techniques and strategies necessary for doing well on the exam. The Law School Admission Council (LSAC) provides a small selection of sample questions with explanations and general guidance free of charge on its website[28] but it also publishes several study guides and practice tests that are available for purchase. In addition, there is a voluminous amount of materials published commercially and an array of available LSAT prep courses.[29] The popularity of LSAT prep materials and courses among those aspiring to go on to law school is not surprising given the importance placed on the LSAT score in the admissions process. Competitors in this market carefully track the performance of their respective clients and use that information to promote their products. In one recent academic study about the effects of reasoning skills training, researchers found that intense preparation for the LSAT produces actual changes in the structure of the brain, and particularly in the connections in areas of the brain important for reasoning.[30]

Currently, there are 202 ABA-accredited law schools in the United States.[31] Table 2.2 presents the top 10 law schools, based on the 2015 *U.S. News & World Report* law school rankings. The UGPA and LSAT scores for the 25th to 75th percentile of students admitted

TABLE 2.2
"Top" U.S. Law Schools

2015 RANK	LAW SCHOOL	2014 GPA 25TH-75TH PERCENTILE	2014 LSAT 25TH-75TH PERCENTILE
1	Yale University	3.82–3.97	170–176
2	Harvard University	3.77–3.95	170–175
3	Stanford University	3.76–3.95	169–173
4 (tie)	Columbia University	3.58–3.81	170–174
4 (tie)	University of Chicago	3.67–3.95	166–172
6	New York University	3.57–3.85	168–172
7	University of Pennsylvania	3.55–3.94	165–171
8	University of Virginia	3.52–3.94	164–170
9	University of California-Berkeley	3.66–3.89	163–169
10 (tie)	University of Michigan-Ann Arbor	3.52–3.82	165–170
10 (tie)	Duke University	3.59–3.84	165–170

Source: usnews.com

TABLE 2.3
"Fourth Tier" U.S. Law Schools

LAW SCHOOL	2013 MEDIAN GPA	2013 MEDIAN LSAT
Valparaiso (Indiana)	3.00	143
Atlanta's John Marshall	2.99	149
Florida Coastal	2.97	144
Thomas M. Cooley (Michigan)	2.96	145
Whittier (California)	2.95	149
St. Mary's (Texas)	2.94	151
Charlotte	2.91	144
Barry (Florida)	2.90	147
Arizona Summit	2.88	144
Thomas Jefferson (California)	2.86	146
La Verne (California)	2.83	147
Southern (Louisiana)	2.82	144

Note: List based on lowest median GPAs.
Source: American Bar Association. http://www.americanbar.org/groups/legal_education/resources/statistics.html

for fall 2014 demonstrates that applicants need to have extremely high grades and test scores to gain admittance to the best schools.[32] For example, getting into a top law school like Yale can be very difficult, where the UGPA is between 3.82 and 3.97—a student who earned virtually all *A*s as an undergraduate—and the LSAT score is between 170 and 176, which ranks the student higher than 98 percent of all test takers.

At the other end of the spectrum are the so-called "fourth tier" schools, those ranked by *U.S. News* in the bottom 50 of ABA-approved law schools. Table 2.3 reports the schools with the lowest median UGPAs and LSAT scores for the 2013 entering class. In general, these schools attract students with a *B* average in their undergraduate coursework and who score between the 30th and 50th percentile on the LSAT. For example, for Thomas Jefferson—a private law school in San Diego, California—the median UGPA for admitted students was 2.86 and the median LSAT was 146. It is plain from these data that there is quite a difference between the students who are admitted to the top schools and those who are admitted to schools with the lowest rankings.

Scholars have argued that law school rankings actually mislead prospective applicants.[33] Specifically, law professor Jeffrey Evans Stake argues that "[r]ankings push law schools to give too much weight to some factors in admissions decisions," particularly UGPA and LSAT score. According to Stake, "[s]chools wanting to move up in rankings will turn down the student with a 3.4 UGPA in engineering from Rose-Hulman in favor of the applicant with a 3.8 UGPA in shuffleboard from Central Ivy State University."[34] According to the Law School Admission Council, while the LSAT helps predict whether a student will do well in law school, a combination of a student's score and UGPA gives a better prediction than either alone. Statistically, for the year 2012, the median LSAT correlation coefficient (the strength of the relationship between LSAT scores and first-year law school grades)[35] at the 152 participating law schools was 0.36, the coefficient for UGPA was 0.26, and the coefficient for LSAT and UGPA combined was 0.47.[36]

Some scholars object to using standardized tests such as the LSAT because they reinforce racial and class privileges.[37] What is the reality? Research has demonstrated that affluent white students perform better on standardized tests (including the LSAT) than their less advantaged or minority peers.[38] For example, one study by education scholar Linda Wightman used data obtained from students who applied to law schools in 1990 and 1991 and from fall 1991 first-year law students in order to examine the likely effects of an admission policy that relied exclusively on the LSAT and UGPA.[39] Wightman's analysis revealed that a mere 41 percent of the students of color who were offered admission to law school during the 1990–1991 application cycle were likely to have been admitted if only their LSAT scores and UGPA were considered.

Diversity

Despite the challenges associated with making admissions decisions, law schools have become more diverse in recent decades. Women, in particular, have made significant inroads in gaining access to the legal profession. For example, in 1947 only 3.5 percent of first-year law school students were women and that percentage moved little over the next 2 decades.[40] But the percentage nearly doubled from 4.9 percent in 1967 to 7.4 percent in 1968. The rates continued to climb thereafter reaching 20 percent in 1973, 30 percent in 1977, 40 percent in 1985, and nearly 50 percent in 2000 and 2001. Since 2002, however, the percentage of women has declined. In 2011, less than 47 percent of first-year students were women, though some schools, such as American University and University of California at Berkeley, had a majority of women law students.[41] Figure 2.1 displays this trend.

HOW DO WE KNOW?

Is the LSAT an Objective, Neutral Method of Admitting Law School Students?

The 1996, 1997, and 1998 applicant pools to the law school at the University of California, Berkeley, provided the data for a study by legal scholar William Kidder that asked whether students of color with the same undergraduate grades systematically score lower on the LSAT than white students.[42] For each applicant, the researcher obtained data on race and ethnicity, undergraduate institution attended, graduation date, cumulative UGPA, age, and LSAT score (120–180 score). Applicant pools from these 3 years were then categorized by undergraduate institution, focusing on applicants from 15 highly selective colleges and universities. African American, Hispanic Americans, Native American, and Asian/Pacific American applicants were matched with white applicants who had approximately the same UGPA (defined as plus or minus 0.10 on a 4.0 scale) from the same undergraduate institution. The study found that students of color had substantially lower LSAT scores compared to white applicants. Specifically, African American applicants were 9.2 points below white applicants, Hispanic Americans 6.8 points below, Native Americans 4.0 points below, and Asian/Pacific American applicants 2.5 points below.[43]

To take into consideration the possibility that there are race-related differences in choice of major (students of color were disproportionately concentrated in "easier" majors) the study also compared students within each of the most common majors. Controlling for major, however, had a negligible impact on the size of the LSAT gap among applicants with equivalent UGPAs.[44] The study concluded that using the LSAT is not a neutral method on which to base admissions decisions and "the continued emphasis on the LSAT acts as an artificial barrier for students of color aspiring to enter the legal profession."[45] This analysis injects a dose of reality and undercuts the myth that the LSAT provides an objective basis for making law school admissions decisions.

Image 2.4 Annette Abbott Adams
This 1914 photograph shows lawyer and judge Annette Abbott Adams (1877–1956) who earned a law degree from the University of California, Berkeley in 1912—a time when very few women were admitted to law school. She was the first woman Assistant U.S. Attorney General (1914–1918) and U.S. Attorney (1918–1920). She had a successful private law practice and went on to serve as a judge on the California Court of Appeal (1942–1952). George Grantham Bain Collection, Prints and Photographs Division, Library of Congress, Washington, D.C.

FIGURE 2.1
Percentage of Women Enrolling in Law School, 1947–2011

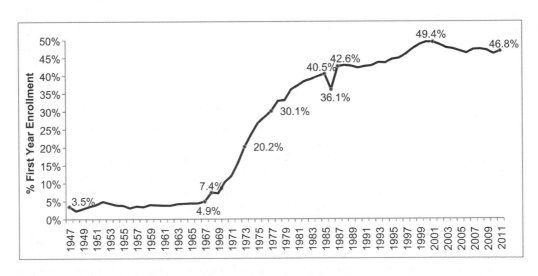

Source: American Bar Association, "First Year and Total J.D. Enrollment by Gender, 1947-2011." http://www.americanbar.org/groups/legal_education/resources/statistics.html

FIGURE 2.2

Percentage of Racial Minorities Enrolling in Law School, 1971–2013

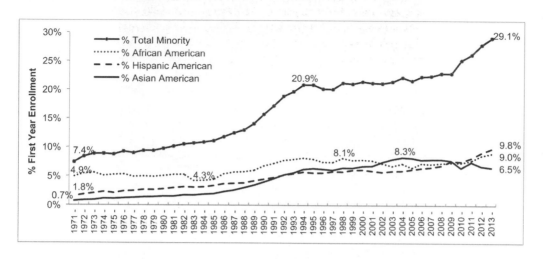

Source. American Bar Association. http://www.americanbar.org/groups/legal_education/resources/statistics.html

There has been much speculation about the recent downward trend and experts have proffered different explanations. Dorian Denburg, president of the National Association of Women Lawyers, suggested that the steady stream of bad news about the difficulties facing women in law is one cause: "Twenty years ago, when you had a lot of women coming out of law school, the ceiling was not as apparent as it is now. You didn't have as many statistics or information."[46] Jessie Kornberg, executive director of Ms. JD—a nonprofit organization that seeks to improve the experiences of women law students and lawyers—agreed that there is a "perception problem." She said that it does not help that there has been "no discernible progress for women in the legal profession in roughly a decade. The number of women in visible leadership positions in law firms and legal departments remains essentially unchanged."[47] Furthermore, Kornberg added that "lawyers in general appear to be an increasingly miserable bunch."[48] Other explanations include concerns about achieving a work-life balance, and interest in other careers that are now more open to women, like the sciences and business.[49]

Over the past several decades, minorities have also made substantial gains in terms of entrée into law schools. Figure 2.2 show the steady increase in racial minorities enrolling in law school. Overall, the percentage of minorities has quadrupled from 7.4 percent in 1971 to 29.1 percent in 2013.[50] The three largest minority groups have also steadily increased. African American enrollment has doubled from a recent low of 4.3 percent in 1984 to a high of 9 percent in 2013. Hispanic American enrollment has grown from less than 2 percent in 1971 to nearly 10 percent in 2013. Finally, Asian/Pacific American enrollment was less than 1 percent in 1971 but steadily grew to a high of 8.3 percent in 2004. Interestingly, Asian/Pacific American enrollment has steadily declined since then to a low of 6.5 percent in 2013. Scholars have suggested this may be the result of a "too many Asians tipping point" whereby admissions committees are discounting the high LSAT scores that Asian/Pacific American applicants are earning compared to whites.[51]

Image 2.5 William H. Hastie
William H. Hastie earned an LL.B. in 1930 and an S.J.D. in 1933 from Harvard Law School. He became the first African American federal judge when he was appointed by President Franklin Roosevelt to the U.S. District Court for the Virgin Islands in 1937. He was also the first African American court of appeals judge when President Harry Truman appointed him to the U.S. Court of Appeals for the Third Circuit in 1949 where Hastie served for 22 years. National Archives and Records Administration.

Affirmative action admissions policies have aided in achieving these overall gains; however, they have not been without controversy and, indeed, have generated a great deal of debate.[52] Almost 35 years ago, in a case dealing with affirmative action in medical school admissions, the Supreme Court invalidated the use of quota systems in which admissions procedures were intended to admit people of particular ethnic or minority groups while excluding the consideration of others.[53] However, many educational institutions continued to use admissions policies that included race as one in a constellation of factors relied upon for making admissions decisions.

The University of Michigan Law School had just such a policy, which was challenged in *Grutter v. Bollinger*.[54] In that case, the U.S. Supreme Court held that the University had a compelling interest in promoting diversity and that an admissions process that took race into account did not violate the U.S. Constitution as long as the applicants were evaluated as individuals and race was used as a "plus" factor in conjunction with other factors.[55] One of the arguments in support of affirmative action is that such policies lead to a diverse student body, which creates a better learning environment.[56] Opponents of affirmative action argue that it does not lead to true diversity because racial diversity does not mean diversity of opinion. According to a recent survey of law students, 91 percent said that they have had serious conversations during law school with students of a different race or ethnicity.[57] At the same time, nearly half of all students (49 percent) never or only sometimes included diverse perspectives (in terms of race, religion, sexual orientation, gender, or political beliefs) in class discussions or writing assignments.[58]

Cost

The cost of attending law school has increased dramatically over the years.[59] The average law school in-state tuition for public school in 1985 was $2,006 per year, while the average in 2011 was $22,116, an increase of over 1000 percent. The average law school tuition for private school in 1985 was $7,526 per year, while the average tuition in 2011 was $39,184, an increase of more than 420 percent. Even controlling for inflation, the increases are staggering: 427 percent for public law schools (in-state tuition) and 149 percent for private law schools. While public law school tuition is generally less costly than private school tuition, when other costs associated with 3 years of law school are factored in, the differences are less pronounced (that is, *both* public and private law schools are expensive).[60] A law school education can cost more than $150,000 since tuition alone has reached more than $50,000 per year at some schools, a figure that does not include the cost of housing, food, books, transportation, and personal expenses.

One common myth about bankrolling law school costs is that students either come from wealthy families who finance their legal education or receive substantial scholarships that ensure that meritorious but less wealthy individuals can still afford to go to law school. The reality, however, is that roughly 80 percent of law students rely on loans as the primary vehicle for financing their legal education. The average amount borrowed for law school has increased as well, with the average increasing by almost 63 percent for public schools from the 2001–2002 academic year to the 2010–2011 academic year ($46,499 to $75,725) and by 78 percent for private schools ($70,147 to $124,950) for the same period.[61] There are both federal government and private loan programs, with the former generally offering low rates and deferring payments until after graduation and the latter varying greatly as to the terms of their loans (depending on the lender and the applicant's credit history). Figures for the 2010 graduating class put average debt levels at $98,500, which translates into monthly loan payments of $1,200 over 10 years.[62] Though there are other repayment options—including 30-year repayment plans, income-based repayment plans that allow lower payments, and loan forgiveness programs offered for government and non-profit employees—the reality is that most law school graduates emerge from law school saddled with debt.

Not surprisingly, there is a good deal of what is termed buyer's remorse among law school students: questioning by students about whether the cost they are incurring in pursuit of a legal education is worth it. For example, according to a 2011 survey of law students in the United States and Canada, 23 percent of those who expect to graduate with more than $80,000 in law school debt say they would not or probably would not attend the same law school if given the opportunity to start over.[63] In addition to loans, there are work-study programs, grants, and scholarships available. Some students are offered partial or even full tuition scholarships from their law schools. These scholarships are generally contingent on the student maintaining a certain GPA—for example, a 3.0—throughout his or her law school career. For students who were high achievers in college, maintaining a 3.0 GPA may seem ridiculously easy. That perception is often an illusion, however, because law schools generally adhere to a mandatory grading curve that can drive down the grades of all students, including the grades of those who were high achievers in college.

CURRICULUM AND TEACHING TECHNIQUES

It does not take long after starting law school for students to hear the old adage: "The first year they scare you to death, the second year they work you to death, and the third year they bore you to death." In this section we will discuss why many law students have come to agree with this sentiment. Specifically, we will explore the Socratic method of law school instruction, the typical law school curriculum, how exams and grading procedures generally work, and extracurricular activities involved in law education.

The Socratic Method

"My professors will teach me the law." This is the myth that first-year law students encounter. Thus, on the first day of law school, students open their laptops or their notebooks, ready to take notes on "the law." The students are waiting "for the professor to fill [them] up with law-knowledge."[64] The reality, however, is that instead of going to the podium and lecturing on the law of contracts or torts or civil procedure, the professor uses the Socratic method, calling on a student and questioning that student at length about the meaning and implications of the cases that were assigned. Although law professors in many schools now assign a group of people to be "on call" for a particular class or call on people in alphabetical order (or even rely on people to volunteer),[65] most law school professors still do not stand up at the podium and teach **"black letter law"** (that is, well-settled legal rules that are not subject to dispute or interpretation).[66] Instead, they teach by asking students not only questions about the particular cases under discussion, but also questions based upon hypothetical fact patterns that are slightly (though meaningfully) different from those cases. Although there has been some claims that the "Socratic method is . . . more myth than reality,"[67] one survey found that 97 percent of first-year law classes are taught using some version of the Socratic method.[68]

Image 2.6 Socrates
This 1750 engraving depicts the Greek philosopher Socrates in dialogue with a group of seated men. A figure of Justice stands behind him. Rather than lecture, law professors routinely employ a dialogue format of questions and answers with their students—similar to the method used by Socrates that now bears his name: the "Socratic method." Prints and Photographs Division, Library of Congress, Washington, D.C.

L. P. Boitard Jnr. del. Sculp.

Typically, the method begins by the professor calling on a student at random and asking about a central argument put forth by the majority opinion in an assigned case. The first step may be to ask the student to paraphrase the argument to ensure she read and has at least a basic understanding of the case. Assuming the student has read the case and can articulate the court's argument, the professor may then ask whether the student agrees with the argument. The professor then follows up by playing devil's advocate, trying to force the student to defend her position by asking additional questions. These subsequent questions can take several forms. Sometimes they seek to challenge the assumptions upon which the student based the previous answer until that answer can no longer be defended. Or the professor may attempt to move a student toward greater specificity, either in understanding a rule of law or a particular case. The professor may attempt to propose a hypothetical situation in which the student's assertion would seem to demand an exception.

Finally, the professor may use the Socratic method to allow students to arrive at legal principles on their own through carefully worded questions that encourage a particular train of thought. When a professor relies upon the Socratic method, there is typically more than one "correct" answer, and more often, no clear answer at all. The primary goal of the Socratic method in the law school setting is to explore difficult legal issues and to teach students the critical thinking skills they will need as lawyers. This method encourages students to go beyond memorizing the facts of a case and instead to focus on the application of legal rules to different fact patterns. A cynical definition of the Socratic method is that it is a "game of 'hide the ball' in which the professor asks questions that he knows the answers to while his students do not. The object of the game is to produce the answer that the professor thinks is correct. If the student fails to answer correctly, personal humiliation follows in various forms."[69]

POP CULTURE

Hollywood Law School

Two major Hollywood films have portrayed the rigors of law school in general and the Socratic method of instruction in particular. *The Paper Chase*, a 1973 film starring John Houseman and Timothy Bottoms, contains several scenes depicting the Socratic method. The first day of class Professor Kingsfield (played by Houseman) promptly begins by questioning a new first-year student, James Hart (played by Bottoms):

Credit: Archive Photos/Stringer

Kingsfield: Mr. Hart, would you recite for us the facts of Hawkins versus McGee? I do have your name right? You are Mr. Hart?

Hart: Yes, my name's Hart.

Kingsfield: You're not speaking loud enough, Mr. Hart. Will you speak up?

Hart:	Yes, my name's Hart.
Kingsfield:	Mr. Hart, you're still not speaking loud enough. Will you stand? Now that you're on your feet, Mr. Hart, maybe the class will be able to understand you. You are on your feet?
Hart:	Yes, I'm on my feet.
Kingsfield:	Loudly, Mr. Hart. Fill the room with your intelligence! Now, will you give us the facts of the case?
Hart:	I haven't read the case.
Kingsfield:	The class assignments for the first day are posted on the bulletin board in Langdell and Austin Halls. You must have known that?
Hart:	No.
Kingsfield:	You assumed this first class would be a lecture, an introduction to the course.
Hart:	Yes, sir.
Kingsfield:	Never assume anything in my classroom. Mr. Hart, I will myself, give you the facts of the case.

Kingsfield explains the nature and purpose of the Socratic method:

In my classroom, there is always another question. Another question to follow your answer. You're on a treadmill. My little questions spin the tumblers of your mind. You're on an operating table. My little questions are the fingers probing your brain. We do brain surgery here. You teach yourselves the law, but I train your mind. You come in here with a skull full of mush and you leave thinking like a lawyer.

Hart's expressions make it clear that he feels like he may be in over his head.

A similar scene takes place in *Legally Blonde*, a 2001 film starring Reese Witherspoon as Elle Woods, an improbable first-year Harvard Law student. On Woods's first day of class, Professor Stromwell, played by Holland Taylor, questions her while the other students, including Woods's rival Vivian Kensington (played by Selma Blair), look on:

Stromwell:	Now, I assume all of you have read pages . . . and are now well versed in subject matter jurisdiction. Who can tell us about Gordon v. Steele? Let's call on someone from the hot zone. Elle Woods?
Woods:	Actually, I wasn't aware that we had an assignment.
Stromwell:	Vivian Kensington. Do you think it's acceptable that Ms. Woods is not prepared?
Kensington:	I don't.
Stromwell:	Would you support my decision to ask her to leave class and to return only when she is prepared?
Kensington:	Absolutely.

Woods awkwardly exits the room. Like Hart in *The Paper Chase*, Woods is made aware that law school can be a tough and bewildering environment.

In the end, both James Hart and Elle Woods master the Socratic method teaching technique and ultimately law school. Overcoming the odds, both become top students—despite the typical Hollywood distraction of love interests who complicate their drive to succeed. While both films are, to some extent, caricatures of the law school experience, they provide a glimpse into what law school is like. Of course there is no substitute for personal experience and prospective law students are well advised to take an undergraduate constitutional law course and sit in on an actual law school class. Law schools welcome inquiries from prospective students and often even have specific days set aside each semester for prospective students to visit campus and attend a class.

There has been a debate over the merits of the Socratic method virtually since it origi-nated. Proponents argue that it forces students to be prepared. If students know they may be called on in class and put on the spot in front of everyone, they are much more likely to read and have an understanding of the material. Also, when the Socratic method is in use, students are forced to think fast and speak publicly, whether they want to or not. Further, by using the Socratic method, a professor is able to teach legal reasoning effectively to a large class. "Students learn legal analysis by doing it, either in their own minds or in an oral exchange with the professor."[70] As one professor at the University of Chicago observes:

> One challenge for law professors is providing an environment of active learning for the students in large classes. A teaching strategy that includes calling on stu-dents without giving them prior notice is the best way I have found to foster critical thinking for all members of such a group. No student is certain before class whether she will be called on to discuss difficult issues or to respond to answers provided by one of her colleagues. She must therefore pay close attention to my discussions with other students so she will be ready to play a meaningful role. Furthermore, the Socratic Method places some responsibility on students to think about the ques-tions silently and participate actively on their own; the element of surprise provides a powerful incentive for them to meet that responsibility. It also encourages stu-dents to prepare for class, which will enable them to learn more from the Socratic dialogue that takes place. The objective is to inculcate in students the rigorous and critical analysis of the arguments that they hear, as well as the practice of assessing and revising their own ideas and approaches in light of new information or different reasoning.[71]

According to Phillip E. Arreda, a former Harvard Law School professor, students learn through the Socratic method what is material and relevant to the understand-ing of a legal problem.[72] Professor Elizabeth Garrett teaches her students "the habit of rigorous and critical analysis of the arguments they hear" and "to learn to reason by analogy" by using the Socratic method.[73] Professor Joseph Dickinson argues that participating "in the process of dialogue by question and answer teaches a student how to function in the legal process that dialogue mirrors. Students learn the law-yer's role by doing it. In this way, students exercise the skills necessary to perform that role and build an understanding of the law."[74] It is not just professors who are proponents of the Socratic method. One third-year law student had the following to say:

> I came to law school to become a lawyer, not just to learn the law. To do that, one must think like a lawyer. Thinking like a lawyer means having a strong grasp of analytical reasoning and the ability to make and defend an argument aloud and in public. To learn to think like a lawyer I need the Socratic method.[75]

Although there are many who extol the benefits of Socratic training, there are numer-ous critics as well. Some argue that it is cruel and psychologically abusive. Specifically, students are subjected to public ridicule if they give the wrong answer,[76] first-year law students feel anxious because they cannot tell which students' answers are right and which are wrong,[77] and it contributes to the dehumanization of law students.[78] Moreover, students feel anxiety because the questions are difficult by design and demand that students think rigorously and analytically.[79] One particularly interesting description of students' responses to the experience is as follows:

During the first year, the law students quickly divide into three groups:

The Active Participants: Overconfident geeks who compete with each other to take up the most airtime pointing out that before law school, when they were Fulbright Scholars, they thought of a question marginally relevant to today's discussion. . . . The Active Participants stop talking completely when first-semester grades come out and they get all *C*'s.

The Back Benchers: Cool dudes who "opt out" of law school's competitive culture and never prepare for class. They sit on the back row, rather than in their assigned seats, so the professor can't find them on the seating chart. . . .

The Terrified Middle Group: People who spend most of their time wondering what the hey is going on, and why don't the professors just tell us what the law is and stop playing "hide the ball" . . . ?[80]

One empirical study estimates that up to 40 percent of law students may experience depression or other problems due to the law school experience.[81] Legal scholar Duncan Kennedy characterizes the Socratic method experience as one where "the professor smil[es] quietly to himself as he prepares to lay [the student's] guts out on the floor yet once again, paternally."[82] Martha Kimes, a law student at Columbia Law School, describes her experience as follows:

The professor asks. You answer. He says, "But what about this? How do you reconcile your answer with this?" You dig deep within yourself and find a response. He then says, "Okay, so how about we twist the facts of the case around, then how would you respond?" This process is then repeated ad nauseam until, at some point, the professor has backed you into a corner and proved that you are nothing but a monumental idiot.[83]

Critics also argue that the Socratic method is especially harsh on women. For example, one study found that men consistently outperform women at the University of Pennsylvania Law School and they partially blame the Socratic method.[84] Specifically, the students at the law school took a survey regarding their views of gender and the law school experience. The study authors found the following:

[M]any women do not "engage" pedagogically with a methodology that makes them feel strange, alienated, and "delegitimated." These women describe a dynamic in which they feel that their voices were "stolen" from them during the first year. Some complain that they can no longer recognize their former selves, which have become submerged inside what one author has called an alienated "social male."[85]

Another study found that 25 percent of the females, compared with only 15 percent of the males, reported feeling a loss of confidence because of the Socratic method experience.[86]

Critics also argue that the Socratic method does not teach practical lawyering skills, instead focusing on the extraction of abstract legal principles. Specifically, the argument is that the real work of a lawyer is solving problems of clients, not exploring abstract legal principles and theories.[87] Thus, students trained by this method are not taught the skills that are necessary to be an effective lawyer. "[L]aw school leaves students unable to tend to the everyday tasks of lawyering because they have not learned the law, only *about* the law."[88]

Typical Law School Curriculum

Students in most law schools study the same core subjects during their first year, including contracts, torts, civil procedure, property, and criminal law. Some schools also offer constitutional law in the first year. Additionally, most law schools require students to take a legal research and writing class in the first year. Some law schools do not follow the traditional curriculum, however. For example, at Georgetown University Law School, students have the option of selecting a first-year curriculum that focuses on history, philosophy, political theory, and economics. Still other schools offer joint-degree programs, such as a J.D. combined with a master's degree (J.D./MA), a master's of business administration (J.D./MBA), or a doctorate (J.D./PhD), that will change and often add to the coursework that students undertake. Furthermore, part-time and evening programs, while allowing students to work and go to school at the same time, generally lengthen the time it takes to complete a law degree from 3 years to 4. Less than half of ABA-approved law schools offer part-time programs and only 10 percent of first-year law students are enrolled part time. For nearly every law student, law school is a full-time endeavor.[89]

At most law schools, first-year classes are divided into multiple sections. The first-year classes combine the sections, with perhaps one or two courses containing just one section. For example, Table 2.4 depicts a sample schedule for Cornell Law School.

TABLE 2.4

Sample Schedule from Cornell Law School, Fall 2009, Section A

Monday		
10:10–11:05	Constitutional Law	Sections AEF
1:25–2:20	Property	Only Section A
Tuesday		
9:05–10:00	Civil Procedure	Sections AE
10:10–11:05	Constitutional Law	Sections AEF
1:25–2:20	Property	Only Section A
2:30–3:25	Lawyering	Only Section A
Wednesday		
10:10–11:05	Constitutional Law	Sections AEF
11:15–12:10	Contracts	Sections ADE
1:25–2:20	Property	Only Section A

(Continued)

TABLE 2.4
(Continued)

Thursday		
9:05–10:00	Civil Procedure	Sections AE
10:10–11:05	Constitutional Law	Sections AEF
1:25–2:20	Property	Only Section A
Friday		
9:05–10:00	Civil Procedure	Sections AE
10:10–11:05	Lawyering	Only Section A
11:15–12:10	Contracts	Sections ADE

At almost every law school, the bulk of the required courses are taken during the student's first year. However, there may be additional required courses that the student will take during the second year; for example, Professional Responsibility. Other than the few required courses, students can take a wide variety of elective courses. One myth is that students should take many bar exam subject-matter courses to help them prepare for the bar exam.[90] However, the reality is that whether there is a relationship between taking these courses and passing the bar exam is still open for debate.[91]

HOW DO WE KNOW?

Does Law School Curriculum Affect Bar Examination Passage?

In order to determine whether there is a relationship between taking law school courses on material that appears on the bar exam and passing the bar exam, legal scholar Douglas Rush and sociology professor Hisako Matsuo examined the performance of all graduates of the Saint Louis University School of Law who graduated between 2001 and 2005 and who took the Missouri bar examination for the first time.[92] There were 827 graduates who took the exam between February 2001 and February 2006. In addition to considering the number of elective, upper division, and bar examination subject-matter classes taken, other variables the scholars took into account included: sex, age, race, undergraduate grade point average (UGPA), LSAT score, Law School Admission Council (LSAC) index score (arrived at by using a formula that applies different weights to the LSAT and UGPA scores and combines the results), graduate's class rank (by quartile) at graduation, and whether the graduate ranked in the bottom 10 percent of his or her graduating class.

The results of a multivariate regression showed that there was a statistically significant relationship between the number of bar examination subject-matter classes taken and bar passage *only* for those graduates who ranked in the third quartile of their law school class. The mean difference in the number of those classes taken by those who passed and those who failed the bar exam for graduates in that quartile was less than one class. Additionally, the results of the study showed that there was no statistically significant relationship between the mean number of bar examination classes taken by graduates in the bottom 10 percent of their law school class who passed the bar exam versus those who failed the bar exam. "Whether taking one additional, upper division, bar examination subject-matter course will have a real world affect [*sic*] of improving bar examination passage rates is open to debate, particularly when the affect [*sic*] is limited to the third quartile of law school graduates."

Exams and Grading

Given their experience as undergraduate students, most uninitiated law students are used to their grades being determined on the basis of multiple components (for example, a combination of a midterm, a final exam, a paper assignment or two, class participation, and perhaps some quizzes or a service learning component). Students are familiar with navigating this sort of structure for evaluation and are usually comforted by the fact that poor performance on any one component will not doom them to failure in a course at the undergraduate level. They know the stakes might be considered higher in law school but nonetheless expect that their efforts over the course of each semester will pay off in the same way as they did in college. The myth that the procedure for evaluation of law students will be some variant of the procedure for evaluation of undergraduates is quickly punctured, however, by the reality that the traditional law school exam is worth 100 percent of the student's grade for the course.

Most often, this high stakes exam consists of a few essay questions the professor writes and can be divided into two types. The first type is the "issue-spotter" essay in which the professor writes a long hypothetical fact scenario in which the student needs to spot the issues and analyze them. The second type of essay question generally asks students to evaluate competing policies. In a hilarious law review article, law professor James D. Gordon III wrote:

> Studies have shown that the best way to learn is to have frequent exams on small amounts of material and to receive lots of feedback from the teacher. Consequently, law school does none of this. Anyone can learn under ideal conditions; law school is supposed to be an intellectual challenge. Therefore, law professors give only one exam, the FINAL EXAM OF THE LIVING DEAD, and they give absolutely no feedback before then. Actually, they give no feedback after then, either, because they don't return the exams to the students.[93]

As undergraduates, law school students were at least passingly familiar with grading curves. They understood them as a means for a professor to adjust grades to compensate for overly difficult exams, paper assignments, and the like. Law school professors also employ grading curves and, indeed, a majority of law schools impose a grading curve on all first-year classes as well as on some upper-level classes. These grading curves set defined, percentage-based limits on how many of each letter grade professors are permitted to assign to students.

For example, Seattle University School of Law has a policy that states: "In all first year courses, with the exception of Legal Writing, the following grade curve is mandatory. In all upper level, multiple section courses taught by more than one professor in the same year, the following grade curve is presumptive."[94] The grading curve requires that 15 to 25 percent of grades are *A-* or above and that, cumulatively: 40 to 50 percent are *B+* and above, 70 to 80 percent are *B* and above, 85 to 95 percent are *C+* and above, and 5 to 15 percent are *C* and below. At Northwestern University, a mandatory curve is applied to all courses with more than 40 enrolled students. Professors in such courses must distribute their grades as follows: *A+* (3–7 percent); *A* (12–15 percent); *A-* (10–15 percent); *B+* (15–30 percent); *B* (20–35 percent); *B-* (10–15 percent); *C+* (0–7.5 percent); *C* (0–7.5 percent); *D/F* (0–7 percent). These kinds of strict grade curves give lie to the myth that law students earn their final grades solely on the basis of their own performance. The reality is that they earn their final grades on the basis of their performance relative to that of their peers. Thus, the undergraduate who is familiar with earning grades based on his own performance or by curves that boost his grades will encounter the harsh law school reality of curves that may (and probably will) harm his grades.

Recently, several top schools have changed their grading policies, either moving away from letter grades or altering the grading curve, permitting professors greater discretion to assign more grades at the top of the curve. For example, Harvard Law School and Stanford Law School have switched from the traditional grade to pass/fail. The *New York Times* reported that Loyola Law School Los Angeles retroactively inflated its grades, adding 0.333 to every grade recorded in the last few years.[95] The goal was to make their students more attractive on the job market. Students at Loyola, for example, before the addition to the grades, had a mean first-year grade of 2.667 compared with the 3.0 or higher of other California schools. Thus, Loyola students were at a distinct disadvantage, especially for highly coveted judicial clerkships that have strict GPA cutoffs.

Extracurricular Activities

While course work certainly comprises the bulk of a law student's legal education, there are other academic programs in which students may engage during their law school years. Most law schools have one or more **law reviews:** scholarly journals that contain articles on the law.[96] Students edit these journals and student editors are generally chosen on the basis of class rank, though an increasing number of schools select editors based on writing competitions. Being selected for law review sends a signal to prospective employers that a law student is not only at the top of his or her class but is also a very good writer.[97] Further, there is some evidence that being a member of law review enhances the likelihood of serving as a clerk for a judge and is associated with an increased likelihood of a student going on to be a legal academic.[98]

In addition to law review, students can participate in a number of other extracurricular pursuits. Moot court competitions allow students to simulate appellate advocacy while mock trial competitions allow students to simulate trial advocacy.[99] Clinical and *pro bono* programs allow students to do actual or simulated legal work with clients and are supervised by faculty. For example, CUNY School of Law requires all third-year students to participate in one of six clinics (e.g., criminal defense, elder law, health law) or one of three concentrations (i.e., intensely supervised external placements in organizations such as the New York State Attorney General Office, the National Labor Relations Board, and the National Employment Law Project). Students can also join any number of organizations and groups such as the ABA Law Student Division;[100] the Asian, African American, Hispanic, and Native American law student associations; or the Federalist Society.[101]

ADMISSION TO THE BAR

Law students are understandably elated once the J.D. is in hand. That elation is likely short-lived, however, since the degree is a necessary but not sufficient credential for the practice of law. Like medicine, law is a profession regulated by state governments. In order to obtain a license to practice, law school graduates must apply to the state for bar admission. Each state has a board of bar examiners. In most states the board of bar examiners is an agency of the state court of last resort,[102] though it is sometimes controlled by the state's bar association. Each state sets its own rules about who can take the bar exam and when. In order to obtain a law license, prospective lawyers must meet two criteria. First, they must show competence to practice law. This generally entails possessing a law degree from an accredited school and passing the state's bar examination. The bar exam is virtually always a 2-day test.[103] The first day is the **Multistate Bar Exam (MBE)**: a standardized 200-question test covering constitutional law, contracts, criminal law, evidence, real property, and torts. The second day consists of essays covering local law on a broader range of subjects. However, an increasing number of states are relying on the Multistate Essay Examination and the Multistate Performance Test instead of the traditional second-day, locally crafted essays. Also, nearly every state requires applicants to pass the Multistate Professional Responsibility Examination. This separate test is offered three times each year.

In addition to demonstrating competence, the second criterion that future lawyers must meet involves character and fitness. As part of demonstrating good character and fitness, applicants are asked for a wealth of background information, including: educational background, school disciplinary actions, employment history, employment misconduct and discharge, involvement in any legal proceedings, neglect of financial responsibilities, motor vehicle violations, any military discharge other than honorable, acts involving dishonesty (fraud, deceit, or misrepresentation), making false statements, and violating court orders. Many states also address mental and chemical or psychological dependency matters. Applicants are understandably nervous about the character and fitness check but each of these areas is qualified by bar examiners by considering the reliability of the information, the applicant's age at the time of occurrence, how recent or serious the conduct was, the circumstances and underlying factors of the occurrence, evidence of rehabilitation, and positive social contributions made by the applicant since the conduct. One of the key qualifiers is the applicant's candor regarding the issue. Applicants who do not fully disclose or otherwise misrepresent past conduct have the most difficulty passing the character and fitness check.

Applicants generally start the bar application process in their final year of law school, though some states begin the process earlier in order to permit more time for the character and fitness check. The cost of the exam varies considerably. For example, the cost is $250 in Indiana but $850 in Illinois.[104] In New York, the fee is $250 for most candidates but $750 for those who qualify to take the bar but studied law in a foreign country.[105] The test may be taken in February or July, with most choosing the latter as it falls after graduation. Each state has different rules for how many times an applicant can take the exam should he or she fail all or part of it the first time. Most states have no limit (e.g., California, Florida, Illinois, Massachusetts, New York, Pennsylvania, and Wisconsin). All other states allow test takers to repeat the exam between three and five times with the exception of Iowa, which only allows two attempts, and Idaho, Utah, and Puerto Rico, each of which permit six attempts. So, Vinny Gambini, played by Joe Pesci in the classic 1992 film *My Cousin Vinny*, could not have secured admission to the bar in Iowa but could have done so in Idaho since it took him six tries to pass the bar exam![106]

Many operate under the mistaken assumption that law students must take the bar exam and practice law in the state in which they attended law school. However, a degree from any ABA-approved law school (regardless of location) will meet any state's education requirement for eligibility to take the bar exam. Hence, a student at an ABA-approved law school outside of New York may still sit for the New York bar exam. Some states, however, allow for other forms of legal education to substitute for a law degree from an ABA-approved school.[107] The most common substitute is a non-ABA approved law school degree. These schools may be state approved or not, and they may offer traditional face-to-face or online instruction. Instead of obtaining a law school education, some states allow those who have obtained their education through studying at a law office to become licensed attorneys. For example, California allows prospective attorneys

Image 2.7 Pennsylvania
Law School
University of Pennsyl-
vania Law School, ca.
1900. Despite its loca-
tion in Philadelphia,
Pennsylvania, most of its
graduates take the New
York state bar exam.
Prints and Photographs
Division, Library of Con-
gress, Washington, D.C.

to attend 2 years of college, obtain 4 years of law-office study, and take a First-Year Law
Students' Examination after the first year in a law office.

While most lawyers practice law in the same state in which they obtained their law
degree, there are many lawyers who choose to leave for a different state after graduation.
For example, most law students who attend Yale Law School in Connecticut and Harvard
Law School in Massachusetts choose to sit for the New York state bar exam. This is not
surprising, of course, as there are many more jobs for attorneys in New York than in those
states and particularly so for graduates of those schools, which are consistently ranked
among the top in the nation. Also sitting for the New York bar are most students from
American University (D.C.), George Washington University (D.C.), Georgetown Univer-
sity (D.C.), Duke University (North Carolina), Vanderbilt University (Tennessee), Uni-
versity of Vermont, University of Virginia, University of Pennsylvania, and University of
Michigan. Other law schools where most students sit for bar exams out-of-state include
Creighton in Nebraska (whose students generally practice in Iowa), Notre Dame in Indiana (whose students generally practice in Illinois), and Widener in Delaware (whose students generally practice in Pennsylvania).

In general, lawyers may only practice in the state in which they hold bar membership.[108]
However, many states allow "admission by motion" for lawyers who have been admitted
to another state's bar and have practiced for a number of years. Out-of-state lawyers who
need to litigate a specific case in another state may petition that state's courts for temporary bar admission for the length of the case. Many states even allow advanced law students to practice when under the supervision of a licensed attorney, often as part of the

law school curriculum. Indeed, that is how *Legally Blonde*'s Elle Woods was permitted to represent accused murderer Brooke Taylor-Windham at trial despite the fact that she was still in law school. Fortunately for Brooke (a well-regarded fitness instructor) Elle was able to secure a courtroom confession from Brooke's stepdaughter without having to reveal where Brook was the day of the murder (having liposuction). On a more serious note, at the federal level, attorneys generally have to be licensed to practice in the state in which the federal district court is located.

Bar associations are the professional membership organizations for attorneys. Each state has its own bar association and, as we have discussed, admittance to the bar is required for attorneys who practice in the state. There are many other national, local, and special-interest bar associations to which attorneys may choose to belong. These groups seek to promote professionalism and legal education among their members and for the public. With nearly 400,000 members, the American Bar Association is the largest of these voluntary organizations. It sponsors programs, research, and conferences on topics ranging from law reform to judicial selection. There are numerous national, state, and local bar associations also that focus on specific groups and interests such as the National Conference of Women's Bar Associations, National Bar Association (originally established in 1925 as the Negro Bar Association), Hispanic National Bar Association, National Asian Pacific American Bar Association, and the National Native American Bar Association.

CONCLUSION

Prospective law students are eager to begin learning the law. They take pre-law courses as undergraduates, not realizing that those courses are often designed for purposes other than to teach them the law. They also compete with other students on their campuses for the best grades and top student leadership positions. They continue competing, this time with students on other campuses, for high LSAT scores, admission to top law schools, and for scholarship dollars. Some earn scores in the 160s, choose among top-tier schools, and have admissions offices bidding for their acceptances, while others struggle to score 150, settle for fourth-tier or non-ABA-approved law schools, and take on considerable debt. Students are quite familiar with competition and hierarchy before they ever step foot in law school.

Once in law school, students do not learn the substance of the law that they expect. Instead they learn how to think, speak, and write like lawyers. They compete with their classmates for high class rankings, invitations to law review and moot court, summer associate positions, and ultimately jobs. Some finish at the top of their classes from prestigious law schools, make law review, have their pick of jobs, and pass the bar on their first try while others struggle to graduate, find it difficult to get jobs that require law degrees or that pay relatively well, and take the bar exam multiple times, if at all. The myth that all lawyers are created equal is plainly tempered by the reality that the legal education process is highly competitive and most prospective attorneys find their place in the hierarchy very early. In the next chapter we will further explicate the myth that all lawyers are created equal through a discussion of lawyers and law practice.

Suggested Readings

James D. Gordon, III. "How Not to Succeed in Law School," *Yale Law Journal*, 100 (6): 1679–1706 (1991). This law review article provides humorous insights into surviving law school, which has attained cult status. The author expands this essay in the book *Law School: A Survivor's Guide* (New York, NY: Harper Perennial, 1994).

Kimes, Martha. *Ivy Briefs: True Tales of a Neurotic Law Student* (New York, NY: Simon & Schuster, 2007). This memoir written by a Columbia Law School student chronicles all 3 years of her law school experience.

Peter F. Lake. "When Fear Knocks: The Myths and Realities of Law School," *Stetson Law Review*, vol. 29, no. 4 (Spring 2000): 1015–1056. This law review article describes 22 myths about, and then discusses, the realities of law school.

Jeffrey Evans Stake. "The Interplay between Law School Rankings, Reputations, and Resource Allocations: Ways Rankings Mislead," *Indiana Law Journal*, vol. 81, no. 1 (Winter 2006): 229–270. This law review article discusses the problems created by the annual rankings of law schools published by the *U.S. News & World Report*.

Robert Stevens. *Law School: Legal Education from the 1850s to the 1980s* (Chapel Hill, NC: University of North Carolina Press, 1983). This book provides a comprehensive history of legal education in America, specifically examining the law school institution and its impact on the legal profession and society.

Scott Turow. *One L: The Turbulent True Story of a First Year at Harvard Law School* (New York, NY: Farrer, Straus and Giroux, 1977). This book chronicles Scott Turow's first year at Harvard Law School, providing both comedic and dramatic insights on the pressures of law school life.

Endnotes

1   Quoted in Sen. Omer Rains, *Back to the Summit: How One Man Defied Death & Paralysis to Again Lead a Full Life of Service to Others* (New York, NY: Morgan James, 2011): 52.

2   Quoted in Nick Ross, *Crime: How to Solve It—And Why So Much of What We're Told Is Wrong* (London, UK: Biteback, 2013).

3   Adapted from Charles M. Fox, *Working with Contracts: What Law School Doesn't Teach You*, Second Edition (New York, NY: Practicing Law Institute, 2008).

4   See, for example, William M. Sullivan, Anne Colby, Judith Welch Wegner, Lloyd Bond, and Lee S. Shulman, *Education Lawyers: Preparation for the Profession of Law* (San Francisco, CA: Jossey-Bass, 2007).

5   Center for Postsecondary Research, Indiana University, *Law School Survey of Student Engagement*, (http://lssse.iub.edu/pdf/2011/2011_LSSSE_Annual_Survey_Results.pdf): 8.

6   Quoted in "Has Legal Education Gone the Way of the Auto Industry?" *NALP Bulletin* (February 2010).

7   "The Inns of Court are a unique learning tradition [in England], a combination of educational institution, boarding facility, and professional association;" Brian J. Moline, "Early American Legal Education," *Washburn Law Journal*, vol. 42, no. 4 (Spring 2003): 775–802, 775. There are currently four Inns of Court in England: Lincoln's Inn, Gray's Inn, Inner Temple, and Middle Temple; J. H. Baker, *The Common Law Tradition: Lawyers, Books and the Law* (London, UK: Hambledon and London, 2003): 3.

8   A. A. Berle, Jr., "Legal Profession and Legal Education," in *The Legal Profession: Responsibility and Regulation*, Geoffrey C. Hazard, Jr. and Deborah L. Rhode, eds (Westbury, NY: Foundation Press, 1988): 9. In the English legal system, as well as in many other common law systems, the legal profession is split between barristers (lawyers who specialize in courtroom advocacy and the drafting of legal pleadings) and soliciters (lawyers who specialize in the handling of day-to-day legal matters for clients).

9   Lawrence Friedman, *A History of American Law* (New York, NY: Simon and Schuster, 1973).

10 Examples of the legal treatises that might have been read include Sir William Blackstone's *Commentaries on the Laws of England* and Associate Justice Joseph Story's *Commentaries on the Constitution of the United States*.

11 Robert Stevens, *Law School: Legal Education from the 1850s to the 1980s* (Chapel Hill, NC: University of North Carolina Press, 1983): 3.

12 Though much of this menial work involved copying legal documents by hand (e.g., deeds, wills, mortgages), it often also involved general housekeeping (e.g., sweeping, stacking firewood) in the

office. See Brian J. Moline, "Early American Legal Education," *Washburn Law Journal*, vol. 42, no. 4 (Spring 2003): 775–802, 781.

13 Lawrence Friedman, *A History of American Law* (New York, NY: Simon and Schuster, 1973): 279.

14 Among the notables who studied with Reeve were three Supreme Court justices, three vice presidents, six members of the Cabinet, 14 governors, 34 state court of last resort judges, and 101 members of Congress; Albert J. Harno, *Legal Education in the United States* (San Francisco, CA: Bancroft-Whitney, 1952): 31.

15 Litchfield ceased operations in 1833 but during its existence was focused exclusively on the actual practice of the law; Brian J. Moline, "Early American Legal Education," *Washburn Law Journal*, vol. 42, no. 4 (Spring 2003): 775–802, 795–796.

16 The United States is a notable exception in this regard. The last LL.B. was awarded by Yale Law School in 1971. See David Perry, "How Did Lawyers Become 'Doctors'?" *New York State Bar Journal*, vol. 84, no. 5 (June 2012): 20–24.

17 Robert Stevens, *Law School: Legal Education in America from the 1850s to the 1980s* (Chapel Hill, NC: University of North Carolina Press, 1987): 7.

18 Anthony T. Kronman, ed., *History of the Yale Law School: The Tercentennial Lectures* (New Haven, CT: Yale University Press, 2004).

19 Jeffrey D. Jackson, "Socrates and Langdell in Legal Writing: Is the Socratic Method a Proper Tool for Legal Writing Courses?" *California Western Law Review*, vol. 43, no. 2 (Spring 2007): 267–308, 270.

20 Socrates the Greek philosopher is the eponym of the Socratic method. Socrates, as portrayed by Plato, was prone to engage his intellectual opponents in a dialogue consisting of a series of questions, with the answer to one question leading into the posing of another question, each designed to tease out the nuances and implications of a given line of reasoning.

21 Susan H. Williams, "Legal Education, Feminist Epistemology, and the Socratic Method," *Stanford Law Review*, vol. 45, no. 6 (July 1993): 1571–1576, 1573.

22 Jeffrey D. Jackson, "Socrates and Langdell in Legal Writing: Is the Socratic Method a Proper Tool for Legal Writing Courses?" *California Western Law Review*, vol. 43, no. 2 (Spring 2007): 267–308, 270.

23 Lawrence Friedman, *A History of American Law* (New York, NY: Simon and Schuster, 1973): 607.

24 The AALS was established in 1900, with 32 law schools as charter members. Those 32 schools accounted for approximately half of the law school students at that time. Association of American Law Schools, "What is the AALS?" http://www.aals.org/about.php.

25 The AALS and ABA's role in law school accreditation looms ever larger but is not without its critics. In particular, some have argued that the rules and standards relied upon by the AALS and ABA in the accreditation process homogenize legal education such that "the law school world [is] a less diverse place than it otherwise would be. The regulations [of the AALS and ABA] represent the conceit that the regulators can tell everyone what type of legal education is right for them— and that the answer is pretty much the same for everyone, regardless of background, of interest, of goals;" Ronald A. Cass, "So, Why Do You Want to Be a Lawyer? What the ABA, the AALS, and the *U.S. News* Don't Know that We Do," *University of Toledo Law Review*, vol. 31, no. 4 (Summer 2000): 573–579, 577.

26 "Law schools consider a variety of factors in admitting their students. The two factors that all candidates present—prior academic performance and the LSAT score—are fundamental to the admission process;" Law School Admission Council and American Bar Association Section on Legal Education and Admissions to the Bar, *ABA-LSAC Official Guide to ABA-Approved Law Schools, 2013 Edition* (Newtown, PA: Law School Admission Council, 2012): 9.

27 Only four sections count toward the score while the fifth is an unscored section of experimental questions being pre-tested for a future exam. Additionally, the writing sample, administered at the end of the test, is not graded, but copies are sent to all law schools to which students apply.

28 The LSAT: LSAT Prep Materials (http://www.lsac.org/jd/lsat/preparing-for-the-lsat).

29 Perhaps the most well-known materials and prep courses are those offered by Kaplan and the Princeton Review. Other popular offerings include those from Testmasters and Powerscore. The

cost of prep courses can be quite significant, ranging from a few hundred dollars for some online packages to a few thousand dollars for personalized, in-person programs.

30 Allyson P. Mackey, Kirstie J. Whitaker, and Silvia Bunge, "Experience-Dependent Plasticity in White Matter Microstructure: Reasoning Training Alters Structural Connectivity," *Frontiers of Neuroanatomy*, vol. 6 (August 2012): 1–9.

31 Of these, 201 confer the J.D. while the remaining ABA-accredited law school (the U.S. Army Judge Advocate General's School) provides a specialized graduate program for officers.

32 According to the American Bar Association, UGPA is based on a 0–4.33 scale.

33 Jeffrey Evans Stake, "The Interplay between Law School Rankings, Reputations, and Resource Allocations: Ways Rankings Mislead," *Indiana Journal of Law*, vol. 81, no. 1 (Winter 2006): 229–270.

34 Ibid., 229–270, 232.

35 A correlation coefficient of 1.00 indicates exact positive correspondence between two measures; that is, increases in one measure correspond exactly to increases in the other measure.

36 Lisa C. Anthony, Susan P. Dalessandro, and Lynda M. Reese, "Predictive Validity of the LSAT: A National Summary of the 2011 and 2012 LSAT Correlation Studies," LSAC (2013).

37 See, for example, Susan Sturm and Lani Guinier, "The Future of Affirmative Action: Reclaiming the Innovative Ideal," *California Law Review*, vol. 84, no. 4 (July 1996): 953–1036; William C. Kidder, "The Rise of Testocracy: An Essay on the LSAT: Conventional Wisdom and the Dismantling of Diversity," *Texas Journal of Women and the Law*, vol. 9, no. 2 (Spring 2000): 167–217; William C. Kidder, "Does the LSAT Mirror or Magnify Racial and Ethnic Differences in Educational Attainment?: A Study of Equally Achieving 'Elite' College Students," *California Law Review*, vol. 89, no. 4 (July 2001): 1055–1124; William C. Kidder, "Affirmative Action Under Attack: The Struggle for Access from *Sweatt* to *Grutter*: A History of African American, Latino, and American Indian Law School Admissions, 1950–2000," *Harvard Blackletter Law Journal*, vol. 19, no. 1 (Spring 2003): 1–41.

38 Frank L. Schmidt and John E. Hunter, "The Validity and Utility of Selection Methods in Personnel Psychology: Practical and Theoretical Implications of 85 Years of Research Findings," *Psychological Bulletin*, vol. 124, no. 2 (September 1998): 262–274; Linda F. Wightman, "The Threat to Diversity in Legal Education: An Empirical Analysis of the Consequences of Abandoning Race as a Factor in Law School Admission Decisions," *New York University Law Review*, vol. 72, no. 1 (April 1997): 1–53.

39 Linda F. Wightman, "The Threat to Diversity in Legal Education: An Empirical Analysis of the Consequences of Abandoning Race as a Factor in Law School Admission Decisions," *New York University Law Review*, vol. 72, no. 1 (April 1997): 1–53.

40 American Bar Association, "First Year and Total J.D. Enrollment by Gender, 1947–2011" (http://www.americanbar.org/content/dam/aba/administrative/legal_education_and_admissions_to_the_bar/statistics/jd_enrollment_1yr_total_gender.authcheckdam.pdf).

41 American Bar Association, "J.D. Enrollment by School" (http://www.americanbar.org/groups/legal_education/resources/statistics.html).

42 William C. Kidder, "Does the LSAT Mirror or Magnify Racial and Ethnic Differences in Educational Attainment?: A Study of Equally Achieving 'Elite' College Students," *California Law Review*, vol. 89, no. 4 (July 2001): 1055–1124.

43 Ibid., Table 1.

44 Ibid., Table 3.

45 Ibid., 1055–1124, 1123.

46 Vivia Chen, "Women Spurn Law Schools," *thecareerist*.com, May 16, 2011.

47 Ibid.

48 Ibid.

49 Amy Farmer, "Are Young Women Turning Their Backs on Law School?" *Perspectives* vol. 18, no. 4 (Spring 2010): 4–7.

50 American Bar Association, "First-Year and Total JD Minority" (http://www.americanbar.org/groups/legal_education/resources/statistics.html).

51 See, for example, William C. Kidder, "Situating Asian Pacific Americans in the Law School Affirmative Action Debate: Empirical Facts about Thernstrom's Rhetorical Acts," *Asian Law Journal*, vol. 7 (December 2000): 29–68.

52 See, for example, Richard O. Lempert, David L. Chambers, and Terry K. Adams, "Michigan's Minority Graduates in Practice: The River Runs through Law School," *Law and Social Inquiry*, vol. 25, no. 2 (Spring 2010): 395–505, and the associated commentary included in that particular volume of the journal.

53 *Regents of the University of California v. Bakke*, 438 U.S. 265 (1978).

54 *Grutter v. Bollinger*, 539 U.S. 306 (2003).

55 The use of race as "plus" factor was being considered yet by the Court in *Fisher v. Univerity of Texas*, 570 U.S. ___ , 133 S. Ct. 2411(2013). In its ruling in that case, dealing with admissions policy at the University of Texas at Austin, the Court sent the case back to the lower court, asserting that the lower court had not applied the appropriate standard of review as established by *Regents of the University of California v. Bakke* and *Grutter v. Bollinger*. The lower court subsequently found in favor of the University.

56 See, for example, Lee Bollinger, "Seven Myths about Affirmative Action in Universities," *Willamette Law Review*, vol. 38, no. 4 (Fall 2002): 535–546.

57 Center for Postsecondary Research, Indiana University, *Law School Survey of Student Engagement* (http://lssse.iub.edu/pdf/2011/2011_LSSSE_Annual_Survey_Results.pdf): 8.

58 Ibid., 9.

59 American Bar Association, "Law School Tuition, 1985–2011" (http://www.americanbar.org/content/dam/aba/administrative/legal_education_and_admissions_to_the_bar/statistics/ls_tuition.authcheckdam.pdf).

60 Brian Z. Tamanaha, *Failing Law Schools* (Chicago, IL: University of Chicago Press, 2012): 108.

61 American Bar Association, "Average Amount Borrowed for Law School, 2001–2010" (http://www.americanbar.org/content/dam/aba/administrative/legal_education_and_admissions_to_the_bar/statistics/avg_amnt_brwd.authcheckdam.pdf).

62 William D. Henderson and Rachel M. Zahorsky, "The Law School Bubble: How Long Will It Last If Law Grads Can't Pay Bills?" *ABA Journal*, January 1, 2012.

63 Center for Postsecondary Research, Indiana University, *Law School Survey of Student Engagement* (http://lssse.iub.edu/pdf/2011/2011_LSSSE_Annual_Survey_Results.pdf): 9.

64 Peter F. Lake, "When Fear Knocks: The Myths and Realities of Law School," *Stetson Law Review*, vol. 29, no. 4 (Spring 2000): 1015–1056, 1022.

65 See, for example, Martha Kimes, *Ivy Briefs: True Tales of a Neurotic Law Student* (New York, NY: Simon & Schuster, 2007).

66 The term "black letter law" is often used interchangeably with "hornbook law." Hornbooks are summaries of the law in particular areas, generally intended as a primer for law school students.

67 Orin S. Kerr, "The Decline of the Socratic Method at Harvard," *Nebraska Law Review*, vol. 78, no. 1 (1999): 113–134, 114.

68 "Most law professor have their own understanding of what the Socratic method means. . . . For many professors, the term 'Socratic' describes a question and answer method in which the professor asks a series of questions of the students, uncovering both preconceptions and cogent legal analysis," Steven I. Friedland, "How We Teach: A Survey of Teaching Techniques in American Law Schools," *Seattle University Law Review*, vol. 20, no. 1 (Fall 1996): 1–28, n. 77.

69 Jennifer L. Rosato, "The Socratic Method and Women Law Students: Humanize, Don't Feminize," *Southern California Review of Law and Women's Studies*, vol. 7, no. 1 (Fall 1997): 37–62, 43.

70 Orin S. Kerr, "The Decline of the Socratic Method at Harvard," *Nebraska Law Review*, vol. 78, no. 1 (1999): 113–134, 116.

71 "The Socratic Method (Green Bag Article)," University of Chicago Law School (http://www.law.uchicago.edu/socrates/soc_article.html).

72 Phillip E. Areeda, "The Socratic Method," *Harvard Law Review*, vol. 109, no. 5 (March 1996): 911–922.

73 "The Socratic Method (Green Bag Article)," University of Chicago Law School (http://www.law.uchicago.edu/socrates/soc_article.html).

74 Joseph A. Dickinson, "Understanding the Socratic Method in Law School Teaching after the Carnegie Foundation's *Educating Lawyers*," *Western New England Law Review*, vol. 31, no. 1 (2009): 97–113, 111.

75 Ann Marie Pedersen, "In Defense of the Oft-Maligned Socratic Method," *National Law Journal*, September 11, 2006.

76 Marina Angel, "Women in Legal Education: What It's Like to Be Part of a Perpetual First Wave or the Case of the Disappearing Woman," *Temple Law Review*, vol. 61, no. 3 (1988): 799–846.

77 Lawrence Silver, "Anxiety and the First Semester of Law School," *Wisconsin Law Review*, vol. 1968, no. 4 (1968): 1201–1218.

78 Maria L. Ciampi, "The I and Thou: A New Dialogue for the Law," *University of Cincinnati Law Review*, vol. 58 (1990): 881–907.

79 Ruta K. Stropus, "Mend It, Bend It, and Extend It: The Fate of Traditional Law School Methodology in the 21st Century," *Loyola University Chicago Law Journal*, vol. 27 (Spring 1996): 449–489.

80 James D. Gordon, III, "How Not to Succeed in Law School," *Yale Law Journal*, vol. 100, no. 6 (April 1991): 1679–1706, 1686–1687.

81 Cathleen A. Roach, "A River Runs through It: Tapping into the Informational Stream to Move Students from Isolation to Autonomy," *Arizona Law Review*, vol. 36 (Fall 1994): 667–699.

82 Duncan Kennedy, "How the Law School Fails: A Polemic," *Yale Review of Law and Social Action*, vol. 1 (Spring 1970): 71–91, 75.

83 Martha Kimes, *Ivy Briefs: True Tales of a Neurotic Law Student* (New York, NY: Simon & Schuster, 2007): 41.

84 Lani Guinier, Michelle Fine, Jane Balin, Ann Bartow, and Deborah Lee Stachel, "Becoming Gentlemen: Women's Experiences at One Ivy League Law School," *University of Pennsylvania Law Review*, vol. 143, no. 1 (November 1994): 1–110.

85 Ibid., 1–110, 4.

86 Joan M. Krauskopf, "Touching the Elephant: Perceptions of Gender Issues in Nine Law Schools," *Journal of Legal Education*, vol. 44, no. 1 (1994): 311–340.

87 Orin S. Kerr, "The Decline of the Socratic Method at Harvard," *Nebraska Law Review*, vol. 78, no. 1 (1999): 113–134.

88 Ruta K. Stropus, "Mend It, Bend It, and Extend It: The Fate of Traditional Law School Methodology in the 21st Century," *Loyola University Chicago Law Journal*, vol. 27 (Spring 1996): 449–489, 461–462.

89 *ABA-LSAC Official Guide to ABA-Approved Law Schools: 2012 Edition* (Newtown, PA: Law School Admission Council, 2011) (http://www.americanbar.org/content/dam/aba/publications/misc/legal_education/2012_official_guide_for_web.authcheckdam.pdf).

90 Douglas K. Rush and Hisako Matsuo, "Does Law School Curriculum Affect Bar Examination Passage? An Empirical Analysis of Factors Related to Bar Examination Passage During the Years 2001 and 2006 at a Midwestern Law School," *Journal of Legal Education*, vol. 57, no. 2 (June 2007): 224–236.

91 Ibid.

92 Ibid.

93 James D. Gordon, III, "How Not to Succeed in Law School," *Yale Law Journal*, vol. 100, no. 6 (April 1991): 1679–1706, 1692.

94 Seattle University School of Law, (http://www.law.seattleu.edu/Academics/Curriculum/Grading.xml).

95 Catherine Rampell, "In Law Schools, Grades Go Up, Just Like That," *New York Times*, June 21, 2010.

96 Law reviews have been the target of a great deal of criticism. In particular, some have argued that the selection of articles for publication is idiosyncratic because it relies on the judgment of often inexperienced law school students rather than the judgment of expert referees. Further, critics have argued that law review editors focus on the minutiae of citations and academic writing style rather than on the substance of the articles submitted. See, for example, Richard A. Posner, "The Future of the Student-Edited Law Review," *Stanford Law Review*, vol. 47 (Summer 1995): 1131–1138.

97 E. Joshua Rosenkranz, "Law Review's Empire," *Hastings Law Journal*, vol. 39, no. 4 (April 1988): 859–926.

98   Dexter Samida, "The Value of Law Review Membership," *University of Chicago Law Review*, vol. 71, no. 4 (Autumn 2004): 1721–1748.

99   Some have questioned the value of moot court, however, finding it too far removed from an actual courtroom experience to teach useful advocacy skills. See, for example, Alex Kozinski, "In Praise of Moot Court—Not!" *Columbia Law Review*, vol. 97, no. 1 (January 1997): 178–197.

100   Membership in the ABA Law Student Division provides access to benefits such as eligibility for ABA writing competitions, judicial internships, and clerkships, as well as subscriptions to the *ABA Journal* and *Student Lawyer* magazine (http://www.americanbar.org/groups/law_students/membership.html).

101   The Federalist Society is a conservative organization that advocates for textualist interpretations of the Constitution and includes divisions for students, faculty, and attorneys (http://www.fed-soc.org/).

102   For example, the State Bar of California is a public corporation located in the judicial branch of the state government and is considered to be an arm of the California Supreme Court.

103   The grueling nature of the standard bar exam (as well as the intensive, often expensive, preparation for taking it that is necessary) have been the subject of much criticism. Critics have also argued, among other things, that the bar exam is an inadequate test of professional competence and has a disparate effect on racial and ethnic minorities. See, for example, Kristin Booth Glen, "When and Where We Enter: Rethinking Admission to the Legal Profession," *Columbia Law Review*, vol. 106 (October 2002): 1696–1740. See, also, William C. Kidder, "The Bar Examination and the Dream Deferred: A Critical Analysis of the MBE, Social Closure, and Racial and Ethnic Stratification," *Law & Social Inquiry*, vol. 29, no. 3 (Summer 2004): 547–589.

104   Student Lawyer, "Bar Exam Directory" (http://www.americanbar.org/publications/student_lawyer/2012–13/nov/2012_2013_bar_exam_directory.html).

105   Ibid.

106   The 2007 documentary film *A Lawyer Walks into a Bar* provides a fascinating perspective on the bar exam. It follows six individuals who struggle to prepare for and pass the California Bar Exam, including one working father who never had sufficent time to prepare and, as a consequence, failed the bar exam 42 times before giving up.

107   For a detailed overview of state legal education requirements, see Erica Moeser and Claire Huismann, eds., "Comprehensive Guide to Bar Admission Requirements, 2012," a joint publication of the National Conference of Bar Examiners and the ABA Section of Legal Education and Admission to the Bar (http://www.ncbex.org/assets/media_files/Comp-Guide/CompGuide.pdf).

108   States in which bar membership is mandatory for the practice of law are said to have an integrated bar. The American Judicature Society began vociferously advocating in favor of the integrated bar beginning in the early twentieth century. Bar unification is intended to enhance the status and professionalism of the legal profession. See, for example, Terry Radtke, "The Last Stage in Reprofessionalizing the Bar: The Wisconsin Bar Integration Movement, 1934–1956," *Marquette Law Review*, vol. 81 (Summer 1998), 1001–1027.

3

THE LEGAL PROFESSION
Lawyers and the Practice of Law

"It is the trade of lawyers to question everything, yield nothing, and talk by the hour."

—Thomas Jefferson, Third President of the United States[1]

"If there were no bad people, there would be no good lawyers."

—Charles Dickens, Social Critic and English Novelist[2]

D r. Milton "Mike" Horowitz was an educated man. He was a World War II veteran, earned a Ph.D. in clinical psychology, worked as the chief psychologist at the University Hospital of Western Reserve in Cleveland, served as the director of professional education at the Reiss-Davis Child Study Center, and was a founding member of the Los Angeles Institute and Society for Psychoanalytic Studies. A smoker since his days in the military, it was not exactly a surprise when Dr. Horowitz was diagnosed with cancer. What was unusual, however, was the type of cancer with which he was diagnosed: mesothelioma. Mesothelioma is a rare form of cancer that develops from cells comprising the protective lining of the human body's internal organs, especially the outer lining of the lungs. There is a very specific profile associated with mesothelioma patients; virtually all such patients have been exposed to asbestos. While asbestos is a naturally occurring substance and mesothelioma is more common in populations located near naturally occurring asbestos,[3] the major risk factor for mesothelioma is working with asbestos (e.g., shipyard workers, heating and construction workers, those employed in the manufacture of asbestos products).[4] There was no evidence of occupational exposure in Dr. Horowitz's case. However, he did claim to have smoked Kent Micronite cigarettes, which had an asbestos filter, and that was the basis of the lawsuit he filed against the Lorillard Tobacco Company, the manufacturer of Kent cigarettes.[5]

The credibility of witnesses is always important in a trial but the credibility of Dr. Horowitz was perhaps especially important in this trial as there was no corroborating evidence to support the plaintiff's testimony regarding his use of Kent Micronite cigarettes.[6] On the witness stand, Dr. Horowitz said he was certain about the timing of his use of Kent cigarettes because he made the switch from unfiltered cigarettes on the recommendation of a doctor he worked with at Western Reserve Hospital. More importantly (as well as more poignantly), the distinctive blue color of the Kent filter was the same color as the eyes of his deceased and beloved father.

During cross-examination, Lorillard's lead trial attorney expended with any pleasantries and dove directly into a barrage of questions directed at Dr. Horowitz. The attorney asked about Dr. Horowitz's medical history. He asked about his history with smoking.

He asked about the side effects of his devastating disease. He asked questions designed to raise doubt about a person's ability to recall events clearly in hindsight. Then, out of the blue, the attorney circled back to the color of Dr. Horowitz's father's eyes. Producing a copy of the citizenship petition signed by Dr. Horowitz's father when his father immigrated to the United States from Austria in 1928, the attorney asked, "Did your father have brown eyes?" The petition clearly listed the eye color as brown. Dr. Horowitz, filled with emotion, responded, "That's what it says, but that's not true. Are you telling me that my father has brown eyes?" "All I'm telling you is that's what it says in this petition," was the attorney's rejoinder, leading Dr. Horowitz to mutter indignantly, "That's ridiculous."

This kind of real-life exchange comports with the common notion of lawyers as articulate (and crafty) advocates arguing eloquently on behalf of their clients before a judge and jury. Despite the fact that the witness, Dr. Horowitz, was a learned man, the tobacco company's trial attorney was able to call his memory into question through a seemingly unrelated issue—the color of his father's eyes. The implication of this line of questioning was plain: if Horowitz could not even recall the color of his father's eyes, how could he possibly recall the color of the filter of the cigarettes he smoked? The lesson of the Horowitz case is that legal disputes can be won or lost by skillful attorneys in the courtroom.

POP CULTURE

To Kill a Mockingbird

The 1962 film *To Kill a Mockingbird* depicts Atticus Finch (played by Gregory Peck, winner of an Academy Award for his performance in this role), a heroic small-town lawyer in the 1930s who is determined to defend a poor black man, Tom Robinson. Robinson, played by Brock Peters who went on to appear in *Star Trek* feature films and *Star Trek: Deep Space Nine*, is accused of having raped a white woman. In the aftermath of the alleged rape, tensions are high in fictional Maycomb, Alabama. Finch uses passion and reason in an attempt not just to sway jurors but also to convince a community that racial prejudice is wrong:

> To begin with, this case should never have come to trial. The state has not produced one iota of medical evidence that the crime Tom Robinson is charged with ever took place. . . . It has relied instead upon the testimony of two witnesses, whose evidence has not only been called into serious question on cross-examination but has been flatly contradicted by the defendant.

Ultimately, Finch demonstrates his wit and skill in what appears to be a kind of theatrical performance. He remains a heroic figure, despite the fact that the jury of racist men ultimately convict Robinson.

To be sure, some attorneys appear in court and some disputes are resolved in a courtroom—and on occasion that resolution is even due to the passionate advocacy of the attorney. Yet the vast majority of law work is done outside the courtroom and the vast majority of cases are settled or plea bargained before they reach the trial stage.[7] This means that the day-to-day job of the typical lawyer is one spent behind a desk, reading, writing, and talking on the phone negotiating. Indeed, if one considers all of the scenes that depict Atticus Finch in *To Kill a Mockingbird*, it is plain to see that lawyers spend most of their time outside of the courtroom. He interacts with others in the community regarding the case in his office, at the jail, around town, and at his home. For example, when Atticus is confronted outside the courtroom by Mr. Ewell, a virulent racist and the father of the woman who has accused Tom Robinson of raping her, Atticus explains, "I've been appointed to defend Tom Robinson and now that he's been charged, that's what I intend doing." In short, much of the work of an attorney—even one who regularly appears in a courtroom—is done outside rather than inside court.

The image of the passionate courtroom attorney is rife with dramatic potential. Think, for example, of Gregory Peck as small-town lawyer Atticus Finch, ardently defending an unjustly accused black man in the Jim Crow–era South in the 1962 movie adaptation of Harper Lee's *To Kill a Mockingbird*. Or, perhaps, of Sam Waterston as *Law & Order*'s Assistant District Attorney Jack McCoy of the New York District Attorney's Office, valiantly trying to persuade a jury to convict a criminal who thought she could get away with murder.

The reality, however, is that courtroom advocacy is not what most lawyers do and those who do regularly appear in court still spend more time working outside the courtroom than they do inside. A lawyer's major job is to provide information and advice to clients to minimize the likelihood of disputes evolving into lawsuits and to keep clients free from unwanted entanglements with government and other businesses and individuals. The primary task of the lawyer is negotiation, particularly negotiation with other lawyers, in an effort to reach settlements and compromises. As a consequence, most legal

MYTH AND REALITY OF LAWYERS AND LAW PRACTICE

MYTH	REALITY
Lawyers work in courtrooms: arguing cases before judges and juries.	Lawyers work in offices: sitting behind desks, reading, writing, and talking on the phone.
Law school graduates work as practicing attorneys.	While most law school graduates work as practicing attorneys, some work in jobs that do not require bar passage or even law degrees.
The legal profession is the province of older white males.	While older white males continue to dominate the profession, gender and racial diversity is on the rise.
Lawyers win or lose cases for their clients at trial.	Lawyers bargain and negotiate in an attempt to stay out of and settle disputes long before they reach trial.
Lawyers have broad knowledge of all legal matters.	Lawyers specialize and know a great deal about the relatively narrow area of the law in which they specialize.
The job of a lawyer is prestigious.	The prestige level of different law jobs varies greatly, with some lawyers holding positions that are far more prestigious than others.
Everyone is entitled to an attorney.	There is no absolute right to legal services and representation unless one is accused of a serious crime.
Lawyers are unhappy.	Lawyers are relatively satisfied.
Legal advice is costly and only the rich can afford attorneys.	Low- or no-cost legal services are available through the contingency fee system, clinics, legal insurance, and legal aid.
Lawyers are unethical shysters.	Lawyers are governed by an enforceable code of ethics by which the vast majority abides.

work is done in offices behind a desk and involves reading, writing, and communicating via e-mail and phone. This is not to imply that courtroom advocacy is unimportant. Indeed, some lawyers specialize in just this component of legal work. But trying to understand the work of lawyers by focusing exclusively on courtroom advocacy is like trying to understand the work of professors by focusing exclusively on classroom lectures. In either case, what is gleaned from such a focus is an incomplete picture at best.

In this chapter we highlight the myths and realities of lawyers and law practice. We begin with a brief discussion of the job market for law school graduates and the overall demographics of the legal profession. **Legal Specialization**—concentrating and becoming expert in a particular area of the law—is a hallmark of the legal profession and we spend considerable time talking about the various ways that lawyers are differentiated from one another in the practice of law. **Legal Prestige**—law work with a good reputation and that is held in high esteem—and specialization go hand-in-hand, and we examine how some law work is more prestigious than other kinds of law work. We pay particular attention to the two most common types of practice settings. We contrast lawyers who work in **private practice**—law work as a business—with lawyers who perform government work in order to highlight the interplay between specialization and prestige. We also discuss whether lawyers are satisfied or dissatisfied with their jobs. Finally, we consider two particularly knotty issues at the intersection of lawyers and clients—the accessibility of legal assistance (high-cost vs. low-cost legal help) and the application of **legal ethics** (standards and rules associated with law work) particularly as applied to the representation of clients.

WHO PRACTICES LAW?

Job Market
Virtually all law school graduates are concerned about their employment prospects. Certainly the dream is to secure a well-paying position at a well-regarded firm, such as was the case for Mitch McDeere, played by Tom Cruise in the 1993 film *The Firm*. (Presumably, however, those dreaming of such a job are hoping that the corruption and murder associated with McDeere's firm are absent in their own employment.) The notion that obtaining a law degree guarantees a job as a lawyer is a myth. Contrast the experience of Tom Cruise's character in *The Firm* with that of Matt Damon's character (Rudy Baylor) in the 1997 film *The Rainmaker*.[8] McDeere found himself in a cushy job right out of the box while Baylor had a hard time finding a job, ending up as a so-called ambulance chaser struggling to make ends meet. While it is true that most J.D.'s will ultimately find positions as practicing attorneys, the reality is that some will work in jobs that do not require bar passage or even law degrees. Consider Figure 3.1, which shows employment statistics for the law school class of 2013 9 months after graduating. Note, first, 11 percent were unemployed while another 4 percent worked in law-school funded positions, which are typically accepted by students who have not found full-time law work. The majority of graduates do some kind of **business law**—law work that applies to persons and businesses engaged in commerce, merchandising, trade, and sales (also known as commercial law)—either in private practice or as in-house legal counsel for businesses. More than four in 10 recent law school graduates go into private practice either as solo practitioners (2 percent) or associates in law firms (40 percent). Nearly 15 percent of graduates obtain jobs in business and industry, including positions in accounting firms, insurance companies, banking and financial institutions, as well as corporations, companies, and

FIGURE 3.1

Employer Types: Law School Graduating Class of 2013

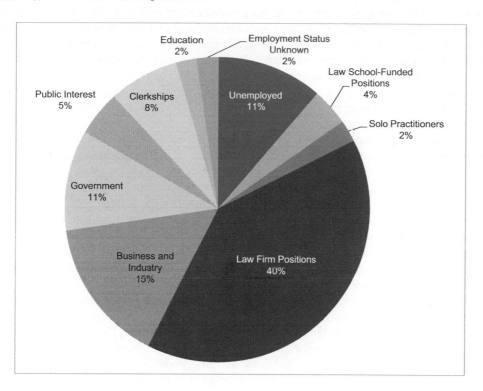

Source: American Bar Association Section on Legal Education and Admissions to the Bar, "Class of 2013 Law Graduate Data." http://www.americanbar.org/groups/legal_education/resources/statistics.html

organizations of all sizes and types such as private hospitals, retail establishments, and consulting and public relations firms.

At the other end of the spectrum is the remaining quarter of graduates who work in relatively low-paying jobs in the government and the **public interest**—law work that furthers interests shared by the entire public or significant segments of it such as discrimination, environmental protection, child welfare, and domestic violence. Just over 10 percent of graduates work in government jobs at all levels and in all branches, including **prosecutors**—government lawyers who institute legal proceedings against defendants in criminal court, the military, government agencies, legislative committees, law enforcement, and social services. Roughly 8 percent of those with law degrees work as **law clerks**—legal assistants who work for state and federal judges for 1 or 2 years conducting research, making recommendations regarding cases, and drafting judicial opinions. Despite the fact that as many as half of incoming law students claim to desire a career in public interest law, only about 5 percent of graduates get jobs as **public defenders** (attorneys who represent individuals accused of crimes), work for **legal aid** (government-funded legal services for those who otherwise cannot afford it), or represent unions, non-profit advocacy groups, or cause-related organizations.

These statistics are reported to the American Bar Association each year by law schools, which survey their graduates 9 months after graduation. While these statistics in the aggregate do provide a picture of legal employment for recent law school graduates writ large, the facts on the ground vary considerably for graduates of specific schools. For example, six law schools reported that 90 percent or more of their 2013 graduates (in the 9 months after graduation) were employed full time in long-term jobs that required bar passage: Virginia, Columbia, NYU, Chicago, Pennsylvania, and Cornell. Yet at the other end of the spectrum, more than 30 schools reported percentages below 40 percent. Excluding Puerto Rican law schools, the five lowest were Thomas M. Cooley in Michigan at 26.9 percent, Whittier in Los Angeles at 26.7 percent, the University of the District of Columbia at 26.3 percent, Golden Gate in San Francisco at 22.8 percent, and North Carolina Central at 22.5 percent of its 2013 graduates employed in full-time, long-term jobs that require bar passage.[9] Plainly, it should be understood that employment prospects for law school graduates can vary substantially depending on many factors, including the schools they graduated from.

As Table 3.1 shows, there is also considerable variation in lawyer salaries depending on the type of employer.[10] For the class of 2013, lawyers working in private practice made the most money with an average salary of $102,590. There is considerable variation, however, with the top quarter earning $160,000 but the bottom quarter making only $58,000. Similar variation exists with the population of attorneys employed by the next most lucrative employer: business. Specifically, lawyers who work for business and industry average $72,934, with the top quarter earning $85,000 and the bottom quarter making $51,000. Academics, law clerks, and government lawyers average just over $50,000 but with less variation than attorneys in private practice. At the low end of the salary spectrum are public interest lawyers who average $46,532.

More broadly, average annual salaries for all lawyers, not just those from the class of 2013, were $131,990 in 2013 according to data from the U.S. Bureau of Labor Statistics.[11] That places lawyers well behind other occupations such as various categories of physicians, who are the top earners (including anesthesiologists, $235,070, and surgeons, $233,150), chief executives ($178,400), petroleum engineers ($149,180), and marketing managers ($133,700). The overall average of $131,990 for lawyers masks a great deal of geographic variation in salaries. For example, the average wage for the 4,540 attorneys in the San Jose-Sunnyvale-Santa Clara, California metro market is $195,530, compared to $136,760 for the 9,820 attorneys in the Dallas-Plano-Irving, Texas area, and $103,500 for the 1,270 attorneys in Jackson, Mississippi.[12] In short, the key word when it comes to attorney employment is variation: there is variation in which law school graduates will get jobs, what kind of jobs they will be, and how much they will be paid to do those jobs.

TABLE 3.1
Salary by Employer Type, Class of 2013

EMPLOYER TYPE	FULL-TIME, LONG-TERM SALARIES			
	MEDIAN	MEAN	25TH PERCENTILE	75TH PERCENTILE
Academic	$50,000	$52,140	$40,000	$60,000
Business	$65,000	$72,934	$51,000	$85,000
Judicial Clerk	$53,000	$52,296	$45,192	$60,000
Private Practice	$95,000	$102,590	$58,000	$160,000
Government	$52,000	$54,641	$42,500	$61,000
Public Interest	$45,000	$46,532	$40,000	$52,000

Source: NALP, "Class of 2013 National Summary Report." http://www.nalp.org/uploads/NatlSummaryChartClassof2013.pdf

Image 3.1 Lawyer Fee
*Lawyers are generally
well paid. This early
eighteenth century
print is critical of the
lawyer who collects his
fee despite the fact that
his clients are disabled.*
Prints and Photographs
Division, Library of
Congress, Washington,
D.C.

The rising costs of a legal education and the less-than-stellar job market in the wake of the Great Recession has led to a controversy in recent years over the job data that law schools report for their graduates.[13] Employment data is one of the key criteria that *U.S. News & World Report* uses to rank schools, and some have charged law schools with deceptive reporting practices. In 2012 a series of lawsuits were filed on behalf of dozens of graduates in multiple states.[14] The suits claimed that schools misled students by advertising higher job placement rates than actually existed. Specifically, the suits claimed that the schools misclassified graduates with temporary or part-time jobs as "fully" employed, omitted information about graduates who did not respond to employment surveys, and created postgraduate job programs to hire their own graduates (for example, hourly temp work in law school admissions offices). Many of the schools defended their rates and reporting procedures, as did the ABA, and most of the suits were dismissed. But other schools pledged reform and worked with an independent organization, Law School Transparency,[15] to provide more accurate data.[16]

The job market is not only tied to the law schools from which lawyers graduated or the type of law graduates choose to practice. Careers in the law are also tied to issues of specialization, prestige, and practice settings. We will spend some time discussing these topics later in the chapter, as both jobs and salaries are dependent on these factors. While students routinely believe they will land high-paying, "big law" type jobs at major firms (like Tom Cruise's character in *The Firm*), the reality of the legal job market is that these positions are not open to many lawyers and there is a wide range of positions for which law school graduates are hired (including as attorneys in tiny practices like Matt Damon's character in *The Rainmaker*).

Lawyer Demographics

Despite the recent downturns in hiring, law school graduates are still getting jobs and the number of lawyers in America continues to rise. Historically, the legal profession was relatively small. Judge Richard Posner argued that the profession, through the 1950s, was a cartel: an anticompetitive club with an exclusionary membership policy.[17] But dramatic growth began occurring in the 1960s spurred by greater demand for legal services. There were many causes for this increased demand, including the creation of new rights and subsidization for criminal defendants and indigent civil plaintiffs, the relaxation of rules of standing to bring lawsuits including class action cases, and increased government regulation in the form of New Deal and Great Society programs.[18] Increased demand coupled with the civil and women's rights movements, allowed racial minorities and women to make inroads into the cartel.[19]

Ultimately, these developments transformed the profession from a tacitly **cooperative** to a **competitive marketplace**. Figure 3.2 demonstrates this sea change from a nation where there was one lawyer for every 886 people in 1930 to one where there is now a single lawyer for every 250 people. Recent data from the ABA indicates that there were over 1,268,000 licensed attorneys in 2013.[20] That represents a percentage increase of 20 percent since 2002 (when the ABA reported 1,049,751 licensed attorneys) and an increase of more than 50 percent since 1992 (when the ABA reported 799,760 licensed attorneys).[21]

Image 3.2 Income Tax Litigation
This November 1913 print "Lawyers at least have plenty to be thankful for" depicts how lawyers will benefit from the legal work that will inevitably result from the ratification of the Sixteenth Amendment making the income tax a permanent fixture of the U.S. tax system. Prints and Photographs Division, Library of Congress, Washington, D.C.

FIGURE 3.2

Number of Americans per Lawyer, 1880–2013

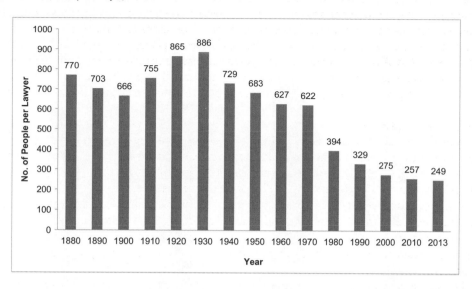

American Bar Association Legal Profession Statistics, 2013. http://www.americanbar.org/resources_for_lawyers/profession_statistics.html
U.S. Census Bureau, 2013. http://www.census.gov/popest/data/national/totals/2013/index.html

TABLE 3.2

Attorneys per State: Five Highest and Lowest, per Capita, 2010

RANK	STATE	# OF ATTORNEYS[a]	POPULATION (1,000s)[b]	ATTORNEYS PER 10,000 RESIDENTS
1	New York	157,778	1,9378	81.4
2	Massachusetts	44,121	6,548	67.4
3	Connecticut	20,309	3,574	56.8
4	Illinois	60,069	1,2831	46.8
5	New Jersey	40,286	8,792	45.8
46	Idaho	3,299	1,568	21.0
47	Arizona	13,384	6,392	20.9
48	North Dakota	1,397	673	20.8
49	South Carolina	9,264	4,625	20.0
50	Arkansas	5,789	2,916	19.9

[a] American Bar Association, "National Lawyer Population by State." http://www.americanbar.org/resources_for_lawyers/profession_statistics.html
[b] U.S. Census Bureau, *Statistical Abstract of the United States: 2012* (Washington, D.C.: Government Printing Office, 2012).

Despite the demise of the legal profession as a cartel and the growth of the legal profession generally, lawyers are not distributed evenly throughout the nation. The over 1.2 million lawyers are dispersed in unequal concentrations across the states, with some states having appreciably more lawyers than others. For example, as reported in Table 3.2, Arkansas has the fewest attorneys per capita (just shy of 20 attorneys for every 10,000 residents) while New York has the most attorneys per capita (slightly more than 81 attorneys

FIGURE 3.3
Percentage of Male vs. Female Attorneys, Selected Years

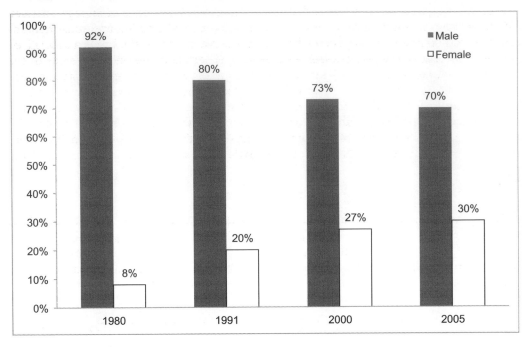

American Bar Association Legal Profession Statistics, 2013. http://www.americanbar.org/resources_for_lawyers/profession_
statistics.html

for every 10,000 residents). As a point of information, the median figure for the 50 states
is 29 attorneys per every 10,000 residents. Not surprising given its role as the nation's
capital, the District of Columbia has an even higher concentration of attorneys, with
49,207 licensed attorneys and a population of 602,000 in 2010.

The legal profession is commonly thought of as the province of older white males.
Indeed, lawyers still overwhelmingly fit this demographic. The median age of licensed
attorneys in the United States in 2005 (the most recent figure available from the ABA) is
49, which represents an increase of 10 years over the prior two and a half decades.[22] The
largest proportion of attorneys (roughly 28 percent) is between the ages of 45 and 54.
Further, though women have come close to parity in terms of enrollment in law school,[23]
in recent years only 30 percent of licensed attorneys have been women. As Figure 3.3
reports, however, that 30 percent is substantially higher than the 8 percent reported in
1980. As for the racial and ethnic profile of lawyers, nearly nine out of ten lawyers are
white, with 4.8 percent African American, 3.7 percent Hispanic, and 3.4 percent Asian/
Pacific American.[24] Thus, while older white males continue to dominate the profession,
there has been increasing diversity in recent decades, particularly in terms of gender.

As this discussion of the legal job market and the demographics of the legal profession
demonstrates, there is considerable diversity in the types of law work available and in the
attorneys who comprise the profession. In the next section, we detail how this has led to
increased specialization. Because lawyers specialize, some law work is viewed as more prestigious than other law work. In short, the legal profession is no longer the monolithic cartel it
once was and is instead a diverse vocation in terms of demographics, law work, and prestige.

ATTORNEY SPECIALIZATION

A common myth about lawyers is that they have broad knowledge of all legal matters. While all lawyers do receive a common core of basic legal training and must demonstrate broad competence to pass the bar exam, the reality is that the law is a specialized profession. That is, lawyers are trained and have expertise in well-defined areas of the law. For example, an attorney might be conversant in corporate mergers and acquisitions but know little about criminal defense law. How many areas of law are there? The legal information website HG.org, an online law and government information site, lists 70 core areas of law broken down into roughly 300 sub-areas of practice, as seen in Table 3.3.[25] How does one make sense of this dizzying list of specialties? Broadly speaking, there are two main fields of law: litigation and transactional law. Consequently, most of the

TABLE 3.3
Legal Specialization—Sub-Areas of Law Practice

Aboriginal People	Bonds Law	Constitutional Law
Administrative Law	Brain Injury Law	Construction Accidents
Admiralty and Maritime Law	Bribery	Construction Injuries
Adoption Law	Burglary	Construction Law
Advertising Law	Bus Accident	Consumer Law
Aerospace Law	Business Formation Law	Contract Law
Agency Law	Business Law	Controlled Substances
Agriculture	Capital Markets	Cooperatives
Alcohol Law	Car Accident	Copyright
Alimony	Case Law	Corporate Finance Law
Alternative Dispute Resolution	Catastrophic Injuries	Corporate Governance
Amnesty	Cell Phone Accident	Corporate Law
Animal Bites	Charitable Organizations	Corporate Taxation
Animals/Wildlife	Child Abduction Law	Counterfeiting
Antitrust Law	Child Abuse	Court Stenography Law
Appellate Practice	Child Custody	Credit Card Fraud
Arbitration	Child Pornography	Credit Law
Arson	Child Support	Creditors Rights
Art and Culture	Child Visitation Law	Criminal Defense
Asbestos Mesothelioma	Children's Rights	Criminal Law
Assault	Citizenship Law	Cyberspace Crimes Law
Asset Protection	Civil Rights	Data Protection
Auto Dealer Fraud	Collaborative Law	Death Penalty
Automobile Accidents	Commercial Law	Debt Recovery Law
Aviation Accidents	Commercial Ship Accidents	Defamation, Libel and Slander
Aviation Law	Commodities, Futures and Options	Defective Drugs Law
Bad Faith Insurance Law	Common Law	Discrimination
Banking Law	Communications	Dispute Resolution
Bankruptcy	Competition Law	Distributorship Law
Battery	Computer Crime	Divorce Law
Biotechnology Law	Computer Law	Domain Names
Birth Injury	Conciliation	Domestic Violence
Blackmail Law	Confidentiality Agreement	Drivers License Reinstatement
Boating Accident	Conflicts of Interest	

(Continued)

TABLE 3.3
(Continued)

Drug Crime	Forestry Law	Leisure Law
Drug Law	Franchising Law	Lemon Law
Drug Testing—Employees	Fraud Law	Litigation
DUI-DWI	Free Speech	Mail Fraud
E-Commerce Law	Gaming Law	Maintenance Law
E-Discovery Law	Gas Law	Manslaughter Law
Economic Deregulation	Gifts	Manufacturing Law
Economics and Law	Government	Maritime
Education Law	Government Affairs	Marketing Law
Elder Law	Government Benefits	Marriage
Election and Political Law	Health Care and Social Law	Mass Tort
Electricity Law	Health Care Law	Media
Embezzlement Law	Homeowners Association	Mediation
Eminent Domain	Homicide	Medical Law
Employee Benefits Law	Human Resources Law	Medical Malpractice
Employee Rights Law	Human Rights Law	Medicare and Medicaid
Employment Discrimination Law	Identity Theft	Medication Errors Law
Employment Law	Immigration	Mergers and Acquisitions
Encryption Law	Immigration Amnesty	Mesothelioma
Energy	Indian Law	Migration Law
Enforcement of Judgments	Indigenous Peoples	Military Law
Entertainment Law	Industrial Injuries	Minerals
Environmental Law	Industrial Law	Mining Regulation
Equal Protection	Information Services	Money Laundering
Equal Rights	Information Technology Law	Mortgage Law
Equine Law	Informed Consent Law	Motor Vehicle Law
ERISA	Inheritance Law	Motorcycle Accident
Estate and Trust	Insolvency Law	Murder Law
Estate Planning Center	Insurance	Mutual Funds
Ethics	Insurance Fraud	Native People
Expropriation	Intellectual Property	Natural Resources
Extortion Law	International Law	Naturalization Law
Extradition Law	Internet Law	Negotiable Instruments
Factoring	Investment Companies Law	Newspapers
Failure to Diagnose Law	Investment Law	Nonprofit Organizations
Family Law	Job Safety	Nuclear Law
Fashion Law	Joint Ventures	Nursing Home Abuse
Federal Administration	Jones Act	Obscenity Law
FELA	Juvenile Crime Law	Oil and Gas Law
Felony	Juvenile Law	Outsourcing Law
Finance Law	Labor and Employment	Patent
Financial Services Law	Land Transport	Paternity Pension
Financing	Land Use	Perjury
Firearms Law	Landlord and Tenant	Personal Injury Law
First Amendment Law	Larceny Law	Personal Property
Fisheries Law	Leasing Personal Property	Pharmaceutical Law
FLSA Overtime Claim	Leasing Real Property	Police Law
Food and Beverages Law	Legal Ethics	Politics and Law
Foreclosure	Legal Malpractice	Practice of Law
	Legal Theory	Premises Liability

Prenuptial Agreement	Residential Real Estate	Testament
Price Control	Retail Law	Theft Law
Printed Media	RICO Law	Torts Law
Prison Administration Law	Risk	Toxic Mold
Prisoner's Rights Law	Robbery	Toxic Torts Law
Prisoners of War Law	Rollover Accident	Trade Investment Law
Privacy	Rule of Law	Trade Regulation
Private Equity Law	Safety, Job-related	Trademark
Private Investigation Law	Sales of Goods and Services	Traffic Law
Privatization Law	Scams	Traffic Ticket Law
Pro Bono Law	Sea Law	Transportation
Probate	Secured Transactions	Truck Accident
Procurement by Government	Securities	Trucking
Products Liability	Securities Fraud	Trusts Law
Professional Liability Law	Separation Law	U.S. Environmental Law
Professional Malpractice	Separation of Church and	U.S. Federal Government
Profit Sharing	State	U.S. State Government
Project Finance Law	Sex Crimes	Unfair Competition
Property Law	Sexual Harassment	Urban Planning
Property Management	Shareholders Rights	Utilities Law
Property, Personal	Ship Registration	Venture Capital
Prostitution Law	Shoplifting	Visa
Public Employment	Shopping Centers	Water
Public Finance	Slip and Fall	Weapons
Public Health Care	Social Security Disability	Welfare
Public Utility	Social Security Law	Whistleblower
Qui Tam, False Claims Act	Social Services	White Collar Crime
Radio/TV	Social Welfare	Wills
Railroad	Special Needs Trust	Wire Fraud
Railroad Accident	Spinal Cord Injury	Women
Rape	Sports Law	Work Permits
Real Estate—Commercial	Spousal Support	Worker Compensation
Real Estate Law	Statutory Law	Workplace Injuries
Real Property	Surgical Errors	Workplace Safety Law
Recreation/Leisure	Syndications	Wrongful Death
Regulatory Law	Taxation	Wrongful Termination
Religious Freedom	Technology and Cyber Law	Zoning Law
Remedies	Telecommunications	

Source: HG.org Law Center, "Areas of Practice." http://www.hg.org/practiceareas.html.

medium and large law firms consist of at least these two major departments (i.e., litigation and transactional law). The practice groups in a litigation department may include employment, securities, product liability, intellectual property, and insurance while a transactional department may include merger and acquisition work, private equity, and real estate transactions.

Litigation lawyers are attorneys who work mainly with lawsuits with the goal of taking cases to court and winning. Litigators resemble more closely the kinds of lawyers most frequently seen on television and in movies. They are the ones who seek to resolve disputes in court. However, the myth does not match the reality. While TV shows and movies show lawyers most often in a courtroom, the truth of litigation is very different: the vast majority of the work of litigators takes place outside the courtroom. They spend their time researching the law, interviewing clients and witnesses, drafting pleadings and writing motions, taking depositions, reviewing documents, analyzing the case based on the law and facts, and negotiating settlements. Furthermore, even when litigators are in court, they spend that time arguing **motions** (a request to a court to obtain an order or ruling directing that some act be done in favor of the applicant) rather than in trial. There are two types of litigation: civil and criminal. A **criminal litigator** works on state or federal prosecution cases (or defends a client accused of a crime) while a **civil litigator** may specialize in one specific area or work in many areas, including personal injury, land-lord-tenant, or contract breaches. Civil litigators also generally represent either plaintiffs or defendants. Additionally, litigators also specialize in either trial or appellate advocacy.[26] There is even further specialization among appellate attorneys, with a very small group of attorneys at the apex of the judiciary who are expert at appellate advocacy before the U.S. Supreme Court.[27]

Transactional lawyers, on the other hand, never see the inside of a courtroom. They spend the majority of their time researching, drafting, negotiating, and advising. Trans-actional lawyers provide day-to-day advice to their clients, such as writing contracts or handling a real estate closing. While there is some overlap between these two large areas, most lawyers, especially in larger law firms, concentrate their practices on one or the other. Solo and small firm practitioners tend to be more generalists and will engage in a mix of transactional work and litigation.

An additional way that attorneys specialize is that they focus broadly on either busi-ness law or **personal law**—law work concerning the legal and financial interests of indi-viduals and families. There are enormous differences between legal matters that pertain to businesses—such as patents, antitrust, and corporate stock—and the common legal problems of individual personal clients—such as wills, divorce, and criminal defense. As a result, most lawyers devote the majority of their time to either business matters or to the problems of individual personal clients, but not to both. There is very little overlap between business law and personal law practice.

Parenthetically, in addition to the broad division between business and personal law, there is a third area of law work (mentioned earlier in the discussion of salaries) that is neither business law nor personal law in a strict sense: public interest law.[28] Many stu-dents enter law school at least considering a career in public interest law[29]—and there are some law schools that are exclusively devoted to training public interest lawyers, such as CUNY School of Law.[30] Ultimately, however, only a very small number of lawyers work in public interest law. Those that do represent various organizations that use the courts (as well as other branches of government) to obtain public policies that they favor. The NAACP Legal Defense Fund, the American Civil Liberties Union, and the National Rifle Association are examples of organizations that seek to influence public policy and the lawyers who work for them litigate cases on behalf of citizens—not simply to win the case for their client, but to change the law in the process.[31] Thus, in *Brown v. Board of Education*,[32] the NAACP Legal Defense Fund certainly won the case for the Brown fam-ily, whose daughters no longer had to walk long distances and across railroad tracks to attend an African American–only public school. But, more importantly, it changed the law in the interest of the larger public as the Court's decision applied to all public schools in the United States.[33]

In addition to the broad categorization of legal work as either transactional or litiga-tion and either business or personal, there is one final way to think about how law work is divided: urban settings versus small town settings. Small-town lawyers are often **solo**

practitioners—attorneys who have their own private law practice—or work in partnership with one or two other attorneys. They handle a broad range of legal matters in order to make ends meet, including personal legal issues such as wills and divorces and local small business matters. Unlike their urban counterparts, small-town lawyers handle their cases from start to finish. The bigger the city, however, the more likely lawyers are to be specialists and to hand the case off to other specialists as the case moves through the stages of litigation.

Subspecialties

There are further subspecialties within the broad specializations just described. For example, in large urban areas there are five major divisions of law practice, each with its own subspecialties, as depicted in Table 3.4. There are business lawyers who concentrate on highly specialized matters affecting large corporations such as antitrust, patents, business taxes, stocks and bonds, corporate banking, and commercial law. Other lawyers handle general corporate matters such as business litigation, business real estate, public utilities, defending against personal injury lawsuits, and civil rights issues. Labor lawyers specialize in the legal relationship between management and unions. Lawyers who work for the government largely deal with criminal matters on the state and local level. Finally, attorneys who handle personal matters for individuals deal with general litigation for their clients: criminal defense, divorce, personal injury on behalf of plaintiffs, real estate, probate (wills and estates), general family law, and personal tax issues. In short, there are countless subspecialties within the broader specializations of law work.

The chances are small that lawyers working in one of these five areas will ever do much work in one of the others. For example, a banking or tax lawyer probably will never do any business litigation or civil rights work, and a tax lawyer virtually never appears in criminal court. Many lawyers never even cross over subspecialties, such as a lawyers who specialize in patent law for investors of computer microprocessors or lawyers who work on new stock offerings for bank corporations. Both legal specialists may work for the same large corporation—or law firm representing that corporation—but they do not practice the same kind of law. Lawyers who represent private individuals are more likely than other lawyers to do a variety of law work, often because they do not have many repeat clients and have to take what they can get. The population size of the community affects the degree of legal specialization. The smaller the community, the less possible it is for lawyers to specialize narrowly.

TABLE 3.4

Types of Urban Law Work

LARGE CORPORATE	GENERAL CORPORATE	LABOR	GOVERNMENT	PERSONAL
Antitrust	Business Litigation	Management	Criminal	General Litigation
Patents	Business Real Estate	Unions	Municipal	Criminal Defense
Business Tax	Public Utilities			Divorce
Stocks/Bonds	Personal Injury (Defense)			Personal Injury
Banking	Civil Rights			(Plaintiff)
Commercial				Real Estate
				Probate
				General Family
				Personal Tax

Specialization and Prestige

A myth related to the notion that lawyers have broad knowledge of the law is the idea that being a lawyer is a prestigious job. As mentioned previously, prestige can be defined as law work with a good reputation and that is held in high esteem. While law work in general may be more prestigious than digging ditches,[34] not all law work carries the same level of prestige. Specialization and prestige go hand in hand. Table 3.5 shows the prestige scores for 30

TABLE 3.5
Prestige Scores and Job Characteristics of Legal Specialties

LEGAL SPECIALTY	PRESTIGE SCORE	INTELLECTUAL CHALLENGE SCORE	RAPIDITY OF CHANGE SCORE	PRO BONO SCORE	ETHICAL CONDUCT SCORE	FREEDOM OF ACTION SCORE
Securities	68	63	62	44	57	39
Tax	67	67	66	43	55	46
Antitrust (Defendants)	65	64	56	40	53	39
Patents	61	56	44	45	62	47
Antitrust (Plaintiffs)	60	65	57	46	47	65
Banking	59	47	42	42	58	35
Public Utilities	59	55	53	48	56	39
General Corporate	59	51	48	44	59	41
Probate	58	45	32	44	57	46
Municipal	56	44	38	45	56	41
Admiralty	55	52	34	42	62	48
Civil Litigation	54	52	48	51	45	55
Labor (Management)	53	52	53	45	46	38
Real Estate	51	45	37	43	48	50
Commercial	49	52	48	46	55	48
Labor (Unions)	49	53	53	51	47	42
Environmental (Defendants)	49	61	65	47	51	43
Personal Injury (Defendants)	48	33	42	43	38	46
Environmental (Plaintiffs)	47	61	65	72	58	66
Civil Rights/Liberties	46	61	65	77	64	70
Criminal (Prosecution)	44	48	56	56	47	53
General Family (Paying)	42	38	41	52	54	55
Criminal (Defense)	41	51	57	57	33	64
Consumer (Creditor)	40	50	60	46	43	41
Personal Injury (Plaintiffs)	38	35	43	43	25	64
Consumer (Debtor)	38	52	59	65	50	62
Condemnations	37	35	36	43	39	49
Landlord-Tenant	37	43	47	55	41	52
Divorce	35	30	45	50	30	54
General Family (Poverty)	34	38	51	76	61	64

Edward O. Laumann and John P. Heinz, "Specialization and Prestige in the Legal Profession: The Structure of Deference," *American Bar Foundation Research Journal*, vol. 2, no. 1 (1977): 155–216, 166–168.

legal specialties as determined by a survey of attorneys. The scores are standardized such that 50 represents the average prestige score across all legal specialties.[35] At the top of the legal heap are corporate lawyers in large business law firms and corporations who specialize in securities, tax, antitrust, and patents. Salaries reflect the level of prestige. In 2012, starting salaries at the top firms for the best new law school graduates who do the most prestigious work climbed to $160,000 with signing bonuses of $10,000 or more.[36] However, attorneys at the bottom of the prestige/specialization ladder—those who handle landlord-tenant disputes, divorces, and general family law—often have problems making ends meet.

In addition to prestige levels, Table 3.5 details a number of other differences across legal specialties. Some areas of the law are more intellectually challenging than others in terms of the legal doctrines, cases, statutes, and regulations involved. The most challenging are tax, antitrust, securities, environmental, and civil rights/liberties. The least challenging

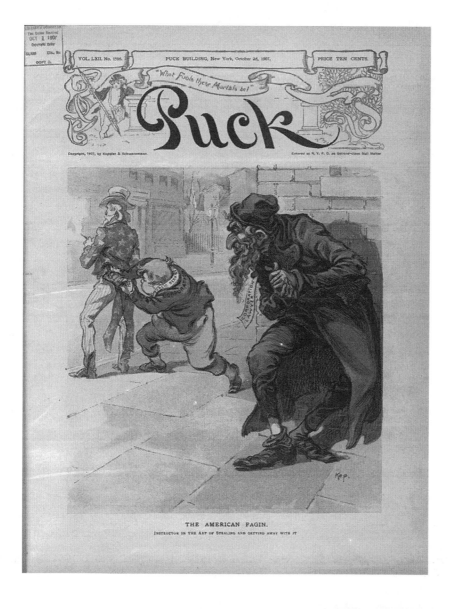

Image 3.3 Corporate Lawyer
This 1907 illustration shows the character Fagin (labeled "Corporation Lawyer") from the Charles Dickens novel Oliver Twist, *watching his protégé, Oliver Twist (labeled "Public Service Corporation"), as he picks the pocket of Uncle Sam on a city sidewalk. Despite the negative imagery, corporate lawyers have high levels of prestige among those in the legal profession.* Prints and Photographs Division, Library of Congress, Washington, D.C.

are divorce, personal injury, condemnation of private property, and general family law. The rapidity of change score reflects how fast the law in a given specialty changes, making it more difficult for lawyers to keep up with new developments. The highest scores on this measure are in the tax, environmental, and civil rights/liberties areas. The areas of the law that have the least rapid changes are probate, admiralty, and condemnations.

Pro bono work is defined as public interest law work done voluntarily by attorneys either for free or for a reduced fee. The *pro bono* score reported in Table 3.5 reflects the extent to which a type of law work is done for the public good versus for profit. The highest scoring specialties for altruistic law work are civil rights/liberties, general family law for the poor, and environmental law on behalf of plaintiffs. The least altruistic are antitrust on behalf of defendants, banking, and admiralty.

Specialties also differ in the level with which they are perceived to engage in ethical versus unethical conduct. The most ethical are thought to be civil rights/liberties, patents, and admiralty while the most unethical are personal injury, divorce, and criminal defense. The perception of the latter group, even among attorneys, may reflect the pervasiveness of the myth that this kind of law work is inherently unethical. Contemporary pop culture contributes to this myth with the depiction of lawyers of dubious ethics such as AMC's *Better Call Saul* centered on sleazy lawyer Saul Goodman, a character first introduced in AMC's *Breaking Bad*.

Finally, the freedom of action score reported in Table 3.5 measures the degree to which lawyers have flexibility to pursue whichever strategic course of action to which their own professional judgments lead (as opposed to being constrained by knowledgeable clients or organizational superiors). The highest rated specialties with regard to freedom of action are civil rights/liberties, environmental on behalf of plaintiffs, and antitrust on behalf of plaintiffs. The most constrained are banking, labor on behalf of management, securities, antitrust on behalf of defendants, and public utilities.

As this discussion about specialization demonstrates, the legal profession is quite diverse in terms of law work. That diversity translates into different practice settings to conduct different law work. In the next section, we contrast lawyers who work in private practice with those who work for the government. While most work in various private practice settings, there are a number of avenues open to attorneys who desire a career in public law work.

PRACTICE SETTINGS

The array of settings in which lawyers work is broad. As Figure 3.4 reports, the vast majority of lawyers (three out of every four) work in private practice. An additional 8 percent are employed in business and industry, including positions in accounting firms, insurance companies, banking and financial institutions, as well as corporations, companies, and organizations of all sizes such as private hospitals, retail establishments, and consulting and public relations firms. Another 8 percent work in government jobs, including in public prosecutor offices, the military, government agencies, legislative committees, and law enforcement. The remaining lawyers are scattered in positions in private associations, the field of education, and the judiciary.

Private Practice

According to the most recent available Census data, there are roughly 169,000 private practice law firms.[37] Not all of these law firms are the same. One key dimension for differentiating among private practice firms is size. Approximately half of the lawyers in private practice work as solo practitioners, as can be seen in Figure 3.5. The distribution of non-solo practice firms is reported in Figure 3.6. Three quarters of non-solo practice firms

FIGURE 3.4
Percentage of Lawyers Working in Specific Practice Settings, 2005

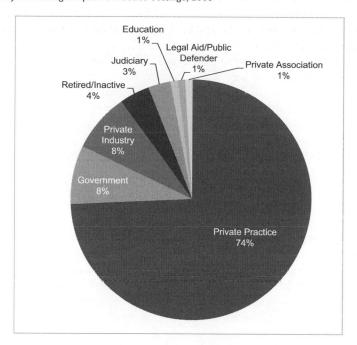

American Bar Association Legal Profession Statistics, 2012. http://www.americanbar.org/resources_for_lawyers/profession_
statistics.html

FIGURE 3.5
Distribution of Private Practitioners Across Firm Sizes, 2005

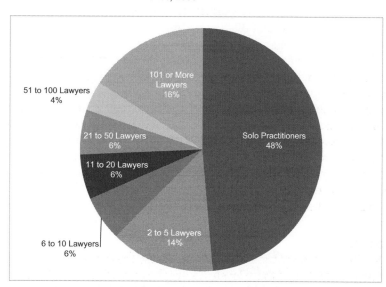

American Bar Association Legal Profession Statistics, 2012. http://www.americanbar.org/resources_for_lawyers/profession_
statistics.html

FIGURE 3.6
Distribution of Firm Sizes, 2005

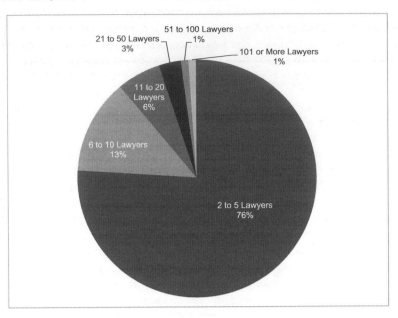

American Bar Association Legal Profession Statistics, 2012. http://www.americanbar.org/resources_for_lawyers/profession_
statistics.html

have between two and five lawyers on staff and another one in eight employ between six
and 10 lawyers. Very few firms (only 2 percent) have more than 50 lawyers on staff but
firms of this size account for 20 percent of all private practice lawyers.

Generally speaking (and as noted earlier), the larger the firm is, the greater the specialization among the attorneys of that firm. Typically, solo practitioners are jacks-of-all-
trades in that they handle a variety of matters for individuals and small businesses. For
example, in the course of a given week, a lawyer working as a solo practitioner might handle a criminal matter (e.g., representing a client charged with a drug offense), a commercial
transaction (e.g., forming a corporation for a client starting a new business), a real estate
issue (e.g., managing the closing for the sale of a client's home), and a tort claim (e.g., filing
suit against an insurance company on behalf of a client). Recent trends among law school
graduates show a steady increase in the percentage of new graduates who opt for the solo
practice route. For example, 6.1 percent of the 2011 law school graduates surveyed by the
NALP established solo practices as compared to just 2.8 percent of 2001 graduates.[38]

The tightening of the job market for attorneys in the recent past largely accounts for
this trend. The legal services sector lost 54,000 jobs from 2008 to 2011.[39] Further, the
overall employment rate for 2011 law school graduates was a mere 85.6 percent, the lowest since the class of 1994.[40] The employment rate is even more dismal if it is limited to
reflect employment in full-time legal work; only 65.4 percent of 2011 law school graduates
reported being employed in full-time legal work. Recent law school grads who were unable
to secure legal employment have had no choice but to become solo practitioners in order
to pursue a legal career. Attorneys at smaller firms are likely to be more like solo practitioners in handling a range of issues. In contrast, at a medium-size law firm an attorney

may be part of, for example, the firm's commercial real estate group and only handle such matters as real estate leases, the buying and selling of property, and real estate financing. At larger firms, attorneys are likely to be even more specialized; for example, they might only review leases and never handle other aspects of commercial real estate.

Typically, the organization of a law firm is centered on the **partners** of the firm. The partners are attorneys who jointly own the firm and direct its legal operations.[41] Understanding how firms are organized and the concept of partnership is important because most attorneys work in private firms and many aspire to the greater prestige and wealth that can come with "making partner."[42] A law firm may be organized in one of several ways. In a general partnership arrangement, the partners share both the profits and the liabilities of the firm. An alternative to the general partnership is the limited liability company (LLC). Under this arrangement, the attorneys who "own" the firm are members of the company but are insulated in that they are not liable to any third-party creditor of the firm. Another alternative is the limited liability partnership (LLP). Like a general partnership, in an LLP the attorneys who "own" the firm are partners but, as in an LLC, the partners are not liable to any third-party creditor of the firm. The partners in an LLP are also not liable for the negligence of any other partner. A much less common arrangement is the professional corporation. Firms using the professional corporation model issue stock to the attorneys, much like with a business corporation.

Associates are attorneys who are employed by the firm with the prospect of becoming partners at some future point, depending on their performance as associates. Associates for larger firms are typically recruited from the ranks of new law school graduates each year and often (but not always) have worked for the firm as a "summer associate" during the summer between their second and third year of law school.[43] Most regular associates are compensated using an approach that relies in whole or in part on the **lockstep model** in which associates receive a fixed salary with increases and bonuses based on length of service. This approach is part of the model originated by Paul Cravath of the white shoe firm[44] of Cravath, Swaine, & Moore[45] at the beginning of the twentieth century.[46] Cravath focused on hiring the best of the best law school graduates and providing intensive training to them over the course of their term as an associate. Under Cravath's up-or-out philosophy, associates who did not meet the standards for becoming a partner after a reasonable amount of time were expected to leave the firm. The average length of time that it takes an associate to become partner varies from firm to firm but one analysis of those who recently made partner at top firms found the average to be 10.5 years.[47]

Firms may use a **single-tier** or **two-tier partnership track**. With a single-tier partnership track, associates who demonstrate themselves to be skilled attorneys capable of generating sustained revenue over a period of years become partners and share in the profits of the firm accordingly, usually under some version of a lockstep model. Beginning in the 1980s, firms began to experiment with two-tiered partnership tracks in which some associates advance to become **equity partners** while others become **non-equity partners**.[48] The former acquire ownership stakes in the firm and share in its profits. In contrast, the latter may acquire limited voting rights but are compensated with a fixed salary. The difference in compensation between equity and non-equity partners is quite substantial. A recent survey of Am Law 200[49] firms found the annual compensation for equity partners to average $896,000 while that of non-equity partners almost 60 percent less than that at a mere $335,000.[50]

The rationale behind the two-tier partnership model is two-fold. First, it is intended to provide a mechanism to reduce shirking on the part of partners. Once made a partner, any individual partner could choose to reduce his efforts since his compensation would be largely based on the profitability of the firm as a whole rather than merely on his efforts.[51] A two-tier partnership model permits those who reliably generate business—particularly the **rainmakers** who are the big-name lawyers bringing in big-money clients—to become equity partners with others who bring value (but not the same value) to the firm becoming non-equity partners. In theory, the result should be higher earnings on a per-equity-partner basis. Second, it offers a mechanism to bypass the up-or-out model by letting associates who do not meet the standards for full equity partnership nonetheless to remain with the firm. The two-tier partnership model has been widely adopted, with at least three out of four firms on the Am Law 200 using it.[52] Adoption has been, however, uneven across the size of firms. While a little more than one-third of firms of 100 or fewer attorneys report using a tiered partnership model, more than half of firms of 251–500 attorneys indicate that they do so.[53] Interestingly, it has been eschewed by many of the most highly prestigious firms.[54] An analysis of the profitability of firms found single-tier firms tend to be more profitable than those with two-tiers and suggested that, in part, single-tier firms are more profitable because they are more likely to be elite firms able to attract client bases that are more lucrative.[55]

The economics of large law firms has yielded another development directed at enhancing profitability: **boutique law firms**. Boutique law firms are very small, single-specialty practices. All the attorneys at a given boutique law firm focus on one particular area of the law. Frequently, boutique firms originate when attorneys who work in a particular practice area of a large firm opt to leave the large firm to establish a much smaller firm concentrated on that particular practice area. For example, in 2010, 15 attorneys from LeClairRyan, a large firm of almost 300 lawyers, left to form a boutique practice focusing on the financial services industry, including representation for government investigations, securities litigation, and arbitration.[56] In the aftermath of 9/11, boutique law firms whose niche was aviation law were active in the efforts to compensate victims and family members for their legal claims. Other examples of the specializations of boutique law firms include immigration, environmental protection, elder care and estate planning, and not-for-profit organizations.

Government Attorneys

Perhaps the most prominent alternative to working in private practice is working as a government attorney at either the state or the federal level. These positions include prosecutors and public defenders, as well as those who serve as attorneys general or in government agencies. **Prosecutors** are attorneys who represent the government and try cases on behalf of the government (or, more accurately, on behalf of the people represented by the government). Prosecution originated as a private matter in England and on the Continent, with victims or their kin responsible for pressing for redress on their own.[57] The American prosecutor had its roots in the Dutch *schout*, English attorney general, and French *procureur publique*,[58] though none of these models served as the exact templates on which the American prosecutor was based.[59] While much of the Continent adopted public prosecution by the sixteenth century,[60] England continued its primary reliance on private prosecution. The American colonists, however, adopted forms of public prosecution early on.[61] Public prosecutors were originally not particularly strong actors in their own right. Over time, however, the American prosecutor evolved "from a weak figurehead to a powerful political figure."[62] Several things contributed to this development, including the fact that, whereas they originally appeared in state constitutional language as part of the judicial branch, they came to be considered executive branch actors.[63]

In addition to trying cases on behalf of the government, prosecutors also play major roles in criminal investigations. For example, they are involved in the development and coordination of strategies in undercover investigations. They seek authorization for eaves-dropping warrants. They subpoena records and testimony pertinent to ongoing investigations. They offer immunity to witnesses in exchange for cooperation on the part of those witnesses. They use **grand juries** (legal bodies consisting of citizens with the authority to conduct official investigations into possible criminal conduct) to investigate complex criminal enterprises including drug trafficking, money laundering, and official corruption. Prosecutors in many jurisdictions are also part of community-based efforts to reduce crime. In particular, **community prosecution** relies on the prosecution of crime identified by the police as well as taking actions intended to address problems before they result in crime, typically in a well-defined geographic area with a focus on public safety and quality-of-life issues.[64] The prosecutorial role in community prosecution, particularly in problem-solving courts (e.g., drug courts), is much more collaborative than in conventional prosecutorial contexts, but prosecutors still perform the traditional functions of prosecutors.[65]

Public defenders are attorneys who are salaried government employees but are responsible for representing indigent criminal defendants. Such clients can also be represented by legal aid societies (not-for-profit agencies) or via court-appointed lawyers; however, public defender offices are the primary source of legal counsel for the indigent. The first public defender's office in the United States began operations in 1914 in Los Angeles County.[66] Depending on the state, the funding of the public defender's office may be at the state level, left to individual counties, or involve a hybrid mechanism drawing from both state-level and county-level coffers.

> Public defender systems have been subject to much criticism because of the problems that some jurisdictions face. Many systems are underfunded, resulting in low salaries for attorneys and insufficient legal and support staff. . . . It appears that one of the biggest problems facing all indigent defense systems is funding. Funding can affect the quality of services provided if there are not enough resources to do the job adequately.[67]

The systematic evidence, however, as to whether those represented by public defenders are disadvantaged in comparison to those represented by privately retained counsel is mixed. For example, an analysis of outcomes for criminal defendants in one northern Florida county found no differences in terms of the likelihood of being placed on probation, the likelihood of being incarcerated, and the length of sentence based on whether the accused was represented by a public defender rather than privately retained counsel.[68] In comparison, another analysis of felony cases in Denver, Colorado, found that those represented by public defenders fared worse in terms of their sentences than those represented by privately retained counsel.[69] Interestingly, the Colorado judge and law professors who conducted that study cautioned against automatically concluding that the quality of representation by public defenders is inferior to that provided by privately retained counsel.

> [M]arginally indigent defendants, with a choice of spending resources on private counsel or claiming indigency and using the services of the public defender, are likely to make that choice depending on the interplay of two factors: the seriousness of the charges and the strength of the prosecution's case. Marginally indigent defendants are most likely to spend resources on a private defense lawyer to defend minor charges for which they are guilty, or, more precisely, for which they know the risk of conviction is high.[70]

As a consequence, public defenders are left representing more defendants with weak cases than are privately retained counsel. If that is the case, then it stands to reason that the outcomes they achieve for their clients in the aggregate are less positive than those achieved by privately retained counsel.

At the federal level, there are two models for public defender services: federal public defender organizations and community defender organizations. The former are federal organizations staffed by federal employees while the latter are not-for-profit organizations (incorporated under state laws) that are supported in part by the federal judiciary. Originally, the Criminal Justice Act (CJA)[71] provided for the compensation of appointed counsel but did not authorize the creation of federal defender organizations. The CJA was amended in 1970 to permit the creation of defender organizations to provide for defense counsel in districts in which a minimum of 200 individuals per year require the appointment of counsel. Two adjacent districts can combine for the purposes of meeting the 200-person threshold so, for example, there is one federal public defender office that covers both North and South Dakota and there is one public defender office that covers both Colorado and Wyoming. Collectively, there are 80 authorized federal defender organizations, each of which is headed by a chief federal public defender. The chief public defender is appointed to a 4-year term by the U.S. court of appeals within which that defender organization is situated.

An **attorney general** is the chief legal officer of a political unit.[72] The office of attorney general in the American context is one that traces it roots to the local attorneys who were appointed to assist the attorney general in England in representing the interests of the Crown in colonial courts. In the aftermath of the Revolution, these positions were transformed into state attorneys general—either by state statute or state constitutional language—but were no longer "local delegates of a central government;" rather, they were representatives of the local government.[73] Though the duties of a given attorney general vary by jurisdiction, commonly, attorneys general are responsible for performing several broad functions, which include: issuing formal opinions to agencies to assist them in conforming their actions to the law; acting as an advocate on behalf of the public with regard to issues such as consumer protection, antitrust, and utility regulation; representing the government and its agencies before the courts; and handling serious criminal prosecutions (though most prosecutions are handled by county-level officials).

Each state has its own attorney general (or equivalent), as do American Samoa, the District of Columbia, Guam, the Northern Mariana Islands, Puerto Rico, and the U.S. Virgin Islands. Among the 50 states, 44 have constitutions that create the office of attorney general, with the remaining states creating the office by statute.[74] In 43 states the attorney general is an elected position. In another five states (Alaska, Hawaii, New Hampshire, New Jersey, and Wyoming), the attorney general is appointed by the government, while the attorney general is elected by the Supreme Court in Tennessee and by secret legislative ballot in Maine. State attorneys general have taken increasingly prominent roles in a range of regulatory issues that were not previously thought to be the province of that office. For example, former New York Attorney General Eliot Spitzer strategically mounted a series of investigations targeted at financial regulation.[75] More generally, state attorneys general have pursued multi-state litigation actions (e.g., tobacco litigation) in the service of advancing consumer protection.[76] Each state attorney general is assisted by a cadre of assistant attorneys general.

At the federal level, the Office of the **Attorney General** was created by the Judiciary Act on September 24, 1789.[77] This makes the U.S. attorney general the fourth position of what is now considered a cabinet-level position created by Congress, though the U.S.

Department of Justice (which the U.S. attorney general heads) was not created until 1870.[78] The Office of the Attorney General has 10 attorneys on staff and is assisted by the Office of the Deputy Attorney General (with a staff of 21) and the Office of the Associate Attorney General (with a staff of 10).[79] The U.S. attorney general is the chief law enforcement officer of the federal government and serves as an advisor to the president, heads of executive departments, and other federal agencies on legal matters.[80] The Office of the **Solicitor General** is also part of the Department of Justice. The solicitor general, whose office has 28 attorneys on staff, supervises and conducts litigation on behalf of the United States in the U.S. Supreme Court. He or she has broad discretion to determine which cases to appeal to the Court and the arguments to be made on behalf of the government before the Court.[81]

In addition to the offices detailed above, attorneys work in a host of other governmental organizations. At the federal level, every government agency employs attorneys, including the Bureau of Prisons; Bureau of Alcohol, Tobacco, Firearms, and Explosives; the U.S. Marshals Service; the Foreign Claims Settlement Commission; and the Office of Tribal Justice. Some of these organizations employ more than 100 attorneys (e.g., the Bureau of Prisons) while others employ 10 or fewer (e.g., the Office of Tribal Justice). These lawyers engage in a wide range of law-related work including formulating regulations consistent with federal legislation, personnel matters, inter-agency coordination, and audits. Similarly, at the state and local level, attorneys work in a wide range of government settings.[82] In some states (e.g., Colorado, Georgia), the attorney general's office provides legal services to most executive agencies. But, in other states (e.g., Illinois, New York), at least some agencies are authorized by law to employ independent in-house counsel and, in a handful of states (e.g., Florida, Wisconsin), virtually every agency has its own in-house counsel. Lawyers can also be found working in a range of capacities in local government. Some, for example, work for city law departments, such as the San Diego City Attorney's Department, which employs 120 attorneys, and Chicago's Law Department, which employs more than 250 attorneys. Others work for city councils or other municipal-level governments, providing legal advice on the day-to-day local government operations as well as drafting legislation, negotiating public contracts, and vetting real estate or other legal agreements. Several aspects of working as an attorney for local government are attractive, including the fact that new lawyers are often entrusted with greater independent responsibilities earlier in their tenure than their counterparts working as law firm associates.

The contrast between private practice and government law work can manifest itself in many ways, including differences in salary, prestige, and future advancement in the profession. Much has been written about how lawyers in general are supposedly unhappy and dissatisfied with their careers. As we turn to this question in the following section, consider whether lawyer happiness depends on practice settings and the type of law work in which a lawyer is engaged. Is there a relationship between how lawyers feel and where they work and what they do?

ARE LAWYERS UNHAPPY?

Headlines such as "More Lawyers Are Less Happy at Their Work, Survey Finds"[83] and "Why So Many Lawyers are Unhappy with Their Jobs"[84] paint a picture of lawyers who are dissatisfied with their careers. *U.S. News & World Report* publishes an annual list of the 100 best jobs in the nation based on job openings, advancement opportunities, career fulfillment, and salary expectations. According to their formula, the top jobs of 2015 were Dentist (#1), Nurse Practitioner (#2), Software Developer (#3), Physician (#4), and Dental Hygienist (#5). At the same time, the job of Lawyer sinks lower in the rankings each year. Specifically, in 2013, the publication ranked Lawyer thirty-fifth out of 100 and the following year it fell out of the top 50 behind such careers as Nail Technician (#49), Maintenance/Repair Worker (#34), Esthetician—a skin care specialist—(#29), and Massage Therapist (#27).[85] In 2015, Lawyer was ranked fifty-third, beating out Massage Therapist (#62) and Maintenance Worker (#55) but still trailing Nail Technician (#52) and Esthetician (#24).[86] It's no wonder there are so many news stories about the comparative unhappiness of lawyers. However, empirical research has called this conventional wisdom into question: lawyers in general are relatively satisfied with their careers.

For example, in a survey of members of the Minnesota bar conducted in 1997 and 1998, three-fourths of the 1,038 respondents "generally agree[d] with the statement 'I am satisfied with the practice of law as a meaningful part of my life.'"[87] Furthermore, the study showed no statistically significant differences between men and women. The responses did show a significant difference across years in practice, with 86 percent of those in practice 31 or more years agreeing with the statement while only 68 percent of those in practice 10 years or less agreeing with the statement. Another study—After the JD (AJD)[88]—reported that 80 percent of respondents were "moderately satisfied" or "extremely satisfied" with their decision to become a lawyer and reported relatively high levels of satisfaction with their jobs.[89] A follow-up study[90] reported that three-quarters of the respondents were moderately or extremely satisfied with their decision to become a lawyer and reported that they were relatively satisfied with their jobs. A new measure of job satisfaction included for the most recent wave of data collection was "Balance of personal life and work," with a mean response rate of 5.13 on a 7-point scale (1 = highly dissatisfied, 7 = highly satisfied). Finally the report found that those in private practice generally were less satisfied than those in government, legal services, and public defender and public interest jobs. Thus, the authors of the report concluded that "contrary to media accounts, AJD respondents in both waves of the study reported generally high levels of satisfaction."[91] Interestingly, a recent study using AJD data focused on level of satisfaction based on the relative prestige of the particular law school the lawyer attended, finding that respondents from the top law schools are the least satisfied with their decision to become a lawyer while those graduating from the lower-tiered law schools are the most satisfied.[92]

HOW DO WE KNOW?

Does Where You Go to Law School Influence Your Career Satisfaction?

In a recent study, sociologist Ronit Dinovitzer and law professor Bryan Garth argue that job satisfaction depends in part on social origins and the credentials related to those origins.[93] They rely on the work of Pierre Bourdieu, who found that class positions explain both which schools students will attend and how well students will fit with the mission of specific schools. "A Bourdieusian approach thereby emphasizes that social stratification is not merely externally produced, but that individuals, through their habitus—the set of practices and dispositions acquired through the repetition of living life—internalize what they can reasonably expect in life and, more important, what they cannot." Thus, the authors examined whether those who have lower career expectations (those attending lower tiered law schools) are more satisfied with their decision to become a lawyer.

The authors relied on the first wave of data from the After the JD study, a national longitudinal survey of law students who graduated in 2000. Specifically, they used data from the national sample of 3,950 respondents. In order to determine respondents' satisfaction with their careers, the authors used responses to the following question: "How satisfied are you with your decision to become a lawyer?" Respondents were given a 5-point scale, ranging from 1 ("extremely satisfied") to 5 ("extremely dissatisfied"). Dinovitzer and Garth subsequently modeled satisfaction as a dichotomous variable, with extremely satisfied equal to 1 and other responses equal to 0. In addition to law school tiers—which were divided into Top 10, Top 11–20, Top 21–40, Top 41–100, Tier 3, and Tier 4—the researchers controlled for other factors that they hypothesized would influence career satisfaction. These factors included demographic factors, such as gender, marital status, and whether the respondent has children; region; practice setting, such as solo practitioner, private firm 2–20, private firm 21–100, private firm 101–250, private firm 251+, government, and business; and salary. The results showed that respondents with children were more likely to report that they are extremely satisfied with their decision to become a lawyer and that, for lawyers working in private practice, the larger the firm, the lower the career satisfaction, with satisfaction decreasing as firm size increases.

Law school tier also influences expressions of career satisfaction, with lawyers graduating from elite law schools significantly less satisfied with their decision to become a lawyer when compared to graduates of fourth-tier schools. Graduates of top-10 schools have the lowest odds of reporting that they were extremely satisfied, followed by graduates of top-20 schools. Respondents graduating from top-40 schools and lower tiers report levels of satisfaction that are no different than respondents from fourth-tier law schools. Finally, the authors found that as salary increases, the odds of being extremely satisfied with the decision to become a lawyer increase as well.

Finally, in a meta-analysis[94] of the research on lawyer satisfaction over a 25-year time period (1984–2007), law professor Jerome Organ reported that the average level of satisfaction among lawyers is 79 percent.[95] Thus, he concluded that "[t]his data confirms what has been stated in several articles: the 'conventional wisdom' regarding the level of dissatisfaction in the legal profession would appear to be somewhat misleading. As a general matter, lawyers are relatively satisfied with their jobs/careers."[96] Furthermore, the author also drew the following conclusions from his analysis of the data: more experienced attorneys are more satisfied than newer attorneys; attorneys in private practice are less satisfied than attorneys working in public interest or for the government; women are generally not less satisfied than men; and that racial minority attorneys are not significantly less satisfied than racial majority attorneys.

When it comes to lawyer satisfaction, the myth is belied by the reality. Despite stories in the popular press about unhappy lawyers, systematic empirical research demonstrates exactly the opposite. Perhaps this should not be surprising given that—as we pointed out earlier in this chapter—lawyers generally enjoy relatively high levels of prestige and income. In addition, as the previous chapter demonstrates, lawyers have spent considerable time, money, and effort in obtaining their law degrees and passing the bar exam. To be sure, while some lawyers are unhappy and have abandoned the profession for different lines of work, the vast majority remains in the profession and are relatively satisfied with that choice.

Having discussed who comprises the legal profession, the types of law work they do, the settings they do it in, and whether or not they are happy with their choices, we now turn to the topic of their clients. Specifically, we discuss who has access to lawyers and the differences between high-cost and low-cost legal help. Ultimately, access to the legal profession is largely a function of money and that has important implications for justice in America. If money can't buy you love, can it buy you legal access, representation, and protection?

ACCESS TO LAWYERS

The notion that everyone is entitled to an attorney is another myth. The reality is that there is no absolute right to legal services or representation, except that those accused of serious crimes are guaranteed an attorney under the Sixth Amendment to the U.S. Constitution, which states: "In all criminal prosecutions, the accused shall enjoy the right . . . to have the assistance of counsel for his defense."[97] The U.S. Supreme Court has made plain that, in both federal and state criminal cases, courts are required to appoint counsel to represent defendants who are unable to retain their own counsel independently, though only if the defendant is actually imprisoned.[98] However, all others are not so entitled. To be sure, the finest lawyers in the country are available to those who can afford to pay. In this sense, money does buy access, and perhaps even a sense of entitlement to legal representation. Yet the poor and middle class have difficulty finding and using lawyers.[99] They do, however, have several low-cost options for obtaining legal help.

High-Cost Legal Help

Most large firms use the **billable-hour** system as the mechanism to charge clients. Under this system, clients are charged for the total hours each lawyer spends on their case, with the hourly rate for each lawyer dependent on his or her experience and expertise. In 2012, the median hourly billing rate (on a firm-wide basis) was $425,[100] up from $324 in 2006.[101] Partners, of course, charge more than associates. For example, in 2007, the top rate at Wilmer Cutler Pickering Hale and Dorr was $1,000 an hour.[102] Even more recently, the top reported rate was almost $1,300 an hour, charged by a real estate investment trust partner in Lock Lord's Dallas office.[103] The overall average number of billable hours required of an associate is 1,879; however, as Table 3.6 reports, there is a nontrivial amount of variation depending on the size of the firm. The majority of firms with more than 250 attorneys require a minimum of 1,900 billable hours per year. In contrast, a mere 16 percent of small firms (those with 50 or fewer attorneys) require 1,900 or more billable hours. Almost half of the very largest firms (those with more than 700 attorneys) mandate 1,950 hours or more. This

TABLE 3.6
Billable Hours Requirement by Firm Size

FIRM SIZE	1,800 BILLABLE HOURS	1,850 BILLABLE HOURS	1,900 BILLABLE HOURS	1,950 BILLABLE HOURS	2,000 BILLABLE HOURS	AVERAGE BILLABLE HOURS REQUIRED
≤ 50	28.0 percent	16.0 percent	6.7 percent	6.7 percent	2.7 percent	1,778
51–100	37.9 percent	25.3 percent	11.6 percent	4.2 percent	8.4 percent	1,846
101–250	28.8 percent	20.9 percent	25.4 percent	9.6 percent	4.0 percent	1,856
251–500	20.6 percent	10.1 percent	31.6 percent	18.9 percent	12.3 percent	1,897
501–700	5.8 percent	31.1 percent	32.6 percent	20.0 percent	10.0 percent	1,899
> 700	7.1 percent	12.4 percent	34.7 percent	30.0 percent	15.9 percent	1,918
All	19.0 percent	18.8 percent	27.2 percent	16.9 percent	9.7 percent	1,879

"Number of Associate Hours Worked Increases at Largest Firms," *NALP Bulletin*, February 2012. http://www.nalp.org/billable_hours_feb2012.

Image 3.4 And They Get Away With It

This 1914 comic strip "The Lawyer – 'And they get away with it'" depicts a man who wants to open a pickle factory and is seeking legal advice from Mister Windbag, a lawyer, who speaks a lot of nonsense, then charges the man $500—the equivalent of nearly $12,000 today. Prints and Photographs Division, Library of Congress, Washington, D.C.

requirement means that associates routinely work more than 8-hour days and on weekends to "make their hours," particularly since "[i]t typically takes at least 50 hours a week to bill an honest[104] 40 hours to a client." Billing at $400 per hour, an associate who bills 2,000 hours earns $800,000 for her firm—generally four times more than the associate's salary. Associates that hit their marks can earn bonuses and pay increases. Partners also maximize the billing for the clients they control as that generally determines the partner's annual share of the firm's profits. Furthermore, partners are reluctant to share responsibility for their most important clients with others in the firm because those clients are the partner's ticket to a more lucrative job in another firm should the partner choose to leave.

There are many critics of the billable-hour system. They point to high-profile instances where firms overcharged clients, such as in a 2010 case against DLA Piper that revealed memos where the firm's lawyers famously wrote one another: "Churn that bill, baby!" and "THAT bill shall know no limits."[105] Steven J. Harper, a former partner at Kirkland & Ellis, said: "The billable-hour system is the way most lawyers in the big firms charge clients, but it serves no one. Well, almost no one. It brings most equity partners in those firms great wealth. Law firm leaders call it a leveraged pyramid. Most associates call it a living hell."[106] Another critic made a distinction between the partners and the associates: "The problem isn't the $1,000-an-hour lawyer who's worth it. It's the $450-per-hour associates who aren't."[107] But reforms such as fixed or flat fees for services performed have not taken hold.[108] In 2010, alternative fee arrangements accounted for only 16 percent of the revenues at the nation's biggest law firms.[109]

Low-Cost Legal Help

There is a common perception that attorneys are expensive and one has to be rich in order to afford one. This perception is, no doubt, at least partially a product of numerous studies that have found that "for the vast majority of legal problems or legal needs of low-income households, and only slightly fewer of the needs of moderate-income household, no one from the household obtained the advice or assistance of an attorney."[110] But, while our discussion above suggests that money can certainly secure top-notch legal counsel, individuals do not necessarily have to have any money to obtain legal services. There are a number of low-cost avenues available. The contingency fee system is the most common way for those who cannot afford an attorney to secure one. Legal clinics and legal insurance also help to meet the legal needs of low-income individuals, and the poor routinely take advantage of a number of legal aid options.

POP CULTURE

Erin Brockovich

In the 2000 film *Erin Brockovich*, Julia Roberts plays a fictionalized real-life legal assistant (the Erin Brockovich of the movie's title) who discovers that a city's water supply has been polluted by a power company. She suspects that the illnesses contracted by a number of individuals and families were caused by the tainted water and convinces her boss, attorney Ed Masry (played by the celebrated actor Albert Finney, who, among other things, voiced two roles in Tim Burton's *The Corpse Bride*), to pursue the matter. When Masry meets with some of the alleged victims, he lays out the case and presents them with a retainer agreement (i.e., contract) for his counsel. The victims are worried that they will not be able to afford his services and one of them asks: "It doesn't say here how much this whole thing's gonna cost us." Masry replies matter-of-factly: "My fee's forty percent of whatever you get awarded." The group is stunned by the figure but earthy, blue-collar Brockovich chimes in both to empathize and to explain why the fee is as high as it is: "Boy, do I know how you feel. First time I heard that number, I said you got to be kidding me. Forty goddamn percent? I'm the one who's injured, and this joker who sits at a desk all day is gonna walk away with almost half my reward?" Masry is visibly nervous at Brockovich's side but she asks: "Then I asked him how much he makes if I didn't get anything?" Masry replies: "Then I don't get anything either." Brockovich concludes: "And I realized, he's taking a chance too." The victims reach for their pens and sign.

Image 3.5 *Erin Brockovich*
Julia Roberts as Erin Brockovich and Albert Finney as Ed Masrey in the movie Erin Brockovich (2000). *The film is an example of how most law work takes place outside a courtroom and how the contingency fee system can allow people access to the legal system who otherwise would not be able to afford it.* Photo by Getty Images.

The scene illustrates both the myth that legal services can only be obtained by the rich and the reality that the contingency fee system is a common option for acquiring low-cost legal help. More generally, the movie also demonstrates the reality that most law work takes place outside the courtroom, with both lawyers and their legal assistants spending considerable time doing research and talking to clients and others involved in their cases.

Private attorneys will often agree to represent clients on a **contingency fee** basis, a model of compensation for legal services that originated in the American context in the nineteenth century.[111] In civil matters, lawyers represent clients for no charge and pay all the legal costs associated with the case. Why would a lawyer do this? Because clients agree to pay the attorney a fee (typically anywhere from 30–40 percent of the monetary award), contingent on the attorney winning the case. From the perspective of a client, there are both pros and cons to the contingency fee system. On the pro side, contingency fees help level the playing field in that injured plaintiffs with little or no money can take on big, deep-pocketed corporations and insurance companies. In this sense, contingency fees provide a vehicle for equal representation in civil matters. Litigants who are not financially well endowed do not have to incur what are often large legal costs as their case wends its way through the legal system. Further, the fact that an attorney is working for a client on a contingency fee basis—and, hence, will receive no compensation if he does not win—serves (at least theoretically) as a powerful incentive for the attorney to put forth all of the effort he can to secure the win.

Still, at least some critics suggest that the contingency fee system is not all that it is cracked up to be as an equalizer of access to legal counsel. One problem is that attorneys play a **gate-keeping** function. It is up to the lawyer to take the case and she may not if the payout will be too low or the case too difficult. For example, a survey of contingency fee practitioners in Wisconsin shows that, over all, lawyers reported accepting cases from only a mean of 46 percent of the potential clients who contacted them.[112] The survey also shows that women lawyers are more selective than men, lawyers with more than 20 years of experience are less selective than those with 20 or fewer years of experience, and selectivity decreases as the lawyer's dependence on contingency fee work goes up. Lack of liability and inadequate damages are the dominant reasons for declining cases, accounting for about 80 percent of the declined cases.

Other problems with the contingency fee system include the fact that the awards can be disproportionate to a lawyer's work. No matter how little lawyers do, they still get the contingency fee, leaving the plaintiff with only two-thirds or less of any monetary award. Imagine an attorney settling a million-dollar case with a single phone call and pocketing over $300,000. That is one expensive phone call! Additionally, lawyers working on a contingency fee basis may well feel a pull to settle big-fee cases. Lawyers may be inclined to settle a case just to get paid, taking the easy way out at the expense of their clients who may have reaped greater rewards had the case gone to trial or been developed further. Yet one more drawback to the contingency fee system is that cases with the potential for creating new law and policy are not applicable if there is no money involved. For example, in a right-to-die case the client's goal is to change the law to be allowed to die. There is no monetary award that is possible. Thus, clients must pay on an hourly basis in these kinds of cases, making the contingency fee system a poor vehicle for policy change.

HOW DO WE KNOW?

The Impact of Fee Arrangement on Lawyer Effort

Economic theory suggests that hourly paid lawyers will spend more than the optimal time on a case and that lawyers paid on a contingent fee will spend less than the optimal time on a case. In other words, lawyers paid by the hour will look for ways to maximize the number of hours they can bill while lawyers paid on a contingency fee basis will look for ways to minimize the number of hours they put in. According to this account, both types of lawyers are attempting to maximize profit. Is this true? A study by political scientist Herbert Kritzer and his colleagues provides a systematic empirical test of these propositions.[113]

Specifically, the authors interviewed 371 hourly fee lawyers and 267 contingency fee lawyers who worked on cases selected randomly from 12 state and federal courts. The authors controlled for (that is, took into account) many factors that are believed to influence lawyer effort. These can be clustered into five categories: (1) the process of interaction among the parties, such as the number of pleadings, briefs, and motions filed by the other side; (2) case characteristics, such as the stakes (for example, the lawyer's estimate of the amount of money the client should have been willing to accept to settle the case); (3) participant characteristics, which include client characteristics (such as whether the client is an individual or an organization) and lawyer characteristics (such as general experience, litigation experience, specialization, craftsmanship); (4) participant goals, which include client goals and lawyer goals; and (5) processing and case management characteristics, such as client control and participation. The authors used the lawyer's hours as the dependent variable in their analyses.

They estimated two separate multivariate models to relate the independent variables to the dependent variable—one for hourly fee lawyers and the other for contingent fee lawyers. For the "average" case (that is, a case where all factors are set at their average values), the hourly fee lawyer spends 50 hours on the case whereas the contingent fee lawyer spends 46 hours on the case. When the research team disaggregated the impact of fee arrangement by the size of stakes (holding all other variables at their average values), they found that contingent fee lawyers put in significantly less time for "small" cases than do hourly fee lawyers, but they put in more time for "big" cases. On a typical $6,000 case (the median case in state courts in 1978 involved about $4,500), the gap was 7 hours.

Additionally, the authors found that the kinds of variables that influenced lawyers differed depending on the fee arrangement:

> Contingent fee lawyers appear to be highly sensitive to the potential productivity of their time and are less affected by craft-oriented factors. This effect can be seen in two variables: craftsmanship and response to opposing party's briefs. The contingent fee lawyer does spend time in response to the opposing side's briefs, but the response involves half as much time per brief as the response of hourly fee lawyers. While the hourly fee lawyer is strongly influenced by commitment to craftsmanship, the contingent fee lawyer is not. On the other hand, the level of effort of contingent fee lawyers goes up at a faster rate as the level of stakes increases than that of hourly fee lawyers. In other words, the contingent fee lawyer appears sensitive to the potential return to be achieved from a case, which is closely related to stakes. The hourly fee lawyer's return from a case is not tied to stakes, and other types of considerations (e.g., the client's goals, the nature of the forum, etc.) have a greater influence.[114]

Thus, the authors did find a gap in the amount of time that a contingency fee lawyer will spend on a "small" case, but they did not know whether this gap affected case outcomes. In any event, even if contingency fee lawyers do spend less time on cases than would hourly fee lawyers, the authors concluded that the client is still benefited by a low-cost, low-risk opportunity to pursue a claim.

Legal insurance and legal clinics are a second category of low-cost legal help. They generally deal with relatively routine matters such as landlord-tenant disputes, wills and contracts, divorces, and criminal cases. **Legal insurance** is similar to limited medical insurance. It is most often obtained through a company or labor union program where individuals pay a monthly fee and can obtain legal advice when necessary. Legal insurance is much less common in the United States compared to, for example, Europe.[115] It is typically most common in jurisdictions that have the English rule (or "loser pays" rule), which requires losing litigants to pay part of or all the legal fees incurred by the winning litigant. **Legal clinics** provide free or low-cost consultations and/or classes that individuals can attend to learn about their legal rights and options. Legal clinics originated as a mechanism for the provision of practical training for law students. For example, the clinical program at the Dedman School of Law at Southern Methodist University provides practical skills training to its students and includes six specialized clinics (Civil Clinic, Criminal Justice Clinic, Federal Taxpayers Clinic, Small Business and Trademark Clinics, W.W. Caruth, Jr. Child Advocacy Clinic, and the Consumer Advocacy Project). Though legal clinics attached to law schools are still common, legal clinics in non-academic settings have proliferated since their origination. For example, the Legal Aid Society of Mid-New York offers Self-Help Divorce Clinic, Self-Help Consumer Law Clinic, and Veterans Clinic. The Chicago Legal Clinic provides educational seminars and legal service in more than a dozen different areas. Legal clinics are much more common than legal insurance.

Image 3.6 Freedman's Bureau
The Reconstruction-era Freedman's Bureau provided federal assistance to ex-slaves including legal representation. This racist poster attacked the agency by depicting whites as hard working and former slaves as lazy and dependent on the government. Rare Book and Special Collection Division, Library of Congress, Washington, D.C.

The final option for low-cost legal help is government-supported legal aid. Though the concept of government-funded legal aid for the poor has its origins in the mid-nineteenth century, it was not until the mid-twentieth century that the concept took hold in the United States.[116] The post-Civil War Freedman's Bureau provided legal representation during Reconstruction for newly freed slaves. Toward the end of the nineteenth century, private charities performed basic legal services for the poor. Slowly, government funding for legal aid took root. It began in New York City in 1876 with the Legal Aid Society of New York and spread throughout the urban areas of the nation. By 1965, there was still no national program. Yet there was some form of legal aid in nearly every major American city. One hundred fifty-seven organizations employed over 400 lawyers with an aggregate budget of nearly $4.5 million.[117] As part of President Lyndon Johnson's War on Poverty, the federal Legal Services Program began in the Office of Economic Opportunity in 1965.[118] In 1974, it was reorganized as the Legal Services Corporation (LSC), providing grants-in-aid to local legal aid organizations, which rely mainly on local, state, and charitable contributions to function.

The overwhelming source of legal aid funding is from **interest on lawyer trust accounts (IOLTA)**, which are bank accounts where lawyers keep clients' money.[119] The interest is distributed to legal aid programs. IOLTA began in the late 1960s and early 1970s to generate funds for legal services for the poor. The idea was that any interest obtained from a lawyer trust account that was not substantial or long term would go to legal aid. Though the legality of IOLTA programs have been challenged in court,[120] today every state and the District of Columbia (plus the U.S. Virgin Islands) operate IOLTA programs. Currently, 44 of these jurisdictions require lawyers to participate in IOLTA while six permit lawyers to opt out of participation and participation is voluntary in two others. In 2007, IOLTA programs generated more than $371 million for legal aid nationwide.[121]

However, because the program's funding is based on interest rates and the health of the legal profession in general, funding can fluctuate. For example, IOLTA funding plummeted to a mere $93.2 million in 2011, a shocking decrease of almost 75 percent from 2007.[122] When the economy is down, legal aid programs are forced to scramble to make up the difference lost from low-yielding IOLTA programs. They lobby state legislatures, request greater support from local law firms, and ask for cuts in filing fees, *pro hac vice* fees (fees collected from an attorney who is not a member of the appropriate bar but is permitted to participate in a particular case in that jurisdiction), and victim funds. In addition, private attorneys are asked to take on more *pro bono* work. Under the worst case scenario, where legal aid firms cannot meet their budgets, they have to lay off attorneys, staff, and start turning away those in need of legal help. In 2008, the president of legal services for New Jersey said that for every million dollars New Jersey loses in money for legal aid services, it must lay off 20 staff members and serve 900 fewer clients.[123]

As the preceding discussion illustrates, money is the driving force in determining whether and how the public gains access to the legal profession. For those who do, there is certainly an expectation that lawyers should always have the best interests of their clients in mind. Yet there is also a perception that lawyers are unethical—particularly compared with other professionals such as medical doctors. In the next section we consider the issue of legal ethics and examine how professional codes are meant to police the attorneys and ensure ethical behavior—particularly when it comes to representing clients. Are lawyers immoral, valueless, liars?

LEGAL ETHICS

Spoiler alert! In the 1997 film *The Devil's Advocate*, Keanu Reeves plays a hotshot defense attorney who joins a slick New York law firm only to find out that his boss is the devil himself. Is it possible to portray attorneys as anything worse than the devil? It is a common myth that lawyers are unethical shysters who bilk their clients for money and manipulate the system on behalf of those they represent even if it subverts truth and justice. While the origins of the term "shyster" are uncertain, one likely derivation is from the German word *scheisser* (literally translated as defecator), which inspired one commentator to observe, "The shyster is indeed excrement, the filthiness of the legal profession."[124] Strong words, indeed, and while there are certainly unethical lawyers—just as there are unethical individuals in all professions—the reality is that legal professionals are governed by an enforceable code of ethics by which the vast majority abide. **Legal ethics** are the standards, rules, and codes of conduct that members of the legal profession are expected to follow and support. In this section we discuss the professional codes that lawyers swear to uphold as well as the ethical issues involved in representing clients.

POP CULTURE

The Devil's Advocate

In the 1997 film *The Devil's Advocate*, we meet a hotshot southern attorney by the name of Kevin Lomax (played by Keanu Reeves, also well known for playing Neo in the Matrix trilogy) who has never lost a case. In the film's opening sequence, we quickly see why. While Lomax does not break the law in order to win cases, he does whatever it takes (including some unsavory things) to win. Even though he knows his client is guilty of child molestation he wins the case through a harsh cross-examination of the victim. Lomax and his wife Mary Ann (played by Academy-Award winning actress Charlize Theron) move to New York City to join a law firm headed by the powerful John Milton (played by iconic actor Al Pacino). Milton is constantly forcing Lomax to question his ethics—both as an attorney and as a husband. Throughout the film, Pacino's character takes the cynical view of the legal profession. He says that "[l]awyers are the devil's ministry" and that the legal profession is "the ultimate backstage pass" and "the new priesthood" for a sinful world. Eventually, Lomax finds out that Milton is literally the devil himself. Milton tells him: "Who, in their right mind . . . could possibly deny that the Twentieth Century was entirely mine?" Ultimately, Lomax—like many attorneys—must choose whether to join the devil and continue engaging in unethical behavior or not. In the end, Lomax declines and is able to go back to the southern courtroom where it all began. This time, rather than destroy the child-molestation victim through a harsh cross-examination, he tells the judge: "Your Honor, I'm terribly sorry, but I can no longer represent my client. I need to be replaced as counsel."

Professional Codes

Every state—with the exceptions of California and Maine—has adopted a version of the ABA's *Model Rules of Professional Conduct*, which covers issues such as client–lawyer relationships, the lawyer as counselor, the lawyer as advocate, transactions with persons other than clients, law firms and associations, public service, communications involving legal services, and maintaining the integrity of the profession. The ABA once prohibited lawyer advertising, the direct solicitation of clients, and aiding the unauthorized practice of law.[125] The U.S. Supreme Court held that these were unlawful limitations on competition among lawyers and the public's access to legal services. For example, in *Bates v. State Bar of Arizona*, the Court struck down a state law that prohibited lawyers from advertising for their services.[126] The Court held that lawyers have a First Amendment right to advertise and that the public would benefit from having more information about legal services. Thus, the justices concluded, state prohibitions "inhibit the free flow of commercial information and keep the public in ignorance."[127]

Currently, the ABA code (and state codes modeled on it) heavily emphasize a lawyer's business relationship with clients: keeping funds that clients have deposited with their lawyers separate from the lawyers' personal money; maintaining client privacy; fully and faithfully representing clients; avoiding conflicts of interest with clients; informing clients

of the progress of their case; and providing *pro bono* work. For example, Rule 1.4 of the Illinois Rules of Professional Conduct deals with communication and states that

> a lawyer shall: (1) promptly inform the client of any decision or circumstance with respect to which the client's informed consent . . . is required by these Rules; (2) reasonably consult with the client about the means by which the client's objectives are to be accomplished; (3) keep the client reasonably informed about the status of the matter; (4) promptly comply with reasonable requests for information; and (5) consult with the client about any relevant limitation on the lawyer's conduct when the lawyer knows that the client expects assistance not permitted by the Rules of Professional Conduct or other law.[128]

Whether lawyers adequately comply with these standards to their clients' satisfaction is another matter.

Ethical codes are enforced at the state level.[129] Most states place regulation of the practice of law with the state supreme court, but the courts, in turn, give most of the responsibility to disciplinary committees of the state bar association.[130] Penalties for ethical violations vary, depending upon the nature and severity of the violation. Law professor Leslie Levin has usefully categorized sanctions into four types: incapacitating sanctions, expressive sanctions, rehabilitative sanctions, and consumer-oriented responses.[131]

Incapacitating sanctions are punishments that serve to protect the public by preventing the offending lawyer from violating professional standards. The most severe incapacitating sanction is **disbarment**: the termination of an attorney's status as an attorney. Another form of incapacitating sanction is **suspension**, which is the temporary removal of an attorney from practice for a specified period of time.

Expressive sanctions are punishments intended to express a message regarding the culpability of the attorney and the level of condemnation attached to the misconduct. The message can be intended for the attorney in question, the legal community, the public, or some combination thereof. The most severe type of expressive sanction involved reprimanding the attorney publicly. A **public reprimand** is a punishment that typically entails publication of the errant attorney's name and misconduct. But expressive sanctions may also be done privately. A **private admonition** punishment usually involves the appearance of the violator before a court or disciplinary body where the admonition is delivered.

Rehabilitative sanctions are punishments based on the notion that human behavior (including attorney behavior) can be reformed given appropriate opportunities for reflection. The most serious form of rehabilitative sanction is **probation** where an attorney is subject to monitoring or limited in some way. Another form of rehabilitative sanction is **mandatory education** in professional responsibility, where an attorney is required to take a class on legal ethics.

Finally, **consumer-oriented responses** are based on a broader conception of the dangers clients face. Attorneys who steal from clients and perpetuate frauds on the court are the most severe forms of endangering clients. Lesser, but far more common, occurrences of attorney shortcomings include neglect, failure to communicate, and incompetence. Thinking of these as dangers faced by legal consumers and attorney discipline as a means of addressing legal consumer complaints puts the focus on restitution and conciliation, as opposed to punishment per se.

Very few complaints result in any sanction by disciplinary committees. For example, in 2000, 114,000 complaints were filed but a mere 4 percent resulted in formal discipline.[132] More recently, almost 118,000 complaints were filed in 2007 but less than 5,000 attorneys were charged with disciplinary violations.[133] Suing an attorney for malpractice is an option but malpractice is very difficult to prove, as well as time consuming and expensive.

States routinely look to improve the conduct of their licensed attorneys. They revise and update their codes—often through committees of the state bar association—and they require attorneys to keep up to date on the latest developments in legal ethics, typically through mandatory continuing legal education classes.[134] In Iowa, for example, attorneys must complete a minimum of 15 credit hours of continuing legal education each year, including a minimum of 3 hours every 2 years devoted exclusively to legal ethics. In California, attorneys must complete 25 credit hours of continuing education, including 4 hours devoted to ethics, 1 hour regarding substance abuse or mental illness that impairs professional competence, and 1 hour directed at the elimination of bias in the profession.

Representing Clients

One ethical area that attorneys routinely struggle with is choosing clients. Every person accused of a serious crime is entitled to a lawyer and the lawyer has an ethical obligation to provide a defense against criminal charges no matter what the crime, be it rape, child molestation, or serial murder. According to ABA rules, attorneys who are appointed to represent clients must do so diligently unless they can show good cause for turning down the appointment. Valid reasons for declining include representation that would result in a violation of the Rules of Professional Conduct or other law, an unreasonable financial burden on the lawyer, or if "the client or the cause is so repugnant to the lawyer as to be likely to impair the client-lawyer relationship or the lawyer's ability to represent the client."[135] To be sure, no one wants an attorney to do less than her best when representing a client and codes of conduct allow attorneys to opt out of situations that they feel will compromise their ability to provide effective counsel and advocacy.

Another area where ethical questions often arise is in trial tactics. Are defense attorneys obligated to do everything the law will allow to win an acquittal or avoid a financial judgment against their client? Or, if the evidence seems clear that the defendant is guilty, should they temper their defense strategy to ensure that justice is done? The ABA rules specify how the lawyer as advocate is expected to behave in all situations. For example, ABA Rule 3.4 states that lawyers shall not alter, destroy, conceal, or obstruct another party's access to evidence; falsify evidence or counsel witnesses to testify falsely; disobey court rules; make frivolous discovery requests during pretrial; or make irrelevant or personal opinion statements at trial.[136]

CONCLUSION

There are countless myths about lawyers: they work exclusively or primarily in courtrooms; they win or lose cases for their clients at trial; they all work as practicing attorneys; women and minorities have little if any chance of breaking into the profession; attorneys have broad knowledge of all legal matters; the job of a lawyer is prestigious; everyone is entitled to an attorney; and attorneys are unethical shysters who put their own interests before those of their clients. While there may be some truth to each of these myths, the reality is—more often than not—substantially different: lawyers work in offices at desks where they read, write, and talk to other lawyers; lawyers bargain and negotiate in an attempt to stay out of court; some law school graduates work in jobs that do not require bar passage or even law degrees; women and minorities continue to make inroads into the legal profession, so much so, that women now comprise half of the new lawyers entering the profession each year; lawyers are specialists who know a great deal about relatively narrow areas of the law; some law jobs are far more prestigious than others; lawyers are generally satisfied with their jobs; there is no absolute right to legal representation; and lawyers are ethical professionals governed by rules and codes of conduct.

The law profession is split into specialized subgroups with little overlap. Broadly speaking, lawyers choose transactional work or litigation, business or personal law, and work in either big cities or small towns. There are hundreds of subspecialties and lawyers who practice in one area will rarely if ever practice in another. Prestige, social status, and income are closely tied to the type of law practiced and the clients represented. Corporate lawyers in large business law firms who specialize in securities, tax, antitrust, and patent law hold the most prestige among legal professionals and also make the most money. Conversely, attorneys at the bottom of the prestige/specialization scale—those handling landlord-tenant disputes, divorces, and general family law—will likely never be rich.

Low-cost legal help is available on a small scale (local, state level) for poor individuals. While there are pros and cons to the contingency fee system, it is a common way for those with little or no money to secure legal representation. Free or low-cost legal clinics and legal insurance are available for relatively routine matters and government-supported legal aid is offered for lower-income individuals.

Ethical standards in the law profession have become somewhat relaxed over time. Attorneys may advertise for their services and solicit clients in ways that were considered unethical prior to the 1970s. State professional codes of conduct—modeled on ABA rules—govern what attorneys may or may not do in the practice of law. Though state supreme courts are the ultimate arbiters of any ethical dispute, state bar associations often conduct hearings and handle discipline when necessary. Still, despite the popular image that attorneys are unethical shysters out to exploit their clients and make as much money as possible, the reality is that only a small percentage of lawyers behave unethically.

Suggested Readings

Alan Dershowitz. *Letters to a Young Lawyer* (New York, NY: Basic Books, 2001). The Harvard law professor writes about the allure of money, fame, and success and how young lawyers can find personally fulfilling legal careers. He addresses the challenges of representing clients with few socially redeeming qualities and reveals some of the "tricks of the trade" that have made him successful in the past.

Steven J. Harper. *The Lawyer Bubble: A Profession in Crisis* (New York, NY: Basic Books, 2013). A critical look at the legal profession, which the author characterizes as one in crisis due to schools obsessed with rankings, law firm partners preoccupied with maximizing profits, and other problems resulting from short-term thinking. The author calls for greater honesty about the legal job market, discusses the financial incentives that drive bad behavior, and charts the problems associated with the billable-hour model.

Robert A. Kagan. *Adversarial Legalism: The American Way of Law.* (Cambridge, MA: Harvard University Press, 2001). Discusses the American legal system's basis on an adversarial model of legal opposition and winners and losers. The author discusses the history of American law and how it relates to broader political developments. He contrasts the American system with other models around the world and argues that, while adversarial legalism has many strengths, it is costly and unpredictable, can alienate citizens, and frustrates justice.

Herbert M. Kritzer. *Risks, Reputations, and Rewards: Contingency Fee Legal Practice in the United States* (Stanford, CA: Stanford University Press, 2004). Comprehensive treatment of the contingency fee system including how lawyers select cases, manage their work, and deal with the pressure to settle.

Nancy Levit and Douglas O. Linder. *The Happy Lawyer: Making a Good Life in the Law* (New York, NY: Oxford University Press, 2010). Details the causes of unhappiness among lawyers and offers suggestions for pursuing happy, fulfilling careers in the law.

Lynn Mather, Craig A. McEwen, and Richard J. Maiman. *Divorce Lawyers at Work: Varieties of Professionalism in Practice* (New York, NY: Oxford University Press, 2001). Explores the day-to-day decisions that lawyers make through an empirical examination of divorce lawyers in New England.

Deborah Rhode. *Pro Bono in Principle and in Practice* (Stanford, CA: Stanford University Press, 2005). Comprehensive treatment of the *pro bono* work in which lawyers engage. Based on a survey of over 3,000 lawyers, the author details how law school experiences and workplace factors impact the decisions lawyers make about *pro bono* work and offers strategies to increase and improve *pro bono* activity.

Cameron Stracher. *Double Billing: A Young Lawyer's Tale of Greed, Sex, Lies and the Pursuit of a Swivel Chair* (New York, NY: HarperCollins, 1999). A witty and engaging legal profession tell-all about the life of a new lawyer at a major Wall Street law firm.

Richard Susskind. *Tomorrow's Lawyers: An Introduction to Your Future* (New York, NY: Oxford University Press, 2013). What will the legal profession look like in the future? This book details a profession that will be characterized by virtual courts, internet-based global legal businesses, online document production, outsourcing, and web-based law practice.

Paul B. Wice. *Public Defenders and the American Justice System* (Westport, CT: Praeger, 2005). Comprehensive treatment of public defenders by contrasting a relatively small system in Newark, New Jersey, with larger operations in New York and Chicago. The author calls for a number of reforms to improve the criminal justice process.

John L. Worrall and M. Elaine Nugent-Borakove, eds. *The Changing Role of the American Prosecutor* (Albany, NY: State University of New York Press, 2008). Collection of essays by scholars who study American prosecutors which details how the job has changed from a largely reactive one to a more proactive job where creative problem solving is necessary to effectively deal with crime.

Endnotes

1   Quoted in S. Jack Horne, *Timing Is Everything* (Salt Lake City, UT: American Book Publishing, 2011): 46.

2   Charles Dickens, *The Old Curiosity Shop* (London, UK: Chapman and Hall, 1841): 113.

3   Xue-lei Pan, Howard W. Day, Wei Wang, Laurel A. Beckett, and Marc B. Schenker, "Residential Proximity to Naturally Occurring Asbestos and Mesothelioma Risk in California," *Journal of Respiratory and Critical Care Medicine*, vol. 172, no. 8 (October 2005): 1019–1025.

4   See, for example, Joshua E. Muscat and Ernst L. Wynder, "Cigarette Smoking, Asbestos Exposure, and Malignant Mesothelioma," *Cancer Research*, vol. 51, no. 9 (May 1991): 2263–2267.

5   *Horowitz v. Raybestos-Manhattan Inc.* was originally heard by the Superior Court of the State of California for the City and County of San Francisco.

6   Adapted from Mark Hansen, "Shook Hardy Smokes 'Em," *ABA Journal*, October 1, 2008.

7   See, for example, Theodore Eisenberg and Charlotte Lanvers, "What is the Settlement Rate and Why Should We Care," *Journal of Empirical Legal Studies* 6 (March 2009): 111–146; George Fisher, *Plea Bargaining's Triumph: A History of Plea Bargaining in America* (Stanford, CA: Stanford University Press, 2003).

8   Both films are based on best-selling books authored by John Grisham.

9   The data can be accessed and analyzed at http://employmentsummary.abaquestionnaire.org.

10 NALP, "Class of 2013 National Summary Report," (http://www.nalp.org/uploads/NatlSummary ChartClassof2013.pdf).

11 U.S. Bureau of Labor Statistics, Overview of BLS Wage Data by Area and Occupation, National Wage Data, for Over 800 Occupations, May 2013 (http://www.bls.gov/oes/current/oes_nat.htm).

12 U.S. Bureau of Labor Statistics, Overview of BLS Wage Data by Area and Occupation, Wage Data by Metropolitan Area, For 375 Metropolitan Statistical Areas (MSAs), 34 Metropolitan Divisions, and Over 170 Nonmetropolitan Areas, May 2013 (http://www.bls.gov/oes/current/oessrcma. htm).

13 Ameet Sachdev, "American Bar Association Taking Steps to Ensure Integrity of Employment Data from Law Schools," *Chicago Tribune*, October 21, 2011.

14 Matthew Shaer, "The Case(s) Against Law School," *New York Magazine*, March 4, 2012.

15 Law School Transparency is a non-profit legal education policy organization (http://www.lawschooltransparency.com). Established in 2009, its mission is to enhance the provision of consumer information regarding legal education, particularly information regarding employment and career prospects for law school graduates.

16 Carl Bialik, "Law-School Jobs Data Under Review," *Wall Street Journal Blogs: The Numbers Guy*, March 16, 2012.

17 Richard Posner, "The Material Basis of Jurisprudence," *Indiana Law Journal*, vol. 69 (Winter 1993): 1–37.

18 See, for example, Richard H. Sander and E. Douglass Williams, "Why Are There So Many Lawyers? Perspectives on a Turbulent Market," *Law & Social Inquiry*, vol. 14, no. 3 (Summer 1989): 431–479; Robert C. Clark, "Why So Many Lawyers? Are They Good or Bad?" *Fordham Law Review*, vol. 61 (November 1992): 275–302.

19 Terence C. Halliday, "Six Score Years and Ten: Demographic Transitions in the American Legal Profession, 1850-1980," *Law & Society Review*, vol. 20, no. 1 (1986): 53–78.

20 ABA Market Research Department, "National Lawyer Population by State–2002-2013" (http://www.americanbar.org/resources_for_lawyers/profession_statistics.html).

21 ABA Market Research Department, "National Lawyer Population by State–1989-2008" (http://www.americanbar.org/resources_for_lawyers/profession_statistics.html).

22 ABA Market Research Department, "Lawyer Demographics Table–Current" (http://www.americanbar.org/resources_for_lawyers/profession_statistics.html).

23 According to the ABA Section of Legal Education and Admissions to the Bar, women constituted 47 percent of total law school enrollment in the 2011–2012 academic year (http://www.americanbar.org/groups/legal_education/resources/statistics.html).

24 ABA Market Research Department, "Lawyer Demographics," (http://www.americanbar.org/resources_for_lawyers/profession_statistics.html).

25 Detailed coverage of legal specialties can be found in National Association for Law Placement, *The Official Guide to Legal Specialties* (Chicago, IL: BarBri Group, 2000).

26 Thomas G. Hungar and Nikesh Jindal, "Observations on the Rise of the Appellate Litigator," *The Review of Litigation*, vol. 29, no. 3 (2010): 511–536.

27 Isaac Unah, *The Supreme Court in American Politics* (New York, NY: Palgrave Macmillan, 2009): 125–126. See also, Richard J. Lazarus, "Advocacy Matters Before and Within the Supreme Court: Transforming the Court by Transforming the Bar," *Georgetown Law Journal*, vol. 96, no. 5 (June 2008): 1487–1564.

28 For a comprehensive survey of public interest law, see Alan K. Chen and Scott Cummings, *Public Interest Lawyering: A Contemporary Perspective* (New York, NY: Aspen, 2012).

29 Robert B. Stover, "The Importance of Economic Supply in Determining the Size and Quality of the Public Interest Bar," *Law & Society Review*, vol. 16, no. 3 (1981–82): 455–480; Howard S. Erlanger, Charles R. Epp, Mia Cahill, and Kathleen M. Haines, "Law Student Idealism and Job Choice: Some New Data on an Old Question," *Law & Society Review*, vol. 30, no. 4 (December 1996): 851–864.

30 Other law schools that place meaningful proportions of their graduating classes each year in public interest law jobs include College of William and Mary Marshall-Wythe School of Law, George Washington University Law School, and Florida State University College of Law. See Staci Zaretsky, "The Best Law Schools for Government and Public Interest Career Placement," *Above the Law*, April 9, 2013 (http://abovethelaw.com/2013/04/the-best-law-schools-for-government-and-public-interest-career-placement/).

31 There is considerably more scholarship devoted to public interest lawyers and firms working on behalf of liberal causes than there is devoted to those working on behalf of conservative causes. One exception is John P. Heinz, Anthony Paik, and Ann Southworth, "Lawyers for Conservative Causes: Clients, Ideology, and Social Distance," *Law & Society Review*, vol. 37, no. 2 (March 2003):

5–50. See also, Lee Epstein, *Conservatives in Court* (Knoxville, TN: University of Tennessee Press, 1985) and Karen O'Connor and Lee Epstein, "The Rise of Conservative Interest Group Litigation," *Journal of Politics*, vol. 45, no. 2 (May 1983): 479–489.

32 347 U.S. 483 (1954).

33 Robert J. Cottrol, Raymond T. Diamond, and Leland B. Ware, *Brown v. Board of Education: Caste, Culture, and the Constitution* (Lawrence, KS: University of Kansas Press, 2002).

34 Arguably the seminal study with regard to occupational prestige, whether of ditch diggers or lawyers, is Donald Treiman, *Occupational Prestige in Comparative Perspective* (New York, NY: Academic Press, 1977).

35 Edward O. Laumann and John P. Heinz, "Specialization and Prestige in the Legal Profession: The Structure of Deference," *American Bar Foundation Research Journal*, vol. 2, no. 1 (1977): 155–216, 166–168. Prestige scores were based on a random sample of 224 Chicago lawyers who were surveyed about their perceptions of prestige and legal specialties. Other legal specialty scores were derived from a survey of Northwestern Law School professors and American Bar Foundation research specialists on the legal profession.

36 David Lat, "The $160K-Plus Club: Which Law Firms Pay the Biggest Starting Salaries?" *Above the Law*, October 22, 2012 (http://abovethelaw.com/2012/10/the-160k-plus-club-which-law-firms-pay-the-biggest-starting-salaries/).

37 U.S. Census Bureau, *Establishment and Firm Size: 2002* (Washington, DC: U.S. Department of Commerce, 2005).

38 National Association for Legal Career Professionals, "Class of 2011 Has Lowest Employment Rate Since Class of 1994," *NALP Bulletin*, July 2012.

39 Anika Anand, "Law School Grads Going Solo and Loving It," NBCNews.com, June 20, 2011 (http://www.msnbc.msn.com/id/43442917/ns/business-careers/t/law-grads-going-solo-loving-it/#.UGb9LDWtmJo).

40 National Association of Legal Career Professionals, "Employment for the Class of 2011–Selected Findings" (http://www.nalp.org/uploads/Classof2011SelectedFindings.pdf).

41 Though in many regards law firms are comparable to corporations, in virtually every case non-lawyers are prohibited from investing in law firms and, as a result, law firms remain privately owned companies. See Larry E. Ribstein, "Ethical Rules, Agency Costs, and Law Firm Structure," *Virginia Law Review*, vol. 84, no. 8 (November 1998): 1707–1759.

42 See generally the blog posts and links about "Making Partner" at *Above the Law* (http://abovethelaw.com/tag/making-partner/).

43 Hiring for summer associate positions takes place in a short period of time during the early fall of students' second (that is, 2L) year and is therefore largely based on first (that is, 1L) year performance. Competition for these coveted positions is intense. Yet even students who have succeeded in obtaining one face uncertainty, as was the case for 30 students who were offered summer associate positions for summer of 2012 at Dewey & LeBoeuf. Dewey & LeBoeuf, created through a merger in 2007, canceled its summer associate program in light of the firm's economic difficulties and the exodus of a significant number of its partners. See Catherine Rampell, "For Law Students, Dewey & LeBoeuf Internships Evaporate," *New York Times*, May 2, 2012.

44 "White shoe" originated as a term to indicate financial or law firms that catered to elite clients. White buckskin shoes with red rubber soles were, at one time, de rigueur at the Ivy League schools the people running these firms attended. The shoes purportedly remained a staple of their wardrobes after these men "went on to become masters of the universe on Wall Street and in the best-known law firms." William Safire, "On Language: Gimme the Ol' White Shoe," *New York Times*, November 9, 1997.

45 Cravath, Swaine, & Moore, located in New York City and established in 1819, is among the most prestigious law firms in the world. For example, a recent survey of law firm associates ranked Cravath second only to the venerable firm of Wachtell, Lipton, Rosen & Katz (http://www.vault.com/company-rankings/law/vault-law-100/).

46 Paul Hoffman, *Lions in the Street: The Inside Story of the Great Wall Street Law Firms* (New York, NY: Saturday Review Press, 1973).

98   The Legal Profession

47   Sara Randazzo, "For This Year's New Partners, Perseverance Pays," *The American Lawyer*, January 13, 2012. The analysis focused on recent partners at Am Law 100 firms. The Am Law 100, which debuted in 1987, consists of the 100 top-grossing firms as tracked by *The American Lawyer*.

48   In fact, interest in moving from a single-tier to a two-tier model was significant enough to prompt the American Bar Association to commission a study about two-tier partnerships and associated alternatives. See Bruce Heintz and Nancy Markham-Bugbee, *Two-Tier Partnerships and Other Alternatives: Five Approaches* (Chicago, IL: American Bar Association, 1986).

49   As its name implies, the Am Law 200 consists of the 200 top-grossing firms as tracked by *The American Lawyer*.

50   Drew Crombs, "Report Shows Pay Gaps Widening Among Partners," *Am Law Daily*, September 18, 2012.

51   Though the method of divvying up firm profits among the partners may rely on the number of billable hours, the incentive to shirk potentially remains since "some partners can free-ride off the business development talents of others;" William D. Henderson, "An Empirical Study of Single-Tier versus Two-Tier Partnerships in the Am Law 200," *North Carolina Law Review*, vol. 84 (June 2006): 1691–1750, 1694.

52   William D. Henderson, "An Empirical Study of Single-Tier Versus Two-Tier Partnerships in the Am Law 200," *North Carolina Law Review*, vol. 84 (June 2006): 1691–1750, 1694.

53   Association for Legal Career Professionals, "Partnership Tiers and Tracks," *NALP Bulletin*, February 2002.

54   For example, while Latham & Watkins and White & Case are elite firms that have adopted the two-tier partnership model, Cravath, Swaine, & Moore; Wachtell, Lipton, Rosen & Katz; and Sullivan & Cromwell remain firmly wedded to the single-tier partnership model.

55   William D. Henderson, "An Empirical Study of Single-Tier Versus Two-Tier Partnerships in the Am Law 200," *North Carolina Law Review*, vol. 84 (June 2006): 1691–1750.

56   Karen Sloan, "Boutiques Split Off from Neal Gerber and LeClairRyan" *National Law Journal*, June 9, 2010.

57   Yue Ma, "Exploring the Origins of Public Prosecution," *International Criminal Justice Review*, vol. 18, no. 2 (June 2008): 190–211, 191–198.

58   Jack M. Kress, "Progress and Prosecution," *Annals of the American Academy of Political and Social Science*, vol. 423 (January 1976): 99–116, 100–104.

59   Yue Ma, "Exploring the Origins of Public Prosecution," *International Criminal Justice Review*, vol. 18, no. 2 (June 2008): 190–211, 198–201.

60   Ibid., 190–211, 198.

61   Angela J. Davis, "The American Prosecutor: Independence, Power, and the Threat of Tyranny," *Iowa Law Review*, vol. 86 (January 2001): 393–465, 448–453. Note that Connecticut became the first colony to entirely eliminate private prosecution in 1704. See John L. Worrall, "Prosecution in America: A Historical and Comparative Account," in *The Changing Role of the American Prosecutor*, John L. Worrall and M. Elaine Nugent-Borakove, eds (Albany, NY: State University of New York Press, 2008): 7.

62   John L. Worrall, "Prosecution in America: A Historical and Comparative Account," in *The Changing Role of the American Prosecutor*, John L. Worrall and M. Elaine Nugent-Borakove, eds (Albany, NY: State University of New York Press, 2008): 5.

63   Ibid., 8.

64   M. Elaine Nugent-Borakove and Patricia L. Fanflik, "Community Prosecution: Rhetoric or Reality?" in *The Changing Role of the American Prosecutor*, John L. Worrall and M. Elaine Nugent-Borakove, eds (Albany, NY: State University of New York Press, 2008).

65   John L. Worrall, "Prosecutors in Problem-Solving Courts," in *The Changing Role of the American Prosecutor*, John L. Worrall and M. Elaine Nugent-Borakove, eds (Albany, NY: State University of New York Press, 2008).

66   Los Angeles County Public Defender, "Our History—The Public Defender Concept—Why and When?" (http://pd.co.la.ca.us/About_history.html).

67   Marian R. Williams, "A Comparison of Sentencing Outcomes for Defendants with Public Defenders Versus Retained Counsel in a Florida Circuit Court," *Justice System Journal*, vol. 23, no. 2 (2002): 249–257, 249.

68 Ibid.

69 Morris B. Hoffman, Paul H. Rubin, and Joanna M. Shepherd, "An Empirical Study of Public Defender Effectiveness: Self-Selection by the 'Marginally Indigent,'" *Ohio State Journal of Criminal Law*, vol. 3 (Fall 2005): 223–255.

70 Ibid., 223–255, 250.

71 18 USC § 3006A.

72 For a broad consideration of the history, operation, and contemporary landscape of attorneys general, see Nancy v. Baker, *Conflicting Loyalties: Law & Politics in the Attorney General's Office, 1789–1990* (Lawrence, KS: University Press of Kansas, 1992).

73 Cornell W. Clayton, "Law, Politics and the New Federalism: State Attorneys General as National Policymakers," *Review of Politics*, vol. 56, no. 3 (Summer 1994): 525–553.

74 Ibid., 525–553: 527.

75 Justin O'Brien, "The Politics of Enforcement: Eliot Spitzer, State-Federal Relations, and the Redesign of Financial Regulation," *Publius*, vol. 35, no. 3 (Summer 2005): 449–466.

76 Colin Provost, "State Attorneys General, Entrepreneurship, and Consumer Protection in the New Federalism," *Publius*, vol. 33, no. 2 (Spring 2003): 37–53.

77 Ch. 20, Sec. 35, 1 Stat. 73, 92–93 (1789).

78 Ch. 150, 16 Stat. 162 (1870).

79 U.S. Department of Justice, "Choose Justice: Guide to the U.S. Department of Justice for Law Students and Experienced Attorneys," *Legal Careers at Justice* (http://www.justice.gov/careers/legal/).

80 For a discussion of the effectiveness and independence of the office of U.S. Attorney General, see David Alistair Yalof, *Prosecution among Friends: Presidents, Attorneys General, and Executive Branch Wrongdoing* (College Station, TX: Texas A&M University Press, 2012).

81 There is a wealth of scholarship devoted to the office of Solicitor General's activities and influence. See, for example, Richard Pacelle, Jr., *Between Law and Politics: The Solicitor General and the Structuring of Race, Gender, and Reproductive Rights Litigation* (College Station, TX: Texas A&M Press, 2003); Michael A. Bailey, Brian Kamoie, and Forrest Maltzman, "Signals from the Tenth Justice: The Political Role of the Solicitor General in Supreme Court Decision Making," *American Journal of Political Science*, vol. 49, no. 1 (January 2005): 72–85; Chris Nicholson and Paul M. Collins, Jr., "The Solicitor General's Amicus Curiae Strategies in the Supreme Court," *American Politics Research*, vol. 36, no. 3 (May 2008): 382–415; Patrick C. Wohlfarth, "The Tenth Justice? Consequences of Politicization in the Solicitor General's Office," *Journal of Politics*, vol. 71, no. 1 (January 2009): 224–237; Ryan C. Black and Ryan J. Owens, *The Solicitor General and the United States Supreme Court: Executive Branch Influence and Judicial Decisions* (New York, NY: Cambridge University Press, 2014).

82 Katie Nihill, "Careers in State and Local Government," Bernard Koteen Office of Public Interest Advising, Harvard Law School (http://www.law.harvard.edu/current/careers/opia/toolkit/guides/documents/statelocal_09.pdf).

83 David Margolick, "More Lawyers Are Less Happy at Their Work, Survey Finds," *New York Times*, August 17, 1990.

84 Dave Cheng, "Why So Many Lawyers Are Unhappy With Their Jobs," *Business Insider*, August 29, 2013 (http://www.businessinsider.com/why-lawyers-are-unhappy-at-work-2013-8).

85 Staci Zaretsky, "The 2014 U.S. News Job Rankings: Being a Lawyer Is Worse Than Being a Nail Technician," *Above the Law*, January 24, 2014 (http://abovethelaw.com/2014/01/the-2014-u-s-news-job-rankings-being-a-lawyer-is-worse-than-being-a-nail-technician/).

86 *U.S. News & World Report*, "The 100 Best Jobs of 2015" (http://money.usnews.com/careers/best-jobs/rankings/the-100-best-jobs).

87 John Sonsteng and David Camarotto, "Minnesota Lawyers Evaluate Law Schools, Training and Job Satisfaction," *William Mitchell Law Review*, vol. 26 (2000): 327–484, 418.

88 After the JD (AJD) is an empirical study of the career outcomes of a group of almost 5,000 new attorneys who graduated from law school in 2000. The AJD study design is longitudinal, following the careers of new lawyers over the first 10 years following law school graduation. The first wave of the study surveyed the lawyers in 2002–2003, the second in 2007–2008, and the third in 2012. A

description of the project, along with access to study data and a bibliography of research using that data, is available at http://www.americanbarfoundation.org/publications/afterthejd.html.

89   Ronit Dinovitzer, Bryant G. Garth, Richard Sander, Joyce Sterling, and Gita Z. Wilder, *After the JD: First Results from a National Study of Legal Careers* (Chicago, IL: The American Bar Foundation and the NALP Foundation, 2004).

90   Ronit Dinovitzer, Robert L. Nelson, Gabriele Plickert, Rebecca Sandefur, and Joyce S. Sterling, *After the JD II: Second Results from a National Study of Legal Careers* (Chicago, IL: The American Bar Foundation and the NALP Foundation, 2009).

91   Ibid., 46.

92   Ronit Dinovitzer and Bryan G. Garth, "Lawyer Satisfaction in the Process of Structuring Legal Careers," *Law & Society Review*, vol. 41, no. 1 (March 2007): 1–50.

93   Ibid.

94   Meta-analysis refers to a method that focuses on combining results from different studies in order to identify patterns among study results.

95   Jerome M. Organ, "What Do We Know About the Satisfaction/Dissatisfaction of Lawyers? A Meta-Analysis of Research on Lawyer Satisfaction and Well-Being," *University of St. Thomas Law Journal*, vol. 8, no. 2 (2011): 225–274.

96   Ibid., 225–274, 262.

97   U.S. Const. amend. VI.

98   The seminal cases with regard to the right to counsel include *Powell v. Alabama* (287 U.S. 45, 1932) in which the Court found that defendants in capital cases had to be provided counsel and *Johnson v. Zerbst* (304 U.S. 458, 1938) in which the Court found that this requirement applied in all federal cases in which a defendant was indigent. The Court extended this requirement to the states in *Gideon v. Wainwright* (372 U.S. 335, 1963). For compelling and accessible retellings of *Gideon v. Wainwright*, see Anthony Lewis, *Gideon's Trumpet* (New York, NY: Vintage Books, 1989) and Lisa A. Wroble, *The Right to Counsel: From Gideon v. Wainwright to Gideon's Trumpet* (Berkeley Heights, NJ: Enslow, 2009).

99   Karen Houppert, *Chasing Gideon: The Elusive Quest for Poor People's Justice* (New York, NY: New Press, 2013).

100   Debra Cassens Weiss, "Highest Partner Billing Rate in New Survey is $1,285 an Hour," *ABA Journal*, December 17, 2012.

101   Leigh Jones, "Large Firms' Billing Rates Continue to Climb," *National Law Journal*, December 11, 2007.

102   Ibid.

103   Debra Cassens Weiss, "Highest Partner Billing Rate in New Survey is $1,285 an Hour," *ABA Journal*, December 17, 2012.

104   Steven J. Harper, "The Tyranny of the Billable Hour" (Op-Ed), *New York Times*, March 28, 2013.

105   Allison Shields, "Are Billable Hours Eroding Trust Between Lawyers and Clients," *Lawyerist.com*, May 17, 2013 (http://lawyerist.com/are-billable-hours-eroding-trust-between-lawyers-and-clients/).

106   Steven J. Harper, "The Tyranny of the Billable Hour," *New York Times*, March 28, 2013.

107   Quoted in Leigh Jones, "Large Firms' Billing Rates Continue to Climb," *National Law Journal*, December 11, 2007.

108   Rachel M. Zahorsky, "Facing the Alternative: How Does a Flat Fee System Really Work?" *ABA Journal*, March 1, 2012.

109   "A Less Gilded Future," *The Economist*, May 5, 2011.

110   Herbert M. Kritzer, "Examining the Real Demand for Legal Services," *Fordham Urban Law Journal*, vol. 37, no. 1 (2009): 255–272.

111   Peter Karsten, "Enabling the Poor to Have Their Day in Court: The Sanctioning of Contingency Fee Contracts, a History to 1940," *DePaul Law Review*, vol. 47, no. 2 (Winter 1998): 231–259.

112   Herbert M. Kritzer, "Contingency Fee Lawyers as Gatekeepers in the Civil Justice System," *Judicature*, vol. 81, no. 1 (July–August 1997): 22–29.

113   Herbert H. Kritzer, William L.F. Felstiner, Austin Sarat, and David M. Trubek, "The Impact of Fee Arrangement on Lawyer Effort," *Law & Society Review*, vol. 19, no. 2 (1985): 251–278.

114 Ibid., 251–278, 271.

115 For a comparative perspective on legal insurance see Matthias Kilian and Francis Regan, "Legal Expenses Insurance and Legal Aid—Two Side of the Same Coin? The Experience from Germany and Sweden," *International Journal of the Legal Professions*, vol. 11, no. 3 (November 2004): 233–255. See, also, Kyung Hwan Baik and In-Gyu Kim, "Contingent Fees Versus Legal Expenses Insurance," *International Review of Law and Economics*, vol. 27, no. 3 (September 2007): 351–361.

116 Earl Johnson, Jr., *Justice and Reform: The Formative Years of the American Legal Services Program* (New Brunswick, NJ: Transaction Books, 1974).

117 Ibid.

118 Mauro Cappelletti and James Gordley, "Legal Aid: Modern Themes and Variations, Part Two: Variations on a Modern Theme," *Stanford Law Review*, vol. 24, no. 2 (January 1972): 387–421, 410–411.

119 The National Association of IOLTA Programs (NAIP) and the ABA Commission on IOLTA oversee the IOLTA Clearinghouse (http://www.iolta.org).

120 *Phillips v. Washington Legal Foundation*, 524 U.S. 156 (1998).

121 Robert J. Derocher, "The IOLTA Crash: Fallout for Foundations," *Bar Leader*, vol. 37, no. 1 (September-October 2012).

122 Terry Carter, "IOLTA Programs Find New Funding to Support Legal Services," *ABA Journal*, March 1, 2013.

123 Julie Kay, "Deep Cuts Slam Legal Aid," *National Law Journal*, October 27, 2008.

124 Ashley Cockrill, "The Shyster Lawyer," *Yale Law Journal*, vol. 21, no. 5 (March 1912): 383–390, 383.

125 J. Gordon Hylton, *Professional Values and Individual Autonomy: The United States Supreme Court and Lawyer Advertising* (Durham, NC: Carolina Academic Press, 1998).

126 433 U.S. 350 (1977).

127 433 U.S. 350, 365 (1977).

128 Illinois Rules of Professional Conduct of 2010, Article VIII, Rule 1.4.

129 An excellent overview of how disciplinary procedures for attorneys have changed over time can be found in Mary M. Devlin, "The Development of Lawyer Disciplinary Procedures in the United States," *Journal of the Professional Lawyer*, vol. 2008 (2008): 359–387.

130 Leslie C. Levin, "The Emperor's Clothes and Other Tales about the Standards for Imposing Lawyer Discipline Standards," *American University Law Review*, vol. 48, no. 1 (October 1998): 1–83.

131 Ibid., 1–83, 20–29.

132 James C. Turner and Suzanne M. Mishkin, "Time for a Whupping: Across the Country, Attorney Discipline Systems Disgrace the Profession," *Legal Times*, August 28, 2003.

133 Jennifer Gerarda Brown and Liana G.T. Wolf, "The Paradox and Promise of Restorative Attorney Discipline," *Nevada Law Journal*, vol. 12 (Spring 2012): 253–315, 258.

134 State-by-state requirements can be found on the American Bar Association's webpage (http://www.americanbar.org/cle/mandatory_cle/mcle_states.html).

135 American Bar Association, "Model Rules of Professional Conduct," Rule 6.2 (http://www.american bar.org/groups/professional_responsibility/publications/model_rules_of_professional_conduct/rule_6_2_accepting_appointments.html).

136 American Bar Association, "Model Rules of Professional Conduct," Rule 3.4 (http://www.american bar.org/groups/professional_responsibility/publications/model_rules_of_professional_conduct/rule_3_4_fairness_to_opposing_party_counsel.html).

4

ORGANIZATION OF COURTS

"The judicial Power of the United States, shall be vested in one supreme Court, and in such inferior Courts as the Congress may from time to time ordain and establish."

—U.S. Constitution, Article III, Section 1

"Do you understand what subject matter jurisdiction is? I didn't think so. Well, due to *habeas corpus*, you and Miss Bonifante had a common law marriage."

—Elle Woods, Law Student, *Legally Blonde*

Located 150 miles east of Dallas, Texas, and 40 miles west of Shreveport, Louisiana, the town of Marshall, Texas—population 23,523—is home to many things: an important civil rights legacy,[1] a large African American population (nearly 40 percent), a substantial pottery industry, the birthplace of boogie woogie music,[2] the Fire Ant Festival (a tongue-in-cheek celebration of the stinging arthropod), the Stagecoach Days festival (highlighting various modes of transportation including the stagecoach), and the Wonderland of Lights (one of the nation's largest light festivals). But it is also home to hundreds of patent lawsuits. Marshall outpaces New York, Washington, D.C., Chicago, and San Francisco when it comes to patent litigation. Quick trials and plaintiff-friendly juries make the historic Harrison County Courthouse in Marshall an attractive place for litigants who come from all over the United States to file their cases in the U.S. District Court for the Eastern District of Texas. Between 2002 and 2006 the number of patent cases skyrocketed from 32 to 234.[3] While 95 percent of the cases are settled before ever reaching the actual trial stage, those who hold patents win nearly 80 percent of the time, compared with a success rate of less than half in New York and an average win-rate of 60 percent nationally. For example, in April 2006, a Marshall jury awarded $73 million to TiVo in its patent infringement lawsuit against EchoStar Communications, the parent company of Dish Network.[4]

How can TiVo—a company based in San Jose, California—file a lawsuit in Marshall, Texas against a company headquartered in Englewood, Colorado? One of the myths involving how courts are organized is that **jurisdiction**—the power or authority of a court to determine the merits of a dispute and grant relief—is clearly defined and that all litigation is local, meaning that court proceedings must take place where the incident in question took place or, at least, where the litigants themselves are located. While this is often true, the reality is that so-called **forum shopping** takes place every day, with litigants seeking to have their legal cases heard in the courts thought most likely to provide a favorable judgment.

A court possesses jurisdiction when it has power over the subject matter of the case (**subject matter jurisdiction**) and over the people who are the plaintiff and defendant (**personal jurisdiction**). Subject matter jurisdiction is important because it limits the

Image 4.1 Old Harrison County Courthouse in Marshall, Texas *Photograph of the old Harrison County Courthouse in Marshall, Texas. Built in 1900, it is the signature landmark of Marshall and is frequently used to represent East Texas in travel literature. The building, noted as being the location of the first sit-ins in Texas, was designed by J. Riely Gordon. It became a historical museum and government office building when a new county courthouse opened in 1964. Today, the new courthouse is home to quick trials and plaintiff-friendly juries making it a national destination for patent lawsuits.* The Lyda Hill Texas Collection of Photographs in Carol M. Highsmith's America Project, Prints and Photographs Division, Library of Congress, Washington, D.C.

power of a court to hear certain kinds of cases. For example, federal bankruptcy courts only hear bankruptcy cases. But there are some matters that involve **concurrent jurisdiction** where two or more courts from different systems have simultaneous jurisdiction over a case. Thus, a party from Illinois may be able to file a breach of contract lawsuit against a party from New York in either a federal district court or a New York state court.

In deciding where to file suit, some plaintiffs will seek jurisdictions that have been sympathetic in the past to comparable claims or who have personnel—namely judges— who are expert in particular types of cases and law. At the federal level, as in the TiVo example, a plaintiff can bring a case in any federal district court where the defendant does business. Thus, in the case of a national company like Dish Network, it is not necessary to file the suit in the federal district court where the company is headquartered—in that case, Colorado. It can be filed in any federal district court. An attorney in Marshall, Samuel F. Baxter, said: "It's not as if you have a situation here where Microsoft is hated or Cisco is spit upon. Whether it happens in Marshall, Texas or Des Moines, Iowa, these lawsuits are going to happen. They might as well happen here."[5]

Likewise, some defendants will seek a change of venue from one state court to another or invoke **removal jurisdiction** to move a case from a state court to a federal court in order to neutralize a plaintiff's perceived advantage because of the jurisdiction. Successfully invoking removal jurisdiction requires that the case could have originally been filed in the federal court. It further requires independent grounds to support the federal court's jurisdiction; for example, the litigants hail from different states and, to avoid bias on the part of the courts of the litigants' respective state courts, the federal district courts are authorized to hear the case.

In theory, forum shopping is allowed and can even be required in some cases in order to ensure justice. The idea is that litigants should be able to have a fair and equal chance at favorably resolving their dispute and that one jurisdiction may be better able to guarantee this over another. This is perhaps most obvious in criminal cases where it may be difficult if not impossible to find an unbiased local jury in a sensational case with substantial media coverage. Indeed, the U.S. Supreme Court has ruled that the Sixth Amendment guarantees that defendants receive a **change of venue**—moving a case from one court to another—whenever it is necessary to ensure an impartial jury.[6] Of course, these decisions are ultimately made by judges.

For example, defense attorneys for accused Boston Marathon bomber Dzhokhar Tsarnaev requested a change of venue arguing that a federal court in Boston could not provide a fair trial given that pretrial publicity was overwhelmingly prejudicial and that virtually everyone in the jury pool in eastern Massachusetts was personally connected to the marathon bombing by running in it, watching it, knowing people who ran or watched it, or lived in parts of the city that were under police lockdown during the search for the suspect.[7] While their motion was denied, judges do grant such requests and not only due to issues of pretrial publicity or personal connection. For example, judges may consider demographic factors such as the race of the accused as compared to the jurisdiction as well as the cost and convenience of changing venues.[8]

Judges often find forum shopping objectionable and some legislators have sought to limit the practice. For example, in 2006 members of Congress introduced a bill that would have required a substantial connection between a business and the court in which a company brings a patent lawsuit. Mark W. Isakowitz, a lobbyist and advocate on behalf of corporations for patent reform, said: "We think the bill will restore more balance in the patent system and remove incentives for plaintiffs to run to one jurisdiction and try to hit the jackpot."[9] Ultimately, that provision was not included in the America Invents Act, the patent reform bill that was passed and signed into law by President Barack Obama in 2011.[10] Thus, all litigants had to do was what they were previously doing: simply state that the company involved in the litigation "did business in" the community where the suit was filed.[11]

As the previous examples suggest, concerns over forum shopping belie the myth that court jurisdiction is clearly defined and that court organization results from neutral choices over institutional design. The reality is far more complex. As this chapter will demonstrate, court organization is political, court jurisdiction is often ambiguous, and attorneys can use these relatively abstruse structures to advantage their clients and disadvantage opponents. Thus, we can think of court organization as one aspect of **adversarial legalism** (a legal style that emphasizes lawyer-dominated litigation for making and implementing public policy as well as resolving disputes), something we will discuss at length in Chapter Six.

In thinking about how courts are organized and the jurisdiction they exercise, it is important to bear in mind that the United States has two types of courts: federal and state. The reason there are two types of courts in the United States is **federalism** (the distribution of exclusive and shared powers between the national and state governments). The Constitution gives certain enumerated (that is, specified) powers to the federal government, while the rest are reserved for the states. Specifically, the Tenth Amendment to the Constitution specifies: "The powers not delegated to the United States by the Constitution, nor prohibited by it to the States, are reserved to the States respectively, or to the people." Generally speaking, this means that powers possessed by the states at the time of the ratification of the Constitution remain with the states unless the Constitution specifically lodges those powers in the federal government or specifically takes them away from the state governments.[12]

As a consequence, both the federal and state governments each need their own court system to apply and interpret their respective laws. In this sense, there are 51 different court systems, each operating side by side under their respective authorities—the 50 different state constitutions and, in the case of the federal government, the U.S. Constitution.[13] Both the federal and state constitutions specifically explain the jurisdiction of their respective court systems. The federal court system deals with issues of law relating to the express or implied powers granted to it by the Constitution (such as bankruptcy laws), while state court systems deal with issues of law relating to those matters the Constitution did not vest responsibility for in the federal government (such as divorce law). But because constitutions do not always specify all aspects of court jurisdiction, much is left to legislative judgment and therefore the political process.

In this chapter we detail the myths and realities surrounding court organization at both the state and federal level. For example, states do not all structure their courts the same way. Some have a relatively simple, streamlined hierarchy while others have a complex system of numerous, specialized courts. Complex systems exemplify the politics of court organization as they make it difficult for litigants to know where to file cases, provide flexibility for attorneys who know how to use the system to their advantage, and resist reform efforts due to local bureaucratic control.

Another major myth involves the difference between trial and appellate courts—the myth being that all courts involve fact finding through witnesses and evidence with juries rendering verdicts. Yet the reality is that trial courts are fact-finding bodies that fit this description while appellate courts have none of these features. Instead, intermediate appellate courts assume that the facts established in trials are true and instead serve as error correction institutions. Appellate judges sit in groups and render their judgments collectively. Courts of last resort—commonly (but not always) called supreme courts—are also appellate courts but they are designed for rule creation through the interpretation of statutes and constitutions.

Ultimately, most of the myths associated with court organization involve the relatively streamlined or complex nature of court systems, the roles of trial versus appellate courts, judges, and the relationship among state and federal courts. While questions about how courts are organized may not be the most exciting ones, much of the myths and misunderstanding about American courts comes from the structure and jurisdiction of courts. Thus, we intend this chapter to provide a considerable dose of reality for those interested in the judicial process.

MYTH AND REALITY IN THE ORGANIZATION OF COURTS

MYTH	REALITY
Court jurisdiction is clearly defined and litigation is local.	Jurisdiction can be ambiguous, allowing litigants to engage in forum shopping to have their cases heard in the most favorable courts.
Court organization involves neutral choices about institutional design.	Court organization is political and largely determined by legislatures.
Federal courts may not consider state cases or matters of state law.	Federal courts can consider state cases or matters of state law under federal question, diversity, and supplemental jurisdiction.

Federal judges serve lifetime appointments.	Though it is rare, federal judges may be impeached and removed from office.
Federal courts of appeals are mandated by the U.S. Constitution.	Federal courts of appeals were created by Congress over a century after the Constitution was adopted.
Each federal case is decided by a single judge.	While trials are conducted by a single judge, courts of appeals judges sit in panels of 3, occasionally *en banc*, and Supreme Court cases are decided by 9 justices.
Courts of appeals decisions are uniform across the nation.	A court of appeals decision is only binding on its geographic jurisdiction and circuit splits happen when two or more courts of appeals reach different decisions in similar cases.
The chief justice is promoted from the ranks of the associate justices and is the longest serving member of the U.S. Supreme Court.	The chief justice is not required to have any prior judicial experience and must be nominated by the president and confirmed by the Senate.
The Supreme Court only hears appellate cases.	The Supreme Court hears original matters involving two or more states.
The federal court system consists of Article III courts: district courts, appeals courts, and the U.S. Supreme Court.	In addition to Article III courts, the federal court system includes specialized courts created under Articles I, II, III, and IV.
Every state organizes its court system the same way.	States vary in term of court organization with some having simple, hierarchical courts while others have complex, convoluted court systems.
Complex court systems are maintained to help facilitate the processing of cases.	Complex court systems are maintained because local administrators do not want to relinquish their authority.
Complex court systems confuse local attorneys who do not know where to file cases.	Complex court systems increase the power of attorneys to choose where to file cases.
Lay judges, such as justices of the peace, lack the legal understanding that professional judges with formal legal education possess.	While the majority of lay judges have similar understanding and make comparable decisions to professional, formally trained judges, some do not and commit serious legal errors and ethical violations.
Appellate courts conduct new trials for losing litigants.	Appellate courts do not conduct trials and instead only hear arguments about law and procedure.
The decisions of state courts of last resort are final and cannot be appealed.	The decisions of state courts of last resort can be appealed to the U.S. Supreme Court if they involve a federal question.
Courts of last resort must decide the cases that are appealed to them.	For the vast majority of cases, courts of last resort choose which cases to decide.
A litigant suing a party from a different state must file the lawsuit in either their home state or the opposition's home state.	Litigants from opposing states may have their case heard in federal court under diversity jurisdiction.

THE JURISDICTION AND ORGANIZATION OF FEDERAL COURTS

In contrast to the heterogeneous and relatively complex state court systems that will be discussed in the second half of this chapter, the federal courts are far less numerous and much easier to understand. In this section we discuss the jurisdiction and structure of the federal court system. There are two key dimensions of federal court jurisdiction. The first is whether a court possesses original or appellate jurisdiction. **Original jurisdiction** refers to the authority of a court to hear a case for the first time. A court exercising original jurisdiction is serving as a trial court. These are the courts typically depicted in popular television crime dramas with dramatic eyewitness testimony and impassioned speeches to juries. In contrast, **appellate jurisdiction** refers to the authority of a court to review a lower court decision to determine if there are errors in process or procedure. Appellate courts are rarely seen in popular culture, giving rise to the mistaken notion that all courts involve witnesses, evidence, and juries. Yet these are features only found in courts of original jurisdiction. Appellate courts feature a group of judges considering arguments made by attorneys.

The second dimension of jurisdiction involves the types of cases to be adjudicated. Federal courts generally hear cases under either **federal question jurisdiction** (the authority to hear cases arising under the U.S. Constitution or federal statutes) or **diversity of citizenship jurisdiction** (the authority to hear cases involving litigants from different states who meet certain conditions). The latter is a powerful tool for litigants whose cases involve state law, and therefore raise no federal questions. Diversity of citizenship jurisdiction can be invoked by plaintiffs when they initially file a case in federal court or by defendants who seek to remove a case from state court so that it may be heard in federal court. There are many differences between federal and state courts that can advantage (or disadvantage) a litigant, not least of which is that federal judges serve for life while state judges are often accountable to their local constituencies through election and retention systems—something we detail in the next chapter.

Table 4.1 compares each type of federal court jurisdiction. Federal question jurisdiction stems from the Constitution while diversity jurisdiction derives from federal law. While there is no minimum amount of money that must be involved under federal questions, diversity cases require that the amount at stake exceed $75,000. While the parties do not have to be from different states when federal questions are raised, they must be in order for diversity jurisdiction to be met. Federal courts also have jurisdiction when the federal government is a party to the case either as plaintiff or defendant.

Table 4.2 shows the number of civil cases filed in recent years in federal district courts by jurisdiction. The data show that while the number of cases involving federal questions has been relatively stable over time, there was a steady increase in diversity cases from 2007 to 2011. This increase was largely due to attorneys choosing federal courts over state

TABLE 4.1
Primary Types of Federal Court Jurisdiction

POSSIBLE BASIS FOR JURISDICTION	FEDERAL QUESTION	DIVERSITY
Source of jurisdiction	Constitution	Federal law
Minimum amount in controversy	None	>$75,000
Must parties be from different states?	No	Yes

TABLE 4.2

U.S. District Courts, Civil Cases Filed by Jurisdiction, 2007–2013

YEAR	U.S. AS PLAINTIFF	U.S. AS DEFENDANT	FEDERAL QUESTION	DIVERSITY OF CITIZENSHIP
2007	9,564	35,900	139,424	72,619
2008	9,649	34,515	134,582	88,457
2009	8,834	34,310	136,041	97,209
2010	8,672	34,365	138,655	101,202
2011	10,797	36,072	141,013	101,366
2012	8,858	38,834	145,007	85,742
2013	7,694	40,545	147,057	89,305

Source: Administrative Office of the U.S. Courts, *Judicial Business* (Washington, DC: Administrative Office of the U.S. Courts, various years).

courts when their cases allowed such a choice, as in asbestos litigation. The decrease in subsequent years was almost entirely in the Eastern District of Pennsylvania, which had over 20,000 fewer asbestos case filings than in prior years. The data also show that the U.S. is roughly five times more likely to be on the receiving end of lawsuits than it is in initiating them. Also, the relatively large increase in plaintiff actions in 2011 was due to an effort to recover on defaulted student loans. We will discuss federal civil caseloads in greater detail in Chapter Six.

Federal Question Jurisdiction

The authority federal courts have to hear cases that raise federal questions derives from Article III, Section 2 of the Constitution, which states, in part, that the "judicial power shall extend to all cases, in law and equity, arising under the Constitution, the laws of the United States, and Treaties made, or which shall be made, under their Authority." While *Marbury v. Madison*[14] was the first case in which the Supreme Court exercised its judicial power to strike down a federal law as unconstitutional, the Court had exercised its judicial power in prior cases involving federal questions—including *Hylton v. United States*[15] in which the justices upheld a federal law as constitutional. Consistent with the language in Article III, the United States Code provides: "The district courts shall have original jurisdiction of all civil actions arising under the Constitution, laws, or treaties of the United States."[16] Thus, if a case involves a federal law, then it can be filed in a federal court. Federal courts also have jurisdiction over cases involving whether a state law violates the federal Constitution.

To illustrate, the laws that govern the rights and obligations of landlords and tenants are typically state (not federal) laws. This means that a dispute between a landlord and tenant over, for example, the necessity of certain repairs and the habitability of an apartment would not give rise to a federal question and, hence, would not be suitable for adjudication in the federal courts. However, there are federal laws pertaining to landlords and tenants that can and do give rise to federal questions. For example, the Fair Housing Act prohibits discrimination in the sale, rental, and financing of dwellings.[17] Accordingly, if a tenant claims that a landlord is discriminating against her due to her race, the case could be brought in federal court because it raises a federal question (the application of the Fair Housing Act).

Another issue pertaining to federal jurisdiction is **habeas corpus**. *Habeas corpus*—Latin for "you may have the body"—is the common law right, codified in federal law,[18] to be free from unlawful incarceration.[19] Federal prisoners, as well as state prisoners, can seek their freedom by filing *habeas corpus* petitions in federal district courts. The Suspension Clause of Article I of the Constitution restricts the ability of Congress to suspend *habeas corpus* except for public safety in cases of rebellion or invasion. Congress has done so only in a handful of instances, such as during the Civil War and the War on Terrorism for certain types of cases.[20] Yet the vast majority of *habeas* petitions involve those convicted of state criminal matters who petition federal courts with claims of ineffective counsel or constitutional rights violations. In recent years, roughly 20,000 *habeas* petitions have been filed in federal district courts each year, with about 1 percent involving capital (murder) cases and 20 percent involving life sentences.[21] Most—about two-thirds—are dismissed on procedural grounds (such as failing to exhaust all potential state remedies) while the other third are dismissed on the merits of the case. The small percentage of petitions that are not dismissed—roughly 2 percent at most—generally result in further proceedings in state courts or, in rare instances, outright release of the prisoner.

POP CULTURE

The Hurricane

Rubin Carter was a professional boxer known as "The Hurricane" for his frenetic style and ferocious punching power. Yet he had been in trouble with the law and in and out of prison since he was first arrested at age 11. One night in 1966, he left a Patterson, New Jersey bar at 2:30 a.m. with another man, John Artis. Police stopped their car because they fit the description of suspects in a murder committed nearby. Specifically, witnesses told police that they saw two African American men carrying weapons leaving the scene of the crime in a white automobile. Carter and Artis were in the neighborhood and were in a white car. Ultimately, they were arrested, tried, convicted, and sentenced to life in prison.

In prison, Carter wrote his autobiography and it was published in 1975.[22] His case became a cause célèbre and many advocated for his release, arguing that his situation was a classic example of racial profiling, a biased police force, and a wrongful conviction.[23] Bob Dylan, who had stopped writing protest songs years earlier, returned to the genre with the top-40 hit "Hurricane" detailing Carter's plight.[24] Dylan also performed a benefit concert at Madison Square Garden that raised $100,000. Carter and Artis received a new trial in New Jersey but were once again found guilty and sent back to prison for life.

The 1999 film based on Carter's story, *The Hurricane*, is instructive for a number of reasons, one of which is its depiction of court jurisdiction. Carter, played by the acclaimed and versatile actor Denzel Washington, makes plain his view that he will never be able to receive a fair trial in New Jersey, largely due to racism

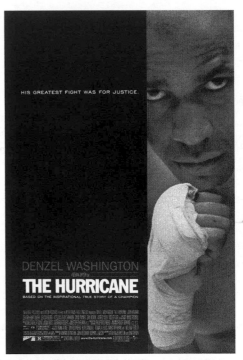

Image 4.2 *The Hurricane*

The Hurricane *is a film depicting how champion boxer Rubin Carter is imprisoned and uses the federal court system to gain his freedom after being convicted by the state of New Jersey for a crime he did not commit.* Photo by John D. Kisch, Separate Cinema Archive, Getty Images.

and the corrupt practices of its criminal justice system. When a group of friends discovers new evidence definitively placing Carter and Artis at the bar during the time of the nearby murders, Carter is told about what they must do procedurally with his case: "The law states we have to take our new evidence back to the original trial judge, and then if he turns us down, we go to the state appeals court." Carter protests:

> No. No. No. No. Listen to me. These people aren't gonna just let that happen. They've made their careers on my case. I'm talking about lawyers, prosecutors, judges who have moved up the ladder on my black back. We don't know what enemies we have out there in this state. We gotta take it out of New Jersey and take it to the federal court.

Carter is told of the risks associated with his plan: "Rubin, if you go into federal court with new evidence that hasn't been heard in the state court, the judge is gonna throw it out. Okay? This is the law." Carter is resolute: "Then we transcend the law. We get back to humanity. You said if we take the new evidence before the federal judge, he's gotta look at it before he throws it out, right? I believe that once he looks at it, he will have seen the truth. Having seen the truth, he can't turn his back on me."

Carter filed for a writ of *habeas corpus* in the U.S. District Court for the District of New Jersey and Judge H. Lee Sarokin (who was appointed by President Jimmy Carter) heard the appeal. As his friends had done previously, Judge Sarokin (played by Rod Steiger in the film) warned Carter:

> This court is not unmoved by your eloquence and passion, but the prosecution is correct. This petition contains new evidence that has not been presented before the State Court of New Jersey, and there is no legal argument that you could make which would allow me to consider it. Therefore, you have two choices before you. I can send this case back to the state court and you can present the evidence; or if you insist on proceeding, this evidence will be lost to you forever.

Carter chose to proceed and was allowed to address the court:

> Thank you, Your Honor. I was, a, um, prizefighter. My job was to take all the hatred and skill that I could muster, and send a man to his destruction. And I did that. But Rubin "Hurricane" Carter is no murderer. Twenty years I've spent locked up in a cage considered a danger to society. Not treated like a human being. Not treated like a person. Counted fifteen times a day. I serve my time in a house of justice, and yet, there's no justice for me. So, I ask you to consider the evidence. Don't turn away from the truth. Don't turn away from your conscience. Please, don't ignore the law. No, embrace that higher principle for which the law was meant to serve: justice. That's all I ask for, Your Honor. Justice.

Subsequently, Judge Sarokin granted the writ, saying that Carter's prosecution was "predicated upon an appeal to racism rather than reason, and concealment rather than disclosure."

Carter was released from prison in 1985. Prosecutors appealed Sarokin's ruling but the U.S. Court of Appeals for the Third Circuit affirmed Sarokin's decision and the U.S. Supreme Court chose not to hear the case. Carter's case raises many questions about the criminal justices process. But it also is instructive for understanding court organization and jurisdiction. Specifically, Carter's *habeas* appeal in federal court is an example of federal question jurisdiction and how state matters can reach federal courts.

Diversity Jurisdiction

Diversity jurisdiction is a form of subject matter jurisdiction. As we noted earlier, it is the authority to hear cases involving litigants from different states who meet certain conditions. Article III of the U.S. Constitution gives Congress the power to permit federal courts to hear diversity cases through legislation authorizing such jurisdiction—currently found in the previously mentioned, United States Code.[25] Congress first exercised that power and granted federal trial courts diversity jurisdiction in the Judiciary Act of 1789. The provision was included because the framers of the Constitution were concerned that if a case is filed in one state, and it involves parties from that state and another state, the state court might be biased toward the party from that state.[26]

Fundamentally and most obviously, diversity jurisdiction requires that the plaintiff and defendant are citizens of different states. Perhaps the most infamous case involving diversity jurisdiction is *Dred Scott v. Sandford*.[27] In that case, the U.S. Supreme Court ruled, among other things, that Dred Scott, a slave, could not invoke federal court diversity jurisdiction to sue for his freedom because neither slaves nor emancipated slaves could be considered citizens of states within the meaning of Article III. The decision was ultimately overturned after the Civil War by the ratification of the Thirteenth Amendment.

Appropriately invoking diversity jurisdiction, however, requires an understanding of the meaning of citizenship under the Constitution. U.S. citizens are citizens of the state in which they are domiciled, which is the state in which they reside and intend to remain. Thus, if a person presently makes her home in Georgia, she is a citizen of Georgia. If that person spends the summer working in Florida and plans to return home to Georgia in September, she would still be a citizen of Georgia. A corporation is treated as a citizen of the state in which it is incorporated as well as the state in which its principal place of business is located. Accordingly, a business incorporated in Delaware with its principal place of business in Illinois cannot invoke the federal courts' diversity jurisdiction to bring suit against citizens of either Delaware or Illinois in the federal courts.

Additionally, complete diversity between and among the parties is required. For example, if a citizen of California files a lawsuit in federal court suing three defendants—a citizen of Georgia, a citizen of California, and a citizen of Maine—the conditions for diversity jurisdiction would not be met. Because there would be citizens of California on both sides of the lawsuit, there would not be complete diversity between the plaintiff and all of the defendants. Diversity is determined at the time the action is filed and on the basis of the residency of the parties at that time. Thus, if a change in domicile occurs after the action is filed, there is no effect on whether federal diversity jurisdiction can be invoked. Additionally, there is an "amount in controversy" requirement. A federal district court has jurisdiction over the subject matter if the plaintiff is suing in good faith for over $75,000.[28] If the statutory amount cannot be satisfied, the case can only be heard in the appropriate state court.

What if one of the parties to a lawsuit is a state? In *Chisholm v. Georgia*[29] the Supreme Court ruled that, under Article III's diversity jurisdiction, a state could be sued in federal court by a citizen from another state. But the decision was quickly overturned by the Eleventh Amendment, which articulated the concept of **state sovereign immunity**—the principle that states cannot be sued in federal court without their consent. Subsequent Supreme Court cases have expounded on the extent of that immunity including *Hans v. Louisiana*[30] (which held that the amendment was applicable to suits involving citizens suing their own state), *New Hampshire v. Louisiana*[31] (which barred suits brought by one state against another when the interests represented are not state interests but are instead interests of the people of the state), and *Monaco v. Mississippi* [32] (which dealt with situations in which states are sued by foreign sovereigns).

However, states may consent to each of these suits and the federal government can subject states to these suits in certain cases depending on the Constitutional authority on which Congress relies. For example, in *Fitzpatrick v. Bitzer*[33] the Court held that

Congress can subject states to these suits under the Fourteenth Amendment's enforcement power. Yet in *Seminole Tribe v. Florida*[34] the Court ruled that Congress could not do so under its Article I powers but made an exception in *Central Virginia Community College v. Katz*[35] by allowing Congress to subject states to suit under Article I's Bankruptcy Clause.[36] Both *Seminole Tribe* and *Katz* were decided by 5-4 votes suggesting that this area of the law may be in flux in the coming years as the Court's membership changes.[37]

Diversity cases require federal courts to apply state law, not federal law, in deciding cases. The U.S. Supreme Court determined in *Erie Railroad Co. v. Tompkins*[38] that the law to be applied in a diversity case is the law of whatever state in which the action was filed. Federal law cannot be applied because there is no federal common law (refer to Chapter One for a discussion of common law). The principle of applying state law in diversity cases is known as the *Erie* Doctrine after this case. The *Erie* Doctrine is problematic according to opponents of diversity jurisdiction who argue that federal courts are simply not the best interpreters of state law.[39] Further, those advocating for the elimination of diversity jurisdiction assert that federal courts have enough responsibilities when it comes to deciding federal cases and would more profitably spend their time deciding federal cases.

Those who argue that diversity jurisdiction is still important point to the continuing need to protect out-of-state litigants. However, empirical evidence on the influence of fear of prejudice on lawyers' choice of forum has been mixed.[40] One survey of Virginia lawyers found that 60 percent of lawyers representing out-of-state plaintiffs gave potential prejudice as a reason for their choice of federal court over state court. In another survey of lawyers, 40 percent reported that they chose federal court because of the local bias fear. However, when Wisconsin lawyers were asked about local bias and the choice of federal versus state court, only 4.3 percent cited that reason as a factor.

Additionally, a federal court can hear a claim that would normally come under the jurisdiction of a state court under a special set of circumstances; in particular, if it is substantially related to a claim already before that court. In such circumstances, the federal court can invoke **supplemental jurisdiction**, thereby handling a state law claim that is substantially related to a federal law claim it is already deciding.[41] The purpose of supplemental jurisdiction is to foster efficiency by having only one trial (rather than one state trial for the state claim and one federal trial for the federal claim). While federal question jurisdiction and diversity jurisdiction are mandatory jurisdictions, supplemental jurisdiction is discretionary and the federal court is not obligated to exercise it. To extend the earlier landlord-tenant example, a tenant's claim that a landlord was negligent, and as a result damaged his car, would normally lie outside of the purview of the federal court. However, if the federal court is handling a federal question claim regarding, for example, discrimination barred by the Fair Housing Act, it could invoke supplemental jurisdiction to handle the negligence claim in conjunction with the Fair Housing Act claim.

Federal courts fall into one of four broad classifications based on the source of their authority under the U.S. Constitution: Article I, Article II, Article III, and Article IV. As the following discussion illustrates, myths about judicial selection, tenure of office, and judicial powers largely stem from conceptions about Article III courts. The reality is that Article I, II, and IV courts are distinct from Article III courts on each of these features and more.[42] Figure 4.1 shows the hierarchical nature of these courts and how they fit together to comprise the American court system.

Article III Courts

Article III courts are the primary courts in the federal system. They derive their power from Article III of the Constitution, which reads, in part: "The judicial power of the United States, shall be vested in one Supreme Court, and in such inferior courts as the Congress may from time to time ordain and establish." These courts include the U.S. district courts, the U.S. courts of appeals, and the U.S. Supreme Court. They also include one specialized court: the U.S. Court of International Trade. Note that the only court whose existence is constitutionally mandated by the language of the Constitution is the Supreme Court.

All judges of Article III courts are appointed by the president, with the advice and consent of the Senate. They serve "during good behavior," which essentially means that they are appointed for life unless they resign, retire, die, or are removed via the impeachment process. **Impeachment** allows for formal charges against a judge (or other federal officeholders) for crimes committed in office. The House of Representatives is the body that decides if an individual should be impeached. It is analogous to indictment in regular court proceedings, with the Senate then determining whether the officeholder should be convicted on those articles of impeachment.

While no U.S. Supreme Court justice has ever been removed from office, there have been eight lower federal court judges who have been impeached by the House and convicted by the Senate. Others have been impeached by the House and either acquitted in the Senate or simply resigned before they could be removed. The latest removal occurred

FIGURE 4.1

U.S. Court System

The American court system is hierarchical in nature and comprised of both federal (on the left side of the diagram) and state (on the right) courts. The white boxes denote trial courts while the shaded boxes signify appellate courts.

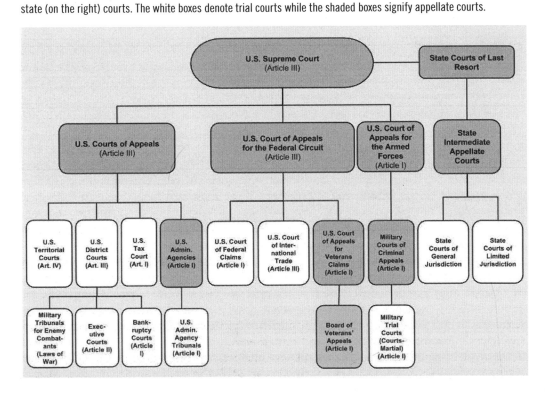

TABLE 4.3
Federal Judges Removed from Office

JUDGE	YEAR OF REMOVAL	OFFICE	REASON
John Pickering	1804	District of New Hampshire	Drunkenness, Unlawful Rulings
West Hughes Humphreys	1862	Eastern, Middle, and Western Districts of Tennessee	Joining the Confederacy
Robert W. Archbald	1913	Third Circuit Court of Appeals	Bribery
Halsted L. Ritter	1936	Southern District of Florida	Embezzlement, Tax Evasion, Ethics
Harry E. Claiborne	1986	District of Nevada	Bribery, Fraud, Tax Evasion
Alcee Hastings	1989	Southern District of Florida	Bribery, Perjury, Racketeering
Walter Nixon	1989	Southern District of Mississippi	Ethics, Perjury
Thomas Porteous	2010	Eastern District of Louisiana	Bribery, Perjury

on December 8, 2010, when the U.S. Senate found Judge C. Thomas Porteous of Louisiana guilty on four articles of impeachment, removing him from the federal bench.[43] He was accused of accepting kickbacks and lying to the Senate and FBI. Still, it is extremely difficult to remove federal judges from office and the low number of such removals suggests that the impeachment process provides no real check on the judiciary except in the most extraordinary circumstances.

U.S. District Courts

The U.S. district courts are the general trial courts (also referred to as courts of original jurisdiction) at the federal level, and most federal cases begin here. Except for a few categories of cases that fall under the jurisdiction of specialized courts, the federal district courts have jurisdiction to hear all types of federal cases, including both civil and criminal cases. There are currently 91 federal judicial districts (673 authorized judgeships)[44] arranged geographically, with each state having at least one district court (see Figure 4.2). The least populous states—such as Idaho, Montana, and Oregon—have one district court with the more populous states having multiple district courts. For example, the three states with the largest populations—California, New York, and Texas—have four judicial districts each. There is also a district court in D.C. and Puerto Rico.[45] In addition to trials, district court judges conduct many other proceedings in court. These include hearings on motions for summary judgment (where there is no dispute as to the material facts of a case and the court determines that one litigant should prevail based on the law) and other motions, calendar calls (appearances before a court to schedule the dates of hearings, trials, etc.), preliminary proceedings in criminal cases (such as arraignment and the setting of bail), hearings on sentencing issues, and *Daubert* hearings regarding expert witnesses.[46] District court judges are also involved in case management efforts, alternative dispute resolutions activities,[47] and settlements.

As we will detail in Chapter Six, the vast majority of cases filed in the U.S. district courts are civil suits. For example, in fiscal year 2013, the total number of cases filed in

FIGURE 4.2

Geographic Boundaries of U.S. District Courts and U.S. Courts of Appeals

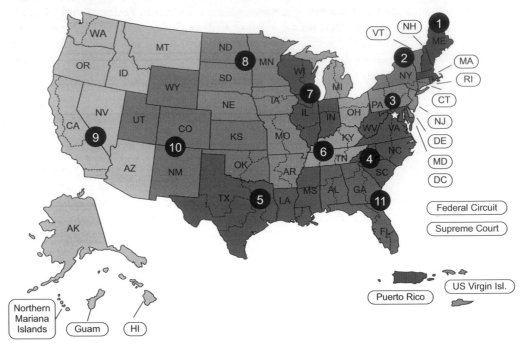

Source: Court Locator, Administrative Office of U.S. Courts, www.uscourts.gov.

the district courts was 375,870 and more than three of every four of those filings (just over 284,604) were civil cases.[48] The largest component of the district courts' civil case docket are personal injury cases, which comprised nearly a quarter of the docket (63,316) in 2013. In terms of the jurisdiction under which cases come to the federal district courts, 147,057 cases (52 percent) on the civil case docket come under the courts' federal question jurisdiction, with another 89,305 cases (31 percent) coming under diversity jurisdiction. Litigants unhappy with the decision in the federal district courts have the option of appealing the adverse ruling to the U.S. courts of appeals.

U.S. Courts of Appeals

The U.S. courts of appeals are the primary intermediate appellate courts in the federal system and are colloquially known as circuit courts. Originally, U.S. Supreme Court justices traveled around the country twice a year visiting a "circuit" of courts in different states, a practice called **circuit riding**.[49] Travel was slow and difficult in the late eighteenth century and the justices loathed riding circuit.[50] They lobbied Congress to end the practice and often missed attending circuit court because of illness or impractical travel conditions. Although Congress passed several laws creating new courts to handle the ever-increasing federal court caseload, Supreme Court justices continued to ride circuit until the 1891 Evarts Act, when Congress created the U.S. Circuit Courts of Appeal.[51] These courts were intended to relieve the workload of the Supreme Court. In 1948, the official name was changed to the U.S. courts of appeals.

These courts are arrayed geographically, each encompassing a set of states, with the entirety of any given state falling within one circuit (see Figure 4.2). There are 11 numbered circuits plus the U.S. Court of Appeals for the D.C. Circuit. The present U.S. Court of Appeals for the Tenth Circuit was carved out of the U.S. Court of Appeals for the Eighth Circuit in 1929, and the present Eleventh was carved out of the Fifth in 1980. There are currently 167 judgeships on the 12 courts of appeals. The number of authorized judges differs across the circuits, ranging from six in the First Circuit to 29 in the Ninth Circuit.

As appellate courts, the courts of appeals only handle cases in which a party has appealed, arguing that a district court judge made an error handling the case. Thus, circuit courts review the work of district court judges and issue decisions based on whether the lower court's decision was correct in terms of process and procedure. The workload of the courts of appeals is substantial, with the average annual number of cases from 2001 to 2011 hovering at just over 60,000. As is the case in the federal district courts, civil cases dominate the docket of the courts of appeals. For example, as Table 4.4 shows, in 2013 over 42,000 cases were appealed to the courts of appeals from the district courts. Of these, over 30,000 (roughly 71 percent) were civil cases.

Image 4.3 William Evarts
Photograph of New York Senator William M. Evarts who sponsored the Judiciary Act of 1891—popularly known as the Evarts Act—that created the U.S. courts of appeals. Brady-Handy Collection, Prints and Photographs Division, Library of Congress, Washington, D.C.

To handle these cases, increasing numbers of judges, clerks, and staff have been added to the courts of appeals over time. Critics argue that rising caseloads and increased bureaucratization have limited the ability of these courts to administer justice. Yet research suggests otherwise. For his book *Inside Appellate Courts*, Jonathan M. Cohen interviewed over 70 appellate judges and law clerks and found that the courts of appeals have been able to maintain a high level of justice and efficiency despite substantial growth.[52] He charts the development of law clerks, the communication among judges, visiting judges, unpublished decisions, and court culture, among other things, as ways in which courts have adapted to effectively handle rising caseloads.

Despite this research, court reformers routinely point to caseloads as a reason for change. Consider the Ninth Circuit Court of Appeals. In 2013, the Ninth Circuit resolved 7,760 cases—more than any other circuit and far more than most of the circuits who resolve less than half that many (see Table 4.4). Similar disparities have persisted for years as have calls to divide the Ninth Circuit to ease the caseload burden.[53] Yet the caseload argument perpetuates the myth that court organization is a neutral exercise designed to improve the functioning of courts. In reality, those who want to divide the Ninth Circuit seek to isolate California, the liberal appellate judges appointed from its ranks, and the liberal decisions they have handed down on environmental, religious, and other controversial areas of the law.[54] Dividing California from the other states and territories in the Ninth Circuit—Alaska, Arizona, Guam, Hawaii, Idaho, Montana, Nevada, Northern Mariana Islands, Oregon, and Washington—would free them from the liberal judges and precedents that they are currently subject to. Thus, the debate over the Ninth Circuit illustrates the reality that issues of court organization are tied to politics.

The courts of appeals rely on **three-judge panels** to process their caseloads. The members of each panel are typically randomly selected, though practices are inconsistent across

TABLE 4.4
Number of Criminal and Civil Courts of Appeals Cases Arising from the U.S. District Courts by Circuit, 2013

CIRCUIT	CRIMINAL CASES	CIVIL CASES	TOTAL CASES
D.C. Circuit	105	514	619
First Circuit	580	720	1,300
Second Circuit	743	2,706	3,449
Third Circuit	587	2,177	2,764
Fourth Circuit	1,403	2,775	4,178
Fifth Circuit	2,320	3,817	6,137
Sixth Circuit	1,148	2,967	4,115
Seventh Circuit	618	1,898	2,516
Eighth Circuit	771	1,603	2,374
Ninth Circuit	1,669	6,091	7,760
Tenth Circuit	454	1,335	1,789
Eleventh Circuit	1,526	3,648	5,174
Total	**11,924**	**30,251**	**42,175**

Source: Administrative Office of the U.S. Courts, *Judicial Business* (Washington, DC: Administrative Office of the U.S. Courts, 2014) Table B-7.

circuits and neutral assignment is not necessarily absolute.[55] The membership of the panels is often not revealed to the attorneys until shortly before oral argument. For example, in the Fifth Circuit, the attorneys are notified 1 week before oral argument, while in the Sixth Circuit, the attorneys are notified 2 weeks before oral argument. Not infrequently, a retired federal judge on "senior status" or an active district court judge will participate on a panel. Though there is evidence to suggest that these "substitute" judges are not fully fungible with the regular, active duty court of appeals judges,[56] the ever-increasing workloads of the courts of appeals (coupled with persistent vacancies on the courts of appeals benches) makes it unlikely that their use will diminish any time soon.

Random selection means that it is possible that any given case might end up before a panel of three conservative judges or possibly three liberal judges. This can lead to very different outcomes as research suggests that judges do base their decisions on ideology, particularly in high-profile cases where the law is relatively ambiguous. Yet a party may ask for a rehearing by all of the circuit court judges. These are known as **en banc** proceedings. However, en banc proceedings in the courts of appeals are not common; for example, in the 12-month reporting period ending September 30, 2011, there were only 51 en banc proceedings in the courts of appeals and two circuits, the First and the Second, had no en bancs.[57] Because the Supreme Court accepts so few cases petitioned to it each year, the implications of a random three-judge-panel process become plain. The luck of the draw at the courts of appeals can go a long way in determining who wins and who loses.

HOW DO WE KNOW?

Does Court Organization Affect the Decisions of Judges?

Given the increasing workload faced by the federal courts of appeals, 28 U.S.C. Section 282 (1988) gives the chief judge of a circuit the authority to designate a district court judge to serve in a temporary capacity as a court of appeals judge. Do these trial court visitors behave differently than their appellate brethren? Two studies address this question.

In the first study, the authors examined district judge participations in more than 1,100 published and unpublished courts of appeals labor law cases.[58] The dependent variable for most of the analyses was whether a judge voted to support the union's legal position on a specific issue in a given case. For another analysis, examining types of judicial participation by each judge, they used a dependent variable that was broken down into four different categories: authoring an opinion, authoring a concurrence, authoring a dissent, or joining the opinion of another judge. The authors coded different independent variables to capture different judicial characteristics, such as background and experience, and also included many control variables to assess potential biases for or against the union. The main variable of interest was whether the judge was a designated district judge.

When they examined differences in types of judicial participation, they found that district court visitors were significantly less likely to author majority opinions or to dissent from majority opinions. Specifically, the probability of authoring a majority opinion was 12 percent for an appellate court judge versus 8 percent for a district court judge and the probability of dissenting was .9 percent for an appellate court judge and only .3 percent for a district court judge. Furthermore, when they examined support for the union's legal position, they found that district court judges did not differ from the support given by appellate court judges. Thus, the authors concluded that district court judges were "largely following the lead of appellate judges on their panels . . ."[59]

In the second study, the authors used the U.S. Courts of Appeals Database to examine opinions from 1970 to 1996 in order to determine whether designated district court judges were too deferential to the courts of appeals judges and whether they compromise the consistency of the law since they are outsiders to the court.[60] The dependent variable indicated the ideological direction of each judge's vote, coded 1 if the vote is liberal and 0 if the vote is conservative. Specifically, the authors used a multiple regression model in order to examine the influences on both liberal or conservative voting and consistent or inconsistent voting. The authors included several independent variables, such as litigant resources, the preferences of the Supreme Court, and the ideological influence of the other panel members.

The authors found that, in the majority of the cases, district court judges were no different than appellate court judges when it came to responding to the preferences of the other judges on the panel. However, in 17 percent of the cases, there was a statistically significant difference between designated judges and regular court of appeals members. In those cases, designated district court judges were far more deferential to their court of appeals colleagues. In terms of consistency of vote choice, the authors found that district court judges were no more inconsistent than the courts of appeals judges.

The judges in one circuit are not bound by the decisions from another circuit, although an opinion written by a different circuit court may be helpful. Thus, one circuit panel may rule differently from another panel in another circuit on the same issue.[61] These **circuit splits** may happen because of geographical, political, or ideological differences. Different circuits have developed reputations when it comes to their ideology. For example, during the George W. Bush administration, the Fourth Circuit was once known as being more conservative than other circuits[62] while the Ninth Circuit tended to be more liberal than other circuit courts.[63] Yet, this can change over time. For example, Democrat Barack Obama was able to appoint six judges to the Fourth Circuit from 2010–2014, giving that court a majority of judges appointed by Democratic presidents. He also appointed seven judges to the Ninth Circuit from 2011–2014 thereby preserving that court's majority of Democratic appointees. Thus, the composition and ideological direction of circuit courts is necessarily determined by the appointment process. Still, circuit splits are important because the Supreme Court is more likely to review a case that involves a circuit split, though circuit splits are not the only factor contributing to the Supreme Court's decision to review a case.[64]

The U.S. Supreme Court

The Supreme Court of the United States is the highest court in the federal system: it is the federal court of last resort. Though we devote an entire chapter to the Supreme Court later in this text, here we provide some basic information. The Supreme Court currently consists of a chief justice and eight associate justices and the members of the Court sit en banc to decide their cases. Though the size of the Court has been set at nine since 1869, Congress has the authority to change the number of justices. The last time there was a serious attempt to enlarge the size of the Court was during the New Deal with President Franklin D. Roosevelt's infamous Court-packing plan.[65] Though the president couched the plan as a means of easing the burden on the elderly justices by allowing for the appointment of an additional justice for each current justice over the age of 70, his clear intention was to tip the balance of the Court in favor of those who would support New Deal legislation. The scheme quickly failed to win the support of the American people or Congress. The position of chief justice (officially, Chief Justice of the United States) is a distinct position on the Court and, though formally the chief justice is considered to have seniority on the Court, it is not a position that is assumed simply on the basis of being the longest serving justice. Rather, for an associate justice to become chief justice, he must be nominated by the president and confirmed by the Senate just like any other individual who might be considered for chief.[66]

The annual term of the Supreme Court runs from the first Monday in October to early summer (usually ending in late June). So, for example, cases decided in February 2015 are considered to have been decided in the 2014 term of the Court. The Supreme Court possesses both original and appellate jurisdiction. The Court has original jurisdiction in cases involving ambassadors and cases involving disputes between states. In practice, however, the Court only exercises original jurisdiction in the latter kind of case. Its original jurisdiction in the former is concurrent with the federal district courts and those are the courts that handle such disputes. The Court only rarely acts pursuant to its original jurisdiction. For example, only six original jurisdiction cases were on the Court's docket in the 2006 term, five in 2007, four in the 2008 term, six in 2009, and four in the 2010 term.[67] One example is the case of *Nebraska v. Wyoming*,[68] which involved a dispute between the two states regarding the apportionment of the waters of a river that flows through Wyoming before entering Nebraska. Another is the case of *New Jersey v. New York*,[69] which centered on disputed ownership of a portion of Ellis Island in New York Harbor. When the Court does act pursuant to its original jurisdiction, it appoints a special master to review the evidence presented and arguments made by the litigants and to make findings and recommendations. The Court then reviews the report of the special master and makes its decision accordingly.[70]

The Supreme Court of the United States.

Image 4.4 Chase Court *The nine justices, seated, of the U.S. Supreme Court photographed with the clerk of the Court, standing, in 1864. Although Congress may set the number of Supreme Court justices, it has remained fixed at nine since the chief justiceship of Salmon P. Chase, seated in the middle.* Prints and Photographs Division, Library of Congress, Washington, D.C.

By far, the most common way for a case to reach the Supreme Court is on appeal from a circuit court or state supreme court.[71] There are technically two different mechanisms for seeking Supreme Court review of a lower court decision: a petition for a writ of appeal and a petition for a writ of *certiorari*. A petition for a **writ of appeal** is filed by a party who is seeking appellate review under the Court's mandatory jurisdiction. Currently, the Court's mandatory jurisdiction is virtually nonexistent, having been scaled back by Congress numerous times over the years, most recently in 1988.[72] Today, the only cases that the Court must hear involve reapportionment, the Civil Rights and Voting Rights Acts, antitrust law, and the Presidential Election Campaign Fund Act.[73] But because there have been very few appeals on these matters in recent years, in practice, the only viable mechanism for those seeking Supreme Court review is through a petition for a **writ of certiorari**—asking the Court to hear a case under its discretionary jurisdiction. That petition outlines the arguments of the litigant as to why the case should be reviewed. Rule 10 of the Supreme Court lists the factors that the Court considers when deciding whether or not to grant a case—the most important of which is a circuit split, meaning that two or more courts have reached conflicting results on an issue. If the Court is persuaded by the petition, it issues a writ of *certiorari*, which is an order by the Supreme Court to the lower court to send all the documents in a case to it so the higher court can review the lower court's decision. The Court operates under the norm of the **Rule of Four**, meaning that at least four justices must agree to accept the case in order for the Court to issue a writ of *certiorari*. In recent years, the Court has received upwards of 8,000 petitions for a writ of *certiorari*. In the 2010 term, for example, the Supreme Court received 9,062 petitions and granted review to a mere 80 of them.

Other Article III Courts

The U.S. Court of International Trade originated as the Board of General Appraisers in 1890, became the U.S. Customs Court in 1926, and was converted into an Article III court in 1956. It was given its current name in 1980. This court has nationwide jurisdiction regarding civil suits against the U.S. government for claims based on any international trade law. Although the court is located in New York City it may also hold hearings in foreign nations. There are currently nine judges on the U.S. Court of International Trade. Judges are appointed by the president, confirmed by the Senate, and have lifetime tenure. Appeals from this court go to the U.S. Court of Appeals for the Federal Circuit.[74]

The U.S. Court of Appeals for the Federal Circuit is a specialized circuit court with national jurisdiction, resulting from a merger of the U.S. Court of Customs and Patent Appeals and the appellate division of the U.S. Court of Claims in 1982. Five of the initial 12 judges came from the former, and seven from the latter. The Federal Circuit hears appeals on most patent issues. It also serves as an appellate court for many of the Article I courts, including the U.S. Court of Federal Claims and the U.S. Court of Appeals for Veterans Claims. Additionally, it hears appeals from some administrative agencies (e.g., Trademark Trial and Appeals Board, Department of Justice Bureau of Justice Assistance). The workload for this court is approximately half administrative law and one-third intellectual property rights, with the rest of its cases involving claims for monetary damages against the United States.[75]

Article I Courts

Article I gives Congress the authority "[t]o constitute Tribunals inferior to the supreme Court." **Article I courts** are also referred to as **legislative courts** because Congress creates them by invoking this authority.[76] Congress has created many different Article I courts over the years. The judges of these courts are generally appointed by the president with the advice and consent of the Senate and hold office for a set number of years—usually 15. However, bankruptcy courts are an exception to this norm.

Bankruptcy courts are Article I courts established by Congress to handle all bankruptcy matters—there are no state bankruptcy courts.[77] Congress established its position of "referee" in the Bankruptcy Act of 1898 to act as administrators in bankruptcy cases. As their responsibilities expanded over the years, Congress ultimately applied the term "judge" to the position in 1973 and formally established bankruptcy judgeships in the Bankruptcy Reform Act of 1978. These judges were appointed by the president and confirmed by the Senate for 14-year terms. However, in *Northern Pipeline Construction Co. v. Marathon Pipe Line Co.*, the Supreme Court ruled that Congress could not grant bankruptcy jurisdiction to independent courts composed of judges who did not have the protections of Article III.[78] In response, Congress amended the law to make bankruptcy courts units of federal district courts and bankruptcy judges appointed by the U.S. courts of appeals for each circuit to each district court within its jurisdiction for renewable 14-year terms. There are currently over 300 bankruptcy judges as authorized by Congress.

Another Article I court is the U.S. Court of Federal Claims located in Washington, D.C. It originated as the Court of Claims in 1855, later became U.S. Court of Claims in 1982, and was renamed the U.S. Court of Federal Claims in 1992.[79] This court has nationwide jurisdiction regarding monetary claims against the United States (e.g., claims

Image 4.5 Court of Claims
Photograph ca. 1940 of the five judges of the U.S. Court of Claims, an Article I court created by Congress. Harris & Ewing Collection, Prints and Photographs Division, Library of Congress, Washington, D.C.

for tax refunds, just compensation for taking of private property, damages for breach of contract, patent and copyright infringement claims against the United States). An interesting example of its jurisdiction occurred when Congress passed the Civil Liberties Act of 1988 and gave the court the power to hear claims related to Japanese-Americans who were held in internment camps during WWII. There are currently 16 judges on the U.S. Court of Federal Claims. Decisions from this court can be appealed to the U.S. Court of Appeals for the Federal Circuit.

The U.S. Tax Court is another Article I court located in Washington, D.C.[80] This court originated as the U.S. Board of Tax Appeals in 1924, then became the Tax Court of the United States in 1942, and was later renamed the U.S. Tax Court in 1969. It has nationwide jurisdiction regarding federal income tax disputes. There are currently 19 judges on the U.S. Tax Court. Although taxpayers may choose to bring an action in any U.S. district court, or in the U.S. Court of Federal Claims, those courts require that the tax be paid first, and that the party then file a lawsuit to recover the contested amount paid. In contrast, litigants who file cases in the U.S. Tax Court can dispute a tax before it has been paid. This variability allows litigants to consider which venue is most advantageous to their case before deciding whether or not to pay a tax. Although the Tax Court is physically located in Washington, D.C., the judges travel nationwide to hear cases. Therefore, appeals from this court go the applicable geographical U.S. Court of Appeals.

Another court that was created by Congress under its Article I power is the U.S. Court of Appeals for Veterans Claims in Washington, D.C.[81] This court handles certain cases arising from the denial of veterans' benefits that are appealed from the Board of Veterans' Appeals. It originated as the U.S. Court of Veterans Appeals in 1988 and was renamed U.S. Court of Appeals for Veterans Claims in 1999. There are currently seven judges on the U.S. Court of Appeals for Veterans Claims. Appeals from this court go to the U.S. Court of Appeals for the Federal Circuit.

Yet another legislative court is the U.S. Court of Appeals for the Armed Forces, also located in Washington, D.C.[82] Born from criticism over the World War II–era military justice system, which was largely based on the court-martial tradition of efficiency and chain of command, Congress created the Court of Military Appeals in 1951 to provide a civilian check on military authority. It was renamed the United States Court of Military Appeals in 1968 and received its current name in 1994. There are currently five judges on the U.S. Court of Military Appeals who serve for 15-year terms. Appeals from this court go to the U.S. Supreme Court.

Except for the rare case that is successfully appealed to the U.S. Supreme Court, the U.S. Court of Appeals for the Armed Forces is the final appellate court for cases arising under the Uniform Code of Military Justice. The Court of Appeals for the Armed Forces reviews decisions from the various military courts of criminal appeals of the services: The Army Court of Criminal Appeals, the Navy-Marine Corps of Criminal Appeals, the Coast Guard Court of Criminal Appeals, and the Air Force Court of Criminal Appeals. These appellate courts in turn review criminal judgments by military trial courts, which are known as **courts-martial**. There are a number of films that portray American court-martial proceedings including the Bruce Willis movie *Hart's War* (2002), *Rules of Engagement* (2000) starring Tommy Lee Jones and Samuel L. Jackson, *The Court-Martial of Billy Mitchell* (1955), and the Humphrey Bogart films *The Caine Mutiny* (1954) and *Across the Pacific* (1942). Films dealing with non-U.S. courts-martial include India's *Shaurya* (2008), the Australian film *Breaker Morant* (1980), and Stanley Kubrick's *Paths of Glory* (1957) starring Kirk Douglas.

Administrative tribunals are also constituted by Congress under its Article I power and perform quasi-adjudicatory functions such as reviewing decisions made by federal agencies like the Department of Labor, Equal Employment Opportunity Commission, or Securities and Exchange Commission. These bodies are staffed with administrative law judges. While most agencies have a few dozen administrative law judges, the Social Security Administration has over 1,400 who resolve over 700,000 cases each year.[83] Recently, it was reported that there was widespread disparity among social security judges in awarding disability benefits. Specifically, dozens of judges awarded benefits in 90 percent of their cases while others denied benefits in more than 80 percent of their cases.[84] In response, the agency began tightening scrutiny over its judges to ensure that benefits are awarded consistently. Still, the decisions of administrative law judges can be appealed within the agency and some may be able to be appealed to Article III courts such as the U.S. courts of appeals, depending on what Congress has specified for each agency.

Article IV Courts

Article IV, Section 3, Clause 2 of the U.S. Constitution gives Congress the "power to dispose of and make all needful rules and regulations respecting the territory or other property belonging to the United States." Pursuant to this authority, Congress has created **Article IV courts** that exercise jurisdiction over U.S. territories: Guam, the U.S. Virgin Islands, and the Northern Mariana Islands.[85] Prior to the transfer of control of the Panama Canal Zone from the United States to Panama, there was also a territorial court with jurisdiction over the Canal Zone (the United States District Court for the Canal Zone) created under Article IV authority. Puerto Rico, too, has a federal district court; however, it is no longer considered a territorial court since, though originally created under Article IV, it is now an Article III court.[86] Unlike with the other federal courts discussed in this chapter, territorial courts not only have jurisdiction over federal matters but also local ones and therefore perform functions similar to what state and local courts do in the 50 states. Like the judges of Article I courts, the judges on territorial courts do not have life tenure but instead have set terms of office as established by Congress—currently 10 years.

Article II Courts

From time to time throughout the nation's history, presidents have set up executive courts to administer justice in territories occupied by the American military during times of war or civil unrest.[87] The first such court was established in the Mexican War of 1846 as part of the provisional government that would become the territory of New Mexico. It heard criminal and civil matters and had appellate review of trial court decisions. Similar occupation courts were established during the Civil War, Spanish-American War, and World War II. There have been many questions surrounding these courts including the extent to which judges should apply U.S. law and local laws in the territories in which the courts reside.

One notable example—the final time an Article II court was constituted—was the U.S. Court for Berlin, which was set up after World War II to hear criminal matters "arising under any legislation in effect in the United States Sector of Berlin if the offense was committed within the area of Greater Berlin."[88] Its decisions could be appealed to the U.S. Chief of Mission—the principal officer in charge of a U.S. diplomatic mission to a foreign country, generally the Ambassador. While it has never happened, it is possible that decisions of Article II courts, or the Chief of Mission, could ultimately be appealed to Article III courts, particularly in criminal matters for individuals seeking *habeas* review.[89]

The only case ever heard by the U.S. Court for Berlin occurred in 1978 when two East German citizens were charged under German law with hijacking a Polish plane and ordering it to land in West Berlin.[90] The U.S. State Department selected U.S. district court Judge Herbert Stern to try the case. In opposition to the preferences of the State Department, Judge Stern employed American trial procedures, empanelled a jury, and allowed a mix of both German and American lawyers to try the case. After the jury convicted one of the defendants, Stern sentenced him to time already served—9 months. At the end of the trial, some citizens of Berlin brought an unrelated lawsuit to Judge Stern in an attempt to stop the U.S. Army from erecting military housing in a public park. The U.S. Ambassador to Germany ordered Stern not to take the case and fired him from the court when he refused to comply. Stern went back to his job on the federal district court and the U.S. Court of Berlin was shut down for good. Stern later wrote a book about his experiences that was made into a film *Judgment in Berlin* (1988) starring Sean Penn and Martin Sheen as Judge Stern.[91]

In his discussion of the Court of Berlin and Judge Stern, political scientist Lawrence Baum offered this insight:

> Another district judge might have behaved differently from Stern, but judicial rebellion was likely for two reasons. First, although the State Department could dismiss a judge of the Court of Berlin, it could not affect the judge's tenure on the federal bench. Second, a judge who was accustomed to independence could hardly be pleased with direction from the executive branch, direction that was highly inconsistent with the self-image of federal judges.[92]

The inability of the executive branch to control Judge Stern suggests that future executives may be reluctant to set up another Article II court going forward. There are serious questions over whether Article II courts are even permissible under the Constitution.[93]

Military commissions or tribunals are both similar to and different from Article II courts.[94] They are similar in that they are established by the president to administer judicial proceedings in wartime. They are different, however, in that they are specifically constituted to impose authority on enemy combatants and civilians hindering the war effort and are recognized by federal statutes under the **laws of war**—international law governing war such as the Geneva Conventions—rather than Article I.[95] Military commissions have been used since the American Revolution and have most recently been constituted to deal with enemy combatants in the War on Terrorism—individuals captured abroad and held at a prison camp at an American military base in Guantanamo Bay, Cuba. These commissions were established by presidential order 2 months after the terrorist attacks of September 11, 2001, and later authorized by Congress in 2006 and again in 2009 after Supreme Court decisions limited the president's unilateral authority to create and run them.[96] Although there is debate about whether noncitizen enemy combatants can petition Article III courts for release under *habeas corpus*, the Supreme Court's decision in *Boumediene v. Bush* states that they may.[97]

THE JURISDICTION AND ORGANIZATION OF STATE COURTS

As we mentioned earlier in this chapter, courts possess both personal and subject matter jurisdiction. The subject matter jurisdiction of state courts is virtually any type of case that does not fall within the exclusive jurisdiction of the federal courts. Examples of cases that fall within the jurisdiction of state courts include: the interpretation of the state constitution; state criminal offenses, which include crimes defined by the state constitution or by state statute, such as murder and theft; and tort and personal injury law, which are civil wrongs in which a person's behavior is claimed to have unfairly caused someone else to suffer loss or harm. Generally, a person who suffers a tortious injury is seeking damages, usually monetary compensation, from the individual responsible for his injuries. Other examples of cases that are usually within the ambit of state court jurisdiction are those that have to do with contract law (in which two or more parties have an agreement that is enforceable by law), family law (such as divorce and child custody), real property law (pertaining to the use, control, and disposition of land and permanent structures), and probate law (the distribution of assets to heirs when an individual dies). Additionally, state courts have jurisdiction over cases involving federal law. The only cases state courts do not have jurisdiction to hear are cases where the defendant is the United States, and those involving certain federal laws, such as antitrust, patent and copyright, bankruptcy, and some maritime law cases. Finally, state courts are not allowed to hear certain specific federal crimes, such as crimes committed on federal property.

States designate courts as having either general or limited jurisdiction. A court of **general jurisdiction** is authorized to hear a broad array of civil and criminal cases (anything that is not committed exclusively to another court). In comparison, a court of **limited jurisdiction** is authorized to hear a narrowly defined set of cases and its jurisdiction may be limited in terms of the substantive issue (e.g., juvenile, probate, or family law cases) or by other means (e.g., small claims courts that are limited to handling civil cases with small dollar amounts at stake). As mentioned earlier with regard to federal courts, a second key dimension of state court jurisdiction is whether a court possesses original or appellate jurisdiction—whether hearing the case for the first time and conducting a trial as in the former case or reviewing the trial court for procedural errors or the validity of the law in question as in the latter.

Although no two state court systems are structured exactly the same way, there are sufficient similarities to provide an example of what a typical state system looks like. The majority of state court systems are patterned on a simple hierarchy: trial courts of limited jurisdiction, trial courts of general jurisdiction, intermediate appellate courts, and state courts of last resort. Some states, however, have more complex systems, with multiple courts of limited and general jurisdiction (and even multiple appellate courts). Figure 4.3 depicts the convoluted nature of New York's judiciary, with its multiple limited jurisdiction trial courts and multiple general jurisdiction trial courts. By way of comparison, Figure 4.4 portrays the relative simplicity of California's system, with its single set of trial courts. Complex systems make it more difficult for litigants to know where to file claims and provide more opportunities for experienced attorneys to use the system to their advantage (by engaging in forum shopping). Reform efforts to simplify and unify state court systems were inspired in the early twentieth century by Roscoe Pound, a noted legal scholar who served for 2 decades as the Dean of Harvard Law School.[98] Those efforts, nurtured and fostered by the American Judicature Society and American Bar Association, did not gain momentum and achieve some measure of success until the latter half of the twentieth century.[99] Over time, an increasing number of states have scrapped complex systems for simple, streamlined ones but local officials are loathe to give up administrative control over their courts and, as a result, court unification remains uneven across the states.[100] Despite this unevenness, there are general characteristics of each type of court—trial court of limited jurisdiction, trial court of general jurisdiction, intermediate appellate court, and court of last resort—that are common across the states. We discuss each, in turn, below.

FIGURE 4.3

New York State Unified Court System

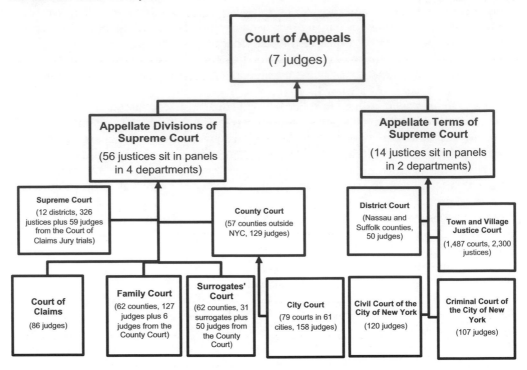

Source: Adapted from *State Court Structure Charts*, National Center for State Court, www.courtstatistics.org and *New York State Unified Court System.* www.courts.state.ny.us/courts/structure.shtml.

State Trial Courts of Limited Jurisdiction

Trial courts of limited jurisdiction—also sometimes referred to as trial courts of special jurisdiction—at the state level are the workhorses of state judiciaries in the sense that they try the vast majority of cases heard in state courts. In 2009, for example, approximately two-thirds of the cases filed in state trial courts were heard in trial courts of limited jurisdiction; that translates into more than 70 million cases,[101] which represents a 10 percent increase since 2000.[102] Common examples of state trial courts of limited jurisdiction include: probate, juvenile, family, traffic, small claims, and municipal courts. For example, a probate court, which is also called a surrogate court in some states, deals with matters pertaining to the administration of estates, while a family court hears cases that relate to family law, such as custody of children, adoption, alimony, and divorce.

These trial courts are often located in or near the county courthouse and are usually presided over by a single judge without a jury; a trial without a jury is known as a **bench trial**. Trial courts of limited jurisdiction may also have the responsibility to handle preliminary matters in felony cases, such as arraigning defendants (formally charging them in criminal complaints), setting bail, and assigning counsel. As a general rule, though state trial courts of limited jurisdiction process large volumes of cases, those cases, while certainly important to the persons involved, are generally not complex. For example, in 2009, state trial courts of limited jurisdiction reported receiving over 43 million traffic

FIGURE 4.4
California Court System

```
        ┌─────────────────────────┐
        │      Supreme Court       │
        │   (7 justices sit en banc) │
        └─────────────────────────┘
                     ↑
        ┌─────────────────────────┐
        │     Court of Appeal      │
        │ (6 districts, 105 justices sit │
        │        in panels)        │
        └─────────────────────────┘
                     ↑
        ┌─────────────────────────┐
        │      Superior Court      │
        │ (58 counties; 1,630 judges; │
        │   392 commissioners and  │
        │         referees)        │
        └─────────────────────────┘
```

Source: Adapted from *State Court Structure Charts*, National Center for State Courts. www.courtstatistics.org and *About California Courts*, California Courts: The Judicial Branch of Government. www.courts.ca.gov/2113.htm.

Image 4.6 Justice of the Peace
This 1940 photo shows a farmer who was at the same time a grade school teacher and justice of the peace in the small town of Chamisal, New Mexico. Prints and Photographs Division, Library of Congress, Washington, D.C.

cases, which represents 61 percent of their overall workload.[103] Such courts are not always courts of record, meaning that there may be no verbatim transcript of the proceedings.

Though it has become much less common over time, state trial courts of limited jurisdiction may be presided over by lay judges (i.e., judges who do not have formal legal training) and may be part time.[104] The venerable justice of the peace is a lay judge that is familiar to most. Historically, they held their positions and exercised authority because of their standing in the community rather than from formal state grants of power. The procedures they followed were informal, reflecting the communities they served. However, professional associations of attorneys—licensed by the state to practice law—viewed lay judging as a threat to the expert administration of justice and, over time, most urban jurisdictions did away with lay judges. But some lay judges did hold on in local communities.

A study comparing both lay and lawyer judges in the state of New York found no significant distinctions in their understanding of due process guarantees or in their approach to exercising discretion.[105] Yet 20 years later, a year-long investigation by the *New York Times* found the opposite, documenting failures and abuses by a number of lay judges over a period of years.[106] The following year, a state commission conducted a thorough review of town and village courts and found that while the majority of lay judges were hardworking, experienced, and adequately dispensing justice, many were not and had committed legal errors, ethical violations, and other abuses.[107] The commission recommended enhancing the education, training, and certification of lay judges and providing all criminal defendants the ability to "opt out" and have their cases heard by an attorney judge rather than a lay judge.[108] Thus, research suggests that if lay judges are to remain in place, they should do so in limited circumstances and under professional supervision.

State Trial Courts of General Jurisdiction

State trial courts of general jurisdiction are the main trial courts in state judiciaries. They have the authority to hear any case outside the jurisdiction of the trial courts of limited jurisdiction, including both civil and criminal cases. In a criminal case, the crime is formally prohibited by the state—hence, it is considered a crime against "the people"—and can involve a fine or a jail term. Civil cases include all other cases and do not involve jail terms. Civil cases may involve the government against an individual or a group for the enforcement of government policies. Civil cases not involving the government are typically conflicts between and among private parties and usually involve torts, debts, or some other conflict involving the transfer of or claim to money. In terms of the substance of their workload, state trial courts of general jurisdiction handle more civil cases than any other type of case, with more than a third of their caseloads devoted to civil cases.[109] The majority of these civil cases have to do with issues pertaining to contracts (e.g., a legally binding agreement for the exchange of goods or services).[110] Criminal cases account for approximately one-fifth of the workload of state trial courts of general jurisdiction.[111] Criminal cases reached an all-time high in 2006 but have been decreasing every year since then.[112]

The trial courts of general jurisdiction are typically organized geographically into judicial districts or circuits using existing geographic boundaries (e.g., county line). The most common names for state trial courts of general jurisdiction are circuit court (e.g., Illinois Circuit Court, Wisconsin Circuit Court), district court (e.g., Texas District Court, North Dakota District Court), and superior court (Arizona Superior Court, Connecticut Superior Court). One judge usually hears these cases—whether in conjunction with a jury or not—and the judge decides the issues of law, meaning that the judge determines which aspects of the law are relevant and how the law is applied. The jury—or the judge if it is a bench trial—is responsible for deciding issues of fact; in other words, the jury evaluates the factual circumstances of the case. These courts are courts of record, meaning that verbatim records are kept and it is those records that will be reviewed by the relevant appellate court for errors in process and procedure in the event of an appeal. Appeals from these courts usually go to the intermediate appellate court, in those states that possess them, or to the state court of last resort, in the absence of an intermediate appellate tribunal.

Research suggests that state trial courts have different organizational cultures—norms, values, and resulting behavior—that have significant implications for the administration of justice.[113] Specifically, court culture can be communal, networked, autonomous, or hierarchical with each culture having different implications for solidarity (independent decision making) and sociability (interaction between chambers). Thus, autonomous cultures have little solidarity or sociability while networked cultures have high levels of each due to their emphasis on collegiality. These cultures persist because there is disagreement between judges and professional court administrators on the appropriate role of the judiciary. This disagreement results in considerable variation across states in how cases are processed. For example, courts that have a hierarchical culture generally process cases in a timely fashion. The downside, however, is that they are viewed by attorneys as less accessible, less fair, and less effective than courts with more diffuse cultures. Thus, issues of organizational culture go hand-in-hand with how courts are structured.

State Intermediate Appellate Courts

The overwhelming majority of states have an intermediate appellate court situated between the trial courts of general jurisdiction and the highest court in the state. Currently, 40 states have intermediate appellate courts[114] and five of these (Alabama, Illinois, New York, Pennsylvania, and Tennessee) have two intermediate appellate courts as part of their judicial structure. The purpose of these courts is to reduce the workload for state courts of last resort by providing a mechanism for fulfilling the commonly understood right to an appeal, thereby enabling the high courts to focus on the development of consistent doctrines and procedures to guide lower courts under their supervision.

The most common name for this intermediate appellate court level is court of appeals (e.g., Indiana Court of Appeals, Alaska Court of Appeals). Other names include appellate division (e.g., New Jersey Appellate Division of the Supreme Court), state appellate court (e.g., Illinois Appellate Court), superior court (e.g., Pennsylvania Superior Court), and intermediate court of appeals (Hawaii Intermediate Court of Appeals). Any party who is not satisfied with the judgment of the state trial court—except in a case where a criminal defendant has been found not guilty—may appeal his or her case to the intermediate appellate court. The total number of incoming cases reported by the states for intermediate appellate courts has hovered around 200,000 in recent years,[115] with four out of every five of the cases handled by state intermediate appellate courts a matter of **mandatory review**, which means the courts have no choice and are required to hear the cases.[116]

Intermediate appellate courts may sit en banc, use panels, or rely on a combination of en banc and panel proceedings. If a court sits en banc, the entire complement of judges on the court hears the case together. When, however, a court uses panels, only a subset of the judges of that court handles the case. Some states, such as Alabama and Tennessee, have separate intermediate appellate courts for civil and criminal matters. Recall that appellate courts do not conduct trials; instead they review the record of the trial court and hear arguments from the attorneys to determine if there was an important error in procedure or interpretation of law at the trial. If so, the decision of the trial court may be reversed and a new trial ordered.[117] More often than not, intermediate-appellate-court decisions are final, as appeal to the state high court from the intermediate appellate court is commonly limited.

State Courts of Last Resort

All states have a final court of appeals. While the most common name is supreme court (e.g., Wisconsin Supreme Court), in some states they are known as courts of appeals (e.g., Maryland Court of Appeals). Every state has one court of last resort except for Texas and Oklahoma, each of which has separate courts of last resort for civil and criminal appeals (yielding 52 separate courts of last resort). Regardless of the nomenclature—the actual name of the court—the state court of last resort has the final word on all state constitutional questions and provides the authoritative interpretation of state statutes. However, if there is a substantial federal question involved, state-court-of-last-resort decisions can be appealed to the U.S. Supreme Court.

To illustrate, consider *Gideon v. Wainwright*.[118] Clarence Earl Gideon was charged with breaking and entering a pool hall to commit a petty larceny, which is the theft of a low-value item or small amount of money. Though Gideon requested the assistance of counsel at trial, the trial court judge declined the request, noting that state law permitted the appointment of counsel only for capital cases—in other words, cases in which the crime may merit the death penalty. The Florida State Supreme Court declined to mandate a new trial and provide counsel. Though the state supreme court was the final authority on the interpretation and application of the state statute regarding the provision of counsel to the indigent, the case implicated the right to counsel embedded in the Sixth Amendment of the federal Constitution.[119] Accordingly, the U.S. Supreme Court did accept the case for review and, in a landmark ruling, determined that the Sixth Amendment's right to counsel was not limited to capital cases.

Collectively, state courts of last resort heard almost 100,000 cases in 2000; however, their workloads have decreased since then and the volume of cases heard in 2009 was approximately 75,000.[120] Those states that have intermediate level appellate courts usually grant **discretionary review** to their court of last resort, which means that the court has the authority to decide which appeals it will consider from among the cases submitted to it. In fact, in 2009, 56 percent of state-court-of-last-resort cases were discretionary, whereas a mere 17 percent were mandatory, with the remainder largely original proceedings and other miscellaneous cases.

Which cases merit review? Generally, it will *not* be those cases that are "fact-bound," or cases that are merely concerned with questions of fact and for which even minor changes in the factual circumstances would mandate an alternative outcome. Instead, a court of last resort's purpose is to interpret the meaning of either the state constitution or state statutes to provide guidance to lower courts. In states that do not have an intermediate level appellate court, however, the court of last resort will generally have mandatory review for all cases petitioned from the state's trial courts.

CONCLUSION

Are the jurisdictions and the way courts are structured limited, uniform, and defined? In this chapter we have explained that while there are certainly well-defined structural differences in the way that courts are organized—for example, between trial and appellate and federal and state courts—there is also considerable overlap, variability, and discretion in choosing which cases to file in which courts. For example, litigants can file federal tax cases in the U.S. district courts, the U.S. Court of Federal Claims, or the U.S. Tax Court. Why does the American legal system allow such variability?

The answer is politics. Diversity jurisdiction, forum shopping, and change-of-venue motions are routinely invoked and employed by attorneys seeking to gain an edge over the competition. Because legislators determine how courts are organized, they are regularly lobbied and held accountable by attorneys and litigants who stand to benefit from jurisdictional options. Lawyers are a politically powerful group. For example, the American Association for Justice—formerly the Association of Trial Lawyers of America—boasts 56,000 members worldwide and has spent millions of dollars each year on political campaigns and lobbying in Washington, D.C., alone.[121] Given the political reality of court organization we should not be surprised that legislative decisions about jurisdiction and structure are as driven by politics as are the decisions that attorneys and litigants make in choosing among courts in which to file their cases.

Suggested Readings

Lawrence Baum. *Specializing the Courts* (Chicago, IL: University of Chicago Press, 2010). The first comprehensive analysis of the growing trend toward specialization in the federal and state court systems.

Jonathan Matthew Cohen. *Inside Appellate Courts: The Impact of Court Organization on Judicial Decision Making in the United States Courts of Appeals* (Ann Arbor, MI: University of Michigan Press, 2002). A comprehensive study of how the organization of a court affects the decisions of appellate judges.

Richard A. Posner. *The Federal Courts: Challenge and Reform*, Revised Edition (Cambridge, MA: Harvard University Press, 1999). Originally published in 1985, this classic book provides a comprehensive evaluation of the federal judiciary, including how caseloads have exploded, and a detailed program of judicial reform.

Doris Marie Provine. *Judging Credentials: Nonlawyer Judges and the Politics of Professionalism* (Chicago, IL: University of Chicago Press, 1986). Historical treatment and contemporary research based on surveys, interviews, and observation demonstrates that there is little significant difference between lay and lawyer judges in their conceptions and administration of justice.

Endnotes

1 For example, a graduate of Wiley College, located in Marshall, was denied admission to the University of Texas Law School due to his race and initiated a lawsuit that ultimately made its way to the Supreme Court. The result was the desegregation of postgraduate studies in Texas by the decision of the Court in *Sweatt v. Painter*, 339 U.S. 629 (1950).

2 Wade Goodwin, "Boogie Woogie: Born in the Backwoods of America," *All Things Considered*, January 17, 2011 (http://www.npr.org/2011/01/17/132963070/boogie-woogie-born-in-the-backwoods-of-america).

3 Julie Creswell, "So Small a Town, So Many Patent Suits," *New York Times*, September 24, 2006.

4 TiVo claimed that EchoStar had infringed on its patent for a particular aspect of DVR technology that permits viewers to record one show while simultaneously watching another.

5 Julie Creswell, "So Small a Town, So Many Patent Suits," *New York Times*, September 24, 2006.

6 *Groppi v. Wisconsin*, 400 U.S. 505 (1971); *Rideau v. Louisiana*, 373 U.S. 723 (1963). See Scott Kafker, "Right to Venue and the Right to an Impartial Jury: Resolving the Conflict in the Federal Constitution," *University of Chicago Law Review*, vol. 52, no. 3 (Summer 1985): 729–750.

7 Katharine Q. Seelye, "Change of Venue Denied for Boston Marathon Bombing Suspect," *New York Times*, January 3, 2015.

8 Mark Hansen, "Different Jury, Different Verdict? A Rehearing on Change of Venue," *American Bar Association Journal*, vol. 78, no. 8 (August 1992): 54–57.

9   Julie Creswell, "So Small a Town, So Many Patent Suits," *New York Times*, September 24, 2006.

10 A key element of the Act changes the basis on which the priority for patent applications is determined from "first to invent" to "first to file." See Jia Lynn Yang, "Senate Passes Patent Bill," *Washington Post*, September 8, 2011.

11 Mark Curriden, "Patent Lawsuits Skyrocket in Texas," *The Dallas Morning News*, February 12, 2013.

12 Questions of federalism have been hotly debated since the founding and continue to this day. See J. Mitchell Pickerill and Cornell W. Clayton, "The Rehnquist Court and the Political Dynamics of Federalism," *Perspectives on Politics*, vol. 2, no. 2 (June 2004): 233–248.

13 Though not a state, the District of Columbia has its own court system that derives its authority from the U.S. Congress with the District of Columbia Court of Appeals as the district's court of last resort for appeals from the Superior Court of the District of Columbia—the local trial court for the district.

14 5 U.S. 137 (1803).

15 3 U.S. 171 (1796).

16 28 U.S.C. Sec. 1331.

17 The Fair Housing Act is the common or popular name for Title VIII of the Civil Rights Act of 1968.

18 28 U.S.C. Sec. 2241.

19 See, generally, Justin J. Wert, *Habeas Corpus in America: The Politics of Individual Rights* (Lawrence, KS: University Press of Kansas, 2011).

20 See Anthony Gregory, *The Power of Habeas Corpus in America: From the King's Prerogative to the War on Terror* (New York, NY: Cambridge University Press, 2013). See, also, Jonathan Hafetz, *Habeas Corpus After 9/11: Confronting America's New Global Detention System* (New York, NY: New York University Press, 2011).

21 Detailed federal judicial caseload statistics are compiled by the Office of Administrative Courts and are available here on its website (http://www.uscourts.gov/Statistics/FederalJudicialCaseload-Statistics.aspx).

22 Rubin "Hurricane" Carter, *The Sixteenth Round: From Number 1 Contender to #45472* (New York, NY: Viking Press, 1974).

23 Paul B. Wice, *Rubin "Hurricane" Carter and the American Justice System* (New Brunswick, NJ: Rutgers University Press, 2000): 89–92.

24 Andrew Cohen, "The Redemption Song of Rubin 'Hurricane' Carter," *The Atlantic*, April 22, 2014.

25 Diversity jurisdiction is currently codified at 28 U.S.C. Sec. 1332.

26 For a systematic assessment of congressional action vis-à-vis diversity jurisdiction, see Brett Curry, "Institutions, Interests, and Judicial Outcomes: The Politics of Federal Diversity Jurisdiction," *Political Research Quarterly*, vol. 60, no. 3 (September 2007): 454–467.

27 60 U.S. 393 (1857).

28 The amount was originally set at $500 and has been increased over time—in 1887 to $2,000, in 1911 to $3,000, in 1958 to $10,000, in 1988 to $50,000, and, since 1996, to $75,000.

29 2 U.S. 419 (1793).

30 134 U.S. 1 (1890).

31 108 U.S. 76 (1883).

32 292 U.S. 313 (1934).

33 427 U.S. 445 (1976).

34 517 U.S. 44 (1996).

35 546 U.S. 356 (2006).

36 Article I, Sec. 8, Cl. 4.

37 See, for example, Ernest A. Young, "State Sovereign Immunity and the Future of Federalism," *The Supreme Court Review*, vol. 1999 (1999): 1–79; John F. Manning, "The Eleventh Amendment and the Reading of Precise Constitutional Texts," *The Yale Law Journal*, vol. 113 (June 2004): 1663–1750; Thomas D. Rowe, Jr., "Exhuming the 'Diversity Explanation' of the Eleventh Amendment," *Alabama Law Review*, vol. 65, no. 2 (2013): 457–472.

38 304 U.S. 64 (1938).

39 Victor E. Flango, "Litigant Choice between State and Federal Courts," *South Carolina Law Review*, vol. 46 (Summer 1995): 961–977.

40 Ibid.

41 Supplemental jurisdiction is codified at 28 U.S.C. Section 1367, which states that courts have supplemental jurisdiction over "all other claims that are so related … that they form part of the same case or controversy."

42 For a discussion of specialized federal courts see Lawrence Baum, *Specializing the Courts* (Chicago, IL: University of Chicago Press, 2011).

43 Jennifer Steinhauer, "Senate, for Just the 8th Time, Votes to Oust a Federal Judge," *New York Times*, December 8, 2010.

44 There are 94 total judicial districts and 677 total authorized judgeships if the Article IV district courts for Guam, Northern Mariana Islands, and U.S. Virgin Islands are included.

45 Congress originally created a territorial court for Puerto Rico under its Article IV authority. In 1966, however, Congress replaced that territorial court with the U.S. District Court for the District of Puerto Rico as an Article III court.

46 In a *Daubert* hearing, the judge determines the validity and admissibility of expert opinion testimony. The name comes from the seminal Supreme Court case of *Daubert v. Merrell Dow Pharmaceuticals* (509 U.S. 579, 1993).

47 As we discuss in greater detail in Chapter Six, alternative dispute resolution processes are designed to aid civil litigants in resolving disputes using vehicles such as arbitration and mediation. ADR processes are typically less costly and take less time than traditional trials. In 1998, Congress mandated that each district court devise and make available at least one ADR mechanism, the most common being mediation.

48 Administrative Office of the United States Courts, Federal Judicial Caseload Statistics, U.S. District Courts (http://www.uscourts.gov/Statistics/JudicialBusiness/2013/us-district-courts.aspx).

49 Joshua Glick, "On the Road: The Supreme Court and the History of Circuit Riding," *Cardozo Law Review*, vol. 24 (April 2003): 1753–1843.

50 Linda Greenhouse, "Riding Circuit with Swamps and Yellow Fever," *New York Times*, November 2, 1990.

51 Though the Evarts Act formally retained the practice of circuit riding for the Supreme Court justices, the workload of the Court precluded the justices from attending circuit courts on anything but an extremely irregular basis. Congress formally eliminated circuit-riding duties in 1911.

52 Jonathan M. Cohen, *Inside Appellate Courts* (Ann Arbor, MI: University of Michigan Press, 2002).

53 See Jonathan D. Glater, "Lawmakers Trying Again to Divide Ninth Circuit," *New York Times*, June 19, 2005.

54 See Frank Tamulonis III, "Splitting the Ninth Circuit: An Administrative Necessity or Environmental Gerrymandering?" *Penn State Law Review*, vol. 112 (Winter 2008): 859–883.

55 J. Robert Brown, Jr., and Allison Herren Lee, "Neutral Assignment of Judges at the Court of Appeals," *Texas Law Review*, vol. 78 (April 2000): 1037–1115.

56 Paul M. Collins, Jr., and Wendy L. Martinek, "The Small Group Context: Designated District Court Judges in the U.S. Courts of Appeals," *Journal of Empirical Legal Studies*, vol. 8, no. 1 (March 2011): 177–205.

57 Administrative Office of the United States Courts, *Judicial Business of the U.S. Courts*, Fiscal Year 2011 (Washington, D.C.: Administrative Office of the United States Courts, 2011): Table S-1.

58 James J. Brudney and Corey Ditslear, "Designated Diffidence: District Court Judges on the Courts of Appeals," *Law and Society Review*, vol. 35, no. 3 (2001): 565–606.

59 Ibid., 565–606, 585.

60 Paul M. Collins, Jr., and Wendy L. Martinek, "The Small Group Context: Designated District Court Judges in the U.S. Courts of Appeals," *Journal of Empirical Legal Studies*, vol. 8, no. 1 (March 2011): 177–205.

61 David E. Klein, *Making Law in the United States Courts of Appeals* (New York, NY: Cambridge University Press, 2002).

62 See John W. Dean, "The New Nattering Nabobs of Negativism Are Gunning for Obama's Judicial Nominees: A Republican Strategy that We Must All Hope Fails," FindLaw's Writ (http://writ.news. findlaw.com/dean/20090417.html). See, also, Deborah Sontag, "The Power of the Fourth," *New York Times Magazine*, March 9, 2003.

63 Bruce Fein, "Race Separation Ratified," *Washington Times*, December 26, 2006; Orrin G. Hatch, "A Circuitous Court: Pledge Decision Is Judicial Activism," *Washington Times*, July 2, 2002. But see, Erwin Chemerinsky, "The Myth of the Liberal Ninth Circuit," *Loyola of Los Angeles Law Review*, vol. 37, no. 1 (Fall 2003): 1–21.

64 Stefanie A. Lindquist and David E. Klein, "The Influence of Jurisprudential Considerations on Supreme Court Decisionmaking: A Study of Conflict Cases," *Law and Society Review*, vol. 40, no. 1 (March 2006): 135–161.

65 For a detailed background of this historical episode, see William E. Leuchtenburg, "The Origins of Franklin D. Roosevelt's 'Court-Packing' Plan," *Supreme Court Review*, vol. 1966 (1966): 347–400. For an analysis of this episode, see Jamie L. Carson and Benjamin A. Kleinerman, "A Switch in Time Saves Nine: Institutions, Strategic Actors, and FDR's Court-Packing Plan," *Public Choice*, vol. 114, no. 3/4 (December 2002): 301–324. See, also, Michael Nelson, "The President and the Court: Reinterpreting the Court-Packing Episode of 1937," *Political Science Quarterly*, vol. 103, no. 2 (Summer 1988): 267–293.

66 See Edward T. Swaine, "The Chief Justice and the Institutional Judiciary," *University of Pennsylvania Law Review*, vol. 154, no. 6 (June 2006): 1709–1728, 1713–1718.

67 Administrative Office of the United States Courts, *Judicial Business of the U.S. Courts*, Fiscal Year 2011 (Washington, DC: Administrative Office of the United States Courts, 2011): Table A-1.

68 515 U.S. 1 (1995).

69 523 U.S. 767 (1998).

70 Michael Coenen, "Original Jurisdiction Deadlocks," *Yale Law Journal*, vol. 118, no. 5 (March 2009): 1003–1012, 1009–1010.

71 Although the Supreme Court will generally not challenge a state court's ruling on an issue of state law, the Court will grant certiorari in cases where the state court's ruling deals with federal law or the U.S. Constitution.

72 Supreme Court Case Selections Act of 1988, 28 U.S.C. Sec. 1254.

73 Robert L. Stern, Eugene Gressman, and Stephen M. Shapiro, "Epitaph for Mandatory Jurisdiction," *ABA Journal*, December 1, 1988.

74 For a detailed look at the history and functions of this court, see Isaac Unah, *The Courts of International Trade: Judicial Specialization, Expertise, and Bureaucratic Policymaking* (Ann Arbor, MI: University of Michigan Press, 1998).

75 For a detailed look at the history and functions of this court, see Steven Flanders, *The Federal Circuit—A Judicial Innovation, Establishing a US Court of Appeals* (New York, NY: Twelve Tables Press, 2010).

76 James E. Pfander, "Article I Tribunals, Article II Courts, and the Judicial Power of the United States," *Harvard Law Review*, vol. 118, no. 2 (December 2004): 643–776.

77 Lawrence Baum, *Specializing the Courts* (Chicago, IL: Chicago University Press, 2011): 194–204.

78 458 U.S. 50 (1962).

79 Lawrence Baum, *Specializing the Courts* (Chicago, IL: Chicago University Press, 2011): 156–160.

80 Ibid., 147–154.

81 Ibid., 160–164.

82 Ibid., 68–71; John T. Willis, "The United States Court of Military Appeals—'Born Again.'" *Indiana Law Journal*, vol. 52, no. 1 (1976): 151–166.

83 Social Security Administration, "Fiscal Year 2012 Budget Overview," February 2011 (http://www. socialsecurity.gov/budget/hist/FY2012/2012BudgetOverview.pdf).

84 Damian Paletta, "Government Pulls in Reins on Disability Judges," *Wall Street Journal*, December 26, 2013.

85 American Samoa is an unincorporated territory of the United States but does not have a federal district court.

86 Congress converted the district court for Puerto Rico into an Article III court in 1966 (80 Stat. 764).

87 See David J. Bederman, "Article II Courts," *Mercer Law Review* vol. 44 (1992-1993): 825–879.

88 *United States v. Tiede*, 86 F.R.D. 227, 238 (1979).

89 See David J. Bederman, "Article II Courts," *Mercer Law Review*, vol. 44 (1992-1993): 825–879, 879.

90 Lawrence Baum, *Specializing the Courts* (Chicago, IL: Chicago University Press, 2011): 66–67.

91 Herbert Stern, *Judgment in Berlin* (New York, NY: Signet, 1984).

92 Lawrence Baum, *Specializing the Courts* (Chicago, IL: Chicago University Press, 2011): 67.

93 See Maryellen Fullerton, "Hijacking Trials Overseas: The Need for an Article III Court," *William and Mary Law Review*, vol. 28 (Fall 1986): 1–87.

94 For a detailed discussion of military tribunals and extended argument against their use, see Louis Fisher, *Military Tribunals & Presidential Power: American Revolution to the War on Terrorism* (Lawrence, KS: University of Kansas Press, 2005).

95 See 10 U.S.C. Sec. 821, Article 21 of the Uniform Code of Military Justice.

96 See *Rasul v. Bush*, 542 U.S. 466 (2004); *Hamdan v. Rumsfeld*, 548 U.S. 557 (2006); Military Commissions Act, P.L. 109-366 (2006); *Boumediene v. Bush*, 553 U.S. 723 (2008); Military Commissions Act, P.L. 111-84 (2009).

97 553 U.S. 723 (2008).

98 Allan Ashman and Jeffrey A. Parness, "The Concept of a Unified Court System," *DePaul Law Review*, vol. 24 (1974): 1–41, 2–5.

99 James W. Douglas and Steven W. Hays, "Judicial Administration: Modernizing the Third Branch," in *Handbook of Public Administration*, Third Edition, Jack Rabin, W. Bartley Hildreth, and Gerald J. Miller, eds (Boca Raton, FL: CRC Press, 2006).

100 Robert W. Tobin, *Creating the Judicial Branch: The Unfinished Reform* (Williamsburg, VA: National Center for State Courts, 1999).

101 Richard C. LaFountain, Richard Y. Schauffler, Shauna M. Strickland, Sarah A. Gibson, and Ashley N. Mason, *Examining the Work of State Courts: An Analysis of 2009 State Court Caseloads* (Williamsburg, VA: National Center for State Courts, 2011): 3.

102 Ibid., 2.

103 Ibid., 3–4.

104 "Evolution of Law Judges: From Kitchens to Courts." *New York Times* October 23, 1994.

105 Doris Marie Provine, *Judging Credentials: Nonlawyer Judges and the Politics of Professionalism* (Chicago: University of Chicago Press, 1986).

106 William Glaberson, "In Tiny Courts of N.Y., Abuses of Law and Power," *New York Times*, September 25, 2006.

107 Special Commission on the Future of the New York State Courts, *Justice Most Local: The Future of Town and Village Courts in New York State*, September 2008 (http://www.nyslocalgov.org/pdf/Justice_Most_Local.pdf).

108 Ibid.

109 Richard C. LaFountain, Richard Y. Schauffler, Shauna M. Strickland, Sarah A. Gibson, and Ashley N. Mason, *Examining the Work of State Courts: An Analysis of 2009 State Court Caseloads* (Williamsburg, VA: National Center for State Courts, 2011): 4.

110 Ibid., 11.

111 Ibid., 4.

112 Ibid., 20.

113 Brian J. Ostrom, Charles W. Ostrom, Jr., Roger A. Hanson, and Matthew Kleiman, *Trial Courts as Organizations* (Philadelphia, PA: Temple University Press, 2007).

114 Of the 40, only the North Dakota Court of Appeals is not permanent. It was first authorized on July 1, 1987 and consists of three temporary judges. This court only hears cases assigned to it by the North Dakota Supreme Court.

115 Richard C. LaFountain, Richard Y. Schauffler, Shauna M. Strickland, Sarah A. Gibson, and Ashley N. Mason, *Examining the Work of State Courts: An Analysis of 2009 State Court Caseloads* (Williamsburg, VA: National Center for State Courts, 2011): 38.

116 Ibid., 41.

117 The appellate court may find that there was error but, nonetheless, decline to invalidate the lower court ruling if it finds that the error was harmless (as opposed to reversible) error. Harmless error is error that the appellate court judges to be insufficient to have affected the outcome of the lower court proceedings.

118 372 U.S. 335 (1963).

119 The relevant portion of the Sixth Amendment reads as follows: "In all criminal prosecutions, the accused shall enjoy the right ... to have the Assistance of Counsel for his defense."

120 Richard C. LaFountain, Richard Y. Schauffler, Shauna M. Strickland, Sarah A. Gibson, and Ashley N. Mason, *Examining the Work of State Courts: An Analysis of 2009 State Court Caseloads* (Williamsburg, VA: National Center for State Courts, 2011): 38.

121 Lobbying data available is available from the Center for Responsive Politics (http://www.opensecrets.org/orgs/summary.php?id=D000000065).

CHOOSING JUDGES

"Personal experiences affect the facts that judges choose to see."

—Sonia Sotomayor, Associate Justice of the U.S. Supreme Court[1]

"Judicial elections powered by money and special interests create the impression, rightly or wrongly, that judges are accountable to money and special interests, not the law. Our judges should never be beholden to any constituency."

—Sandra Day O'Connor, Former Associate Justice of the U.S. Supreme Court[2]

In July of 1991, Florynce "Flo" Kennedy, a staunch feminist and civil rights activist, addressed the conference of the National Organization for Women in New York City. The topic of Kennedy's remarks: the importance of defeating the nomination of Clarence Thomas, who a mere 4 days before had been nominated for a seat on the United States Supreme Court by President George H.W. Bush. A flamboyant personality with a reputation for sometimes-outrageous comments, Kennedy exclaimed, "We're going to bork him. We're going to kill him politically. . . . This little creep, where did he come from?"[3] Though Kennedy did not originate the term "to bork,"[4] it was certainly in keeping with her colorful style.

The *Oxford Dictionary* defines the term to "bork" as to "obstruct (someone, especially a candidate for public office) through systematic defamation or vilification."[5] This verb, which debuted in the *Dictionary* in March 2002, comes from the name of Robert Bork, whose nomination to the Supreme Court in 1987 was rejected following unfavorable publicity for his allegedly extreme views. Within hours after President Ronald Reagan announced Judge Bork's nomination, Senator Edward Kennedy of Massachusetts attacked Bork in a speech on the floor of the Senate:

Robert Bork's America is a land in which women would be forced into back alley abortions, blacks would sit at segregated lunch counters, rogue police could break down citizens' doors in midnight raids, school children could not be taught about evolution, writers and artists could be censored at the whim of government, and the doors of the federal courts would be shut on the fingers of millions of citizens for whom the judiciary is—and is often the only—protector of the individual rights that are the heart of our democracy.

[I]n the current delicate balance of the Supreme Court, his rigid ideology will tip the scales of justice against the kind of country America is and ought to be.[6]

Image 5.1 Reagan and Bork
President Ronald Reagan meeting with Judge Robert Bork in the White House residence, October 9, 1987. Bork's nomination to the U.S. Supreme Court was defeated in the Senate 42-58. Ronald Reagan Presidential Library Archives, U.S. Government Work.

Additionally, liberal interest groups took swift action to block the confirmation, with over 150 organizations uniting in opposition against Bork. They used a sophisticated media strategy, which involved targeted radio announcements, video news releases, and newspaper advertising.[7] In fact, Gregory Peck, the actor who played the heroic lawyer Atticus Finch in the classic film *To Kill a Mockingbird*, did the voice-over on a television ad opposing Bork.[8]

At the time of his nomination, Bork was a sitting judge on the United States Court of Appeals for the D.C. Circuit, and had developed a reputation as an ardent conservative. He rejected an expansive interpretation of the Constitution, and instead embraced a legal philosophy that emphasized interpreting the Constitution on the basis of the intent of the framers—an approach that generally supports conservative positions on constitutional issues. Although Bork had a stalwart conservative record, he described himself as a moderate during the confirmation hearings and backed away from strong statements he had made in the past. He held firm to his criticisms of the Court's rulings that found a right to privacy in the Constitution, although he did try to temper and reframe his prior opposition to the Civil Rights Act and mute his antagonism toward applying the Equal Protection Clause outside of the context of racial discrimination. Senators accused Bork of undergoing a "confirmation conversion" in order to win Senate support.[9] Ultimately, the Judiciary Committee voted 9–5 to reject Bork's nomination and on October 23, 1987, the Senate voted 58–42 to reject him, earning Bork the dubious distinction of being the nominee with the largest margin of defeat of any Supreme Court nominee in history.[10]

Why was Bork rejected? First, as already noted, Bork's ideology was perceived as extreme despite his efforts to portray himself as part of the mainstream. Second, the 1986 election had produced a substantial Democratic legislative majority in the Senate. This resurgence in the Democratic opposition, coupled with the Iran Contra hearings,[11] severely limited the Reagan Administration's ability to counter the opposition forces effectively. Third, the vacancy to which Bork was nominated was one created by the departure of Justice Lewis F. Powell, Jr. Powell was seen as the Court's centrist "swing vote" and his replacement had the potential to significantly alter the ideological balance on the Court. Finally, some observers suggested that Bork's lengthy and candid answers led to his rejection by the Senate (and they also argued that this has prompted subsequent nominees to be more evasive and less candid during their confirmation hearings).[12] Of course, it was probably of no help to Bork that he was infamously connected with the Watergate scandal because he fired the special prosecutor in charge of investigating the break-in at Democratic Party headquarters at the Watergate Hotel.[13]

The reality of the spectacle and drama that accompanied Bork's nomination, and its ultimate defeat, is quite at odds with the myth that judging is an apolitical enterprise and, hence, the only thing that should matter is a candidate's professional qualifications. To be sure, an individual's competence, integrity, and temperament all clearly matter. For example, G. Harrold Carswell, who served both as a federal district court judge in Florida and as a judge on the United States Court of Appeals for the Fifth Circuit, failed to secure confirmation to the Supreme Court when he was nominated by President Nixon. With the extraordinary rate at which his decisions were reversed on appeal and his generally lackluster career, the best his supporters could say about Carswell was that "[e]ven if he were mediocre, there are a lot of mediocre judges and people and lawyers. They are entitled to a little representation, aren't they, and a little chance? We can't have all Brandeises, Frankfurters, and Cardozos."[14] But whereas a lack of professional merit may be sufficient to prevent a candidate from ascending to the bench, professional merit alone is *not* sufficient to ensure that a candidate *will* ascend to the bench. The various processes by which the state and federal benches are staffed are surely intended to maximize the quality of judges. But—as the discussion that follows should make clear—a host of other factors also matters for understanding how and why judges come to the bench. In short: politics matters.

In this chapter we detail the myths and realities of choosing judges. Many of the myths are based on a misunderstanding of the structure of the American judiciary, which includes lifetime tenure for (most) federal judges[15] and separate, distinct systems in each of the states involving various forms of appointment, retention, and tenure systems. At the federal level, while presidents have generally had success in placing their nominees on the bench, the Senate is also an important actor and is influential throughout the process. At the state level, elections have attempted to bring a level of popular accountability to the process but have been harshly criticized for compromising judicial independence. At the same time, questions over judicial diversity, quality, and legitimacy are crucial to understanding the politics inherent in choosing judges.

MYTH AND REALITY IN CHOOSING JUDGES

MYTH	REALITY
There is a single method that is best for selecting judges.	Various judicial selection methods represent a trade-off between judicial independence and popular accountability.
Because judging is an apolitical enterprise, judges are selected based on their professional qualifications.	While professional qualifications matter to a certain extent, judging is a political enterprise and political considerations drive the judicial selection process.
Judges are appointed by the president.	The president has no power over state and local judges and only has the power to nominate federal judges.
The president is solely responsible for nominating federal judges.	While presidents technically nominate federal judges, home-state senators are influential in the process—particularly at the lower-court level—and can single-handedly derail a nomination.
Federal judges retire due to old age.	Federal judges time their departures with favorable political climates to maximize the appointment of like-minded successors.
Senators question judicial nominees to gain information that will help them vote on confirmation.	Senators have multiple goals when questioning nominees, including bolstering or hampering the nominee's chances of confirmation, alerting the nominees and the public to issues they care about, and appealing to constituencies including interest groups.
Supreme Court nominees are evasive when answering questions during confirmation hearings.	Research shows that recent nominees are only slightly less candid than in the past and the perception of greater evasiveness is a function of more probing questions posed by senators during the hearings and greater explicitness of nominees in declining to respond.
Confirmation is a *pro-forma* process of rubber-stamping judicial nominees.	The Senate often delays, blocks, rejects, and otherwise derails judicial nominees—particularly when the president's party is in the minority and does not control the Senate, the president's approval rating is low, and the president is in his last year in office.
All judges are appointed.	While all federal judges are appointed, states employ various methods to select judges including gubernatorial appointment, legislative appointment, popularly contested election, and merit selection.
Once on the bench, judges serve for life.	While most federal judges have life tenure, nearly every state requires judges who want to remain in office to stand for retention either by election or re-appointment.

As recent films and TV shows portray, the judiciary is racially diverse and African Americans in particular dominate the ranks of judges.	The judiciary is dominated by white males with women and racial minorities particularly underrepresented on state courts of last resort.
The type of selection method has no effect on the gender and racial makeup of the judiciary.	Research shows that appointment and merit-based systems lead to greater diversity than do elective methods.
The type of selection method has no effect on judicial quality.	Research suggests that, by some measures, appointment and merit-based systems enhance judicial quality.
Judicial elections disadvantage incumbents.	While vulnerable, unpopular incumbents can lose to well-funded challengers, incumbents who are not unpopular and who spend as much as their opponents have a good chance at retaining their seats.
Public confidence in the judiciary is harmed when judges campaign for office like other politicians.	While campaign contributions do harm judicial legitimacy, judicial campaigning in general, including position taking on issues and policy pronouncements, does not.
Judicial candidates who raise money will be biased in favor of campaign contributors.	Despite the occasional high-profile incident, there is no systematic evidence that judicial votes are influenced by campaign contributions.

SELECTING FEDERAL JUDGES

Presidents do not simply appoint judges. Judges for the federal bench must be nominated by the president and confirmed by the Senate on a majority vote. A **nomination** is the formal selection of a candidate by the president that is sent, in writing, to the Senate. **Confirmation** is the formal process used by the Senate to approve or reject a nomination. The pertinent language in the Constitution appears in Article II: the president "shall nominate, and by and with the Advice and Consent of the Senate, shall appoint Ambassadors, other public Ministers and Consuls, Judges of the supreme Court, and all other Officers of the United States, whose Appointments are not herein otherwise provided for, and which shall be established by Law."[16] Technically, this language does not directly speak to the issue of the selection of judges for lower federal courts but the presumption from the outset has been that the same selection process applies, at least for courts created by Congress under its authority in Article III. Recall from our discussion in the previous chapter that Congress is also given the authority to create courts under Article I. Congress is free to use the same process for selecting Article I judges as the Constitution mandates for Article III judges, but Congress can also stipulate an alternative selection process for staffing them.

The mechanism of advice and consent was the constitutional compromise struck by those who advocated for exclusive congressional appointment power and those who wanted exclusive presidential appointment authority.[17] The former were wary of concentrating too much power in the hands of the president because of their experience with the British crown while the latter were much less skittish about the possibility of excessive presidential authority and much more sanguine about the democratic commitments of occupants of the presidential office. Problematically, however, the language embedding this compromise in the Constitution has a great deal of ambiguity. What, precisely, constitutes the **advice and consent** of the Senate? Is the Senate's role simply a consultative one, with its consent merely a formality? Or, is the Senate's role a meatier one, requiring the active and engaged participation of senators in the decision to confirm (or not) presidential nominees to the bench? Presidents, of course, tend to take the former view, with senators, not surprisingly, advancing the latter perspective.

Though the process for selecting individuals to fill vacancies on the Supreme Court bench is constitutionally indistinguishable from the process that transpires in the selection of most lower federal court judges, presidents have historically devoted much more of their time and energy to staffing the Supreme Court versus the lower federal court bench. This makes sense given the greater importance attributed to appointments to the nation's highest court. The Supreme Court is, after all, the final arbiter on the interpretation of the Constitution. Further, appointments to the Supreme Court can and do serve expressive purposes for presidents. For example, they may communicate presidential attention to particular constituencies, whether that appointment is of the first African American to the Court (Thurgood Marshall by President Lyndon Johnson), the first

Image 5.2 Justices O'Connor, Sotomayor, Ginsburg, and Kagan *Presidents make judicial nominations for expressive purposes such as appealing to women or racial minorities. The first four women appointed to the U.S. Supreme Court are (from left) Justices Sandra Day O'Connor, Sonia Sotomayor, Ruth Bader Ginsburg, and Elena Kagan.* Steve Petteway, Collection of the Supreme Court of the United States.

woman to the Court (Sandra Day O'Connor by President Ronald Reagan), or the first Latina to the Court (Sonia Sotomayor by President Barack Obama). Or, they may be used to promote and foster the political identity a president is attempting to cultivate, as was the case with President Richard Nixon's appointment of law-and-order Warren Burger and President Bill Clinton's appointments of political moderates Ruth Bader Ginsburg and Stephen Breyer.

In addition to the greater policy and political import attached to Supreme Court nominations, another key reason that presidents have spent much more time on nominations to the high court is that senators have historically expected (and demanded) a more active role in the process of selecting lower court judges. In particular, **senatorial courtesy** is an informal norm that gives senators representing the state corresponding to a lower federal court vacancy (that is, the home-state senators) the power to hold up a nomination, potentially indefinitely—thereby defeating it without a formal vote by the full Senate.[18] "In its narrowest and most exact sense, 'senatorial courtesy' requires that the body of senators be guided in its action on a nomination by the attitudes of the senators from the state immediately affected by such nomination."[19] In practice, this has meant that presidents generally demonstrate deference to home-state senators (particularly to home-state senators of their own parties) when selecting nominees for the lower federal courts.[20]

Because federal district courts are situated within state boundaries, there are two home-state senators responsible for each district court vacancy with the exception of the District of Columbia, which is, of course, not a state. Since the geographic boundary of a court of appeals encompasses more than one state—with the exception of the United States Court of Appeals for the District of Columbia, which covers only the District of Columbia—technically no single state's senators could claim to be the home-state senators for a vacancy on the court of appeals. Historically, however, particular seats on a circuit have been considered to "belong to" particular states and, hence, senatorial courtesy matters for court of appeals judgeships as well.[21]

President Barack Obama explained the difference between the Supreme Court and lower-court appointment process in terms of visibility:

> My sense is that the Senate necessarily has to treat the Supreme Court nomination process differently than the circuit or district court nomination process—higher profile, people are paying attention. They have the sense 'All right, this is big,' which means that some of the shenanigans that were taking place in terms of blocking appointments, stalling appointments, I think are more difficult to pull off during a Supreme Court nomination process.[22]

According to this logic, a Supreme Court nomination comes with increased scrutiny and constituent pressure on senators—most of who will inevitably stand for reelection and whose behavior and votes on Supreme Court nominees could be used against them by opponents.

Political scientists have dubbed the link between legislative behavior and voters the "electoral connection."[23] The potential of reprisals at the ballot box—particularly for vulnerable or electorally marginal senators[24]—distinguishes highly visible Supreme Court confirmations from those to the relatively low-profile lower courts. Studies show that there is indeed an electoral connection for Senate votes on Supreme Court nominees.[25] Thus, it is not surprising that presidents might treat the Supreme Court nomination process differently.

In recent years, however, presidents have increasingly seen lower court appointments as a way to further their policy goals. As a result, they have exercised increasing control over lower court nominations—particularly at the court of appeals level—generally at the expense of senatorial influence.[26] The increasing politicization of the process is often traced to the Reagan administration generally and the Bork nomination specifically. Longtime Senate Judiciary Committee member Charles Grassley (R-IA) said in 2014: "It all starts with Bork."[27]

Incoming and new presidential administrations designate staff and move quickly to compile lists of potential nominees for vacancies that need to be filled. For example, President-elect Barack Obama knew he would have at least three dozen judicial vacancies to fill as he prepared to take office during the months after his election in November 2008. By the end of his first year as president, he was facing more than 100 vacancies as large numbers of sitting judges departed. Of course this was not surprising given that the Democrats also controlled the Senate and liberal, retirement-eligible judges had been waiting through 8 years of Republican president George W. Bush's administration for a Democratic president. Thus, the nomination process for the federal judiciary begins as soon as a presidential candidate wins election.

With presidents placing greater weight on lower court nominations, the process of staffing the federal judiciary is becoming increasingly singular. Indeed, recent Supreme Court nominees John Roberts, Clarence Thomas, David Souter, Robert Bork, Douglas Ginsburg, and Antonin Scalia were all appointed to the U.S. courts of appeals by the same president who soon thereafter nominated them to the U.S. Supreme Court. Thus, these Supreme Court nominees had already been vetted by the same White House and confirmed by the same or recent Senate once before.

If presidents are drawing on the lower courts for potential Supreme Court nominees, it makes sense that they make their lower court nominations with future elevations in mind—building a farm team, to use a baseball analogy. Indeed, one might stretch the logic to apply to other preparatory offices that require Senate confirmation, such as Elena Kagan's appointment as U.S. Solicitor General. Conversely, Supreme Court nominees who have not successfully navigated the process in the past may have difficulty gaining confirmation, as was the case with White House Counsel Harriet Miers. Senators are well aware that some lower court nominees in particular are being groomed for nomination to the U.S. Supreme Court. Because of this potential, these lower court nominees are blocked from even receiving a vote in the Senate—a process we will detail later in the chapter. In recent years, Republicans thwarted Obama's court of appeals nominees Caitlin Halligan and Goodwin Liu and Democrats blocked Bush's court of appeals nominee Miguel Estrada—all widely viewed as on the fast track to the Supreme Court, until their paths were blocked. In short, the process of appointing federal judges is rife with politics.

The Nomination Process

Regardless of the level of federal court on which a vacancy arises, the process for filling that vacancy follows a common path. Figure 5.1 shows the steps involved in the nomination phase. First, and most obviously, a sitting jurist is promoted to a higher court, resigns, retires, or dies—thereby creating a vacancy. In rare instances, a vacancy opens on the federal courts when a judge is impeached and convicted.[28] Vacancies are also created when Congress periodically authorizes new judgeships for the federal courts. For example, in 2002, Congress created eight new permanent judgeships on the U.S. district courts.[29]

FIGURE 5.1
Federal Judicial Nomination Process

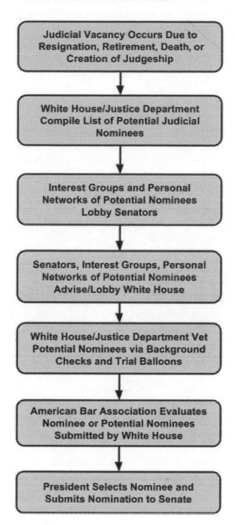

Still, most vacancies arise due to retirement and it is commonly assumed that the reason judges retire is simply because of old age. The myth of old age retirement is perpetuated by jurists who routinely cite it as the reason for their departures. Justice Thurgood Marshall famously responded, "I'm old!" when asked by reporters why he was leaving the Supreme Court. The reality, however, is that the retirement decisions of judges are political in that they try to time their departures to coincide with like-minded presidents.[30] In recent years, sitting Supreme Court justices have publicly admitted as much. For example, Justice Ruth Bader Ginsburg even went so far as to say that she has not only considered the president but also the Senate in making her departure decision. Just over 1 month before the Democrats would lose their narrow Senate majority in the 2014 midterm elections—a widely predicted outcome—Ginsburg remarked: "If I resign anytime this year, [Obama] could not successfully appoint anyone I would like to see in the Court."[31]

Furthermore, once federal judges reach age 65 and have served on the federal bench for 15 years, they may retire in "senior status," continue to draw their full salaries, and continue to participate in as many cases on lower federal courts as they wish. Given this, it makes little sense for federal judges *not* to retire once they become eligible and feel the timing is right politically to maximize their influence of having a like-minded successor appointed to succeed them. Thus, life tenure has politicized the departure process: it gives federal judges considerable flexibility and power to shape the federal judiciary by influencing who their successors will be.

POP CULTURE

The Pelican Brief

Fade in on a mob of angry protestors outside the U.S. Supreme Court. Justice Rosenberg (played by Hume Cronyn) sits in a wheelchair staring down from inside the Court building. He asks Gray Grantham (played by Denzel Washington), a journalist who is there to interview him off the record if any of the signs have his name on them and what they say. Grantham answers: "The usual. Death to Rosenberg. Retire Rosenberg. Cut off the oxygen." Rosenberg replies: "That's my favorite. Of course, you did pretty good by me your last time out: 'Rosenberg equals the government over business, the individual over government, the environment over everything, and the Indians, oh, give them whatever

Image 5.3 *The Pelican Brief*
Denzel Washington and Julia Roberts in The Pelican Brief *(1993), a film that dramatizes the importance of the succession process on the U.S. Supreme Court.* Photo by Ken Regan/Warner Bros./Getty Images.

they want.'" Grantham explains that he was quoting an unnamed senior White House official—who Rosenberg assumes is the president. The Justice makes clear that he disapproves of the president, the implication being that he has no plans to retire and allow the president to appoint his successor.

Later that night, Justice Rosenberg is home—surrounded by a mountain of medicine bottles—when an assassin enters his residence and shoots him in cold blood. Soon thereafter, a second member of the Court—Justice Jensen—is strangled to death at an adult movie house. The next morning the president addresses the American people to assure them that those responsible for the murders will be found. Law student Darby Shaw (played by Julia Roberts) and her law professor (with whom she is having an affair) puzzle over the connection between the two justices and who might want them both dead. They know that the White House was hoping to replace Rosenberg but Shaw asks: "So why Jensen? This president nominated him. He and Rosenberg had almost nothing in common. That's what they should look for: decisions on which they both agreed."

After days of comparing the votes of the two justices, the law student-cum-sleuth comes up with a theory: the two seemingly ideologically unrelated justices (Jensen was a conservative and Rosenberg a liberal) have one thing in common—they both voted against business concerns in environmental cases. Shaw says that Jensen "wrote three majority opinions protective of the environment" and suggests that the murders were motivated by "old-fashioned material greed—a case that involves a great deal of money." She writes a legal brief arguing that the president's new nominees will be less supportive of the environment, ensuring that the Court would vote in favor of an oil tycoon who had lost at the lower court level in a case involving drilling in the marshes of Louisiana, the home of the brown pelican. Ultimately, with the help of reporter Grantham, Shaw discovers that the tycoon was behind the killings and, in a Watergate-like plot twist, the president and his chief of staff sought to cover up their association with him.

Despite its far-fetched plot involving the murder of two Supreme Court justices, *The Pelican Brief* (1993)—based on the 1992 John Grisham novel—illustrates the high stakes surrounding judicial vacancies. Research shows that presidents are strategic in appointing justices who will further their policy goals. Presidents are largely successful in placing their nominees on the bench and justices generally vote consistently with the preferences of their appointing presidents. So it turns out that Darby Shaw was on to something: judicial vacancies—particularly in the U.S. Supreme Court—have real policy consequences, not only for environmental issues as portrayed in the film, but for all issues that come before the Court. Maybe Shaw will pass the bar after all.

Once a vacancy occurs, lobbying for the position begins in earnest. Interest groups and the personal networks of potential nominees contact both the White House and the Senate to urge consideration of specific individuals. Senators also lobby the White House and the White House reaches out to senators, interest groups, and others. This should not be surprising given that the Constitution gives the Senate the power of "advice" as well as "consent." Whether the White House genuinely considers any of this advice, however, is a different matter.

As the White House draws up its short list of candidates, the vetting stage of the process heats up. This involves intense scrutiny of potential nominees, supervised by top presidential aides, usually from the White House Counsel's Office and the Department of Justice. Even potential nominees who have already been through the process or who the White House has already placed on internal short lists will undergo additional scrutiny. Potential nominees complete extensive personal data questionnaires and are subject to background checks by the FBI. No administration wants to be caught off guard, as the Reagan administration was when Douglas Ginsburg—their next choice after Bork's rejection—was said to have smoked pot with his students or the George H.W. Bush administration's experience with sexual harassment allegations against Clarence Thomas. Any potential negative that a nominee may have will inevitably reflect poorly on the administration—particularly at the highly visible Supreme Court level.

The American Bar Association's Standing Committee on the Federal Judiciary is also involved in the evaluation of candidates, though the timing of that participation has varied depending upon the president.[32] Prior to the Reagan administration, the names of potential nominees were provided to the ABA before the president settled on a candidate. Presidents Bill Clinton and Barack Obama relied on the same timing for ABA involvement. In contrast, Reagan, George H.W. Bush, and George W. Bush provided the names of their nominees after selection but before formal nomination.

Over time, the ABA's involvement in the nomination process has become controversial, with charges that the Standing Committee shows bias against conservative candidates.[33]

Presidents have three main agendas or goals when selecting their nominees: personal, partisan, and policy.[34] When a president nominates an individual for personal reasons, such as to please a friend or associate, he is said to be motivated by a **personal agenda**. For example, President George W. Bush's 2005 Supreme Court nomination of his longtime friend and advisor Harriet Miers was largely seen as a reward for her personal loyalty. Bush was forced to withdraw her nomination after much criticism including charges of "cronyism."[35] In comparison, the **partisan agenda** refers to the situation in which a president uses nominations to further support for his party or for himself. One reason President Dwight Eisenhower selected William Brennan to replace Justice Sherman Minton, for example, was because Brennan was Catholic and "the Catholic vote [was viewed] as vital."[36] Finally, when the president nominates someone he believes will further the substantive policy objectives of his administration, he is being guided by a **policy agenda**. Thus, he chooses someone whose ideology or policy preferences are similar to his own.[37] For example, in 2010 President Obama nominated Elena Kagan (often called his "ideological twin") while in 2005 President George W. Bush nominated Samuel Alito, a judge known for his conservative rulings on abortion, federalism, discrimination, and religion in public spaces.

Systematic analyses of the process by which nominees for the Supreme Court[38] and for the lower federal courts[39] are selected suggest that presidents are strongly motivated by their policy preferences when deciding on a nominee but that they are very aware of the political context within which they are making that choice. That is, presidents behave strategically with regard to whom they select (as well as the timing of their nominations) because they know that they must secure the cooperation of the Senate if they are to have their nominees confirmed. Interestingly, presidents occasionally make **recess appointments** to bypass the Senate. In these instances, presidents are able to immediately and unilaterally fill vacancies without Senate confirmation. But they may only do so when the Senate has not been in session for a sufficient length of time—roughly 10 days or more[40]—and their appointees may only serve until the end of the next session of the Senate, roughly the end of the next calendar year, unless the Senate confirms them beforehand. Historically, presidents have become increasingly reluctant to use recess appointments to fill judicial vacancies and the Senate has made it clear that they will be especially skeptical of such appointments when considering whether to permanently confirm them.[41]

Thus, although we like to think that the best qualified and most deserving people are selected for the federal bench, the reality is that the nomination process was designed to be and is in fact a political process. Presidents have political goals in selecting nominees and employ various strategies to see that their nominees ascend to the bench. The confirmation process is no less political.

The Confirmation Process
Once a nomination is made and the name of the nominee has been transmitted to the Senate, it is referred to the Senate Judiciary Committee. The **blue slip procedure**, an institutionalized manifestation of senatorial courtesy, looms large when it comes to understanding what happens (or does not happen, as the case may be) in the Judiciary Committee.[42] Since the early 1900s, both home-state senators for a circuit or district

FIGURE 5.2
Federal Judicial Confirmation Process

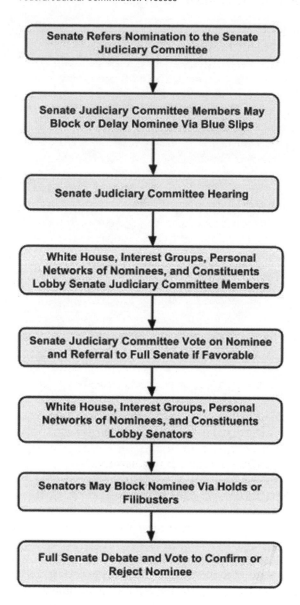

court nominee have received a form printed on blue paper (hence the term "blue slip") from the chair of the Senate Judiciary Committee (see Image 5.4). The form asks the home-state senators for their views as to the suitability of the nominee. A senator may return the blue slip noting an objection, return the blue slip noting support, or decline to return the blue slip at all.

What is meant by a senator failing to return a completed blue slip has depended on the blue slip policy set by each chair of the Judiciary Committee; sometimes it has meant

Image 5.4 Blue Slip
*One of the earliest
existing blue slips in the
records of the Senate
shows Senator Thomas
Hardwick's objection
to the nomination
of U.V. Whipple for
appointment to the U.S.
District Court, April 11,
1917.* Records of the
U.S. Senate, National
Archives.

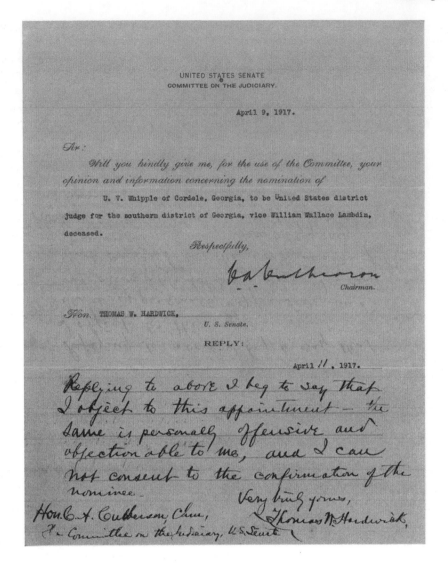

that the senator declining to return the blue slip has an objection to the nominee, while at other times it has meant that the senator has no objection. Likewise, what happens when a blue slip is not returned (or is returned noting an objection to the nominee) has also varied. For example, under the chairmanship of Democratic Senator James O. Eastland of Mississippi (1956–1978), if a blue slip was not returned by one of the home-state senators, all committee action on a nomination came to a halt. On Eastland's retirement, Democratic Senator Edward Kennedy of Massachusetts took over as chair in 1979 and said that the non-return of a blue slip would not necessarily be enough to preclude the Committee from moving forward.[43] Though each new chair of the Committee has set his own parameters for blue slips, systematic analysis of the blue slip procedure has demonstrated that senators can use it to derail (or at least significantly delay) the confirmation process for lower federal court judges. However, the blue slip can also serve as a positive tool in that those returned with endorsements can enhance the likelihood of nominee success in the Judiciary Committee and on the floor of the Senate.[44]

If action on a nomination does move forward, the next step is a **committee hearing** where a small group of senators formally question a nominee and vote on whether or not to recommend confirmation to the full Senate. Hearings for nominees to the district courts or courts of appeals are generally perfunctory affairs, drawing little controversy and garnering little media coverage.[45] Hearings for nominees being considered for the Supreme Court are quite different. Harlan Fiske Stone, nominated by President Calvin Coolidge in 1925, was the first Supreme Court nominee to testify in person before the Senate Judiciary Committee.[46] Most subsequent nominees went back to the historical practice of refusing to testify—or in some cases were not even asked—with a few exceptions: President Franklin Roosevelt's nominees Felix Frankfurter, Frank Murphy, and Robert Jackson who appeared before the committee in 1939, 1940, and 1941 respectively.[47] Beginning with President Dwight Eisenhower's nomination of John Marshall Harlan II in 1955, every Supreme Court nominee has testified in person before the Senate Judiciary Committee.[48]

Typically, a Supreme Court confirmation hearing begins with a statement by the chair of the Judiciary Committee. Other members of the committee follow with preliminary statements, and then the nominee is introduced to the committee by a panel of "presenters." At this point, the nominee makes an opening statement, which is followed by questioning of the nominee by members of the committee. The chair begins the questioning and is followed by the ranking minority member; the remaining members then ask questions in descending order of seniority, alternating between majority and minority members. Each senator has a time limit for his or her questions and, when the first round of questioning is complete, the committee begins a second round. At the discretion of the committee chair, more rounds may follow.[49]

Various purposes may be served by questioning the nominee. Some senators may be undecided about how they will vote and so they question the nominee as a means of acquiring information to help them make their choice. Thus, they may question the nominee about their professional qualifications, character, understanding of the Constitution, and the role of the judiciary to glean the information they need. Other senators may already be decided as to how they are going to vote and so they question the nominee in order to enhance the likelihood of the nominee's success or, alternatively, secure the nominee's defeat. Senators may also use the hearings to make the nominee aware of certain legal or policy concerns they have, or they may use their questioning to make the public aware of particular issues, or even use the hearings to advocate their personal policy preferences. Since 1981, with Sandra Day O'Connor's hearing, all hearings have been televised. Thus, senators may use the hearings to ask questions that might appeal to their constituencies, including various interest groups.

What actually happens at confirmation hearings? Consider the following responses by President Obama's nominee Elena Kagan to questions by Republican senators about whether her judicial philosophy would be liberal, like the justice she clerked for—Thurgood Marshall: "[My] politics would be, must be, have to be completely separate from my judging. . . . The courts are open to all people and will listen respectfully with attention to all claims. I love Justice Marshall. He did an enormous amount for me. But if you confirm me to this position, you will get Justice Kagan. You won't get Justice Marshall."[50] Another line of questioning involved the controversial Affordable Care Act, known as "Obamacare," and whether the nominee thought it was constitutional. While she declined to address the specific case—one that was likely to and ultimately did come before the

Supreme Court—she made plain that she believed that Congress possessed broad regulatory authority: "[The Commerce Clause] grants broad deference to Congress in this area [and] assumes that Congress knows what is necessary to regulate the country's economy."[51] Kagan's testimony illustrates how politics drives the hearings.

In a recent study, law professor Lori Ringhand and political scientist Paul Collins, Jr., conducted a content analysis of the transcripts of confirmation hearings for Supreme Court nominees and coded every question from a senator and every response by a nominee.[52] They found that the number of comments at the hearings has increased over time. For example, from 1939 to 1981, the average number of comments made by senators was 253 and the average number of comments made by nominees was 181. In comparison, since Chief Justice William Rehnquist's hearing in 1986, the average number of comments made by senators was 987 and the average number of comments made by nominees was 749. They also found that three issues have dominated the hearings: civil rights, judicial philosophy, and criminal justice. Taking senator and nominee comments together, 29.8 percent of all of the comments are about civil rights, 12.4 percent are about judicial philosophy, and 8.6 percent are about criminal justice.

Some court observers have argued that Supreme Court nominees are less forthcoming than they used to be at their confirmation hearings, evading questions they think will hurt their chances, particularly since Robert Bork's disastrous experience.[53] Some scholars, however, dispute the idea that nominees have become cagier during the hearings. Political scientists Sean Farganis and Justin Wedeking, for example, analyzed the questions asked of and the responses given by nominees and found that recent nominees are only slightly less candid than in the past.[54] Their analysis suggests that the perception of greater evasiveness is a function of more probing questions posed by senators and greater explicitness of nominees in declining to respond: "[I]t is not that nominees since Bork have adopted a more evasive posture when it comes to the hearings, but rather that they are being asked more difficult questions more often."[55] However, any lack of candor by the nominee does not influence his level of support from the members of the Senate Judiciary Committee. Since 1981, when the hearings were first televised, senators have been influenced more by partisanship and ideology than by whether the nominee was forthcoming.

Following questioning, the committee takes a vote on whether to send the nomination to the Senate floor with a favorable recommendation.[56] If a majority fails to vote in the affirmative, a second vote may be taken to send the nomination to the Senate floor without recommendation. If a majority again fails to vote for this motion, in the case of lower court nominees, the nomination dies in committee, the full Senate has no opportunity to consider it, and it is returned to the president. For Supreme Court nominees, however, a negative committee vote does not prevent a nomination from moving to the full Senate for consideration. For example, prior to the full Senate's rejection of Robert Bork, the Senate Judiciary Committee voted 9–5 to send his nomination to the Senate floor with an unfavorable recommendation.[57] The committee was split 7–7 on sending Clarence Thomas's nomination to the full Senate with a favorable recommendation but voted 13–1 to send it to the floor without recommendation.

If a nomination makes it out of committee, the process moves to the full Senate. It is at this point that every senator, rather than simply the members of the Senate Judiciary Committee, may formally weigh in on a nominee. Senators have the power to delay or derail a nominee through the use of anonymous or secret **holds**. This tactic allows a single senator to secretly keep the chamber from consideration of a nominee. Because Senate rules require unanimous consent before the chamber can consider matters on its calendar, any senator can inform his party leaders that he has an objection to moving forward.

Senators are in effect making a threat that they will not grant unanimous consent to move forward and possibly more. Sarah Binder of the Brookings Institution explained: "A hold is a threat to filibuster, it's a statement to your leader that says when this nomination comes to the floor, I'm going to object."[58] Holds have been repeatedly used by both parties to stall and block lower court nominees. In recent years the Senate has amended its rules to make public, after a certain number of days, the names of senators placing holds on nominees. But senators have found a way around this by "tag-teaming" a hold: one senator places a hold and then withdraws the hold before his or her name is made public and another places a new hold and so on. Senators are reluctant to end the practice because it is a way to exact policy and other concessions from party leaders.

Once the Senate begins consideration of a nomination, senators may use another parliamentary tactic to delay or block a nominee. The **filibuster** is a legislative maneuver that effectively continues the debate on the nomination and delays—perhaps indefinitely—a confirmation vote. Filibusters can effectively quash a nomination unless 60 senators vote to end debate, which is called a **cloture** vote. The film *Mr. Smith Goes to Washington* (1939) dramatizes the procedure with Jimmy Stewart taking to the Senate floor to speak for countless hours in order to force his colleagues to change their minds on approving a piece of legislation he opposes. While individual senators can still attempt to hold the floor through indefinite speeches, as long as 41 senators agree to continue debating, there is no need to literally keep talking on the floor. The nomination will simply stall and die.

Only one filibuster has ever been successfully used against a Supreme Court nominee: the Republican filibuster of lame-duck President Lyndon Johnson's nomination of Justice Abe Fortas for chief justice in 1968. The story is instructive of how politics pervades the succession process.[59] Johnson had decided not to seek reelection and, following the assassination of Democratic candidate Robert F. Kennedy, it appeared likely that Republican candidate Richard Nixon would win the election. Chief Justice Earl Warren was hoping to retire under a Democratic president. But with future Democratic prospects weakened, Warren informed Johnson that he would retire on confirmation of his successor. Johnson moved quickly to nominate Fortas—his longtime crony who he had previously appointed to the Court as an associate justice.

Most Democrats, who held the majority and who were supported by some Republicans, hoped to confirm Fortas—one of the Court's more liberal members—before the election. However, most Republicans and conservative southern Democrats knew that if they could delay or block the nomination, Nixon would be able to name a conservative chief justice should he win the presidency. Accordingly, the latter coalition filibustered Fortas's nomination; preventing him from receiving a vote from the full Senate. Ultimately, Nixon won election, appointed Warren Burger as the new chief justice (an office Republicans have held even since), and Fortas was forced to resign due to allegations of financial misconduct. Since Fortas, all other attempts to filibuster Supreme Court nominees have failed, such as the effort by Democrats to filibuster President Ronald Reagan's nomination of William Rehnquist for chief justice in 1986.[60]

As mentioned earlier in the chapter, filibusters have been used successfully by both parties to block lower court and other presidential nominees. After decades of criticism by both parties that the process had become unduly partisan, the Senate changed its rules in 2013. Specifically, the Democrat-controlled Senate voted 52–48—with every Republican voting no—to end the use of filibusters for most presidential nominations, including those to the courts of appeals and district courts, but not to the Supreme Court and not for legislation. In the past, major Senate rule changes had required the approval of two-thirds of the Senate and because this change was passed by a simple majority it was known as the "nuclear option."[61] The effect was significant: lower court nominees would only need a majority vote rather than the 60 that was previously required in order to cut off debate and proceed to a vote. Thus, a narrow Senate majority of less than 60—which was what the Democrats had in 2013–2014—was able to end debate with a majority vote and confirm previously blocked lower court nominees. Interestingly, this change also affected holds as it was easier to call the bluff of senators who would threaten to vote against ending debate and threaten to filibuster. Whether future Senate majorities continue these reforms or go even further remains to be seen. Will the nuclear option be employed for legislation? Supreme Court nominees? In this sense, the Senate may be in the process of transforming itself to a more majoritarian body, similar to the House of Representatives.

Despite the power of the Senate in the appointment process, presidents have generally been successful in placing their nominees on the federal bench. Since 1789, of the 160 nominations to the Supreme Court, 124 have been confirmed (77.5 percent). The 36 unsuccessful nominations (22.5 percent) represent 31 individuals whose names were sent to the Senate by presidents, with some of the 31 individuals nominated more than once. Table 5.1 lists the Supreme Court nominations officially submitted to the Senate since Earl Warren's selection in 1954. The results demonstrate that the Senate is by no means a rubber stamp for the president with a number of recent nominees being withdrawn or rejected.

Why has the Senate confirmed some nominees and not others? Whether the Senate confirms a nominee depends on a variety of factors, with qualifications, politics, and ideology each playing an important role. With regard to qualifications for nominees to the U.S. Supreme Court, a recent study by political scientists and legal scholars Lee Epstein and Jeffrey Segal offers valuable insight.[62] The researchers gathered votes cast by every senator for every Supreme Court nominee beginning in 1954 and then analyzed the extent to which the perception of the nominee's qualifications influenced those votes. They found that a highly qualified nominee would receive about 45 more votes (if all 100 senators voted) than one who was perceived as unqualified. "This may well explain why certain nominees who were very liberal (e.g., William J. Brennan) or very conservative (e.g., Antonin Scalia) sailed through the Senate. Despite their political outlooks, they received the highest possible merit rating, and senators—even those on the other side of the ideological fence—may have found it difficult to justify voting against them."[63] Research by other scholars regarding the relationship between qualifications and confirmation for nominations to the lower federal court bench likewise indicates that qualifications matter, though they appear to be more consequential for how quickly a nominee is confirmed than for whether a nominee is confirmed.[64]

Politics, too, obviously plays a role in whether a nominee is confirmed by the Senate. When the president's party controls the Senate, 90 percent of Supreme Court nominees have been confirmed, compared to 59 percent during periods of divided government.[65] Additionally, when the president is in his last year of office, and presumably has the least influence over senators, the Senate has only confirmed 56 percent of Supreme Court nominees (compared to an 87 percent success rate for presidents during their first 3 years of office).[66] Presidents who enjoy high approval ratings also enjoy greater success in securing the confirmation of their Supreme Court nominees. Specifically, 98 percent of nominees have been confirmed when the president has high approval ratings versus less than 80 percent when the president has low approval ratings.[67]

Senators also take into account their constituents when they are casting a vote for or against the nominee. Specifically, if the senators' constituents are ideologically distant from the nominee, they are less likely to vote to confirm.[68] In one study that examined the effects of African American constituency size and the proximity of reelection on

TABLE 5.1
Supreme Court Nominations, 1954–2010

NOMINEE	TO REPLACE	PRESIDENT	NOMINATED	VOTE[a]	RESULT	DATE
Elena Kagan	Stevens	Obama	05/10/2010	63-37	Confirmed	08/05/2010
Sonia Sotomayor	Souter	Obama	06/01/2009	68-31	Confirmed	08/06/2009
Samual Alito, Jr.	O'Connor	Bush II	11/10/2005	58-42	Confirmed	01/31/2006
Harriet Miers	O'Connor	Bush II	10/07/2005	—	**Withdrawn**	10/28/2005
John Roberts, Jr.[b]	Rehnquist	Bush II	09/06/2005	78-22	Confirmed	09/29/2005
John Roberts, Jr.[c]	O'Connor	Bush II	07/29/2005	—	**Withdrawn**	09/06/2005
Stephen Breyer	Blackmun	Clinton	05/17/1994	87-9	Confirmed	07/29/1994
Ruth Bader Ginsburg	White	Clinton	06/14/1993	96-3	Confirmed	08/03/1993
Clarence Thomas	Marshall	Bush I	07/08/1991	52-48	Confirmed	10/15/1991
David Souter	Brennan	Bush I	07/25/1990	90-9	Confirmed	10/02/1990
Anthony Kennedy	Powell	Reagan	11/30/1987	97-0	Confirmed	02/03/1988
Robert Bork	Powell	Reagan	07/01/1987	42-58	**Rejected**	10/23/1987
Antonin Scalia	Rehnquist	Reagan	06/24/1986	98-0	Confirmed	09/17/1986
William Rehnquist[b]	Burger	Reagan	06/20/1986	65-33	Confirmed	09/17/1986
Sandra Day O'Connor	Stewart	Reagan	08/19/1981	99-0	Confirmed	09/21/1981
John Paul Stevens	Douglas	Ford	11/28/1975	98-0	Confirmed	12/17/1975
William Rehnquist	Harlan	Nixon	10/22/1971	68-26	Confirmed	12/10/1971
Lewis Powell Jr.	Black	Nixon	10/22/1971	89-1	Confirmed	12/06/1971
Harry Blackmun	Fortas	Nixon	04/15/1970	94-0	Confirmed	05/12/1970
G. Harrold Carswell	Fortas	Nixon	01/19/1970	45-51	**Rejected**	04/08/1970
Clement Haynsworth, Jr.	Fortas	Nixon	08/21/1969	45-55	**Rejected**	11/21/1969
Warren Burger[b]	Warren	Nixon	05/23/1969	74-3	Confirmed	06/09/1969
Homer Thornberry[d]	Fortas	Johnson	06/26/1968	—	**No Action**	—
Abe Fortas[b]	Warren	Johnson	06/26/1968	—	**Withdrawn**	10/04/1968
Thurgood Marshall	Clark	Johnson	06/13/1967	69-11	Confirmed	08/30/1967
Abe Fortas	Goldberg	Johnson	07/28/1965	Voice	Confirmed	08/11/1965
Arthur Goldberg	Frankfurter	Kennedy	08/31/1962	Voice	Confirmed	09/25/1962
Byron White	Whittaker	Kennedy	04/03/1962	Voice	Confirmed	04/11/1962
Potter Stewart	Burton	Eisenhower	01/17/1959	70-17	Confirmed	05/05/1959
Charles Whittaker	Reed	Eisenhower	03/02/1957	Voice	Confirmed	03/19/1957
William Brennan, Jr.	Minton	Eisenhower	01/14/1957	Voice	Confirmed	03/19/1957
John Harlan	Jackson	Eisenhower	01/10/1955	71-11	Confirmed	03/16/1955
John Harlan[e]	Jackson	Eisenhower	11/09/1954	—	**No Action**	—
Earl Warren[b]	Vinson	Eisenhower	01/11/1954	Voice	Confirmed	03/01/1954

[a] Vote tally # votes in favor - # votes against; a voice vote means that the names and numbers of those voting in favor or against were not recorded.
[b] Nominated for the position of chief justice.
[c] Withdrawn when Chief Justice Rehnquist died; renominated for position of chief justice.
[d] Withdrawn when nomination of Fortas to position of chief justice was withdrawn since Fortas then retained his position of associate justice.
[e] Congress adjourned before taking action.
Source: www.senate.gov/pagelayout/reference/nominations/Nominations.html

the confirmation vote for Clarence Thomas, the authors found that for a senator facing reelection, the impact of race was striking. As the percentage of African Americans in the state constituency increased from 0 percent, to 10 percent, to 20 percent, the likelihood of a senator voting for Thomas increased from 1 percent, to 15 percent, to 78 percent. If the percentage of African Americans in the state constituency was 30 percent, a moderate Democrat facing reelection was 99 percent certain to vote for Thomas.[69]

As discussed in the previous section on the nomination phase of the appointment process, interest groups also play an important role in the confirmation phase. Interest groups provide information to senators and their constituents about how nominees will likely behave if they are confirmed. Interest groups can therefore have an effect at various points throughout the confirmation phase: after the formal nomination is made in an attempt to influence a senator's decision whether or not to delay or block the nominee via the blue slip process, prior to the judiciary committee hearing to discuss questioning strategy, after the hearing but prior to the vote to discuss what transpired at the hearing and how the committee member will vote, and before full Senate debate and vote to again influence whether senators might delay or block a nominee at this point and ultimately how senators will vote.

The failure of recent Supreme Court nominations illustrates the power of interest groups. For example, President George W. Bush was forced to withdraw his nomination of Harriet Miers prior to her confirmation hearing due to pressure from conservative interest groups such as Concerned Women for America. The pro-life group accused Miers of supporting people and groups who "undermine respect for life and family" and after her withdrawal said, "We are assured that the president will keep his promise to nominate a strict constructionist."[70] The television ad opposing Robert Bork that was mentioned at the start of this chapter was paid for by the liberal interest group People for the American Way. Research shows that interest group lobbying, either for or against a nominee, affects senators' confirmation votes.[71]

HOW DO WE KNOW?

Do Senators Base Their Confirmation Votes on Ideology or Qualifications?

Did the Bork nomination prompt senators to cast votes for future nominees based on ideology as opposed to qualifications? According to John Maltese:

> The defeat of Robert Bork's 1987 Supreme Court nomination was a watershed event that unleashed what Stephen Carter has called "the confirmation mess." There was no question that Bork was a highly qualified nominee. He was rejected not because of any lack of qualification, or any impropriety, but because of his stated judicial philosophy: how he would vote as a judge.[72]

Thus, the conventional wisdom is that the Bork nomination "generated a seismic change in confirmation politics . . . "[73] But is this true? In order to ascertain whether this conventional wisdom is, in fact, correct, Epstein and her colleagues analyzed the votes of senators from Hugo Black's nomination in 1937 through John G. Roberts's nomination in 2005.[74] Their dependent variable was whether the senator voted yes or no. Their main independent variables were: (1) lack of qualifications, which is the degree to which senators perceive the candidate as qualified for office, a measure derived from a content analysis of newspaper editorials written at the time of the nomination until the vote by the Senate; (2) strong president, which is measured by whether the president's party controlled the Senate and whether he was not in his fourth year of office; (3) same party, which denotes whether the senator is of the same political party as the president; (4) ideological distance between the senator and the nominee; and (5) interaction between ideological distance and qualifications.

First, legal scholar Lee Epstein and her colleagues confirmed that ideology and qualifications are crucial factors when it comes to voting for Supreme Court nominees. For example, the predicted probability of a senator voting for a moderately qualified nominee is only 0.06 when the nominee and the senator are ideological extremes; however, that number increases to 0.90 when the nominee and the senator are ideologically close. When a nominee is perceived as highly unqualified and the ideological distance is set at the mean, the likelihood of a senator voting to confirm is only 0.18 whereas the predicted probability increases to 0.92 when the nominee is highly qualified.

Next, the researchers assessed whether the balance between ideological distance and lack of qualifications has shifted since 1987, when Bork was defeated. Thus, they separately analyzed nominations both before and since Bork's and they also estimated two sets of models for each of the 25 nominees between Vinson in 1946 and Kennedy in 1987. They found that the importance of ideology has increased over time, but that this emphasis on ideology did not begin with Bork, but began in the late 1950s. They also found that the coefficient for ideological distance increases from -1.93 for all nominees prior to Bork to -6.64 for all nominees after and including Bork. Substantively, this means that prior to Bork's nomination, senators were willing to vote in favor of moderately qualified candidates if the ideological distance between them and the nominee was no greater than 0.74 but after Bork, a moderately qualified nominee needs to be as close to a senator as 0.29 in order to receive a yes vote. Even if the nominee is highly qualified, "the ideological cut-off point for a yea vote for these candidates was a relatively distant 1.02 prior to the Bork nomination; with the Bork nomination that figure reduces substantially, to 0.37."[75] Thus, although the trend toward greater attention to ideology did not begin with Bork, ideological distance matters more since Bork. However, qualifications still matter as well.

The confirmation rate for nominees to the federal district courts and courts of appeals has averaged roughly 80 percent since the Truman Administration, with nominations to the district courts enjoying a slightly higher confirmation rate for most of that time.[76] Interestingly, the Senate has taken an increasing amount of time to process lower court nominees in the past several decades, which reflects the increasing politicization of the process. For all but a few congressional terms up to the last few years of the Reagan Administration, the time from nomination to final Senate action—confirmation, rejection, or return to the president upon the Senate's adjournment—averaged 60 days or less. With rare exception since then the Senate has doubled, tripled, and quadrupled the amount of time it has taken to deal with nominations to the lower federal court bench.[77]

The likelihood of confirmation (and the timing of final senatorial action) for a nominee to a lower federal court judgeship is influenced by a variety of factors. On average, nominees with higher ABA ratings[78] and those who are white men fare better in the confirmation process.[79] As with Supreme Court nominees, aspects of the political environment matter as well, including divided government and nomination later in a presidential term (both of which dampen the likelihood of confirmation success).[80] In their recent study, political scientists Nancy Scherer, Brandon Bartels, and Amy Steigerwalt suggested that the key to understanding the likelihood of and timing for confirmation, at least for nominees to the court of appeals bench, is understanding the role of interest groups.[81] While they are not the only scholars to suggest that interest groups have transformed the lower federal court confirmation process,[82] they do offer a unique theory as to how and why interest groups matter. This team of researchers argued that, given the multiple demands on senators' time and the lesser salience of lower federal court nominations, interest groups serve as fire alarms, alerting senators to potentially problematic nominees, thereby increasing their salience and inducing senators to pay greater attention. Under those conditions, confirmation becomes less likely and lengthy delay in the senatorial processing of nominations becomes more likely. In a separate study, Amy Steigerwalt found that many nominees are blocked for private political reasons that have nothing to do with ideology and that senators may use their support for or opposition to nominees as bargaining chips to garner votes for their positions on unrelated issues.[83]

Diversifying the Federal Bench

An increasingly important issue in staffing the federal courts is the extent to which the bench reflects the diversity of the nation—particularly with regard to gender and race. Historically, all federal judges were white males—perhaps not surprising given that white males were making the selections, and formal and informal bars excluded women and racial minorities from the legal profession generally and its upper echelons specifically. It was not until the 1930s that women and racial minorities were represented in the federal judiciary. The first woman appointed to the federal bench was Florence Allen who was appointed to the Sixth Circuit Court of Appeals by Democratic President Franklin Roosevelt in 1933. Burnita Shelton Matthews was the first woman appointed to a federal trial court when Democratic President Harry Truman selected her for the U.S. District Court for the District of Columbia in 1949. William H. Hastie was the first African American appointed to the federal bench when Roosevelt selected him for the U.S. District Court of the Virgin Islands. He later became the first African American on the federal appellate bench when Truman appointed him to the U.S. Court of Appeals for the Third Circuit in 1950.

Despite these breakthroughs during the Roosevelt and Truman administrations, Figure 5.3 shows that subsequent presidents were slow to increase diversity. Gains were

FIGURE 5.3

Gender and Racial Diversity on the Federal Bench: Presidential District Court and Appellate Court Nominations, 1952-2014

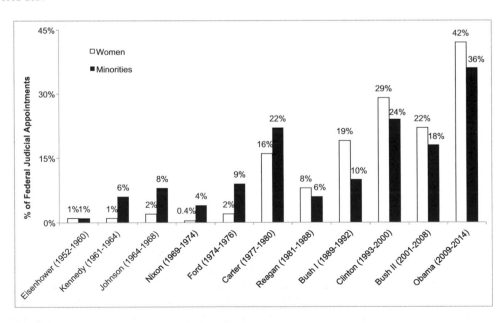

Source: Jeffrey Toobin, "The Obama Brief: The President Considers His Judicial Legacy," *The New Yorker*, October 27, 2014. http://www.newyorker.com/magazine/2014/10/27/obama-brief

relatively miniscule from the Dwight Eisenhower through Gerald Ford administrations. Democratic President Jimmy Carter was the first modern president to make significant inroads in diversifying the bench with women comprising 16 percent of his nominees and minorities 22 percent. While Republican Presidents Ronald Reagan and George H.W. Bush nominated substantially fewer minorities, Bush nominated a higher percentage of women than Carter had. Democratic president Bill Clinton bested Carter's numbers with women making up nearly one-third of his nominees (29 percent) and racial minorities one-quarter (24 percent). While diversity declined slightly under Republican president George W. Bush, his successor—Democratic President Barack Obama—has substantially diversified the federal bench. Through the first 6 years of his presidency, women comprised 42 percent of his nominees and minorities 36 percent. For the first time in history, white men did not make up a majority of a president's judicial nominees.

With 2 years remaining in his presidency, Obama commented on his focus beyond women and African Americans: "I think there are some particular groups that historically have been underrepresented—like Latinos and Asian Americans—that represent a larger and larger portion of the population. And so for them to be able to see folks in robes that look like them is going to be important. When I came into office, I think there was one openly gay judge who had been appointed. We've appointed ten."[84] Through his first 6 years Obama nominated more Hispanics (33) and more Asian Americans (21) than any president before him. He also appointed the first Native American woman when the Senate confirmed Diane Humetewa, a Hopi, to the U.S. District Court of Arizona in 2014.[85] It is plain that diversifying the federal bench has become increasingly important to presidents.

SELECTING STATE JUDGES

What is the best way to select judges? The 50 states have experimented with a range of selection mechanisms in an effort to balance issues of judicial independence and democratic accountability. On the one hand, we want judges to be independent in the sense that they are not dependent on any individual or group that might exert some influence on their decisions, and instead will apply the law fairly. Yet on the other hand, we also want judges to be accountable to the public in the sense that they do not exercise power arbitrarily, or in ways that undermine the judicial system they have sworn to uphold, and will render decisions that reflect public values.

The federal system falls on the independence side of the ledger as judges are appointed for life. In *Federalist No. 78*, Alexander Hamilton argued that granting life tenure to judges would guarantee an independent judiciary free from political influence; capable of invalidating legislative acts at odds with the Constitution: "In a monarchy it is an excellent barrier to the despotism of the prince; in a republic it is a no less excellent barrier to the encroachments and oppressions of the representative body. And it is the best expedient which can be devised in any government, to secure a steady, upright, and impartial administration of the laws."[86] Anti-federalists decried Hamilton's proposal and wanted to copy the English model where judges were accountable to the legislature. Writing under the pseudonym "Brutus," New York Judge Robert Yates wrote: "There is no power above them, to control any of their decisions. There is no authority that can remove them, and they cannot be controlled by the laws of the legislature. In short, they are independent of the people, of the legislature, and of every power under heaven. Men placed in this situation will generally soon feel themselves independent of heaven itself."[87] Of course Hamilton's argument won out and life tenure has been in place since the founding.

Life tenure largely explains why the nomination and confirmation process is so crucial and so infused with politics: it is the only time the public and their representatives will be able to directly influence the federal judiciary. Yet, as we detail in this section of the chapter, nearly every state has come to reject this method for choosing their judges. Thus, the notion that the process for selecting federal judges—lifetime appointment on executive nomination and legislative confirmation—is the best method is plainly not the case.

Unlike the selection process for federal judges, which has been largely unchanged, at least formally, since the nation's founding, the history of state judicial selection has been characterized by successive waves of reforms, with advocates for change first championing elections and then merit-selection methods. Some scholars have argued that the original impetus for popular election of judges was not only the result of pressure for judicial accountability but also a function of the legal profession's desire to enhance the power and authority of the judiciary, which would gain a popular base of support to serve as a counterweight against executive and legislative bases of power.

The impetus for these reforms has been the changing understanding of whether the more pressing problem was compromised judicial independence or weakened democratic accountability. Figure 5.4 shows that in addition to gubernatorial appointment (with or without required senatorial confirmation), states currently use legislative appointment, popularly contested election (either partisan or nonpartisan), and merit selection.

The variation across the states (including within each general method of judicial selection) embodies the principle of federalism, with each state free to experiment with alternative methods of judicial selection to determine which method best suits its needs. The variation also reflects the lack of consensus as to the best means of striking the balance between judicial independence and judicial accountability. Popularly contested elections

FIGURE 5.4
State Judicial Selection Methods

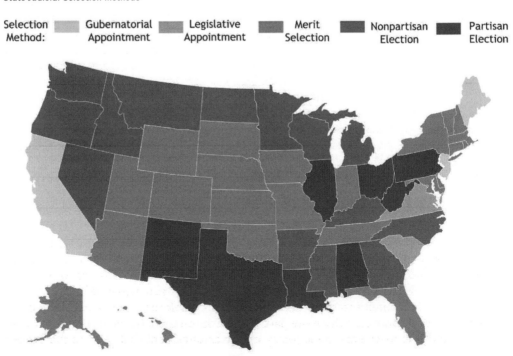

Selection Method: Gubernatorial Appointment   Legislative Appointment   Merit Selection   Nonpartisan Election   Partisan Election

tie judges closer to voters, enhancing judicial accountability. Appointment mechanisms loosen the ties between voters and judges, giving them greater independence; however, they may simply substitute accountability to political elites for accountability to the voters. Merit selection blends appointive and elective mechanisms, with the intention of striking a balance between independence and accountability.

Each state's constitution prescribes the method by which its judges will be selected. There are, however, two caveats. First, in several states the constitution stipulates the method of selection for some but not all judges. So, for example, the Idaho constitution stipulates the method of selection for the members of its highest court (the Idaho Supreme Court) and its trial courts of general jurisdiction (the Idaho District Court) but not for its intermediate appellate court (the Idaho Court of Appeals). This makes sense given that Idaho's high court and trial courts of general jurisdiction were created by the state's constitution but its intermediate appellate court was created by statute in 1980. Second, the constitutional language often leaves room for legislative discretion. This is the case in Mississippi, a state in which the constitution stipulates that the selection of its judges must be via election but does not specify whether those elections must be partisan or nonpartisan. In partisan elections, the party affiliation of the candidate is indicated on the ballot, whereas in nonpartisan elections it is not. Accordingly, when Mississippi moved from partisan to nonpartisan elections in 1994, no constitutional amendment was required and the Mississippi legislature made the change simply via statute.[88] The result of the variation in state constitutional language regarding judicial selection means that each state can (and has) put its unique stamp on the general type of selection mechanism in use.

Gubernatorial Appointment

Prior to the Revolutionary War, the King selected the judges who presided in the American colonies, much to the consternation of the colonists themselves. They saw it as yet one more instance of arrogant power on the part of the King and were especially disgruntled at what they saw as the complete and entire dependence of colonial judges on the King. For example, whereas the individual colonial assemblies originally paid for judicial salaries, in 1773 the British Parliament made a provision for their payment directly from the National Treasury.[89] The ensuing uproar about this arrangement among the colonists was intense enough that the Declaration of Independence referenced it: "He [the King] has made judges dependent on his will alone for the tenure of their offices, and the amount and payment of their salaries." In the aftermath of the Revolution, with the colonial ire at royal abuses still fresh, only a few states involved the governor in the selection of judges, with most states lodging that authority in the state legislatures.

At present, three states—California, Maine, and New Jersey—use **gubernatorial appointment** for at least some judges. In this system, the governor appoints judges, and that choice must be confirmed. In California, members of the state high court (California Supreme Court) and intermediate appellate court (California Court of Appeals) are appointed by the governor for 12-year terms but must be confirmed by the Commission on Judicial Appointments. The Commission—consisting of the California chief justice, the senior presiding judge of the court of appeals for the judicial district to which an appointment is being considered, and the state attorney general—holds public hearings about the appointee and reviews his or her record before making a decision. In the absence of a favorable decision on the part of the Commission, the governor's appointee cannot take office. Maine and New Jersey use an arrangement that mimics the process

Image 5.5 King George
III Statue at Bowling
Green
*Engraving depicting
the American "Sons of
Freedom" pulling down
the statue of King George
III at Bowling Green,
New York City, July 1776.
Colonial judges were
appointed by the King
and when he shifted the
payment of their salaries
from colonial assemblies
to the English National
Treasury, Americans
were so outraged that
they listed this develop-
ment as one of their grievances in the Declaration
of Independence. Accord-
ingly, early Americans
were skeptical of guber-
natorial appointment of
state judges.* Prints and
Photographs Division,
Library of Congress,
Washington, D.C.

PULLING DOWN THE ⬥⬥⬥ STATUE OF GEORGE III.
BY THE SONS OF FREEDOM.

for the selection of federal court judges: governors nominate individuals who must be confirmed by the state senate. In Maine, a joint standing committee on the judiciary of the Maine legislature makes a recommendation as to whether the gubernatorial appointee should be confirmed, with the committee's recommendation becoming final unless a super majority of two-thirds of the state senate votes to reject the recommendation.

Legislative Appointment

Just as gubernatorial appointment represents a vestige of history, so too does legislative appointment; eight of the original 13 states initially relied on some form of **legislative appointment**.[90] In this system, the legislature chooses judges. Currently, however, only two states, South Carolina and Virginia, rely on this mechanism to staff their courts. In the case of South Carolina, the state legislature is aided by the Judicial Merit Selection Commission. The Commission was created in 1997 and consists of 10 members. Three members are appointed by the Speaker of the House from among the currently serving members of the General Assembly, with two more appointed by the Speaker from the general public. The Chair of the Senate Judiciary Committee appoints three additional members, with the final two appointments made by the President Pro Tempore of the Senate. Of those five appointees, three must be currently serving members of the General Assembly and two must be from the general public. In practice, this means the Speaker of the House appoints members of the House and the President Pro Tempore appoints members of the Senate, with the members of the general public coming from the ranks of the legal profession. The Commission screens potential candidates for the bench and the legislature is limited to the selection of Commission-approved candidates.

Virginia, too, vests the selection of its judges in the state legislature. While the South Carolina legislature is obligated to select individuals screened by the Judicial Merit Selection Commission, the Virginia legislature is not similarly bound. However, each legislative chamber has a Courts of Justice Committee and there is a Joint Judicial Advisory Committee that serves as an informal screening mechanism for the Virginia legislature. The leadership of the upper and lower chambers of the Virginia legislature selects the members of the Advisory Committee. Though the recommendation of the Advisory Committee is not binding on the state legislature, candidates must secure a majority vote in both chambers. If a vacancy on a court arises when the legislature is not in session, the governor may appoint an individual to fill that vacancy; however, such appointees must be legislatively elected at the next legislative session. When the governorship and both chambers of the state legislature are controlled by the same party, gubernatorial appointments to judgeships that arise when the legislature is not in session are subsequently routinely elected by the legislature. Such unified government, however, has been on the decline and, as a consequence, interparty hostility between governors of one party and legislative majorities of the other has made legislative election of gubernatorial-appointed judges anything but certain.

Popularly Contested Election

Popularly contested election, a method of judicial selection where the voters choose judges, first fully emerged during the era of Jacksonian democracy.[91] This period, so-named because of its association with President Andrew Jackson and his partisans, was characterized by an emphasis on popular democracy; i.e., a focus on the direct and immediate involvement of citizens in electoral processes and governance.[92] When it came to judicial selection, old models of gubernatorial or legislative appointment smacked of elitism to the Jacksonians, who were displeased with judges who were increasingly striking down popularly enacted laws.[93] In addition to pressure for judicial accountability, the legal profession sought to enhance the power and authority of the judiciary by gaining a popular base of support to serve as a counterweight against executive and legislative bases of power.[94]

Accordingly, reformers pushed for the direct election of judges.[95] Mississippi was the first state to move to popular election of its state supreme court justices, switching from legislative appointment to popular election in 1832.[96] The popular election of judges was wildly popular in the late nineteenth and very early twentieth centuries: every new state admitted to the Union between 1846 and 1912 adopted popular election for its judiciary.[97]

There are two variants of popularly contested elections: partisan elections and nonpartisan elections. A significant majority of all states use one or the other of these mechanisms to staff all or some of their courts. In the case of **partisan elections,** candidates for judgeship are selected by their respective political parties, generally via primary elections. A notable exception is New York, in which judicial candidates for the major trial court (confusingly named the New York Supreme Court even though it is not an appellate court) are selected via party conventions. Primary voters for these judgeships in New York are not voting for judicial candidates but, instead, for convention delegates who then select the candidates who will run in the general election.[98] The names of the candidates for judicial office selected via partisan election appear on the ballot along with their partisan affiliation.[99] Louisiana has an interesting twist on the partisan election. It uses a blanket primary in which all candidates appear on the primary ballot with their partisan affiliation noted and the two candidates who receive the most primary votes, regardless of partisan affiliation, appear on the general election ballot.

In contrast, **nonpartisan elections** are those in which candidates' partisan affiliations are omitted from the ballot. Initial efforts to change from partisan to nonpartisan elections came during the Progressive Era, a period during which efforts at social, economic, and political reform were rife.[100] Progressive reformers saw the move to nonpartisan elections as a means of lessening the influence of party bosses and party machines and, concomitantly, enhancing the influence of the public at large.[101] Nonpartisan elections were also seen as having the potential to enhance the prestige of judiciaries by, hopefully, moving the focus from how politically connected candidates were to how well qualified they were. More recent switches to nonpartisan elections have been concentrated in southern states such as Arkansas and Georgia.[102] Most commonly, states that use nonpartisan elections for the selection of some or all of their judges start the process with a nonpartisan primary, with the two candidates receiving the most votes during the primary then advancing to the general election where, once again, they appear on the ballot sans an indication of their partisan affiliation. Michigan represents a unique variant on the nonpartisan election mechanism in that, while the general election is nonpartisan, those candidates seeking to oust an incumbent or contest an open seat can appear on the general election ballot only if they are nominated at a party convention or secure sufficient signatures on a nonpartisan nominating petition.[103]

Merit Selection (Missouri Plan)

Merit-selection systems are hybrid systems that blend appointment and election in an attempt to incorporate democratic accountability but temper it to avoid unduly compromising judicial independence. The idea is that the judiciary should be composed of qualified and independent judges and therefore they should be selected from the most talented lawyers available, they should not have to engage in political campaigns, and they should be secure in their positions as long as they do their jobs well. Merit plans were the brainchild of Albert M. Kales, a law professor on the faculty of Northwestern Law School and a co-founder of the American Judicature Society.[104] Kales proposed that a nonpartisan judicial nominating commission be responsible for screening the qualifications of applicants and, based on that screening process, submit a list of recommended candidates for consideration by the chief judge of the court on which a vacancy arose. Under the Kales Plan, after the person so appointed served for a specified period of time, he would then be subject to a retention election in which the voters would determine whether he should be retained in office or not. If voters did not choose to retain a sitting judge, then the chief judge would appoint another individual from a list submitted, again, by the judicial nominating commission. Harold Laski, a prominent British political scientist, proposed a modification of the Kales Plan in which the appointing authority would be the governor (rather than the chief judge).

The Kales-Laski Plan earned the endorsement of the American Bar Association in 1937 and, 3 years later, Missouri amended its constitution to provide for a merit-selection

Image 5.7 Harold Laski *Law professor Albert M. Kales and British political scientist Harold Laski (pictured) devised a merit-selection system for judges that blended both appointment and election. Merit plans are often called "Missouri Plans" after the first state that adopted the merit-selection system proposed by Kales and Laski.* Harris & Ewing Collection, Prints and Photographs Division, Library of Congress, Washington, D.C.

mechanism for the selection of virtually all of its judges, becoming the first state to adopt the plan. As a result, the moniker **Missouri Plan** is often used to refer to merit-selection systems. Currently, states that rely on the Missouri Plan to staff their benches have a nonpartisan nominating commission that screens candidates and the governor then selects from the list of candidates recommended by the commission, as originally envisioned in the Kale-Laski Plan. Judges subsequently run in retention elections to remain in office.

The nominating commission is obviously the key feature of the Missouri Plan. Most commissions include a combination of sitting judges, lawyers, and non-lawyer members. The process by which members of these commissions are chosen varies, though typically state bar associations, state legislators, state governors, and sitting judges are involved (in various combinations depending upon the state).[105] State bar associations are particularly involved in the selection of lawyers to serve on nominating commissions, while governors are more influential in the selection of non-lawyer members of these commissioners.[106] In addition, non-lawyer commissioners are more likely than lawyer commissioners to have served as an officer in a political party or as a public official.[107] However, all nominating commissions are charged with soliciting and reviewing applicants for judicial vacancies. The recruitment of applicants takes a variety of forms. Though nominating commissions most often focus their recruitment efforts on publication through state and local bar association outlets (e.g., newsletters, websites), recruitment efforts also involve combing through the recommendations of labor unions, trade associations, prominent attorneys, and public officials, as well as personal efforts on the part of commissioners to solicit applications.[108]

The Retention of State Court Judges

There are only a few states in which judges, once they ascend to the bench, are there for life (or until retirement). Judges on the state high court benches of Massachusetts and New Hampshire serve until the age of 70. Judges on Rhode Island's court of last resort enjoy lifetime tenure, making Rhode Island the only state whose judges share this characteristic with federal judges serving on Article III courts.[109] The other 47 states have adopted various approaches to how judges are retained in office once their terms of service end. The majority of states use an electoral method for retention. Most obviously, states using a version of the Missouri Plan rely on **retention elections** in which voters are not choosing between two candidates (the incumbent and a challenger) but, rather, whether the incumbent should be retained in office. Basically, voters are presented with the question, "Should Judge X be retained in office, Yes or No?" In many states, judicial retention elections are fairly low profile. Most judges are retained in these elections, although recently that number has declined. In the 1980s the margin of approval for state judges in retention elections was 76.8 percent whereas in 1994, the margin of approval was 60.1 percent.[110]

The states that select their judges via nonpartisan elections require judges to stand for reelection against a challenger in another nonpartisan election. Similarly, the states that rely on partisan elections to staff their benches tend to require judges to stand for reelection against a challenger in a partisan election. Exceptions to this general tendency include Illinois, New Mexico, and Pennsylvania, states that use partisan elections for the election of their appellate and trial court judges but then use retention elections to determine whether judges should remain in office.

The fact that the method of initial selection is not necessarily the same as the method of retention in any given state is what results in such a dizzying array of arrangements by which state benches are staffed. Table 5.2 reports the method of appointment and

TABLE 5.2

Selection and Retention of State Court of Last Resort Judges

METHOD OF SELECTION	METHOD OF RETENTION	STATES
Gubernatorial Appointment	Retention Election	California[a]
Gubernatorial Appointment with Nominating Commission	Retention Election	Alaska, Arizona, Colorado, Florida, Indiana, Iowa, Kansas, Missouri, Nebraska, Oklahoma, South Dakota, Tennessee, Wyoming
	N/A	Massachusetts[b], New Hampshire[c]
Gubernatorial Appointment with Legislative Confirmation	Gubernatorial Appointment with Legislative Confirmation	Maine, New Jersey
Gubernatorial Appointment with Nominating Commission and Legislative Confirmation	Gubernatorial Appointment with Nominating Commission and Legislative Confirmation	Connecticut, Delaware, New York
	Judicial Nominating Commission	Hawaii
	Legislative Retention	Vermont
	N/A	Rhode Island[d]
	Retention Election	Maryland, Utah
Legislative Appointment	Legislative Retention	South Carolina, Virginia
Nonpartisan Election	Nonpartisan Election	Arkansas, Georgia, Idaho, Kentucky, Michigan, Minnesota, Mississippi, Montana[e], Nevada, North Carolina, North Dakota, Oregon, Washington, Wisconsin
Partisan Election	Partisan Election	Alabama, Louisiana[f], Ohio[g], Texas, West Virginia
	Retention Election	Illinois, New Mexico, Pennsylvania

Source: American Judicature Society, Judicial Selection in the States (http://www.judicialselection.us/).

[a] Nomination must be confirmed by Commission on Judicial Appointments.

[b] No retention method as judges serve during good behavior until age 70.

[c] Appointment officially made by the Executive Council, a constitutionally authorized, executive advisory body whose members are chosen via partisan elections. No retention method as judges serve during good behavior until age 70.

[d] No retention method as judges have lifetime tenure during good behavior.

[e] Retention election in the event of an unopposed incumbent.

[f] All candidates appear on the same primary ballot with partisan affiliation noted; top two vote getters appear on general election ballot.

[g] Candidates chosen through partisan primaries but partisan affiliation omitted from general election ballot.

Council of State Governments, *The Book of the States*, volume 42 (Lexington, KY: Council of State Governments, 2010)

retention for state courts of last resort judges in each state. Hawaii and Vermont are perhaps particularly interesting in that each has adopted its own unique combination of selection and retention. As is the case in several other states, governors in Hawaii and Vermont appoint members of the bench but they must select from a set of candidates recommended by their respective nominating commissions and their appointees can only take their place on the bench if they secure legislative confirmation.

In Hawaii, however, retention in office after the initial 10-year term is dependent on the Judicial Selection Commission. The Commission—a nine-member body with a mix of attorney and non-attorney members who are selected variously by legislative leaders, the governor, the state bar association, and the chief justice—reviews the records of incumbent judges who have indicated that they wish to remain in office and makes a decision as to retention on the basis of its investigation. In Vermont, retention is dependent on the state legislature. In particular, the Judicial Retention Committee is an eight-member joint-standing committee of the two chambers of the state legislature and it undertakes the review of incumbent judges on behalf of the legislature. The recommendation of the Committee is advisory rather than binding and the legislature then votes, with each member of the upper and lower chambers receiving one vote, to determine whether a judge should be retained.

Consequences of Different Methods of Selection/Retention

As noted earlier, a state's choice of mechanism by which to staff its judiciary represents an attempt to find a balance between judicial independence and democratic accountability. Each choice comes with associated consequences that are directly tied to the trade-off between independence and accountability. Of particular interest in this regard are the relationships between selection mechanisms and diversity on the bench, selection mechanisms and judicial quality, and the role of money in judicial selection and its effects on judicial legitimacy in the eyes of the public.

JUDICIAL SELECTION IN THE STATES: DIVERSIFYING THE BENCH

State courts are noted as (and often criticized for) lacking diversity. For example, an analysis by political scientists Mark Hurwitz and Drew Lanier found that, in 2005, African Americans constituted a mere 8 percent of state court of last resort judges and women comprised only 27 percent.[111] Furthermore, although every state had seated its first woman on the state high court bench by 2009, 19 states had yet to seat their first African American justice on the state supreme court by that time.[112] Court observers and scholars have put forth several arguments as to why this lack of diversity is problematic. Two loom particularly large. The first is that descriptive representation is a prerequisite for substantive representation.[113] In other words, it is important to have the full range of backgrounds, experiences, and perspectives present on the courts to ensure adequate representation of diverse interests. The second is that a lack of diversity erodes public confidence in the courts and threatens their legitimacy.[114]

When Lawrence Baca, who represented the Native American Bar Association, recounted his first trial experience as an attorney in South Dakota, he stated:

> I stepped into the courtroom. . . . [T]he judge was white, the state attorney general who was there to defend the right of the state to disallow Indians to run for office was also white. The county attorney defending the right to disallow this young man the right to run for office was also white. . . . The courtroom clerk, the courtroom reporter, all white males. . . . I felt alone. I had a serious question as to whether there could be justice in that courtroom.[115]

Image 5.8 Judge Mary Bartelme
This ca. 1910–1915 photo shows Mary Bartelme (1866–1954), the first woman judge elected to the Circuit Court of Cook County (Chicago), suffragist, reformer of the juvenile justice system, and co-founder of the Chicago Business Woman's Club. Despite the electoral success of Judge Bartelme and many other women who have run for judicial office, research shows that while gubernatorial appointment and merit-selection systems are most advantageous for women obtaining judgeships, the lack of gender diversity on the bench persists. Prints and Photographs Division, Library of Congress, Washington, D.C.

These concerns have motivated several scholars to tackle the question of how methods of judicial selection shape the descriptive characteristics of state judiciaries.

The Fund for Modern Courts found that selection via gubernatorial appointment and merit-selection systems advantaged women when it came to obtaining judicial office.[116] In a more recent analysis, political scientists Kathleen Bratton and Rorie Spill found that selection via appointment does enhance the likelihood of a woman being placed on the bench; however, that advantage is conditional. It is conditional in the sense that a vacancy on a court is most likely to be filled by a woman when the method of selection is appointment and there is no other woman serving on that bench.[117] In one study, the authors found that states that used merit selection are more likely to choose minorities and women.[118] In 2008, approximately 50 percent of all minority and women judges on courts of last resort, and at least 25 percent of minority and women judges on lower courts, were chosen through a merit-selection process. Additionally, Democratic governors were more likely than Republican governors to appoint minorities and women to the bench. Approximately 17 percent of judges appointed by Democratic governors on a court of last resort in 2008 were minorities whereas almost 9 percent of judges appointed by Republican governors on a court of last resort were minorities.

POP CULTURE

Why Do African Americans Dominate the Hollywood Bench?

In the Coen Brothers's screwball comedy *Intolerable Cruelty* (2003), a dramatic courtroom scene between attorney Miles Massey—played by George Clooney—and witness Marilyn Rexroth—played by Catherine Zeta-Jones—takes place before African American Judge Marva Munson who is portrayed by Isabell O'Connor. As with their depiction of the other characters in the film—such as the shyster lawyer, gold-digging paramour, or wealthy playboy businessman—the Coens exaggerate Hollywood tropes to the extreme, not to perpetuate but to disparage them. Thus, they consciously choose to criticize Hollywood's stereotypical portrayal of the sassy, cynical, disinterested African American judge. After every objection during the ludicrous courtroom scene, Judge Munson exclaims matter-of-factly: "I'm going to allow it." Finally, when the buffoonery reaches its apex, as the wealthy playboy businessman leaps into the witness stand to strangle the pretentious witness, attorney Freddie Bender—played by Richard Jenkins—says: "Objection, your Honor! Strangling the witness!" Judge Munson coolly replies: "I'm going to allow it."

This brilliant send-up would be funny enough with anyone playing the judge. But in choosing an African American, the Coens double the laughter because the audience is so familiar with Hollywood's stereotypical use of African American jurists beginning in the 1990s: Morgan Freeman as Judge Leonard White in *The Bonfire of the Vanities* (1990), Paul Winfield as Judge Larren Lyttle in *Presumed Innocent* (1990), J.A. Preston as Judge Julius Alexander Randolph in *A Few Good Men* (1992), James Earl Jones as Judge Isaacs in *Sommersby* (1993), Alfre Woodard as Judge Miriam Shoat in *Primal Fear* (1996), Danny Glover as Judge Tyrone Kipler in *The Rainmaker* (1997), Whoopi Goldberg as the judge in *The Adventures of Rocky and Bullwinkle* (2000), Francesca P. Roberts as Judge Marina R. Bickford in *Legally Blonde* (2001), Myra Lucretia Taylor as Judge Frances Abarbanel in *Changing Lanes* (2002), Ossie Davis as Judge Buchanan in *She Hate Me* (2004), Oprah Winfrey as Judge Bumbleton in *Bee Movie* (2007), Reggie Baker as Judge Fullbright in *The Lincoln Lawyer* (2011), and Sharon Wilkins as Judge Lee in *Win Win* (2011).

African American judges populate the small screen, too, with James Avery as Judge Phillip Banks in *The Fresh Prince of Bel-Air* (1990), Ossie Davis as both Judge Farris in *The Stand* (1994) miniseries and Judge Harry Roosevelt in the short-lived show *The Client* (1995–1996), Iris Little Thomas as Judge Barbara Lusky in seven episodes of *Law & Order* (1999–2009), Myra Lucretia Taylor as Judge Suzanne Michaels in the *Law & Order* spinoff *Conviction* (2006), and Patricia R. Floyd as Judge Rochelle Desmond in six episodes of *Law & Order* (2006–2009). As with Davis and Taylor, it is not uncommon for African Americans to play judges in multiple projects. For example, Albert Hall first played Judge Seymore Walsh in five episodes of *The Practice* in 1998. He returned as the same judge for a whopping 51 episodes of *Ally McBeal* (1998–2002). But he has also played judges in the TV movie *Swing Vote* (1999), the TV series *Half & Half* (2003) and *Private Practice* (2010), and the daytime soap operas *The Young and the Restless* (2004) and *Days of Our Lives* (2010).

But the widespread use of African American jurists in dramatic fare has also crossed over to the most recent Hollywood trend: reality TV. Specifically, African American "judges" now "preside" over "cases" once heard by whites like original reality TV Judge Joseph Wapner and the men who followed him on *The People's Court*: former New York City Mayor Ed Koch and Judge Jerry Scheindlin. Now, viewers tune in to watch Judge Joe Brown, Judge Greg Mathis, Judge Glenda Hatchett, Judge Lynn Toler, and Judge Mablean Ephriam (who also appeared as a judge in Tyler Perry's *Madea* films).

Why do African Americans dominate the Hollywood bench? Scholars have demonstrated that the film and television industry has a long history of patronizing racial minorities—and African Americans in particular—with one-dimensional, smaller roles where they play street-wise authority figures who support and aid in the on-screen journeys of complex white lead characters. Some have even gone so far as to call this trope the "magical negro."[119] In the case of judges in particular, African American jurists do little judging while running their courts in a stern, orderly, and often disinterested fashion. Yet there is always a crucial point where they must be sassy and hard-nosed in providing common-sense solutions to the white folks.

Ultimately, Hollywood's depiction of the African American judge is a doubly damaging myth. On the one hand, Hollywood thinks it is being progressive and exhibiting diversity by casting African American judges. Yet it is reinforcing long-standing stereotypes about the "magical negro" and that African American jurists are one-dimensional, street-wise helpers of whites. At the same time, Hollywood gives the impression that African Americans dominate the judiciary, particularly at the trial court level. Yet statistics have long demonstrated that whites—and white males in particular—continue to dominate the ranks of judges.

In another study, political scientist Greg Goelzhauser found that the use of nominating commissions enhances the likelihood that an African American justice will assume a seat on a state supreme court. This comports with the idea that nominating commissions are often tasked with enhancing diversity on the courts. Goelzhauser also found that the use of a partisan selection mechanism makes the ascension of an African American to the bench more likely, provided that the electorate is sufficiently liberal.[120] Political scientists Lisa Holmes and Jolly Emrey pay special attention to a little-considered but potentially quite consequential feature of elective systems: interim appointments.[121] In particular, Holmes and Emrey examined the effect of interim appointments in states that use elective methods to select their judges but permit governors to make appointments to fill vacancies that arise due to the retirement, resignation, or death of an incumbent judge.[122] They found, first, that over half of the judges in elective states from 1964 to 2004 originally came to the bench via gubernatorial appointment. Further, they found that interim appointments have been more effective in initially diversifying courts than elections have been.

JUDICIAL SELECTION IN THE STATES: JUDICIAL QUALITY

Proponents of merit selection argue that it screens out unqualified applicants and identifies the most qualified, resulting in a higher quality judiciary. Although supporters acknowledge that it does not completely eliminate politics from the process, they argue that it minimizes the role of political, partisan, and special interests. In order to assess the comparative quality of merit-selected judges versus popularly elected judges, scholars have used a variety of approaches.

Some studies have compared elected and appointed judges when it comes to the *potential* for quality judicial work. For example, political scientists Henry Glick and Craig Emmert [123] found that the number of years of practicing law and prior judicial service for judges was fairly equal across all judicial selection systems, while merit-selected and gubernatorially appointed judges were somewhat more likely than elected judges to have attended prestigious undergraduate or law schools. A totally different way to measure judicial quality was used in a study examining the nature and severity of judicial disciplinary actions.[124] The author found that merit-selected judges were disciplined less often than elected judges, and that when they were disciplined, merit-selected judges were less likely to receive the most severe sanction and more likely to receive the least severe sanction. Thus, there is some support for the claims advanced by merit-selection supporters.

Still another study measured the quality of state judicial systems by using a survey-based ranking of state legal liability systems conducted by the U.S. Chamber of

Commerce.[125] Specifically, the ranking is derived from a random survey of approximately 1,000 lawyers throughout the United States who were asked to evaluate states they were familiar with on such criteria as judicial impartiality, judicial competence, and overall treatment of tort and contract litigation. Their answers were then used to construct the overall ranking. States selecting judges through appointment are ranked higher in judicial quality than states selecting judges through election (61 v. 54 on a scale of 0–100). Also, states with nonpartisan elections were ranked higher than states with partisan elections (57 v. 48). Thus, lawyers perceive that judicial quality suffers when elections are used to select judges—consistent with the claims of merit-selection proponents.

A recent study examined the quality of judges' performance on the bench. Legal scholars Stephen Choi, G. Mitu Gulati, and Eric Posner [126] found that appointed judges write "better" opinions, as indicated by the number of out-of-state citations, but that elected judges write more opinions and thus are more productive. However, they found no difference between elected and appointed judges when it comes to independence, as measured by their willingness to write opinions that disagree with a judge who shares their party affiliation. But Hall found that where state supreme court justices are subject to reelection, perceived constituent values can suppress the expression of dissent in highly salient issues.[127] Thus, what some scholars see as a lack of judicial quality may be a strategic attempt to minimize electoral opposition in order to retain their seats.

Indeed research demonstrates a strong link between electoral competition and judicial behavior.[128] For example, political scientist Melinda Hall found that decisions to sentence defendants to death were affected by both general electoral conditions and the personal experiences judges have had with electoral politics.[129] Do such findings suggest a lack of quality or merely the kind of accountability that elections are supposed to produce?

JUDICIAL SELECTION IN THE STATES: MONEY, LEGITIMACY, AND CONSTITUENT INFLUENCE

Those opposed to electoral methods of judicial selection point to their supposed deleterious effects. For example, in a well-known speech he delivered to the American Bar Association in 1906, Roscoe Pound asserted that "putting courts into politics, and compelling judges to become politicians, in many jurisdictions has almost destroyed the traditional respect for the bench."[130] The argument is that judges should not have to stand for election because raising campaign funds creates an appearance of impropriety given that judges are receiving money from contributors who may appear before them. The American Bar Association recently recommended that the system of electing judges should be replaced by merit-based systems. "Money is the elephant in the room on judicial selection. It raises serious questions, such as how much money is required for judicial election, from whom does it comes, what is the public perception, and so on."[131]

State judicial elections have become more contested, competitive, and expensive over time.[132] As political scientist Chris Bonneau reported, the average contested race for state supreme court justice in 1990 saw campaign spending of just over $360,000. But, in 2004, that spending more than doubled to just over $890,000.[133] A 2004 election for a seat on the Illinois Supreme Court is an illustrative example.[134] Loyd Karmeier and Gordon Maag engaged in a vicious and acrimonious campaign, spending a combined total of approximately $10 million. Television advertisements accounted for $5 million alone in spending, with three-quarters of the campaign ads attack or contrast ads. What is the effect of campaign spending? Research shows that partisan elections reduce campaign costs while nonpartisan elections increase campaign spending.[135] Because voters are not able to rely on party labels in a nonpartisan race, candidates are forced to spend money to inform voters in an attempt to win support. The main vehicle for informing voters is television advertising in general and attack ads—commercials criticizing opponents—in particular.[136] Research shows that while attack ads have little to no effect in partisan elections, attack ads run by challengers in nonpartisan races are effective in increasing voter turnout and decreasing incumbency advantage.[137]

Also, the more expensive and contentious the race in general, especially in statewide partisan elections, the more likely it is that voters will participate.[138] The findings on voter participation are particularly important given that judicial elections are often low-information affairs that many potential voters choose to abstain from casting a vote in. **Roll-off** is the phenomenon of voters not completing a ballot with a selection in each contest, particularly at the bottom of the ballot for lesser-known offices and candidates. Voter roll-off in judicial elections is significant with about one-quarter of voters who make selections in high-information races such as president, senator, or governor choosing to skip contests for state supreme court seats.[139] Roll-off is even higher—more than one-third—in contests for lower-level judgeships.[140] Thus, research suggests that roll-off can be mitigated and turnout increased through greater competition and spending on judicial elections.

HOW DO WE KNOW?

Can Challengers Defeat Incumbent Judges by Outspending Them?

What is the effect of campaign spending on judicial elections? Does money buy votes? Can challengers guarantee victory by outspending incumbent judges who must stand for reelection? One of the criticisms of judicial elections is that they fail to live up to their supposed purpose of judges being held accountable for their decisions. This is argued to be the case because electoral outcomes may be dictated by factors such as political party affiliation or who spent the most money rather than issues, substantive evaluations, or other meaningful considerations relevant to the judiciary. Thus, the accountability that elections are supposed to produce is not occurring. Does research support these claims?

As political scientist Chris Bonneau examined contested incumbent-challenger state supreme court elections from 1990 to 2004 in 18 of the 22 states that elect justices on either a partisan or nonpartisan ballot. He collected data on both the characteristics of the elections and of the candidates as well as the campaign expenditures for each election. The dependent variable was the percentage of the vote received by the incumbent state supreme court justice. The key independent variables were the amount spent by the incumbent and amount spent by the challenger. Other independent variables included the quality of the challenger as measured by prior judicial experience and previous electoral success; the electoral context, including whether the incumbent had to run in a primary election, whether there was a history of competitive high court elections in that state, and the murder rate in the state for the year prior to the election; and institutional arrangements, including whether the election was partisan or nonpartisan, whether the election was statewide or held in a district within the state, and the length of the term of office. Based on previous research on legislative elections, Bonneau hypothesized that, all else being equal, the more money spent by the challenger, the lower the incumbent's electoral support.

His empirical analysis found support for a number of his independent variables with the incumbent's electoral fortunes harmed by quality challengers, the presence of a close prior state supreme court race, and the institutional arrangements of partisan election systems and district races. As to the key explanatory variables, he found that, similar to both national and state legislative elections, the amount of spending by incumbents did not increase their percentage of the vote. However, also like legislative elections, campaign spending by challengers did substantially diminish the incumbency advantage. Specifically, for every 1 percent increase in challenger spending, the incumbent's level of electoral support decreased by almost 1.8 percentage points.

These results mean that challengers can increase their level of support by spending more money while the incumbents cannot. Bonneau concluded that, "when deciding whom to support, voters behave in judicial elections much as they do in other elections. Thus, campaign spending (at least by challengers) can lead to enhanced electoral competition and this promotes electoral accountability."[141]

Critics of judicial elections suggest that incumbent judges are unfairly disadvantaged by elections, particularly nonpartisan races. While research suggests that campaign spending by challengers does in fact promote electoral competition by diminishing incumbency advantage,[142] this does not necessarily mean that challengers who outspend or spend as much as incumbents will always win. To be sure, some judges are unpopular and are therefore vulnerable to losing their seats. At the same time, potential challengers are strategic and will be reluctant to run against incumbent judges who are not vulnerable. Research shows that incumbent judges, who are not unpopular and who spend as much as challengers, generally retain their seats, all things being equal.[143] Thus, while money does not guarantee victory, it can make races more competitive.

But do judicial elections, and the money spent on them, damage the reputation of judges and the judiciary in general? Critics of judicial elections argue that public confidence in the judiciary is harmed when judges campaign for office like other politicians by raising campaign contributions, airing attack ads, and making policy pronouncements. Former Supreme Court Justice Sandra Day O'Connor devoted considerable time after leaving the Court to crusade against judicial elections: "You just can't have a fair and impartial system if you have cash in the court."[144] Does the public agree?

First, research shows that personal experience affects perception. Specifically, members of the public who have past experience as parties to litigation—as criminal defendants or on either side of civil cases— are much less supportive of courts in general than those who have no experience.[145] Similarly, those who perceive that the procedures used by the judicial system are unfair have less confidence in judges and courts than those who perceive that procedures are fair.[146] Finally, those who reside in partisan election states have less confidence in courts than those who have no experience with partisan judicial elections—though this may be conditioned on education level.[147] Thus, the legitimacy of judges and courts appears to depend on personal experience.

Given these findings, we would reasonably expect that in a litigious society, such as the United States, negative perceptions of judges and courts would be the rule. Yet, research suggests that, while judicial campaign contributions and ads personally attacking opponents do harm perceptions of legitimacy, policy pronouncements and position taking on issues do not.[148] In this sense, judicial races do not inherently delegitimize courts. It depends on how they are conducted. If they are run like legislative campaigns—particularly with regard to fundraising and personal, as opposed to policy, attacks—public confidence in the institution, perhaps already shaken by personal experience, may be harmed.

Interestingly, the potential delegitimizing effects of campaigns exist despite the fact that there is no systematic evidence that judges' votes are influenced by campaign contributions. Of course there have been high-profile instances of judicial corruption, such as the sensational 1970s resignations of four justices of the Florida Supreme Court, two of who attempted to fix cases in lower courts on behalf of campaign contributors.[149] Safe-guards in the form of judicial ethics canons and statutes with professional and even criminal sanctions have been put in place—often following such incidences—to ensure that judges do not participate in cases where they have a conflict of interest.[150] In *Caperton v. Massey*, the U.S. Supreme Court held that the Due Process Clause of the Fourteenth Amendment requires judges to **recuse** themselves—take no part in the consideration of the case—not only when they have a demonstrated conflict of interest or bias but also when there is a probability of bias due to the unique nature of the case in question.[151] Despite these checks against judicial impropriety, the very act of raising private campaign funds appears to create the public perception of corruption. Indeed, public opinion polls from partisan election states show that more than 80 percent of adults believe that campaign contributions to judges running for election significantly influence the subsequent decisions they make.[152]

In order to rid the process of the corrupting influence—real or perceived—of private fundraising, some states have opted for public financing for judicial campaigns. But research suggests that total spending by candidates has not diminished[153] and public financing has no bearing on what candidates say. A number of states have attempted to constrain the messages of judicial candidates by prohibiting them from commenting on issues that they could rule on if elected. However, the U.S. Supreme Court ruled 5–4 in *Republican Party of Minnesota v. White* that judicial candidates have free-speech rights to announce their views on disputed legal and political issues.[154]

Ultimately, it is up to the candidates to decide how to spend their campaign funds and what messages to convey. It is certainly possible for judicial candidates to accept public financing, take positions on issues, and refrain from negative campaigning without substantially harming their chances of winning and delegitimizing the judiciary. Thus, research suggests that judicial elections—depending on how they are conducted—can increase democratic accountability without harming the legitimacy of law, courts, and judges in the eyes of the public.

CONCLUSION

The process of selecting federal and state judges involves much more than placing the most qualified individuals on the bench. Although a candidate's professional qualifications clearly matter, it is a myth to think that only the most learned and accomplished legal minds don the black robes of the judiciary. A host of other factors also matter for understanding how and why judges ascend to the bench. The reality is that the process of choosing judges is a political one.

With regard to staffing the federal judiciary, presidents may be motivated by a personal agenda, partisan agenda, or policy agenda when deciding whom to nominate, and whether a nominee is confirmed by the Senate depends on a variety of factors, with qualifications, politics, and ideology each playing an important role. The role of interest groups in influencing the process has been particularly important and their support can both enhance and hinder a potential candidate's chances of becoming a federal judge. The federal bench has become increasingly diverse in recent years with women and racial minorities making inroads into an institution that, despite these developments, continues to be dominated by white males.

States use different selection mechanisms in an effort to balance issues of judicial independence and democratic accountability. Historically, states have moved from executive and legislative appointments to popular elections and, most recently, merit systems that attempt to fuse features of both approaches. Appointment and merit-based systems lead to greater diversity and, by some measures, enhanced judicial quality. On the other hand, judicial elections increase competition and accountability without substantially harming judicial legitimacy.

In all, the various methods Americans use to choose their judges suggests that no one system is plainly the best. Not only does each selection method present a potential trade-off between independence and accountability, each system has different implications for diversity, quality, and legitimacy. Regardless of the specific method, judicial selection at both the federal and state levels is infused with politics. Why? Because the process of judging is itself political.

Suggested Readings

Henry Abraham. *Justices, Presidents, and Senators: A History of U.S. Supreme Court Appointments from Washington to Bush II*, Fifth Edition (Lanham, MD: Rowman & Littlefield, 2007). Classic history of the politics surrounding every Supreme Court nomination since the nation's founding.

Chris W. Bonneau and Melinda Gann Hall. *In Defense of Judicial Elections* (New York, NY: Routledge, 2009). Comprehensive study of state supreme court elections demonstrating that expensive and contentious judicial elections increase voter turnout, partisan elections reduce campaign costs while nonpartisan elections increase spending, and that while money helps challengers it does not guarantee victory.

Lee Epstein and Jeffrey A. Segal. *Advice and Consent: The Politics of Judicial Appointments* (New York: Oxford University Press, 2005). Comprehensive study of the federal judicial appointment process illustrating how the process has always been a highly contentious and political affair with the Senate Judiciary Committee, American Bar Association, the media, and interest groups playing key roles.

James L. Gibson. *Electing Judges: The Surprising Effects of Campaigning on Judicial Legitimacy* (Chicago, IL: University of Chicago Press, 2012). Case study of the 2006 Kentucky election based on public surveys finding that judicial campaign contributions leads to perceptions of bias and illegitimacy but that judicial candidates taking positions on policy issues do not.

Sheldon Goldman. *Picking Federal Judges: Lower Court Selection from Roosevelt through Reagan* (New Haven, CT: Yale University Press, 1997). Details how nine presidents over a period of 56 years selected lower federal court judges.

Nancy Scherer. *Scoring Points: Politicians, Activists, and the Lower Federal Court Appointment Process* (Stanford, CA: Stanford University Press, 2005). Explores how the lower federal court appointment process has become politicized in the modern era where patronage was replaced by policy-oriented appointments.

Amy Steigerwalt. *Battle Over the Bench: Senators, Interest Groups, and Lower Court Confirmations* (Charlottesville, VA: University of Virginia Press, 2010). Offers a new analytic framework for understanding when lower court nominations become contested and shows when and how key actors, particularly interest groups, can influence nominations.

Matthew J. Streb, ed. *Running for Judge: The Rising Political, Financial, and Legal Stakes of Judicial Elections* (New York, NY: New York University Press, 2007). Collection of essays that analyze state judicial elections, including topics such as the history of judicial elections, electoral competition during races, and the increasing importance of campaign financing.

Endnotes

1 Sonia Sotomayor, "A Latina Judge's Voice," *Berkeley La Raza Law Journal*, vol. 13 (2002): 87–93.
2 Sandra Day O'Connor, "Remarks," Legislative Summit, National Conference of State Legislatures, August 12, 2013 (http://www.ncsl.org/research/civil-and-criminal-justice/general-session-sandra-day-oconnor-video.aspx).
3 John H. Fund, "Chavez's Crime? Helping the Needy," *Wall Street Journal*, January 9, 2001.
4 William Safire, "Judge Fights," *New York Times Magazine*, May 27, 2001.

5   Oxford Dictionary Online (http://www.oxforddictionaries.com/us/definition/american_english/online).

6   133 Cong. Rec. S9188-S9189 (daily ed. July 1, 1987) (statement of Senator Edward Kennedy).

7   Joyce A. Baugh, *Supreme Court Justices in the Post-Bork Era: Confirmation Politics and Judicial Performance* (New York, NY: Peter Lang, 2002).

8   The television ad is available for viewing on YouTube (http://youtu.be/NpFe10lkF3Y).

9   Lee Epstein and Jeffrey A. Segal, *Advice and Consent: The Politics of Judicial Appointments* (New York, NY: Oxford University Press, 2005): 86.

10 Denis Steven Rutkus and Maureen Bearden, "Supreme Court Nominations, 1789–2010: Actions by the Senate, the Judiciary Committee, and the President," Congressional Research Service Report for Congress RL 33225 (Washington, DC: Congressional Research Service, 2010): Table 1.

11 These hearings investigated a secret operation to sell weapons to Iran (in violation of an embargo that was in place) with the hopes of securing the release of American hostages being held by Iranian terrorists in Lebanon. President Reagan's credibility was severely undermined when he publicly and vehemently denied the existence of the operation. The plot only thickened when it was found that substantial amounts of the money paid by Iran for the weapons had been diverted to support the Contras, anti-Communist rebels in Nicaragua.

12 Stephen L. Carter, "The Confirmation Mess," *Harvard Law Review*, vol. 101, no. 6 (April 1988): 1185–1201.

13 Bork was Solicitor General at the time and, given the resignations of Attorney General Elliot Richardson and Deputy Attorney General William Ruckelshaus, was the acting head of the Department of Justice. Richardson and Ruckelshaus had resigned because they refused to comply with President Nixon's order to fire the special prosecutor.

14 "The Supreme Court: A Seat for Mediocrity?" *Time*, March 30, 1970, 22.

15 As we noted in the previous chapter on the organization of courts, judges who serve on federal courts created by other than under the auspices of Article III do not enjoy lifetime tenure.

16 Art. II, Sec. 2, §2.

17 See Keith E. Whittington, "Presidents, Senates, and Failed Supreme Court Nominations," *Supreme Court Review*, vol. 2006, no. 1 (2006): 401–438, 405–406. See, also, John F. Manning, "Separation of Powers as Ordinary Interpretation," *Harvard Law Review*, vol. 124, no. 8 (June 2011): 1939–2040, 2002–2003.

18 For more about the role of senatorial courtesy in the lower federal court confirmation process, see Lauren Cohen Bell, "Senatorial Discourtesy: The Senate's Use of Delay to Shape the Federal Judiciary," *Political Research Quarterly*, vol. 55, no. 3 (September 2002): 589–608. For a systematic analysis of the historical use of the blue slip, see Janet Box-Steffensmeier, Charles Campisano, Kevin M. Scott, and Connie C. Shen, "Senate Obstruction: A Senator's Decision on Whether to Use a Blue Slip," paper presented at the annual meeting of the Midwest Political Science Association, Chicago, IL, April 11–14, 2013.

19 Kenneth Cole, "Mr. Justice Black and 'Senatorial Courtesy,'" *American Political Science Review*, vol. 31, no. 6 (December 1937): 1113–1115, 1113.

20 See, for example, Micheal W. Giles, Virginia A. Hettinger, and Todd Peppers, "Picking Federal Judges: A Note on the Policy and Partisan Selection Agendas," *Political Research Quarterly*, vol. 54, no. 3 (September 2001): 623–641. But, see, Sarah A. Binder and Forrest Maltzman, "The Limits of Senatorial Courtesy," *Legislative Studies Quarterly*, vol. 29, no. 1 (February 2004): 5–22. Note that the norm of senatorial courtesy is not limited to lower federal court judgeships. The first instance of senatorial courtesy in practice involved President George Washington's appointment of a naval officer in Georgia. See Joseph P. Harris, *The Advice and Consent of the Senate: A Study of the Confirmation Appointments by the United States Senate* (Berkeley, CA: University of California Press, 1958). Senatorial courtesy is also not limited to federal appointments, as the New Jersey Senate, too, relies on the norm of senatorial courtesy. See Tonja Jacobi, "The Senatorial Courtesy Game: Explaining the Norm of Informal Vetoes in Advice and Consent Nominations," *Legislative Studies Quarterly*, vol. 30, no. 2 (May 2005): 193–217.

21 Micheal W. Giles, Virginia H. Hettinger, and Todd Peppers, "Picking Federal Judges: A Note on Policy and Partisan Selection Agendas," *Political Research Quarterly*, vol. 54, no. 3 (September 2001): 623–641, 628–629.

22 Quoted in Jeffrey Toobin, "The Obama Brief: The President Considers His Judicial Legacy," *The New Yorker*, October 27, 2014.

23 David R. Mayhew, *Congress: The Electoral Connection* (New Haven, CT: Yale University Press, 1974); Richard F. Fenno, *Home Style: House Members in Their Districts* (Boston, MA: Little, Brown, 1978); Morris P. Fiorina, *Representatives, Roll Calls, and Constituencies* (Lexington, MA: D.C. Heath, 1974).

24 Classic studies of the "marginality hypothesis" of legislative behavior include: Duncan MacRae, "The Relation Between Roll Call Votes and Constituencies in the Massachusetts House of Representatives," *American Political Science Review*, vol. 46, no. 4 (December 1952): 1046–1055; Lewis A. Froman, Jr., "The Importance of Individuality in Voting in Congress," *Journal of Politics* vol. 25, no. 2 (May 1963): 324–332; Barbara Sinclair Deckard, "Electoral Marginality and Party Loyalty in House Roll Call Voting," *American Journal of Political Science*, vol. 20, no. 3 (August 1976): 469–481; and John L. Sullivan and Eric M. Uslaner, "Congressional Behavior and Electoral Marginality," *American Journal of Political Science*, vol. 22, no. 3 (August 1978): 536–553.

25 Jonathan P. Kastellec, Jeffrey R. Lax, and Justin H. Phillips, "Public Opinion and Senate Confirmation of Supreme Court Nominees," *Journal of Politics*, vol. 72, no. 3 (July 2010): 767–784; Robert J. McGrath and James A. Rydberg, "The Marginality Hypothesis and Supreme Court Confirmation Votes in the Senate," unpublished manuscript, December 19, 2013 (http://www.academia.edu/4188839/The_Marginality_Hypothesis_and_Supreme_Court_Confirmation_Votes_in_the_Senate).

26 See, for example, David S. Law, "Appointing Federal Judges: The President, the Senate, and the Prisoner's Dilemma," *Cardozo Law Review*, vol. 26, no. 2 (2005): 479–523.

27 Jeffrey Toobin, "The Obama Brief: The President Considers His Judicial Legacy," *New Yorker*, October 27, 2014.

28 The House has voted to impeach fourteen federal judges. Eight of the fourteen were convicted by the Senate and removed from office: John Pickering (1804), West Humphreys (1862), Robert Archibald (1912), Halsted Ritter (1936), Harry Claiborne (1986), Alcee Hastings (1989), Walter Nixon (1989), and G. Thomas Porteous (2010). All of these eight were judges serving on the federal district courts, except for Archibald who was a judge on the (now defunct) Commerce Court of the United States. See Emily Field Van Tassel, "Resignations and Removals: A History of Federal Judicial Service—And Disservice—1789–1992," *University of Pennsylvania Law Review*, vol. 142, no. 1 (November 1993): 333–430, 424–425.

29 At the same time, Congress created seven new temporary judgeships on the district courts. Most often, but not always, judgeships that are created on a temporary basis are subsequently converted into permanent judgeships.

30 Artemus Ward, *Deciding to Leave: The Politics of Retirement from the United States Supreme Court* (Albany, NY: State University of New York Press, 2003).

31 Jeffrey Toobin, "The Obama Brief: The President Considers His Judicial Legacy," *The New Yorker*, October 27, 2014.

32 Sheldon Goldman, *Picking Federal Judges: Lower Court Selection from Roosevelt through Reagan* (New Haven: Yale University Press, 1997): 323–327.

33 Susan Navarro Smelcer, Amy Steigerwalt, and Richard L. Vining, "Bias and the Bar: Evaluating the ABA Ratings of Federal Judicial Nominees," *Political Research Quarterly*, vol. 65, no. 4 (December 2012): 827–840.

34 Sheldon Goldman, *Picking Federal Judges: Lower Court Selection from Roosevelt through Reagan* (New Haven: Yale University Press, 1997): 3–4.

35 David Greenberg, "Supreme Court Cronyism: Bush Restarts a Long and Troubled Tradition," *Slate*, October 5, 2005.

36 Seth Stern and Stephen Wermiel, *Justice Brennan: Liberal Champion* (New York, NY: Houghton Mifflin Harcourt Publishing Company, 2010): 76.

37 Christine L. Nemacheck, "Selecting Justice: Strategy and Uncertainty in Choosing Supreme Court Nominees," in *New Directions in Judicial Politics*, Kevin T. McGuire, ed. (New York, NY: Routledge, 2012).

38 Christine L. Nemacheck, *Strategic Selection: Presidential Nomination of Supreme Court Justices from Herbert Hoover through George W. Bush* (Charlottesville, VA: University of Virginia Press, 2007).

39 Tajuana Massie, Thomas G. Hansford, and Donald R. Songer, "The Timing of Presidential Nominations to the Lower Federal Courts," *Political Research Quarterly*, vol. 57, no. 1 (March 2004): 145–154.

40 See *N.L.R.B. v. Noel Canning*, 573 U.S. __ (2014).

41 See, for example, Scott E. Graves and Robert M. Howard, *Justice Takes a Recess: Judicial Recess Appointments from George Washington to George W. Bush* (Lanham, MD: Lexington, 2009); David R. Stras and Ryan W. Scott, "Review Essay: Navigating the New Politics of Judicial Appointments," *Northwestern University Law Review*, vol. 102, no. 4 (Fall 2008): 1869–1917, 1906–1910.

42 Sara Binder, "Where Do Institutions Come From? Exploring the Origins of the Senate Blue Slip," *Studies in American Political Development*, vol. 21, no. 1 (Spring 2007): 1–15.

43 Nancy Scherer, *Scoring Points: Politicians, Activists, and the Lower Federal Court Confirmation Appointment Process* (Stanford, CA: Stanford University Press, 2005): 187.

44 Janet Box-Steffensmeier, Charles Campisano, Kevin M. Scott, and Connie C. Shen, "Senate Obstruction: A Senator's Decision on Whether to Use a Blue Slip," paper presented at the annual meeting of the Midwest Political Science Association, Chicago, IL, April 11–14, 2013.

45 Roy B. Flemming, Michael C. Macleod, and Jeffrey Talbert, "Witnesses at the Confirmations? The Appearance of Organized Interests at Senate Hearings of Federal Judicial Appointments, 1945–1992," *Political Research Quarterly*, vol. 51, no. 3 (September 1998): 617–631; Nancy Scherer, Brandon L. Bartels, and Amy Steigerwalt, "Sounding the Fire Alarm: The Role of Interest Groups in the Lower Federal Court Confirmation Process," *Journal of Politics*, vol. 70, no. 4 (October 2008): 1026–1039.

46 John Anthony Maltese, *The Selling of Supreme Court Nominees* (Baltimore, MD: Johns Hopkins University Press, 1995): 93.

47 Ibid., 107.

48 Ibid., 109.

49 Denis Steven Rutkus and Maureen Bearden, "Supreme Court Nominations, 1789–2010: Actions by the Senate, the Judiciary Committee, and the President," Congressional Research Service Report for Congress RL 33225 (Washington, DC: Congressional Research Service, 2010).

50 Amy Goldstein and Alec MacGillis, "Kagan Makes Bipartisan Appeal in Supreme Court Confirmation Hearings," *Washington Post*, June 30, 2010.

51 Ibid.

52 Lori A. Ringhand and Paul M. Collins, Jr., "May It Please the Senate: An Empirical Analysis of the Senate Judiciary Committee Hearings of Supreme Court Nominees, 1939–2009," *American University Law Review*, vol. 60, no. 3 (February 2011): 589–641.

53 Stephen L. Carter, "The Confirmation Mess," *Harvard Law Review*, vol. 101, no. 6 (April 1988): 1185–1201.

54 Dion Farganis and Justin Wedeking, "'No Hints, No Forecasts, No Previews': An Empirical Analysis of Supreme Court Nominee Candor from Harlan to Kagan," *Law and Society Review*, vol. 45, no. 3 (September 2011): 525–559.

55 Ibid., 525–559, 554.

56 For a discussion of the committee voting process and historical outcomes for lower court nominees, see Barry J. McMillion, "U.S. Circuit and District Court Nominations: Senate Rejections and Committee Votes Other Than to Report Favorably, 1939–2014." Congressional Research Service, R40470, May 29, 2014 (https://www.fas.org/sgp/crs/misc/R40470.pdf).

57 Senate Judiciary Committee votes on Supreme Court nominations from 1971–present can be found an the Committee's webpage (http://www.judiciary.senate.gov/nominations/supreme-court/committee-votes).

58 Amanda Becker, "Senators' Use of 'Anonymous Hold' Contributes to Backlog of Stalled Judicial Nominations," *Washington Post*, September 27, 2010.

59 Laura Kalman, *Abe Fortas: A Biography* (New Haven, CT: Yale University Press, 1990).

60 Sheldon Goldman, *Picking Federal Judges: Lower Court Selection from Roosevelt Through Reagan* (New Haven, CT: Yale University Press, 1997): 316.

61 Paul Kane, "Reid, Democrats Trigger 'Nuclear' Option: Eliminate Most Filibusters on Nominees," *Washington Post*, November 21, 2013.

62 Lee Epstein and Jeffrey A. Segal, *Advice and Consent: The Politics of Judicial Appointments* (New York, NY: Oxford University Press, 2005).

63 Ibid., 103.

64 Nancy Scherer, Brandon L. Bartels, and Amy Steigerwalt, "Sounding the Fire Alarm: The Role of Interest Groups in the Lower Federal Court Confirmation Process," *Journal of Politics*, vol. 70, no. 4 (October 2008): 1026–1039.

65 Lee Epstein and Jeffrey A. Segal, *Advice and Consent: The Politics of Judicial Appointments* (New York, NY: Oxford University Press, 2005): 107.

66 Ibid., 108.

67 Ibid.

68 Jeffrey A. Segal, Charles M. Cameron, and Albert D. Cover, "A Spatial Model of Roll Call Voting: Senators, Constituents, Presidents, and Interest Groups in Supreme Court Confirmations," *American Journal of Political Science*, vol. 36, no. 1 (February 1992): 96–121.

69 L. Marvin Overby, Beth M. Henschen, Michael H. Walsh, and Julie Strauss, "Courting Constituents? An Analysis of the Senate Confirmation Vote on Justice Clarence Thomas," *American Political Science Review*, vol. 86, no. 4 (December 1992): 997–1003.

70 Michael A. Fletcher and Charles Babington, "Miers, Under Fire from Right, Withdrawn as Court Nominee," *Washington Post*, October 28, 2005.

71 Gregory A. Caldeira and John R. Wright, "Lobbying for Justice: Organized Interests, Supreme Court Nominations, and the United States Senate," *American Journal of Political Science*, vol. 42, no. 2 (April 1998): 499–523.

72 John Anthony Maltese, "Anatomy of a Confirmation Mess: Recent Trends in the Federal Judicial Selection Process," JURIST Online Symposium, University of Pittsburgh School of Law, April 15, 2004 (http://jurist.law.pitt.edu/forum/symposium-jc/maltese-printer.php).

73 Lee Epstein, René Lindstädt, Jeffrey A. Segal, and Chad Westerland, "The Changing Dynamics of Senate Voting on Supreme Court Nominees," *Journal of Politics*, vol. 68, no. 2, (May 2006): 296–307.

74 Ibid.

75 Ibid., 303.

76 Lee Epstein and Jeffrey A. Segal, *Advice and Consent: The Politics of Judicial Appointments* (New York, NY: Oxford University Press, 2005): Figure 4.2.

77 Lauren Cohen Bell, "In Their Own Interest: Pressure Groups in the Federal Judicial Selection Process," in *Exploring Judicial Politics*, Mark C. Miller, ed. (New York, NY: Oxford University Press, 2009): Table 3.2.

78 Wendy L. Martinek, Mark Kemper, and Steven R. Van Winkle, "To Advise and Consent: The Senate and Lower Federal Court Nominations, 1977–1998," *Journal of Politics*, vol. 64, no. 2 (May 2002): 337–361.

79 Nancy Scherer, Brandon L. Bartels, and Amy Steigerwalt, "Sounding the Fire Alarm: The Role of Interest Groups in the Lower Federal Court Confirmation Process," *Journal of Politics*, vol. 70, no. 4 (October 2008): 1026–1039.

80 Ibid.; Wendy L. Martinek, Mark Kemper, and Steven R. Van Winkle, "To Advise and Consent: The Senate and Lower Federal Court Nominations, 1977–1998," *Journal of Politics*, vol. 64, no. 2 (May 2002): 337–361.

81 Nancy Scherer, Brandon L. Bartels, and Amy Steigerwalt, "Sounding the Fire Alarm: The Role of Interest Groups in the Lower Federal Court Confirmation Process," *Journal of Politics*, vol. 70, no. 4 (October 2008): 1026–1039.

82 Lauren Cohen Bell, *Warring Factions: Interest Groups, Money and the New Politics of Senate Confirmation* (Columbus, OH: The Ohio State University Press, 2002); Lauren Cohen Bell, "In Their Own Interest: Pressure Groups in the Federal Judicial Selection Process," *Exploring Judicial Politics*, Mark C. Miller, ed. (New York, NY: Oxford University Press, 2009).

83 Amy Steigerwalt, *Battle Over the Bench: Senators, Interest Groups, and Lower Court Confirmations* (Charlottesville, VA: University of Virginia Press, 2010).

84 Jeffrey Toobin, "The Obama Brief: The President Considers His Judicial Legacy," *The New Yorker*, October 27, 2014.

85 Michael Kiefer, "First Native American Woman Confirmed as Federal Judge," *USA Today*, May 16, 2014.

86 Although there are many published collections of *The Federalist Papers* that include additional commentary and analysis—such as Jacob E. Cooke, ed., *The Federalist* (Middletown, CT: Wesleyan University Press, 1961)—the original essays can be accessed online through the Library of Congress (http://thomas.loc.gov/home/histdox/fedpapers.html).

87 *The Antifederalist Papers*, No. 78–79. While the collected essays have been published in various forms with commentary and analysis—including Herbert J. Storing, ed., *The Anti-Federalist* (Chicago, IL: University of Chicago Press, 2006)—the original essays can be accessed online through various websites (e.g., http://www.thefederalistpapers.org/anti-federalist-papers).

88 Daniel Becker and Malia Reddick, *Judicial Selection Reform: Examples from Six States* (Des Moines, IA: American Judicature Society, 2003): 27–33.

89 Joseph H. Smith, "An Independent Judiciary: The Colonial Background," *University of Pennsylvania Law Review*, vol. 124, no. 5 (May 1976): 1104–1156.

90 Sari S. Escovitz, *Judicial Selection and Tenure* (Chicago, IL: American Judicature Society, 1975): 4.

91 Larry C. Berkson, "Judicial Selection in the United States: A Special Report," *Judicature*, vol. 64, no. 4 (October 1980): 176–193, 176.

92 The archetypal examples of direct democracy mechanisms are the initiative and the referendum. Citizens who secure enough signatures on a petition can have a proposed state law or state constitutional amendment placed on the ballot (for the initiative process) or a proposal to repeal a law previously enacted by the state legislature (for the referendum process) to be voted upon by the electorate.

93 Chris W. Bonneau and Melinda Gann Hall, *In Defense of Judicial Elections* (New York, NY: Routledge, 2009): Chapter 1.

94 See, for example, Kermit L. Hall, "Progressive Reform and the Decline of Democratic Accountability: The Popular Election of State Supreme Court Judges, 1850–1920," *American Bar Foundation Research Journal*, vol. 9, no. 2 (April 1984): 345–369.

95 Paul D. Carrington, "Judicial Independence and Democratic Accountability in Highest State Courts," *Law and Contemporary Problems*, vol. 61, no. 3 (Summer 1998): 79–126, 89–90.

96 After a 40-odd-year dalliance with gubernatorial appointment with legislative approval in the late 1800s and very early 1900s, Mississippi returned to popular election and, since 1994, uses nonpartisan elections for the selection of most of its judges.

97 Kermit L. Hall, "Progressive Reform and the Decline of Democratic Accountability: The Popular Election of State Supreme Court Judges, 1850–1920," *American Bar Foundation Research Journal*, vol. 9, no. 2 (April 1984): 345–369, 346–347.

98 Mark S. Hurwitz, "Judge Lopez Torres and New York's Trial Judge Nominating Process," *Justice System Journal* vol. 28, no. 2 (May 2007): 243–246.

99 The state statute mandating the party convention system was the subject of a U.S. Supreme Court case, *New York Board of Elections v. Lopez Torres* (552 U.S. 196, 2008). Margarita Lopez Torres was a judge on the Kings County civil court and claimed that party leaders opposed her nomination for a seat on the New York Supreme Court because she declined to engage in patronage politics. She—along with other candidates who had been unsuccessful in securing the nomination of their party, voters who had supported these candidates, and a public-interest organization called Common Cause—was able to obtain an injunction from the federal district court that required the use of a direct primary to select party nominees for the general election. Though that injunction was affirmed by the U.S. Court of Appeals for the Second Circuit, it was struck down and the challenge to the convention system invalidated by the Supreme Court because, in the Court's words, "None of our cases establishes an individual's constitutional right to have a 'fair shot' at winning the party's nomination" (552 U.S., 196, 205). See Linda Greenhouse, "Supreme Court Rebuffs a Challenge to New York's Way of Picking Its Judges," *New York Times*, January 17, 2008.

100 Maureen A. Flanagan, *America Reformed: Progressives and Progressivisms, 1890s-1920s* (Chicago, IL: Oxford University Press, 2006).

101 Members of the legal profession were especially agitated by partisan elections because they saw them as democratic beards intended to disguise the unfettered power of party bosses to select judges. See F. Andrew Hanssen, "Learning about Judicial Independence: Institutional Change in the State Courts," *Journal of Legal Studies*, vol. 33 (June 2004): 431–473, 449–450. In fact, their disgruntlement with partisan judicial elections contributed to the creation of bar associations.

102 There have been southern voices of dissent, for example, in Georgia, in the aftermath of a heated state supreme court race in 2004. Though the race was ostensibly nonpartisan, players in both major parties were quite active, leading the governor and others to suggest that partisan elections would be preferable to elections that were formally nonpartisan but in practice partisan. See Matthew J. Streb and Brian Frederick, "Judicial Reform and the Future of Judicial Elections," in *Running for Judge: The Rising Political, Financial, and Legal Stakes of Judicial Elections*, Matthew J. Streb, ed. (New York, NY: New York University Press, 2007): 210–211.

103 Mark S. Hurwitz, "Selection System, Diversity and the Michigan Supreme Court," *Wayne Law Review*, vol. 56 (Fall 2010): 691–704, 701–703.

104 Rachel Paine Caufield, "How the Pickers Pick: Finding a Set of Best Practices for Judicial Nominating Commissions," *Fordham Urban Law Journal*, vol. 34, no. 1 (2006): 163–202.

105 American Judicature Society, *Judicial Merit-selection: Current Status* (Chicago, IL: American Judicature Society, 2003).

106 Rachel Paine Caufield, *Inside Merit-selection: A National Survey of Judicial Nominating Commissioners* (Chicago, IL: American Judicature Society, 2012): 15.

107 Ibid.

108 Ibid., 22.

109 Federal judges serving on courts created by Congress under its authority under Article I (rather than Article III) have more limited terms of office. So, for example, the five judges who serve on the U.S. Court of Appeals for the Armed Forces serve 15-year terms.

110 Malia Reddick, "Merit-selection: A Review of the Social Scientific Literature," *Dickinson Law Review*, vol. 106 (Spring 2002): 729–745.

111 Mark S. Hurwitz and Drew Noble Lanier, "Explaining Judicial Diversity: The Differential Ability of Women and Minorities to Attain Seats on State Supreme and Appellate Courts," *State Politics and Policy Quarterly*, vol. 3, no. 4 (Winter 2003): 329–352.

112 Greg Goelzhauser, "Diversifying State Supreme Courts," *Law and Society Review*, vol. 45, no. 3 (September 2011): 761–781.

113 Descriptive representation refers to the congruence of relevant characteristics (e.g., race, ethnicity, gender) between representatives and those they represent while substantive representation refers to the situation in which representatives advance constituents' interests. See Hanna Pitkin, *The Concept of Representation* (Berkeley, CA: University of California Press, 1967).

114 Kathleen A. Bratton and Rorie L. Spill, "Existing Diversity and Judicial Selection: The Role of the Appointment Method in Establishing Gender Diversity in State Supreme Courts," *Social Science Quarterly*, vol. 83, no. 2 (June 2002): 504–518. See, also, Mark S. Hurwitz and Drew Noble Lanier, "Explaining Judicial Diversity: The Differential Ability of Women and Minorities to Attain Seats on State Supreme and Appellate Courts," *State Politics and Policy Quarterly*, vol. 3, no. 4 (Winter 2003): 329–352.

115 Quoted in Lawyers' Committee for Civil Rights Under Law, "Answering the Call for a More Diverse Judiciary: A Review of State Judicial Selection Models and Their Impact on Creating a More Diverse Judiciary," *Report of the Judicial Independence and Access to the Courts Project* (June 2005): 5.

116 Fund for Modern Courts, *The Success of Women and Minorities in Achieving Judicial Office* (New York, NY: Author, 1985).

117 Kathleen A. Bratton and Rorie L. Spill, "Existing Diversity and Judicial Selection: The Role of the Appointment Method in Establishing Gender Diversity in State Supreme Courts," *Social Science Quarterly*, vol. 83, no. 2 (June 2002): 504–518.

118 Malia Reddick, Michael J. Nelson, and Rachel Paine Caufield, "Racial and Gender Diversity on State Courts: An AJS Study," *Judges' Journal*, vol. 48, no. 3 (Summer 2009): 28–32.

119 Gary Crowdus and Dan Georgakas, "Thinking About the Power of Images: An Interview with Spike Lee," *Cinéaste*, vol. 26, no. 2 (2001): 4–9; Matthew W. Hughey, "Cinethetic Racism: White Redemption and Black Sterotypes in 'Magical Negro' Films," *Social Problems*, vol. 56, no. 3 (August 2009): 543–577; Cerise L. Glenn and Landra J. Cunningham, "The Power of Black Magic: The Magical Negro and White Salvation in Film," *Journal of Black Studies*, vol. 40, no. 2 (November 2009): 135–152.

120 Greg Goelzhauser, "Diversifying State Supreme Courts," *Law and Society Review*, vol. 45, no. 3 (September 2011): 761–781

121 Lisa M. Holmes and Jolly A. Emrey, "Court Diversification: Staffing the State Courts of Last Resort through Interim Appointments," *Justice System Journal*, vol. 27, no. 1 (2006): 1–13.

122 All states but two that elect their judges permit governors to make interim appointments. The two exceptions are Illinois and Louisiana. See Lisa M. Holmes and Jolly A. Emrey, "Court Diversification: Staffing the State Courts of Last Resort through Interim Appointments," *Justice System Journal*, vol. 27, no. 1 (2006): 1–13, 1.

123 Henry R. Glick and Craig Emmert, "Selection Systems and Judicial Characteristics: The Recruitment of State Supreme Court Judges." *Judicature*, vol. 70, no. 4 (December-January 1987): 228–235.

124 Malia Reddick, "Judging the Quality of Judicial Selection Methods: Merit Selection, Elections, and Judicial Discipline." American Judicature Society (http://www.judicialselection.us/uploads/documents/Judging_the_Quality_of_Judicial_Sel_8EF0DC3806ED8.pdf).

125 Russell S. Sobel and Joshua C. Hall, "The Effect of Judicial Selection Processes on Judicial Quality: The Role of Partisan Politics," *Cato Journal*, vol. 27, no. 1 (Winter 2007): 69–82.

126 Stephen J. Choi, G. Mitu Gulati, and Eric A. Posner, "Professionals or Politicians: The Uncertain Empirical Case for an Elected Rather Than Appointed Judiciary," *Journal of Law, Economics, and Organizations*, vol. 26, no. 2 (August 2010): 290–336.

127 Melinda Gann Hall, "Electoral Politics and Strategic Voting in State Supreme Courts," *Journal of Politics*, vol. 54, no. 2 (May 1992): 427–446; Melinda Gann Hall, "Constituent Influence in State Supreme Courts: Conceptual Notes and a Case Study," *Journal of Politics*, vol. 49, no. 4 (1987): 1117–1124.

128 See, for example, Paul Brace and Melinda Gann Hall, "The Interplay of Preferences, Case Facts, Context, and Structure in the Politics of Judicial Choice," *Journal of Politics*, vol. 59, no. 4 (November 1997): 1206–1231; Paul Brace and Melinda Gann Hall, "Studying Courts Comparatively: The View from the American States," *Political Research Quarterly*, vol. 48, no. 1 (March 1995): 5–29; Paul Brace and Melinda Gann Hall, "Neo-Institutionalism and Dissent in State Supreme Courts," *Journal of Politics*, vol. 52, no. 1 (February 1990): 54–70.

129 Melinda Gann Hall, "Justices as Representatives: Elections and Judicial Politics in American States," *American Politics Quarterly*, vol. 23, no. 4 (October 1995): 485–503.

130 Quoted in Matthew J. Streb, "The Study of Judicial Elections," in *Running for Judge: The Rising Political, Financial, and Legal Stakes of Judicial Elections*, Matthew J. Streb, ed. (New York, NY: New York University Press, 2007): 10.

131 American Bar Association Commission on the 21st Century Judiciary, *Justice in Jeopardy* (Chicago, IL: American Bar Association, 2003): 125.

132 Chris W. Bonneau, "Patterns of Campaign Spending and Electoral Competition in State Supreme Court Elections," *Justice System Journal*, vol. 25, no. 1 (2004): 21–38.

133 Chris W. Bonneau, "The Dynamics of Campaign Spending in State Supreme Court Elections," in *Running for Judge: The Rising Political, Financial, and Legal Stakes of Judicial Elections*, Matthew J. Streb, ed. (New York, NY: New York University Press, 2007): 63.

134 Matthew J. Streb, "The Study of Judicial Elections," in *Running for Judge: The Rising Political, Financial, and Legal Stakes of Judicial Elections*, Matthew J. Streb, ed. (New York, NY: New York University Press, 2007), 1.

135 Chris W. Bonneau and Melinda Gann Hall, *In Defense of Judicial Elections* (New York, NY: Routledge, 2009): Chapter 2.

136   For an extended treatment of the effect of campaign spending in state supreme court elections, see Melinda Gann Hall, *Attacking Judges: How Campaign Advertising Influences State Supreme Court Elections* (Redwood City, CA: Stanford University Press, 2014).

137   Ibid.

138   Chris W. Bonneau and Melinda Gann Hall, *In Defense of Judicial Elections* (New York, NY: Routledge, 2009): Chapter 3.

139   Melinda Gann Hall and Chris W. Bonneau, "Mobilizing Interest: The Effects of Money on Ballot Roll-Off in State Supreme Court Elections," *American Journal of Political Science*, vol. 52, no. 3 (July 2008): 457–470; Melinda Gann Hall, "Ballot Roll-Off in Judicial Elections: Contextual and Institutional Influences on Voter Participation in the American States," paper presented at the Annual Meeting of the American Political Science Association, Atlanta, GA, September 2–5, 1999.

140   Larry Aspin, William K. Hall, Jean Bax, and Celeste Montoya, "Thirty Years of Judicial Retention Elections: An Update," *Social Science Journal*, vol. 37, no. 1 (January 2000): 1–17, 12.

141   Chris W. Bonneau, "The Effects of Campaign Spending in State Supreme Court Elections." *Political Research Quarterly*, vol. 60, no. 3 (September 2007): 489–498, 490.

142   Chris W. Bonneau, "The Effects of Campaign Spending in State Supreme Court Elections." *Political Research Quarterly*, vol. 60, no. 3 (September 2007): 489–498.

143   Chris W. Bonneau and Melinda Gann Hall, *In Defense of Judicial Elections* (New York, NY: Routledge, 2009): Chapter 4.

144   Leslie Larson, "Sandra Day O'Connor Decries Letting 'Cash in the Court' with Judicial Elections," *New York Daily News*, July 11, 2014.

145   Sara C. Benesh, "Understanding Public Confidence in American Courts," *Journal of Politics*, vol. 68, no. 3 (August 2006): 697–707; James P. Wenzel, Shaun Bowler, and David J. Lanoue, "The Sources of Public Confidence in State Courts," *American Politics Research*, vol. 31, no. 2 (March 2003): 191–211. Note that these studies reach different conclusions with regard to those who have experience serving as jurors.

146   Sara C. Benesh, "Understanding Public Confidence in American Courts," *Journal of Politics*, vol. 68, no. 3 (August 2006): 697–707.

147   Benesh found selection-method effects while Wenzel and his colleagues suggested that higher education levels condition the effects of selection-methods on public confidence. See also Damon M. Cann and Jeff Yates, "Homegrown Institutional Legitimacy: Assessing Citizens' Diffuse Support for State Courts," *American Politics Research*, vol. 36, no. 2 (March 2008): 297–329.

148   James L. Gibson, *Electing Judges: The Surprising Effects of Campaigning on Judicial Legitimacy* (Chicago, IL: University of Chicago Press, 2012); James L. Gibson, "Challenges to the Impartiality of State Supreme Courts: Legitimacy Theory and 'New-Style' Judicial Campaigns," *American Political Science Review*, vol. 102, no. 1 (February, 2008): 59–75; James L. Gibson, Jeffrey A. Gottfried, Michael X. Delli Carpini, and Kathleen Hall Jamieson, "The Effects of Judicial Campaign Activity on the Legitimacy of Courts: A Survey-Based Experiment," *Political Research Quarterly*, vol. 64, no. 3 (September 2011): 545–558.

149   Martin A. Dyckman, *A Most Disorderly Court: Scandal and Reform in the Florida Judiciary* (Gainesville, FL: University Press of Florida, 2008).

150   See, for example, Abraham Abramovsky and Jonathan I. Edelstein, "Prosecuting Judges for Ethical Violations: Are Criminal Sanctions Constitutional and Prudent, or Do They Constitute a Threat to Judicial Independence?" *Fordham Urban Law Journal*, vol. 33, no. 3 (March 2006): 727–774.

151   556 U.S. 868 (2009).

152   Charles G. Geyh, "Why Judicial Elections Stink," *Ohio State Law Journal*, vol. 64, no. 1 (2003): 43–79.

153   Chris W. Bonneau and Melinda Gann Hall, *In Defense of Judicial Elections* (New York, NY: Routledge, 2009): Chapter 5.

154   536 U.S. 765 (2002).

CIVIL LAW

"As a general rule never take your whole fee in advance, nor any more than a small retainer. When fully paid beforehand, you are more than a common mortal if you can feel the same interest in the case, as if something was still in prospect for you, as well as for your client."

—Abraham Lincoln, Lawyer and Sixteenth President
of the United States[1]

"It's the perfect definition of a settlement. Both parties felt they didn't get what they wanted."

—David Geffen, Music Mogul and Partner at
DreamWorks Studios[2]

Did you hear the one about the old lady who spilled McDonald's coffee on herself, sued, and won millions of dollars?[3] Ridiculous—right? For most people this story illustrates everything that is wrong with the legal system in America. How can a person get millions of dollars for spilling coffee on herself? In fact, however, the case illustrates how the media can distort the legal process,[4] how individual narratives can dominate an issue, and how the myths about civil law to which people ascribe are a far cry from the complexity of reality. Does the case (and its implications for civil law) seem any different knowing that McDonald's required its franchisees to serve coffee at 180–190 degrees Fahrenheit, which can cause third-degree burns in mere seconds?[5] Or that the company had received more than 700 complaints in the decade prior to the accident, settling similar cases of scalding injuries by paying more than half a million dollars? Does it matter that the 79-year-old woman who brought the suit suffered severe burns on her pelvic region that required skin grafts, 8 days of hospitalization, and two years of medical treatment? Or that she asked the company for $20,000 to cover her medical expenses but the company only offered $800? Does it matter that after she hired an attorney, but before trial, the company declined to settle the matter for $90,000 and further rejected a mediator's suggestion of $225,000? Or that the jury's punitive damage award of $2.7 million was based on one or two days of the company's coffee revenues, and that the judge later reduced this amount to $480,000? What about the fact that, on appeal, the parties ultimately settled out of court for an undisclosed amount? Does it matter that McDonald's and other retailers continue to sell their coffee at scalding temperatures?[6]

Whatever one might think of the merits of the case, it is plain from the contextual details that the suit was about far more than someone suing a large corporation to

Image 6.1 McDonald's
*The McDonald's coffee
case is perhaps the most
important example of
the myths associated
with civil litigation.*
saknakorn/
Shutterstock.com.

make a quick buck. Nonetheless, the simplified version has been fodder for comedians,[7] television sitcoms,[8] commercials,[9] and popular songwriters,[10] while critics and legal reformers continually cite it as an example of America's growing thirst for frivolous lawsuits by opportunistic lawyers and their greedy clients. In this sense, the case has become a hegemonic (that is, dominant) narrative for civil litigation reformers that is difficult for their opponents to counter.[11] Yet the reality is that the case was neither frivolous nor part of a trend. In fact, the evidence suggests that only a small minority of injured parties file a **tort suit** (a case in which one party sues another for an alleged injury or harm).[12] Further, data from the National Center for State Courts demonstrates that tort cases represent less than 6 percent of all civil caseloads, a percentage that has been declining over time.[13] Instead, contract and small-claims cases combine for about three-fourths of all civil cases.[14] In short, the myth regarding the prevalence of tort litigation is contradicted by the reality that such suits constitute only a small proportion of civil litigation.

The notion that civil litigation in America is a growing trend driven by opportunism, manipulation, and greed is a powerful myth that distorts reality and distracts policymakers and their constituents from focusing on real issues involving both civil law and larger policy matters.[15] In contrast to the greed myth, the scholarly community has investigated the structural developments in American society that cause Americans to seek recourse in the civil justice system. Legal scholar Lawrence Friedman argued that there is a growing cultural expectation of "total justice" in America—that is, of recompense for all injuries and losses.[16] Friedman and others have charted an American legal culture shift from low expectations regarding rights in the nineteenth century—as social and private insurance for disasters was virtually nonexistent—to a modern culture of high expectations for compensation for all injuries and losses that are not the victim's fault—driven by medical, technical, and social developments.[17] Thus, the expansion of legal rights and protections only serves to increase expectations for total justice.[18]

Building on Friedman's work, legal scholar Robert Kagan explained that, while litigiousness is also present in other advanced industrialized countries, unlike in these nations, the U.S. is dominated by **adversarial legalism**. Adversarial legalism is a legal style that emphasizes lawyer-dominated litigation for making and implementing public policy in addition to resolving disputes:

> Adversarial legalism encourages and facilitates the articulation of new justice-claims and ideas. Ready recourse to a politically responsive judiciary enables dissenters to attack the official dogma of government officials, corporate toxicologists, medical experts, highway planners, and penologists. Repeatedly, adversarial legalism has enabled political underdogs to demand just rights from the government, first and foremost in the case of the civil rights movement, but also in the quest for more equitable electoral districts, more humane conditions in prisons and mental institutions, and more compassionate welfare administration.[19]

In other nations, Kagan argues, adversarial litigation is constrained and judges and bureaucrats professionally manage public policy.[20]

The cause of adversarial legalism in America is twofold.[21] First, as already noted, the expectation for total justice has grown over time. Second, the basic governmental structure in the United States—a particularly decentralized and fragmented system of separation of powers[22] and federalism[23] based on a "deep distrust of centralized authority and . . . [a] glorified view of self-reliance"[24]—limits the ability of the American state to meet these demands through centralized administrative institutions. This means that lawyers, as opposed to judges or other bureaucrats, have filled the void, and not simply through litigation itself but also through threats and perceived threats of litigation that significantly influence how organizations behave. Indeed, political scientist Thomas Burke has characterized the American system as one that produces political incentives for activists, interest groups, and policymakers to encourage litigious policies.[25] Thus, we should not be surprised that research shows that, for political reasons, Congress generally chooses to allow private litigation to be the vehicle for policy enforcement rather than delegating authority to a regulatory agency.[26]

The effects of adversarial legalism are complex. On the one hand, it has provided groups who might not otherwise have access to the system opportunities to influence public policy through litigation—something we discuss in greater detail later in this chapter. Thus, American tort law is more responsive to popular pressures for social change and for holding big business and the government accountable.[27] At the same time, the costs of adversarial legalism are high, both monetarily (as lawyers routinely take 40 percent or more of damage awards[28]) and structurally (as the system promotes contentiousness, uncertainty, delay, and unpredictability). Regardless of the costs and benefits of this system in the abstract, it is quite clear that the judiciary, and particularly lawyers, have become a critical part of the American process of governance.

MYTH AND REALITY IN CIVIL LAW

MYTH	REALITY
Civil lawsuits are driven by manipulative lawyers and individual greed.	Civil litigation is inherent in the decentralized American governmental system that forces individuals to take their grievances to court.
Litigiousness is a growing problem.	The vast majority of disputes never end up in court and civil litigation rates have been stable for decades (and recently have been in decline).
Modern tort law developed because of opportunistic lawyers.	Modern tort law developed because the government failed to protect people from the hazards of the industrial revolution.
Civil litigation involves individuals seeking monetary damages from large corporations.	Civil litigation can be a tool for social change.
Tort cases dominate civil caseloads.	Tort cases represent a small percentage of civil caseloads.
Most tort cases go to trial and the numbers are increasing.	Few tort cases are resolved through trial and the number is declining.
Injured victims always win at trial and are awarded large damages.	Injured victims often lose at trial and, if they prevail, awards are often modest.
Punitive damage awards are common and large.	Punitive damages are rarely awarded and modest in amount.
Alternative Dispute Resolution processes such as mediation and arbitration are neutral, independent, and fair.	Alternative Dispute Resolution processes favor repeat players and "haves" particularly when set "in house" or with private third parties.
Class action suits advantage plaintiffs.	Although class action suits can benefit plaintiffs, the use of binding arbitration has largely neutralized any plaintiff advantage.

COPING WITH DISPUTES

How do disputes arise? It is not remarkable to observe that people can disagree over just about anything (including how exams are graded and what constitutes a reasonable number of pages for a college-level reading assignment). Disputes over politics are settled at the ballot box. Disagreements over sporting teams are settled on the playing field. And disputes about the best film are resolved at the Oscars—at least according to members of the Academy of Motion Picture Arts and Sciences! Disputes are commonplace. But only a small fraction of disputes result in a court case being filed.[29]

A **civil dispute** is a legal disagreement between two or more principle individuals or organizations. Divorce, child custody, failure to pay for services rendered (or failure to provide services for which payment has been rendered), defective products, wrongdoing

by business associates, medical malpractice, and injuries sustained in automobile accidents are all examples of civil disputes. Unlike criminal matters, where the state initiates
the dispute against an individual for violating the law, civil matters are typically between
two or more private parties—usually over monetary issues or the performance of duties—
and generally do not involve the state as a formal party to the dispute.[30] In general, civil
matters fall into three categories: torts, contracts, and property.

Torts are wrongful acts (not involving the breach of an agreement, which falls under
contracts), whether intentional or accidental, from which injury occurs to another. The
goals of tort law are to provide compensation to the victim as well as to deter others from
engaging in the same harmful behavior.[31] Injured parties often seek damages for loss of
earnings, pain and suffering, and present and future medical expenses. Common examples of torts include trespass, assault, battery, negligence, products liability, and intentional infliction of emotional distress. So, for example, if the latex gloves Dexter Morgan
(Miami-Metro Police Department forensic blood spatter expert during the day and serial
killer at night) wore to avoid leaving evidence when he dispatched his victims in the
Showtime series *Dexter* gave him an allergic reaction, he might have grounds to file a tort
case against the manufacturer of said latex gloves.

Contracts are legally enforceable agreements containing one or more promises. For a
contract to be considered valid or legally binding, there must be an offer, the acceptance
of the offer, and consideration—that is, something of value must be promised in exchange
for a specific action or nonaction (e.g., one party must pay a price and one person must
provide goods or services for that price). Some (though not all) contracts must to be in
writing in order to be legally enforced.[32] Common examples of contracts include residential leases, employment agreements, and bills of sale for personal property such as an
automobile. Whether written or oral, a contract that obligates an individual to do something illegal—such as steal a roommate's property to fence for money to defray the costs
of a friend's spring break trip to South Padre Island—is never enforceable.

Property law deals with ownership and is divided into two categories: real property
and personal property. **Real property** consists of land and objects permanently attached
to land, with all other property considered **personal property** (or, alternatively, **chattel
property**). So, for example, if lumber is merely sitting in a pile on a piece of property then
it is not considered real property but, instead, is considered personal property. If, however, that lumber is used to construct a fence on the property then it is, indeed, considered part of the real property constituted by the land on which it is built. Questions as to
whether something is permanently attached to land (and hence real property as opposed
to personal property) are answered on the basis of how attached the property in question
is. So, for example, the Fleetwood Bounder RV used by Walter White and Jesse Pinkman
for cooking meth in the HBO series *Breaking Bad* would not have been considered part
of the real property constituted by Jesse's house when it was parked in the driveway. But,
if Walter and Jesse had made modifications to the RV to make it inoperable, poured a
foundation for it in Jesse's backyard, and permanently attached it to that foundation it
would, indeed, have been considered real property.

In terms of the law, it is important to understand how disputes emerge and are transformed before they enter the legal system, meaning before attorneys are contacted and
lawsuits are filed. As illustrated in Figure 6.1, there are three stages in the emergence
and transformation of disputes: 1) **naming**, 2) **blaming**, and 3) **claiming**.[33] First, a party
must realize that a particular experience has been injurious—i.e., naming. A party may
have either a perceived or unperceived injury. Perceived injuries are readily observ-
able such as a broken arm, property damage, or a defective product. In these cases it is

FIGURE 6.1
Early Stages of the Civil Dispute Process: Emergence and Transformation

relatively easy to name the injury. Unperceived injuries are those that are not so obvious, such as local residents getting cancer from a tainted water supply, shipyard workers getting sick from asbestos in the workplace, or homebuyers who are subject to unfair loan contracts. The injury has occurred (or is in process) but the person suffering it has not (yet) perceived it.

The process of transforming unperceived injuries to perceived injuries is arguably the most crucial part of the civil litigation process as it determines both the level and kind of disputing that will ultimately make it to courts. For example, historically shipyard workers took for granted that they would have trouble breathing after 10 years of installing insulation and only viewed their condition as injurious when asbestosis became an acknowledged "disease" and the basis of a claim for compensation.[34] The evidence demonstrates that individuals from groups with lower status (socioeconomic status or otherwise) are more likely to perceive and identify discrimination in the workplace than are those from groups with comparatively higher status.[35] For example, racial and ethnic minorities—particularly African Americans and Hispanics—are more likely to perceive workplace discrimination than are whites. Other examples include women in comparison to men, married people in comparison to non-married people, parents in comparison to non-parents, union members in comparison to non-union members, and government workers compared to private sector workers.[36] Thus, the interaction of individual characteristics with institutional settings determines whether experiences will be perceived as injurious or not. Further, similar research shows that this is true not only at the naming stage but throughout the entire dispute process.[37]

The second stage in the emergence and transformation of disputes occurs when a perceived injurious experience becomes a grievance—i.e., blaming. Blaming "takes place

Image 6.2 Asbestos
This February 1942 photograph was published with the following caption: "Transformer manufacture. It's a formidable task, but Jack Hassel can wind one of these asbestos insulated low volts coils in a day. Essential to America's war efforts, these asbestos coils are used in air cooled transformers which are explosion-proof, hence advantageous for use in ships, mines and large buildings. Westinghouse, Sharon, Pennsylvania." Should workers who handled asbestos be compensated for their injuries by the companies they worked for? Prints and Photographs Division, Library of Congress, Washington, D.C.

when the perceived injury becomes a grievance that is attributed to the fault of another individual or social entity. The attribution of fault is an indication that the injury has become a grievance."[38] The injured party feels wronged and desires that the party at fault do something in response. A dramatized illustration of blaming is depicted in the early part of *Erin Brockovich*, starring Julia Roberts as the eponymous character of the 2000 film. Erin is tasked with reading some real estate files pertaining to Pacific Gas & Electric's (PG&E) offer to purchase the home of Donna Jensen, who resided in Hinkley, California, near a compressor station owned and operated by the power company. Though Jensen had several tumors and her husband suffered from Hodgkin's Disease,[39] they did not connect their medical conditions with the chromium they knew was used by PG&E at the compressor station. Nor did other Hinkley residents who were part of the cancer cluster in the area. Only after extensive investigative work by Brockovich did those affected engage in blaming.

Finally, a claim is transformed into a dispute when it is rejected in whole or in part. "Rejection need not be expressed by words. Delay that the claimant construes as resistance is just as much a rejection as is a compromise offer (partial rejection) or an outright refusal."[40] In one key scene in *Erin Brockovich*, Julia Robert's character undertakes the grueling task of getting all 634 plaintiffs to agree to binding **arbitration**—submission of the dispute to a third party whose decision is final—rather than proceeding to court. When asked by an incredulous colleague how she was able to accomplish this Herculean task, Erin flippantly says, "I just went out there and performed sexual favors. Six hundred and thirty-four blow jobs in five days. . . . I'm really quite tired." Flippancy aside, however, her efforts were motivated by the fact that PG&E could engage in endless appeals and other tactics to delay settlement. A settlement did not need to be expressly rejected by PG&E for the claim to be transformed into a dispute.

Research has long demonstrated that only a small fraction of injurious experiences ever mature into disputes.[41] Attrition occurs at the earliest stages of the process for a host of reasons: experiences may not be perceived as injurious, perceptions may not ripen into grievances, and grievances may only be voiced to friends and family but not to the individual the aggrieved person has determined is at fault. Given the high attrition rate for injurious experiences, it is somewhat surprising that at any given time roughly half of all low- and middle-income households in the U.S. are engaged in a civil matter that has risen to the level of a dispute, with some states and communities having even higher rates.[42] The most common disputes focus on personal finances and consumer issues such as problems with creditors, insurance companies, being denied credit, and tax difficulties. Similarly common are housing and real property issues, including unsafe living conditions, utility disputes, landlord-tenant disagreements, and real estate transactions. People also routinely deal with community and regional matters, including inadequate police and other municipal services, environmental hazards, and opposition to the location of facilities. Family and domestic issues including divorce and child support are also prevalent, as are employment issues such as job discrimination, working conditions, and compensation and benefits. Also relatively common are personal or economic injury matters, wills and estates, and health-related matters.[43]

What happens to these disputes? Just as in the earliest stages of the dispute process there is once again a high level of attrition moving from the dispute stage to the lawsuit stage.[44] An attorney is consulted in merely one in three of all disputes. In another third, no action is taken at all. Individuals handle approximately one in four disputes on their own initiative without involving or engaging the legal process in any way. Finally, about one out of every 10 times, individuals seek advice from someone not involved in the legal process, such as a friend, family member, or work associate. Thus, the civil justice system plays no formal role in two-thirds of the civil disputes that arise among low- and moderate-income people.[45] That proportion is far higher if injuries and grievances that do not mature to the dispute stage are included. Simply consulting an attorney would likely change this situation and make legal action more common since research demonstrates that lawyers can provide information about choices and consequences of which clients may have been previously unaware; offer a forum for testing the reality of the client's perspective; help identify, explore, organize, and negotiate client problems; and give emotional and social support to clients.[46]

Family and domestic matters account for roughly three-fourths of civil disputes. At the other end of the spectrum, only one-fourth to one-third of disputes involving health, employment, financial, consumer, housing, property, personal, or economic injury are brought to the civil justice system.[47] The most common reasons that individuals give for not involving the civil justice system is that it would not help the situation, it would cost too much, the issue was not really a problem, and they could handle it on their own.[48]

Legal reformers have engaged in substantial efforts over time to equalize access for people of low and moderate incomes to the later stages of the dispute process. For example, advocates have argued for waivers of court costs, the creation of small-claims courts, and provisions for legal aid and *pro bono* services.[49] Note that these reforms, because they seek to facilitate the transformation of disputes into lawsuits, do nothing to transform injurious experiences into grievances or grievances into disputes, hence, they do not touch the vast majority of civil problems in society. It is not surprising, then, when research continually demonstrates that, contrary to the popular myth, very few aggrieved persons in the supposedly litigious U.S. ever seek redress.[50]

ALTERNATIVES TO GOING TO COURT: TAKING YOUR LUMPS, VIOLENCE, AND ADR

Parties seeking a resolution short of litigation have essentially two categories of options: 1) individual methods and 2) Alternative Dispute Resolution processes. The appeal of each of these methods can change as the process unfolds. For example, the response of an adversary may change the perception of the dispute. Alternatively, counseling may drain the dispute of moral content and diffuse the responsibility for problems. Or, delay, frustration, and despair may produce a change in objectives. Consider, for example, victims of job discrimination who often want the job or the promotion at the outset of a dispute but later become willing to settle for money based on what happens during the stages of the conflict.

The first individual method for resolving a dispute short of filing a lawsuit is simply to ignore it—so called "taking your lumps"—and/or withdraw from the situation.[51] People who blame themselves for an experience are not as likely to see it as injurious. And, if they do, they are less likely to give voice to a grievance about it and attribute blame. Indeed, one argument is that "the cult of competence, the individualism celebrated by American culture, inhibits people from acknowledging—to themselves, to others, and particularly to authority—that they have been injured, that they have been bettered by an adversary [citations omitted]."[52] And those who do blame themselves (at least in part) but nonetheless voice grievances are less likely to claim an injury and ask for redress by the party they perceive is to blame. In turn, when the claim is rejected, the individual who feels at least partially responsible for the perceived injurious experience in the first place is more likely to take her lumps at the dispute stage rather than contact an attorney and/or file a lawsuit.

The other individual method that people sometimes resort to rather than filing a lawsuit is violence: verbal abuse, vandalism, and assault.[53] The aggrieved party may perceive that this tactic will "let off steam" and defuse the conflict.[54] The opposite, however, is almost always the case. Direct confrontation, much like litigation, is likely to intensify feelings and focus blame. In other words, violence is likely to inflame the situation (not to mention open the door for criminal behavior in an effort to "let off steam"). An illustration of this can be seen in the 2002 Paramount film *Changing Lanes*. The protagonists of the film, played by acclaimed actors Ben Affleck and Samuel L. Jackson, engage in a vicious cycle of retribution after a car accident rather than pursue a civil action. Both, however, are left worse off because of it.

In recent years there has been marked growth in **Alternative Dispute Resolution** (ADR) as a substitute for going to court (or resorting to violence).[55] In the broadest sense, ADR is any means of settling a dispute outside the courtroom. Generally it takes one of three forms: negotiation, mediation, and arbitration. The most common form of ADR is **negotiation**, either on one's own behalf or through an attorney.[56] Negotiation is a give-and-take discussion with the goal of settling a dispute.[57] Though it may take place with or without an attorney, negotiation may be more effective with an attorney present since the threat of filing a lawsuit—implicit when dealing with lawyers—is likely to cause a party to take a claim more seriously and reach a settlement in order to stay out of court. Negotiation usually involves a face-to-face meeting and has the advantage of being wholly controlled by the parties or the attorneys without third-party intervention. This means that the parties have nothing to risk by negotiating; if negotiation fails, then mediation or arbitration are still available options.

Mediation is the attempt to settle a legal dispute through active participation of a third party (mediator) who works to find points of agreement and shepherd those in conflict to a mutually agreeable and fair result.[58] Mediators are neutral third parties who are trained in negotiation techniques that bring the parties together in an attempt to reach a settlement. Generally, a mediator will identify issues, explore possible bases for agreement, discuss the consequences of reaching an impasse, and encourage each party to accommodate the interests of the other party by finding a middle ground.[59] Mediated settlement proposals are not legally binding and must be acceptable to both sides. In other words, a mediated settlement does not preclude going to court and both parties to the mediation must voluntarily agree to accept the mediated settlement for it to be definitive. As an illustrative example, employee disputes in the workplace can be handled through various mediating structures in unions and firms such as grievance procedures, peer review forums, open-door policies, and employee assistance programs.[60]

Arbitration is more formal than mediation and, unlike mediation, is generally legally binding.[61] The binding nature of arbitration means that it carries greater risk for the parties than does negotiation or mediation, though perhaps not as much risk as formal litigation and a trial. In practice, arbitration is much like a simplified version of a trial that involves limited **discovery**—the formal process by which parties to a suit exchange information regarding the evidence and witnesses to be presented at trial—and simplified **rules of evidence**—the rules that control whether, when, and how evidence may be introduced before the adjudicator.[62] Hearings last a few hours a day for a few days or a week, followed by deliberation on the part of the arbitrator (or arbitrators[63]) and the issuance of a written decision that is generally not made public.

There are three categories of arbitration.[64] The first is **in-house arbitration**, in which a business has its own internal arbitration system. Businesses see them as valuable tools for controlling legal costs. However, many view in-house arbitration systems with deep suspicion. As one ADR consultant observed, "Some in-house arbitration programs are unaware of due process protocols and there is a belief that the playing field is not level."[65] For example, employees do not enjoy the opportunity to choose their own representation or have the document access necessary to prepare for the proceeding. The second is arbitration by independent third parties in forums funded by the business or industry in question.[66] For example, California's consumer protection law providing consumers with compensation for cars that repeatedly fail quality and performance standards (i.e., lemon law) requires that disputes are resolved in one of three forums that are administered by third parties but that are funded by automobile manufacturers. Finally, the third is **court-annexed** arbitration, which arises when the court diverts certain cases (after the suit has been filed but before a trial takes place) to arbitration rather than trial.[67] Generally, civil cases subject to court-annexed arbitration are those with smaller dollar amounts at stake and the arbitrators are drawn from pre-approved lists maintained by the court.[68]

Federal and state laws govern arbitration and it has long been used in labor, construction, and securities regulation.[69] Arbitration has increasingly been used by other businesses, as well, and it is now more common than not for individuals to find binding arbitration clauses in the fine print of contracts they are required to sign with banks,[70] nursing homes,[71] brokerage houses,[72] cell phone providers,[73] and even pest exterminators.[74] The same is true with regard to many websites (e.g., Amazon) and some social media platforms (e.g., Instagram). For example, the terms of service for Tinder,[75] a matchmaking site that uses geolocation to identify possible matches within a specified area of the user, includes the following language:

> By using the Service in any manner, you agree to the above arbitration agreement. In doing so, **YOU GIVE UP YOUR RIGHT TO GO TO COURT** to assert or defend any claims between you and the Company (except for matters that may be taken to small-claims court). **YOU ALSO GIVE UP YOUR RIGHT TO PARTICIPATE IN A CLASS ACTION OR OTHER CLASS PROCEEDING.** Your rights will be determined by a **NEUTRAL ARBITRATOR, NOT A JUDGE OR JURY**.[76]

The debate over mandatory arbitration has been heated and even more so in the wake of several controversial Supreme Court rulings in which the Court upheld the use of mandatory arbitration provisions.[77] In addition to the unease critics have with the mandatory nature of such provisions, the controversy is fueled by concerns that in-house and industry-funded arbitrators are not neutral but, instead, favor commercial interests. The assumption of legislatures and the Supreme Court is that they are, indeed, neutral and independent. As the Court declared in 1987: "[T]he streamlined procedures of arbitration do not entail any consequential restrictions on substantive rights."[78] The neutrality of arbitrators is assumed to be safeguarded by professional training and norms, including the general philosophy in ADR to operate under a "consensus" rather than "adversary" philosophy.[79]

There is research to suggest, however, that the neutrality of arbitration is more myth than reality and that, instead, arbitration processes are used as a weapon in the battle between opposing interests, with repeat players and "haves" (those with resources) benefiting at the expense of one-shotters and "have nots" (those without resources).[80] For example, arbitration clauses may not only bar virtually all judicial relief but may also allow companies to select the arbitrators and the location of the arbitration, exclude certain recoveries (e.g., punitive damages), shorten the statute of limitations to arbitrate a claim, minimize discovery, and eliminate any appeals.[81] Research by legal scholar Shauhin Talesh suggests that private, third-party arbitration does, indeed, favor repeat players and "haves," whereas government-run arbitration more fairly balances the opposing interests, even if it is not as neutral as litigation in terms of the outcomes.[82] In short, it is a myth that mediation and arbitration are automatically fair and neutral mechanisms of dispute resolution. The structure of ADR mechanisms plays an important role in determining whether the process is neutral and fair.

HOW DO WE KNOW?

Is There a Repeat Player Effect in Arbitration?

To assess whether repeat players enjoy an advantage over others when it comes to arbitration, industrial relations scholar Alexander J.S. Colvin analyzed employment arbitration outcomes in 1,213 American Arbitration Association (AAA) cases that resulted in awards from 2003–2007.[83] Colvin hypothesized that employers have advantages in employment arbitration because larger employers (more likely to be repeat players) have greater resources available to devote to cases, including the ability to hire better defense counsel. In addition, employers who are repeat players are more likely to have greater expertise with arbitration, expertise that can advantage them in the arbitration process. Additionally, arbitrators may be biased in favor of employers because they hope to be selected as an arbitrator by the employer in future cases, which Colvin describes as a repeat-employer-arbitrator bias. In order to test these hypotheses, Colvin identified those with more than one case in his data set as repeat employers. He then identified all cases in which the same arbitrator heard more than one case involving the same employer, creating repeat-employer-arbitrator pairings.

Colvin found that there is indeed a repeat employer effect, with employees winning 31.6 percent of cases involving one-shot employers compared to winning only 16.9 percent of cases involving repeat employers. In addition, Colvin found a substantial difference in the amount of damage awards: the mean damage award in cases involving one-shot employers was $40,546 as compared to the mean damage award of only $16,134 in cases involving repeat employers. In short, employees fared better in arbitration against one-shot employers both in terms of the likelihood of winning and the amount of the damage award. Colvin next analyzed the pairings of repeat employer and arbitrators. To separate out the general advantages of repeat employers, Colvin specifically focused only on the cases involving repeat employers. What he found was that the rate at which employees won was 18.6 percent for cases that did not involve a repeat-employer-arbitrator pairing and 12.0 percent for cases that did involve such a pairing. However, Colvin found no statistically significant difference in the mean damage award between the two pairings (repeat-employer-arbitrator versus nonrepeat-employer-arbitrator).

Finally, Colvin estimated regression models for employee wins and award amounts in order to identify the independent effect of each factor on the outcomes of interest; that is, the effect of each independent variable on the dependent variable controlling for the effect of the other independent variables. Each dependent variable (employee win and damages award amount) was regressed on the repeat employer, repeat-employer-arbitrator pairing, and employee self-representation independent variables. The models also included controls for possible changes over time and took into account employer-specific effects. The results showed that the chance of an employee win was 48.6 percent lower where the employer in the arbitration case was a repeat employer and 40.2 percent lower where the employer and the arbitrator were involved in more than one case together in the data set. Award amounts were significantly lower as well. What does this suggest? That the myth of arbitrators as neutral third parties is belied by the empirical evidence.

OBSTACLES TO ACCESSING THE COURTS

The normative ideal is of courts that are open and equally accessible to all: "One of the basic principles, one of the glories of the American system of justice is that the courthouse door is open to everyone—the humblest citizen, the indigent, the convicted felon, the illegal alien."[84] Notwithstanding this normative ideal, however, there are several factors that may serve as barriers to litigants seeking redress for a civil matter in the courts: financial costs, aversion to lawyers, emotional costs, daunting rules and procedures, and perceptions of unfairness. Each of these, singularly and in combination, can lead a litigant to settle a case or forego taking action all together. We discuss each in turn below.[85]

To begin with, going to court is a costly proposition. The cost for an attorney is an important part of it but there are numerous other costs associated with the process, including filing fees, witness fees, and the costs of sending notices to opponents. It might stand to reason, then, that an individual's income level would be predictive of the decision to seek out an attorney and file court cases, particularly given that government-funded legal aid (particularly for civil cases) in the U.S. is minimal.[86] While some research outside of the U.S. context does show such a relationship,[87] studies that focus on the American context suggest that income level makes little difference vis-à-vis the decision to enlist a lawyer to deal with a dispute or other legal need.[88] Instead, the decision depends on the nature of the dispute, with individuals across the income spectrum choosing to forego lawyers at about the same rates. In other words, high-, middle-, and low-income individuals are all more likely to consult a lawyer for some disputes (such as divorce, real estate, wills, and estates) than for others (such as community/municipal services or health care). Consequently, the costs of lawyers and filing fees can be obstacles to going to court for any American, regardless of income—it simply depends on the substance of the case.

Moreover, individuals may have an aversion to lawyers for any number of reasons. They may be discouraged by their own (or others') past experiences with legal representation.[89] For example, research by sociologist Ellen Berrey and her colleagues found that over half of all plaintiffs who filed employment discrimination claims thought their lawyers were incompetent.[90] Another study, by socio-legal scholars Austin Sarat and William L.F. Felstiner, suggested that the relationship between divorce lawyers and their clients is best characterized as one of differing views, avoidance of conflict, and talking past one another (hardly conducive to the cultivation of fond feelings about the legal profession).[91] Hollywood can also be a powerful influence for the perception that lawyers do not have their clients' best interest at heart, as the attorneys portrayed in the George Clooney film *Michael Clayton* demonstrate.[92]

Aversion to lawyers is only heightened by research that suggests that not all lawyers look out for the best interests of their clients. Lawyers can exercise considerable power and influence over their clients by maintaining control over the course of litigation and discouraging clients from seeking second opinions or taking their business elsewhere.[93] Further, lawyers may "cool out" (that is, counsel against aggressive action and in favor of compromise and conciliation) clients who have legitimate grievances, such as in a consumer case where the lawyer is reluctant to press a claim for fear of offending a potential business client.[94] In tort litigation lawyers may offer package deals to claims adjusters[95] and divorce lawyers may recommend costly litigation rather than engage in difficult and unprofitable negotiations about reconciliation.[96] Lawyers may reject requests for assistance or provide only minimal help to clients, depending on who the client is, with individuals, the poor, the disabled, ethnic and racial minorities, and young people disadvantaged at the expense of corporations, the wealthy, the nondisabled, ethnic and racial majorities, and older people.[97] The result may be a distaste for lawyers that leads a potential litigant to accept the status quo rather than engage a lawyer; in effect, choosing the lesser of two evils from the litigant's perspective.

A third deterrent to using courts to resolve civil matters is the emotional cost involved in the process. As one scholar observed, "Short of physical violence, litigation is taken to be one of the worst kinds of social interaction."[98] Litigation takes more time than alternative methods of settling disputes and litigants may not want to spend the time entailed in preparing for and participating in a trial. It encourages litigants to focus on the past at the expense of the present, to focus on fault and blame rather than taking responsibility for their own lives, and fosters a polarized, black-and-white thought process. Also, because of the nature of the adversarial system, lawyers are focused on challenging and tearing down the opposition rather than uncovering the truth, per se. Thus, attorney behavior may be emotionally trying on litigants who will have to answer all types of questions, in writing and orally at depositions as well as on the witness stand. As a result, litigants may experience an emotional gain from settling: they can get over it and move on with their lives. One recent example is the settlement reached by the family of James McNair, a close friend of former *Saturday Night Live* and *30 Rock* star Tracy Morgan. Morgan and McNair were driving in a car that was hit by a Walmart truck. McNair was killed and his family agreed to a settlement instead of going to trial. The family's lawyer was quoted as saying, "Whenever you have a situation like this, you always have mixed emotions, but the family could not be happier to have this piece done and try to move on with their lives."[99]

Additionally, the procedures, official language, and special knowledge of the court system can often seem daunting to the layperson and he may, therefore, choose not to contact attorneys or go to court. As we discuss later in the chapter, each step of the litigation process is often complex. For example, merely filing a complaint involves far more than having an attorney submit a document to the court. Because the document outlines the case against the defendant, the plaintiff must necessarily spend time with the attorney identifying the parties involved, establishing the legal claims, relating the facts that give rise to the claims, and determining relief, such as paying damages or requiring a particular action be taken. And, this is only the first step of the process!

POP CULTURE

Michael Clayton

The 2007 film *Michael Clayton* (nominated for an Academy Award) starring George Clooney (also nominated for an Academy Award) depicts a pack of money-hungry, unethical lawyers who engage in manipulative behavior, indulge in illegal drugs, and fail to come anywhere near to faithfully representing their clients. We follow George Clooney's character, a well-paid "fixer" attorney (the Michael Clayton of the film title) whose gambling debts and work at an unethical law firm drive him to question the system. He is tasked with aiding a fellow attorney—Arthur Edens played by celebrated English actor Tom Wilkinson—who is defending an agriculture conglomerate's use of harmful pesticides. Edens goes off his meds—stripping in the middle of taking a deposition and running out into a snowy parking lot—and is unwilling to continue the case. As the film progresses, the audience learns that Edens has done this before and Clayton must try to coax him back to the case. In one exchange, Clayton explains to Edens: "You are the senior litigating partner of one of the largest, most respected law firms in the world. You are a legend." Eden responds: "I'm an accomplice!" Clayton tries to reason with him: "You're a manic-depressive!" Edens realizes his importance to the firm and the kind of clients they represent and retorts: "I am Shiva, the god of death."

George Clooney
Credit: James Devaney/WireImage

This less than savory depiction of lawyers is not made any better by the actions of the general counsel for the agriculture conglomerate. Karen Crowder (played by Tilda Swinton, who won the Academy Award for Best Supporting Actress for her work in this role) first contracts to have Edens killed when she learns he has come into possession of a document incriminating her firm. She then tries to have Clayton killed as well once his suspicions are aroused about the incriminating document. Barely escaping the assassins she hired, Clayton confronts Crowder about the incriminating document and her efforts to have him killed. He further advances the tawdry image of lawyers when he says, "I'm not the guy you kill. I'm the guy you buy! Are you so fucking blind that you don't even see what I am?" In the exchange, he goads Crowder into making an offer of $10 million for his silence. Clayton has no intention of accepting the offer and reveals that the conversation was heard by law enforcement via his cell phone. But Clayton is no hero; just a shady lawyer with a gambling problem who owes money to the mob and simply wants to stop Crowder from continuing her efforts to have him (permanently) eliminated.

Finally, if individuals do choose to litigate, ample scholarship suggests that they will likely find the process unfair—even if they begin the process optimistically. For example, plaintiffs in employment discrimination suits find the process less than appealing because they face significant obstacles in properly defending their claims, rarely get a final ruling based on the substantive merits of the case, and see the process as unfairly biased in favor of the defendant-employers.[100] Interestingly, even employer-defendants feel the process is unfair because they perceive that employees have the power to initiate what they consider "meritless" suits that force the company to respond, thereby wasting time and other resources. Society may cherish the myth of the courthouse as freely accessible to all but the reality of financial costs, aversion to attorneys, emotional costs, daunting rules and procedures, and perceived unfairness of the process can deter individuals with meritorious claims from seeking justice through the civil court system.

WHY USE THE CIVIL COURTS?

Despite the obstacles outlined above, some parties nonetheless do choose to litigate for a variety of reasons. For example, individuals may avail themselves of the civil courts because the parties feel that there is something serious at stake—in a word, honor. Historian Peter Charles Hoffer examined the roots of American litigiousness in the colonial era and found that, while lawsuits were certainly about legal issues such as property rights, the reason these disputes went to court instead of being resolved outside of the legal system was because the parties felt that they had to defend their honor in the face of what they believed to be unjust claims. "Honor is at stake—the honor of the litigants, the honor of the litigators. And honor seems to prevent a satisfactory conclusion of the dispute. Honor makes disputants irreconcilable."[101] In this sense, Hoffer suggests that little has changed in terms of what drives Americans to use the courts. Litigants fully believe that their honor—and the honor of those like them—is at stake and settling a dispute through compromise would be an admission that they were not absolutely in the right.

Parties may also choose to avail themselves of the civil courts because they simply overestimate their chances of winning.[102] To be sure, everyone wants to win. But even if lawyers carefully explain to clients that their chances of prevailing in court are slim to none, litigants may nonetheless choose to believe otherwise. For example, research by legal scholar Arthur Best and consumer behavior expert Alan Andreasen shows that consumers from higher socioeconomic backgrounds have higher levels of dissatisfaction with their purchases than do individuals from lower socioeconomic backgrounds. It is not that the goods and services are worse, but that the expectations are higher.[103] This can lead to disputes and, subsequently, litigation based on unreasonable expectations.

Yet another reason individuals turn to civil courts is because they have little to lose or see no other choice. For example, some individuals find themselves short when it comes time to pay the rent and just do not have the money to do so. Thus, if a landlord orders a tenant to vacate a property for failure to pay rent, the tenant may willingly go to court rather than face homelessness in order to benefit from the delays that the litigation process may entail. In this scenario, the tenant has little or nothing to lose and much to gain by using the courts. And, sometimes courts are simply seen as the last resort—the only remaining avenue left for resolving a dispute once other avenues have been exhausted. Regardless of how litigants feel about attorneys or the civil litigation process generally, they know that using the court system will inevitably bring the dispute to a resolution— one way or another. This is particularly true of individuals who have attempted to settle before going to court and feel that they have been more than fair in their settlement offers. If the opposing party behaves in an unreasonable way, courts may be the only way to resolve the dispute. But it is also true for those seeking a divorce or filing for bankruptcy, for example. The only means to secure a divorce decree or to have one's debts discharged through bankruptcy is, in fact, to go to court.

PROMOTING SETTLEMENT: PROCESSING CIVIL SUITS

Trials hold a mythic place in the American judicial system and are what most often come to mind as the major forum for resolving disputes, including civil disputes. In reality, however, most disputes are settled in the preliminary stages of litigation long before a trial takes place. The path to trial includes several steps that help to promote negotiation and settlement. These preliminary steps are the province of lawyers using special procedures and discourse that may be difficult for clients to fully grasp. The result is that disputants may change their attitudes and be much more willing to settle as they learn that they themselves will have a minimal role in the litigation process.[104] Furthermore, delays (which are common in many civil courts[105]) only exacerbate the situation, further alienating litigants and increasing the chances of settlement. As we noted above, some litigants do proceed toward trial but cases can still be settled at any time prior to the verdict.

Table 6.1 shows the typical stages in processing civil suits for damages. Each of these steps involves time, money, and effort that litigants may not be willing to invest. The person who brings the civil suit is known as the **plaintiff** and the person being sued is referred to as the **defendant**. Filing the **complaint** commences an action against the defendant. The complaint must include a wealth of information: the names and addresses of the parties; information that establishes that the court has jurisdiction over the parties (**personal jurisdiction**) as well as jurisdiction over the subject matter of the case (**subject matter jurisdiction**); a list of the allegations and statement of facts, along with the **cause of action**, which explains the legal theories that form the basis of the lawsuit; and the damages being sought.[106]

Next, the defendant is notified that she is being sued. This is referred to as **service of process** and involves delivering a copy of the complaint and a **summons,** the official notice of a lawsuit from a court. A summons typically includes a warning to the defendant that a **default judgment** (judgment in favor of one party due to the failure of the other

TABLE 6.1
Typical Stages of the Processing of Civil Suits for Damages or Restitution

1. Filing of Complaint by the plaintiff
2. Serving of process on the defendant
3. Filing an answer to the complaint by defendant
4. Discovery of evidence: depositions, interrogatories, and document production
5. Pretrial conference and motions
6. Trial
7. Verdict of liability and remedy
8. Post-trial motions: for judgment notwithstanding the verdict, to set aside the verdict
9. Compliance with or enforcement of the judgment

party to take required action) can be awarded unless she responds within a specified period of time. Service of process is considered a crucial step in civil proceedings because the due process of law protected by the Fifth and Fourteenth Amendments prohibits legal action against an individual who has not been given proper notice. As a practical matter, a party to a suit who is not formally served is not bound by any decision in the case.

Service of process can take one of three forms, depending upon the laws of the jurisdiction within which the court operates. **Personal service** (also referred to as actual service) means that there is in-person delivery of the summons to the defendant. **Substituted service** refers to methods (other than personal service) that make it likely that the defendant will be informed of the proceedings. For example, some jurisdictions permit delivery of the summons and complaint to other responsible adults living at the defendant's residence. And, in some states, substituted service can take the form of affixing the documents to the entrance of the defendant's home and then mailing a copy via registered mail (sometimes referred to as "nail and mail" service). Finally, under limited circumstances some jurisdictions permit service of process via **constructive service** (also called service by publication), which is publication of a public notice in a newspaper. The individual who actually serves process varies by jurisdiction. Some jurisdictions have a designated court official (e.g., marshal, bailiff) that is responsible. Others permit private process servers (e.g., private investigators) but they may be subject to training and licensing requirements. One comedic pop culture example of a private process server is the character played by Seth Rogen in the 2008 film *Pineapple Express*, Dale Denton. Dale, a pot smoker and slacker, witnesses a murder when he arrives to serve process on what turns out to be a drug lord. Hijinks ensue in this 'bromance' as Dale and his drug dealer, Saul Silver played by James Franco, are chased by a corrupt cop and other assorted bad guys. Presumably, most process servers do not have such exciting lives.

The next stage of the civil litigation process is initiated by the defendant's **answer**, which is the defendant's formal, written response to the complaint. In his answer, the defendant addresses each of the claims asserted by the plaintiff, admitting or denying each point of the complaint (or indicating that he has insufficient knowledge to admit or deny). The defendant's answer may also provide an **affirmative defense**; i.e., legal reasons why the defendant is not liable for the plaintiff's damages. The defendant may actually concede to the facts alleged by the plaintiff but attempt to demonstrate other facts that excuse what would otherwise be considered wrongful actions. For example, the defendant may assert that the statute of limitations has expired. The defendant may also raise a **counterclaim** in the answer, which is appropriate when the defendant has a cause of action against the plaintiff arising out of the same set of facts that gave rise to the plaintiff's claim. If the defendant counterclaims, the plaintiff then files a pleading called the **reply,** in which she admits, denies, or raises defenses against the factual allegations contained in the counterclaim. A plaintiff's reply to a defendant's counterclaim is analogous to a defendant's answer to a plaintiff's complaint.

Discovery is the process by which the parties disclose all relevant facts and documents to the other side prior to trial and it constitutes the next stage in the run up to a civil trial.[107] Discovery can include **interrogatories** and **oral depositions**. Interrogatories are lists of written questions requiring written answers under oath. Oral depositions are out-of-courtroom statements made under oath that are reduced to writing for later use in court or for discovery purposes. Discovery can also involve the **production of documents**, which is the exchange of all documents that each party has the right to see related to the case. Critics of the contemporary use of the discovery process have argued that it can be abusive and expensive.[108] Moroever, the potential for discovery to be burdensome (especially for those with fewer resources at their disposal) has only been enhanced by the technological advances that have yielded burgeoning amounts of electronic information (e.g., electronic messages, databases, voicemail).[109] Indeed, an industry of "e-discovery" consultants has sprung up in response.[110] Onerous or not, however, "[b]y enabling litigants to acquire relevant information that otherwise may be unavailable to them, discovery serves the interests of procedural justice and facilitates enforcement of the society policy choices embodies in controlling substantive law."[111]

There are also additional proceedings that come before a trial but can shape what subsequently happens at trial (or, possibly, facilitate a pretrial settlement). A **pretrial conference** is a meeting between the parties to a case and a judge or magistrate. **Status conferences** (also referred to as early conferences), which occur soon after initial pleadings (e.g., complaint, answer) have been filed, are intended to aid the presiding judge to manage the case (e.g., set a timeline for pretrial activities, set a tentative trial date). The purpose of **issue conferences**, which occur later in the process if a settlement has not been reached, is to foster agreement between the lawyers in a case on undisputed facts or points of law. Both status and issue conferences are directed at expediting the disposition of the case, encouraging settlement of the case, and helping to improve the quality of the trial through preparation.[112] Pretrial motions are made by attorneys asking the court to rule on particular matters, such as a defendant's motion to dismiss the case (because the complaint is deficient in some way) or motion for summary judgment (because the facts are undisputed and there is no need for a trial).

There are numerous facets of civil trials, including jury selection, opening statements, direct and cross-examination of witnesses, closing arguments, jury instructions, jury deliberation, and, ultimately, a verdict. Though we discuss each of these facets in greater detail in Chapter Eight, here we touch on civil juries and the standard of proof in civil cases. The Federal Rules of Civil Procedure require that a federal civil jury must have no less than six and no more than 12 jurors; the standard size of a federal civil jury is six.[113] Further, the Rules also require that "[u]nless the parties stipulate otherwise, the verdict must be unanimous and must be returned by a jury of at least 6 members."[114] States have a good deal of discretion when it comes to determining the size of civil jury trials so it is no surprise that the size (and unanimity requirements) in civil cases vary considerably across the states. For example, less than half of the states require 12-person civil juries, and approximately half allow for non unanimous verdicts.[115] It is important to bear in mind that the jury in a civil trial is making a determination as to whether the defendant is liable or not liable. The jury is not making a determination of guilt or innocence as it is in a criminal case. If the jury fails to reach a unanimous or super majority verdict, it is considered a **hung** or **deadlocked jury**. In the event of a hung jury, the judge may declare a mistrial (i.e., a trial that is not successfully completed but, instead, is terminated before the verdict is returned) and dismiss the case or start the trial stage all over again.

The standard of proof in civil cases is a **preponderance of the evidence**.[116] This means that the facts asserted are more likely to be true than not true. In other words:

> [T]he plaintiff has to persuade the fact finder that the existence of the facts giving rise to her or his alleged legal right is more probable than their nonexistence. . . . In a somewhat more formal formulation, the rule means that the plaintiff has to establish a case with a probability exceeding .5. Finally, the rule has been interpreted as requiring that the best explanation of the evidence favors the plaintiff [citations omitted].[117]

Though it is not difficult to articulate the meaning of the preponderance-of-the-evidence standard at a conceptual level, its application in practice can be less than obvious. For example, one study asked judges and jurors to quantify the preponderance-of-the-evidence standard as a percentage probability (that is, what percentage of the evidence in favor of the plaintiff would be necessary to meet the preponderance-of-the-evidence standard). For judges, the median value was 55 percent probability while for jurors the median value was 75 percent.[118] This suggests that both judges and jurors (but especially jurors) place a heavier burden of proof on plaintiffs than is called for by the preponderance-of-the-evidence standard that is to govern the disposition of civil cases.

The verdict in a civil trial does not represent the end of the civil trial process. There can be any number of **post-trial motions**, motions permitted after the rendering of a verdict requesting an alteration in the verdict.[119] Common post-trial motions include a motion for a new trial and a motion for relief from judgment. On particularly interesting kind of post-trial motion is a motion for **judgment notwithstanding the verdict** (JNOV).[120] "Of all the forms of posttrial relief available to litigants, a JNOV has the potential to most dramatically influence the trial court outcome."[121] Why? Because a JNOV asks the judge to decide that reasonable people could not have reached the verdict that the jury has reached and to set aside the jury verdict, replacing it with one that favors the losing party. Post-trial motions are not uncommon. One recent study found that the verdicts or judgments in a sizable minority of cases are challenged via post-trial motions.[122] The analysis in this study also revealed that product liability and medical malpractice cases were more likely to be associated with post-trial motions but that there was little difference in the propensity for seeking post-trial relief between business plaintiffs and individual plaintiffs.

The final stage in the civil litigation process involves **compliance with** or **enforcement of the judgment**. This commonly involves collection of money damages. That process starts with the drafting of the judgment, which is sent to the clerk's office for entry in court records after it has been signed by the judge. Once entered, a copy of the judgment and notice of entry is typically served on the **judgment debtor** (the litigant responsible for paying the award amount) by the **judgment creditor** (the litigant who has been awarded the judgment). If the judgment debtor refuses to follow the court order or cannot afford to pay the amount then the judgment creditor must take additional steps to enforce the judgment. For example, he could pursue wage garnishment or hire a collection attorney. In addition, there may be appeals with which to deal. We discuss the appellate process in depth in Chapter Nine.

WHO GOES TO COURT? REPEAT PLAYERS AND ONE-SHOTTERS

Earlier in this chapter we discussed the advantages repeat players possess relative to one-shotters in arbitration, one form of ADR. We consider repeat players and one-shotters again here, this time with regard to their propensity to go to court.[123] As their name suggests, one-shotters use courts only rarely, such as the spouse in a divorce case or the auto-injury claimant. They are typically individuals whose cases may either have high tangible stakes relative to their total worth or claims so small that the cost of enforcing them outweighs any possible benefit. Repeat players, on the other hand, use courts regularly as part of their business activity. Some examples include insurance companies, banks, and corporations. They are typically the larger of the parties in a dispute and the stakes in any given case are smaller for them relative to their total worth. Repeat players have the resources to pursue their long-term interests even if individual cases seem relatively small. Because of these differences, repeat players have numerous built-in advantages over one-shotters, advantages that make it likely that they will prevail in any dispute.[124]

To begin with, repeat players have experience. They have been previously involved in litigation on similar and related matters and, as a consequence, they are able to structure transactions and construct records that work to their advantage. For example, they know what provisions to include in a rental contract to safeguard their interests. Further, repeat players have expertise of their own (in part gleaned from their experience) and ready access to specialists with even more expertise. The fact that they have litigated so many cases means that they enjoy economies of scale; i.e., low start-up costs in any given case. For example, insurance companies employ claim adjustors in routine negotiations, obviating the need to resort to expensive professionally qualified outside experts on a case-by-case basis. Moreover, repeat players have ongoing relationships with court personnel. Those relationships can yield subtle advantages over one-shotter opponents. For example, the creditor who appears weekly in small claims court and gets to know the clerk responsible for scheduling cases may find cases are more likely to be scheduled at the creditor's convenience.[125] In addition, repeat players have credibility that comes from their previous experience in the court. The reputations that they have accrued gives their bargaining positions credibility in a way that one-shotters cannot hope to match. Of course, one potential advantage for one-shotters is that the very fact that they will not have ongoing dealings with their opponent or the court means that they have the opportunity to act irrationally and say or do virtually anything without fear of reprisal in the next case.

A further advantage enjoyed by repeat players is the fact that they can play the odds, so to speak, by adopting strategies to maximize their gains over a long series of cases even if it involves the risk of loss in some cases. Repeat players are aided in their ability to do this because one-shotters are more likely to adopt a strategy of minimizing their probability of a maximum loss if the stakes are high (as they often are for one-shotters). And, repeat players not only hope to win the cases at hand but they also expend resources to influence the making of the relevant rules that apply to their business or industry in order to facilitate their causes in the future. Thus, repeat players lobby and do so persuasively because of their accumulated expertise. Similarly, unlike one-shotters, who are concerned with only winning their individual case, repeat players want to influence the outcomes of future cases of the same kind. This means repeat players may settle cases where they expect unfavorable rule outcomes and can elect to adjudicate or appeal those cases that they think will produce favorable rules. As a result, the body of precedents—cases capable of influencing outcomes in future cases—will be relatively skewed toward favoring repeat players. Indeed, repeat players may act in concert with other repeat players to gain favorable common litigation rules, which only compounds their advantage.

As the discussion of repeat players and one-shotters demonstrates, a legal system that is formally neutral between "haves" and "have nots" plainly advantages the former at the expense of the latter. Table 6.2 illustrates how some well-known examples of civil litigation fit into the repeat player–one-shotter dichotomy and include some examples from criminal law by way of comparison.

In Box I—one-shotters v. one-shotters—the most common kind of cases are divorce cases, with the vast majority of them uncontested. There is little interest in the long-term state of the law, as in custody cases, which are almost always *ad hoc* and instrumental to the individual case. There are few appeals, little expenditure of resources on

TABLE 6.2
Taxonomy of Litigation by Strategic Configuration of Parties

		INITIATOR, CLAIMANT	
		One-Shotter	Repeat Player
DEFENDANT	One-Shotter	*Box I: One-Shotter v. One-Shotter* Parent v. Parent (Custody) Spouse v. Spouse (Divorce) Family v. Family Member (Insanity Commitment) Family v. Family (Inheritance) Neighbor v. Neighbor Partner v. Partner	*Box II: Repeat Player v. One-Shotter* Prosecutor v. Accused (criminal) Finance Co. v. Debtor Landlord v. Tenant I.R.S. v. Taxpayer Condemnor v. Property Owner
	Repeat Player	*Box III: One-Shotter v. Repeat Player* Welfare Client v. Agency Auto Dealer v. Manufacturer Injury Victim v. Insurance Company Tenant v. Landlord Bankrupt Consumer v. Creditor Defamed v. Publisher	*Box IV: Repeat Player v. Repeat Player* Union v. Company Film Distributor v. Censorship Board Developer v. Suburban Municipality Purchaser v. Supplier Regulatory Agency v. Firms of Regulated Industry

Source: Marc Galanter, "Why the 'Haves' Come Out Ahead: Speculations on the Limits of Legal Change," *Law & Society Review*, 9 (1974): 95–160, 107.

rule development, and legal doctrine is remote from common practice and popular attitudes. Box II—repeat players v. one-shotters—constitutes most of the litigation in America and generally deals with claims that arise from regular business activity. Cases are often settled informally based on possible litigation outcomes. The state of the law is important to repeat players but not to one-shot defendants. In addition, the law tends to be favorable to repeat players, such as creditors, police, and draft boards. Box III—one-shotters v. repeat players—consists of infrequent types of cases such as those where a one-shotter attempts to create leverage on an organization, as with the case of a fired employee. The exception is personal injury matters, which are unique due to easy access to the system through contingency fees; i.e., one-shotters do not have to invest their resources upfront to litigate. Litigation involving personal injury from auto accidents is relatively routine, with settlements geared to possible litigation outcomes. One-shotters generally have no interest in rule development while repeat players are greatly interested.

Finally, Box IV provides common examples of litigation involving repeat player v. repeat player. On its face, this arrangement would seem to involve little litigation as it would logically be in the interests of repeat players to come to collective agreements to avoid costly litigation. Yet there are some special cases that do not conform to this idea. First, some repeat players have fundamental cultural commitments and use litigation to vindicate values (who is right) as opposed to securing tangible stakes (who gets what). Organizations that sponsor church-state litigation are examples of repeat players who seek to vindicate values; for example, the strict separation of church and state. Second, the government is another special type of repeat player because, unlike other organizations, the government cannot withdraw future association from other parties the way that other organizations can withdraw membership. The government will necessarily continue to have ongoing relations with the other parties and therefore both seek to externalize decisions to courts. The final special type of repeat player is the repeat player who does not deal with the other repeat player regularly. An example would be two insurance companies who regularly litigate but rarely against each other. Like with the government, there is nothing from which to withdraw in these disputes, and both parties use the courts to resolve a unique issue such as a one-time deal that fell through. Although litigation among repeat players is relatively rare, when it does occur, considerable resources are spent on rule development, appeals, and the development of doctrinal law.

Based on this litigation typology, a general profile of civil litigation and the factors associated with it emerges. The vast majority of litigation occurs in Box II and much less in Box III. Most of the litigation in these boxes involves mass processing of routine disputes between parties who are strangers and between whom there is a disparity in size. One party is organized and professional in the sense that they engage in litigation for a living and therefore have strategic advantages. There are little in the way of informal controls and the relationships between the parties are defined by official rules that the parties seek to manipulate to their advantage. Conversely, Boxes I and IV involve much more infrequent and individualized litigation between parties of the same general magnitude. They have ongoing relationships and informal controls that make litigation less likely in general and only when relationships lose future value. When they do litigate, parties in this situation prefer courts to adjudicate claims, particularly when they seek to vindicate conflicting values.

LITIGATION RATES

Has there been a litigation explosion in America? The popular myth would have us believe so.[126] However, the empirical evidence shows that U.S. litigation rates have been relatively stable and, by some measures, have even declined over time.[127] For example, law professor Marc Galanter has demonstrated that, while periodic surges in litigation do happen from time to time, the general rise in litigation in nearly every area of the law has barely kept up with population increases.[128] If the reality is that litigation rates have not exploded (and are, in fact, essentially only keeping up with population increases) then calls for reform based on the litigation explosion myth may be misguided. In this section we examine the data—for both state and federal courts—on the cases filed, the cases resolved at the trial stage, and appeals. The results largely confirm what prior research suggests: by almost any measure, there has not been a litigation explosion in America.

Civil Litigation Rates in State Courts

Consider, first, what civil case numbers in state courts look like. Figure 6.2 shows that the total civil caseload for all 50 state courts has increased in recent years from just fewer than 16 million cases in 2001 to just fewer than 19 million cases in 2010. It also shows that there have been some periods of decline over that period: from 2003 to 2005 and from 2009 to 2010. Of course, as a general matter, we might expect caseloads to grow given that population increases over time. Figure 6.3 takes into account changes in population and shows that, while there has been an increase from 5,461 cases filed per 100,000 people in 2001 to 6,063 in 2010, the increase is so limited that it is more accurate to conclude that caseloads have been essentially stable over time.

FIGURE 6.2

Civil Cases in State Courts, 2001–2010

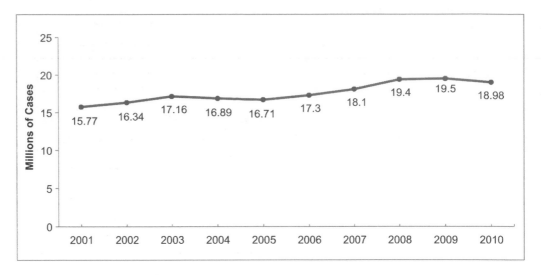

Source: "Examining the Work of State Courts: An Analysis of 2010 State Court Caseloads," National Center for State Courts, Court Statistics Project, 2012.

FIGURE 6.3

Civil Cases per 100,000 Population in State Courts, 2001–2010

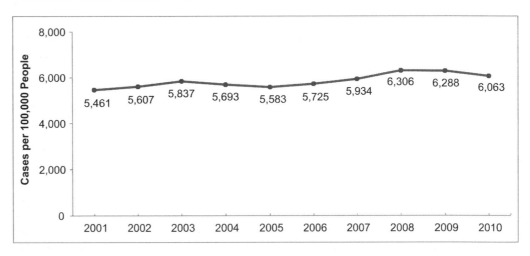

Source: "Examining the Work of State Courts: An Analysis of 2010 State Court Caseloads," National Center for State Courts, Court Statistics Project, 2012.

Figure 6.4 reports the types of civil cases filed in state courts of general jurisdiction in 2010. By far the most common type of civil cases are those involving contracts (e.g., seller plaintiff/debt collection, buyer plaintiff, landlord-tenant), which make up the vast majority of civil dockets (61 percent). Both probate (estates of deceased

FIGURE 6.4

Composition of Civil Trials in State Courts in the Nation's 75 Most Populous Counties: 1992–2005

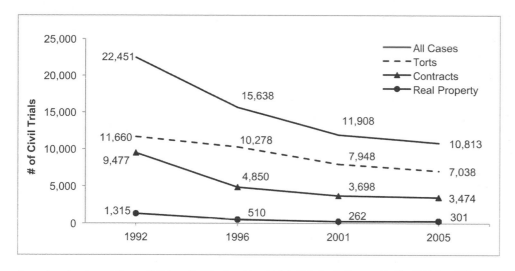

Source: Lynn Langton and Thomas H. Cohen, *Civil Bench and Jury Trials in State Courts*, Bureau of Justice Statistics, 2005.

persons) and small claims (tort, contract, and real property cases with low monetary stakes) each make up 11 percent of state court caseloads. Tort cases (e.g., automobile, malpractice, product liability), which reformers point to as the scourge of the civil litigation system, only comprise 6 percent of cases in state courts. Real property (e.g., condemnation, title disputes) and mental health cases only account for 2 percent each. "All other" civil cases include civil appeals, *habeas corpus*, nondomestic restraining orders, tax cases, writs, and other civil matters and each make up a small fraction of civil caseloads.

Table 6.3 compares types of civil cases across various states arrayed from states with the highest percentage of contract cases to the states with the smallest such percentage. As with the overall data on case types, contracts generally dominate civil litigation in most states and comprise more than three out of four civil cases filed in Kansas, North Carolina, Colorado, and Mississippi. At the other end of the spectrum, only one out of three cases on the civil dockets in Washington and Hawaii deals with contracts, but those two states also had the highest percentage of real property cases—20 percent and 16 percent respectively. There are also differences across a number of other categories such as small claims, comprising roughly 40 percent of civil caseloads in Connecticut and Oregon but only 1 percent or less in New Hampshire and Rhode Island, which in turn have the highest percentage of tort cases—20 percent and 25 percent respectively. Also of note, not all general jurisdiction courts have jurisdiction over all civil cases. For example, six of these 17 courts do not process any of their state's small-claims cases, three states have separate probate courts to handle those matters, and six states process their mental health cases in a limited jurisdiction court. In short, how states structure their court systems and the policies they put in place regarding civil litigation can have a significant effect on caseloads.

As we have discussed, simply because a case is filed it does not mean that it will necessarily go to trial. Indeed, most cases are settled before they are filed and most cases

TABLE 6.3
Comparison of Civil Case Composition in State Courts, 2010

STATE	TOTAL CASES	CONTRACT	PROBATE	SMALL CLAIMS	TORT	REAL PROPERTY	MENTAL HEALTH	ALL OTHER CIVIL
Kansas*	193,402	81%	5%	4%	2%	1%	2%	6%
North Carolina	106,166	78%	1%	n/j	10%	3%	n/j	9%
Colorado	130,716	77%	9%	n/j	4%	1%	4%	5%
Mississippi	27,611	75%	n/j	n/j	14%	1%	n/j	11%
Missouri*	317,613	69%	7%	4%	5%	1%	5%	10%
Utah	125,670	67%	4%	15%	2%	7%	2%	4%
New Jersey	1,004,778	65%	21%	5%	6%	<1%	n/j	1%
North Dakota*	35,633	57%	14%	15%	1%	1%	5%	7%
Minnesota	211,898	48%	5%	24%	2%	3%	2%	16%
Maine	47,225	46%	n/j	24%	2%	1%	2%	25%
Connecticut	149,029	44%	<1%	43%	10%	1%	n/j	3%
Alabama	51,723	40%	3%	n/j	16%	1%	n/j	39%
Oregon	193,458	40%	5%	39%	3%	<1%	4%	9%
Rhode Island	11,286	38%	<1%	<1%	25%	7%	n/j	30%
New Hampshire	7,864	37%	n/j	1%	20%	5%	<1%	38%
Washington	102,813	31%	19%	n/j	9%	20%	10%	11%
Hawaii	12,998	23%	17%	n/j	9%	16%	5%	30%

Note: Data reflect courts of general jurisdiction; "n/j" indicates no jurisdiction over that case type which are handled in courts of limited jurisdiction.
* = states that process all civil cases in their general jurisdiction courts.

Source: R. LaFountain, R. Schauffler, S. Strickland, and K. Holt, *Examining the Work of State Courts: An Analysis of 2010 State Court Caseloads,* National Center for State Courts, 2012.

FIGURE 6.5

Civil Jury Trial Awards in State Courts in the Nation's 75 Most Populous Counties: 1992–2005

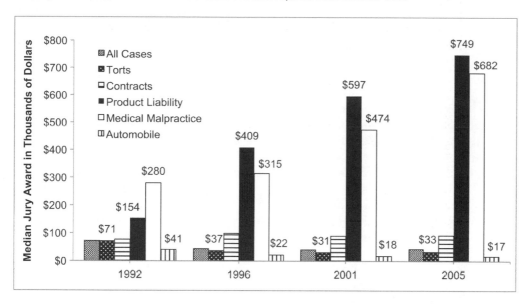

Source: Lynn Langton and Thomas H. Cohen, *Civil Bench and Jury Trials in State Courts*, Bureau of Justice Statistics, 2005.

that are filed are settled before they reach the trial stage. Figure 6.4 shows a general decline in civil trials—both jury trials and bench trials—based on a sample of the 75 most populous counties over time for all case types. Specifically, tort cases have declined from 11,660 in 1992 to 7,038 in 2005—a decrease of 40 percent. Contract cases have gone down from 9,477 in 1992 to 3,474 in 2005—a decline of 63 percent. And real property cases have decreased from 1,315 in 1992 to 301 in 2005—a 77 percent reduction. In all, these three case types have declined from 22,451 in 1992 to 10,813 in 2005—a 52 percent decrease. Given that Figure 6.2 shows that case filings have remained relatively stable over time, we can conclude that the decrease in trials is a result of more cases being settled prior to trial.

Systematic evidence shows that plaintiffs win more than half (56 percent) of all civil trials concluded in state courts. Based on samples from, again, the 75 most populous counties, Figure 6.5 shows how trends in civil jury awards have either risen or declined over time. Overall, civil jury awards declined from a median award of $72,000 in 1992 to $43,000 in 2005. Tort cases decreased from $71,000 to $33,000 but contract cases increased from $77,000 to $92,000. Yet not all types of tort or contract cases were treated equally. For example, jury awards in automobile cases declined 59 percent from $41,000 in 1992 to $17,000 in 2005. On the other hand, product liability awards increased 387 percent from a median award of $154,000 in 1992 to $749,000 in 2005. Similarly, medical malpractice awards grew 144 percent from $280,000 in 1992 to $682,000 in 2005. Thus, while case filings have been relatively stable and trials have declined over time, many categories of civil cases have seen large increases in jury awards—further fueling the myth of litigiousness.

Civil Litigation Rates in Federal Courts

How does the picture in state courts compare to that in federal courts? Figure 6.6 shows that the number of civil cases filed in district courts has generally been stable over time with a slight upward trend from 236,391 in 1994 to 284,604 in 2013. Yet, as with state court caseloads, there are ups and downs throughout with periods of growth, most notably from 1994–1997 and from 2007–2011. There was a decline in federal court civil cases from 1999–2001 and from 2011–2013, with the highest number of civil cases filed in district court occurring in 2011 (289,252). Figure 6.7 shows trends in civil case composition over time. While most categories are relatively stable, two stand out. First, the number of contract cases was on the rise from 1994 to 2000, reaching an apex of 53,625 filings. This was primarily due to the decision of the U.S. Department of Education to intensify efforts to submit defaulted student loans for collection.[129] However, contract cases have been in steady decline since then, totaling only 28,571 in 2013, despite a temporary increase beginning in 2005 due to thousands of additional contract insurance cases filed in the Eastern District of Louisiana as a result of Hurricane Katrina and in the Southern District of New York related to the 2001 terrorist attacks in New York City.

Second, tort cases (the vast majority of which involve personal injury and product liability) have ebbed and flowed with considerable variation. For example, tort cases were in steady decline from 1996–2001 and then nearly doubled from a low of 33,663 in 2000 to 62,919 the following year. What accounted for this spike? Most of the

FIGURE 6.6

Civil Cases in Federal District Courts, 1994–2013

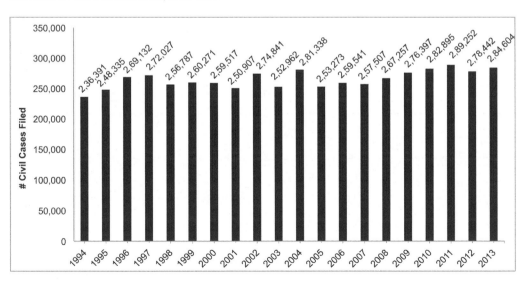

Note: Data reflect civil cases commenced during the 12-month period ending March 31 of each year.

Sources: www.uscourts.gov;
http://www.uscourts.gov/uscourts/Statistics/JudicialBusiness/2013/appendices/C02ASep13.pdf;
http://www.uscourts.gov/uscourts/Statistics/JudicialBusiness/2008/appendices/C02ASep08.pdf;
http://www.uscourts.gov/uscourts/Statistics/JudicialBusiness/2003/appendices/c2a.pdf

FIGURE 6.7

Civil Case Composition in Federal District Courts, 1994–2013

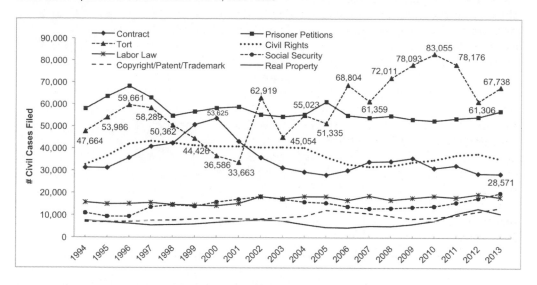

Note: Data reflect civil cases commenced during the 12-month period ending March 31 of each year.

Sources: www.uscourts.gov;
http://www.uscourts.gov/uscourts/Statistics/JudicialBusiness/2013/appendices/C02ASep13.pdf;
http://www.uscourts.gov/uscourts/Statistics/JudicialBusiness/2008/appendices/C02ASep08.pdf;
http://www.uscourts.gov/uscourts/Statistics/JudicialBusiness/2003/appendices/c2a.pdf.

increase—22,671 cases—was due to plaintiffs alleging injuries from asbestos in auto-motive break pads, particularly in the Northern District of Ohio (up 9,105 filings from the prior year) and Eastern District of Virginia (up 3,253 cases), against the "Big Three" automakers (Ford, General Motors, and Daimler/Chrysler) and Honeywell International. Many of the other tort cases, such as those in the Eastern District of Pennsylvania (up 1,794 cases), involved the plaintiffs alleging injurious side effects from the anti-cholesterol drug Baycol made by the Bayer Company.[130] Another spike occurred from 51,335 cases in 2005 to 68,804 cases the following year and was again largely caused by the filing of 14,000 asbestos cases—this time in a single court.[131] Similar increases in 2008–2010 were also largely a result of asbestos claims. However, tort cases fell after that. Thus, variation in tort filing in the past 2 decades has largely been due to asbestos litigation and not because of other tort categories, such as medical malpractice (as we will discuss at the end of the chapter).[132]

Figure 6.8 compares the number of civil cases to the total number of cases filed in federal appellate courts. Overall, the total number of all appeals cases has slightly increased over time from 51,991 in 1996 to 56,475 in 2013. Yet the numbers spiked in 2004 at 68,473. The steady decline since then has been due, in part, to a decrease in administrative agency appeals, mostly from the Board of Immigration Appeals.[133] It is also attributable to a decline in prisoner appeals, specifically cases filed seeking sentence reductions in response to *Blakely v. Washington* (2004)[134] and *United States v. Booker* (2005),[135] in which the Supreme Court held that only facts admitted by a defendant or decided by

FIGURE 6.8

Civil Cases in Federal Appellate Courts, 1992–2013

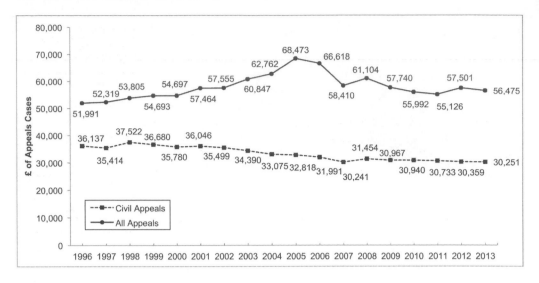

Note: Data reflect cases appealed from U.S. District Courts, administrative agencies, and bankruptcy courts and include original proceedings. Cases from the U.S. Court of Appeals for the Federal Circuit are excluded.

Source: www.uscourts.gov

the jury may be used to calculate or enhance a sentence. Another contributing factor are the changes in sentencing for low-level crack cocaine offenses in 2007 by the U.S. Sentencing Commission and the Fair Sentencing Act of 2010.[136] But what is perhaps most interesting is that the number of civil cases has steadily diminished from 36,137 in 1996 to 30,251 in 2013. It is plain from these data that, while civil cases make up a majority of the federal appellate docket, those cases represent only a small percentage (11 percent) of the total number of civil cases filed in district court. For example, in 2013, there were 271,950 civil cases filed in district court but only 30,251 (11 percent) were appealed. Of course most of the cases filed in district court are settled before ever reaching the trial stage. Still, the fact remains: nine out of 10 civil cases filed in federal trial courts never reach an appellate court.

Figure 6.9 compares trends in civil cases filed in federal appellate courts with criminal appeals included for comparison purposes. In nearly all respects, appeals in civil matters have been remarkably stable in recent years and have even exhibited slight declines in some areas, such as prisoner petitions and private civil cases. And, while there was a dramatic rise in appeals from administrative agencies beginning in 2001, there has been a steady decrease in recent years. Thus, federal appellate data do not lend support to the notion that America has experienced an explosion of litigiousness.

How do American litigation rates compare to similar advanced, industrial nations? By almost any measure, the U.S. is by no means an overly litigious nation. Table 6.4 shows that, while the U.S. has more suits filed than comparable nations, the U.K. is not far behind (5,806 vs. 3,681). France has more judges per capita than the U.S. (12.5 vs. 10.8).

FIGURE 6.9

Composition of Civil Cases Filed in Federal Appellate Courts, 1992–2013

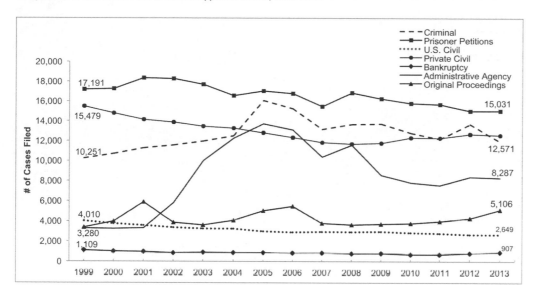

Note: Data reflect cases appealed from U.S. District Courts, administrative agencies, and bankruptcy courts and include original proceedings. Cases from the U.S. Court of Appeals for the Federal Circuit are excluded.

Source: www.uscourts.gov

TABLE 6.4

Litigation Rates in Comparative Perspective

	AUSTRALIA	CANADA	FRANCE	JAPAN	U.K./ENGLAND	U.S.
Suits Filed (per 100,000 people)	1,542	1,450	2,416	1,768	3,681	**5,806**
Judges (per 100,000 people)	4.0	3.3	**12.5**	2.8	2.2	10.8
Lawyers (per 100,000 people)	357	26	72	23	251	**391**
Automobile Insurance (percent GDP)	0.8	1.4	0.9	0.7	0.9	**1.5**
Automobile Insurance (U.S.$ per car)	664	**1,574**	786	754	927	1,464
Cost of Contract Action (percent of value)	21	22	17	**23**	**23**	14

Source: J. Mark Ramseyer and Eric B. Rasmusen, "Comparative Litigation Rates," The Harvard John M. Olin Discussion Paper Series, Discussion Paper No. 681, November 2010. http://www.law.harvard.edu/programs/olin_center/papers/pdf/Ramseyer_681.pdf

Image 6.4 Press Outside Supreme Court on Obamacare Decision
Litigants hold a press conference on the steps of the U.S. Supreme Court the morning of the Court's announcement upholding the Affordable Care Act in National Federation of Independent Business v. Sebelius *(2012). The National Federation of Independent Business (NFIB) is an interest group representing over 350,000 small businesses in the U.S. Through their Small Business Legal Center, the group litigates for small business in the courts. They explain that they do what federal and state NFIB lobbyists do, but instead of lobbying legislators they lobby judges through briefs and oral arguments in court. They tell judges how the decision they make in a given case will impact small businesses nationwide.* U.S. government work.

Australia has about the same number of lawyers that the U.S. has per capita (357 vs. 391). Canada spends about the same amount of money as the U.S. on auto insurance as a percentage of Gross Domestic Product (1.4 vs. 1.5) and per car ($1,574 vs. $1,464). Both Japan and England spend far more on contract actions than the U.S. as a percentage of the contract's value (23% vs. 14%), with all nations spending more than the United States. A fair characterization, then, is that America may be near the top on some measures of litigiousness it is by no means an outlier.

CLASS ACTION LAWSUITS

Class action lawsuits allow a named plaintiff or plaintiffs to represent the interests of many people (who are not formally named as parties in the suit but are in the same situation) against a defendant for injuries caused by common actions or inactions.[137] Common class actions include environmental issues such as preventing pollution and maintaining clean water; finance matters concerning predatory lending and breaches of securities law; employment issues involving wage and hour laws, sexual harassment, discrimination, and hostile work places; civil rights involving police department misconduct; the treatment of people with disabilities by major corporations; product defects, including automobile safety; and dangerous drugs and pharmaceutical devices, such as contraceptives and surgical materials. One recent illustrative example is the class action suit filed to challenge racial discrimination in the selection of bachelors and bachelorettes on the ABC shows *The Bachelor* and *The Bachelorette*.[138] Another is the class action suit filed against Facebook for its launch of Beacon, an advertising program that permitted the transmission of consumer-related information between Facebook and partner retailers without the permission of Facebook users.[139] It also allowed some consumer-related information to be automatically posted on Facebook newsfeeds, as one man found out when his purchase of an engagement ring from Overstock.com was made public on Facebook, thereby ruining his surprise marriage proposal plans.

Class actions have a number of benefits compared to individual suits. For example, there are lower overall litigation costs since they are divided among class members. Such cost sharing opens the door for plaintiffs to seek relief for small amounts of money. The amount of harm that any single individual may have experienced—such as systematic small overcharges on a phone bill—would likely make an individual claim too costly to pursue. But in the aggregate, the individual claims may add up to a substantial amount of money, making a class action lawsuit an effective way to obtain remedies from the company. One example of this is *Robbins v. Lower Merion School District*, a 2000 case involving schools secretly using webcams in school-issued laptops to spy on students at home.[140] As one of the attorneys explicitly noted, "[s]ince the damage suffered by individual class members may be relatively small," individual litigation would be too costly, making a class action the only viable option.[141]

Class action suits also enhance efficiency and uniformity in several ways. For example, they enhance judicial efficiency in the sense that one judge in one court can simultaneously handle a large volume of claims as compared to the situation with individual suits that would exponentially occupy the time of countless courts and judges. Class action suit also yield greater uniformity for similarly situated plaintiffs in terms of their opportunities to receive damages and in the amount of recoveries (as compared to separate litigation) for two reasons. First, those plaintiffs who file earlier have a greater likelihood of receiving compensation if a defendant is being sued by multiple independent plaintiffs, with those plaintiffs who are late to the party running the risk of the defendant no longer being able to pay (or pay as much) in damages for those later suits. And, second, there is no guarantee that different judges and different courts will produce consistent rulings in individual suits (regardless of the similarity of the plaintiffs). Similarly, there will also be greater uniformity for defendants in the sense that they will have one (not multiple) rulings to consult in determining how to follow the law going forward.

Finally, class actions insulate the suit from becoming moot. Determining whether a case has become moot or not requires a court to determine whether the matter underlying the case is beyond the reach of the law.[142] For example, if a named plaintiff in an individual case dies while proceedings are on going that individual case may be rendered moot but that would not be the case in a class action suit with multiple plaintiffs. To further illustrate, consider the case of Marco DeFunis, who was denied admission to the University of Washington School of Law.[143] He challenged that denial, arguing that it was the result of an affirmative action policy that favored minority applicants. However, while the case was pending, DeFunis was admitted to the law school and was close to graduating so his suit challenging his original denial of admission was considered moot by the time it reached the U.S. Supreme Court. Compare the situation DeFunis found himself in to that of Norma McCorvey (the Jane Roe of *Roe v. Wade*[144]). Though the case was not originally a class action, McCorvey's attorneys had amended the suit to make it one.[145] Hence, even though McCorvey had already given birth when the Court took up the appeal in her case, the class action status saved it from being considered moot.

Just as there are advantages to class actions there also disadvantages. For example, the majority of the plaintiffs lack control over the case. The named representatives of the class are the ones who make the decisions about the case, such as when and for how much to settle. Thus, a plaintiff in the class who is not a named party does not have a say in when or whether to settle or continue litigating. For example, the settlement Facebook made over Beacon resulted in the payment of about $2.3 million in attorney fees plus another $6.5 million to create a new privacy organization, the Digital Trust Fund. Seven Facebook users objected to the settlement, noting that it offered no compensation directly to users, and brought suit to invalidate the settlement but did not prevail.[146]

Additionally, class action suits may settle for compensation that is not in the form some plaintiffs would like. Some may prefer that the defendant take some affirmative action (i.e., enhance its privacy policies and controls) while others prefer that the defendant pay cash awards. One increasingly criticized form of settlement is the so-called **coupon settlement**.[147] With a coupon settlement, plaintiffs receive coupons or rebates for products and services rather than a cash award. What seems galling to many plaintiffs is that the value of the settlement is inflated by overstating the anticipated number of class members, with the result being that the plaintiffs' attorney fees (which are based on the value of the settlement) are likewise inflated beyond any reasonable relation to the financial benefit the plaintiffs themselves receive. Regardless, of the basis for the objection to a settlement, however, the fact remains that only one or a few plaintiffs in a case (the named plaintiffs) have much to say about whether a settlement is accepted or not.

And, finally, if the plaintiffs' attorney is not an effective advocate or the named class representatives do not have strong claims, individual members of the class may find themselves on the losing side of a case that they might have won if they had proceeded as individual plaintiffs. If a plaintiff had opted out of the class at the outset, then he would be entitled to file suit individually, but the right to do so is eliminated if the plaintiff remains part of the class. Thus, eligible individuals must weigh the pros and cons of deciding whether to join a class action or not.

It is not surprising that banks, insurance companies, and other potential corporate defendants do not like class actions—unless of course they enter into favorable settlements with collusive attorneys.[148] In response to the growth of class action suits, these companies have adopted a number of tactics to counteract this development, including compelling binding arbitration through take-it-or-leave-it contracts with consumers, employees, and others as we previously discussed in this chapter. Despite criticisms that such practices are unfair,[149] they have been sustained by courts that see arbitration as an effective and fair way to resolve disputes.[150]

Taxpayer's suits are similar to class action suits in that individuals claim to represent an entire class of similarly situated persons—in this case taxpayers. Individual taxpayers—or organized taxpayer groups—file lawsuits against the state or federal government—or specific governmental agency—on behalf of all taxpayers against government spending that is thought to be unlawful.[151] The U.S. Supreme Court held in *Flast v. Cohen*[152] that taxpayers have **standing**—legally protectable stake or interest that an individual has in a dispute that entitles him to bring the controversy before the court—to prevent the unconstitutional use of funds. In that case, Florance Flast and others filed a suit against Wilbur Cohen, the Secretary of Health, Education, and Welfare, arguing that spending taxpayer funds on religious schools violated the Establishment Clause of the First Amendment. Many state laws grant individuals the right to sue local officials to recover money that has been wrongfully spent. However, in recent years defendants have found ways to narrow the definition of taxpayer and standing to make it more difficult for suits to go forward—particularly at the federal level.[153] Yet it is also true on the local level. For example, in California—a state that explicitly authorizes taxpayer suits by statute—a state court recently held that only individuals who pay property taxes—as opposed to income, gas, or sales taxes—can bring taxpayer suits because, unlike other groups, they have a greater interest in government action.[154] Still, taxpayer suits can be a powerful tool for ordinary citizens to not only check government spending but to also engage the policy-making process.

ISSUES IN CIVIL DISPUTES: LITIGIOUSNESS AND TORT REFORM

The hot coffee case that began this chapter has been a lightning rod for the debate over tort reform as the issue of so-called "frivolous lawsuits" continues to be one that polarizes the legal profession and the nation. Should individuals be able to sue large corporations? Should companies be "punished" by large punitive damage awards? If so, how should those awards be determined and should they be capped? Where you stand on these questions is largely determined by whether you think the U.S. is an overly litigious nation. Scholars have found that concerns about litigiousness tend to focus on personal injury lawsuits even though such cases are rare compared to other areas of civil litigation such as contract actions, which are both far more numerous are generally viewed with approval.[155] What causes this skewed perception? At the broadest level, the myth is driven by the changing conception of society—for example, from a farming to manufacturing to industrial to technological economy, from a racially homogenous population to a diverse one, from an older generation to a younger one—and the resulting contentious relationship between "insiders" and "outsiders" in society. The media only serve to exacerbate these root causes.[156]

Thus, the popular myth of litigiousness is more broadly a commentary on dissatisfaction with the changing realities of modern American society. The myth persists as part of a larger symbolic effort by "insiders" to preserve a sense of meaning and coherence in the face of social changes they find threatening and confusing. Thus, **tort reform**—proposed changes in the civil justice system that would reduce tort litigation or damages—is popular to the extent that it is seen as a solution, even if only a partial one, to the problem of living in a world that has lost the innocence and simplicity it is thought to have had. Ironically, to the extent that tort reform takes place, the broader changes that drive tort reformers will only persist. Thus, tort reform will never solve the larger issue of the perception of lost innocence.

Robert Kagan argues that tort reform measures such as placing caps on damages are unlikely to change the nation's broader legal style of lawyer-dominated litigation.[157] Instead, Kagan proposes following the lead of other nations by enhancing the power of bureaucrats and judges. But Kagan is skeptical that such reforms are possible given the "legal parochialism" of American elites who he argues are largely unaware of what takes place outside the U.S. context. Building on Kagan's work, political scientist Thomas Burke has categorized anti-litigation efforts into two broad categories: discouragement policies and replacement policies.[158] Discouragement policies seek to decrease the amount of litigation in some way. The tort reform movement is an example of an anti-litigation effort that advocates discouragement policies. Specifically, tort reform centers around the caps on damage awards. Replacement reforms, on the other hand, seek to replace a category of litigation with an alternative non-litigation mechanism. An example of a replacement reform is the September 11th Victim Compensation Fund to provide victims of the 9/11 terrorist attacks with compensation without them having to resort to litigation. Other examples include no-fault auto insurance and state-run workers' compensation schemes. Thus, policymakers interested in litigation reform have a choice between discouragement

Image 6.5 Protesters and Police in Grant Park Protesters and police in Grant Park, Chicago, IL, 1968. *The popular myth of litigiousness is more broadly a commentary on dissatisfaction with the changing realities of modern American society. The myth persists as part of a larger symbolic effort by "insiders" to preserve a sense of meaning and coherence in the face of social changes they find threatening and confusing.* Exhibit from the case *United States v. Dellinger*, August 28, 1968, National Archives, Chicago, IL.

and replacement legislation. Yet, research shows that even when there is broad agreement among policymakers, legal professionals, and experts that a form of litigation—such as asbestos claims—is inefficient and unfair to both victims and businesses, political obstacles, such as Senate filibusters and political polarization, can thwart policy change.[159]

Law professor Carl Bogus argues that lawsuits are good for America, a beneficial adjunct to government regulation that is not as easily manipulated by big business.[160] He argues that modern tort law actually developed because of government failure to pass legislation to protect people from the hazards of the industrial revolution. Litigation and courts gave rise to safety measures when elected officials refused to act. In his examination of asbestos tort litigation, Jeb Barnes has argued that given the information and political constraints on legislators and rule-makers, courts can be a fruitful if not ideal forum for policy making.[161] Charles Epp has demonstrated how activists used the threat of legal liability and lawsuit publicity to induce bureaucratic reforms of police brutality, workplace sexual harassment, and playground safety through innovative managerial ideas such as intricate rules, employee training, and managerial oversight.[162]

In all, questions about whether there has been a litigation explosion or whether tort reform is needed serve only to distract from the larger issue of what the role of litigation in society should be and how it relates to the larger policy-making process. Given that civil litigation is currently the mechanism by which harmed persons seek justice, yet only one in eight people who suffer serious injury from medical malpractice sue and only about five in 100 who believe they have been discriminated against at work file a claim, it would seem that the current system has failed to provide justice. Such conclusions become even starker when one considers that even if plaintiffs decide to file a suit, 95 percent lose on appeal.[163]

CONCLUSION

The myth that the American civil litigation process is one of hyper-litigiousness driven by greedy and manipulative lawyers and litigants is a powerful one. Yet the reality is that going to court is usually the last thing people do to settle disputes. Most injurious experiences never even reach the level of disputes, let alone formal lawsuits, and even if they do end up in the legal system they will likely settle without formal trials. Thus, there may be too *little* legal conflict in the U.S., rather than too much. The overly litigious perspective is often driven by the "haves" and the repeat players who would rather avoid conflict as well as courts who may necessarily have limited resources to handle large volumes of litigation. Shifting the focus from these entities to the "have nots" and one-shotters suggests that under-litigiousness may be what is actually occurring.

But not all civil litigation is driven by money and business. Interest groups use courts to make political, social, and economic demands on others and to influence broad government policies that affect many people. Test cases, class actions, taxpayer's suits, and *amicus* briefs are common ways that organized interests access courts to not only win cases on behalf of litigants but to change the law. Thus, the civil litigation process provides a judicial alternative to the political process of elections and lobbying executives and legislatures to achieve social change.

Tort reform carries the risk that people will be deprived of the help they need and that government has failed to provide. The myth that people use the civil justice system to make a quick buck obscures the reality that many times it is used as a last resort by desperate individuals. If the myth of large and growing numbers of people suing for frivolous reasons persists, the result will inevitably be that it will be harder for individuals with legitimate concerns to bring cases to court and obtain justice through the civil process.

Suggested Readings

Thomas F. Burke. *Lawyers, Lawsuits, and Legal Rights: The Battle Over Litigation in American Society* (Berkeley, CA: University of California Press, 2002). This book interrogates the perception that Americans are litigious, using evidence from the Americans with Disabilities Act, California no-fault auto insurance, and the Vaccine Injury Compensation Act to make the argument that it is not Americans but American public policy that is litigious.

Charles R. Epp. *The Rights Revolution: Lawyers, Activists, and Supreme Courts in Comparative Perspective* (Chicago, IL: University of Chicago Press, 1998). An examination of the rights revolution as a function of advocacy group influence, the establishment of governmental enforcement agencies, growth in the financial and legal resources available to ordinary citizens, and strategic planning on the part of grass roots organization.

Sean Farhang. *The Litigation State: Public Regulation and Private Lawsuits in the U.S.* (Princeton, NJ: Princeton University Press, 2010). This volume investigates the role of private lawsuits in the implementation of federal statutes, making a powerful argument that the explosion of private lawsuits to enforce federal law has been fostered by the deep ideological polarization between the president and Congress over the past half century.

William Haltom and Michael McCann. *Distorting the Law: Politics, Media, and the Litigation Crisis* (Chicago, IL: University of Chicago Press, 2004). Relying on interviews, systematic analysis of newspapers, and case studies of the McDonald's coffee case and tobacco litigation, the authors demonstrate how distorted understandings of tort litigation have contributed to the myth that the U.S. is litigious and burdened by frivolous lawsuits and ridiculous settlements.

Robert A. Kagan. *Adversarial Legalism: The American Way of Law* (Cambridge, MA: Harvard University Press, 2003). This book offers a compelling evaluation of American legal culture, characterizing it as one dominated by lawyers and litigation, and providing a rich historical and cross-national comparative perspective.

Endnotes

1   Roy P. Basler, ed., *The Collected Works of Abraham Lincoln*, Volume 2 (New Brunswick, NJ: Rutgers University Press, 1953): 82.

2   Bernard Weinraub, "The Media Business; Disney Settles Bitter Suit with Former Studio Chief," *New York Times*, July 8, 1999.

3   *Liebeck v. McDonald's Restaurants* (Bernalillo County, N.M. Dist. Ct., August 18, 1994). Dan Shaw,
    "Coffee, Tea or Ouch?" *New York Times*, October 12, 1994.

4   See William Haltom and Michael McCann, *Distorting the Law: Politics, Media, and the Litiga-
    tion Crisis* (Chicago, IL: University of Chicago Press, 2004). But also see Joshua C. Wilson and
    Erin Ackerman, "'Tort Tales' and TV Judges: Amplifying, Modifying, or Countering the Antitort
    Narrative?" *Law & Society Review*, vol. 46, no. 1 (March 2012): 105–135, suggesting that reality
    TV judge shows present a view of the civil law system that largely treats plaintiffs' claims as legit-
    imate and showcases the majority of defendants as wrongdoers. Nonetheless, they also find that
    the dramatic qualities of these shows limit their potential as narratives to counter the anti-tort
    and anti-ligation stories.

5   Andrea Gerlin, "A Matter of Degree: How a Jury Decided that a Coffee Spill Is Worth $2.9 Million,"
    Wall Street Journal, September 1, 1994.

6   For a thorough discussion of the case, see Chapter Six in William Haltom and Michael McCann,
    Distorting the Law: Politics, Media, and the Litigation Crisis (Chicago, IL: University of Chi-
    cago Press, 2004). See, also, the 2011 HBO documentary film *Hot Coffee* (http://www.hotcoffeet-
    hemovie.com) and the 2013, 12-minute *New York Times* video on the case (http://www.nytimes.
    com/video/us/100000002507537/scalded-by-coffee-then-news-media.html).

7   On his eponymously named CBS show *Late Night with David Letterman*, the host included the
    following on his Top Ten List of Dr. Kevorkian Tips for Summer on the June 29, 1995 broadcast:
    "Number Four: Take a bunch of friends to McDonald's and pour scalding coffee on each other." Jay
    Leno, host of NBC's *The Tonight Show*, also referenced the case for jokes on his show. See Mark
    B. Greenlee, "Kramer v. Java World: Images, Issues, and Idols in the Debate over Tort Reform,"
    Capital University Law Review, vol. 26 (1997): 701–738, 702.

8   In the October 5, 1995 episode of the NBC sitcom *Seinfeld*, which starred comedian Jerry Seinfeld,
    Kramer (one of Jerry's friends) initiates a case against a coffee shop after he spills coffee on himself
    in a theater. Despite the fact that Kramer burnt himself while sneaking into the theater (rather than
    pay for admission) and that the minor burn he suffered was quickly remedied by a single appli-
    cation of a medicinal balm, Kramer's lawyer is confident he has a strong case. However, Elaine,
    another of Jerry's friends, asks, " . . . [W]ho ever heard of this anyway? Suing a company because
    their coffee is too hot? Coffee is supposed to be hot."

9   For example, Mercedes Benz ran a commercial for a new four-wheel drive vehicle depicting the
    vehicle maneuvering over rough terrain while a child hands a cup of hot tea to his grandmother.
    And, Sprint aired a commercial in which Emmy-winning, Academy Award–nominated Candice
    Bergen places an order at a drive-through window saying, "Large coffee. Make sure the lid's on this
    time." See Mark B. Greenlee, "Kramer v. Java World: Images, Issues, and Idols in the Debate over
    Tort Reform," *Capital University Law Review*, vol. 26 (1997): 701–738, fn. 14.

10 Toby Keith, a popular American country music singer and songwriter, included the following lyric
    referencing the case in his number one hit "American Ride": "Spill a cup of coffee, make a million
    dollars." See Bonnie Bertram, "Storm Still Brews Over Scalding Coffee," *New York Times*, October
    25, 2013.

11 On the concept of narratives see Patricia Ewick and Susan S. Silbey, "Subversive Stories and
    Hegemonic Tales: Toward a Sociology of Narrative," *Law & Society Review*, vol. 29, no. 2 (1995):
    197–226.

12 Deborah R. Hensler, M. Susan Marquis, Allan F. Abrahamse, Sandra H. Berry, Patricia A. Ebener,
    Elizabeth G. Lewis, E. Allan Lind, Robert J. MacCoun, Willard. G. Manning, Jeannette A. Rogowski,
    and Mary E. Vaiana, *Compensation for Accidental Injuries in the United States* (Santa Monica,
    CA: Rand, 1991). Tom Baker, *The Medical Malpractice Myth* (Chicago, IL: University of Chicago
    Press, 2005).

13 Richard Y. Schauffler, Robert C. LaFountain, Shauna M. Strickland, and Kathryn Holt, Examining
    the Work of State Courts: An Analysis of 2010 State Court Caseloads (Williamsburg, VA: National
    Center for State Courts, 2012): 10.

14 Ibid.

15 See, for example, Walter K. Olson, *The Litigation Explosion: What Happened When America Unleashed the Lawsuit* (New York, NY: Dutton, 1991); Philip K. Howard, *The Death of Common Sense: How Law Is Suffocating America* (New York, NY: Random House, 1994).

16 Lawrence M. Friedman, *Total Justice* (New York, NY: Russell Sage, 1994). But this does not mean rights consciousness is inevitable and only bound to expand over time. For example, research on rights consciousness in northern Thailand suggests it may be diminishing, with ordinary people increasingly relying on new forms of religiosity to justify inaction. See David M. Engel and Jaruwan S. Engel, *Tort, Custom, and Karma: Globalization and Legal Consciousness in Thailand* (Stanford, CA: Stanford University Press, 2010). See, also, David M. Engel, "Vertical and Horizontal Perspectives on Rights Consciousness," *Indiana Journal of Global Legal Studies*, vol. 19, no. 2 (Summer 2012): 423–455.

17 For a review of the extensive literature on rights consciousness see Stuart A. Scheingold, *The Politics of Rights: Lawyers, Public Policy, and Political Change*, Second Edition (Ann Arbor, MI: University of Michigan Press, 2004). For the legal history of the development of tort law and its relationship to industrialization and economic development during the nineteenth and early twentieth centuries, see Randolph Bergstrom, *Courting Danger: Injury and Law in New York City, 1870–1910* (Ithaca, NY: Cornell University Press, 1992); Lawrence M. Friedman and Thomas D. Russell, "More Civil Wrongs: Personal Injury Litigation, 1901–1910," *American Journal of Legal History*, vol. 34, no. 3 (July 1990): 295–314; Arthur F. McEvoy, *The Triangle Shirtwaist Factory Fire of 1911: Social Change, Industrial Accidents, and the Evolution of Commonsense Causality* (Chicago, IL: American Bar Association,1994); Donald W. Rogers, "From Common Law to Factory Laws: The Transformation of Workplace Safety Law in Wisconsin before Progressivism," *American Journal of Legal History*, vol. 39, no. 2 (April 1995): 177–213; Christopher L. Tomlins, *Law, Labor, and Ideology in the Early American Republic* (New York, NY: Cambridge University Press, 1993); Barbara Young Welke, *Recasting American Liberty: Gender, Race, Law, and the Railroad Revolution, 1865–1920* (New York, NY: Cambridge University Press, 2001); John Fabian Witt, *The Accidental Republic: Crippled Workingmen, Destitute Widows, and the Remaking of American Law* (Cambridge, MA: Harvard University Press, 2004). For the legal history of mid-twentieth century tort law development see John Fabian Witt, *Patriots and Cosmopolitans: Hidden Histories of American Law* (Cambridge, MA: Harvard University Press, 2007).

18 This should not be confused with Kenner's line of popular DC Comics characters produced under the rubric *Batman: Total Justice*. The *Total Justice* characters were engaged in combating evildoers and nefarious villains. They did not take a side in debates over tort reform.

19 Robert A. Kagan, "Adversarial Legalism and American Government," *Journal of Policy Analysis and Management*, vol. 10, no. 3 (Summer 1991): 369–406, 375.

20 Despite Kagan's assertions, some literature suggests that other nations may be becoming more adversarial. See, for example, Eric A. Feldman, "Blood Justice: Courts, Conflict, and Compensation in Japan, France, and the United States," *Law & Society Review*, vol. 34, no. 3 (2000): 651–702; Jefferey M. Sellers, "Litigation as a Local Political Resource: Courts in Controversies over Land Use in France, Germany, and the United States," *Law & Society Review*, vol. 29, no. 3 (1995): 475–516; C. Neal Tate and Torbjorn Vallinder, *The Global Expansion of Judicial Power* (New York, NY: New York University Press, 1995).

21 Robert A. Kagan, "Adversarial Legalism and American Government," *Journal of Policy Analysis and Management*, vol. 10, no. 3 (Summer 1991): 369–406, 389–397.

22 Separation of powers as in the distribution of power across the separate branches of the national government.

23 Federalism as in the distribution of power between levels of government; that is, the states and the federal government.

24 Daphne Eviatar, "Is Litigation a Blight, or Built In?" *New York Times*, November 23, 2002.

25 Thomas F. Burke, *Lawyers, Lawsuits, and Legal Rights: The Battle Over Litigation in American Society* (Berkeley, CA: University of California Press, 2002).

26 Sean Farhang, *The Litigation State: Public Regulation and Private Lawsuits in the U.S.* (Princeton, NJ: Princeton University Press, 2010).

27 See, for example, Peter H. Schuck, *Agent Orange on Trial: Mass Toxic Disasters in the Courts* (Cambridge, MA: Harvard University Press, 1986).

28 See, for example, Anya Sostek, "Attorney Says Contingency Fee Frequently Isn't the Best Bet," *Pittsburgh Post-Gazette*, April 9, 2012. See also Steven Garber, Michael D. Greenberg, Hilary Rhodes, Xiaohui Zhuo, and John L. Adams, "Do Noneconomic Damages Caps and Attorney Fee Limits Reduce Access to Justice for Victims of Medical Negligence?" *Journal of Empirical Legal Studies*, vol. 6, no. 4 (December 2009): 637–686, 655.

29 For one lively and engaging accounting of dispute resolution without resort to the legal system, see Robert C. Ellickson, *Order Without Law: How Neighbors Settle Disputes* (Cambridge, MA: Harvard University Press, 1991).

30 This does not mean that governments cannot be parties in a civil suit. For example, when he was New York Attorney General, Eliot Spitzer filed a civil suit on behalf of the State of New York against GlaxoSmithKline, a pharmaceutical company giant, charging that the company had engaged in fraud by concealing negative information about Paxil, an antidepressant. See Gardiner Harris, "Spitzer Sues a Drug Maker, Saying It Hid Negative Data," *New York Times*, June 3, 2004. Another example is the civil suit filed by a group of protestors in Missouri against the City of Ferguson and its police department for wanton and excessive force. See Taylor Wofford, "Ferguson Slapped with $40 Million Civil Rights Lawsuit," *Newsweek*, August 29, 2014. In the former scenario the government was the plaintiff in a civil suit, while in the latter, government was the defendant in a civil suit.

31 Jules L. Coleman, *Risks and Wrongs* (New York, NY: Cambridge University Press, 1992). See, also, William M. Landes and Richard A. Posner, *The Economic Structure of Tort Law* (Cambridge, MA: Cambridge University Press, 1987).

32 Though oral contracts can be as legally binding as a written contract, it is often much more difficult to demonstrate exactly what was agreed upon with an oral contract and, hence, harder to prevail when seeking to have the contract legally enforced.

33 William L.F. Felstiner, Richard L. Abel, and Austin Sarat, "The Emergence and Transformation of Disputes: Naming, Blaming, Claiming . . . ," *Law & Society Review*, vol. 15, no. 3/4 (1980–1981): 631–654. See, also, Richard E. Miller and Austin Sarat, "Grievances, Claims, and Disputes: Assessing the Adversary Culture," *Law & Society Review*, vol. 15, no. 3/4 (1980–1981): 525–566.

34 William L.F. Felstiner, Richard L. Abel, and Austin Sarat, "The Emergence and Transformation of Disputes: Naming, Blaming, Claiming . . . ," *Law & Society Review*, vol. 15, no. 3/4 (1980–1981): 631–654, 635.

35 Elizabeth C. Hirsh, "The Strength of Weak Enforcement: The Impact of Discrimination Charges, Legal Environments, and Organizational Conditions on Workplace Segregation," *American Sociological Review*, vol. 74, no. 2 (April 2009): 245–271; Derek R. Avery, Patrick F. McKay, and David C. Wilson, "What Are the Odds? How Demographic Similarity Affects the Prevalence of Perceived Employment Discrimination," *Journal of Applied Psychology*, vol. 93, no. 2 (2008): 235–249; Vincent J. Roscigno, *The Face of Discrimination: How Race and Gender Impact Work and Home Lives* (Lanham, MD: Rowman and Littlefield, 2007); Tom A. Smith, *Measuring Racial and Ethnic Discrimination* (Washington, DC: National Academies Press, 2004).

36 Elizabeth Hirsh and Christopher J. Lyons, "Perceiving Discrimination on the Job: Legal Consciousness, Workplace Context, and the Construction of Race and Discrimination," *Law & Society Review*, vol. 44, no. 2 (June 2010): 269–298.

37 Beth A. Quinn, "The Paradox of Complaining: Law, Humor, and Harassment in the Everyday Work World," *Law & Social Inquiry*, vol. 25, no. 4 (October 2000): 1151–1185; Patricia A. Gwartney-Gibbs and Denise H. Lach, "Gender and Workplace Dispute Resolution: A Conceptual and Theoretical Model," *Law & Society Review*, vol. 28, no. 2 (1994): 265–296.

38 Cynthia Ann Gonzales, *Taking It to Court: Litigating Women in the City of Valencia, 1550–1600*, unpublished dissertation (Tucson, AZ: University of Arizona, 2008): 109.

39 Hodgkin's Disease is a cancer that originates in white blood cells. D-Roc the Executioner (guitarist with Ice-T's band Body Count) and Michael C. Hall (who starred in Showtime's *Dexter* and, before

that, HBO's *Six Feet Under*) are two examples of well-known celebrities who have been diagnosed with the disease. D-Roc died from it while Hall is in remission.

40 William L.F. Felstiner, Richard L. Abel, and Austin Sarat, "The Emergence and Transformation of Disputes: Naming, Blaming, Claiming . . . ," *Law & Society Review*, vol. 15, no. 3/4 (1980–1981): 631–654, 636.

41 See, for example, Arthur Best and Alan Andreasen, "Consumer Response to Unsatisfactory Purchases: A Survey of Perceiving Defects, Voicing Complaints, and Obtaining Redress," *Law & Society Review*, vol. 11, no. 4 (Spring 1977): 701–742, 708–711; S. B. Burman, H. G. Genn, and J. Lyons, "The Use of Legal Services by Victims of Accidents in the Home—A Pilot Study," *Modern Law Review*, vol. 40, no. 1 (January 1977): 47–57; Deborah R. Hensler, M. Susan Marquis, Allan F. Abrahamse, Sandra H. Berry, Patricia A. Ebener, Elizabeth G. Lewis, E. Allan Lind, Robert J. MacCoun, Willard. G. Manning, Jeannette A. Rogowski, and Mary E. Vaiana, *Compensation for Accidental Injuries in the United States* (Santa Monica, CA: Rand, 1991); Tom Baker, *The Medical Malpractice Myth* (Chicago, IL: University of Chicago Press, 2005).

42 American Bar Association, *Report on the Legal Needs of the Low- and Moderate-Income Public* (Chicago, IL: American Bar Association, 1994): Table 3–1. See, more generally, Hazel Genn, *Paths to Justice: What People Do and Think about Going to Law* (Oxford, UK: Hart Publishing, 1999); Rebecca L. Sandefur and Aaron C. Smyth, *Access Across America: First Report of the Civil Justice Infrastructure Mapping Project* (Chicago, IL: American Bar Foundation, 2011).

43 American Bar Association, *Report on the Legal Needs of the Low- and Moderate-Income Public* (Chicago, IL: American Bar Association, 1994): Chart 2. See, also, Rebecca L. Sandefur, "The Impact of Counsel: An Analysis of Empirical Evidence," *Seattle Journal for Social Justice*, vol. 9, no. 1 (February 2010): 51–95.

44 American Bar Association, *Report on the Legal Needs of the Low- and Moderate-Income Public* (Chicago, IL: American Bar Association, 1994): Chart 3.

45 Ibid.

46 See Robert H. Mnookin and Lewis Kornhauser, "Bargaining in the Shadow of the Law: The Case of Divorce," *Yale Law Journal*, vol. 88, no. 5 (April 1979): 950–997, 985; Carrie Menkel-Meadow, "The Transformation of Disputes by Lawyers: What the Dispute Paradigm Does and Does Not Tell Us," *Journal of Dispute Resolution*, vol. 1985 (1985): 25–44.

47 American Bar Association, *Report on the Legal Needs of the Low- and Moderate-Income Public* (Chicago, IL: American Bar Association, 1994): Charts 4, 5, and 6.

48 Ibid., Chart 7.

49 See, for example, Richard L. Abel, "Socializing the Legal Profession: Can Redistributing Lawyers' Services Achieve Social Justice?" *Law & Policy Quarterly*, vol. 1, no. 1 (January 1979): 5–51; Eric H. Steele, "The Historical Context of Small Claims Courts," *Law & Social Inquiry*, vol. 6, no. 2 (April 1981): 293–376; Scott L. Cummings, "The Politics of Pro Bono," *UCLA Law Review*, vol. 52, no. 1 (October 2005): 1–149; Deborah L. Rhode, *Pro Bono in Principle and Practice: Public Service and the Professions* (Stanford, CA: Stanford University Press, 2005).

50 Richard L. Abel, "The Real Tort Crisis—Too Few Claims," *Ohio State Law Journal*, vol. 48 (Spring 1987): 443–467; Frank A. Sloan and Chee Ruey Hsieh, "Injury, Liability, and the Decision to File a Medial Malpractice Claim," *Law & Society Review*, vol. 29, no. 3 (1995): 413–435; Tom Baker, *The Medical Malpractice Myth* (Chicago, IL: University of Chicago Press, 2005): 22–44.

51 Marc Galanter, "Why the 'Haves' Come Out Ahead: Speculations on the Limits of Legal Change," *Law & Society Review*, vol. 9, no. 1 (Autumn 1974): 95–160, 124–125.

52 William L.F. Felstiner, Richard L. Abel, and Austin Sarat, "The Emergence and Transformation of Disputes: Naming, Blaming, Claiming . . . ," *Law & Society Review*, vol. 15, no. 3/4 (1980–1981): 631–654, 652. See, also, Arthur Best and Alan Andreasen, "Consumer Response to Unsatisfactory Purchases: A Survey of Perceiving Defects, Voicing Complaints, and Obtaining Redress," *Law & Society Review*, vol. 11, no. 4 (Spring 1977): 701–742, 709; Carrie Menkel-Meadow, *The 59th Street Legal Clinic: Evaluation of an Experiment* (Chicago, IL: American Bar Foundation, 1979): 40.

53 See Sally Engle Merry, "Going to Court: Strategies of Dispute Management in an American Urban Neighborhood," *Law & Society Review*, vol. 13, no. 4 (Summer 1979): 891–925. With regard to civil

litigation as an alternative to violence, see J.A. Jolowicz, "Civil Litigation: What's It For?" *Cambridge Law Journal*, vol. 67, no. 3 (November 2008): 508–520, 509–511.

54 For a broader consideration of human psychology in dispute resolution, see Neil Vidmar, "Justice Motives and Other Psychological Factors in the Development and Resolution of Disputes," in *The Justice Motive in Social Behavior: Adapting to Times of Scarcity and Change*, Melvin J. Lerner and Sally C. Lerner, eds (New York, NY: Springer, 1981).

55 See Jerome T. Barrett and Joseph Barrett, *A History of Alternative Dispute Resolution: The Story of a Political, Social, and Cultural Movement* (San Francisco, CA: Jossey-Bass, 2004). See, also, Christine Harrington, *Shadow Justice: The Ideology and Institutionalization of Alternatives to Court* (Westport, CT: Greenwood Press, 1985).

56 Negotiation could also involve additional parties (such as a union representative) but those third parties are not responsible for structuring the negotiation and are no more privileged than the other participants in the negotiation.

57 Jacqueline M. Nolan-Haley, *Alternative Dispute Resolution in a Nutshell*, Fourth Edition (St. Paul, MN: West Academic, 2013): Chapter 2.

58 See Jacqueline M. Nolan-Haley, "Court Mediation and the Search for Justice Through Law," *Washington University Law Quarterly*, vol. 74, no. 1 (1996): 47–102, 57–63; Jacqueline M. Nolan-Haley, *Alternative Dispute Resolution in a Nutshell*, Fourth Edition (St. Paul, MN: West Academic, 2013): Chapter 3.

59 See, for example, Robert A. Baruch Bush and Joseph P. Folger, *The Promise of Mediation: The Transformative Approach to Conflict*, Revised Edition (San Francisco, CA: Jossey-Bass, 2004); Martin E. Latz, "Give and Take: In Mediation, It Is Important to Negotiate Effectively with the Mediator," *ABA Journal*, vol. 87, no. 12 (December 2001): 66; Sally Engle Merry and Neal Milner, *The Possibility of Popular Justice: A Case Study of Community Mediation in the United States* (Ann Arbor, MI: University of Michigan Press, 1994).

60 Alexander J.S. Colvin, "The Relationship between Employment Arbitration and Workplace Dispute Resolution Procedures," *Ohio State Journal on Dispute Resolution*, vol. 16 (2001): 643–668.

61 Nonbinding arbitration is much like standard binding arbitration in terms of procedure. In terms of outcomes, the awards made in nonbinding arbitration may not be binding but they have the potential to be binding since most state-sponsored ADR programs that include nonbinding arbitration provide that the award will be final unless one of the parties requests a trial. For a general discussion of arbitration, see Jacqueline M. Nolan-Haley, *Alternative Dispute Resolution in a Nutshell*, Fourth Edition (St. Paul, MN: West Academic, 2013): Chapter 4.

62 See Jan Paulsson, *The Idea of Arbitration* (New York, NY: Oxford University Press, 2013) for a general discussion of arbitration and its place in the legal process, as well as a consideration of the ethical dimensions of an arbitrator's authority.

63 Rather than a single arbitrator there may be a panel of three, with one selected by the parties on either side of the arbitration and the third selected by the two chosen by the parties.

64 Lauren B. Edelman, "Legal Environments and Organizational Governance: The Expansion of Due Process in the American Workplace," *American Journal of Sociology*, vol. 95, no. 6 (May 1990): 1401–1440; Lauren B. Edelman, "Legal Ambiguity and Symbolic Structures: Organizational Mediation of Civil Rights Law," *American Journal of Sociology*, vol. 97, no. 6 (May 1992): 1531–1576; Lauren B. Edelman and Mark C. Suchman. "When the 'Haves' Hold Court: Speculations on the Organizational Internalization of Law," *Law & Society Review*, vol. 33, no. 4 (1999): 941–991; Marc Galanter and John Lande, "Private Courts and Public Authority," *Studies in Law, Politics & Society*, vol. 12 (1992): 393–415; Carrie Menkel-Meadow, "Do the 'Haves' Come out Ahead in Alternative Judicial Systems? Repeat Players in ADR," *Ohio State Journal on Dispute Resolution*, vol. 15, no. 1 (1999): 19–61; John R. Sutton, Frank Dobbin, John W. Meyer, and W. Richard Scott, "The Legalization of the Workplace," *American Journal of Sociology*, vol. 99, no. 4 (January 1994): 944–971.

65 Marc Ferris, "In Business; Reaching Out to a Third Party," *New York Times*, January 27, 2002.

66 Shauhin A. Talesh, "How Dispute Resolution System Design Matters: An Organizational Analysis of Dispute Resolution Structures and Consumer Lemon Laws," *Law & Society Review*, vol. 46, no. 3 (September 2012): 463–496.

67 John P. McIver and Susan Keilitz, "Court-Annexed Arbitration: An Introduction," vol. 14, no. 2 (1991): 123–132, 251–256.

68 To avoid infringing on the parties' right to a trial by jury, most court-annexed arbitration includes provision for a trial at the conclusion of the arbitration process if a party so desires.

69 The Federal Arbitration Act (Pub.L. 68–401, 43 Stat. 883) applies not only in federal jurisdiction but state jurisdictions, too, when what is at issue involves interstate commerce.

70 Caroline E. Mayer, "Arbitration Left ID Theft Victim with $27,000 Bill," *Washington Post*, February 24, 2005.

71 Michelle Andrews, "Signing a Mandatory Arbitration Agreement with a Nursing Home Can Be Troubling," *Washington Post*, September 17, 2012.

72 Tara Siegel Bernard, "Taking a Broker to Arbitration," *New York Times*, July 19, 2014.

73 David Lazarus, "Bill Aims to Restore Consumers' Right to Sue," *Los Angeles Times*, October 18, 2011.

74 Elizabeth G. Thornburg, "Contracting with Tortfeasors: Mandatory Arbitration Clauses and Personal Injury Claims," *Law and Contemporary Problems*, vol. 67, no. 1 (Winter 2004): 253–278, 259–260. More generally, see Jean R. Sternlight, "Panacea or Corporate Tool? Debunking the Supreme Court's Preference for Binding Arbitration," *Washington University Law Quarterly*, vol. 74, no. 3 (1996): 637–712, 638; Katherine Van Wezel Stone, "Mandatory Arbitration of Individual Employment Rights: The Yellow Dog Contract of the 1990s," *Denver University Law Review*, vol. 73, no. 4 (1996): 1017–1050.

75 Launched in 2012 on the University of Southern California campus, Tinder is an application that uses information from users' Facebook pages to match users in a given geographical location. See Nick Bilton, "Tinder, the Fast-Growing Dating App, Taps an Age-Old Truth," *New York Times*, October 29, 2014. Tinder has been criticized as shallow for its focus on physical appearance; Carson Griffith, "On One Phone App, Looks Are Everything," *New York Times*, April 24, 2013.

76 Tinder, "Terms of Use," September 1, 2013, http://www.gotinder.com/terms (accessed February 1, 2015).

77 See, for example, *AT&T Mobility v. Concepcion* (563 U.S. 321, 2011) and *CompuCredit Corp. v. Greenwood* (132 S. Ct. 665, 2012).

78 *Shearson/American Express, Inc. v. McMahon*, 482 U.S. 220, 232 (1987).

79 Robert A. Baruch Bush, "Mediation and Adjudication, Dispute Resolution and Ideology: An Imaginary Conversation," *Journal of Contemporary Issues*, vol. 3, no. 1 (1989–1990): 1–33; Robert A. Baruch Bush and Joseph P. Folger, *The Promise of Mediation: Responding to Conflict through Empowerment and Recognition* (San Francisco, CA: Jossey-Bass, 1994).

80 See, for example, Christine Harrington, *Shadow Justice: The Ideology and Institutionalization of Alternatives to Court* (Westport, CT: Greenwood Press, 1985).

81 For a discussion of court cases sustaining these provisions see Jean R. Sternlight, "Panacea or Corporate Tool? Debunking the Supreme Court's Preference for Binding Arbitration," *Washington University Law Quarterly*, vol. 74, no. 3 (1996): 637–712, 638.

82 Shauhin A. Talesh, "How Dispute Resolution System Design Matters: An Organizational Analysis of Dispute Resolution Structures and Consumer Lemon Laws," *Law & Society Review*, vol. 46, no. 3 (September 2012): 463–496.

83 Alexander J.S. Colvin, "An Empirical Study of Employment Arbitration: Case Outcomes and Processes," *Journal of Empirical Legal Studies*, vol. 8, no. 1 (March 2011): 1–23.

84 *NAACP v. Meese*, 615 F. Sup. 200, 205–206 (D.D.C. 1985).

85 The discussion that follows is based, in part, on Henry Robert Glick, *Courts, Politics & Justice*, Third Edition (New York, NY: McGraw-Hill, 1993).

86 Erik Eckholm and Ian Lovett, "A Push for Legal Aid in Civil Cases Finds Its Advocates," *New York Times*, November 21, 2014.

87 For a review of the comparative literature on this topic see Kuo-Chang Huang, Chang-Ching Lin, and Kong-Pin Chen, "Do Rich and Poor Behave Similarly in Seeking Legal Advice: Lessons from Taiwan in Comparative Perspective," *Law & Society Review*, vol. 48, no. 1 (March 2014): 193–223, 195–197.

88 Leon H. Mayhew and Albert J. Reiss, Jr., "The Social Organization of Legal Contracts," *American Sociological Review*, vol. 34, no. 3 (June 1969): 309–318; Barbara A. Curran, *The Legal Needs of the Public: The Final Report of a National Survey* (Chicago, IL: American Bar Foundation, 1977); Herbert M. Kritzer, "To Lawyer or Not to Lawyer: *Is* that the Question?" *Journal of Empirical Legal Studies*, vol. 5, no. 4 (December 2008): 875–906.

89 John Ruhnka and Steven Weller with John A. Martin, *Small Claims Courts: A National Examination* (Williamsburg, VA: National Center for State Courts, 1979); Barbara A. Curran, *The Legal Needs of the Public: The Final Report of a National Survey* (Chicago, IL: American Bar Foundation, 1977): 234–239.

90 Ellen Berrey, Steve G. Hoffman, and Laura Beth Nielsen, "Situated Justice: A Contextual Analysis of Fairness and Inequality in Employment Discrimination Litigation," *Law & Society Review*, vol. 46, no. 1 (March 2012): 1–36.

91 Austin Sarat and William L. F. Felstiner, *Divorce Lawyers and Their Clients: Power & Meaning in the Legal Process* (New York, NY: Oxford University Press, 1995).

92 More generally, see Michael Asimow, "How I Learned to Litigate at the Movies," *American Bar Association Journal*, vol. 94, no. 8 (August 2008): 48–53.

93 Douglas Rosenthal, *Lawyer and Client: Who's in Charge?* (New York, NY: Russell Sage, 1974): 112–113; Eric H. Steele and Raymond T. Nimmer, "Lawyers, Clients, and Professional Regulation," *American Bar Foundation Research Journal*, vol. 1, no. 3 (1976): 917–1019, 956–962.

94 Stewart Macaulay, "Lawyers and Consumer Protection Laws," *Law & Society Review*, vol. 14, no. 1 (Autumn 1979): 115–171.

95 Douglas Rosenthal, *Lawyer and Client: Who's in Charge?* (New York, NY: Russell Sage, 1974): 103; Murray L. Schwartz and Daniel J. B. Mitchell, "An Economic Analysis of the Contingent Fee in Personal-Injury Litigation," *Stanford Law Review*, vol. 22, no. 6 (June 1970): 1125–1162, 1133.

96 Hubert O'Gorman, *Lawyers and Matrimonial Cases: A Study of Informal Pressures in Private Professional Practice* (New York, NY: Columbia University Press, 1963): 146.

97 See, for example, Dorothy L. Maddi and Frederic R. Merrill, *The Private Practicing Bar and Legal Services for Low-Income People* (Chicago, IL: American Bar Foundation, 1971): 17–19; Joel F. Handler, Ellen Jane Hollingsworth, and Howard S. Erlanger, *Lawyers and the Pursuit of Legal Rights* (New York, NY: Academic Press, 1978): Chapter 5.

98 Cary Coglianese, "Litigating with Relationships: Disputes and Disturbances in the Regulatory Process," *Law & Society Review*, vol. 30, no. 4 (1996): 735–766, 736.

99 Dareh Gregorian, "Family of Tracy Morgan's Friend James McNair, Killed in June Crash, Settles Suit with Walmart," *Daily News*, Wednesday January 21, 2015.

100 Ellen Berrey, Steve G. Hoffman, and Laura Beth Nielsen, "Situated Justice: A Contextual Analysis of Fairness and Inequality in Employment Discrimination Litigation," *Law & Society Review*, vol. 46, no. 1 (March 2012): 1–36.

101 Peter Charles Hoffer, "Honor and the Roots of American Litigiousness," *American Journal of Legal History*, vol. 33, no. 4 (October 1989): 295–319, 306.

102 See, for example, William M. O'Barr and John M. Conley, "Lay Expectations of the Civil Justice System," *Law & Society Review*, vol. 22, no. 1, (1988): 137–162; John Bronsteen, Christopher Buccafusco, and Jonathan S. Meyer, "Hedonic Adaptation and the Settlement of Civil Lawsuit," *Columbia Law Review*, vol. 108, no. 6 (October 2008): 1516–1549; and J.J. Prescott, Kathryn E. Spier, and Albert Yoon, "Trial and Settlement: A Study of High-Low Agreements," *Journal of Law and Economics*, vol. 57, no. 3 (August 2014): 699–746.

103 Arthur Best and Alan Andreasen, "Consumer Response to Unsatisfactory Purchases: A Survey of Perceiving Defects, Voicing Complaints, and Obtaining Redress," *Law & Society Review*, vol. 11, no. 4 (Spring 1977): 701–742.

104 William H. Simon, "The Ideology of Advocacy: Procedural Justice and Professional Ethics," *Wisconsin Law Review*, vol. 1, no. 1 (1978): 29–144, 98, 115.

105 See, for example, Liz Navrati, "Pa. Reducing Backlog of Civil Cases, Chief Justice Says," *Pittsburgh Post-Gazette*, September 29, 2014; Michael Booth and Mary Pat Gallagher, "Vacancies, Backlogs Growing, But Christie Not Sole Factor," *New Jersey Law Journal*, August 14, 2014; Maura Dolan, "Cutbacks in

California Court System Produces Long Lines, Short Tempers," *Los Angeles Times*, May 20, 2014; and Gary Martin, "Vacancies, Backlogs Plague Federal Judiciary," *Houston Chronicle*, March 1, 2013;

106   Under limited circumstances, an audiovisual work might also be incorporated into a complaint. See Aimee Woodward Brown, "Pleading in Technicolor: When Can Litigants Incorporate Audiovisual Works into Their Complaints?" *University of Chicago Law Review*, vol. 80, no. 2 (Summer 2013): 1269–1307.

107   For a brief history of the rules of discovery and various reform efforts, see Jeffrey W. Stempel, "Ulysses Tied to the Generic Whipping Post: The Continuing Odyssey of Discovery 'Reform,'" *Law and Contemporary Problems*, vol. 64, no. 2/3 (Spring-Summer 2001): 197–252, 201–217.

108   See, for example, Richard E. Best, "Taming the Discovery Monster," *California Litigation*, vol. 18, no. 3 (December 2005); Edward Hartnett, "Taming *Twombly*, Even after *Iqbal*," *University of Pennsylvania Law Review*, vol. 158, no. 2 (January 2010): 473–516.

109   See Martin H. Redish, "Electronic Discovery and the Litigation Matrix," *Duke Law Journal*, vol. 51, no. 2 (November 2001): 561–628. See, also, Bradley T. Tennis, "Cost-Shifting in Electronic Discovery," *Yale Law Journal*, vol. 119, no. 5 (March 2010): 1113–1121.

110   John Markoff, "Armies of Expensive Lawyers, Replaced by Cheaper Software," *New York Times*, March 4, 2011. But see Barbara Rose, "Boom and Bust: E-Discovery Industry Seeing Slower Growth, More Mergers," *ABA Journal*, vol. 95, no. 8 (August 2009): 29–30.

111   Martin H. Redish, "Electronic Discovery and the Litigation Matrix," *Duke Law Journal*, vol. 51, no. 2 (November 2001): 561–628, 563.

112   See, for example, Jeffrey A. Parness, "Thinking Outside the Civil Case Box: Reformulating Pretrial Conference Laws," *Kansas Law Review*, vol. 50 (January 2002): 347–374.

113   Fed. R. Civ. P. 48(a).

114   Fed. R. Civ. P. 48(b).

115   David B. Rottman and Shauna M. Strickland, *State Court Organization, 2004* (Washington, DC: U.S. Department of Justice, Bureau of Justice Statistics, 2006): Table 42.

116   For a comparative perspective on the burden of proof in civil cases see Kevin M. Clermont and Emily Sherwin, "A Comparative View of Standards of Proof," *American Journal of Comparative Law*, vol. 50, no. 2 (Spring 2002): 243–275.

117   Eyal Zamir and Ilana Ritov, "Loss Aversion, Omission Bias, and the Burden of Proof in Civil Litigation," *Journal of Legal Studies*, vol. 41, no. 1 (January 2012): 165–207.

118   Rita James Simon and Linda Mahan, "Quantifying Burdens of Proof: A View from the Bench, the Jury, and the Classroom," *Law & Society Review*, vol. 5, no. 3 (February 1971): 319–330.

119   Thomas H. Cohen, "When Is the Verdict or Judgment Final?: An Examination of Posttrial Activity in Civil Litigation," *Justice System Journal*, vol. 32, no. 1 (2011): 62–87, 63–64.

120   Other post-trial motions include requests to modify court fees and costs and to correct errors that occurred at trial.

121   Thomas H. Cohen, "When Is the Verdict or Judgment Final?: An Examination of Posttrial Activity in Civil Litigation," *Justice System Journal*, vol. 32, no. 1 (2011): 62–87, 63.

122   Ibid.

123   Marc Galanter, "Why the 'Haves' Come Out Ahead: Speculations on the Limits of Legal Change," *Law & Society Review*, vol. 9, no. 1 (Autumn 1974): 95–160.

124   The discussion below is adapted from Marc Galanter, "Why the 'Haves' Come Out Ahead: Speculations on the Limits of Legal Change," *Law & Society Review*, vol. 9, no. 1 (Autumn 1974): 95–160.

125   Arguably the ultimate repeat player in the federal judiciary is the Solicitor General. See Richard L. Pacelle, *Between Law and Politics: The Solicitor General and the Structuring of Race, Gender, and Reproductive Rights Litigation* (College Station, TX: Texas A&M University Press, 2003).

126   For a particularly assertive promotion of the litigation explosion thesis see Walter K. Olson, *The Litigation Explosion: What Happened When American Unleashed the Lawsuit* (New York, NY: Truman TalleyBooks, 1992). For a discussion of the various reforms that have been advanced to combat the purported litigation explosion, see Michael D. Johnston, "The Litigation Explosion, Proposed Reforms, and Their Consequences," *BYU Journal of Public Law*, vol. 21, no. 1 (Fall 2006): 179–207.

127 See, for example, Joel B. Grossman and Austin Sarat, "Litigation in the Federal Courts: A Comparative Perspective," *Law & Society Review*, vol. 9, no. 2 (1975): 321–346; Lawrence M. Friedman and Robert V. Percival, "A Tale of Two Courts: Litigation in Alameda and San Benito Counties," *Law & Society Review*, vol. 10, no. 2 (1976): 267–301; Wayne V. McIntosh, "One Hundred Fifty Years of Dispute Settlement: A Court Tale," *Law & Society Review*, vol. 15, no. 3/4 (1980–1981): 823–848; Wayne McIntosh, "Private Use of a Public Forum: A Long Range View of the Dispute Processing Role of Courts," *American Political Science Review*, vol. 77, no. 4 (December 1983): 991–1010; Marc Galanter, "Reading the Landscape of Disputes: What We Know and Don't Know (and Think We Know) About Our Allegedly Contentious and Litigious Society," *UCLA Law Review*, vol. 31 (October 1983): 4–71; Marc Galanter, "The Day After the Litigation Explosion," *Maryland Law Review*, vol. 46, no. 1 (1986): 3–39; Marc Galanter, "Beyond the Litigation Panic," *Proceedings of the Academy of Political Science*, vol. 37, no. 1 (1988): 1–30; Richard Turbin, "Statistics Challenge Public Perception," *Pacific Business News*, February 8, 1998; and Marc Galanter, "An Oil Strike in Hell: Contemporary Legends About the Civil Justice System," *Arizona Law Review*, vol. 40, no. 3 (Fall 1998): 717–752.

128 Marc Galanter, "Reading the Landscape of Disputes: What We Know and Don't Know (and Think We Know) About Our Allegedly Contentious and Litigious Society," *UCLA Law Review*, vol. 31 (October 1983): 4–71.

129 Administrative Office of the United States Courts, *1998 Annual Report of the Director: Judicial Business of the U.S. Courts* (Washington, DC: U.S. Government Printing Office, 1999): 26.

130 Administrative Office of the United States Courts, *2002 Annual Report of the Director: Judicial Business of the U.S. Courts* (Washington, DC: U.S. Government Printing Office, 2003): 17–19.

131 Administrative Office of the United States Courts, *2006 Annual Report of the Director: Judicial Business of the U.S. Courts* (Washington, DC: U.S. Government Printing Office, 2007): 13.

132 For a comprehensive discussion of asbestos litigation see Jeb Barnes, *Dust-Up: Asbestos Litigation and the Failure of Commonsense Policy Reform* (Washington, DC: Georgetown University Press, 2011).

133 Administrative Office of the United States Courts, *2011 Annual Report of the Director: Judicial Business of the U.S. Courts* (Washington, DC: U.S. Government Printing Office, 2012), 12, 14.

134 542 U.S. 296 (2004).

135 543 U.S. 220 (2005).

136 P.L. 111–220.

137 For a general introduction, see Richard H. Klonoff, *Class Actions and Other Multi-Party Litigation in a Nutshell* (Eagan, MN: West, 2007). See, also, Deborah Hensler and Erick K. Moller, *Class Action Dilemmas: Pursuing Public Goods for Private Gain* (Santa Monica, CA: Rand, 2000)

138 Eileen Finan, "Bachelor and Bachelorette Sued for Alleged Racial Discrimination," *People*, April 19, 2012.

139 The case, *Lane v. Facebook*, was filed in the U.S. District Court for the Northern District of California. It was settled prior to going to trial.

140 The case was filed in the U.S. District Court for the Eastern District of Pennsylvania, but was settled prior to going to trial.

141 Larry King and Bonnie L. Cook, "Family in Laptop Controversy Is No Stranger to Legal Disputes," *Philadelphia Inquirer*, February 25, 2010.

142 For an informative discussion of mootness see Evan Tsen Lee, "Deconstitutionalizing Justiciability: The Example of Mootness," *Harvard Law Review*, vol. 105, no. 3 (January 1992): 603–669.

143 *DeFunis v. Odegaard*, 416 U.S. 312 (1974).

144 410 U.S. 113 (1973).

145 Marian Faux, *Roe v. Wade: The Untold Story of the Landmark Supreme Court Decision that Made Abortion Legal* (New York, NY: Scribner, 1988): 139–140.

146 Pat Murphy, "$9.5 Deal in Facebook Class Action Deemed 'Adequate,' Says 9th Circuit," *Lawyers Weekly*, September 24, 2012.

147 Steven B. Hantler and Robert E. Norton, "Coupon Settlements: The Emperor's Clothes of Class Actions," *Georgetown Journal of Legal Ethics*, vol. 18 (Fall 2005): 1343–1358.

148 See Richard B. Schmitt, "The Deal Makers: Some Firms Embrace the Widely Dreaded Class Action Lawsuit," *Wall Street Journal*, July 18, 1996; Deborah R. Hensler, Nicholas M. Pace, Bonnie Dombey-Moore, Elizabeth Giddens, Jennifer Gross, and Erik Moller, *Class Action Dilemmas: Pursuing Public Goals for Private Gain* (Santa Monica, CA: Rand, 1999).

149 See, for example, Jean R. Sternlight, "As Mandatory Binding Arbitration Meets the Class Action, Will the Class Action Survive?" *William and Mary Law Review* 42 (2000): 1–126.

150 See, for example, *AT&T Mobility v. Concepcion*, 563 U.S. 321 (2011).

151 For a general overview see "Taxpayers' Suits: A Survey and Summary," *The Yale Law Journal* 69 (1960): 895–924.

152 *Flast v. Cohen*, 392 U.S. 83 (1968).

153 See, for example, Anne Abramowitz, "A Remedy for Every Right: What Federal Courts Can Learn from California's Taxpayer Standing," *California Law Review* 98 (2010): 1595–1629.

154 Bob Egelko, "Taxpayers Not Equal in Suits Against Government," *SFGate.com*, May 24, 2014. http://www.sfgate.com/news/article/Taxpayers-not-equal-in-suits-against-government-5500914.php. The ruling can be accessed here: http://www.courts.ca.gov/opinions/documents/A138949.PDF

155 David M. Engel, "The Oven Bird's Song: Insiders, Outsiders, and Personal Injuries in an American Community," *Law & Society Review* 18 (1984): 551–582; Wayne McIntosh, "150 Years of Litigation and Dispute Settlement: A Court Tale," *Law & Society Review* 15 (1980–1981): 823–848; Lawrence M. Friedman and Robert V. Percival, "A Tale of Two Courts: Litigation in Alameda and San Benito Counties," *Law & Society Review* 10 (1976): 267–301.

156 See William Haltom and Michael McCann, *Distorting the Law: Politics, Media, and the Litigation Crisis* (Chicago, IL: University of Chicago Press, 2004); David M. Engel, "The Oven Bird's Song: Insiders, Outsiders, and Personal Injuries in an American Community," *Law & Society Review* 18 (1984): 551–582, footnote 4.

157 Robert A. Kagan, *Adversarial Legalism: The American Way of Law* (Cambridge, MA: Harvard University Press, 2003).

158 Thomas F. Burke, *Lawyers, Lawsuits, and Legal Rights: The Battle Over Litigation in American Society* (Berkeley, CA: University of California Press, 2002).

159 Jeb Barnes, *Dust-Up: Asbestos Litigation and the Failure of Commonsense Policy Reform* (Washington, DC: Georgetown University Press, 2011).

160 Carl T. Bogus, *Why Lawsuits are Good for America: Disciplined Democracy, Big Business, and the Common Law* (New York, NY: New York University Press, 2003).

161 Jeb Barnes, "In Defense of Asbestos Tort Litigation: Rethinking Legal Process Analysis in a World of Uncertainty, Second Bests, and Shared Policy-Making Responsibility," *Law & Social Inquiry* 34 (2009): 5–29.

162 Charles R. Epp, *Making Rights Real: Activists, Bureaucrats, and the Creation of the Legalistic State* (Chicago, IL: University of Chicago Press, 2009).

163 Thomas F. Burke, *Lawyers, Lawsuits, and Legal Rights: The Battle Over Litigation in American Society* (Berkeley, CA: University of California Press, 2002).

7

CRIMINAL LAW

"Every kind of peaceful cooperation among men is primarily based on mutual trust and only secondarily on institutions such as courts of justice and police."

—Albert Einstein, Theoretical Physicist and Winner of the Noble Prize in Physics[1]

"The only power any government has is the power to crack down on criminals. Well, when there aren't enough criminals, one makes them. One declares so many things to be a crime that it becomes impossible for men to live without breaking laws."

—Ayn Rand, Novelist and Philosopher[2]

In 1992, 18-year-old Antonio Yarbough and 15-year-old Sharrif Wilson were arrested as suspects in the stabbing and strangling murders of Yarbough's mother, his 12-year-old sister, and another 12-year-old girl in their Brooklyn, New York, residence.[3] Police questioned Wilson and offered the teenager a lighter sentence if he testified against Yarbough. Although Wilson and Yarbough were in Manhattan at the time medical examiners identified as the victims' likely time of death, Wilson confessed that he and Yarbough committed the murders.[4] In his confession, Wilson said that Yarbough's mother did not approve of the fact that the two men were lovers and that they killed her to get money for drugs.[5] Years later, Wilson recalled: "I was young, afraid, not used to being in the precinct and the justice system. I didn't know much then. It was pretty easy for them to coerce me into giving false statements."[6] Over two decades after their conviction and imprisonment, both Yarbough and Wilson were exonerated after testing revealed that DNA under Yarbough's mother's fingernails matched DNA found on another murder victim from 1999—long after the men had entered prison. Investigators ultimately confirmed that there was no physical evidence linking the men to the crime and prosecutors admitted that the new DNA evidence created substantial reasonable doubt about their guilt. After being freed, Yarbough knelt to pray and said, "It feels good to be vindicated."[7]

The exoneration of Yarbough and Wilson was part of Brooklyn District Attorney Kenneth P. Thompson's review of hundreds of murder convictions. Thompson took office in January 2014 after campaigning, in part, on the promise to engage in more active and aggressive review of cases of wrongful or questionable conviction.[8] Most of the cases reviewed thus far have stemmed from "mistakes and misconduct by police and prosecutors in the violent, drug-plagued 1980s and 1990s"[9]—including coerced confessions, witness intimidation, use of questionable witnesses, reliance on discredited detectives, and prosecutorial misconduct.[10] A coalition involving various advocacy groups, defense attorneys, Legal Aid, and the Innocence Project—which seeks to use DNA evidence to overturn wrongful convictions—worked with the district attorney to devise a protocol for reviewing cases. A similar process was used in Dallas County, Texas, and the result was that 25 men were exonerated through DNA evidence.[11]

The criminal justice process—as the name implies—is supposed to produce just results where proof of guilt is required for conviction. Yet, numerous examples illustrate that there are considerable flaws in the system that can lead to the arrest, trial, conviction, imprisonment, and even the execution of innocent persons.[12] For example, the execution of Cameron Todd Willingham in Texas was the subject of a PBS *Frontline* documentary "Death By Fire" that cast considerable doubt on his arrest and conviction for the death of his children in a house fire.[13] Police and prosecutors maintained that he deliberately set the fire in a satanic ritual to murder his three daughters: a 2-year-old toddler and 1-year-old twins.[14] Yet fire experts insist that the fire was an accident and that the girls' father had nothing to do with it. Just before he received the lethal injection Willingham stated: "I am an innocent man convicted of a crime I did not commit. I have been persecuted for twelve years for something I did not do."[15]

The previous examples highlight the tension between procedural and substantive justice.[16] **Procedural justice** is about the fairness of the dispute resolution process.[16] This involves equal and fair access to attorneys and courts as defined by constitutional provisions and statutory guarantees. The right to an attorney, right to remain silent, right to trial, and right to be judged by a jury of one's peers are hallmarks of procedural justice. Thus, even if an innocent person is found guilty, an argument can be made that procedural justice is met if these procedural guarantees are fulfilled. **Substantive justice**, on the other hand, involves the fairness of the outcome, regardless of the process used to arrive at that outcome. "In systems of substantive justice, the ideal is to decide particular cases on the basis of their individual merits or to refer to substantive goals, rather than to abstract rules."[17] An illustration of this is from the classic courtroom drama *And Justice for All*, a 1979 film starring Al Pacino—after his appearances in *The Godfather* and *The Godfather Part II* but before his appearance in *Scarface*—as criminal defense lawyer Arthur Kirkland. Blackmailed into defending a judge he dislikes against a brutal rape charge, Pacino's character opts to forego procedural justice in favor of substantive justice when the judge admits to him that he is, in fact, guilty of the crime. As the trial begins, Kirkland exclaims in open court, "My client . . . should go right to fucking jail! The son of a bitch is guilty!"

Scholarly research indicates that procedural justice has a major influence on individuals' satisfaction with outcomes and their evaluation of legal authorities in the criminal process. In particular, work by legal scholar and psychology professor Tom Tyler involving a telephone survey of a random sample of Chicago residents suggests that the more individuals perceive authorities to be acting fairly, honestly, and ethically, the more likely they are to be satisfied with the criminal justice system (regardless of the substantive outcome).[18] Similarly, the more individuals are afforded opportunities for representation ("the degree to which parties affected by a decision are allowed to be involved in the decision-making process")[19] and error correction ("the existence of opportunities to correct unfair or inaccurate decisions"),[20] the more satisfied with the criminal justice system they are. Note that procedural justice is intended to foster substantive justice (fair processes should be more likely to yield fair outcomes) but fair processes cannot guarantee a substantively just result.

The criminal process is filled with myths. Film and television police and courtroom dramas portray an action-packed, slick justice system filled with glamour and excitement where smart, ethical individuals triumph over corruption to ensure fair outcomes.[21] Think of, for example, Hilary Swank's portrayal of a loyal sister determined to do anything (including becoming a lawyer) to demonstrate her brother's innocence despite his conviction on murder charges in the 2010 film *Conviction*. Further, the news media cover sensational crime as infotainment rather reporting on police departments as complex governmental agencies.[22] One particularly extreme example of this is the Investigation Discovery network, a cable television network that debuted in the United States in 2008. Its schedule consists entirely of crime reporting shows like *Sex Sent Me to the Slammer*, *Beauty Queen Murders*, and *Wives with Knives*. Additionally, the proliferation of "reality" television from *Cops* to *Judge Judy* to Court TV has led to the perception that all problems in society are ultimately legal ones to be resolved by specialists in settings wholly separate from politics.[23]

The reality is that the criminal justice process is often a political one typified by a hurried assembly line; a daily grind that is often aptly characterized as one of incompetence, abuse, errors, and injustices.[24] In pop culture we encounter many archetypes. The African American or Hispanic boy caught in a spiral of punishment and incarceration; the young police officer under pressure to make arrests and who is in over his head in the face of gang-controlled, street-corner drug businesses; the low-paid, over-worked public defender who pleads most of his clients guilty with little knowledge about their circumstances; the elected prosecutor who habitually declines to pursue significant cases; and the exasperated judge who sets outrageous bail for negligible crimes.[25] A recent analysis of the first 250 wrongfully convicted people to later be exonerated by DNA testing revealed a troubling pattern of evidence corrupted by suggestive eyewitness procedures, coercive interrogations, unsound and unreliable forensics, shoddy investigative practices, cognitive bias, and poor lawyering.[26] Since very few crimes involve biological evidence that can be tested using DNA, these findings suggest a reality in which there are many more innocent persons who were subject to the same practices but will never be exonerated. In sum, these realities have led to what one scholar has called "the collapse of American criminal justice."[27]

MYTH AND REALITY IN CRIMINAL LAW

MYTH	REALITY
The criminal justice process produces substantive justice where proof of guilt is required for conviction.	The criminal justice process guarantees procedural justice but not substantive justice, and unjust convictions can result from coerced confessions, intimidated or untrustworthy witnesses, prosecutorial misconduct, and corrupt law enforcement.
People who are victimized by crime routinely report the incidents to police.	Many victims of crime, and most victims of violent crime, do not contact police because they fear reprisal, lack faith in the police, and believe the issue is personal or trivial.
Police file reports for all crimes to which individuals alert them.	Police can make it difficult for individuals to report crime and police fail to file written reports due to political pressure to keep crime statistics low.
Reported crimes result in police making an arrest.	Most reported crimes do not result in arrests and remain unresolved.

People have similar experiences when they come into contact with the police, particularly during traffic stops.	Males and racial minorities have greater contact with the police and in traffic matters have higher incidences of stops, searches, arrests, and use of force.
Automated traffic cameras promote driver safety and innocent motorists are able to effectively appeal unjust tickets.	Automated traffic cameras are local revenue generators where motorists have little chance of contesting alleged violations.
The procedures of the criminal process ensure that only the guilty will ultimately be punished.	The process itself is often the punishment, particularly for those accused of minor crimes.
The bail process gives all individuals the opportunity to be released from jail pending trial.	Males and racial minorities are less likely to be released on bail than females and whites.
Sentences are handed down equally for all individuals convicted for the same crimes.	Racial minorities are more likely to receive harsher and longer sentences than whites who commit the same crimes.
Most criminal cases go to trial.	Nearly all criminal cases—95 percent—are plea bargained and never reach trial.
Plea bargaining is the result of caseload pressure.	Plea bargaining is a legal norm and part of the local legal culture that occurs regardless of caseload pressure.
Individuals who are accused of committing similar crimes are treated equally during the plea bargaining process.	Racial minorities are less likely to receive a reduced charge during plea bargaining compared to whites.

Many victims do not report crime.[28] As a result, we start this chapter with a discussion of how and why crimes are reported and investigated. Police are the initial point of contact for the public and we discuss the controversies surrounding traffic stops, searches, and the use of force. Do the police treat people differently because of their race? There is systematic evidence to demonstrate that they do and that racial disparities exist throughout the criminal process. For example, African Americans are more likely to be arrested, prosecuted, convicted, and imprisoned, and, further, have difficulty finding employment after their imprisonment and are much less likely to have confidence in the justice system (particularly the police).[29] In fact, one third of African American males born in 2001 will spend time in prison[30] and African Americans are much more likely to be incarcerated than whites. For example, in 2010, 678 white males per 100,000 white U.S. residents were incarcerated compared to 4,347 African American males per 100,000 African American residents.[31] These disparities exist not because of differences in crime or drug use, as some have theorized, but primarily from drug and crime control policies that disproportionately affect African Americans and other racial minorities.[32] Viewed through this lens, the American criminal justice system functions as a contemporary system of racial control, a system that formally gives lip service to the principle of colorblindness but does not conform to that principle in practice.[33]

REPORTING AND INVESTIGATING CRIME

The purpose of criminal law is to maintain social order.[34] The penalties and punishments associated with violating criminal law—material deprivations in the form of fines and incarceration—are thought to deter individuals from committing crimes.[35] But research suggests that in addition to these state-imposed costs, individuals also obey the law because there are socially imposed costs for failing to do so.[36] Specifically, self-imposed shame or guilt feelings, as well as embarrassment and loss of respect in the eyes of others, can also deter individuals from breaking the law. Despite these legal and social controls, crimes occur every day but the vast majority do not involve the police because victims are often not inclined to report them. Violent victimizations (which include rape or sexual assault, robbery, aggravated and simple assault) not reported to the police were at the rate of 14 per 1,000 persons in 2012.[37] Similar to violent crime, the rate of property crime (which includes household burglary, theft, and motor vehicle theft) not reported to police was 102 per 1,000 households.[38] According to the National Crime Victimization Survey (NCVS), victims may not report crime for a variety of reasons, "including fear of reprisal or getting the offender in trouble, believing that police would not or could not do anything to help, and believing the crime to be a personal issue or trivial."[39] In a special report covering 2006–2010, Bureau of Justice Statistics (BJS) statistician Lynn Langton and her colleagues reported that 52 percent of all violent victimizations, or an annual average of 3,382,200 violent victimizations, were not reported to the police.[40] Forty-four percent of these went unreported to the police because the victim reported the crime to another official (for example, a guard, manager, or school official). Eighteen percent were not reported to the police because the victim did not believe the crime was important enough. From 2006 to 2010, the category with the highest percentage of unreported crime was household theft (67 percent) and rape or sexual assault (65 percent), while the lowest percentage was motor vehicle theft (17 percent). The BJS special report also noted that victims were less likely to report a crime if it was committed by someone the victim knew well as compared to the situation in which it was committed by a stranger.

Complicating matters is the fact that sometimes a victim attempts to report a crime but the police do not file an official report.[41] More than half a dozen police officers in New York City cited departmental police pressure to keep crime statistics low as one reason for failing to officially record a crime.[42] According to Paul J. Browne, the police department's spokesperson, these alleged failures to take a report of a crime are investigated by the Internal Affairs Bureau. However, there are other ways that crime reports are discouraged. One example is the New York City police department policy instituted in 2009 requiring robbery victims to go to the station house to give their reports directly to a detective or patrol supervisor. One police commander noted that a consequence was that "[a] police report wouldn't get made because they make you wait in the police station for hours."[43] What these examples illustrate is the fact that crime reporting can be a political issue. Given that elected officials often campaign on "tough on crime" platforms, it is easy to see how crime statistics could affect the public's perception of candidates.

The politics of crime reporting becomes even more crucial when we consider the fact that, even when individuals do contact the police and the police file formal reports, they nonetheless often go unsolved. To illustrate, the Federal Bureau of Investigation (FBI) reported that only 47 percent of violent crimes and 19 percent of property crimes

Image 7.1 The Endless Game
This 1906 illustration shows a game of chess between a hand labeled "Political Pull" showing a cufflink labeled "Brass Check" and a hand labeled "Reform." The chess board is labeled "[Depar]tment of Police" and some of the squares are labeled "Race Track, Suburbs, White Lights, Gambling District, Goatville, Financial District, Tenderloin, Red Light District, Lonely Beat, [and] Hell's Kitchen." The police officers, some in plainclothes, are labeled "Crooked Captain, Inspector, Sleuth, 'Fixed' Captain, Honest Captain, Grafting Captain, Honest Inspector, Plainclothes Man, [and] Sergeant." Though the print depicts the politics of policing in the early twentieth century in New York City, can you think of contemporary examples of police departments being influenced by larger political issues? Prints and Photographs Division, Library of Congress, Washington, D.C.

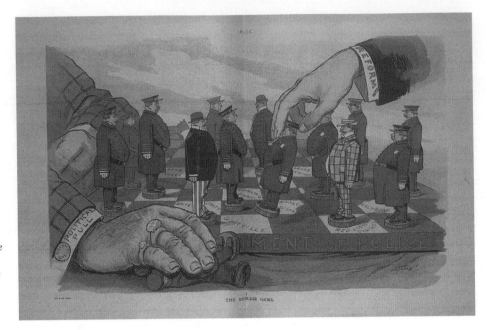

were cleared by arrest or exceptional means in 2012.[44] Parenthetically, exceptional means include such circumstances as the offender's death or the refusal of a victim to cooperate with the prosecution after the offender has been identified. When considering violent crimes, 63 percent of murder offenses, 40 percent of forcible rape offenses, 28 percent of robbery offenses, and 56 percent of aggravated assault offenses were cleared. The upshot is that most reported crime—including much violent crime—does not even result in an arrest.

POLICE CONTACT WITH THE PUBLIC: GUILTY UNTIL PROVEN INNOCENT?

Though virtually every adult has been exposed to depictions of the police in popular culture (for example, Officer Rhodes in the 2011 film *Bridesmaids*) and has seen police officers at least from afar (for example, standing on the roadside next to a car being ticketed), less than one in five members of the public have had direct contact with the police.[45] For example, in 2005 an estimated 19.1 percent of U.S. residents (over the age of 15) had face-to-face contact with the police and in 2008 that estimate dropped to 16.9 percent. In 2008, hands down the most common reason for face-to-face police contact was being a driver involved in a traffic stop, which accounted for 44.1 percent of the contacts.[46] The next most common reason was to report a crime or other problem to the police (20.9 percent), followed by involvement in a traffic accident (12.2 percent). Other reasons included having the police provide assistance or service (6.3 percent), contact while the police are investigating a crime (5.6 percent), and being a passenger in a car stopped during a traffic stop (2.9 percent).

The normative expectation is that the police are there "to protect and to serve"[47] and, hence, they are supposed to uphold the law equally and treat all individuals fairly without

TABLE 7.1

Incident to a Traffic Stop: Searches, Arrests, and Force by Race, 2008

SEARCHED	PERCENT OF DRIVERS
Blacks/African Americans	12.3
Hispanics/Latinos	5.8
Whites	3.9
ARRESTED	
Blacks/African Americans	4.7
Hispanics/Latinos	2.6
Whites	2.4
FORCE THREATENED OR USED	
Blacks/African Americans	3.4
Hispanics/Latinos	1.6
Whites	1.2

Note: The study covered police contacts with the public during 2008 and was based on interviews by the U.S. Census Bureau with people age 16 or older.
Source: Christine Eith and Matthew R. Durose, "Special Report: Contacts between Police and the Public, 2008," Bureau of Justice Statistics, October 2011, Tables 13, 14, and 18. http://www.bjs.gov/content/pub/pdf/cpp08.pdf

regard to gender or race. Yet statistics from the BJS demonstrate the reality that an individual's contact with the police is conditioned by both gender and race.[48] For example, in 2008 male drivers were stopped at slightly higher rates than female drivers, with about 10 percent of male drivers and 7 percent of female drivers stopped by police.[49] Though police were equally likely to issue tickets to men and women in traffic stops—55.9 percent of men and 54.9 percent of women who were stopped were ticketed—men were more likely than women to be arrested following a traffic stop (3.5 percent versus 1.4 percent).[50] Police were also more likely to conduct a search if the driver was male than if the driver was female (7.4 percent versus 1.6 percent).[51] In short, men are more likely to be pulled over for traffic stops and more likely to be arrested pursuant to a traffic stop than are women.

In terms of race, the BJS data report that white, African American, and Hispanic drivers were stopped by police at comparable rates (8.4 percent, 8.8 percent, and 9.1 percent, respectively).[52] As Table 7.1 shows, however, African American drivers were three times as likely as white drivers and two times as likely as Hispanic drivers to be searched during a traffic stop. Further, African American drivers were almost twice as likely than whites and Hispanic drivers to be arrested during a traffic stop (4.7 percent versus 2.4 percent and 2.6 percent, respectively) and significantly more likely to have force against them threatened or used (3.4 percent versus 1.2 percent and 1.6 percent respectively). These kind of disparities have generated a good deal of controversy for decades,[53] resulting in the phrase "driving while black" becoming part of the public discourse[54] and inspiring artistic expression like Jay-Z's 2004 hit "99 Problems" from *The Black Album*.[55]

Image 7.2 Above the Law
*This 1907 illustration
shows a dark and gloomy
landscape where the
police have imposed
martial law conditions
on the laboring class and
punish violators with
impunity, while, at the
top, those responsible for
the deplorable working
and living conditions
stand on a cloud labeled
"Immunity." What does
this depiction tell us
about popular perception
of the police at the time?
Does the public have a
similar perception of the
police today?* Prints and
Photographs Division,
Library of Congress,
Washington, D.C.

POP CULTURE

Crash

The 2004 film *Crash*, which won the Academy Award for Best Picture,[56] portrays a series of intertwining stories that deal with race and the law. In one scene, a white police officer by the name of John Ryan, played by Matt Dillon, conducts a traffic stop. He pulls over Cameron and Christine Thayer, an African American couple played by Terrance Howard and Thandie Newton, whom he observes engaging in oral sex in a luxury SUV. The well-dressed couple is laughing playfully when Ryan first approaches the car and asks to see Cameron Thayer's license and registration. Ryan then asks Thayer to step out of the car and begins conducting a sobriety test on him. Christine Thayer becomes increasingly upset, protesting that her husband does not drink. When she opens the door to exit the vehicle she is warned by the officer to stay in the car. When Christine disobeys the officer's order, he resorts to force against the Thayers, conducting a frisk of Christine that is closer to a physical assault than a pat down. She yells at the officer: "Fuck you! That's what this is all about isn't it? You thought you saw a white woman blowing a black man and that just drove your little cracker ass crazy." The scene is consistent with social science research that shows that racial minorities are not treated equally with whites during police contact—specifically during traffic stops.[57]

In another story line, Rick Cabot, a white district attorney played by Brendan Fraser, must deal with the political fallout from being carjacked by two African American men. He talks the matter over with his African American chief of staff, a woman by the name of Karen played by Nona Gaye: "Why did these guys have to be black? I mean, why? No matter how we spin this, I'm either gonna lose the black vote or I'm gonna lose the law-and-order vote." Karen reassures him: "You're worrying too much. You have a lot of support in the black community." "All right. If we can't duck this thing, we're gonna have to neutralize it. What we need is a picture of me pinning a medal on a black man." The scene illustrates the political side of law enforcement. Prosecutors are elected officials and the evidence suggests that they are not immune to electoral pressure.[58] Is it possible that Cabot picked Karen—an African American woman—to be his chief advisor for this very reason?

Image 7.3 Jail the Only Remedy
This 1902 illustration "Jail the Only Remedy" shows an automobile driver who broke the traffic laws and has been placed in jail with other criminals. Caption: "Fines are a farce when dealing with the auto law breaker." Should traffic violations be punished by jail time? Prints and Photographs Division, Library of Congress, Washington, D.C.

Recently, smart phone apps have been released that are designed to aid people who want to secretly record the police.[59] For example, the American Civil Liberties Union (ACLU) of New Jersey released an app called Police Tape, which disappears from the phone's screen when the recording begins (to avoid alerting officers that they are being taped) and sends a copy of the recording to the ACLU-New Jersey.[60] The New York Civil Liberties Union also released an app called Stop and Frisk Watch.[61] The app facilitates filming with audio, stopping when the device is shaken and prompting users to take a survey to record details about the incident. It also has a function that lets the user know when others using the app in the area are recording police activity: "This function is especially useful for community groups who monitor police activity."[62] Police Tape and Stop and Frisk Watch are merely two of numerous such apps. Some other apps of this kind include features such as live streaming and geolocation.[63]

Not surprisingly, many law enforcement agencies have not been thrilled with citizens recording police action. And, indeed, there have been numerous arrests of individuals filming policing incidents.[64] Regardless, recent court decisions have affirmed the right of citizens to do so. For example, a federal appeals court struck down an Illinois law that made it illegal for citizens to audio-record police officers while on duty, finding it to be a violation of the First Amendment.[65] According to the U.S. Court of Appeals for the Seventh Circuit, the state statute being challenged in this case impermissibly restricted a medium that is commonly used for communicating information and ideas and, further, any governmental interest in protecting conversational privacy[66] is not implicated when police officers are performing duties in public places.[67] The scholarly research suggests that video recordings by citizens can constrain the ability of law enforcement to offer alternative explanations for purported police abuses.[68]

Recently, drivers have been increasingly confronted with automated cameras capturing alleged traffic violations rather than police officers stopping drivers. Critics accuse localities of being less concerned with traffic safety and more interested in raising revenue.[69] One official in Washington, D.C., explained "You are guilty until you have proven yourself innocent. . . . That has worked well for us."[70] Washington, D.C., raised $172 million from traffic cameras in 2013 alone. Lon Anderson, of the American Automobile Association (AAA), explained that he was in favor of punishing people who speed or who run red lights because they are a danger to other motorists. But, he went on to assert, that other supposed violations have nothing to do with safety and are therefore unjust: "We've got these cameras that are ticketing you for going an inch over the stop line, or making a rolling right on red, or unintentionally running a red light by two-tenths, three-tenths of a second. . . . It's a system run wild."[71] Columnist Dana Milbank explained that even when he provided adjudicators proof of his innocence for various violations, he did not receive justice (either procedural or substantive): "I sent in photos and a video showing that I had not parked in an 'emergency' zone as the ticket indicated—appeal denied, no explanation. I sent photos and a video showing that I had not parked in a 'motorcycle' space as the ticket said—appeal denied no explanation." Milbank's conclusion? "That . . . D.C. official was wrong. In Washington, you aren't guilty until proved innocent. You're just guilty."[72]

This discussion of the reality of police contact with the public has important implications for the legitimacy of law enforcement. The empirical evidence demonstrates that the public's perception of police legitimacy is based on the perceived fairness of the procedures used by the police.[73] If police contact with the public results in a lack of procedural justice, social control in the form of people following norms, rules, and laws will be jeopardized. But police contact is only the first step of the criminal process after a crime has been committed, as is illustrated in Figure 7.1. In the next section we detail the

FIGURE 7.1
Early Stages of the Criminal Justice Process

Prosecutorial
Discretion

↑

Booking

↑

Arrest

↑

Filing Report

↑

Contact with Police

↑

Criminal Offense

remaining steps, each of which bears further on public perceptions of procedural justice and, therefore, on the legitimacy of the criminal justice process.

CRIMINAL JUSTICE PROCESS: IS THE PROCESS THE PUNISHMENT?

In his classic 1979 book *The Process Is the Punishment*, legal scholar Malcolm Feeley demonstrated how the criminal process was so taxing for defendants to wade through— particularly for those accused of relatively minor crimes—that they would rather resolve cases quickly and informally than spend time and money moving through each stage of the formal process.[74] Specifically, Feeley argued that the real costs for those accused of crimes were not the fines and prison sentences handed down by courts but lost wages from missed work, commissions to bail bondsmen, attorney's fees, and wasted time. He found that both prosecuting and defense attorneys agreed that the pretrial process was enough to "teach the defendant a lesson," suggesting that informal practices such as plea bargaining—something we will address at length in the next section—mean more than is commonly thought. Procedural justice itself may actually be more unjust than a quick substantive outcome resulting from a guilty plea. As we continue to detail the numerous steps in the criminal justice process, consider whether a defendant would rather resolve a relatively minor case quickly or see it through to its formal conclusion.

The first step in the process for law enforcement involves detecting and investigating criminal offenses. The police must determine whether a crime was committed and who committed the crime. As we discussed previously, this may involve victims contacting the police and filing a report. But it may also involve so-called **victimless crimes** (such as prostitution, gambling, or drug use), crimes in which the actions at issue do not directly harm other individuals but are nonetheless illegal.[75] In these instances, law enforcement initiates the investigation on its own.

Once the police have established that there is **probable cause** to believe that an individual has committed a crime, they may **arrest** that individual (known as the **suspect**) without a warrant or obtain an **arrest warrant** from a judge. The express language of the Fourth Amendment constitutionally requires probable cause:

> The right of the people to be secure in their persons, houses, papers, and effects, against unreasonable searches and seizures, shall not be violated, and no warrants shall issue, but upon probable cause, supported by oath or affirmation, and particularly describing the place to be searched, and the persons or things to be seized.[76]

Probable cause is an abstract concept, and members of the U.S. Supreme Court themselves have at times struggled to agree as to its meaning.[77] But, generally speaking, to meet the threshold for probable cause the police must have enough facts that would lead a reasonable person to believe that the suspect committed a crime. Or, as the Court has said, "[P]robable cause exists where the facts and circumstances within their [the officers'] knowledge and of which they had reasonably trustworthy information [are] sufficient in themselves to warrant a man of reasonable caution in the belief that an offense has been or is being committed."[78] One possible interpretation of the Fourth Amendment is that for an arrest to be constitutional under the Constitution it must be pursuant to the issuance of an arrest warrant (a judge's order to law enforcement officers to arrest and bring to jail a person charged with a crime). Though the Court favors arrests pursuant to an arrest warrant, a warrantless arrest is not automatically invalid.[79] Most obviously, if a crime takes place in an officer's presence an arrest warrant is not required.

At the time of her arrest, the arrestee is searched, with any weapons, contraband, or evidence relating to a crime removed from the arrestee. The Fourth Amendment applies to these searches; however, the Court has found a warrantless search incident to a lawful arrest permissible in the interests of officer safety, to prevent a suspect's escape, and to avoid the destruction of evidence.[80] Originally, the Court gave law enforcement broad authority to search an arrestee and her premises, but ultimately the Court has limited that particular exception to the warrant requirement to a search of the arrestee and the area within her immediate control. Warrantless arrests are permissible, according to the Court, for even minor offenses. So, for example, when Gail Atwater neglected to buckle her preschool children into their car seats, she was arrested without a warrant despite the fact that the offense came with a fine of only $25 to $50.[81]

Following arrest and search, the arrestee is transported to a police station to undergo the **booking process**. That process consists of a series of steps that records information about an arrestee and results in an official arrest record. The arrestee's name, time of arrival, and offense are noted in the police blotter or log. Subsequently, the arrestee is photographed, which produces the infamous "mug shots" that serve as physical documentation of the arrestee at the time of the arrest. The arrestee's personal belongings (for example, wallets, money, cell phones, medications) are removed from the arrestee and catalogued. Fingerprinting is the next step and is intended to aid in both the identification of the arrestee and for purposes of comparison with crime scene evidence. Though all arrestees are subject to body searches, the most invasive of these searches (strip searches, body cavity searches) are typically performed only for those who will be held in prison. Depending upon the jurisdiction and the seriousness of the offense, the arrestee may also have a DNA sample taken (via a cheek swab).[82] Such DNA samples have helped to close many unsolved crimes, however, the Court's rationale for permitting them is based on their value in arrestee identification: "[T]aking and analyzing a cheek swab of the arrestee's DNA is, like fingerprinting and photographing, a legitimate police booking procedure that is reasonable under the Fourth Amendment."[83] Once the booking process is complete, the arrestee is typically placed in some kind of holding cell.

There are three types of crimes classified by legislatures according to their seriousness: infractions, misdemeanors, and felonies. **Infractions** are petty offenses punishable by small fines; that is, they are "noncriminal offense[s] in penal law, municipal codes, or other substate authority."[84] Because they do not result in jail sentences, defendants charged with an infraction do not have a right to jury trial. Defendants may hire attorneys but the state is not required to provide them for defendants who cannot afford them. Minor traffic violations are the most common type of infraction. Other common examples, depending upon the jurisdiction, include jaywalking, littering, building code violations, fishing without a license, drinking alcohol in public spaces, walking a dog off a leash, and possession of less than one ounce of marijuana.

Misdemeanors are typically defined as "an offense for which statutorily authorized punishment does not exceed one year in jail."[85] Punishment for misdemeanors is not, however, limited to jail but, rather, can also include fines, probation, community service, and restitution for victims. Misdemeanor defendants are entitled to a jury trial and, if the offense is one that results in the possibility of jail time, they are also entitled to a state-appointed attorney if they cannot afford to pay for their own.[86] In theory, this right to counsel supports the notion (read: the myth) that all defendants are equal before the law. The reality of the situation is quite different, however, because "[e]ven the best-run state [public defender] programs lack enough money to provide competent lawyers for all indigent defendants who need them."[87] Examples of misdemeanors, which vary from jurisdiction to jurisdiction, include petty theft, trespassing, vandalism, disorderly conduct, public intoxication, and prostitution.

Felonies are the most serious crimes and typically involve physical harm (or the threat thereof) to victims. They can also include white-collar crimes[88] (such as embezzlement and insider trading) and fraud schemes (such as bank fraud and credit card fraud). Second or third offenses that would otherwise be misdemeanors can be elevated to felonies. So, for example, in the state of Texas a first or second DWI offense is considered a misdemeanor while a third such offense is considered a felony. Punishments for felonies include prison sentences from 1 year to life without parole and, for the most serious felonies such as murder, even the death penalty.[89] Defendants are entitled to a jury trial and a court-appointed attorney, though this was not always the case for state crimes. The U.S. Supreme Court had previously held that the right to counsel was crucial when a defendant was charged with a capital crime (that is, a crime for which the death penalty could be imposed),[90] however, it did not extend the right to counsel for state felonies until the well-known case of *Gideon v. Wainwright*.[91] The story behind *Gideon* was recounted in the best-selling book *Gideon's Trumpet*[92] and subsequently adapted for a made-for-television movie of the same name starring acclaimed actor Henry Fonda (father of Jane and Peter Fonda and grandfather of Bridget Fonda). Examples of felonies include murder, rape, assault, battery, and arson. As these distinctions among infractions, misdemeanors, and felonies demonstrate, contemporary society categorizes crime seriousness based on violence rather than other factors (such as betrayal of trust), even though some have argued that the latter do the most damage to society.[93]

Figure 7.2 shows criminal caseloads in all state courts over time based on data collected by the National Center for State Courts (NCSC).[94] Overall, caseloads increased

FIGURE 7.2
Criminal Caseloads in the States, 2001–2010

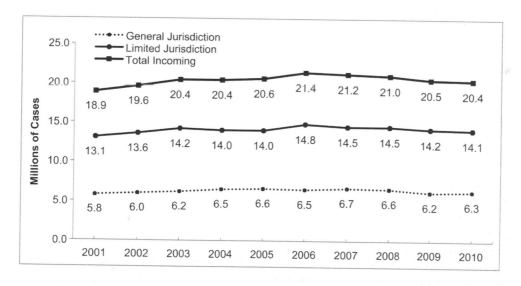

Source: R. LaFountain, R. Schauffler, S. Strickland, and K. Holt, *Examining the Work of State Courts: An Analysis of 2010 State Court Caseloads* (National Center for State Courts, 2012). http://www.courtstatistics.org/~/media/Microsites/Files/CSP/DATA%20PDF/CSP_DEC.ashx

FIGURE 7.3
Misdemeanor Arrest Composition in States, 1998

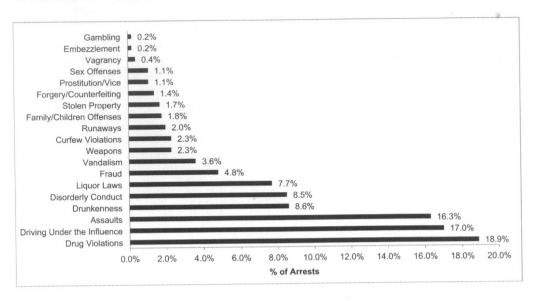

Source: Thomas Cohen, "Caseload Highlights, Examining the Work of State Courts, Volume 6, Number 2: A Renewed Interest in Low-Level Crime," (National Center for State Courts, 2000). http://cdm16501.contentdm.oclc.org/cdm/ref/collection/criminal/id/40

from 18.9 million in 2001 to 20.4 million in 2010, though there were slight declines beginning in the middle of the decade.[95] There are four times as many arrests for misdemeanors and, as Figure 7.3 shows, most misdemeanor arrests are for drug violations (19 percent), driving under the influence (17 percent), assaults (16 percent), drunkenness (9 percent), disorderly conduct (9 percent), and liquor law violations (8 percent). At the other end of the spectrum, there are very few arrests made—1 percent or less—for prostitution, sex offenses, vagrancy, embezzlement, and gambling. Arrest rates are not necessarily a reflection of crimes committed but instead of a jurisdiction's priorities in criminal law enforcement. For example, in recent years there has been a community justice movement in many cities—also known as the "Broken Windows" notion of crime control—that attempts to reduce violent crime by aggressively policing minor criminal behavior such as vandalism, drug possession, and disorderly conduct.[96] Thus, to the extent that elected officials such as governors, legislatures, and prosecutors prioritize different types of crime, the police will respond accordingly through their power to make arrests.

States vary in the strategies they adopt to manage criminal cases. As we discussed in Chapter Four, states model their judiciaries as either single-tired or two-tired systems.[97] States with single-tiered criminal courts (such as California, Iowa, Missouri, and Vermont) process all criminal cases in courts of general jurisdiction. Other states (such as Arizona, Michigan, Nevada, and Utah) used a two-tiered system with criminal courts of general and limited jurisdiction. In these systems, the general jurisdiction courts usually deal with felonies while limited jurisdiction courts specialize in misdemeanors. These courts can go by different names depending on the state. For example, in Michigan criminal courts of limited jurisdiction are called district courts or municipal courts while courts of general jurisdiction are called circuit courts.

FIGURE 7.4

Felony Cases in General Jurisdiction State Courts, 2001–2010

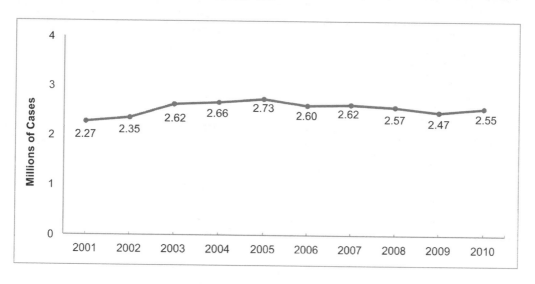

Source: Court Statistics Project, National Center on State Courts. http://www.courtstatistics.org/Criminal.aspx

Figure 7.4 shows the number of felony cases filed in state courts of general jurisdiction over time based on information collected by the NCSC's Court Statistics Project (CSP).[98] The data show that the number of felony cases increased steadily from 2.27 million in 2001 to 2.73 million in 2005 but, like the overall numbers, felonies have also declined since then to 2.55 million in 2010. Table 7.2 shows the types of felony cases filed in the 75 largest counties.[99] Overall, drug offenses comprise the largest percentage (one third) of felony arrests. Property offenses—which include burglary, larceny, and fraud—are the next most common, comprising 29 percent of felony arrests. Violent crimes make up one quarter of felony arrests and largely consist of assault and violent robbery cases. Interestingly, murder and rape, the most severe violent crimes, make up 1 percent or less each of all felony arrests. Finally, public-order crimes such as those involving automobiles and weapons comprise 13 percent of felonies.

Figure 7.5 shows that the criminal caseload in federal district courts has fluctuated over time with increases from 61,242 cases in 2000 to 70,746 in 2004, declines to 66,629 in 2007, increases to 79,551 in 2011, and subsequent declines to 69,449 in 2013.[100] Figure 7.6 shows how various types of criminal cases also reflect this pattern with increases from 2008 through 2011 and declines since. Interestingly, immigration cases grew the most over this time period, moving from just under 20,000 cases in 2008 to over 30,000 by 2011. Three out of four immigration cases were filed in the five southwestern border district courts: the Southern District of Texas, Western District of Texas, District of Arizona, Southern District of California, and District of New Mexico.[101] The increases in immigration cases were the result of a 2005 executive branch decision under the George W. Bush Administration to change the way the U.S. Border Patrol treated immigrants. Specifically, prior to the change, immigrants apprehended by the Border Patrol were largely allowed to voluntarily return to Mexico without penalty. After 2005, the Border Patrol used new strategies

TABLE 7.2

Felony Case Composition in State Courts: 75 Largest Counties, 2009

MOST SERIOUS ARREST CHARGE	NUMBER	PERCENT
Drug Offenses	**18,220**	**32.6%**
Trafficking	8,287	14.8%
Other Drug	9,933	17.8%
Property Offenses	**16,241**	**29.1%**
Burglary	4,819	8.6%
Larceny/Theft	4,700	8.4%
Fraud	1,887	3.4%
Forgery	1,458	2.6%
Motor Vehicle Theft	1,439	2.6%
Other Property	1,937	3.5%
Violent Offenses	**13,938**	**24.9%**
Assault	6,469	11.6%
Robbery	3,782	6.8%
Rape	584	1.0%
Murder	374	0.7%
Other Violent	2,728	4.9%
Public-Order Offenses	**7,504**	**13.4%**
Driving-Related	2,324	4.2%
Weapons	2,052	3.7%
Other Public-Order	3,128	5.6%
All Offenses	**55,902**	**100%**

Note: Data for specific arrest charge were available for 99.7% of all cases. Detail may not sum to total due to rounding.
Source: Bureau of Justice Statistics, State Court Processing Statistics, 2009. http://www.bjs.gov/content/pub/pdf/fdluc09.pdf

FIGURE 7.5

Criminal Cases in Federal District Courts, 2000–2013

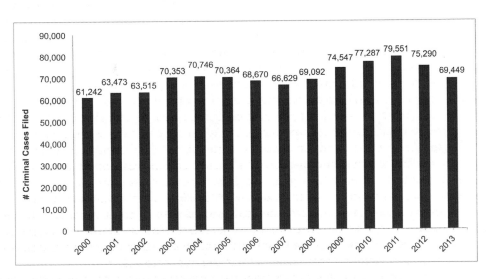

Note: Data reflect criminal cases commenced during the 12-month period ending March 31 of each year.
Source: Federal judicial caseload statistics, www.uscourts.gov

FIGURE 7.6

Criminal Case Composition in Federal District Courts, 2008–2013

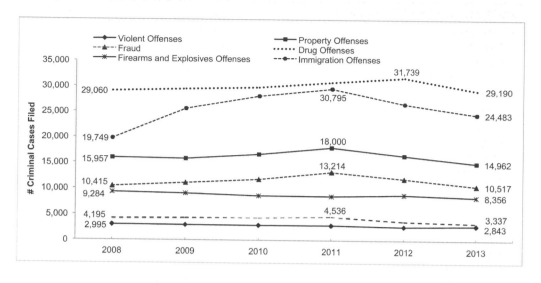

Note: Data reflect civil cases commenced during the 12-month period ending March 31 of each year; data do not include petty offenses decided by magistrates; prior to 2008 categories for criminal offenses were modified rendering prior data not comparable; minor categories excluded include embezzlement, sex offenses, justice system offenses, bribery, money laundering, RICO, racketeering, extortion, gambling, and regulatory offenses.
Source: Federal judicial caseload statistics, www.uscourts.gov

including arresting and charging immigrants for unlawful reentry into the United States, a crime that is accompanied by a prison sentence.[102] As these trends illustrate, criminal caseloads are reflective of government policy.

Prosecutorial discretion is the power of the state to formally charge suspects with criminal offenses or, alternatively, to forgo filing formal charges and release suspects from custody. As we also discuss in Chapter Eight, **prosecutors** have a variety of titles (e.g., District Attorney, State's Attorney) and are employed by the government. They serve the state or jurisdiction that employs them, review arrest reports from police officers, and decide when to press charges and when to drop a case. Prosecutors generally do not conduct their own investigations, relying instead on law enforcement. A prosecutor can opt to drop a case for a variety of reasons, including a lack of evidence or because the police followed improper procedures during the investigation or arrest (for example, lack of probable cause, failing to obtain a warrant). The discretion that prosecutors wield in this regard generated a push for no-drop (or evidence-based) prosecution, particularly in the area of domestic violence (though critics of such policies have raised concerns about the harms they might impose on crime victims).[103] In *United States v. Armstrong* the U.S. Supreme Court found unlimited prosecutorial discretion to be constitutional.[104] Despite formal jurisdictional boundaries, there are cooperative programs between federal and state prosecutors in overlapping geographical areas that further enhance prosecutorial power beyond the discretion they wield in their own jurisdictions.[105]

It is not hyperbole to say that prosecutors are the most powerful officials in the criminal justice system—so much so that their authority has been likened to a sovereign's

TABLE 7.3
Formal Steps in the Criminal Justice Process

1. Detecting and Investigating Criminal Offenses
2. Making Arrests with Probable Cause or an Arrest Warrant
3. Searching the Arrestee
4. Booking, including Photographing, Fingerprinting, and Holding Cell
5. Prosecutorial Discretion to Either Press Charges or Drop the Case
6. Filing the Complaint Against the Accused Alleging a Crime
7. Defendant's First Appearance before Magistrate Judge Including Appointment of a Public Defender and Setting Bail for the Defendant
8. Preliminary Hearing—Adversarial Proceeding to Determine Probable Cause
9. Grand Jury—Group of Citizens Convened to Decide Whether Prosecution Is Appropriate
10. Filing of Information—The Formal Accusation of the Criminal Offense
11. Arraignment—Hearing During Which Defendant Makes a Plea to the Charges Against Him
12. Pretrial Motions—Defense Attorney Asks Judge to Exclude Evidence or Change the Venue for the Trial
13. Trial—Adversarial Proceeding to Establish the Facts in the Case
14. Verdict—Determination of Guilt by a Judge or Jury
15. Sentencing—Punishment for the Accused Including Fines, Conditional Release, or Incarceration
16. Appeal—Losing Litigants Ask an Appellate Court to Overturn the Trial Outcome

power to grant exemptions from the reach of valid law.[106] Yet, because they are elected, they are subject to considerable political pressure and workload strain.[107] There are two categories of decisions that prosecutors make when deciding whether or not to prosecute.[108] The first type involves a prediction about success. The prosecutor asks, "*Can* I prosecute this case successfully?" Toward this end the prosecutor takes into account the sufficiency of the evidence, witness problems, and other legal factors. The second type of decision that prosecutors make involves the desirability and appropriateness of prosecution. They ask, "*Should* I try to prosecute successfully?" Considerations for this question include considering whether the suspect is morally culpable and whether there are adequate alternatives to formally charging the suspect. Answering the "should" question also involves thinking about how overworked or overwhelmed the prosecutor's office is, if it would be impractical to take the case, and the possibility of bad press resulting from charging the suspect.[109]

Mandatory minimum sentencing laws—laws that require prison terms of a particular length for individuals convicted of certain crimes—have increased the power of prosecutors but have resulted in unequal treatment of defendants and victims. Critics have argued that cases involving well-off victims are often prosecuted more vigorously than are those with economically and socially disadvantaged victims.[110] Further, wealthy defendants frequently enjoy more lenient plea bargains than poor defendants.[111] Moreover, because it is rare for a case to ever reach the trial stage, the hidden, nonpublic decisions that prosecutors make at the beginning of the criminal process are the most determinative of whether justice is realized. In an attempt to shift power away from police and prosecutor discretion, some jurisdictions have adopted mandatory arrest and prosecution policies, which have resulted in increased convictions through plea bargaining.[112] At the same time, as work by law and economics scholar David Bjerk suggests, prosecutors often lower charges to avoid the application of **three-strikes laws** (a type of mandatory minimum sentencing in which repetitions of particular crimes by an individual result in harsher penalties). Specifically, "prosecutors become almost twice as likely to prosecute three-strikes arrestees for lesser misdemeanor crimes not covered by the [three-strikes] laws."[113] But evidence has emerged to suggest that mandatory minimum sentencing may not be the panacea that reformers hoped in terms of defendants taking responsibility for their actions.[114] Further, critics of such sentencing policies point out that they often result in punishments that are too harsh to fit the crime and that they have contributed to soaring prison populations.[115] The 2013 film *Snitch*, starring Dwayne Johnson (former professional wrestler and a prominent regular in three films in the *Fast and Furious* franchise), dramatizes the lack of substantive justice critics argue results from three-strikes and other mandatory minimum sentencing laws.

When a prosecutor exercises her discretion and opts to press charges, the next step in the process is filing the **complaint**, which is the initial charging instrument. Note that some jurisdictions do include provisions for the filing of private criminal complaints (for example, Pennsylvania). Such privately filed criminal complaints are arguably throwbacks to the private prosecutions common in the nation's early history (as discussed in Chapter Three). They are rare. A complaint includes the allegation that the accused committed a specific act constituting a violation of a criminal statute at a particular place and time. The victim or the investigating officer (referred to as the **complainant**) signs the complaint, swearing under oath that he or she believes the factual allegations contained in the complaint are true. Once the complaint has been filed, the arrestee is now considered a defendant.

Within 24 or 48 hours of being arrested the accused must be presented before a magistrate. A **magistrate judge** is a minor judicial officer having limited jurisdiction to hear certain cases. Since this is the defendant's initial appearance as a defendant, this proceeding is known as the **first appearance**. The rights of the defendant and the content of the proceedings of the first appearance will vary depending on the jurisdiction but, generally speaking, the magistrate informs the defendant of his rights and appoints counsel at this stage. If the defendant was arrested without a warrant, the magistrate judge will also determine whether probable cause exists for the offense charged in the complaint. This is often referred to as **_Gerstein_ review** because in *Gerstein v. Pugh* the U.S. Supreme Court held that "the Fourth Amendment requires a judicial determination of probable cause as a prerequisite to extended restraint of liberty following arrest."[116] Though in *Gerstein* the Court did not specify how soon after an arrest such a determination was required, in a later case the Court indicated that probable cause determinations should be within 48 hours to avoid being considered excessive delay.[117] Note that the probable cause determination is not synonymous with the first appearance. If a defendant was arrested pursuant to an arrest warrant, then the probable cause determination was already made and *Gerstein* review is not necessary as part of the first appearance.

If a felony defendant is not represented by an attorney at the first appearance, the magistrate will make the defendant aware of his right to be represented by an attorney, including the fact that the state will provide an attorney if the defendant cannot afford one. A **criminal defense lawyer** represents a person charged with a crime. Some criminal defense lawyers specialize in defending those facing drug-related crimes while others specialize in defending those facing drunk driving charges—Driving Under the Influence (DUI) or Driving While Intoxicated (DWI). Another means of specialization among criminal defense lawyers is the division between those who focus on defending clients charged with misdemeanors (think Jimmy McGill of AMC's *Better Call Saul* played by Bob Odenkirk) and those who focus on defending clients charged with felonies (think of Saul Goodman, the identity later taken on by Jimmy McGill, of AMC's *Breaking Bad*). Some criminal defense lawyers are privately retained while others, known as **public defenders**, are salaried government employees responsible for representing **indigent persons** (those who cannot afford their own attorneys) charged with crime. As discussed in Chapter Three, court-appointed attorneys may represent indigent criminal defendants though public defender offices provide the majority of legal representation for the indigent. Regardless of the criminal defense specialty and whether the attorney is privately retained or a public defender, the defense attorney's goal in representing the accused is not to prove that the accused is innocent, but to be an advocate for her client and represent the client throughout the process.

During the first appearance, the magistrate will make a determination about pretrial release. According to a BJS study of the 75 largest counties in the U.S., roughly six out of 10 felony defendants are released before trial.[118] Pretrial release may be conditioned on nonfinancial or financial requirements, a combination of both or neither. As the BJS study reports, approximately one-third of felony defendants are **released on recognizance (ROR)**, meaning they are released based only on their promise to appear in court as required (that is, no financial or nonfinancial requirements are imposed).[119] Nonfinancial requirements include such things as the imposition of a curfew and travel restrictions. For example, when Chris Paciello, former boyfriend of *Modern Family* co-star Sofia Vergara and accused member of the Bonnano crime family, was released on bail in 2000, he was required to live at his mother's house in Staten Island,[120] subject to 24–7 video surveillance, and barred from owning a cell phone.[121] In another example, when John A. Gotti, the son of the Gambino crime family boss, was released on bail in 1998, he was required to remain in his home, wear an electronic ankle bracelet, have his calls monitored, and pay for a security guard to be posted outside his home.[122] Other examples of things that could be required as a condition of bail include participation in anger management classes, periodic drug testing, and staying away from the victim of the alleged crime. Some of the more creative nonfinancial bail requirements have included requiring an alleged robber to read and write book reports every day and requiring a domestic violence defendant to buy flowers for his wife and take her out bowling.[123]

Financial release options require a person to post **bail**, a form of cash or property that the court holds while the disposition of the charges against a criminal defendant are pending in exchange for releasing the defendant from custody. It is intended as an incentive for a criminal defendant to show up for all of his required court proceedings, since failing to show can result in the forfeiture of the bail amount and the issuance of a warrant authorizing the defendant's arrest. The judge is responsible for setting the bail amount; however, for guidance they often rely on **bail schedules**, which are listings of charges and their associated standard bail amounts.[124] Posting bail is accomplished through one of several different types of bonds. **Cash bonds** require the criminal defendant (or someone on behalf of the criminal defendant) to pay the full dollar amount of the bail set by the judge. **Deposit bonds** permit the criminal defendant to pay only a percentage of the bail amount. In Illinois, for example, the deposit bond system requires the defendant to post

10 percent of the face value of the bond. If the defendant fails to appear, not only is the deposit forfeited, the defendant is also responsible for the full value of the bond. **Property bonds** permit the criminal defendant to put up property as collateral. More specifically, the defendant submits a property deed to the court to permit it to place a lien on the property, which may be worth quite a bit more than the dollar amount of the bail.

The most common type of bond, however, is a **surety bond**, also referred to as bail bonds.[125] They involve for-profit bail bonding companies providing a promissory note to the court for a nonrefundable fee paid by the defendant. Though commercial bail bonding is little known outside of the U.S. context (the only other jurisdiction with a meaningful bail bond industry is the Philippines), it is quite common domestically, with only four states (Illinois, Kentucky, Oregon, and Wisconsin) banning it.[126] A surety bond can be used for any amount of bail, but it is especially useful when the defendant cannot afford to pay his or her bail. Bail agents, or bail bondsmen as they are commonly known, are backed by a special type of insurance company called a surety company and pledge to pay the full value of the bond if the defendant fails to appear in court. In return, the bail agent charges the client (the criminal defendant) a 10 percent premium on the amount of the bail and collects some sort of collateral. A bail agent usually has an opportunity to recover a defendant if he fails to appear in court. In such cases, bounty hunters are employed to find the defendant.

As the popular reality television show *Dog the Bounty Hunter* illustrates, bail agents such as Duane "Dog" Chapman may also be bounty hunters. Running for eight seasons on the A&E network, the show chronicled the professional and personal life of Chapman and his extended family. In an interesting twist, Chapman himself jumped bail when he fled Mexico after being released from jail. Chapman had captured a convicted rapist who was living under an assumed identity in Puerto Vallarta, Mexico, and was taking him back to the United States. Bounty hunting is illegal in Mexico, however, and he and his team were jailed when Mexican authorities intercepted them.[127] Another example from pop culture is Stephanie Plum. She is the very unlikely bounty hunter featured as the main character in a popular fiction series by Janet Evanovich, with each book title incorporating a number (*One for the Money, Two for the Dough, Three to Get Deadly*, etc.).[128] Stephanie is an ordinary young woman from Trenton, New Jersey, who works for her smarmy cousin Vinny in his bail bond business and whose mishaps include repeatedly having her car blown up by a rotating cast of villains. The real Dog Chapman and the fictional Stephanie Plum depict a gritty but exciting profession.[129] The work of most bail bondsmen, however, is much more pedestrian. They help to get defendants and lawyers to the right courtroom at the right time, facilitate information sharing among court actors, help defendants obtain release from pretrial detention, work with police to keep defendants in jail by refusing to provide bail and, conversely, lessen pretrial punishment by bailing out police informants quickly.[130]

The professional bail bond industry has, however, been subject to much criticism.[131] Some, for example, have pointed out that private bail bonding undermines the logic of bail. Since the criminal defendant has put up only a fraction of the actual bail amount, the incentive to show up for required court appearances is diminished.[132] This is true even if it is the defendant's family or friends who have provided the funds for a surety bond. Other critics have argued that the system disadvantages the poor.[133] The "glaring weakness [of the bail system] is that it discriminates against poor defendants, thus running directly counter to the law's avowed purpose of treating all defendants equally."[134] Though this critique is not limited to surety bonds, per se, the fact that the fee paid to a bondsman is nonrefundable even if the defendant meets all of his obligations to show up for court proceeding means that those who must resort to a surety bond (because they cannot afford to post bail otherwise) incur a financial cost that is not incurred by those who have sufficient funds and/or property to post bail without resort to a surety bond. A related criticism is that bondsmen may decline to work with clients whose bail is small because there will be little profit involved in making the bond.[135] Perhaps the strongest criticism of the professional bail bond industry is that it lodges too much discretion to "exercise powers of custody" in nongovernmental actors.[136] Reports of overly aggressive tactics, such as when a trio of female bounty hunters from Lipstick Bounty Hunters was alleged to have blinded a prospective detainee with a rubber bullet,[137] and misidentifications that lead to detention of the wrong individuals[138] serve to illustrate this concern.

Setting bail requires the magistrate to consider the seriousness of the alleged offense along with other information relating to the offender, such as prior criminal history and community ties. All but four states permit the judge to consider not just the risk of a defendant not showing up for trial but also the risk to public safety.[139] If the magistrate imposes a financial condition and the defendant cannot meet that condition, the defendant will be held in custody in a jail and will remain there until either he can pay the bail or there is a final disposition of the charges. According to BJS data, from 1990 to 2004, 62 percent of felony defendants in state courts in the 75 largest counties were released on bail.[140] Among defendants who were to receive pretrial release, one in six were denied bail while the remaining five in six had bail set but the defendant did not meet the financial conditions.[141] Not surprisingly, the higher the amount of bail, the lower the probability of release.[142] As with police contact, the empirical evidence indicates that the bail process does not appear to be administered to individuals equally. BJS statisticians Thomas Cohen and Brian Reaves undertook a multivariate analysis that showed Hispanics were less likely than non-Hispanic defendants to be released on bail, even when controlling for factors such as the offense with which the defendant was charged and the defendant's criminal history.[143] Further, they found that males were less likely than females to be released.[144]

Following the first appearance, the next step in a felony case is the **preliminary hearing**. During the preliminary hearing, the judge determines whether there is probable cause to believe that the defendant committed the crime charged in the complaint. Recall that probable cause is about whether there are sufficient facts for a reasonable person to believe that the defendant committed the crime with which she has been charged. Although the magistrate will already have determined that probable cause exists at the initial appearance, the preliminary hearing is an adversarial proceeding in which both sides are represented by counsel. The preliminary "hearing's adversarial procedures promote a more reliable determination of probable cause than the speedy ex parte review [that is, without representation of the defendant] at the initial appearance."[145] Typically, the prosecution presents its key witnesses and the defense will cross-examine those witnesses. The defense also has the right to present its own witnesses and may occasionally do so.

If the judge determines that probable cause is lacking, the case is dismissed. In most states, if the judge determines that there is probable cause, the prosecutor then files an **information** document with the clerk of the court and the case is set for trial. The information is the formal accusation of a criminal offense. In the federal system and in some states, the case moves from the preliminary hearing to a **grand jury**.[146] A grand jury is a panel of citizens that a court convenes for the purpose of determining whether to proceed with the prosecution of someone suspected of a crime.[147] The size of a grand jury varies across jurisdictions, with federal grand juries consisting of between 16 and 23 jurors and state grand juries consisting of between 12 and 23 jurors. At the federal level, a grand jury is required by the terms of the Fifth Amendment, which reads, in part, "No person shall be held to answer for a capital, or otherwise infamous crime, unless on presentment or indictment of a grand jury . . . "[148] If the grand jury finds that there is probable cause, an **indictment** (also referred to as a true bill) is issued against the defendant and the case is bound over for trial. Not infrequently, the decisions of grand juries are controversial. In 2014, for example, the lack of grand jury indictment against the Ferguson, Missouri, police officer who shot and killed an unarmed black teenager generated a maelstrom of protests and violence.[149] Similarly, the 2014 decision of a New York grand jury not to charge a white officer who killed an unarmed black man using a chokehold, despite the fact that the incident was caught on videotape, generated waves of protest.[150]

The next step in the process is the **arraignment**. The arraignment is the proceeding at which a judge informs the defendant of the charges against him, the defendant is advised of his rights, and the defendant is asked to enter a plea. As we will discuss at length in the next section, it is at this point that plea bargaining between the defense attorney and the prosecution takes place. Of course if a plea agreement is reached, a trial will not be necessary. If an agreement is not reached, the defense attorney may file various pretrial motions. For example, the defense attorney might file a motion to exclude unlawfully seized evidence from the trial pursuant to the **exclusionary rule**. The exclusionary rule emerged over a series of U.S. Supreme Court cases interpreting the Fourth Amendment's protection against unreasonable searches and seizures.[151] Generally speaking, and with important exceptions, the exclusionary rule requires the exclusion of evidence from trial that was obtained in violation of the Fourth Amendment.[152] Another example of a pre-trial motion that a criminal defense attorney might file is a motion to change the location of the trial.[153] The Sixth Amendment reads, in part, "In all criminal prosecutions, the accused shall enjoy the right to . . . an impartial jury . . . "[154] The Supreme Court has found that the impartiality of a jury may sometimes only be guaranteed through a change of venue. "If there has been extensive pretrial publicity . . . the risk of prejudice to the defendant in the district where the crime was committee may be so great that . . . remedies [other than a change of venue] are inadequate to protect his right to an impartial jury."[155] This is the logic behind, for example, the efforts of Boston Marathon bombing suspect Dzhokhar Tsarnaev's defense team to change the venue for his trial out of Boston.[156]

The next step in the criminal process is the **trial**. As we detail in Chapter Eight, there are numerous steps in criminal trials, including jury selection, opening statements, direct and cross examination of witnesses, closing arguments, jury instructions, jury deliberation, and, ultimately, a **verdict** (the formal finding of fact, which translates, in criminal cases, to a choice of guilty or not guilty). As legal scholar Daniel Givelber and criminologist Amy Farrell demonstrate, acquittals represent a one-time failure by the prosecution to persuade a jury of guilt beyond a reasonable doubt rather than a positive indication that the defendant did not commit the crime.[157] If the defendant is convicted, the next step is **sentencing**, which generally takes place at the same time or immediately after the verdict. Basically, three different types of sentences are available: financial sanctions, such as fines or restitution orders; some form of release into the community, such as probation or house arrest; or incarceration in a jail (for lesser sentences) or prison (for longer sentences).[158] Financial sanctions may be difficult to collect because offenders are unable or unwilling pay. For example, from 2004 to 2013 the U.S. Department of Justice was only able to collect $21.2 billion (22 percent) arising from criminal cases and enforcement actions leaving $97 billion uncollected during that period.[159]

One key dichotomy is indeterminate versus determinate sentences. An **indeterminate sentence** is one in which an individual is imprisoned for a minimum to a maximum period, but may be released by a parole board before the maximum time is served. An example of an indeterminate sentence is 20 years to life. Indeterminate sentences may be handed down for felony convictions, where punishment includes incarceration in a state prison, but they are not generally used when the crime is less serious. The principle behind indeterminate sentences is the hope that prison will rehabilitate some offenders, warranting earlier release than for those who do not become rehabilitated. Furthermore, the prospect of early release gives a prisoner an incentive to behave while in prison. Critics of indeterminate sentencing argue that it puts too much power into the hands of the parole board, leading to arbitrary and discriminatory results.[160]

Determinate sentences, on the other hand, are fixed sentences without parole. For example, a sentence of 6 months in the county jail is determinate because the prisoner will spend no more than 6 months in jail. Sometimes, however, early parole is allowed and judges still retain some leeway in setting the exact term of the sentence. Widely used prior to 1920, determinate sentences largely disappeared with the advent of the rehabilitative model.[161] Yet, determinate sentences reappeared in some states beginning in the mid-1970s. Conservatives saw a return to determinate sentences as a solution to what they saw as a too-lenient judicial system that released still-dangerous offenders. Liberals felt that it could solve the problem of racial, gender, and economic disparity in sentencing. Yet, many states found that determinate sentences solved neither of these problems. Scholars have argued that reforms should instead focus on substance abuse and mental health treatment as well as vocational and educational programs.[162]

As we discussed earlier in this chapter, in recent decades judges have been limited by legislatures that have passed mandatory minimum statutes, three-strikes laws that impose harsher sentences at the moment of a third felony conviction,[163] and general sentencing guidelines. Research shows that these kinds of legislative enactments have been driven by social and political concerns rather than objective research by legal scholars or criminal policy experts. Specifically, the law enforcement lobby and conservative interest groups and politicians aligned in the 1970s and 1980s to politicize crime—fueled by the public's alarm over a threatening African American drug trade, declining morality and discipline within the family, and increases in the diversity of society—and inaugurated a new era of punishment and incarceration that some have termed a "prison state."[164]

Sentencing guidelines provide structure at the criminal-sentencing stage by specifically defining offense and offender elements that should be considered in each case. After considering these elements using a grid or worksheet scoring system, the guidelines recommend a sentence or sentence range. Although the goals of guidelines vary, an underlying theme is that offenders with similar offenses and criminal histories be treated alike. But guidelines vary in terms of whether they are promulgated by the legislature or judiciary, when judges must follow the recommendations, and what rights are afforded to those who disagree with imposed guideline sentences. Thus, even when guidelines are in place, there is still room for discretion and disparities. Organizational norms change slowly, even after formal law changes, and sentencing disparities persist even after the passage of sentencing guidelines, mandatory minimums, and three-strikes laws.[165]

The Federal Sentencing Guidelines were adopted in 1984 to counter widespread disparities in federal sentencing. One study showed that the expected difference in sentence length between judges fell from 17 percent (4.9 months) in 1986–1987 to 11 percent

SUPERLATIVE PROVOCATION.

RUBE ROUNDUP.—Yes, your Honor, I admit I shot the tenderfoot, but he asked *me* to play a game of "ping-pong" with him.
LEAD GULCH JUSTICE.—Discriminatin' sarcumstances. When he gets out o' the hospittle I 'll see thet you get the justice of his commitment. Next case.

Image 7.4 Judge Pronounces Verdict in County Courtroom

This 1902 illustration shows a country court-room scene with a judge pronouncing a verdict based on testimony of the cowboy standing in front of the clerk's desk. Caption: "Rube Roundup—Yes, your Honor, I admit I shot the tenderfoot, but he asked me to play a game of ping-pong with him. / Lead Gulch Justice—Discriminatin' sarcumstances. When he gets out o' the hospittle I'll see thet you get the justice of his commitment. Next case." Should sentences be determined by legislatures, judges, or juries? Prints and Photographs Division, Library of Congress, Washington, D.C.

(3.9 months) in 1988–1993.[166] Another study found that the sentencing judge accounted for 2.32 percent of the variation in sentences in 1984–1985, but only 1.24 percent of the variation in sentences under the Guidelines in 1994–1995.[167] However, the Guidelines were struck down in *United States v. Booker*.[168] In *Booker*, the United States Supreme Court found that the mandatory application of the Guidelines violated defendants' Sixth Amendment right to a jury trial and rendered the Guidelines advisory. Subsequent Supreme Court cases diminished the effect of the Guidelines by reducing the degree of appellate scrutiny applied to sentences both within and outside the range provided by the Guidelines.[169] A recent study conducted by legal scholar Crystal Yang addressed whether greater judicial discretion after *Booker* has impacted inter-judge sentencing disparities.[170] Yang found that inter-judge sentencing disparities have doubled since the Guidelines became advisory.[171]

There has been a great deal of scholarship investigating the role of race in the sentencing of convicted defendants. In 2000, a review of 40 studies reported that a majority of them found that race affects the incarceration decision, and nearly one-quarter found evidence that race affects sentence length.[172] For example, economics scholar David Mustard examined the impact of race on the incarceration and sentencing decisions of federal judges, including controls for income as well as interaction terms for race and income, race and education, and race and criminal history. He found that African Americans are more likely to be incarcerated and receive longer sentences.[173] Another study, exploiting the random assignment of cases to judges in Cook County, Illinois, found statistically significant, between-judge variation in incarceration rates between African American and white defendants, though not in sentence lengths.[174] However, a study of sentencing under California's Three Strikes law found that not only have sentences become harsher, particularly in politically conservative counties, but also that African Americans received longer prison sentences.[175] Sentences of life without parole

Image 7.5 The In and Out of Our Penal System *This 1909 print "The In and the Out of our Penal System" shows criminals on the left entering a prison labeled "Penitentiary" with a statue of "Justice" and on the right leaving the prison after serving their sentences and given papers labeled "Freedom" where they are confronted by a large hand above a city with a wall labeled "Ex-Convicts Not Wanted." Given that there are racial disparities in sentencing, what are the implications for racial minorities who leave the prison system?* Prints and Photographs Division, Library of Congress, Washington, D.C.

are disproportionately imposed on racial minorities leading scholars to call it "America's new death penalty."[176]

A number of studies have found differences among minority racial groups—particularly between African Americans and Hispanics. One study, using data on Pennsylvania sentencing practices, compared the sentence outcomes of white, African American, and Hispanic defendants.[177] The authors found that Hispanic defendants were treated more harshly than white defendants and even more harshly than African American defendants in incarceration decisions and sentence-length decisions.[178] This pattern held for drug as well as for nondrug defendants. Specifically, compared with white defendants, African Americans were 6 percent more likely and Hispanics 18 percent more likely to be incarcerated in nondrug cases.[179] Also, African American defendants received sentences about 3 months longer than whites did, and Hispanic defendants received sentences about 10 months longer than white defendants and 7 months longer than African American defendants.[180] Why have Hispanics been treated more harshly than other minority groups? Some have argued that there is a "citizenship penalty" with noncitizens sentenced more harshly than citizens, which explains the majority of the increase in Hispanic–white sentencing disparity over the past 2 decades.[181]

Following sentencing, losing litigants may choose to appeal the result to a higher court. As we detail in Chapter Nine, there are numerous steps and various issues involved in the appellate process. In all, very few cases are appealed, appellate courts only consider matters of law and procedure rather than facts, and losers in criminal cases generally have a poor chance of winning in a higher court. Thus, the outcomes that result from the criminal trials are almost always final.

Figure 7.7 shows that criminal cases make up less than one-third of the federal appellate docket, which is dominated by civil matters. While criminal appeals rose from just

FIGURE 7.7
Criminal Cases in Federal Appellate Courts, 1992–2013

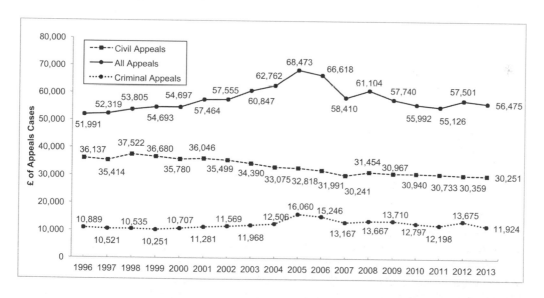

Note: Cases from the U.S. Court of Appeals for the Federal Circuit are excluded.
Source: Federal judicial caseload statistics, www.uscourts.gov

FIGURE 7.8
Criminal Case Composition in Federal Appellate Courts, 2008–2013

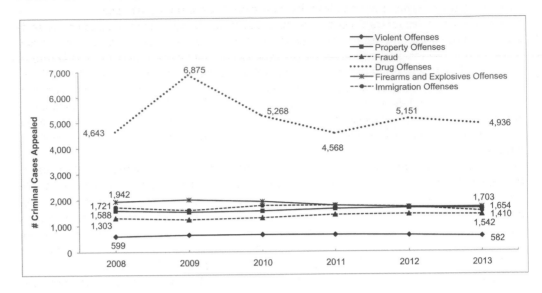

Note: Data reflect criminal appeals commenced during the 12-month period ending March 31 of each year; prior to 2008 categories for criminal offenses were modified rendering prior data not comparable; minor categories excluded include embezzlement, sex offenses, justice system offenses, bribery, money laundering, RICO, racketeering, extortion, gambling, regulatory offenses, and traffic offenses.
Source: Federal judicial caseload statistics, www.uscourts.gov

under 11,000 cases in 1996 to just over 16,000 cases by 2005, they subsequently declined to fewer than 12,000 by 2013. As we discuss in Chapter Nine, the record caseload in 2005 was driven by the U.S. Supreme Court's decisions in *Blakely v. Washington*[182] and *United States v. Booker*[183] holding that a defendant's punishment must be based on facts submitted by a jury and proved beyond a reasonable doubt and that appellate court judges had the power to review those sentences for "reasonableness." Figure 7.8 shows the composition of criminal appeals over time. While each major criminal category remained relatively stable from 2008 to 2013, drug appeals increased dramatically in 2009. This growth was the result of appeals in crack cocaine cases affected by an amendment to the sentencing guidelines issued by the U.S. Sentencing Commission on November 1, 2007. Specifically, the amendment reduced penalties for most crack cocaine offenses and became retroactive on March 3, 2008.[184] Thus, changes in criminal appeal caseloads have resulted from changes in the law—either by legislatures, administrative agencies, or judges.

PLEA BARGAINING

Despite the ubiquity of popular depictions of courtroom proceedings, it is a myth that criminal matters are adjudicated through trials. Nearly every criminal case—approximately 95 percent—is resolved through plea bargaining.[185] **Plea bargaining** is the negotiation of an agreement between a prosecutor and a defendant whereby the defendant is permitted to plead guilty to a lesser charge or to the original charge with less than the maximum sentence. Unlike in the formal procedural due-process setting, where guilt and sentencing are decided separately, in the informal plea bargaining process these decisions are made together through a determination among the attorneys about a case's "worth."[186] Thus, plea bargains follow the "going rate" for similar past cases.

A good deal of scholarship demonstrates that legal characteristics—such as the seriousness of the current offense, prior record, strength of the evidence, the use of a public or private defender, and the detention status of the offender—increase the likelihood that a defendant will plead guilty.[187] Pretrial detention has a strong effect on the decision to offer and accept pleas. Those who are taken into custody are more likely to accept a plea and are less likely to have their charges dropped.[188] Further, some extralegal characteristics make it more likely that a defendant will not receive a reduced plea charge. For example, African Americans are less likely to receive a reduced charge compared to whites.[189]

There are three types of pleas bargains. A **charge bargain** involves reducing the charge to a less serious offense in exchange for a guilty plea. For example, in exchange for a guilty plea there may be a reduction in the charge from rape to sexual assault. A **sentence bargain** involves the prosecutor agreeing to recommend a lighter sentence in exchange for a guilty plea. For example, the prosecutor might recommend that the defendant serve three years of a possible seven-year sentence. Either side may begin the negotiation, but it is within the prosecutor's discretion whether to offer a plea bargain. There is also **implicit plea bargaining**, in which defendants are informed that if they go to trial and are convicted, they will be punished more severely than if they agree to a plea.

Historians agree that plea bargaining was nonexistent before 1800; began to appear as a result of industrialization, immigration, and urbanization prior to the Civil War; and continued to gain traction during the end of the nineteenth century, despite the skepticism of judges that the practice gave prosecutors too much authority over case outcomes.[190] But with the growth in complex civil cases and tort law at the end of the century and into the next—which we discuss in Chapter Six—judges began to see the benefits of efficiently settling civil cases without trial. This mindset carried over into the criminal process, particularly in the 1920s as federal courts faced large numbers of prohibition cases and legal actors including police, prosecutors, and judges became more professionalized through formal legal training.[191] Plea bargaining soon became the norm. But it was not until 1970 that the United States Supreme Court affirmed the necessity of plea bargaining as long as it was voluntary.[192] The Court again affirmed and even advocated plea bargaining in *Santobello v. New York*.[193] According to the Court:

> Disposition of charges after plea discussions is not only an essential part of the process but a highly desirable part for many reasons. It leads to prompt and largely final disposition of most criminal cases; it avoids much of the corrosive impact of enforced idleness during pretrial confinement for those who are denied release pending trial; it protects the public from those accused persons who are prone to continue criminal conduct even while on pretrial release; and, by shortening the time between charge and disposition, it enhances whatever may be the rehabilitative prospects of the guilty when they are ultimately imprisoned.[194]

The Court has also ruled that the Sixth Amendment of the Constitution safeguards the right of a criminal defendant to an effective lawyer during plea bargain negotiations, as well as when the defendant gives up the right to a trial and accepts a plea offer. The Supreme Court extended that constitutional guarantee to cases in which the defendant rejects a favorable plea offer and goes to trial because of ineffective counsel. In *Missouri v. Frye*,[195] the Court found that defense counsel had been ineffective in not communicating plea offers to the defendant, resulting in the defendant pleading guilty to a felony instead of a misdemeanor. In *Lafler v. Cooper*,[196] the parties involved conceded the fact of deficient performance on the part of the defense attorney. The prosecutor offered the defendant a 51–85-month sentence in exchange for pleading guilty to a charge of assault with intent to murder. The defendant rejected the offer after his attorney told him that the prosecution would not be able to establish intent to murder because the victim had been shot below the waist. The defendant rejected the plea offer, was convicted, and received a mandatory minimum 185–360-month sentence, which was three-and-a-half times greater than he would have received under the plea.

The process of plea bargaining has three stages to it.[197] First, plea offers are made and assessed by the attorneys based on the value of the case—the seriousness of the crime, the strength of the evidence, and the defendant's background—and factors associate with temporary postponements—namely how long the accused may remain incarcerated before resolution of the case. Prosecutors decide whether cases are "light" or "serious" by considering the sentence most likely to be imposed.[198] A light case has a high probability of probation and little chance of prison. A serious case is one that likely involves prison. Furthermore, cases are considered either **dead bang cases**—those with a high chance of conviction—or **reasonable doubt cases**—those where the evidence does not clearly connect the defendant to the crime and there is a chance of complete acquittal.

The second step in the plea bargaining process is the negotiation of the terms of the plea bargain. These negotiations may include threats of delays through continuances or by setting trial dates. Legal scholar Douglas Maynard has argued that attorneys use stories or narratives to negotiate by telling what happened when a defendant was charged with an offense.[199] These narratives include a story entry device (including the name of the case and a synopsis), the story itself (which may contain background information and details the actions taken by the parties involved), and finally a denial or explanation of the defendant's behavior by the defense attorney. With the use of that narrative, the attorneys exchange offers and counteroffers about shorter sentences, dismissal of second or third counts, or reduced charges. Each side is seeking to make a deal, trying to arrive at a mutually agreeable outcome that gives each side something it would like.

The third step in the plea bargaining process is when the defense attorney counsels the defendant by educating him or her about reasonable expectations in the case. The defendant makes her desires concerning the outcome of the case known to her attorney, and the attorney and client discuss the options. Defense attorneys have an affirmative obligation to look out for the best interests of their clients during the plea bargaining process and this includes providing sound advice as to the advisability of accepting the plea offer on the table.[200] Of course, the final decision always rests with the client, even though many clients are reluctant to make a decision and mistakenly expect their attorneys to decide for them.

Though they do not necessarily emerge in a neat and tidy sequence, these three steps constitute a recurring process that can repeat itself multiple times throughout the stages of litigation as prosecutors and defense attorneys—and theoretically, victims and the accused—constantly decide whether a case should be settled immediately or proceed further. For example, sometimes the defense attorney counsels the defendant prior to receiving a plea offer from the prosecutor and sometimes the attorneys negotiate the terms of the plea deal before the defense attorney confers with the defendant. Regardless of the sequence, however, with rare exceptions plea offers are made and considered, there is some form of negotiation, and defense attorneys consult defendants prior to making a decision.

HOW DO WE KNOW?

Are Public Defenders as Effective as Private Lawyers?

A recent study examined whether public defenders are as effective as private lawyers when it comes to how long a defendant is sentenced.[201] The study authors proposed a theory about plea bargaining taking into account the incentives of prosecutors and rooted in the workload differences between public defenders and private attorneys. Prosecutors who are faced with two otherwise identical cases—one with lots of potentially time-consuming motions and one with fewer such motions—and the time to try only one of them, will plea bargain the one with more motions. Because they are overworked, public defenders file fewer potentially time-consuming pretrial motions than is the case for private counsel. Accordingly, private lawyers will receive more favorable plea bargains than public defendants.

In order to test this theory, the authors examined sentence outcomes in every felony case filed in Denver, Colorado, in 2002. For each case, they compared the actual sentence a defendant received to the maximum sentence he or she faced. They used two different dependent variables: (1) absolute sentence reduction, in which they simply subtracted the sentence received from the sentence faced; and (2) percentage sentence reduction, in which they divided the absolute sentence reduction by the total sentence faced. The main independent variable of interest was the number of all motions filed in the case. However, the authors were unable to differentiate between pretrial motions from post-conviction motions, and they were also unable to tell whether it was a defense motion or a prosecution motion. As a consequence, they simply counted all motions filed in the case. To justify that measurement decision, the authors argued that the range of prosecution motions is rather limited and that there is no reason to believe that prosecutors file more or fewer motions depending on whether the defense lawyer is a public defender or private lawyer. Accordingly, the number of motions filed by the prosecution will tend to cancel each other out case to case, "leaving the total motions filed as a reasonably good relative indicator of the number of motions filed by the defense."[202]

The authors found that, when controlling for the seriousness of the charge, the average public defender client was sentenced to almost three more years of incarceration than clients of the average private lawyer. On this basis, the authors concluded that public defenders are less effective than private lawyers. But is it because private lawyers file more motions than public defenders? On the contrary, the authors found that, even after controlling for the seriousness of the charge, public defenders filed marginally more motions than private lawyers (about one motion per case). The authors went on to speculate that the reason public defenders are less effective (that is, their clients have longer sentences) is because of self-selection on the part of the defendants. Simply put, public defenders attract less winnable cases. A guilty defendant, especially one who is charged with a less serious crime, will not waste his money on a private attorney, but an innocent defendant, especially one who is charged with a serious crime, will somehow find the money. The authors call the former "marginally indigent defendants."

How long do cases take to get resolved through plea bargaining? The median time from arrest to adjudication—which almost always results from a plea agreement—for felony defendants in 2009 was 4 months, 1 month longer than in 1998.[203] Murder cases take the longest, on average, to be resolved (more than 1 year), while motor vehicle theft and drug offenses other than trafficking are the quickest (taking less than 3 months to resolve).[204] The median time from arrest to adjudication was shorter for detained defendants (2 months) than for those released prior to case disposition (5.5 months).[205]

Supporters of plea bargaining argue that it allows defendants to acknowledge guilt and assume responsibility for their actions; it allows victims to gain a sense of closure, knowing the defendant will be punished but at the same time the victim avoids going through a trial; and it allows greater flexibility and more efficient allocation of resources in the criminal justice system by allowing judges, prosecutors, and defense attorneys to reduce caseloads—the **caseload pressure hypothesis**. While research on the caseload pressure hypothesis is

mixed, there is considerable evidence that plea bargaining results from legal norms rather than caseload pressure.[206] New courtroom personnel including prosecutors and defense attorneys join a local legal culture and learn to plea bargain from the existing culture.

POP CULTURE

A Few Good Men

A Few Good Men
Credit: Mondadori Portfolio via Getty Images

In the 1992 film *A Few Good Men*, Tom Cruise plays a cocky and ambitious lawyer, fresh out of Harvard Law School who takes a job as an attorney in the Navy Judge Advocate General's (JAG) Corps. We learn that the lawyer Cruise plays, Lt. Daniel Kaffee, is only in the Navy to fulfill the dream of his dead father and that he will soon depart for a high-paying position in a major law firm. Kaffee has never seen the inside of a courtroom but has quickly established a reputation as a smart, effective lawyer due to his plea bargaining prowess. His knowledge of the intricacies of the process and past cases gives him the ability to know what the outcomes of new cases will be.

Early in the film we see how skillful Kaffee is at negotiating deals for his clients—even while he's playing softball. An opposing attorney (Lt. Dave Spradling, played by Matt Craven) asks him: "We were supposed to meet in your office 15 minutes ago to talk about the McDermot case. You're stalling on this thing. We get this done right now, or I mean it . . . I'm going to hang your boy." After a couple jokes from Kaffee, Spradling says: "I'm going to charge him with possession and being under the influence while on duty. You plead guilty I recommend 30 days in the brig with loss of rank and pay." Kaffee counters: "It was oregano. . . . It was 10 dollars worth of oregano." Spradling: "Yeah, but your client thought it was marijuana." Kaffee: "My client's a moron; that's not against the law." Spradling protests: "I have people to answer to just like you do. I'm going to charge him." Kaffee continues to mock him: "With what? Possession of a condiment?" Kaffee finally gets serious: "I tried to help you out of this but if you ask for jail time I'm going to file a motion to dismiss." Spradling: "You won't get it." Kaffee: "I will get it. And if the MTD is denied I'll file a motion *in limine* seeking to obtain an evidentiary ruling in advance and after that I'm going to file against pretrial confinement and you're going to spend the next three months going blind on paperwork because a Signalman Second Class bought and smoked a dime bag of oregano." Spradling, clearly shaken, offers: "B misdemeanor 20 days in the brig." Knowing he has won, Kaffee counters: "C misdemeanor 15 days restricted duty."

Next, Kaffee is assigned to defend two young Marines who have been accused of murdering a colleague. Kaffee is quick to work out a plea bargain with the prosecuting attorney (Capt. Jack Ross played by Kevin Bacon). Indeed, we later learn that the case was specifically assigned to Kaffee so a plea would be reached and the sensational case would remain private. When Kaffee and Ross first discuss the case, Kaffee asks: "What are we looking at?" Ross replies: "They plead guilty, we drop the conspiracy and the conduct unbecoming. Twenty years they're home in half that time." Kaffee counters: "I want 12." Ross: "Can't do it." Kaffee attempts to persuade Ross that his case is weak: "They called the ambulance." Ross replies: "Look, I don't care if they called the Avon lady. They killed a Marine." Kaffee again challenges Ross's case: "Rag was tested for poison. The autopsy, the lab reports, all say the same thing: maybe, maybe not." Ross replies: "The Chief of Internal Medicine for Guantanamo Bay Naval Hospital says he's sure." With Kaffee on his way to Cuba to investigate the matter, Ross concedes: "Look, I'm going to give you the 12 years." But Ross warns Kaffee that he's wasting his time going to Guantanamo Bay and asks: "We got a deal?" But having gotten Ross to agree to his terms, Kaffee is still going to Cuba: "I'll talk to you when I get back."

Ultimately, Kaffee has a change of heart, takes the case to trial, and in a dramatic courtroom confession, gets the military base commander (Col. Nathan R. Jessup played by Jack Nicholson) to admit on the witness stand that he ordered the Marines to take action against the Marine who was killed. Kaffee demands: "I want the truth!" Jessup replies: "You can't handle the truth!" The early plea bargaining scene over oregano shows how a good defense attorney can use the plea bargaining process as a check on overzealous or incompetent prosecutors. But the dramatic ending illustrates how over-eager attorneys intent on plea bargaining may subvert justice if they fail to put in the effort required to defend their clients.

Plea bargaining has been criticized on the grounds that it unfairly causes criminal defendants to waive their Fifth, Sixth, and Fourteenth Amendment rights: "Instead of establishing a defendant's guilt and sentence through an impartial process with a complete investigation and an opportunity for the defense to present its case, prosecutors take on the role of judge and jury, making all determinations based on the probability of whether they will win or lose at trial."[207] The most important criticism of plea bargaining is that it is coercive, with allegations that prosecutors induce defendants to forfeit their rights out of fear of being punished with additional charges and a harsher sentence if they do not plead guilty. The argument is that innocent, risk-averse defendants may not be willing to risk going to trial and receiving a severe sentence and instead will plead guilty to ensure a more lenient sentence.[208] Indeed, research shows that guilty pleas are secured primarily through granting concessions to defendants.[209] This means that law enforcement and prosecutors have an incentive to overcharge or "throw the book" at defendants so that they may later grant concessions and secure guilty pleas.[210]

Do innocent people plead guilty? The evidence suggests that most court actors assume that, because they were arrested, defendants must have done something wrong and are not entirely innocent.[211] Although it is unclear how many defendants who are convicted through pleading guilty are actually innocent of the charged offenses, many agree that there is an **innocence problem**—the possibility that innocent defendants accept discounted plea offers to avoid the risk of severe sentences, which compromises the legitimacy of the entire criminal justice system. Other scholars and observers, however, believe that plea bargaining's innocence problem is exaggerated. One study examining exonerations in the United States from 1989 to 2003 found that approximately 6 percent (20 of 340 exonerees) had pleaded guilty.[212] Regardless of innocence or guilt, as research by Feeley and others suggests, defendants may see that the just result comes from simply avoiding the formal process through a quick plea bargain.[213]

CONCLUSION

The notion that the criminal justice process is fair or just is a myth. Criminal convictions are regularly overturned because of coerced confessions, questionable witnesses, overzealous prosecutors, and corrupt law enforcement. Many victims of crime, and most victims of violent crime, fail to contact police who sometimes make it difficult to report crime. Police are subject to political pressure from elected officials resulting in police failure to file reports in many cases. The extant research shows that most crimes that are reported do not result in arrests and remain unresolved. Further, statistics make clear that there are gender and racial differences when it comes to contact with the police, stops, searches, arrests, use of force, plea bargaining, bail, and sentencing. Plea bargaining dominates the criminal process with very few cases resulting in trial. These realities raise serious questions about whether we can reasonably conclude that justice is served in the criminal process.

Reformers have offered a number of solutions to improve the system, including an end to the war on drugs; downgrading some minor misdemeanors to violations payable by fines; more leniency in term of pretrial release; rapid processing of cases; less plea bargaining and more trials with local juries; less prosecutorial discretion with laws that accurately define what prosecutors seek to punish; an equal-protection guarantee to make prosecution and punishment less discriminatory; and focusing on drug treatment, mental health, vocational training, and education to tackle the problem of crime at its root causes. Of course these solutions are subject to the political process. Criminal justice reforms are no different from other areas of public policy: they are only possible to the extent that the American people look beyond the myths to a realistic view of the criminal process and decide for themselves how justice should be served.

Suggested Readings

Angela J. Davis. *Arbitrary Justice: The Power of the American Prosecutor* (New York, NY: Oxford University Press, 2009). A critical exploration of the power of American prosecutors, this text considers the unequal treatment of defendants and victims that can arise through the abuse of prosecutorial discretion.

Malcolm M. Feeley. *The Process Is the Punishment: Handling Cases in a Lower Criminal Court* (New York, NY: Russell Sage Foundation: 1979, 1992). This now-classic book lays bare the inner workings of criminal courts, in the process arguing that the much-maligned pretrial process of plea bargaining is not punitive but, rather, helps defendants minimize the time and money they must spend in dealing with the court.

Jon B. Gould. *The Innocence Commission: Preventing Wrongful Conviction and Restoring the Criminal Justice System* (New York, NY: New York University Press, 2007). A recounting of the creation and first years of operation of the Innocence Commission for the state of Virginia, which uses a dozen wrongful conviction cases as the vehicles for demonstrating how and why wrongful convictions happen and how the prisoners in question were exonerated.

Milton Heumann. *Plea Bargaining: The Experiences of Prosecutors, Judges, and Defense Attorneys* (Chicago, IL: University of Chicago Press, 1981). A careful inquiry into the history and dynamics of plea negotiation, which makes a strong case against the conventional wisdom that plea bargaining is a product of caseload pressures.

Michael J. Nelson. "Responsive Justice? Retention Elections, Prosecutors, and Public Opinion," *Journal of Law and Courts*, vol. 2, no. 1 (Spring 2014): 117–152. A systematic analysis of the responsiveness of prosecutors and judges to constituent preferences, which finds that both actors are attentive to the preferences of their electoral constituents.

Micahel Tonry, *Punishing Race: A Continuing American Dilemma* (New York, NY: Oxford University Press, 2011). An analysis of the pattern of different experiences between African American and white men in the criminal justice system, which forcefully argues that the patterns are a function of drug and crime control policies that disproportionately affect African Americans.

Endnotes

1 Quoted in "Albert Einstein Warns of Dangers in Nuclear Arms Race," *NBC News*, February 12, 1950.
2 Ayn Rand, *Atlas Shrugged* (New York, NY: Random House, 1957).
3 Vivian Yee, "As 2 Go Free, Brooklyn Conviction Challenges Keep Pouring In," *New York Times*, February 6, 2014.
4 Ibid.

5 Sean Gardiner and Alison Fox, "Two New York Men Freed After Decades in Prison," *Wall Street Journal*, February 7, 2014.

6 Vivian Yee, "As 2 Go Free, Brooklyn Conviction Challenges Keep Pouring In," *New York Times*, February 6, 2014.

7 Ibid.

8 Sean Gardnier, "Brooklyn District Attorney Kenneth Thompson Takes on Wrongful Convictions," *Wall Street Journal*, August 8, 2014.

9 Vivian Yee, "As 2 Go Free, Brooklyn Conviction Challenges Keep Pouring In," *New York Times*, February 6, 2014.

10 Matthew McKnight, "No Justice, No Peace," *New Yorker*, January 6, 2015.

11 Molly Hennessy-Fisk, "Dallas County District Attorney a Hero to the Wrongfully Convicted," *Los Angeles Times*, May 8, 2012.

12 See, more generally, Jon B. Gould, *The Innocence Commission: Preventing Wrongful Conviction and Restoring the Criminal Justice System* (New York, NY: New York University Press, 2007); Lola Vollen and Dave Eggers, eds, *Surviving Justice: America's Wrongfully Convicted and Exonerated* (San Francisco, CA: McSweeney's, 2005); Innocence Project, *Lessons Not Learned: New York State Leads in the Number of Wrongful Convictions but Lags in Policy Reforms that Can Prevent Them* (New York, NY: Innocence Project, 2009).

13 PBS, "Death By Fire," *Frontline*, October 19, 2010 (http://video.pbs.org/video/1618590505/).

14 David Grann, "Trial by Fire," *New Yorker*, September 7, 2009; PBS, "Death By Fire," *Frontline*, October 19, 2010 (http://video.pbs.org/video/1618590505/).

15 Steve Mills and Maurice Possley, "Texas Man Executed on Disproved Forensics," *Chicago Tribune*, December 9, 2004.

16 E. Allan Lind and Tom R. Tyler, *The Social Psychology of Procedural Justice* (New York, NY: Springer, 1988). See, also, Tom R. Tyler and Yuen Huo, *Trust in the Law: Encouraging Public Cooperation with the Police and Courts* (New York, NY: Russell Sage, 2002).

17 Allan Horwitz and Michael Wasserman, "Formal Rationality, Substantive Justice, and Discrimination: A Study of Juvenile Court," *Law and Human Behavior*, vol. 4, no. 1/2 (1980): 103–115.

18 Tom R. Tyler, "What is Procedural Justice? Criteria Used by Citizens to Assess the Fairness of Legal Procedures," *Law & Society Review*, vol. 22, no. 1 (1988): 103–136.

19 Ibid.,103–136, 105.

20 Ibid.

21 See Michael Asimow and Shannon Mader, *Law and Popular Culture: A Course Book* (New York, NY: Peter Lang, 2004).

22 See Jerome H. Skolnick and Candace McCoy, "Police Accountability and the Media," *American Bar Foundation Research Journal*, vol. 9, no. 3 (Summer 1984): 521–557. See, also, Ray Surette, *Media, Crime, and Criminal Justice: Images, Realities, and Policies*, Fifth Edition (Stamford, CT: Cengage, 2014).

23 Elayne Rapping, *Law and Justice as Seen on TV* (New York, NY: New York University Press, 2003).

24 See Malcolm M. Feeley, *The Process Is the Punishment: Handling Cases in a Lower Criminal Court* (New York, NY: Russell Sage, 1979, 1992); Edward Conlon, *Blue Blood* (New York, NY: Riverhead, 2005); Steve Bogira, *Courtroom 302: A Year Behind the Scenes in an American Criminal Courthouse* (New York, NY: Vintage, 2006); Peter Moskos, *Cop in the Hood: My Year Policing Baltimore's Eastern District* (Princeton, NJ: Princeton University Press, 2009); Amy Bach, *Ordinary Injustice: How America Holds Court* (New York, NY: Picador, 2010).

25 See Victor M. Rios, *Punished: Policing the Lives of Black and Latino Boys* (New York, NY: New York University Press, 2011); Amy Bach, *Ordinary Injustice: How America Holds Court* (New York, NY: Picador, 2010).

26 Brandon L. Garrett, *Convicting the Innocent: Where Criminal Prosecutions Go Wrong* (Cambridge, MA: Harvard University Press, 2012).

27 William J. Stuntz, *The Collapse of American Criminal Justice* (Cambridge, MA: Harvard University Press, 2011).

28 See, for example, Samuel L. Myers, Jr., "Why Are Crimes Underreported? What Is the Crime Rate? Does It 'Really' Matter?" *Social Science Quarterly*, vol. 61, no. 1 (June 1980): 23–43; Dean G. Kilpatrick, Benjamin E. Saunders, Lois J. Veronen, Connie L. Best, and Judith M. Von, "Criminal Victimization: Lifetime Prevalence, Reporting to Police, and Psychological Impact," *Crime & Delinquency*, vol. 33, no. 4 (October 1987): 479–489; Rodrigo R. Soares, "Crime Reporting as a Measure of Institutional Development," *Economic Development and Cultural Change*, vol. 52, no. 4 (July 2004): 851–871.

29 See, for example, Michael Tonry, *Punishing Race: A Continuing American Dilemma* (New York, NY: Oxford University Press, 2011). See, also, Devah Pager, *Marked: Race, Crime, and Finding Work in an Era of Mass Incarceration* (Chicago, IL: University of Chicago Press, 2007).

30 Michael Tonry, *Punishing Race: A Continuing American Dilemma* (New York, NY: Oxford University Press, 2011): ix.

31 Pew Research Center, "Demographic & Economic Data, by Race," *Social & Demographic Trends*, August 22, 2013 (http://www.pewsocialtrends.org/2013/08/22/chapter-3-demographic-economic-data-by-race/#incarceration).

32 See, for example, Kenneth B. Nunn, "Race, Crime and the Pool of Surplus Criminality: Or Why the 'War on Drugs' Was a 'War on Blacks,'" *Journal of Gender, Race, and Justice*, vol. 6 (Fall 2002): 381–445; Faye S. Taxman and James M. Byrne, "Racial Disparity and the Legitimacy of the Criminal Justice System: Exploring the Consequences for Deterrence," *Journal of Health Care for the Poor and Underserved*, vol. 16, no. 4 (November 2005): 57–77; Michael Tonry and Matthew Melewski, "The Malign Effects of Drug and Crime Control Policies on Black Americans," *Crime and Justice*, vol. 37, no. 1 (2008): 1–44; Ian F. Haney Lopez, "Post-Racial Racism: Racial Stratification and Mass Incarceration in the Age of Obama," *California Law Review*, vol. 98, no. 3 (June 2010): 1023–1074.

33 For a broader consideration of this position, see Michelle Alexander, *The New Jim Crow: Mass Incarceration in the Age of Colorblindness* (New York, NY: The New Press, 2012).

34 Henry M. Hart, Jr., "The Aims of the Criminal Law," *Law and Contemporary Problems*, vol. 23, no. 3 (Summer 1958): 401–441; Samuel I. Shuman, "Responsibility and Punishment: Why Criminal Law," *American Journal of Jurisprudence*, vol. 1, no. 1 (1970): 25–63; Roger Bowles, Michael Faure, and Nuno Garoupa, "The Scope of Criminal Law and Criminal Sanctions: An Economic View and Policy Implications," *Journal of Law and Society*, vol. 35, no. 3 (September 2008): 389–416.

35 See, for example, Avinash Singh Bhati and Alex R. Piquero, "Estimating the Impact of Incarceration on Subsequent Offending Trajectories: Deterrent, Criminogenic, or Null Effect?" *Journal of Criminal Law and Criminology*, vol. 98, no. 1 (Fall 2007): 207–253; David S. Abrams, "Estimating the Deterrent Effect of Incarceration Using Sentencing Enhancements," *American Economic Journal: Applied Economics*, vol. 4, no. 4 (October 2012): 32–56.

36 Harold G. Grasmick and Robert J. Bursik, Jr., "Conscience, Significant Others, and Rational Choice: Extending the Deterrence Model," *Law & Society Review*, vol. 24, no. 3 (1990): 837–862; Ronet Bachman, Raymond Paternoster, and Sally Ward, "The Rationality of Sexual Offending: Testing a Deterrence/Rational Choice Conception of Sexual Assault," *Law & Society Review*, vol. 26, no. 2 (1992): 343–372; Daniel S. Nagin and Raymond Paternoster, "Enduring Individual Differences and Rational Choice Theories of Crime," *Law & Society Review*, vol. 27, no. 3 (1993): 467–496; Raymond Paternoster and Sally Simpson, "Sanction Threats and Appeals to Morality: Testing a Rational Choice Model of Corporate Crime," *Law & Society Review*, vol. 30, no. 3 (1996): 549–584; Amitai Etzioni, "Social Norms: Internalization, Persuasion, and History," *Law & Society Review*, vol. 34, no. 1 (2000): 157–178; Sally S. Simpson and Nicole Leeper Piquero, "Low Self-Control, Organizational Theory, and Corporate Crime," *Law & Society Review*, vol. 36, no. 3 (2002): 509–548.

37 Jennifer Truman, Lynn Langton, and Michael Planty, "Bulletin: Criminal Victimization, 2012," Bureau of Justice Statistics, October 2013 (http://www.bjs.gov/content/pub/pdf/cv12.pdf): 1.

38 Ibid.

39 Ibid., 4.

40 Lynn Langton, Marcus Berzofsky, Christopher Krebs, and Hope Smiley-McDonald, "Special Report: Victimizations Not Reported to the Police, 2006–2010," Bureau of Justice Statistics, August 2012 (http://www.bjs.gov/content/pub/pdf/vnrp0610.pdf).

41 See, for example, William K. Rashbaum, "Retired Officers Raise Questions on Crime Data," *New York Times*, February 6, 2010. In addition to declining to take a police report from crime victims, there are numerous documented instances of police reports being "scrubbed" by characterizing incidents as less serious than they were. See, for example, Ben Poston, "Crimes Underreported by Police Include Robbery, Rape," *Milwaukee Journal-Sentinel*, August 25, 2012, and David Bernstein and Noah Isackson, "The Truth about Chicago's Crime Rates," *Chicago Magazine*, April 7, 2014.

42 Al Baker and Joseph Goldstein, "Police Tactic: Keeping Crime Reports Off the Books" *New York Times,* December 30, 2011.

43 Ibid.

44 Federal Bureau of Investigation, "Offenses Cleared," *Crime in the United States, 2012* (Fall 2013) (http://www.fbi.gov/about-us/cjis/ucr/crime-in-the-u.s/2012/crime-in-the-u.s.-2012/offenses-known-to-law-enforcement/clearancetopic.pdf).

45 Christine Eith and Matthew R. Durose, "Special Report: Contacts between Police and the Public, 2008," Bureau of Justice Statistics, October 2011 (http://www.bjs.gov/content/pub/pdf/cpp08.pdf).

46 Ibid., Table 2

47 The "To Protect and To Serve" motto originated with the Los Angeles Police Academy and later became the official motto of the entire Los Angeles Police Department. Many other police jurisdictions have adopted it as well. It is a common trope in movies (such as the eponymously named 1992 movie starring C. Thomas Howell about corrupt cops) and television (such as the eponymously named November 6, 2002, episode of *The Twilight Zone* starring Usher as a police officer trying to protect a prostitute).

48 Christine Eith and Matthew R. Durose, "Special Report: Contacts between Police and the Public, 2008," Bureau of Justice Statistics, October 2011, (http://www.bjs.gov/content/pub/pdf/cpp08.pdf).

49 Ibid., Table 9

50 Ibid., Table 13

51 Ibid., Table 14

52 Ibid., Table 9

53 David Kocieniewski, "Study Suggests Racial Gap in Speeding in New Jersey," *New York Times*, March 21, 2002; Gary Webb, "Driving While Black," *Esquire*, June 29, 2007; Howard Witt, "Highway Robbery? Texas Police Seize Black Motorists' Cash, Cars," *Chicago Tribune*, March 20, 2009; Ben Poston, "Racial Gap Found in Traffic Stops in Milwaukee," *Milwaukee Journal Sentinel*, December 3, 2011; Charles R. Epp, Steven Maynard-Moody, and Donald P. Haider-Markel, *Pulled Over: How Police Stops Define Race and Citizenship* (Chicago, IL: University of Chicago Press, 2014); Victoria Bekiempis, "Driving While Black in Ferguson," *Newsweek*, August 14, 2014; Jeremy Gorner, "Chicago Police Stop Black Motorists More, ACLU Finds," *Chicago Tribune*, December 26, 2014.

54 The phrase seems to have first appeared in print in a May 1990 article in the *New York Times*. The article focused on the strained relations between residents and law enforcement in Teaneck, New Jersey in the aftermath of the shooting of an African American youth by a white officer. One resident was quoted as saying, "We get arrested for D.W.B. . … You know, driving while black." See Tim Golden, "Doubts Link Residents and Police in Teaneck: Residents and Police Share Lingering Doubts in Teaneck," *New York Times*, May 21, 1990.

55 For an analysis of "99 problems" that is both educational and entertaining, see Caleb Mason, "Jay-Z's *99 Problems*, Verse 2: A Close Reading with Fourth Amendment Guidance for Cops and Perps," *Saint Louis University Law Journal*, vol. 56 (Winter 2012): 567–585.

56 *Crash* beat out *Brokeback Mountain* for the Oscar that year. The win was controversial, with some suggesting that the gay love story in *Brokeback Mountain* made Academy Award voters uncomfortable. See, for example, Kenneth Turan, "'Brokeback' Dreams Crash and Burn as the Academy's Voters Play It Safe," *Los Angeles Times*, March 6, 2006. *Crash* was also controversial in the sense

that Angelenos disagreed sharply as to whether the film distorted the reality of race relations in Los Angeles. See, for example, Cara Mia DiMassa, "Differing Views of Race in L.A. Collide in 'Crash,'" *Los Angeles Times*, March 2, 2006.

57 See, for example, John Knowles, Nicola Persico, and Petra Todd, "Racial Bias in Motor-Vehicle Searches: Theory and Evidence," *Journal of Political Economy*, vol. 109, no. 1 (2001): 303–329. See, also, Greg Ridgeway, "Assessing the Effect of Race Bias in Post-Traffic Stop Outcomes Using Propensity Scores," *Journal of Quantitative Criminology*, vol. 22, no. 1 (March 2006): 1–29.

58 See, for example, David Boerner, "Prosecution in Washington State," *Crime and Justice*, vol. 41, no. 1 (2012): 167–210. See, also, Michael J. Nelson, "Responsive Justice? Retention Elections, Prosecutors, and Public Opinion," *Journal of Law and Courts*, vol. 2, no. 1 (Spring 2014): 117–152.

59 Alexis C. Madrigal, "Policing the Police: The Apps That Let You Spy on the Cops," *The Atlantic*, June 21, 2011.

60 Elinor Mills, "ACLU App Lets Android Users Secretly Tape the Police," *CNET Magazine*, July 5, 2012 (http://news.cnet.com/8301–1009_3–57467073–83/aclu-app-lets-android-users-secretly-tape-the-police/).

61 New York Civil Liberties Union, "Stop and Frisk Watch App" (http://www.nyclu.org/app).

62 Ibid.

63 For example, Cop Block, whose tagline is "Badges Don't Grant Extra Rights," lists roughly two dozen of these kinds of apps (http://www.copblock.org/).

64 Ray Sanchez, "Growing Number of Prosecutions for Videotaping the Police," *ABC News*, July 19, 2010; Eric Badia and John Marzulli, "Student Arrested for Filming Outside of Brooklyn Police Stationhouse: Suit," *Daily News*, November 6, 2013; Jason Henry, "Covina Officer Probed Over Arrest of Man Filming Police Activity," *San Gabriel Valley Tribune*, July 26, 2014; James Queally, "Philadelphia Police Sued by ACLU, Which Says Filming Led to Arrests," *Los Angeles Times*, September 19, 2014.

65 *ACLU v. Alvarez*, 679 F.3d 583 (7th Circuit 2012).

66 Protection of conversational privacy is at the heart of legislation that governs, for example, under what conditions a phone conversation can be recorded or surveillance software can be used on shared computers. For a broad discussion of the parameters of conversational privacy see Mary McThomas, *The Dual System of Privacy Rights in the United States* (New York, NY: Routledge, 2012).

67 Though the case was appealed to the U.S. Supreme Court, the Court declined to grant review, thereby leaving the circuit court ruling in place.

68 See, for example, Forrest Stuart, "Constructing Police Abuse after Rodney King: How Skid Row Residents and the Los Angeles Police Department Contest Video Evidence," *Law & Social Inquiry*, vol. 36, no. 2 (Spring 2011): 327–353.

69 See, for example, Erin Mulvaney and Dug Begley, "Opposition Putting a Stop to Red Light Cameras," *Houston Chronicle*, April 24, 2013; Maggie Clark, "Red-Light Cameras Generate Revenue, Controversy," *USA Today*, October 15, 2013; and John R. Quain, "On Alert for Red-Light Cameras," *New York Times*, December 6, 2013.

70 Dana Milbank, "D.C.'s War on Motorists," *Washington Post*, September 15, 2014.

71 Ibid.

72 Ibid.

73 Jason Sunshine and Tom R. Tyler, "The Role of Procedural Justice and Legitimacy in Shaping Public Support for Policing," *Law & Society Review*, vol. 37, no. 3 (2003): 513–548.

74 Malcolm M. Feeley, *The Process is the Punishment: Handling Cases in a Lower Criminal Court* (New York, NY: Russell Sage, 1979, 1992).

75 What does and does not constitute a victimless crime is subject to much debate. See Robert F. Meier and Gilbert Geis, *Victimless Crime? Prostitution, Drugs, Homosexuality, Abortion* (Los Angeles, CA: Roxbury, 1997).

76 U.S. Constitution, Amend. IV.

77 Cynthia Lee, "Package Bombs, Footlockers, and Laptops: What the Disappearing Container Doctrine Can Tell Us about the Fourth Amendment," *Journal of Criminal Law and Criminology*, vol. 100, no. 4 (Fall 2010): 1403–1494, 1408–1414.

78 *Carroll v. United States*, 267 U.S. 132, 162 (1924).

79 A discussion of the origination and evolution of the Fourth Amendment's meaning, including a discussion of the emergence of exceptions to the warrant requirement, can be found in Thomas N. McInnis, *The Evolution of the Fourth Amendment* (Lanham, MD: Lexington Books, 2009). See also Cynthia Lee, *Searches and Seizures: The Fourth Amendment: Its Constitutional History and Contemporary Debate* (Amherst, NY: Prometheus Books, 2011).

80 *Chimel v. California*, 395 U.S. 752 (1969).

81 *Atwater v. City of Lago Vista*, 532 U.S. 318 (2001).

82 Adam Liptak, "Justices Allow DNA Collection After an Arrest," *New York Times*, June 3, 2013.

83 *Maryland v. King*, 186 L. Ed. 2d 1, 53 (2013). For a critique of the line of reasoning included in this case, see Tracey Maclin, "*Maryland v. King: Terry v. Ohio* Redux," *Supreme Court Review*, vol. 2013, no. 1 (2013): 359–404.

84 Issa Kohler-Hausmann, "Misdemeanor Justice: Control without Conviction," *American Journal of Sociology*, vol. 199, no. 2 (September 2013): 351–393, 352.

85 Ibid.

86 This is true even if the punishment that is imposed is a suspended sentence. See *Alabama v. Shelton*, 535 U.S. 654 (2002).

87 Lincoln Caplan, "The Right to Counsel: Badly Battered at 50," *New York Times*, March 9, 2013.

88 The term was coined by sociologist Edwin H. Sutherland in 1939. See John Braithwaite, "White Collar Crime," *Annual Review of Sociology*, vol. 11 (1985): 1–25, 2.

89 On the death penalty, see Stuart Banner, *The Death Penalty: An American History* (Cambridge, MA: Harvard University Press, 2003); Hugo Adam Bedau and Paul Cassell, eds, *Debating the Death Penalty: Should America Have Capital Punishment? The Experts on Both Sides Make Their Case* (New York, NY: Oxford University Press, 2005); Raymond Paternoster, Robert Brame, and Sarah Bacon, *The Death Penalty: America's Experience with Capital Punishment* (New York, NY: Oxford University Press, 2007); and David Garland, *Peculiar Institution: America's Death Penalty in an Age of Abolition* (Cambridge, MA: Belknap Press, 2012).

90 See, for example, *Powell v. Alabama*, 287 U.S. 45 (1932).

91 *Gideon v. Wainwright*, 372 U.S. 335 (1963).

92 Anthony Lewis, *Gideon's Trumpet* (New York, NY: Vintage Books, 1965).

93 See Paul G. Chevigny, "From Betrayal to Violence: Dante's Inferno and the Social Construction of Crime," *Law & Social Inquiry*, vol. 26, no. 4 (Autumn 2001): 787–818.

94 Robert C. LaFountain, Richard Y. Schauffler, Shauna M. Strickland, and Kathryn A. Holt, *Examining the Work of State Courts: An Analysis of 2010 State Court Caseloads* (Williamsburg, VA: National Center for State Courts, 2012).

95 Ibid., 19.

96 See James Q. Wilson George Kelling, "Broken Windows: The Police and Neighborhood Safety," *The Atlantic*, March 1, 1982; George Kelling and Catherine Coles, *Fixing Broken Windows: Restoring Order and Reducing Crime in Our Communities* (New York, NY: Free Press, 1996); Hope Corman and Naci Mocan, "Carrots, Sticks, and Broken Windows," *Journal of Law and Economics*, vol. 48, no. 1 (April 2005): 235–266. The evidence as to the effectiveness of broken-window policing is limited. See John E. Eck and Edward R. Maguire, "Have Changes in Policing Reduced Violent Crime? An Assessment of the Evidence," in *The Crime Drop in America*, Alfred Blumstein and Joel Wallman, eds (New York, NY: Cambridge University Press, 2000) and Bernard E. Harcourt and Jens Ludwig, "Broken Windows: New Evidence from New York City and a Five-City Social Experiment," *University of Chicago Law Review*, vol. 73, no. 1 (Winter 2006): 271–320.

97 The Court Statistics Project, a project of the National Center for State Courts, maintains an interactive website that permits users to examine the structure of courts in each state (http://www.courtstatistics.org/Other-Pages/State_Court_Structure_Charts.aspx).

98 The Court Statistics Project DataViewer is an interactive application that allows users to access caseload data for the 50 states, D.C., and Puerto Rico (http://www.ncsc.org/Sitecore/Content/Microsites/PopUp/Home/CSP/CSP_Criminal).

99 Brian A. Reaves, "Felony Defendants in Large Urban Counties, 2009–Statistical Tables," Bureau of Justice Statistics, December 2013.

100 See Administrative Office of the U.S. Courts, *Federal Judicial Caseload Statistics*, Various Years: Table D.

101 Administrative Office of the U.S. Courts. *Federal Judicial Caseload Statistics, 2009*: (http://www.uscourts.gov/Viewer.aspx?doc=/uscourts/Statistics/FederalJudicialCaseloadStatistics/2009/front/MarJudBus2009.pdf).

102 See Michael T. Light, Mark Hugo Lopez, and Ana Gonzalez-Barrera, "The Rise of Federal Immigration Crimes: Unlawful Reentry Drives Growth," *Pew Research Center: Hispanic Trends*, March 18, 2014 (http://www.pewhispanic.org/2014/03/18/the-rise-of-federal-immigration-crimes/) and Marc R. Rosenblum, "Border Security: Immigration Enforcement Between Ports of Entry," *Congressional Research Service Report*, May 3, 2013 (http://fas.org/sgp/crs/homesec/R42138.pdf.). See, also, Anna O. Law, *The Immigration Battle in American Courts* (New York, NY: Cambridge University Press, 2010).

103 Cheryl Hanna, "No Right to Choose: Mandated Victim Participation in Domestic Violence Prosecutions," Harvard Law Review, vol. 109, no. 8 (June 1996): 1849–1910; Kalyani Robbins, "No-Drop Prosecution of Domestic Violence: Just Good Policy, or Equal Protection Mandate?" *Stanford Law Review*, vol. 52, no. 1 (November 1999): 205–233; Robert C. Davis, Barbara E. Smith, and Caitilin R. Rabbitt, "Increasing Convictions in Domestic Violence Cases: A Field Test in Milwaukee," *Justice System Journal*, vol. 22, no. 1 (2001): 61–72.

104 517 U.S. 456 (1996).

105 See, for example, Lisa L. Miller and James Eisenstein, "The Federal/State Criminal Prosecution Nexus: A Case Study in Cooperation and Discretion," *Law & Social Inquiry*, vol. 30, no. 2 (April 2005): 239–268.

106 See Malcolm M. Feeley, *The Process is the Punishment: Handling Cases in a Lower Criminal Court* (New York, NY: Russell Sage Foundation: 1979, 1992); Robert M. Emerson, "Case Processing and Interorganizational Knowledge: Detecting the 'Real Reasons' for Referrals," *Social Problems*, vol. 38, no. 2 (May 1991): 198–212; David T. Johnson, "The Organization of Prosecution and the Possibility of Order," *Law & Society Review*, vol. 32, no. 2 (1998): 247–308; Austin Sarat and Conor Clarke, "Beyond Discretion: Prosecution, the Logic of Sovereignty, and the Limits of Law," *Law & Social Inquiry*, vol. 33, no. 2 (June 2008): 387–416; John L. Worrall and M. Elaine Nugent-Borakove, eds, *The Changing Role of the American Prosecutor* (New York, NY: State University of New York Press, 2008); Daniel S. Medwed, *Prosecution Complex: America's Race to Convict and Its Impact on the Innocent* (New York, NY: New York University Press, 2013).

107 See, for example, Ian M. Gomme and Mary P. Hall, "Prosecutors at Work: Role Overload and Strain," *Journal of Criminal Justice*, vol. 23, no. 2 (1995): 191–200.

108 Austin Sarat and Conor Clarke, "Beyond Discretion: Prosecution, the Logic of Sovereignty, and the Limits of Law," *Law & Social Inquiry*, vol. 33, no. 2 (2008): 387–416.

109 For considerations of the trade offs prosecutors might consider, see Eric Rasmusen, Manu Raghav, and Mark Ramseyer, "Convictions versus Conviction Rates: The Prosecutor's Choice," *American Law and Economics Review*, vol. 11, no. 1 (Spring 2009): 47–78.

110 Angela J. Davis, *Arbitrary Justice: The Power of the American Prosecutor* (New York, NY: Oxford University Press, 2009).

111 Ibid.

112 Richard A. Oppel, Jr., "Sentencing Shift Gives New Leverage to Prosecutors," *New York Times*, September 25, 2011.

113 David Bjerk, "Making the Crime Fit the Penalty: The Role of Prosecutorial Discretion under Mandatory Minimum Sentencing," *Journal of Law and Economics*, vol. 48, no. 2 (October 2005): 591–625, 593.

114 See, for example, Keith Guzik, "The Forces of Conviction: The Power and Practice of Mandatory Prosecution upon Misdemeanor Domestic Battery Suspects," *Law & Social Inquiry*, vol. 32, no. 1 (March 2007): 41–74.

115 Barbara S. Vincent and Paul J. Hofer, *The Consequences of Mandatory Minimum Prison Terms: A Summary of Recent Findings* (Washington, DC: Federal Judicial Center, 1994); Charlie Savage, "Justice Dept. Seeks to Curtail Stiff Drug Sentences," *New York Times*, August 12, 2013.

116 420 U.S. 103, 114 (1975).

117 *County of Riverside v. McLaughlin*, 500 U.S. 44 (1991).

118 Thomas H. Cohen and Brian A. Reaves, "Special Report: Pretrial Release of Felony Defendants in State Courts," Bureau of Justice Statistics, November 2007: 1 (http://www.bjs.gov/content/pub/pdf/prfdsc.pdf).

119 Ibid., 2

120 The terms of his pretrial release did permit him to move to his Florida home at a later date.

121 Alan Feuer, "$15 Million Bail in Murder Case with a Celebrity Glow," *New York Times*, January 8, 2000.

122 Joseph Berger, "John Gotti's Son Is Freed on Bail of $10 Million," *New York Times*, October 2, 1998.

123 Dan Markel and Eric J. Miller, "Op-Ed: Bowling, as Bail Condition," *New York Times*, July 13, 2012.

124 Bail schedules can vary considerably from jurisdiction to jurisdiction, with identical offenses associated with quite different bail amounts. See, for example, Leigh Martinez, "Meeks Arrest Highlights San Joaquin County's Unusually High Bail Schedule," *CBS Sacramento*, July 7, 2014.

125 Eric Helland and Alexander Tabarrok, "The Fugitive: Evidence on Public versus Private Law Enforcement from Bail Jumping," *Journal of Law and Economics*, vol. 47, no. 1 (April 2004): 93–122, 94. For a history of the professional bail bonds system, see Holly Joiner, "Private Police: Defending the Power of Professional Bail Bondsmen," *Indiana Law Review*, vol. 32 (1999): 1413–1435, 1414–1416.

126 Adam Liptak, "Illegal Globally Bail for Profit Remains in U.S.," *New York Times*, January 29, 2008.

127 David Carr, "Bounty Hunter Arrested in '03 Case," *New York Times*, September 15, 2006; David Carr, "A Cornered Pit Bull: Bounty Hunter Becomes Prey," *New York Times*, September 18, 2006.

128 The first in the series was published by St. Martin's Press in 1994. The most recent (*Top Secret Twenty-One*) came out in 2014.

129 Other films in which bail bondsmen characters play the central or important roles include: *Midnight Run* starring Robert De Niro (1988), *Jackie Brown* starring Pam Grier (1997), *Domino* starring Keira Knightly (2005), and *The Bounty Hunter* starring Jennifer Aniston and Gerard Butler (2010). Bob Fett, featured prominently in *Star Wars Episode V: The Empire Strikes Back*, is also a bounty hunter, albeit an interstellar one.

130 Mary A. Toborg, "Bail Bondsmen and Criminal Courts," *Justice System Journal*, vol. 8, no. 2 (1983): 141–156; Richard A. Gambitta and Barry Paul Hitchings, "Bail Bond Forfeiture Enforcement: The Mechanism and the Mirage," *American Journal of Criminal Law*, vol. 11, no. 3 (November 1983): 233–292; Eric Helland and Alexander Tabarrok, "The Fugitive: Evidence on Public versus Private Law Enforcement from Bail Jumping," *Journal of Law and Economics*, vol. 47, no. 1 (April 2004): 93–122.

131 For a general critique of the bail bond system, see Justice Policy Institute, *Bail Fail: Why the U.S. Should End the Practice of Using Money for Bail* (Washington, DC: Justice Policy Institute, 2012). See, also, "Bail and Its Discrimination Against the Poor: A Civil Rights Action as a Vehicle of Reform," *Valparaiso University Law Review*, vol. 9, no. 1 (Fall 1974).

132 See, for example, the concurrence of Judge J. Skelly Wright of the U.S. Court of Appeals for the District of Columbia in *Pannell v. United States* (320 F.2d 698).

133 John Eligon, "For Poor, Bail System Can Be an Obstacle to Freedom," *New York Times*, January 9, 2011.

134 President's Commission on Law Enforcement and the Administration of Justice, *The Challenge of Crime in a Free Society* (Washington, DC: United States Government Printing Office, 1967): 131.

135 For a general discussion of this criticism, see Holly Joiner, "Private Police: Defending the Power of Professional Bail Bondsmen," *Indiana Law Review*, vol. 32 (1999): 1413–1435, 1417–1418. See, also, Brian Montopoli, "Is the US. Bail System Unfair?" *CBS News*, February 8, 2013 (http://www.cbsnews.com/news/is-the-us-bail-system-unfair/).

136 Holly Joiner, "Private Police: Defending the Power of Professional Bail Bondsmen," *Indiana Law Review*, vol. 32 (1999): 1413–1435, 1418.

137 Lawrence Dechant, "'Lipstick Bounty Hunters' Face Accusations After Confrontation at Arby's," *ABC News*, April 5, 2013 (http://abcnews.go.com/blogs/headlines/2013/04/lipstick-bounty-hunters-face-accusations-after-confrontation-at-arbys/).

138 See, for example, Claire, Galofaro, "Trial Set for Bristol Bounty Hunters Accused of Arresting the Wrong Man," *News Channel 11*, June 5, 2011.

139 Russ, Buettner, "Top Judge Says Bail in New York Isn't Safe or Fair," *New York Times*, February 6, 2013.

140 Thomas H. Cohen and Brian A. Reaves, "Special Report: Pretrial Release of Felony Defendants in State Courts," Bureau of Justice Statistics, November 2007: 1 (http://www.bjs.gov/content/pub/pdf/prfdsc.pdf).

141 Ibid.

142 Ibid.

143 Ibid.

144 Ibid.

145 Peter Arenella, "Reforming the Federal Grand Jury and the State Preliminary Hearing to Prevent Conviction without Adjudication," *Michigan Law Review*, vol. 78, no. 4 (February 1980): 463–585, 484.

146 For detailed information about the history and contemporary operation of grand juries, see Charles Doyle, *The Federal Grand Jury* (Hauppauge, NY: Nova Science Publishers, 2008). For critiques of the grand jury system, see Blanche Davis Blank, *The Not So Grand Jury: The Story of the Federal Grand Jury System* (Lanham, MD: University Press of America, 1993) and Roger Roots, "Grand Juries Gone Wrong," *Richmond Journal of Law and the Public Interest*, vol. 14, no. 2 (Fall 2010): 331–356. For a fun fictional read about grand juries, see Scott Turow's legal thriller *The Burden of Proof* (New York, NY: Farrar Straus Girroux, 1990), which was subsequently adapted into a television miniseries aired on ABC in 1992.

147 There are used for other purposes. For example, more than a dozen states use grand juries to inspect youth detention facilities, jails, or prisons. Further, a sizable number of states rely on them to investigate the conduct of public officials and political corruption. See the interactive data app maintained by the National Center for States Courts http://www.ncsc.org/sco#), specifically the section entitled "Grand Juries: Composition and Functions."

148 U.S. Constitution, Amend. V.

149 Chico Harlan, Wesley Lowery, and Kimberly Kindy, "Ferguson Police Officer Won't Be Charged in Fatal Shooting," *Washington Post*, November 25, 2014.

150 Tina Susman, "New York Grand Jury Decides Not to Indict Police Officer in Chokehold Death," *Los Angeles Times*, February 18, 2015.

151 See, in particular, *Weeks v. United States* (232 U.S. 383, 1914), *Wolf v. Colorado* (338 U.S. 25, 1949), and *Mapp v. Ohio* (367 U.S. 643, 1961).

152 For example, evidence obtained in violation of the Fourth Amendment may nonetheless be admissible if the evidence would ultimately have been discovered anyway under the Doctrine of Inevitable Discovery (see *Nix v. Williams*, 467 U.S. 431, 1984).

153 Scott Kafker, "The Right to Venue and the Right to an Impartial Jury: Resolving the Conflict in the Federal Constitution," *University of Chicago Law Review*, vol. 52, no. 3 (Summer 1985): 729–750.

154 U.S. Constitution, Amend. VI.

155 Scott Kafker, "The Right to Venue and the Right to an Impartial Jury: Resolving the Conflict in the Federal Constitution," *University of Chicago Law Review*, vol. 52, no. 3 (Summer 1985): 729–750, 750.

156 Milton J. Valencia, "Dzhokhar Tsarnaev's Defense Team Again Seeks New Venue," *Boston Globe*, January 22, 2015.

157 Daniel Givelber and Amy Ferrell, *Not Guilty: Are the Acquitted Innocent?* (New York, NY: New York University Press, 2012)

158 For a historical discussion of imprisonment and a critique of the practice as one of social control rather than punishment, see Michel Foucault, *Discipline and Punish: The Birth of the Prison*, trans. Alan Sheridan (New York, NY: Random House, 1979).

159 Michael Rothfeld and Brad Reagan, "Prosecutors Are Still Chasing Billions in Uncollected Debts: Justice Department and Other Financial Watchdogs Face Challenges Pursuing Judgments," *Wall Street Journal*, September 17, 2014.

160 For an overview of the sentencing reform movement, see Cassia C. Spohn, *How Do Judges Decide: The Search for Fairness and Justice in Punishment*, Second Edition (Thousand Oaks, CA: Sage, 2009).

161 Ibid.

162 See, for example, Joan Petersilia, *When Prisoners Come Home: Parole and Prisoner Reentry* (New York, NY: Oxford University Press, 2009).

163 See, for example, Franklin E. Zimring, Gordon Hawkins, and Sam Kamin, *Punishment and Democracy: Three Strikes and You're Out in California* (New York, NY: Oxford University Press, 2003).

164 See, for example, Tom R. Tyler and Robert J. Boeckmann, "Three Strikes and You Are Out, but Why? The Psychology of Public Support for Punishing Rule Breakers," *Law & Society Review*, vol. 31, no. 2 (1997): 237–266; Doris Marie Provine, *Unequal under Law: Race in the War on Drugs* (Chicago, IL: University of Chicago Press, 2007); Bert Useem and Anne Morrison Piehl, *Prison State: The Challenge of Mass Incarceration* (New York, NY: Cambridge University Press, 2008); Vanessa Barker, *The Politics of Imprisonment: How the Democratic Process Shapes the Way America Punishes Offenders* (New York, NY: Oxford University Press, 2009); Mona Lynch, *Sunbelt Justice: Arizona and the Transformation of American Punishment* (New York, NY: Oxford University Press, 2009); Michelle Brown, *The Culture of Punishment: Prison, Society, and Spectacle* (New York, NY: New York University Press, 2009); Michael C. Campbell, "The Emergence of Penal Extremism in California: A Dynamic View of Institutional Structures and Political Processes," *Law & Society Review*, vol. 48, no. 2 (June 2014): 377–409.

165 See, for example, Malcolm Feeley, and Sam Kamin, "The Effect of 'Three Strikes and You're Out' on the Courts: Looking Back to See the Future," in *Three Strikes and You're Out: Vengeance as Public Policy*, David Shichor and Dale K. Sechrest, eds (Thousand Oaks, CA: Sage, 1996); Mona Lynch and Marisa Omori, "Legal Change and Sentencing Norms in the Wake of *Booker*: The Impact of Time and Place on Drug Trafficking Cases in Federal Court," *Law & Society Review*, vol. 48, no. 2 (June 2014): 411–445.

166 James M. Anderson, Jeffrey R. Kling, and Kate Smith, "Measuring Interjudge Sentencing Disparity: Before and After the Federal Sentencing Guidelines," *Journal of Law & Economics*, vol. 42, no. 2 (1999): 271–307.

167 Paul J. Hofer, Kevin R. Blackwell, and R. Barry Ruback, "The Effect of the Federal Sentencing Guidelines on Inter-Judge Sentencing Disparity," *Journal of Criminal Law & Criminology*, vol. 90, no. 1 (Fall 1999): 239–306.

168 543 U.S. 220 (2005).

169 *Rita v. United States*, 551 U.S. 338 (2007); *Gall v. United States*, 552 U.S. 38 (2007); *Kimbrough v. United States*, 552 U.S. 85 (2007).

170 Crystal S. Yang, "Have Inter-Judge Sentencing Disparities Increased in an Advisory Guidelines Regime? Evidence from *Booker*," *NYU Law Review*, vol. 89, no. 4 (October 2014): 1268–1342.

171 Ibid.

172 Cassia C. Spohn, "Thirty Years of Sentencing Reform: The Quest for a Racially Neutral Sentencing Process," *Criminal Justice*, vol. 3 (2000): 427–501.

173 David B. Mustard, "Racial, Ethnic, and Gender Disparities in Sentencing: Evidence from the U.S. Federal Courts," *Journal of Law and Economics*, vol. 44, no. 1 (April 2001): 285–314.

174 David S. Abrams, Marianne Bertrand, and Sendhil Mullainathan, "Do Judges Vary in Their Treatment of Race?" *Journal of Legal Studies*, vol. 41, no. 2 (June 2012): 347–384.

175 John R. Sutton, "Symbol and Substance: Effects of California's Three Strikes Law on Felony Sentencing," *Law & Society Review*, vol. 47, no. 1 (March 2013): 37–72.

176 Charles J. Ogletree, Jr. and Austin Sarat, eds, *Life without Parole: America's New Death Penalty?* (New York, NY: New York University Press, 2012).

177 Darrell Steffensmeier and Stephen Demuth, "Ethnicity and Judges' Sentencing Decisions: Hispanic-Black-White Comparisons," *Criminology*, vol. 39, no. 1 (February 2001): 145–178.

178 Ibid.

179 Ibid.

180 Ibid.

181 Michael T. Light, "The New Face of Legal Inequality: Noncitizens and the Long-Term Trends in Sentencing Disparities across U.S. District Courts, 1992–2009," *Law & Society Review*, vol. 48, no. 2 (June 2014): 447–478.

182 542 U.S. 296 (2004).

183 543 U.S. 220 (2005).

184 Administrative Office of the U.S. Courts, *Federal Judicial Caseload Statistics: 2009* (Washington, DC: Administrative Office of the U.S. Courts, 2009).

185 Sean Rosenmerkel, Matthew Durose, and Donald Farole, *Felony Sentences in State Courts, 2006* (Washington, DC: Bureau of Justice Statistics, 2009); U.S. Sentencing Commission, *2012 Sourcebook of Federal Sentencing Statistics*: Figure C (http://www.ussc.gov/sites/default/files/pdf/research-and-publications/annual-reports-and-sourcebooks/2012/FigureC.pdf).

186 Malcolm M. Feeley, *The Process is the Punishment: Handling Cases in a Lower Criminal Court* (New York, NY: Russell Sage Foundation: 1979, 1992).

187 Dean J. Champion, "Private Counsels and Public Defenders: A Look at Weak Cases, Prior Records, and Leniency in Plea Bargaining," *Journal of Criminal Justice*, vol. 17, no. 4 (1989): 253–263; Jon'a Meyer and Tara Gray, "Drunk Drivers in the Courts: Legal and Extra-Legal Factors Affecting Pleas and Sentences," *Journal of Criminal Justice*, vol. 25, no. 2 (1997): 155–163; Gail Kellough and Scot Wortley, "Remand for Plea: Bail Decisions and Plea Bargaining as Commensurate Decisions," *British Journal of Criminology*, vol. 42, no. 1 (2002): 186–210; Jeffery T. Ulmer and Mindy S. Bradley, "Variation in Trial Penalties among Serious Violent Offenses," *Criminology*, vol. 44, no. 3 (August 2006): 631–670.

188 Gail Kellough and Scot Wortley, "Remand for Plea: Bail Decisions and Plea Bargaining as Commensurate Decisions," *British Journal of Criminology*, vol. 42, no. 1 (2002): 186–210.

189 Ibid.; Jeffery T. Ulmer and Mindy S. Bradley, "Variation in Trial Penalties among Serious Violent Offenses," *Criminology*, vol. 44, no. 3 (August 2006): 631–670.

190 See, for example, Albert W. Alschuler, "Plea Bargaining and Its History," *Law & Society Review*, vol. 13, no. 2 (1979): 211–245; Mary E. Vogel, "The Social Origins of Plea Bargaining: Conflict and the Law in the Process of State Formation, 1830–1860," *Law & Society Review*, vol. 33, no. 1 (1999): 161–246; George Fisher, *Plea Bargaining's Triumph: A History of Plea Bargaining in America* (Stanford, CA: Stanford University Press, 2004).

191 See, for example, Lawrence M. Friedman, "Plea Bargaining in Historical Perspective," *Law & Society Review*, vol. 13, no. 2 (1979): 247–259; John F. Padgett, "Plea Bargaining and Prohibition in the Federal Courts, 1908–1934," *Law & Society Review*, vol. 24, no. 2 (1990): 413–450.

192 *Brady v. United States*, 397 U.S. 742 (1970).

193 404 U.S. 257 (1971).

194 404 U.S. 257, 261 (1971).

195 132 5. Ct. 1399 (2012).

196 132 5. Ct. 1399 (2012).

197 See Debra S. Emmelman, "Trial by Plea Bargain: Case Settlement as a Product of Recursive Decisionmaking," *Law & Society Review*, vol. 30, no. 2 (1996): 335–360.

198 Lynn M. Mather, *Plea Bargaining or Trial? The Process of Criminal Case Disposition* (Lexington, MA: Lexington Book, 1979).

199 Douglas W. Maynard, "Narratives and Narrative Structure in Plea Bargaining," *Law & Society Review*, vol. 22, no. 3 (1988): 449–482.

200 See, for example, *Lafler v. Cooper*, 132 5. Ct. 1399 (2012). See, also, Laurie L. Levenson, "Peeking Behind the Plea Bargaining Process: *Missouri v. Frye* & *Lafler v. Cooper*," *Loyola of Los Angeles Law Review*, vol. 46, no, 2 (2013): 457–490.

201 Morris B. Hoffman, Paul H. Rubin, and Joanna M. Shepherd, "An Empirical Study of Public Defender Effectiveness: Self-Selection by the 'Marginally Indigent,'" *Ohio State Journal of Criminal Law*, vol. 3 (Fall 2005): 223–255.

202 Ibid.

203 Brian A. Reaves, "Felony Defendants in Large Urban Counties, 2009–Statistical Tables," Bureau of Justice Statistics, December 2013 (http://www.bjs.gov/content/pub/pdf/fdluc09.pdf).

204 Ibid.

205 Ibid.

206 Malcolm M. Feeley, *The Process Is the Punishment: Handling Cases in a Lower Criminal Court* (New York, NY: Russell Sage Foundation: 1979, 1992); Milton Heumann, *Plea Bargaining: The Experiences of Prosecutors, Judges, and Defense Attorneys* (Chicago, IL: University of Chicago Press, 1981); Malcolm M. Feeley, "Plea Bargaining and the Structure of the Criminal Process," *Justice System Journal*, vol. 7 (1982): 338–354; John D. Wooldredge, "An Aggregate-Level Examination of the Caseload Pressure Hypothesis," *Journal of Quantitative Criminology*, vol. 5, no. 3 (September 1989): 259–283; Malcolm D. Holmes, Howard C. Daudistel, and William A. Taggart, "Plea Bargaining Policy and State District Court Caseloads: An Interrupted Time Series Analysis," *Law & Society Review*, vol. 26, no. 1 (1992): 139–160; Malcolm M. Feeley, "Legal Complexity and the Transformation of the Criminal Process: The Origins of Plea Bargaining," *Israel Law Review*, vol. 31 (1997): 183–222.

207 Tina Wan, "The Unnecessary Evil of Plea Bargaining: An Unconstitutional Conditions Problem and a Not-So-Least Restrictive Alternative," *Review of Law and Social Justice*, vol. 17 (Fall 2007): 33–61.

208 See, for example, Richard L. Lippke, *The Ethics of Plea Bargaining* (New York, NY: Oxford University Press, 2011).

209 See, for example, Thomas Church, Jr., "Plea Bargains, Concessions and the Courts: Analysis of a Quasi-Experiment," *Law & Society Review*, vol. 10, no. 3 (Spring 1976): 377–401.

210 On the relationship between prosecutors and the police see Robert M. Emerson, "Case Processing and Interorganizational Knowledge: Detecting the 'Real Reasons' for Referrals," *Social Problems*, vol. 38, no. 2 (May 1991): 198–212.

211 Malcolm M. Feeley, *The Process Is the Punishment: Handling Cases in a Lower Criminal Court* (New York, NY: Russell Sage Foundation: 1979, 1992).

212 Samuel R. Gross, Kristen Jacoby, Daniel J. Matheson, Nicholas Montgomery, and Sujata Patil, "Exonerations in the United States 1989 through 2003," *Journal of Criminal Law & Criminology*, vol. 95, no. 2 (Winter 2005): 523–560.

213 Malcolm M. Feeley, *The Process Is the Punishment: Handling Cases in a Lower Criminal Court* (New York, NY: Russell Sage Foundation: 1979, 1992); David L. Shapiro, "Should a Guilty Plea Have Preclusive Effect?" *Iowa Law Review*, vol. 70 (1984): 27–51; Jeffrey T. Ulmer, "Trial Judges in a Rural Court Community: Contexts, Organizational Relations, and Interaction Strategies," *Journal of Contemporary Ethnography*, vol. 23, no. 1 (April 1994): 79–108; Daniel Givelber, "Meaningless Acquittals, Meaningful Convictions: Do We Reliably Acquit the Innocent?" *Rutgers Law Review*, vol. 49 (Summer 1997): 1317–1396.

8

TRIALS

"Never accept a juror whose occupation begins with a P. This includes pimps, prostitutes, preachers, plumbers, procurers, psychologists, physicians, psychiatrists, printers, painters, philosophers, professors, phoneys, parachutists, pipe-smokers, or part-time anythings."

—William Jennings Bryan, U.S. Congressman and Former Secretary of State[1]

"A jury consists of twelve persons chosen to decide who has the better lawyer."

—Robert Frost, American Poet[2]

Jennifer Thompson was a 22-year-old undergraduate at Elon University in Burlington, North Carolina. A bright student with a straight-A average, Jennifer was focused on maintaining good grades and planned on marrying her boyfriend, Paul, after college. One day in July 1984, after having spent the afternoon with Paul, going out to dinner with him that evening, and then accompanying him to a party, Jennifer returned home to her off-campus apartment and went to bed. A short while later, she was awoken by an intruder who put a knife to her throat and raped her. Jennifer decided that she would outsmart her rapist and remember everything about him: "My first plan was to try to get information, and to try to look at him so that if there was any type of mark or a tattoo or a scar that I would have a better idea of how to identify him. . . . I was trying to see as much of him as I could to see if there was [sic] any tattoos or any scars or unusual jewelry or a part in the hair, anything that I could use for information to identify him."[3]

Jennifer was ultimately able to escape from her attacker after the rape, convincing him to let her get a drink of water as a ruse and then running out the back door of her apartment. After neighbors let her in and the police arrived, Jennifer was taken to a local hospital where medical personnel used a rape kit to gather evidence pertaining to the assault.[4] She then helped police put together a composite sketch at the police station. Several days later, Jennifer returned to the police station to look at a photo lineup of possible suspects. She recalled:

[Police] Detective [Mike] Gauldin told me not to feel compelled to make an identification, to take as long as I needed. . . . The detectives stood behind me, and I went through each picture slowly and carefully. The stakes felt awfully high.

My heart raced on adrenaline. I assumed they must have had a suspect. Why would they want me to drive all this way if they didn't? All I had to do was pick him out. And if I failed to do that, would he go free? Would he find me?

Most were easily eliminated, and I narrowed it down to two. When I looked at one photo, the image of the man . . . came back so violently I thought I would be sick right there. The memory was too sharp and clear.

"Yeah. This is the one," I said, pointing to the picture. "I think this is the guy."

"You 'think' that's the guy?" asked [Detective Ballard Sullivan, known as] Sully.

"It's him," I said, clarifying.

"You're sure?" asked Gauldin.

"Positive."

They asked me to date and initial the back of the photo, and then they did, too.

"Did I do OK?" I asked.

Sully and Gauldin looked at each other. Relief washed over me.

"You did great, Ms. Thompson."

It had taken me five minutes.[5]

Eleven days after the rape, Jennifer Thompson picked a man out of a physical lineup. "As always, I wanted to know how I had done. 'We thought that might be the guy,' said [Detective Mike] Gauldin. 'It's the same person you picked from the photos.' My knees nearly gave out from under me. *We got him*."[6] During the trial, Thompson identified the defendant, Ronald Cotton, as the man who raped her. Subsequent jury deliberations took a mere 4 hours and led to a verdict of guilty, after which Ronald Cotton was sentenced to life in prison plus 50 years.

Eyewitness identification such as that of Jennifer Thompson is often very persuasive evidence in both civil and criminal trials.[7] For example, one study recorded verdicts in the mock trial of a defendant charged with a grocery store robbery in which the owner and his granddaughter were killed.[8] Some jurors for the mock trial were told that there were no eyewitnesses to the crime, while others were told that the store clerk had testified to seeing the shooting. When jurors in the mock trial were told that there were no eyewitnesses, only 18 percent of them voted to find the defendant guilty. When jurors were told that there was an eyewitness, however, the percentage of guilty verdicts increased to 72 percent. Even when the purported eyewitness was demonstrated to be legally blind—the defense attorney established that the clerk had not been wearing glasses on the day of the robbery and that his vision was so bad that he could not see the face of the robber from where he stood—68 percent of the jurors still voted to convict when told there was an eyewitness. There is just something about eyewitness identification that constitutes compelling evidence for many judges and jurors. As *60 Minutes* correspondent Lesley Stahl observed in an investigative report about the Cotton rape case:

> It's a cliché of courtroom dramas—that moment when the witness is asked "Do you see the person who committed the crime here in this courtroom before you?" It happens in real courtrooms all the time, and to jurors, that point of the finger by a confident eyewitness is about as damning as evidence can get.[9]

It certainly was for Ronald Cotton.

Two years after the original trial, Cotton secured a new trial based on evidence from another attack that occurred the night Jennifer Thompson was raped. At that new trial, Cotton's defense attorney introduced testimony about another man—a fellow inmate by the name of Bobby Poole who had allegedly told other prisoners that he was the one who raped Jennifer Thompson. Once on the witness stand, however, Poole denied the claim that he was the real perpetrator of the crime, and Thompson testified once again that Cotton was her rapist. Nine years later, Cotton was watching the O.J. Simpson trial on television when he heard about DNA testing. He asked for DNA testing and the results demonstrated that Cotton was, as he had asserted all along, innocent of the rape of which he had been convicted. As for Bobby Poole, the man Thompson swore she had never seen before, the DNA evidence identified him as the actual rapist. The story of Ronald Cotton is not an isolated incident. According to the Innocence Project,[10] eyewitness misidentification plays a role in more than 7 out of 10 convictions overturned through DNA testing.[11] The upshot is that the mechanism on which we rely for determining guilt and innocence and meting out justice—the trial—can be flawed and, at least some of the time, those flaws can lead to a miscarriage of justice.

Trials are intended to serve the purpose of sorting out truth and pretense, fact and fiction. To do this, judges and juries consider the evidence presented by each side in the criminal or civil case being adjudicated. That evidence may include physical evidence (such as footprints, x-rays, and drug paraphernalia), documents (such as medical examiner reports, rental leases, and safety inspection records), and testimony (such as that of a police officer, forensic specialist, or witness to a crime). The legal rules and processes for the gathering and introduction of evidence are extensive and are intended to ensure fairness in the adversarial process that a trial represents. The ultimate objective is to arrive at the truth of what occurred. But what happens when the evidence presented—like eyewitness testimony—may be unreliable?

Certainly, the attorneys' role in a trial is to engage in the vigorous questioning of witnesses and to challenge the judge and jurors to critically consider the evidence presented. This is the very stuff that inspires the dramatic trial moments depicted in virtually every episode of the popular dramas *The Good Wife* (starring Julianna Margulies as the wife of a politician jailed in the aftermath of a sex scandal who becomes a junior associate at a prestigious firm in Chicago) and *Damages* (starring Glenn Close as a ruthless but brilliant lawyer who serves as a mentor to a talented novice attorney). Further, trial scenes are unquestionably some of the most riveting moments in movies such as *The Exorcism of Emily Rose*, a fictionalized account of a real-life trial of a priest for the death of a girl on whom he was performing an exorcism. As we discussed in prior chapters, the heated exchange between Tom Cruise and Jack Nicholson in *A Few Good Men* gave rise to the persistent meme "You can't handle the truth," subsequently used as parody in episodes of *Seinfeld* and *The Simpsons*. But, with rare exceptions, real-life trials are neither quite so dramatic nor quite as likely to generate meme-worthy phrases.[12]

What happens during a trial? What is the role of the jury in a trial? What is the role of the judge in a trial? What kinds of evidence do attorneys bring to bear in making their arguments? How do judges and juries make decisions? In this chapter, we examine the stages of the trial court process, from the opening statements to the closing arguments. We detail the common myths about trials including the reliability of eyewitness testimony—as the case discussed at the start of this chapter illustrates—and the role of attorneys, judges, and juries. With regard to the latter, we discuss the use of scientific jury selection (SJS) and the controversial phenomenon of jury nullification, in which a jury acquits a defendant despite believing that defendant to be guilty of the charges brought against her. In all, there are many myths about trials that can lead the public to misunderstand both how trials are conducted and the role that trials play in the judicial process.

MYTH AND REALITY IN TRIALS

MYTH	REALITY
Every criminal defendant is entitled to a jury trial.	Criminal defendants are only entitled to a jury trial when charged with serious offenses, which typically means offenses that carry sentences of more than 6 months incarceration.
Eyewitness identification is reliable.	Eyewitness misidentification has played a role in nearly 75 percent of convictions overturned through DNA testing.
Larger juries are better than smaller juries.	While larger juries are more representative, have greater memory recall, spend more time deliberating, are less likely to be hung, and are more predictable, smaller juries give larger awards, convict as often but of lesser charges, and are more efficient by reducing person-days across selection, trial, and deliberations.
Judges do better than juries.	While judges and juries agree in three out of four cases, plaintiffs in civil matters are more likely to win, and recover more in damages, if a case is decided by a judge.
Jury pools are only drawn from voter registration lists.	Jury pools are drawn from many sources including voter registration lists, driver's license or state identification card lists, property tax roles, unemployment compensation lists, and public welfare lists among others.
The right to a jury of one's peers guarantees the defendant a jury composed of people who have similar background characteristics such as race, gender, age, and occupation.	The right to a jury of one's peers only guarantees an unbiased jury drawn from a broad cross-section of the jurisdiction where the case will be tried.
Attorneys, using scientific jury selection techniques, can predict how jurors will vote.	Scientific jury selection is only better than conventional methods in certain types of cases such as those involving drugs, as opposed to murder where conventional methods are just as effective.
Juries receiving the nullification instruction will be more likely to use their power of nullification.	When the jury is sympathetic toward the defendant, nullification instructions lead to a greater tendency to acquit. However, when the defendant is unsympathetic, nullification instructions lead to a greater tendency to convict.

A SHORT HISTORY OF JURIES

The American jury system has its roots in medieval England. Specifically, King Henry II created periodic courts known as **courts of assize** (or assizes) to resolve disputes over land and inheritances.[13] Twelve freemen (referred to as "twelve good men and true")[14] were assembled to state, under oath, their knowledge of the identity of the true property owner or heir, based on a preexisting knowledge of the facts. In other words, these bodies were "self-informing" and not dependent on the introduction and consideration of evidence presented by others. By 1215, with the signing of the Magna Carta by King John, these panels were also used to determine innocence or guilt in criminal cases.[15] Previously, criminal prosecutions were privately initiated: "In their simplest

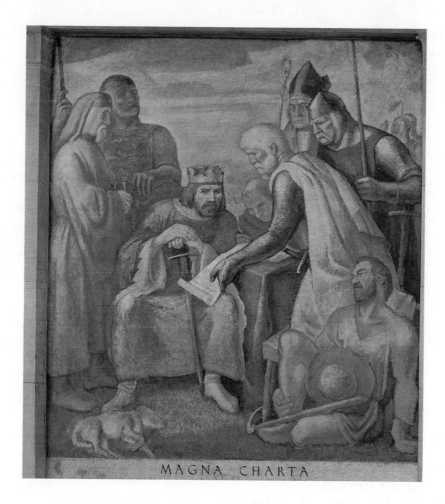

MAGNA CHARTA

Image 8.1 Magna Carta
In 1937 Boardman Robinson painted this depiction of King John I signing the Magna Carta in 1215. The oil painting is in the stairway of the Great Hall of the U.S. Department of Justice building in Washington, D.C. The Magna Carta was the basis for many American rights and liberties including the right to trial by jury in criminal matters. Photographs in the Carol M. Highsmith Archive, Prints and Photographs Division, Library of Congress, Washington, D.C.

form, these prosecutions—appeals—began with a formal complaint by the injured party. The accused—the appellee—denied the accusation. Proof was made by judicial combat between the appellor and the appellee."[16] By the fifteenth century, jurors began hearing evidence presented at trial rather than being expected to come to court with preexisting knowledge.[17] However, they were still permitted to base their verdict on their own personal knowledge as well as the evidence they heard in court.[18]

Subsequently, jury trials achieved a lofty status in the English judicial system as safeguards against heavy-handed authorities and excessive punishment. *Bushel's Case*,[19] dating from 1670, represents a critical juncture in the continued exaltation of jury trials in England (and, ultimately, in the United States).[20] Contrary to the Conventicle Act, which forbade religious assemblies other than assemblies gathered under the auspices of the Church of England, William Penn (a Quaker who would later found Pennsylvania) and William Mead[21] (a fellow Quaker and law student) commenced to preach about their faith on London's Gracechurch Street.[22] Though Penn and Mead were arrested and brought to trial, the jury declined to find the defendants guilty of unlawful assembly.[23] Members of the jury, including Edward Bushel,[24] were then promptly found in contempt of court and imprisoned because the judge disagreed with the verdict. Bushel declined to pay the fine that would have set him free and, instead, he sought an order for his release from a superior court. There, Chief Justice Sir John Vaughan ruled that it was contrary to reason to permit a jury to be punished on the basis of a verdict it returned:

> If a Judge, having heard the evidence given in Court . . . should tell the jury upon this evidence, that the law is for the plaintiff or for the defendant, and they are under pain of fine and imprisonment to find accordingly . . . trial by jury would be but a troublesome delay . . . and no use in determining right and wrong.[25]

In other words, Chief Justice Vaughan wanted to know what the point of having a jury is if it cannot exercise independence in reaching its verdict? If a judge can tell a jury how it must rule, then the jury is no more than window dressing.

The jury system traveled from England to the American continent with the very first settlers and rapidly became entrenched in the colonial legal system. In fact, the right to a jury trial in the United States (at least in criminal cases) technically predates the first English settlement in that King James I's charter to the Virginia Company (in 1606) included that guarantee as a promise to those who settled Jamestown.[26] Both civil and criminal trials in Virginia were by jury less than 20 years later and, over the course of the next 9 decades, Delaware, Massachusetts, New Hampshire, New Jersey, Pennsylvania, Rhode Island, and South Carolina adopted the use of jury trials.[27] In 1727, Delaware borrowed language from the Magna Carta, providing:

> That no free man within this government shall be taken or imprisoned, or disseized of his freehold or liberties, or be outlawed or exiled, or other ways hurt, damnified or destroyed, nor to be tried or condemned but by the lawful judgment of his twelve equals, or by the laws of England, and of this government.[28]

In short, the right to a jury trial (at least in criminal cases) was widespread in the colonies. However, though jury trials were considered part of what Sir William Blackstone referred to as "the grand bulwark of [every Englishman's] liberties,"[29] they were not always respected as independent actors in the cases brought by the Crown against colonists, much to the considerable consternation of those colonists. That includes one John Peter Zenger, whose riveting tale was the subject of a live teleplay aired in the early 1950s on CBS.[30]

Zenger was a printer and publisher residing in New York. Zenger published the *New York Weekly Journal* and was highly critical of William Cosby, the newly appointed colonial governor who arrived in New York in 1732. Shortly after his arrival, Cosby wrangled with the acting governor over his salary and ended up removing the chief justice of the colony's supreme court. When Zenger published articles taking the new governor to task for these and other actions, Cosby condemned the newspaper and Zenger was charged with seditious libel (i.e., writing deemed by the legal authority to foster contempt for the established order). After having his first counsel removed from the case for being held in contempt of court, Zenger spent the better part of 9 months in prison before going to trial. During that time the case garnered more and more public attention. It came to represent the cavalier disregard of the Crown and its agents for the rights of their colonial subjects. Zenger's attorneys never argued that their client had not printed the articles; they were in effect acknowledging that Zenger had violated the law as charged. What they did argue, however, is that the statements were true and, hence, they could not be considered libel. The members of the jury were persuaded, despite the fact that the judge had ordered them to find Zenger guilty if they believed that he printed the stories in

"By no means," exclaimed Hamilton, in his clear, thrilling, silvery voice. "It is not the bare printing and publishing of a paper that will make it a libel; the words themselves must be libelous, that is, false, scandalous, and seditious, else my client is not guilty." Page 558

Image 8.2 The Trial of John Peter Zenger
This late nineteenth century engraving depicts attorney Andrew Hamilton defending publisher John Peter Zenger before a jury. The caption reads: "By no means," exclaimed Hamilton, in his clear, thrilling, silvery voice, "It is not the bare printing and publishing of a paper that will make it a libel. The words themselves must be libelous, that is, false, scandalous, and seditious, else my client is not guilty." Prints and Photographs Division, Library of Congress, Washington, D.C.

question. The Zenger case is widely celebrated as a key development in freedom of the press. However, it also represents an important step in the consecration of the jury trial as a key element of American liberty.

With jury decisions such as the one that found Zenger not guilty, and as tensions between the Crown and the colonies continued apace, it became ever more obvious to the monarchy and Parliament that independent juries were a real impediment to the enforcement of English statutes in the colonies. As a consequence, they looked for ways to circumvent reliance on trial juries. One prominent example was the Stamp Act of 1765, for which enforcement authority was lodged in the Admiralty Courts. This had the effect of eliminating trial by jury when violations of the infamous Stamp Act arose.[31] The American colonies were not amused. Indeed, the First Continental Congress included the right to a jury trial in its Declaration of Rights in October of 1774: "[T]he respective colonies are entitled to the common law of England, and more especially to the great and inestimable privilege of being tried by their peers of the vicinage [neighborhood or district], according to the courts of that law."[32] Prior to the Constitutional Convention, the only protection common to virtually every colony's governing document was the inclusion of the right to a jury trial in criminal cases.[33] Given its importance in the colonial era, it is unsurprising that the right to a jury trial was one of the protections enshrined in the U.S. Constitution.

THE CONSTITUTION AND THE RIGHT TO A JURY TRIAL

There is not one, not two, but three parts of the U.S. Constitution that reference trial by jury: Article III, the Sixth Amendment, and the Seventh Amendment. The jury trial language in the first two pertains to criminal trials while the language in the third relates to civil trials. Article III reads, in part, "The trial of all crimes . . . shall be by jury . . ."[34] Compare that language with that contained in the Sixth Amendment: "In all criminal prosecutions, the accused shall enjoy the right to a speedy and public trial, by an impartial jury of the State and district wherein the crime shall have been committed."[35] The language in Article III appears more stringent (i.e., criminal defendants *must* have a jury trial), while the language of the Sixth Amendment appears more permissive (i.e., criminal defendants *may* have a jury trial if they so desire). The Sixth Amendment (like all of the amendments that comprise the Bill of Rights) automatically and directly applies at the federal level. The same was not true with regard to the state level until the Court's ruling in *Duncan v. Louisiana* (1968).[36] In that case, the Supreme Court found that the right to a jury trial in criminal cases was part and parcel of due process of law and, accordingly, that states were bound by the jury requirement "in all criminal cases which—were they to be tried in a federal court—would come within the Sixth Amendment's guarantee."[37]

The language in the *Duncan* case suggests that not every criminal defendant (at either the state or federal level) is entitled to a jury trial. But that is clearly at odds with a prevalent myth that criminal defendants have a right to a jury trial in *every* criminal case. Given the inherent drama in the idea of two lawyers facing off—making impassioned arguments replete with stirring references to fairness and justice—it is not surprising that courtroom dramas are staples on both the big and little screens. That popular media prevalence fosters the notion that trials are essential for discerning the guilt or innocence of a defendant. Given how crucial trials are for securing truth (at least according to television programs and movies), surely the right to a jury trial must be guaranteed for every person accused of a crime. Surely not. That myth does not match the reality of Sixth Amendment jurisprudence. Indeed, despite the plain language of the Sixth Amendment—which indicates that it applies to *all* criminal prosecutions—the Supreme Court has consistently held that a right to jury trial is constitutionally required only for "serious" criminal offenses.[38]

So, what distinguishes between serious and nonserious criminal offenses? As discussed in the previous chapter, an offense is considered "serious" if the potential punishment for the crime is greater than 6 months imprisonment, although additional statutory and regulatory penalties may make a crime "serious" even if the potential imprisonment is less than 6 months. For example, in *Blanton v. North Las Vegas*, the Court noted that the presumption is that an offense is petty (and, hence, does not constitutionally mandate a jury trial) if the maximum prison sentence is no more than 6 months unless the defendant "can demonstrate that any additional statutory penalties, viewed in conjunction with the maximum authorized period of incarceration, are so severe that they clearly reflect a legislative determination that the offense in question is a 'serious' one."[39]

In the *Blanton* case, the possible penalties for the DUI offense with which the defendant was charged included (in addition to a possible 6-month period of incarceration), a 90-day license suspension, 48 hours of community service while dressed in clothing identifying him as a DUI offender, and a $1,000 fine. The Court was not persuaded that these additional possible penalties were more severe than the potential 6-month sentence itself and, hence, declined to find that they were indications that the legislature saw the offense as one serious enough to warrant a jury trial. But the principle that additional penalties could raise an offense to a level of seriousness requiring a jury trial (despite imprisonment of 6 months or less) remained in effect.

Of course, states can provide the right to a jury trial even when not mandated by the Constitution, since "[i]t is elementary that States are free to provide greater protections in their criminal justice systems than the Federal Constitution requires."[40] That is, though no state can provide less protection than mandated by the federal Constitution (as interpreted by the U.S. Supreme Court), any state that wishes to can provide more protection. Many state constitutions do contain analogues to the Sixth Amendment that provide broader jury trial provisions than those found in that amendment. Language in the constitution of North Carolina affords one example: "No person shall be convicted of any crime but by the unanimous verdict of a jury in open court."[41] Even in situations in which the state constitutional language is nearly identical to that in the U.S. Constitution, the state court of last resort's interpretation of the state constitution may yield broader protection than the Supreme Court's interpretation of the Sixth Amendment.[42] As a consequence, a defendant facing a misdemeanor charge for running a red light in Nevada, for example, cannot insist on a jury trial but the same criminal defendant in Texas can.

In contrast to the language of Article III and the Sixth Amendment, the language of the Seventh Amendment addresses civil trials:

> In Suits at common law, where the value in controversy shall exceed twenty dollars, the right of trial by jury shall be preserved, and no fact tried by a jury, shall be otherwise re-examined in any Court of the United States, than according to the rules of the common law.[43]

The Court's interpretation of this constitutional language relies on a "historical test" to distinguish among the types of claims that fall under the strictures of the Seventh Amendment.[44] Though there is a good deal of nuance to that historical test, the gist of it is that the Court considers whether the **cause of action** (i.e., the set of facts being used to justify suit to obtain money, property, or the enforcement of a right against another) is a cause of action that would have been understood to require a jury trial under the common law at the time of the ratification of the Constitution.[45] Though it has found the right to a jury trial as protected by the Sixth Amendment to apply to state as well as federal criminal cases, the Court has repeatedly declined to find the Seventh Amendment's jury protection for civil cases to apply to the states.[46] This means that individual state constitutions and statutes govern the right to a jury trial at the state level.[47] Most states do, however, include provisions for jury trials in their constitutions for many kinds of civil cases above the level of small-claims court.

Both civil and criminal defendants have substantial (though not completely unfettered) discretion to waive the right to a trial by jury and, instead, opt for a **bench trial**—a trial heard before a judge without a jury. One reason that litigants may prefer a bench trial is because they feel they have a better chance of winning with the judge than they have with a jury. This could be because the judge is perceived to be predisposed to certain outcomes, either because she has ruled that way in the past or because she is perceived to be sympathetic to the litigants' position. Indeed, in the extreme, as discussed in Chapter Four, there have been instances in the past of judges taking bribes and engaging in other illegal and unethical behavior in exchange for favorable rulings. But beyond seeing judges as likely to decide in their favor, criminal and civil litigants may have other motivations for eschewing trial by jury.

Image 8.3 The Kept Judge
This 1908 illustration shows two men, one labeled "Political Boss" and the other labeled "Special Privilege" with copies of "Blank Injunctions" in his pocket, helping a diminutive judge write a "Dictated Decision." In the background, Justice is partially obscured by a note that states "Remember Thy Creator." What does this depiction tell us about litigants choosing between a bench or jury trial? Prints and Photographs Division, Library of Congress, Washington, D.C.

For example, a criminal defendant concerned with negative publicity or charged with an especially gruesome crime may see waiving his or her right to a jury trial and having a bench trial preferable.[48]

> On the one hand, going with a bench trial could reduce the defendant's chances of a favorable outcome because in a jury trial the defense can win by getting a verdict of acquittal or a hung jury whereas in a bench trial there was [sic] certain to be a verdict one way or the other. Also, in a jury trial the prosecution has to convince all twelve jurors beyond a reasonable doubt that they should vote to convict while in a bench trial the trial judge is the only juror to be convinced. On the other hand, a jury might harbor considerable antipathy toward . . . [a criminal defendant] because of his gruesome and unprovoked killing of a . . . [sympathetic victim,] whereas a seasoned trial judge usually can put aside emotion and assess the defendant and his defense dispassionately.[49]

At present, Rule 23 of the Federal Rules of Criminal Procedure permits a federal criminal defendant to waive a jury trial if she waives that right in writing, the government consents, and the court in question approves.[50] At the state level, the extent to which a criminal defendant possesses the prerogative to waive a jury trial varies across the states. In some states, a defendant can opt for a bench rather than a jury trial only with the consent of the state (e.g., Indiana).[51] In other states, the approval of the court is required (e.g., Georgia).[52] In still others, discretion to waive a jury trial is lodged entirely in the defendant himself (e.g., Illinois).[53]

With regard to civil cases, a litigant may find a bench trial preferable to a jury trial for several reasons. Chief among them are, first, the technical complexity of the underlying issues giving rise to the case and, second, the (perceived) uncertainty and unpredictability of jury trial outcomes. Some litigation, such as antitrust or securities litigation, is inherently complex by virtue of the sheer volume of evidence as well as the number of laws and standards to be applied to that evidence.[54] Juries are often characterized as not being up to the task in such instances, whereas presumably better-equipped judges are. As for unpredictability and uncertainty, critics have charged:

> Often awards have little relationship to the seriousness of the injury. There is no way to predict how a jury will rule on a particular set of facts. . . . Often awards bear no relationship to economics losses. . . . [T]oday juries often make awards regardless of the "fault" of anyone—out of sympathy for an injured person. . . . [T]oo often juries appear to award on [the] basis of emotion as opposed to facts and/or realistic evaluation of case circumstances.[55]

Rule 38 of the Federal Rules of Civil Procedure provides that a party to a civil case (in the federal courts) can demand a jury trial for all issues in a case or only for specified issues (that are subject to the right of jury).[56] Most states have chosen to pattern their rules for civil procedure on the federal rules[57] so it is not surprising that state-level rules about jury trial waivers are largely comparable to those found at the federal level.[58]

JURY SIZE AND VERDICT RULES

The common law understanding of a jury was of a 12-person jury—the "twelve good men and true" of medieval England. However, in *Williams v. Florida* the Supreme Court held that a 12-person jury is not an absolute requirement under the Sixth Amendment in a criminal case:

> [T]he essential feature of a jury obviously lies in the interposition between the accused and his accuser of the common-sense judgment of a group of laymen, and in the community participation and shared responsibility which [*sic*] results from the group's determination of guilt or innocence. The performance of this role is not a function of the particular number of the body which [*sic*] makes up the jury. To be sure the number should probably be large enough to promote group deliberations, free from outside attempts at intimidation, and to provide a fair possibility for obtaining a representative cross section of the community. But we find little reason to think that these goals are in any meaningful sense less likely to be achieved when the jury numbers six, than when it numbers 12. . . . [C]ertainly the reliability of the jury as a factfinder hardly seems likely to be a function of its size.[59]

Despite not being constitutionally required, the 12-person jury is nonetheless relied upon in federal criminal cases[60] and all state felony cases.[61] With regard to non-felony criminal trials in the states, however, almost one-third of general jurisdiction trial courts and close to nine out of 10 of limited jurisdiction trial courts hearing misdemeanor cases permit juries of six.[62] Jury sizes in criminal cases other than six or 12 are rare. Virginia currently uses seven-person juries for misdemeanors while Ohio uses eight-person juries for such cases. In comparison, Arizona uses eight-person juries for both misdemeanors and felonies, except for cases involving the death penalty or when a sentence of 30 years or more is being sought, in which case a 12-person jury is required.[63] The Supreme Court declared juries of less than six people for criminal cases unconstitutional in *Ballew v. Georgia*.[64]

From a constitutional perspective, whether a jury verdict must be unanimous is dependent, in part, on the size of the jury being used. For example, in 1972 the Court held that unanimity was not required for a criminal conviction in the states, upholding a 9–3 jury verdict in one case[65] and a 10–2 jury verdict in another.[66] However, if the jury consists of only six persons, a unanimous verdict is required.[67] Even so, federal statutes require a unanimous verdict in both felony and misdemeanor federal cases and virtually all states require unanimous verdicts in felony cases.[68] The two exceptions are Louisiana and Oregon. Both of these states require unanimity for misdemeanor cases (which rely on six-person juries). Louisiana requires unanimity in the jury verdict for capital cases but permits 10–2 jury verdicts in specified types of felony cases. Oregon permits 11–1 or 10–2 verdicts for murder or aggravated murder trials. When a sufficient number of jurors cannot agree on the verdict, the result is a **hung jury**, also known as a **deadlocked jury**. The result is a **mistrial**; i.e., a trial that is not successfully completed but, instead, is terminated before a verdict is returned.[69] In the event of a mistrial, the prosecutor must decide whether to go forward and try the case yet again with a new jury.[70]

The Seventh Amendment's jury provision for civil cases does not require a 12-person jury.[71] The Federal Rules of Civil Procedure stipulate that a civil jury must have no less than six and no more than 12 jurors, though the standard size of a federal civil jury is six.[72] The Rules also specify that "[u]nless the parties stipulate otherwise, the verdict must be unanimous and must be returned by a jury of at least 6 members."[73] One recent example of an instance in which the parties on both sides agreed to accept a non-unanimous verdict involved a defamation case brought by Jesse Ventura. Jesse "The Body" Ventura embarked on a colorful career as a wrestler and commentator in the World Wrestling Federation after having served in the Navy during the Vietnam War. Later, he pursued an acting career (uttering his famous catchphrase "I ain't got time to bleed" in the 1987 movie *Predator* with Arnold Schwarzenegger) and, ultimately, a political career (serving as the governor of Minnesota from 1999 to 2003). Ventura filed a defamation lawsuit against the estate of a Navy SEAL who had written a book that included an episode depicting Ventura in a very poor light. Though not identified by name in the book, the author later identified Ventura publicly, leading to Ventura's defamation suit. The *New York Times* reported:

> In the hours before the verdict was announced, lawyers on both sides agreed to accept something short of a unified verdict without knowing which way the jury was leaning. On Monday, the fifth day of deliberation, the jury had sent word to the judge that it did not believe it could agree to a single verdict, so the lawyers began considering the possibility of a less-than-unanimous verdict while facing the likelihood of a deadlock that could have forced a new trial. "That was a strategic call, which seemed appropriate at the time," . . . said [an attorney representing the Navy SEAL's estate] after the verdict was announced.[74]

In short, litigants may opt to accept a non-unanimous verdict if they think the verdict will go their way and they want to avoid a mistrial. Perhaps not surprising, given that the Supreme Court has not made the Seventh Amendment applicable to the states and, accordingly, states have a freer hand in experimenting with civil juries, size and unanimity requirements in civil cases vary considerably across the nation.[75] For example, civil juries in Oregon consist of six jurors when damages are $10,000 or less and can be as few as four in Utah when damages are less than $20,000. In North Dakota, the size of a civil jury is set at six, unless either party demands a jury of nine. Broadly speaking, less than half of the states require 12-person civil juries, and about half of the states allow for non-unanimous verdicts.

DOES JURY SIZE MATTER?

The myth is that a larger jury, specifically a 12-person jury, is better than a smaller jury. After all, if two heads are better than one, then surely the power of the transitive property means that 12 heads are better than, say, six. But are larger juries, in reality, better than smaller juries? How well the myth matches up with the reality depends on what we mean by "better." Three criteria, in particular, stand out in this regard: "correctness" of the verdict, quality of jury deliberation, and representativeness of the jury. The Marquis de Condorcet was an eighteenth century French philosopher and mathematician who was among the first (perhaps *the* first) to apply the tools of mathematical analysis to assess the accuracy of juries in determining the correct verdict.[76] The (vastly oversimplified) gist of his mathematical demonstration (known as Condorcet's jury theorem) is that more jurors are better than fewer jurors assuming that each juror has more than a 50 percent chance of accurately determining the actual innocence or guilt of a defendant. That is a useful mathematical assumption but not necessarily one that comports with the reality of juries made of actual flesh and blood human beings. Further, Condorcet demonstrated that, if each juror has less than a 50 percent change of accurately determining the actual innocence or guilt of a defendant then more jurors is not better and, in fact, the optimal jury is a jury of one!

Needless to say, there has been a bevy of mathematicians, legal scholars, attorneys, judges, and legal observers who have devoted their energies to puzzling out the optimal jury size to maximize "correct" verdicts. One line of research is based on the notion that "the function of a jury is to serve as a proxy for society. In ancient Greece every citizen of the polis served on the jury. In the modern worlds this is impractical, so we settle for juries of 12. . . . [Accordingly,] the most objective measure of a jury's success is whether it agrees with what society would have decided."[77] There is some appeal in thinking about jury accuracy in this way when we contemplate notorious jury verdicts such as the acquittals of O.J. Simpson for the slaying of his ex-wife and her friend, LAPD officers for the beating of Rodney King, and Casey Anthony for the murder of her 2-year-old daughter. Those verdicts were at odds with the opinions of a substantial proportion of the American people.[78] They just felt "wrong" in some way to a large swath of the public.

Probability theory and statistics can be useful for determining how often juries are likely to disagree with society. The Cliffs Notes version of the mathematical calculations is that the likelihood of a jury disagreeing with society is less than 1.5 percent for every jury margin the Supreme Court has upheld (e.g., 6 to 1, 10 to 2).[79] To be sure, this view of a "correct" verdict as being one that corresponds to the judgment of society is not uncontroversial. As one critic has asked, what constitutes the relevant society? The nation? The state? The county? The city?[80] Further, if the fulcrum on which guilt versus innocence rests is simply what society (however defined) thinks the outcome should be, then juries are little more than varnish and a public opinion poll would be as accurate as (if not more) and certainly more efficient than would be juries. Normatively, juries are supposed to be bodies whose *deliberations* are what are thought to lead to the "correct" or "accurate" verdict. This suggests that determining whether larger or smaller juries are better may be more about the quality of their deliberations.

One potential surrogate for the quality of deliberations is how long juries deliberate. To be sure, the length of time a group of people talk is not always indicative of how productive the conversation was, as any student who has been part of a class discussion with long-winded peers (never faculty!) who seem to simply enjoy hearing themselves talk can attest. But as law and psychology scholars Michael Saks and Molly Marti observe in their meta-analysis of 17 empirical studies of jury size, any "time difference may . . . reflect more substantive deliberation: the sharing of more facts, more ideas, and more challenges to the tentative conclusions of others. . . . To the extent that longer deliberations contain more information, they probably are better deliberations."[81] On this measure, larger juries fare better than smaller juries in that the former take longer to deliberate than do the latter, though the differences are modest.[82] A more specific aspect of the quality of jury deliberations has to do with memory recall. Almost 40 years ago, sociologist and legal scholar Richard Lempert argued persuasively that memory recall is greater among jurors serving on 12-person juries as compared to juries comprised of six or eight members:

> [I]f memory is important, a large group is more likely to contain members who recall crucial facts at each stage of the problem-solving activity [that the determination of guilt or innocence represents]. Thus, larger juries are likely to be superior to smaller juries where memory or a good understanding of facts and instructions is crucial to the deliberative process.[83]

Image 8.4 Women Jurors
Larger jury sizes are thought to help guarantee representativeness. However, women were virtually nonexistent on juries in 1902 when Charles Dana Gibson, creator of the famous "Gibson Girls," drew this caricature for Life. *On rare occasions, however, women were called to serve in cases that involved female defendants. Despite the fact that juries are selected from voter rolls and the passage of the Nineteenth Amendment qualified women as "electors," the states did not immediately pass legislation to include them for jury selection. As late as 1942 only 28 state laws allowed women to serve as jurors, but they also gave them the right to claim exemption based on their sex. The Civil Rights Act of 1957 gave women the right to serve on federal juries, but not until 1973 could women serve on juries in all 50 states.* Prints and Photographs Division, Library of Congress, Washington, D.C.

Presumably, the quality of deliberation is enhanced when a jury collectively has a better handle on the facts, evidence, instructions, and arguments pertinent for those deliberations. So, on this score, larger juries are better than smaller juries.

A third point of departure for assessing whether larger or smaller juries are better is on the basis of their representativeness. The underlying notion is that representativeness is essential for impartiality; i.e., a jury that is a representative cross-section of the community will be less prone to bias and prejudice. According to the Supreme Court:

> The American tradition of trial by jury, considered in connection with either criminal or civil proceedings, necessarily contemplates an impartial jury drawn from a cross-section of the community. . . . This does not mean, of course, that every jury must contain representatives of all the economic, social, religious, racial, political and geographical groups of the community; frequently such complete representation would be impossible. But it does mean that prospective jurors shall be selected by court officials without systematic and intentional exclusion of any of these groups.[84]

In practice, this means that juries are second-order diverse in that random selection of jurors means "a number of juries will look nothing like the population from which they are drawn . . . because random assignment generates a set of juries that falls roughly along a normal distribution curve."[85] One now-classic study, relying on probability theory, argued that, in a community with a 10 percent minority population, one or more minorities would be represented on 72 percent of 12-person juries, but only 47 percent of six-person juries could be expected to contain one or more minorities.[86]

The main argument given for reducing the size of juries is that doing so will save time and money and improve the efficiency of the courts.[87] According to one study, if courts reduced the jury size from 12 to six (with two alternates each), they would reduce the amount spent on jury fees by approximately 40 percent.[88] If jury size were reduced from 12 to eight (with the addition of two alternates) the amount spent on jury fees would be reduced by 29 percent.[89] Furthermore, reducing the jury size from 12 to eight would reduce person-days[90] across the selection, trial, and deliberation stages by 28 percent.[91] On the other hand, critics of reducing jury sizes note that there is evidence that smaller juries are more unpredictable. For example, according to one study by an international team of psychology and organizational science scholars in the civil context, smaller juries show more variability in their awards and will, on average, bestow larger awards than will 12-person juries.[92] Another study, this one conducted by an interdisciplinary team of scholars from the legal academy, psychology, and political science, found that six-person juries convict criminal defendants as often as 12-person juries, but that smaller juries more often convict criminal defendants of lesser charges.[93]

JUDGE VERSUS JURY

As discussed earlier in this chapter, a defendant has some discretion to waive his right to a jury trial. When a defendant or litigant does waive that right, the judge then sits in substitution of the jury as the fact finder; i.e., the result is a bench trial. One myth is that judges will do better than juries because judges are more likely to reach verdicts based on the evidence and be less susceptible to extralegal influences. What is the reality? Do judges' decisions differ from juries' decisions? The short answer is that sometimes they do and sometimes they do not.

One of the earliest rigorous assessments of the difference between the decision making of judges and that of juries appeared in *The American Jury*—"[the] monograph [that] began the modern field of jury studies"[94]—almost 50 years ago.[95] Authors Harry Kalven, Jr. (a noted legal scholar at the University of Chicago) and Hans Zeisel (a sociologist and public opinion polling expert) set out to engage in a comprehensive study of the American jury.[96] To do so, they analyzed jury trial statistics, observed jury trials in action, developed experimental jury simulations, and conducted post-trial interviews with jurors. They also asked judges in thousands of actual cases how they would have decided the case had it been a bench trial rather than a jury trial. Kalven and Zeisel then compared those reports to the actual verdicts issued by juries.[97] With regard to civil cases, the research team found two particularly interesting patterns. First, they found that judges agreed with the jury verdicts regarding liability a sizable majority of the time (almost 80 percent of the time).[98] But, second, they found that judges would have awarded more money for damages than did the juries in 39 percent of the cases and less money for damages in 52 percent of the cases.[99] In short, judges and juries more often than not agreed as to liability but judges favored smaller awards overall compared to juries.[100]

In making the choice to forgo a jury trial in favor of a bench trial, civil litigants may be relying on a conventional wisdom about the relative abilities of judges and juries to jettison biased information from their decision-making calculus:

> Much of modern American civil procedure is premised upon the assumption that judges and jurors operate quite differently when dealing with potentially biasing influences during the course of litigation. Judges are generally depicted as masters of their biases, capable of controlling both their feelings and their reaction to whatever may transpire during the course of proceedings. . . . Jurors are not accorded anything like the same latitude. The operative assumption seems to be that jurors are vulnerable to biasing influences in a wide range of settings and that the justice system needs a variety of prophylactic measures for protection whenever it relies on lay decision makers.[101]

Certainly there is both anecdotal and systematic evidence that jurors do have difficulty in putting testimony and attorney statements that are to be stricken from the record completely out of their minds. For example, jurors in the trial of Drew Peterson for the murder of his ex-wife, Kathleen Savio, were instructed to forget any number of things, including what they had heard about a bullet a neighbor thought was a warning from Peterson, a pathologist at the crime scene who hopped into the bathtub where Savio died, and a protection order Savio may have considered against her ex-husband.[102] They were also instructed to disregard the prosecution's suggestion that the defendant had solicited a hit man to kill Savio. Striking such information from a juror's mind (or, at least, from his decision calculus) is easier said than done! But is this any different for judges? The myth is that it is, indeed, different for judges.

Legal scholar Stephan Landsman and psychology professor Richard Rakos undertook an empirical investigation of this conventional wisdom. Specifically, they asked a set of Ohio judges and a set of individuals from a jury pool to read a description of a product liability case and answer some questions to assess their reactions to the case.[103] Some groups of participants in the experiment were given a description of the case that included no biasing material while others were given a description that included either biasing material with a judicial decision to exclude it or biasing material with a judicial decision to admit it. What the research team found when they analyzed the responses of the participating judges and members of the jury pool is that the two groups of participants reacted comparably to material to which they were exposed and that was subsequently deemed inadmissible. In addition, both groups were less likely to find the civil defendant liable when material with the potential to damage the defendant's case was not introduced. The evidence demonstrated that the pattern of verdicts for each group (judges and juries) was the same; both were related to their exposure to the damaging evidence.[104] The myth of judges as superior to jurors in their ability to ignore biasing information is just that, a myth.

With regard to criminal cases, Kalven and Zeisel also offered unique empirical leverage over the differences (or similarities, as the case may be) between judges and juries. They found that the level of agreement between judges and juries was high with the judge and jury agreeing 75 percent of the time as to the outcome for the criminal defendant.[105] In examining the criminal cases in which the jury and the judge disagreed, the research team found an intriguing asymmetry: in 3 percent of cases the jury convicted when the judge would have acquitted, while in 19 percent of cases the jury acquitted when the judge would have convicted.[106] By way of explanation for the leniency of juries relative to judges, these scholars pointed to different defendant characteristics identified by judges that may have led the juries to sympathize with the defendants; for example, gender, attractiveness, and remorse. A more recent study conducted by scholars from Cornell University, the University of Delaware, and the National Center for State Courts gathered new data to partially replicate the Kalven and Zeisel study.[107] They reported rates of judge-jury agreement that are largely comparable to those reported by Kalven and Zeisel. Like Kalven and Zeisel, they found that juries are more likely to acquit when judges would convict than they are to convict when judges would acquit. Because of the newer study's research design—which included surveys of not only judges but of attorneys and jurors as well—the research team was able to tease out the nuances of judge-jury agreement. In particular, what they found is that judges are more likely to convict than are juries when the strength of the evidence is in the middle range. That is, judges have a lower threshold than do juries for conviction.[108]

Another useful window into differences between judges and juries is the comparison of "win rates": Do plaintiffs win more often before judges or juries? Legal scholars

Kevin Clermont and Theodore Eisenberg analyzed a large number of state court trials and examined just that.[109] In their comparison of outcomes in bench and jury trial, using data archived by the Administrative Office of the United States Courts, Clermont and Eisenberg looked at outcomes in federal civil cases from 1979 to 1989. Though for most case types there were few differences in plaintiff win rates in bench and jury trials, they did find that plaintiffs were more likely to win (and recovered more in damages) in products liability, medical malpractice, and motor vehicle cases.[110]

Yet another valuable perspective on the differences between judges and juries is gained by considering differences in the damages they award in civil cases. For example, Eisenberg and another research team with which he worked found that judges and juries do not differ when it comes to awarding **punitive damages**; i.e., damages awarded to deter the defendant (or others) from behaving in the same manner in the future rather than to compensate the plaintiff, per se.[111] In addition, they found that the ratio of punitive damages to **compensatory damages** (i.e., damages awarded to a plaintiff to replace what he or she lost) was approximately the same for judges and juries.[112] In other words, the amount of punitive damages per "unit" of compensatory damages awarded by a judge was comparable to those awarded by a jury.[113] However, this research team did find that the punitive damages awarded by juries were more variable.[114]

Scholars have also considered whether judges and juries differ in terms of their sentencing behavior in criminal cases. In one experimental study, legal scholars Shari Diamond and Loretta Stalans asked state judges in Illinois and a sample of individuals who had reported for jury duty to assign sentences to criminal offenders in four different mock cases.[115] Participants read a presentencing investigation report and watched a tape of the sentencing hearing for each of the four cases. They were also provided a range of sentencing options. Despite the fact that two-thirds of the lay respondents thought that Illinois judges were too lenient,[116] the sentences the lay respondents handed down were, most of the time, more lenient than those handed down by the judges![117]

HOW DO WE KNOW?

Do Judges Differ from Juries?

Do judges differ from juries? In a partial replication of the classic Kalven and Zeisel study,[118] law professor Theodore Eisenberg and his colleagues used a criminal database assembled by the National Center for State Courts (NCSC) to consider just this question.[119] This database provides systematic information on more than 300 trials in four different locations: the Central Division, Criminal, of the Los Angeles County Superior Court, California; the Maricopa County Superior Court, in Phoenix, Arizona; the Bronx County Supreme Court, New York; and the Superior Court of the District of Columbia.[120]

Instead of relying on information only elicited from the judges to ascertain why judges and juries disagree, questionnaires were administered to both judges and jurors. Judges were given questionnaires both before the jury verdict and after the jury verdict. The questionnaire that was administered before the jury verdict was delivered asked what verdict the judge completing the questionnaire would reach if it was a bench trial. It also asked the judge to evaluate the strength of the evidence favoring conviction (on a scale of one to seven); the evidentiary complexity of the case (on a scale of one to seven); and, the legal complexity of the case (on a scale of one to seven). The questionnaire administered to the judge after the jury verdict was delivered gathered information about the judge's reaction to the verdict. The jurors, too, were given questionnaires asking about evaluation of the strength of the evidence and evidentiary complexity, among other things.

The following table reports the judge-jury agreement rates on convictions from the NCSC Data versus the Kalven and Zeisel data:[121]

	JURY ACQUITS	JURY CONVICTS
A. NCSC Data		
Judge acquits	13 percent	6 percent
Judge convicts	19 percent	62 percent
B. Kalven & Zeisel Data		
Judge acquits	14 percent	3 percent
Judge convicts	19 percent	64 percent

As reported, there was an overall 75-percent agreement rate in the replication study, compared to a 78-percent agreement rate in the Kalven and Zeisel study. Similarly, jurors in both studies were more likely to disagree with a judge's decision to convict than with a judge's decision to acquit; in both studies jurors opted to acquit when judges would have convicted 19 percent of the time. However, the jurors in the replication study had a greater tendency to convict when the judge would acquit (6 percent) compared to the jurors in the Kalven and Zeisel study (3 percent).

When the authors of the contemporary study examined why judges and jurors disagreed, they found that evaluations of the evidentiary strength accounted for the disagreements.[122] Specifically, when the judge regarded the evidence as weak, the judge tended to convict less than did the jury. When the jury regarded the evidence as weak, the jury would acquit in nine cases in which the judge would convict, and the judge would acquit in only two cases in which the jury would convict. When the evidence was regarded as being of medium strength—regardless of which observer classified it as such—the judge was more prone to convict than the jury. Finally, when the evidence was regarded as strong by the judge, the judge would convict 15 defendants that the jury acquitted. When the jury regarded the evidence as strong, the judge would convict in two cases in which the jury acquitted, while the jury convicted in three cases that the judge would have acquitted. Thus, juries were found to require stronger evidence to convict than judges. However, evidentiary complexity did not appear to explain the differences between judge and juries.

What the empirical evidence shows is that, in fact, judges do differ from juries. While it is true that judges and juries agree as to conviction roughly three out of every five times, almost one out of every five times a judge is more likely to convict when a jury would acquit. The empirical evidence also demonstrates that the reason for these differences is attributable to the fact that juries require a stronger evidentiary basis for conviction than do judges. In short, judges and juries are not fully fungible because judges are tougher than juries when it comes to criminal defendants.

SEQUENCE OF A JURY TRIAL

In this section, we outline and discuss the different stages of the jury trial, with Table 8.1 summarizing the sequence of a jury trial.

Jury Selection

In jury trials, the first step is the selection of jurors. The set of prospective jurors is known as the **jury pool** or the *venire*. One common misconception is that the jury pool is drawn only from voter registration rolls. While voter registration rolls are certainly one important

TABLE 8.1
Sequence of a Jury Trial

1. Selection of a Jury
2. Opening Statements
   a. Plaintiff's attorney (or prosecuting attorney for a criminal case)
   b. Defendant's attorney
3. Testimony of Witnesses and Presentation of Evidence
   a. Plaintiff's attorney (or prosecuting attorney for a criminal case)
      i.   Direct examination of plaintiff's witnesses by plaintiff's attorney
      ii. Cross-examination of plaintiff's witnesses by defendant's attorney
      iii. Redirect examination of plaintiff's witnesses by plaintiff's attorney
   b. Defendant's attorney
      i.   Direct examination of defendant's witnesses by defendant's attorney
      ii. Cross-examination of defendant's witnesses by plaintiff's attorney
      iii. Redirect examination of defendant's witnesses by defendant's attorney
   c. Plaintiff's attorney may present rebuttal witnesses and defendant's attorney may
      cross-examine them.
4. Closing Arguments
      i.   Plaintiff's attorney (or prosecuting attorney for a criminal case)
      ii. Defendant's attorney
      iii. Plaintiff's attorney (or prosecuting attorney) to close the case
5. Jury Instructions Presented to the Jury
6. Jury Deliberations
7. Verdict of Jury

source of names for the *venire*, those wishing to avoid jury duty are not "safe" from jury duty just because they avoid registering to vote! Generally speaking, names for the jury pool come from (in addition to voter registration rolls) lists of those with a driver's license or a state identification card. The same is true for federal jury pools; i.e., lists of registered voters and those with driver's licenses or state identification cards in the particular judicial district are used to construct the *venire*. In some jurisdictions, however, these sources are supplemented with names from property tax rolls, unemployment compensation recipient lists, and public welfare recipient lists.[123] To be qualified to serve on a jury, individuals typically must be U.S. citizens, residents of the judicial district in question, at least 18 years old, and English speaking. Those who have been convicted of felonies are usually (though not always) disqualified from service as a juror.[124]

One special case of disqualification is related to service on a jury for a criminal case in which the prosecutor is seeking the death penalty. Those who categorically object to the death penalty in a case in which the prosecutor is seeking that penalty or, alternatively, those who see the death penalty as mandated in all cases of capital murder can be disqualified from service. Note that mere opposition to the death penalty is not an automatic disqualification; as long as the potential juror would consider the death penalty despite his own personal convictions he is not automatically disqualified. Similarly, a potential juror in favor of the death penalty who, nonetheless, would consider life imprisonment instead of the death penalty is also not automatically disqualified.[125]

Though legal scholars and normative democratic theorists may celebrate the jury as an essential part of the American judicial system,[126] quite often those called for jury duty feel less than celebratory. Lucky for them (but perhaps not so lucky for society), there is a plethora of advice readily available to those who wish to avoid jury duty, including a Wikihow site easily located online.[127] Why is jury duty so disdained by the public? Descriptions of actual jury service often paint a dismal picture of the experience. It can be a lengthy[128] and dull process. One critic noted:

> Under the best of circumstances, jury duty is about as enjoyable as being trapped in an elevator with a Ronco salesman. You're yanked away from your job or domestic responsibilities, stuck in an airless bunker with lawyers who flunked out of charm school, forced to work with strangers and paid only a minimal stipend—and all this can go on for weeks or even months.[129]

Of course, concerns such as losing time at work or school and arranging for childcare are very real, and the potential for major disruption in both professional and personal life are nothing at which to laugh. It certainly does not help that the pay for jury service is paltry, averaging less than $21 per day nationwide.[130] Every jurisdiction does provide at least some grounds for an individual to be (legitimately) excused from service as a juror. For example, those called for jury service in the federal district courts may seek to be excused on the basis of age (being over 70 years old), having already recently served on a federal jury (within the past 2 years), or service as a volunteer firefighter, rescue squad, or ambulance crew.[131] Perhaps a more glamorous reason for being excused is for being famous, as was the case for Madonna, who was excused from jury service in New York in July of 2014 to avoid creating a distraction for the court.[132]

Pop culture is likely another contributor to the low esteem with which jury service is held. Numerous popular television shows have included episodes in which a character talks derisively about being called for jury duty and goes to great lengths to avoid having to serve.[133] For example, Liz Lemon, a character on the NBC comedy *30 Rock*, tried to avoid jury duty by wearing a Princess Leia costume and claiming clairvoyant powers. On an episode of *Curb Your Enthusiasm*, Larry David attempts to be excused from serving as a juror by claiming to have been the victim of a "serious" crime: "My cousin once stole an Almond Joy from me. It was quite upsetting at the time."[134] In *Runaway Jury*, a character played by John Cusack (Jeffrey Kurr who is using the alias of Nicholas Easter) fakes trying to get out of jury service on the basis of a low-stakes video game challenge in which he wants to compete. That is a pretty lame excuse but no less lame (and transparently false) than some real-life excuses offered by potential jurors:

> One woman on . . . [a] jury panel explained she had been taught in her church not to sit in judgment of others, and that only God could do that. She said serving on a jury that would judge somebody of a crime would go against her religion. . . . When the questioning continued, a man who was two positions behind her in the alphabetically-ordered venire piped up loudly, "Me, too!" He continued, "What she said. I don't judge others. It's my religion." In response to a series of questions, he stayed with his answer, even though it was clear to the judge, attorneys, and observers that he had leapt on her statement because it was so compelling and tried to make it his.[135]

Antipathy towards jury duty is not a contemporary development, however, as an observation about juries written almost a century ago demonstrates. In 1916, the wickedly funny journalist and satirist H.L. Mencken wrote, "A jury is a group of twelve men who, having lied to the judge about their hearing, health, and business engagements have failed to fool him."[136]

TABLE 8.2
Who Conducts *Voir Dire* in State Courts?

VOIR DIRE CONDUCTED:	JURISDICTIONS
Predominantly or Exclusively by a Judge	AZ, DC, DE, MA, MD, ME, NH, NJ, SC, UT
Predominantly or Exclusively by an Attorney	AK, AL, AR, CT, FL, GA, IA, IN, KS, LA, MO, MT, NC, ND, NE, OR, RI, SD, TN, TX, VT, WA, WY
Equally Judge and Attorney	CA, CO, HI, ID, IL, KY, MI, MN, MS, NM, NV, NY, OH, OK, PA, VA, WI, WV

Source: Gregory E. Mize, Paula Hannaford-Agor, and Nicole L. Waters, *The State-of-the-States Survey of Jury Improvement Efforts: A Compendium Report* (Williamsburg, VA: National Center for State Courts, 2007): Table 21.

Winnowing the jury pool down to an actual trial jury relies on ***voir dire***, which translates from Latin (*verum dicere*) as "to see and speak the truth." At its most basic, *voir dire* is the preliminary stage of the trial during which prospective jurors are questioned to determine their suitability to serve as jurors on the particular case. The removal from the jury of disqualified individuals and those who are not likely to be impartial is the objective. The attorneys or the judge may be responsible for questioning potential jurors during *voir dire*. Although attorney-conducted *voir dire* is common in state courts and judge-conducted *voir dire* is the norm in federal courts, there is still substantial variation across states, as can be seen in Table 8.2. Who conducts *voir dire* matters because the empirical evidence suggests that jurors are generally more candid in response to questions from attorneys than they are to questions from judges.[137] Additionally, attorneys are generally more knowledgeable about their own cases and, therefore, they are better suited to compose questions on issues pertaining to their case than are judges.[138]

Usually at least some questions are posed to the full panel of prospective jurors, with jurors answering the questions by raising their hands. This is more common with judge-conducted *voir dire* questioning. An alternative is for each person to be questioned individually in the jury box, moving from juror to juror until the entire *venire* panel has been questioned. This is the more common approach in attorney-conducted *voir dire* questioning. The nature of the questions that a prospective juror might be asked ranges broadly. Sometimes, the relevance of the questions being asked often seems tenuous (e.g., what books they have read recently, favorite movies, the bumper stickers on their cars[139]) but courts have granted broad latitude to lawyers asking questions "far beyond the specific facts of the case being litigated in an effort to ferret out any possibility that a juror may be predisposed to view the evidence in a certain way."[140]

This trend has generated a good deal of criticism for the encroachment on juror privacy that it represents.[141] That criticism reaches a crescendo when notorious incidents arise, such as when the *Wall Street Journal* and *New York Post* publicized the name of a juror they said flashed an "O.K." sign to the defense attorneys in a civil suit.[142] Subsequently, the juror received an anonymous phone call and note chastising her for her purported support of the defense, with the result that the judge declared a mistrial. Another notorious example transpired in the high profile California murder trial of Scott Peterson for the murder of his pregnant wife and unborn child.[143] Media outlets identified jurors by the license plates on their cars and reporters hounded jurors with questions, even calling them at home, trying to break a story. Other legal observers have argued that providing too much anonymity to jurors threatens the press and the public's right to monitor judicial proceedings.[144] Opponents of (partially or fully) anonymous juries also argue that it compromises the purpose of *voir dire*, thereby undermining the Sixth Amendment's guarantee of an impartial jury.

Given that the Sixth Amendment guarantees "an impartial jury of the state and district wherein the crime shall have been committed" *voir dire* is important in order to ensure that a broad representation of the community serves on the jury. A jury of one's peers does not, however, mean a jury consisting of people who are as much like the defendant in question as possible. So, when Raymond Teller (the talking member of the magic duo Penn and Teller) sued Dutch magician Gerard Dogge for stealing one of his (copyrighted) magic tricks, Dogge was disappointed to find that his argument for a jury comprised entirely of magicians was not persuasive to the presiding judge.[145] Although the accepted purpose of *voir dire* is to ensure impartiality, most attorneys nonetheless seek to empanel a jury that is favorable to their client's case and use *voir dire* as a vehicle for gathering information.[146] Additionally, attorneys use *voir dire* to educate jurors on the facts and the law and to influence the jurors before the start of the trial, planting in the minds of potential jurors a particular argument, or at the very least creating a good rapport with the jury.

There are two types of challenges an attorney can invoke if she wishes to strike an individual from the jury during *voir dire*: **challenge for cause** and **peremptory challenge**. Fundamental to the notion of a fair and just trial is the principle that litigants have the right to an unbiased and impartial jury. Recall the language of the Sixth Amendment: "In all criminal prosecutions, the accused shall enjoy the right to a speedy and public trial, by an impartial jury . . . "[147] If the attorney believes that a juror is biased, and therefore represents a threat to the impartiality of the jury, the attorney may request that the juror be dismissed for cause. To do so, there must be a specific reason to believe that the juror cannot be impartial. For example, potential jurors who themselves have been crime victims, have a financial stake in the outcome, or personally know someone involved in the case (e.g., one of the litigants, one of the attorneys) are all candidates for being stricken for cause. Though the attorneys on each side have an unlimited number of challenges for cause, it is the judge who makes the determination as to whether a prospective juror challenged for cause will actually be dismissed.

Scholars Mary Rose and Shari Diamond used an experimental design to assess judges' decisions with regard to this part of *voir dire*.[148] To do so, they developed a set of scenarios (abstracted from their own court observations and review of appellate cases) that included information about a prospective juror, including biographical details that had at least the potential to raise concerns about impartiality, as well as information about the prospective juror's own assessment of his ability to be impartial. Participants in the study, who were asked to indicate whether they thought the juror in question should be excused for cause due to bias, included not only judges but also defense attorneys and prosecutors. Among the most interesting findings reported by the study's authors is that for judges (but not for either group of attorneys), how confident jurors were in stating that they could be impartial mattered. Specifically, the more confident jurors were in that self-assessment, the less likely judges were to say they would strike them for cause.

Why would that matter for a judge's assessment of a juror's capacity for impartiality but not for an attorney's assessment in that regard? There is no obvious connection between self-confidence and impartiality. What Rose and Diamond suggest (in part) is that judges may be more exacting in their assessment of jurors than attorneys because there is a lot of uncertainty associated with the decision to strike a juror for cause and it is the judge (not the attorneys) who is responsible for that decision. "Faced with a need to rule in the face of uncertainty, judges may view an imperfect cue as far preferable to

no cue."[149] One implication of this finding is that calls for the reduction or elimination of peremptory challenges, which implicitly assume that challenge for cause determinations made by a judge will result in more impartial juries, may be mistaken in that assumption. Judges are less likely to strike confident-sounding jurors but whether confident-sounding jurors are better able to be impartial is an open question.

In contrast to challenges for cause, **peremptory challenges** can be exercised for no stated reason, even if it is just the "gut feeling" of the attorney.[150] The number of peremptory challenges is limited by statute and varies from state to state. For example, in California, both the prosecution and the defense are given 20 peremptory challenges when the defendant is being tried for an offense punishable by death.[151] The number drops to 10 per side for most other criminal cases but there are only six per side permitted if the offense in question is punishable by a jail term of 90 days or less.[152] Six is also the limit for civil cases in California. Compare this to the situation in Wisconsin. Wisconsin limits each side in a criminal case to four peremptory challenges, six per side if the crime with which the defendant has been charged is punishable by life imprisonment.[153] Litigants in civil suits in Wisconsin are generally entitled to three peremptory challenges per side.[154] At the federal level, each side is entitled to 20 peremptory challenges in capital cases and three in misdemeanor cases.[155] The prosecution has six and the defendant has 10 peremptory challenges at their disposal for noncapital felony cases. As for federal civil cases, in those cases each side is granted three peremptory challenges.[156]

Attorneys typically strike jurors perceived to be biased against their case, basing their decisions on information they receive from the *voir dire*, jury questionnaire, juror research, or even on stereotypes. For example, Clarence Darrow, a famous American trial attorney, employed an extensive set of stereotypes as part of his jury selection strategy. Darrow gave the following advice:

> Let us assume that we represent one of "the underdogs" because of injuries received, or because of an indictment brought by what the prosecutors name themselves, "the state." Then what sort of men will we seek? An Irishman is called into the box for examination. There is no reason for asking about his religion; he is Irish; that is enough. We may not agree with his religion, but it matters not, his feelings go deeper than any religion. You should be aware that he is emotional, kindly, and sympathetic. If he is chosen as a juror, his imagination will place him in the dock; really, he is trying himself. You would be guilty of malpractice if you got rid of him, except for the strongest reasons.
>
> An Englishman is not so good as an Irishman, but still, he has come through a long tradition of individual rights, and is not afraid to stand alone; in fact, he is never sure that he is right unless the great majority is against him. The German is not so keen about individual rights except where they concern his own way of life; liberty is not a theory, it is a way of living. Still, he wants to do what is right, and he is not afraid. He has not been among us long, his ways are fixed by his race, his habits are still in the making. We need inquire no further. If he is a Catholic, then he loves music and art; he must be emotional, and will want to help you; give him a chance.
>
> If a Presbyterian enters the jury box and carefully rolls up his umbrella, and calmly and critically sits down, let him go. He is cold as the grave; he knows right from wrong, although he seldom finds anything right. He believes in John Calvin and eternal punishment. Get rid of him with the fewest possible words before he contaminates the others; unless you and your clients are Presbyterians you probably are a bad lot, and even though you may be a Presbyterian, your client most likely is guilty
>
> If possible, the Baptists are more hopeless than the Presbyterians. . . . [Y]ou do not want them on the jury, and the sooner they leave the better. The Methodists are worth considering; they are nearer the soil. Their religious emotions can be transmuted into love and charity. They are not half bad; even though they will not take a drink, they really do not need it so much as some of their competitors for the seat next to the throne. If chance sets you down between a Methodist and a Baptist, you will move toward the Methodist to keep warm.
>
> Beware of the Lutherans, especially the Scandinavians; they are almost always sure to convict. Either a Lutheran or Scandinavian is unsafe, but if both in one, plead your client guilty and go down the docket. He learns about sinning and punishing from the preacher, and dares not doubt. A person who disobeys must be sent to hell; he has God's word for that.[157]

Though Darrow's approach is easy to caricature and is off putting due to the gross generalizations upon which it relies, any number of modern jury consultants think there is a good deal to be gained by lawyers who pay attention to the "subtlety of observation" that underlies Darrow's advice.[158]

The ambit of discretion for the exercise of peremptory challenges is not without limits. Lawyers are prohibited from exercising their peremptory challenges based solely on the race,[159] sex,[160] or national origin[161] of a prospective juror. If an attorney believes that the opposing side is using peremptory strikes for prohibited reasons, the attorney can object and lodge what is known as a *Batson* challenge from the 1986 case of *Batson v. Kentucky*.[162] James Batson, an African American convicted by an all-white jury of burglary and receipt of stolen goods, challenged his conviction on the basis of the *voir dire* process in his case.[163] During *voir dire*, several potential jurors were excused for cause by the judge. Based on the relevant Kentucky Rules of Criminal Procedure, the prosecuting attorney was permitted six peremptory challenges while the defense attorney was permitted nine. Each side exhausted its complement of peremptory challenges; among the six members of the *venire* peremptorily challenged by the prosecutor were all four African American *veniremen*. The defense attorney made a motion to discharge the entire jury, claiming that the exclusion of all four African American *veniremen* by the prosecution represented a violation of Batson's right to a jury of his peers (as guaranteed by the Sixth and Fourteenth Amendments) and the equal protection of the laws (as guaranteed by the Fourteenth Amendment). The trial judge declined to grant that motion, the trial commenced, and Batson was convicted.

Subsequently, Batson's case was appealed to, first, the Kentucky Supreme Court and, then, the U.S. Supreme Court. There, in the U.S. Supreme Court, Batson was victorious.[164] The Court's ruling was especially noteworthy because, in finding for Batson, the Court overruled the precedent it had set in *Swain v. Alabama*.[165] In *Swain*, the Court held that a defendant had to demonstrate the systematic exclusion of a group of jurors from the *venire* to invoke the Sixth and Fourteenth Amendments' protections. In *Batson*, however, the Court made it easier to challenge the *voir dire* process as unconstitutional by permitting a defendant to challenge it by making a *prima facie* case for purposeful discrimination relying solely on the record in his or her own case. In other words, someone challenging the use of the peremptory challenge does not have to demonstrate a systematic use of the peremptory challenge for discriminatory purposes throughout a jurisdiction. This does not mean, however, that African American *venireman* can never be struck through the use of a peremptory challenge, even if the result is an all-white jury. If there is a race-neutral reason for the peremptory challenge then it is permissible. The same is true with regard to the use of peremptory challenges that result in the removal of potential jurors on the basis of gender or national origin. "Thus, the peremptory challenge serves as a safety valve in the selection process; it allows lawyers to tinker around the edges, but not to remake the jury completely."[166]

Over the last three decades, **scientific jury selection** (SJS) has become a very lucrative business[167] and reliance on it has become routine in large jury trials.[168] SJS has been defined as "the application of behavioral and social scientific principles to the selection of jurors most sympathetic to a particular side in a court case . . ."[169] and "a process by which statistical analysis is used to test for relationships between juror characteristics and attitudes about . . . [a] case."[170] No longer exclusively of interest to lawyers and judges, SJS has been popularized in fiction and films such as best-selling author John Grisham's novel *Runaway Jury*, which was subsequently adapted into a film of the same name. The ubiquity of SJS is such that one Boston lawyer asserted, "[N]o self-respecting lawyer will go through the process of jury selection in an important case without the assistance of highly paid trial consultants."[171] Further, law professor Franklin Strier observed, "[I]t's gotten to the point where if you don't hire one [that is, a trial consultant] as a big attorney, you could be sued for incompetence."[172]

POP CULTURE

Runaway Jury

In the 2003 film *Runaway Jury*—based on the best-selling novel by John Grisham—Gene Hackman plays jury consultant Rankin Fitch, who asserts that "trials are too important to be left up to juries." His cynicism invokes an image of jury consultants as ruthless manipulators who subvert justice for a price by using SJS to find jurors who will guarantee that his clients win. Fitch is opposed by attorney Wendall Rohr (played by award-winning actor Dustin Hoffman), who represents a woman suing a gun manufacturer that she claims is responsible for the murder of her husband, Jacob Wood. Wood (played by Dylan McDermott in an uncredited role) died when a disgruntled and mentally unbalanced former employee of a stock brokerage firm returned to the company and opened fire using a gun manufactured by Vicksburg Firearms. The widow sues Vicksburg Firearms because the gun makers knew the store that sold the gun was ignoring federal regulations for gun sales.[173]

Rohr's conventional approach to jury selection involves relying on his keen intuition about potential jurors to identify those he thinks can be fair and impartial. Fitch, on the other hand, is a realist who ruthlessly uses science and the latest technology—even hidden-camera surveillance—to ferret out who the potential jurors are and, therefore, how they will vote in the case. He explains: "You think your average juror is King Solomon? No, he's a roofer with a mortgage. He wants to go home and sit in his Barcalounger and let the cable TV wash over him. And this man doesn't give a single, solitary droplet of shit about truth, justice, or your American way."

Ultimately, the film pits Fitch's SJS against Rohr's conventional methods. John Cusack plays a key juror—Jeffrey Kurr who is using the alias of Nicholas Easter—over whom Rankin and Rohr are battling. Will Rankin's research prove predictive of Easter's behavior as a juror or will Rohr's faith in the juror's basic honesty win the day? Why is Jeffrey Kurr using the alias of Nicholas Easter? Does he have his own, hidden agenda? Can either Rankin or Rohr uncover it? While the film portrays SJS as an unethical, even illegal practice, it is widely used in civil litigation and by defense attorneys in criminal trials who represent wealthy clients. While the film suggests that it is a virtually infallible technique for the selection of sympathetic jurors, the reality is that it is not perfect and its success depends on the type of case that is being litigated.

Although jury selection consultants are now more likely to be hired in civil cases rather than in criminal cases, SJS had its start in the latter. The 1971 Harrisburg Conspiracy Trial involved seven antiwar protesters charged with plotting to destroy draft records and blow up steam tunnels in Washington, D.C.[174] The seven included Father Philip Berrigan, a Roman Catholic priest who, along with his brother Father Philip Berrigan, had been identified by FBI Director Herbert Hoover as the leaders of a militant anarchist group. Social psychologist Richard Christie, sociologist Jay Schulman, and several of their colleagues with expertise in survey research aided the defense in selecting the jury that, ultimately, could not come to a unanimous decision, resulting in a hung jury and the acquittal of the defendants.[175] The team conducted both phone and face-to-face interviews in Harrisburg, Pennsylvania, where the trial was to take place. The extensive pretrial research enabled the consulting team to identify key characteristics of respondents that were related to attitudes toward the case. The survey results revealed that religious affiliation and education were key predictors of respondents' attitudes. With this information in hand, the defense attorneys conducted *voir dire* with profiles of ideal and non-ideal jurors in mind, permitting them to maximize the value of their peremptory challenges to exclude potential jurors who did not fit the profile they desired.

Originally, jury selection consultants were academic researchers interested in studying the relationship between potential jurors' life experiences, demographic characteristics, and attitudes on various issues, on the one hand, and the choices they would make if empanelled on a jury, on the other hand. Sociologists, psychologists, and communications, public opinion, and marketing scholars were particularly interested in the topic. Indeed, the first consulting group (the National Jury Project[176]) was established by one of the academics who consulted on the selection of the jury in the Harrisburg Conspiracy Trial (Jay Schulman).[177] In the late 1970s and 1980s, however, the field developed into a full-time profession for many practitioners. This is reflected in the 1982 establishment of the American Society of Trial Consultants—a professional society with a code of ethics and a research foundation, not to mention over 400 members.[178]

Practitioners of SJS rely on a varied set of tools and techniques. Chief among them are telephone surveys, mock juries, shadow juries, and post-trial interviews.[179] The most commonly relied upon tool is the **telephone survey**.[180] The survey is administered to a representative sample of the individuals in the community from which a jury is likely to be drawn and includes three general types of questions. The first type of question asks potential jurors background questions about such things as age, sex, occupation, and the like. The second type of question measures beliefs and attitudes that may be associated with a favorable or unfavorable verdict. The third type of question involves reading a brief description of the case (or a related hypothetical case) and then asking the potential juror to vote as if she was an actual juror in the case. The jury consultant then analyzes these responses to determine which background characteristics correlate with favorable attitudes and verdict preferences. This information is then used to create the juror profiles that help the attorneys select the jurors.

Mock juries are also part of a jury consultant's toolkit. Mock juries are a form of focus group in which a group of individuals are hired and told about key elements of the case. Attorneys use these mock juries to test their presentation style and refine trial strategies before the trial begins. In this sense, mock juries are like a "full dress rehearsal" before the actual trial.[181] In the sensational O.J. Simpson murder trial, both the prosecution and defense used mock juries prior to the actual jury selection for the case. In this sense, the case had already been tried over and over again by both sides before the actual trial even began. It was reported that the mock juries were either hung or returning not guilty verdicts.[182] In one of the prosecution's mock trials held in Phoenix, Arizona, a majority of the almost dozen and a half mock jurors felt the prosecution did not have enough evidence to convict Simpson. One local truck driver who was paid $125 to participate said, "There is no murder weapon, no eyewitness, nothing to really tie him to the scene. More, or less, it's inconclusive."[183] Another mock juror, a real estate agent, said, "They asked if we could find him guilty of Murder 1 if there was just circumstantial evidence. They asked, if we found DNA and it was this and that, could you find him guilty? . . . It would be hard for me to find him guilty from what they told me in that room."[184] Given the mock jury results, it is not surprising that the prosecution failed to convict Simpson.[185]

A related but distinct tool is the **shadow jury**, which is a surrogate jury that sits in the actual courtroom and is exposed to the real trial.[186] The shadow jury originated in a federal antitrust suit brought against IBM by California Computer Products of Anaheim. IBM enlisted the assistance of a trial consultant who trained six surrogate jurors (chosen to reflect the characteristics of the actual jurors).

These surrogate jurors then became participants, observing everything the actual jurors observed, hearing everything the jurors heard, and suffering the same admonitions. They left the courtroom whenever the actual jurors did and viewed themselves and their conduct in every sense as real jurors.

Both the actual and the surrogate jurors followed the admonition not to discuss the trial with anyone and not to discuss lawyers, witnesses, evidence, or their ideas about the case. They formed their opinions on what was presented to them as admissible evidence and not on anything they had learned or heard prior to the trial.[187]

Typically, the consultants and/or attorneys debrief shadow jurors, such as those used in the IBM case, at the end of each day, providing feedback about the evidence, witnesses, and attorneys. The information gleaned from the shadow jurors each day allows the attorneys to identify weaknesses in their case and adjust accordingly. It can also facilitate informed decisions about the ordering and preparation of witnesses on the part of the attorneys. One high profile case in which a shadow jury contributed to a successful defense was the trial of eccentric millionaire Robert Durst, who was acquitted of murder though he admitted that he dismembered a neighbor's body and disposed of the body parts in Galveston Bay.[188]

Unlike the tools and techniques discussed to this point, the primary purpose of **post-trial juror interviews** is not to aid the attorneys in the immediate case but, instead, are intended to help guide and inform juror selection in future cases. Consultants interview actual jurors and inquire about how jurors felt about the evidence that was presented, their attitudes toward the parties, the jurors' decision-making process, and the content of their deliberations.[189] These post-trial interviews serve diagnostic purposes because they provide information about the accuracy of the consultant's theory of the case and predictions about the behavior and decisions of individual jurors. They can be particularly helpful because the evidence suggests that jurors are not always forthcoming about potential biasing experiences or attitudes during *voir dire* but are more candid in post-trial interviews.[190] Consultants can look for patterns based on that information and leverage it for more informed jury selection in future cases.

The myth is that, by using SJS techniques, attorneys can use juror characteristics to predict how the juror will vote. What is the reality? Does SJS work? Researchers have investigated whether SJS is effective in both mock jury studies and actual trial studies. The estimates of the variance in verdict decisions based on using SJS techniques such as surveys of demographic and personality variables range from 5 percent to 15 percent.[191] However, this "value added" is based on an improvement over a random selection of jurors, which does not happen in a real courtroom given that attorneys use traditional selection techniques based on common sense or stereotypes about the associations between juror demographic characteristics and verdict behavior.

SJS has been criticized for undermining the jury system, being ineffective, and suffering from a lack of regulation.[192] Specifically, critics claim that using these techniques actually eliminates intelligent potential jurors from the panel.[193] Additionally, critics argue that it infringes on a defendant's constitutional rights because it produces a jury that is not impartial.[194] Another criticism is that it unfairly favors the rich because jury consultants are so expensive.[195] Thus, in criminal cases, wealthy defendants who can afford it—such as O.J. Simpson—can benefit from SJS while those who cannot afford it may be disadvantaged, particularly if the prosecution employs SJS (though that is relatively rare due to budgetary constraints routinely faced by prosecutors). In civil cases, corporations and institutions with deep pockets can regularly take advantage of SJS while individuals can only hope that their attorneys have the money to pay for SJS up front as the vast majority work on the contingency fee system and will only get paid after the case is resolved. In all, while jury selection can be a long and involved process, it is only the beginning as trials involve numerous phases.

HOW DO WE KNOW?

Is Scientific Jury Selection Effective?

Is SJS effective? Lots of attorneys rely on it and lots of SJS practitioners make lots of money from it. In one study, 96 potential jurors were recruited from evening classes at the University of Toledo.[196] Forty-eight "defense lawyers" were recruited from students in the University of Toledo Law School. The study participants were randomly assigned and then trained in the social science method (SSM) or conventional method (CM) of choosing jurors. Comparisons were then made over four separate criminal cases.

Participants in the SSM group were shown a 90-minute lecture in the SSM technique, which included the relationship between authoritarianism and the propensity to convict. The lawyers were also provided reprints of relevant articles concerning the SSM to read. They were then given profiles of possible jurors ranging from a profile of the "most friendly juror" to the "most unfriendly juror." These profiles were based on an attitude questionnaire given to 205 students in the evening classes at the University of Toledo. This questionnaire was designed to measure potential jurors' attitudes regarding the criminal cases to which the lawyers were assigned. All lawyers trained in the SSM were instructed to use that method when they were selecting their jurors.

Defense lawyers in the CM group were given a lecture on juror selection methods conventionally used by trial lawyers and were assigned appropriate articles to read. Additionally, a videotaped lecture from a local trial lawyer was shown, which included his reflections and experiences. Finally, the defense lawyers were exposed to actual courtroom *voir dire* sessions, where they observed well-known local attorneys conducting *voir dire* using the conventional method and were then shown a videotape of a *voir dire* examination of potential jurors and were asked to select a jury. They were then given feedback as to how accurate their choices were. All lawyers trained in the CM were instructed to use that method when they were selecting their jurors.

In order to select the criminal cases, 60 students in different psychology classes were asked to read accounts of 22 different crimes. Then a calculation was made of their standard, beyond which there was no longer a reasonable doubt of guilt. That standard of reasonable doubt was then correlated with their authoritarianism score. The students were also given a survey questionnaire, which collected demographic and attitudinal information. Two cases, the sale of illegal drugs and a military court martial, were chosen because there was a strong relationship between probable guilty verdicts and the attitudinal and personality variables. A case involving a murder was chosen because there was a moderate-to-weak predictive relationship between a probable guilty verdict and the attitudinal and personality variables. Finally, a case involving drunk driving was chosen because there was no significant relationship between the various predictive variables and probable guilty verdict.

The defense lawyers then conducted *voir dire* and were told their job was to predict the juror's probable verdict using a 6-point scale. The jurors listened to an audiotape of the case and then each indicated his or her verdict on that same 6-point scale. The SSM group was more successful in predicting jurors' verdicts in the drug and court martial cases. Lawyers using the CM were more successful in predicting jurors' verdicts in the murder case. Neither method had an advantage in the drunk-driving case. Given the fact that these were law students instead of actual attorneys with courtroom experience or jury selection consultants who have a methodological and statistical background, there are obviously validity concerns. However, there is some evidence that the effectiveness of the SSM is dependent on the type of case. Specifically, when the predictive relationships used by the SSM are relatively strong, the SSM is effective. However, the CM is better when those predictive relationships are weak or absent.

Opening Statement

The **opening statement** provides the trial attorney with the opportunity to explain the evidence to the judge or jury and to describe the issues that will be presented during the trial. But the purpose is not merely descriptive. Rather, the objective is to persuade. "It is an awesome opportunity to inoculate the jury and deliver a detailed narrative that personalizes . . . [the] client and states . . . [the] client's cause in a manner that epitomizes . . . [the] theory. The opening statement, if properly presented, should persuade, and in some instances move the jury to tears."[197] In other words, during the opening statement, the goals of the attorney are to grab the attention of the judge or jury, explain the anticipated evidence, and advance the theory of the case by advocating for the attorney's client. An opening statement presents facts and opinions that the attorney plans to introduce into evidence during the trial. "One conservative 'test' to determine whether an attorney can include information during opening is to determine whether a witness, a document or some other form of evidence will provide such information. If the answer is yes, the statement may be made during opening; if no, then that statement is probably inappropriate and objectionable."[198]

Presentation of the Evidence

After the opening statement, the prosecution in a criminal case or the plaintiff in a civil case presents her evidence to the judge or jury. This occurs through the questioning of witnesses. **Direct examination** is the questioning of a witness during a trial that is conducted by the side for which that person is acting as a witness. Witnesses for the prosecution may include people such as the arresting police officer in a criminal case as well as the victims and eyewitnesses to the alleged crime. During direct examination, attorneys are prohibited from asking **leading questions**—questions framed in such a way as to suggest the answer—because it is the witness who must testify, not the attorney. To illustrate, consider the difference between these two questions: (1) "Were you at the defendant's house on the night of January 1st?" (2) "Where were you at on the night of January 1st?" The former is a leading question because it suggests the answer—the defendant's house—while the latter does not and prompts the witness to state where she was free of suggestive influences. There are exceptions to this general rule, such as bringing out preliminary matters and questioning a **hostile witness**, i.e., a witness who is antagonistic to the position of the party calling the witness.[199]

Cross-examination, in contrast to direct examination, is the interrogation of a witness that is called by the opposing party. Thus, after the prosecutor or plaintiff's attorney questions a witness, the defense may cross-examine, or question, the witness. There are two types of cross-examination: **supportive cross** and **discrediting cross**. Supportive cross is cross-examination in which the attorney is questioning the witness to support the cross-examiner's case. It involves questioning the witness to bolster the cross-examiner's theory of the case and to assist in the development of favorable aspects of the case not fully developed in the direct examination. Discrediting cross (sometimes referred to as destructive cross) is cross-examination in which the attorney is questioning the witness to discredit that or another witness. More broadly, it is intended to undercut the persuasive value of the opponent's evidence. The scope of cross-examination is generally limited to the subject matter of direct examination and issues of credibility.[200]

Once the prosecution or plaintiff has presented her case through direct examination of her witness, the defense may then present his case through direct examination of witnesses for the defense. Just as the defense attorney was permitted to cross-examine each

Image 8.6 Cross Exa-
mination of a Witness
*This 1818 British engrav-
ing illustrates a cross-
examination in a crim-
inal proceeding. The
attorney asks: "The Lady
cried out Murder you
say—now Madam—look
at his Lordship and tell
me on your oath—did
she cry out, _murder_?
Or _further_?—answer
that question." What
does this image tell us
about the reliability of
eyewitness testimony?*
Prints and Photographs
Division, Library of
Congress, Washington,
D.C.

Cross examination of a witness in a case of Crim Con.

of the prosecution or plaintiff's witnesses, the prosecution or plaintiff has the prerogative to cross-examine each of the defense witnesses. After the defense completes its case, the prosecution or plaintiff has the option of introducing rebuttal evidence, again through directly questioning witnesses followed by cross-examination by the defense.

Closing Argument

During the closing argument, the trial attorney has a final opportunity to explain the evidence, explain the law applicable to the evidence, and explain the reasons why the jury or judge should find in favor of his client.

> The spotlight is on. The audience is hushed, anxious. . . . Now it's time to orate, to persuade, to prove to judge and jury that you have been correct for all the many past weeks.
>
> It's closing argument, time to break the bounds of evidentiary and black-robed restraint, time to jump up and down, rant and rave. Time to make sense of the intellectual and emotional roller coaster the jury has been riding. Time to make the complex simple, time to convince the jury that you are right, that they should decide for you, if not your client.
>
> Sure, closing arguments are fun. This is the reason you entered law school—at last, you can dance around the courtroom and perform; you can be Gregory Peck as Atticus Finch. The judge has finally shut up, your opposing counsel's whiny objections will be limited, and some of the jurors may even be awake—you hope.[201]

During the closing argument the trial attorney is continuing to tell the story that was first presented during the opening statement, a story that summarizes the factual theories and evidence of a case and is intended to move the jurors or the judge to render a favorable verdict. The facts and opinions presented during the trial, the reasonable inferences that can be made from the evidence, the narrative of the story underlying the case, the law and legal theories, and anecdotal references can all make their way into the closing argument. And, of course, a (hopefully) persuasive call to rule in favor of the party represented by the attorney making the closing argument.[202] Though it generally takes up only a tiny fraction of any given trial, the importance of the closing argument is hard to overstate. It is the last opportunity the attorneys have to tell jurors what is important, and why, for their deliberations. It is the last opportunity to remind jurors of the evidence and explain why it should lead to a verdict in their favor. It is the last opportunity to "give the jurors the ammunition they need to argue your case effectively to the other jurors."[203]

Jury Instructions

Once the closing arguments have concluded but before the jury adjourns to the jury room to deliberate, the judge provides guidance as to the relevant laws that jurors should follow when deciding the case. In giving these **jury instructions**, the judge will typically state the issues in the case and define any terms or words that may not be familiar to the jury. The judge will also discuss the standard of proof that jurors should apply to the case, advise jurors how to evaluate the evidence and weigh the credibility of witnesses, and may read sections of applicable laws. The purpose of the jury instructions is to provide the necessary legal knowledge jurors need to do their job. Problematically, "[w]hile the instructions are meant to teach jurors the relevant law, they are not typically drafted with the jurors' education in mind, nor do they generally offer much guidance to jurors for applying that law to the facts they have just heard and reach a decision."[204] The social scientific research on point makes clear that jurors often experience difficulty in understanding the instructions given to them.[205] For example, in one study, roughly two out of every five subjects believed circumstantial evidence had no value, despite receipt of instructions to the contrary.[206] In that same study, the research team found that approximately one out of every five subjects felt that a defendant should be convicted if there was equal evidence to support a verdict of guilty as there was to support a verdict of innocent.[207]

Jury Deliberation

After receiving the instructions and hearing the closing arguments, the jury begins deliberating in the jury room. In most states, the first step is electing one of the jurors as the foreperson.[208] The **foreperson** presides over discussions and votes of the jurors, and he or she often delivers the verdict. In some states, the jury may take exhibits introduced into the record and the instructions from the judge into the jury room. Scholars have identified two primary styles of jury deliberation: **evidence-driven deliberations** and **verdict-driven deliberations**.[209] The former are deliberations that focus on the review of the facts of the case, the evidence presented, and the judicial instructions. They have high levels of participation among jurors and tend to be wide-ranging in terms of what is included in the discussion.[210] Verdict-driven deliberations, however, are narrowly focused on the final outcome. They typically entail frequent polling of the jurors and are characterized as rife with pressure to conform to the majority.[211]

If the jury cannot come to a decision by the end of the day, the judge may **sequester** the jurors, which means they will spend the night in a hotel and be kept from all contact with other people, as well as from newspapers and news reports. However, in most cases, the jury will be allowed to go home at night and the judge will instruct the jurors not to read or watch reports of the case in the news. Additionally, they will be instructed not to discuss the case while they are outside of the jury room. If the jurors cannot agree on a verdict, a **hung jury** results, which means the case is not decided. The result is a mistrial and, as discussed earlier, it may be tried again at a later date before a new jury, assuming the plaintiff or the government decides to pursue the case. Interestingly, verdict-driven deliberations are also more likely to result in a hung jury than are evidence-driven deliberations.[212]

Verdict

As we discussed in the previous chapter, there are two different standards of proof upon which a jury (or a judge in a bench trial) must rely: **a preponderance of the evidence** and **beyond a reasonable doubt**. Which standard applies depends upon the kind of case. Civil cases rely on a preponderance of the evidence while criminal cases involve beyond a reasonable doubt. The former is a lower standard of evidence than is the latter; i.e., it is easier for a plaintiff to meet the preponderance-of-the-evidence standard in a civil case than it is for a prosecutor to meet the beyond-a-reasonable-doubt standard in a criminal case. A preponderance of the evidence means that whichever side has the greater weight of evidence is to prevail. Another way to say this is that whichever party has just enough (or more) evidence to make it more likely than not that what the party is seeking to demonstrate is true is the party that should win. In a criminal case, the burden is on the prosecution to convince the jury or judge that the defendant is guilty beyond a reasonable doubt. Simply put, this means that the jury or judge must be convinced (by the prosecutor) that there is no reasonable doubt that the defendant committed the crime. Defendants do not have to prove their innocence. If a defendant is found not guilty, the defendant is released and the government may not appeal. If the defendant is found guilty, the judge determines the defendant's sentence, either according to federal sentencing guidelines issued by the United States Sentencing Commission if it is a federal case or by state statute if it is a state case.

When a jury returns a verdict of not guilty, despite believing that the defendant is guilty on the basis of the evidence, the jury has engaged in **jury nullification**. Basically, the jury disregards (or purposefully misapplies) the law in reaching its verdict. The colonial-era Zenger case discussed earlier in this chapter is an example of jury nullification. Jury nullification was not uncommon vis-à-vis the Fugitive Slave Act, which was part of the Compromise of 1850 intended to avert succession of the southern states.[213] Jury nullification was widespread with regard to prosecutions under the National Prohibition Act.[214] There are many reasons a jury may acquit a clearly guilty (on the basis of the evidence) defendant. The jury may believe that, although the defendant's behavior was technically illegal, it was somehow justified on moral or ethical grounds. Or the jury may believe that the defendant acted under compulsion or diminished capacity in a way that is not taken into account by the law. Finally, the jury may nullify if the usual penalty is too severe or if they feel that the defendant has already suffered enough.

A contemporary instance of jury nullification was depicted in the final season of HBO's *The Wire*. Set in the inner city of Baltimore, each of the five seasons of *The Wire* had a unique theme: public housing, unions, politics, schools, and the drug war. On the show, Maryland State Senator Clay Davis (played by Isiah Whitelock, Jr., who also has a recurring role as General George Maddox on HBO's *Veep*) was an unapologetic hustler with deep ties in his home community. Those ties included close relationships with drug

POP CULTURE

12 Angry Men

By far the most important film ever made about juries is the classic 1957 drama *12 Angry Men*, directed by Sidney Lumet, a recipient of the Academy Award for Lifetime Achievement.[215] An all-star cast of classic character actors play the jurors, including Lee J. Cobb as the angry conservative (Juror #3), E.G. Marshall as the intellectual conservative (Juror #4), Jack Klugman as the poor liberal (Juror #5), and Jack Warden as the blue-collar baseball fan (Juror #7). The jurors begin their deliberations on an unbearably hot day in a jury room with nonfunctional air conditioning. The trial for which they are deliberating is the trial of a boy with a criminal record who has been accused of murdering his abusive father. At the

12 Angry Men
Credit: Silver Screen Collection/Getty Images

outset, the verdict seems cut and dried to 11 of the 12 jurors: guilty! But one lone juror holds out—Henry Fonda, the dispassionate liberal (Juror #8).

Over the course of the film we see the jurors debate the evidence, sometimes in excruciating detail. They even engage in a reenactment (in the jury room) of an elderly witness's hobbling from his bed to his apartment door to ascertain whether, in fact, the witness could have gotten to the door as fast as he claimed he had when he testified at the trial. Over time, the jurors reveal their biases, turn on one another, and eventually come to change their minds about the case as Fonda's character convinces them that there is reasonable doubt about whether the boy committed the murder. With three jurors still willing to convict, Fonda as Juror #8 explains: "It's always difficult to keep personal prejudice out of a thing like this. And wherever you run into it, prejudice always obscures the truth. I don't really know what the truth is. I don't suppose anybody will ever really know. Nine of us now seem to feel that the defendant is innocent, but we're just gambling on probabilities—we may be wrong. We may be trying to let a guilty man go free, I don't know. Nobody really can. But we have a reasonable doubt, and that's something that's very valuable in our system. No jury can declare a man guilty unless it's sure."

The deliberations depicted in this film are certainly framed for dramatic effect. It is, after all, a movie and those making it wanted it to engage the audience. Nonetheless, the dialogue among the jurors in *12 Angry Men* is useful for students of jury trials in two regards. First, the deliberations depicted in the film begin very much as verdict-driven deliberations but evolve into evidence-driven deliberations. There are early calls for polling and the pressure for conformity is intense, first for Fonda's Juror #8 and then for subsequent jurors who one by one find themselves moving from a verdict of guilty to one of not guilty. Second, the jurors engage in a good deal of discussion, and sometimes vicious fighting, about what the standard of evidence (beyond a reasonable doubt) means in practice. As we noted in the discussion of the standards of evidence, the meaning of the beyond-a-reasonable-doubt standard (or the preponderance-of-the-evidence standard, for that matter) does often elude jurors. The plain language with which they are articulated is belied by the complexity of discerning their meaning in practice.

dealers and kingpins. Indicted for siphoning money earmarked for community projects, Davis did not deny he had taken the money. But he argued melodramatically and passionately that he had done so only to use the money to help individuals in his community do things like pay their utility bills and buy coats for their children. He concluded, "And if a jury of my peers—you all—deem it right and true for me to walk out of here an upright and justified man, well, I ain't gonna lie to you. I'm gonna do the same damn thing tomorrow and the day after that, and the day after that, until they lay me out at March's Funeral Home and truck me off to Mt. Auburn."[216] The evidence of the senator's guilt was unequivocal but the jury acquitted him; a classic (if fictionalized) instance of jury nullification.

In 1972 the federal courts grappled with the issue of jury nullification in *United States v. Dougherty*.[217] The particular issue was whether it was appropriate for a trial court judge to decline to issue a nullification instruction to the jury, something that had been requested by the defense attorney. Although Judge Harold Leventhal, writing for the majority, recognized the jury's power to nullify, he expressed concern that explicitly telling the jury about its power would encourage the jury to decide cases on reasons other than the evidence:

> What makes for health as an occasional medicine would be disastrous as a daily diet. The fact that there is widespread existence of the jury's prerogative, and approval of its existence . . . does not establish as an imperative that the jury must be informed by the judge of that power. On the contrary, it is pragmatically useful to structure instructions in such ways that the jury must feel strongly about the values involved in the case, so strongly that it must itself identify the case as establishing a call of high conscience, and must independently initiate and undertake an act in contravention of the established instructions. This requirement of independent jury conception confines the happening of the lawless jury to the occasional instances that does not violate, and viewed as an exception may even enhance, the over-all normative effect of the rule of law. An explicit instruction to a jury conveys an implied approval that runs the risk of degrading the legal structure requisite for true freedom, for an ordered liberty that protects against anarchy as well as tyranny.[218]

In effect, the court simultaneously recognized (and even exalted) the role of jury nullification but urged caution and restraint when it comes to encouraging juries to exercise that prerogative.

In dissent, Judge David Bazelon argued that there was no reason to think that jurors would abuse this power because they were specifically told about it. According to Judge Bazelon:

> It is important to recognize the strong internal check that constrains the jury's willingness to acquit. Where defendants seem dangerous, juries are unlikely to exercise their nullification power, whether or not an explicit instruction is offered. Of course, that check will not prevent the acquittal of a defendant who may be blameworthy and dangerous except in the jaundiced eyes of a jury motivated by a perverse and sectarian sense of values. But whether a nullification instruction would make such acquittals more common is problematical, if not entirely inconceivable. In any case, the real problem in this situation is not the nullification doctrine, but the values and prejudice that prompt the acquittal. And the solution is not to condemn the

nullification power, but to spotlight the prejudice and parochial values that underlie the verdict in the hope that public outcry will force a re-examination of those values, and deter their implementation in subsequent cases. Surely nothing is gained by the pretense that the jurors lack the power to nullify, since that pretense deprives them of the opportunity to hear the very instruction that might compel them to confront their responsibility.[219]

The majority opinion of *United States v. Dougherty* represents the myth that juries receiving the nullification instruction will be more likely to use their power of nullification than juries that do not receive the instruction, guided not by law but their emotions and personal bias. This is known as the **chaos hypothesis**.

What is the reality? In one study, experiments were designed to explore the effects of jury nullification instructions in three different mock trials: a murder of a grocery store owner during a robbery, a vehicular homicide involving drunk driving, and a euthanasia case in which a nurse was accused of killing a terminally ill patient who asked to die.[220] In each case, there was clear evidence that the defendant was guilty. Mock jurors were given one of three sets of instructions: standard instructions that did not mention their power to nullify the law; instructions that informed them of their right to nullify, but in a subtle way; and "radical nullification instructions" that explicitly informed jurors that they had the right to nullify the law. The analysis of the participants' decisions indicated that jurors hearing the radical nullification instructions were less likely to find the defendant guilty in the euthanasia case, and more likely to find the defendant guilty in the vehicular homicide case. However, the type of instructions given did not affect the verdicts in the murder case.

Additionally, by employing content analysis of the juries' deliberations, the study showed that juries discussed the evidence less and focused more on the instructions, characteristics of the defendant, and personal experiences of the jurors when they were given the radical nullification instructions. Thus, the study's author concluded that when the jury is sympathetic toward the defendant, nullification instructions "liberate" the jury from the evidence in reaching their verdicts, leading to a greater tendency to acquit. However, when the defendant is unsympathetic, nullification instructions lead to a greater tendency to convict. This supports Judge Bazelon's dissenting opinion, in which he argued that a jury would not acquit a dangerous defendant. In a different study by the same researcher, the author showed that, even if the nullification information comes from the defense attorney, the jury is more likely to acquit a sympathetic defendant.[221] However, when the prosecution challenges the defense attorney, reminding the jurors of their duty to following the law regardless of how they feel personally, the tendency for the jury to acquit was dampened.

Juries may not only ignore the law in criminal cases but they may also interpret the judge's instructions in civil cases to produce an outcome deemed (by them) to be fair. For example, in one study, researchers conducted experiments that examined jury decision making when decision outcome-determinative negligence rules led to outcomes perceived to be unfair.[222] Although civil juries are generally "blindfolded," meaning that they do not receive information such as whether the defendant has liability insurance, different negligence standards in tort trials are outcome-determinative legal rules. For example, in a contributory negligence state, if the plaintiff is determined to be negligent at all, the plaintiff is precluded from receiving any damages. In contrast, in a comparative negligence state, the jurors must reduce the monetary award according to the percentage of negligence contributed by the plaintiff. In this study, mock jurors were presented with a product-design case in which the defendant was clearly responsible for the plaintiff's injuries, but the plaintiff was also partly at fault. Juries were more likely to absolve the plaintiff of all responsibility when they were given the contributory negligence instruction versus the comparative negligence instruction. Thus, when prescribed outcomes violate norms of distributive justice, juries can restore a sense of fairness to actual outcomes.

CONCLUSION

Trials hold an exalted position in the American judicial system and are cherished as institutions critical to ensuring justice. Trials do not, however, guarantee that justice will be served. Despite, or perhaps because of, their importance in the public mind, there are any number of myths that have been attached to trials. Preeminent among these myths is the notion that every criminal defendant has a right to a jury of his peers. But, as we have discussed, not all criminal defendants are entitled to a jury trial; only those accused of serious crimes, though the penalties for many "not serious" crimes may still be substantial. Further, despite constitutional guarantees designed to ensure a fair and impartial jury, there are a number of threats to the achievement of this constitutional ideal. Many potential jurors finagle (often creatively) to get out of jury duty. Jury consultants are explicitly hired to facilitate the selection of jurors likely to be favorable to one side or the other in a case (read: not impartial). Peremptory challenges can be used in discriminatory ways. The result is something quite a bit less than the exemplar we hold in our collective conscious.

Suggested Readings

Shari Seidman Diamond. "Scientific Jury Selection: What Social Scientists Know and Do Not Know," *Judicature*, vol. 73, no. 4 (December-January 1990): 178–183. The author considers the effectiveness of scientific jury selection (SJS), arguing that the greatest utility comes when consultants aid attorneys in developing clear and persuasive trial presentations.

Paula L. Hannaford. "Making the Case for Juror Privacy: A New Framework for Court Policies and Procedures," *Judicature*, vol. 85, no. 1 (July-August 2001): 18–25. The author considers the myriad issues associated with maintaining the privacy of jurors, provides an overview of the eclectic set of policies courts have adopted, and proposes a model framework that courts can use to balance juror privacy and the need for impartial juries.

Roger Haydock and John Sonsteng. *Trial: Theories, Tactics, Techniques* (St. Paul, MN: West, 1991). This volume provides a discussion of a host of specific tactics and techniques that are useful for practitioners preparing for and participating in trial.

Randolph N. Jonakait. *The American Jury System* (New Haven, CT: Yale University Press, 2006). This book provides coverage of the development and operation of the American jury system, including a comparison to other countries as well as a consideration of how movies, news media, and books depict juries.

Harry Kalven, Jr. and Hans Zeisel. *The American Jury* (Boston, MA: Little, Brown, and Company, 1966). A classic book on the American jury that offers a general theory of decision making by juries and a systematic analysis of differences between judges and juries in the decisions they render.

Ross D. Levi. *The Celluloid Courtroom: A History of Legal Cinema* (Westport, CT: Praeger, 2005). This guide to the genre of legal cinema draws attention to how the idealized courtroom reflects how the justice system is viewed, and argues that legal movies depict a justice system less corrupt and more fair than we find in reality.

Jennifer Thompson-Cannino and Ronald Cotton. *Picking Cotton: Our Memoir of Injustice and Redemption* (New York, NY: St. Martin's Press, 2009). A memoir written jointly by a man who was wrongly convicted of rape and the woman who accused him of the rape, demonstrating the weakness of human memory and the consequences of that weakness in the criminal justice system.

Endnotes

1   Quoted in Audrey Cleary, "Scientific Jury Selection: History, Practice, and Controversy," *Concept*, vol. 28 (2005): 1–17, 11.

2   Quoted in Kevin P. Durkin and Colin H. Dunn, "Building Your Case for the Jury," *Litigation*, vol. 36, no. 3 (Spring 2010): 43–47, 43.

3   Frontline, "What Jennifer Saw," *PBS.org*, February 25, 1997 (http://www.pbs.org/wgbh/pages/frontline/shows/dna/interviews/thompson.html).

4   A rape kit contains the supplies necessary for collecting evidence of a sexual assault as part of a forensic medical exam. It typically includes such items as swabs, combs, and blood collection devices as well as bags and envelopes for the collection and storage of possible physical evidence that may have transferred to the victim before, during, or after the assault.

5   Jennifer Thompson-Cannino and Ronald Cotton, *Picking Cotton: Our Memoir of Injustice and Redemption* (New York, NY: St. Martin's Press, 2009): 32–33.

6   Ibid., 37.

7   See, for example, Lauren O'Neill Shermer, Karen C. Rose, and Ashley Hoffman, "Perceptions and Credibility: Understanding the Nuances of Eyewitness Testimony," *Journal of Contemporary Criminal Justice*, vol. 27, no. 2 (May 2011): 183–203.

8   Elizabeth F. Loftus, James M. Doyle, and Jennifer E. Dysart, *Eyewitness Testimony: Civil and Criminal*, Fourth Edition (Newark, NJ: LexisNexis, 2007): 123–124.

9   Lesley Stahl, "Eyewitness: How Accurate Is Visual Memory?" *60 Minutes*, March 8, 2008 (http://www.cbsnews.com/news/eyewitness-how-accurate-is-visual-memory/).

10 The Innocence Project is a non-profit legal clinic started by Barry Scheck and Peter Neufeld, lawyers who served on the defense team for O.J. Simpson. It is associated with Yeshiva University's Benjamin N. Cardozo School of Law, at which Scheck is a professor.

11 Innocence Project, "Understand the Causes: Eyewitness Misidentification" (http://www.innocenceproject.org/understand/Eyewitness-Misidentification.php).

12 One possible exception is the phrase "If it doesn't fit, you must acquit," uttered by Simpson defense attorney Johnnie Cochran during closing arguments in reference to the fact that the gloves found at the scene and presumed to have been worn by the killer of Simpson's ex-wife Nicole Brown and her friend Ronald Goldman were too small to fit Simpson's hands. See David Margolicklos Angeles, "Simpson's Lawyer Tells Jury that Evidence 'Doesn't Fit,'" *New York Times*, September 28, 1995.

13 Roger D. Groot, "The Early-Thirteenth-Century Criminal Jury," in *Twelve Good Men and True: The Criminal Trial Jury in England, 1200–1800*, J.S. Cockburn and Thomas A. Green, eds (Princeton, NJ: Princeton University Press, 1988): 5.

14 Freemen are those who possess the civil and political rights that belong to the people under a free government. Obviously, this excludes indentured servants and slaves.

15 The Magna Carta (translated from Latin as the Great Charter) represented a key step in the development of the rule of law in England. It limited royal authority by proclaiming certain rights and liberties as belonging to non-serf subjects of the King and requiring the application of the law before punishment could be imposed (as opposed to the imposition of punishment merely by the King's will). See, J.C. Holt, *Magna Carta*, Second Edition (New York, NY: Cambridge University Press, 1992). Non-serfs were thus protected from arbitrary action on the part of the King and, as a consequence, embraced the Magna Carta. Serfs were, understandably, likely indifferent at best.

16 Roger D. Groot, "The Early-Thirteenth-Century Criminal Jury," in *Twelve Good Men and True: The Criminal Trial Jury in England, 1200–1800*, J.S. Cockburn and Thomas A. Green, eds (Princeton, NJ: Princeton University Press, 1988): 4.

17 The movement away from self-informing juries was largely a function of the increasingly impersonal social relations that accompanied demographic changes due to both acute (e.g., the Great Plague) and gradual (e.g., urbanization) forces. See, for example, John H. Langbein, Renée Lettow Lerner, and Bruce P. Smith, *History of the Common Law: The Development of Anglo-American Legal Institutions* (New York, NY: Aspen, 2009): 224–227.

18 Sir William Searle Holdsworth, *History of English Law, Volume 1* (Boston, MA: Little, Brown, and Company, 1922): 333–336.

19 124 E.R. 1006 (1670).

20 Eberhard P. Deutsch, "Hugh Latimer's Candle and the Trial of William Penn," *American Bar Association Journal*, vol. 51, no. 7 (July 1965): 624–631, 627–631.

21 In some sources, Mead is spelled with an additional "e," as in Meade.

22 Scott Turow, "Best Trial; Order in the Court," *New York Times*, April 18, 1999.

23 *King v. Penn and Mead*, 6 St. Tr. 951 (1670).

24 In some sources, Bushel is spelled with an additional "l," as in Bushell.

25 John Vaughan, "The Opinion of Sir John Vaughn, Chief Justice of the Court of Common Pleas, on the 9th of November, 1670, When the Case of Edward Bushell, One of the Jurors in the Famous Case of Penn and Mead, Came to be Argued on Writ of Habeas Corpus," *Belfast Monthly Magazine*, vol. 8, no. 42 (January 1812): 27–28, 27.

26 Harold M. Hyman and Catherine M. Tarrant, "Aspects of American Trial Jury History," in *Jury System in America: A Critical Overview*, Rita James Simon, ed. (Los Angeles, CA: Sage, 1975): 24.

27 Randy J. Holland, "State Jury Trials and Federalism: Constitutionalizing Common Law Concepts," *Valparaiso University Law Review*, vol. 38, no. 2 (Spring 2004): 373–403, 377.

28 Quoted in Randy J. Holland, "State Jury Trials and Federalism: Constitutionalizing Common Law Concepts," *Valparaiso University Law Review*, vol. 38, no. 2 (Spring 2004): 373–403, 377–378.

29 Quoted in T. Ward Frampton, "The Uneven Bulwark: How (and Why) Criminal Jury Trial Rates Vary by State," *California Law Review*, vol. 100, no. 1 (February 2012): 183–222, 184.

30 The following discussion is adapted from Paul Finkelman, *A Brief Narrative of the Case and Trial of John Peter Zenger* (New York, NY: Bedford/St. Martin's Press, 2010).

31 Randy J. Holland, "State Jury Trials and Federalism: Constitutionalizing Common Law Concepts," *Valparaiso University Law Review*, vol. 38, no. 2 (Spring 2004): 373–403, 378.

32 Quoted in Rachel E. Barkow, "Recharging the Jury: The Criminal Jury's Constitutional Role in an Era of Mandatory Sentencing," *University of Pennsylvania Law Review*, vol. 152, no. 1 (November 2003): 33–127, 53.

33 Randolph N. Jonakait, *The American Jury System* (New Haven, CT: Yale University Press, 2006): 21.

34 U.S. Constitution, Art. III, § 2.

35 U.S. Constitution, Amend. VI.

36 391 U.S. 145 (1968).

37 391 U.S. 145, 149 (1968).

38 *District of Columbia v. Clawans*, 300 U.S. 617 (1937); *Baldwin v. New York*, 399 U.S. 117 (1970).

39 489 U.S. 538, 543 (1989).

40 *California v. Ramos*, 463 U.S. 992, 1013–1014 (1983).

41 N.C. Constitution, Art. I, § 24 (2010).

42 Such is the case in Alaska where the state constitutional language mirrors the federal constitutional language but, nonetheless, has been interpreted as affording broader protections. This is in contrast to, for example, Missouri and Pennsylvania, where the trial by jury guarantee included in those state constitutions provides nothing more and nothing less than what is guaranteed by the Sixth Amendment. See T. Ward Frampton, "The Uneven Bulwark: How (and Why) Criminal Jury Trial Rates Vary by State," *California Law Review*, vol. 100, no. 1 (February 2012): 183–222, 200–201.

43 U.S. Constitution, Amend. VII.

44 James L. "Larry" Wright and M. Matthew Williams, "Remember the Alamo: The Seventh Amendment of the United States Constitution, the Doctrine of Incorporation, and State Caps on Jury Awards," *South Texas Law Review*, vol. 45, no. 3 (Summer 2004): 449–542, 466–473.

45 James Oldham, "On the Question of a Complexity Exception to the Seventh Amendment Guarantee of Trial by Jury," *Ohio State Law Journal*, vol. 71, no. 5 (January 2010): 1031–1053.

46 See, for example, *Walker v. Suvinet*, 92 U.S. 90 (1875); *Minneapolis & St. Louis R.R. v. Bombolis*, 241 U.S. 211 (1916); and *Hardware Dealers' Mutual Fire Ins. Co. of Wisconsin v. Glidden*, 284 U.S. 151 (1931). The historical evidence strongly suggests that the original purpose of the Seventh Amendment was to serve as a check on the federal judiciary. Anti-federalists were concerned that the federal courts would absorb state judiciaries and that federal judges, "these life-tenured robed

autocrats[,] would soon bring the federal power down upon the necks of poor debtors every-where;" Paul D. Carrington, "The Seventh Amendment: Some Bicentennial Reflections," *University of Chicago Legal Forum*, vol. 1990 (1990): 33–86, 34.

47 Only the constitutions of Louisiana and Colorado do not include some version of a right to a civil jury trial. See Renée Lettow Lerner, "The Failure of Originalism in Preserving Constitutional Rights to Civil Jury Trial," *William & Mary Bill of Rights Journal*, vol. 22, no. 3 (March 2013): 811–880, 812 fn. 4.

48 Fred Anthony DeCicco, "Waiver of Jury Trials in Federal Criminal Cases: A Reassessment of the 'Prosecutorial Veto,' " *Fordham Law Review*, vol. 51, no. 5 (1983): 1091–1112, 1091–1092.

49 Hugh Anthony Levine, *Everyday Murders: Trials on Two Coasts Told by the Prosecutor* (Bloom-ington, IN: Xlibris, 2009).

50 Fed. R. Crim. P. 23(a).

51 *Alldredge v. State*, 156 S.E. 2d 888 (1959).

52 *Palmer v. State*, 25 S.E. 2d 295 (1943).

53 *Illinois v. Spegal*, 125 N.E. 2d 468 (1955).

54 Maralynne Flehner, "Jury Trials in Complex Litigation," *St. John's Law Review*, vol. 53, no. 4 (Summer 1979): 751–774, 752.

55 North Carolina Hospital Association quoted in Eric Helland and Alexander Tabarrok, "Runaway Judges? Selection Effects and the Jury," *Journal of Law, Economics & Organization*, vol. 16, no. 2 (October 2000): 306–333, 307–308.

56 Fed. R. Civ. P. 38.

57 John B. Oakley and Arthur F. Coon, "The Federal Rules in States Courts: A Survey of State Court Systems of Civil Procedure," *Washington Law Review*, vol. 61, no. 3 (October 1986): 1367–1428; John B. Oakley, "A Fresh Look at the Federal Rules in State Courts," *Nevada Law Journal*, vol. 3, no. 2 (Winter 2002/2003): 354–387.

58 Pound Civil Justice Institute, "State Constitutional Provisions, Statutes, and Court Decisions on Trial by Jury," *2011 Forum for State Appellate Court Judges* (http://www.poundinstitute.org/sites/default/files/docs/2011%20judges%20forum/2011%20Forum%20State%20Jury%20Trial%20Provi-sions.pdf). See, also, Eric J. Hamilton, "Federalism and the State Civil Jury Rights," *Stanford Law Review*, vol. 65, no. 4 (April 2013): 851–900.

59 399 U.S. 78, 100 (1970).

60 In addition to 12 regular jurors, there are also typically from one to six alternate jurors on a federal criminal trial jury who can replace regular jurors as the need arises (e.g., due to illness, disqualification).

61 Ron Malega and Thomas H. Cohen, *State Court Organization, 2011* (Washington, DC: U.S. Department of Justice, Bureau of Justice Statistics, 2011): Table 10.

62 Ibid.

63 David B. Rottman and Shauna M. Strickland, *State Court Organization, 2004* (Washington, DC: U.S. Department of Justice, Bureau of Justice Statistics, 2006): Table 42.

64 435 U.S. 223 (1978).

65 *Apodaca v. Oregon*, 406 U.S. 404 (1972).

66 *Johnson v. Louisiana*, 406 U.S. 356 (1972).

67 *Burch v. Louisiana*, 441 U.S. 130 (1979).

68 David B. Rottman and Shauna M. Strickland, *State Court Organization, 2004* (Washington, DC: U.S. Department of Justice, Bureau of Justice Statistics, 2006): Table 42.

69 A hung jury is not the only potential cause of a mistrial. Other events that could result in a mistrial include the death of a juror while the trial is proceeding and juror misconduct, such as having improper contact with one of the parties to the case. Prosecutorial action could also lead to a mistrial if, for example, the prosecutor makes improper remarks during a trial that cannot be rem-edied by an appropriate jury instruction on the part of the judge.

70 A retrial after a mistrial does not necessarily violate the Fifth Amendment's prohibition against double jeopardy, according to the Court's ruling in *United States v. Perez*, 22 U.S. 579 (1824). In that case the Court said that when a judge has to declare a mistrial as a "manifest necessity" the

Double Jeopardy Clause does not preclude a retrial. What constitutes "manifest necessity"? The Court said that "it is impossible to define all the circumstances" that would be considered manifest necessity but "the power [of judges to declare a mistrial and permit a new trial] ought to be used with the greatest caution, under urgent circumstances, and for very plain and obvious causes," *United States v. Perez*, 22 U.S. 579, 580 (1824).

71 *Colgrove v. Battin*, 413 U.S. 149 (1973).

72 Fed. R. Civ. P. 48(a).

73 Fed. R. Civ. P. 48(b).

74 Monica Davey, "$1.8 Million for Ventura in Defamation Case," *New York Times*, July 29, 2014.

75 David B. Rottman and Shauna M. Strickland, *State Court Organization, 2004* (Washington, DC: U.S. Department of Justice, Bureau of Justice Statistics, 2006): Table 42.

76 Condorcet was a supporter of, among other things, public education and equal rights for women. His writings are considered part of the Age of Enlightenment. Unfortunately for Condorcet, though he was a champion of liberal causes, he ran afoul of powerful forces in post-revolutionary France. After hiding out from authorities for several months, he was arrested and imprisoned, dying mysteriously either by suicide or murder (depending on who was recounting his death). Ironically, there was no trial. See, generally, Edward Goodell, *The Noble Philosopher: Condorcet and the Enlightenment* (Buffalo, NY: Prometheus, 1994).

77 Dana Mackenzie, "What's the Best Jury Size?" *Slate*, April 25, 2013.

78 Frank Newport, "Fifth Anniversary of Nicole Brown Simpson and Ron Goldman Murders Finds Americans Still Pointing at O.J. Simpson," *Gallup*, June 14, 1999 (http://www.gallup.com/poll/3781/fifth-anniversary-nicole-brown-simpson-ron-goldman-murders-find.aspx); Seth Mydans, "The Police Verdict: Los Angeles Policemen Acquitted in Taped Beating," *New York Times*, April 30, 1992; Paul Duggan, "Casey Anthony and the Court of Public Opinion," *Washington Post*, July 5, 2011.

79 George C. Thomas III and Barry S. Pollack, "Rethinking Guilt, Juries, and Jeopardy," *Michigan Law Review*, vol. 91, no. 1 (October 1992): 1–33.

80 Stanton D. Krauss, "Thinking Clearly about Guilt, Juries, and Jeopardy," *Indiana Law Journal*, vol. 70, no. 3 (July 1995): 921–927.

81 Michael J. Saks and Mollie Weighner Marti, "A Meta-Analysis of the Effects of Jury Size," *Law and Human Behavior*, vol. 21, no. 5 (October 1997): 451–467, 458.

82 Ibid.

83 Richard O. Lempert, "Uncovering 'Nondiscernable' Differences: Empirical Research and Jury-Size Cases," *Michigan Law Review*, vol. 73, no 4 (March 1975): 643–708, 686–687.

84 *Thiel v. Southern Railway Co.*, 328 U.S. 217, 220 (1946).

85 Heather K. Gerken, "Second-Order Diversity," *Harvard Law Review*, vol. 118, no. 4 (February 2005): 1099–1196, 1112.

86 Hans Zeisel, " . . . And Then There Were None: The Diminution of the Federal Jury," *University of Chicago Law Review*, vol. 38, no. 4 (Summer 1971): 710–724.

87 Nicole L. Waters, *Does Jury Size Matter? A Review of the Literature* (Williamsburg, VA: National Center for State Courts, 2004).

88 Ibid., 2.

89 Ibid.

90 The workday for one person is the equivalent of a person-day.

91 G. Thomas Munsterman, Janice T. Munsterman, and Steven D. Penrod, *A Comparison of the Performance of Eight- and Twelve-Person Juries* (Arlington, VA: National Center for State Courts, 1990): 91.

92 James H. Davis, Lorne Hulbert, Wing Tung Au, Xiao-ping Chen, and Paul Zarnoth, "Effects of Group Size and Procedural Influence on Consensual Judgments of Quantity: The Examples of Damage Awards and Mock Civil Juries," *Journal of Personality and Social Psychology*, vol. 73, no. 4 (October 1997): 703–718.

93 Victor H. Polk, Jr., Brian Hayden, and Edward N. Beiser, "Do Smaller Juries Convict Fewer Defendants?" *Judicature*, vol. 61, no. 5 (November 1977): 225–229.

94 Valerie P. Hans and Neil Vidmar, "The American Jury at Twenty-Five Years," *Law & Social Inquiry*, vol. 16, no. 2 (Spring 1991): 323–351.

95 Harry Kalven, Jr. and Hans Zeisel, *The American Jury* (Boston, MA: Little, Brown, and Company, 1966).

96 The Chicago Jury Project, as the larger project from which *The American Jury* drew was known, also included Fred Strodtbeck, a sociologist with special expertise in small group processes. See Valerie P. Hans and Neil Vidmar, "The American Jury at Twenty-Five Years," *Law & Social Inquiry*, vol. 16, no. 2 (Spring 1991): 323–351, 324.

97 A more contemporary example of a judge-jury agreement study is John B. Attanasio, "Forward: Juries Rule," *Southern Methodist Law Review*, vol. 54 (2001): 1681–1689, 1684.

98 Harry Kalven, Jr. and Hans Zeisel, *The American Jury* (Boston, MA: Little, Brown, and Company, 1966): 63.

99 Ibid., 65.

100 See also Roselle L. Wissler, Allen J. Hart, and Michael J. Saks, "Decision-Making about General Damages: A Comparison of Jurors, Judges, and Lawyers," *Michigan Law Review*, vol. 98, no. 3 (December 1999): 751–856; and, Jennifer Robbennolt, "Punitive Damage Decision Making: The Decisions of Citizens and Trial Court Judges," *Law and Human Behavior*, vol. 26, no. 3 (June 2002): 315–341.

101 Stephan Landsman and Richard F. Rakos, "A Preliminary Inquiry into the Effect of Potentially Biasing Information on Judges and Jurors in Civil Litigation," *Behavioral Sciences and the Law*, vol. 12, no. 2 (April 1994): 113–126, 113–114.

102 Cynthia Dizikes and Stacy St. Clair, "Jury Is Out on Whether Barred Statements in Peterson Trial Will Be Ignored," *Chicago Tribune*, August 18, 2012.

103 The judges who participated in the study were drawn from those attending an annual Ohio Judicial Conference in Columbus, Ohio. The members of the jury pool who participated were drawn from the Cuyahoga County Court of Common Pleas jury pool who were waiting for *voir dire*. Stephan Landsman and Richard F. Rakos, "A Preliminary Inquiry into the Effect of Potentially Biasing Information on Judges and Jurors in Civil Litigation," *Behavioral Sciences and the Law*, vol. 12, no. 2 (April 1994): 113–126, 120.

104 Stephan Landsman and Richard F. Rakos, "A Preliminary Inquiry into the Effect of Potentially Biasing Information on Judges and Jurors in Civil Litigation," *Behavioral Sciences and the Law*, vol. 12, no. 2 (April 1994): 113–126, 125.

105 Harry Kalven, Jr. and Hans Zeisel, *The American Jury* (Boston, MA: Little, Brown, and Company, 1966): 58.

106 Ibid., 59.

107 Theodore Eisenberg, Paula L. Hannaford-Agor, Valerie P. Hans, Nicole L. Waters, and G. Thomas Munsterman, "Judge-Jury Agreement in Criminal Cases: A Partial Replication of Kalven and Zeisel's *The American Jury*," *Journal of Empirical Legal Studies*, vol. 2, no. 1 (March 2005): 171–206.

108 Theodore Eisenberg, Paula L. Hannaford-Agor, Valerie P. Hans, Nicole L. Waters, and G. Thomas Munsterman, "Judge-Jury Agreement in Criminal Cases: A Partial Replication of Kalven and Zeisel's *The American Jury*," *Journal of Empirical Legal Studies*, vol. 2, no. 1 (March 2005): 171–206, 173.

109 Kevin M. Clermont and Theodore Eisenberg, "Trial by Jury or Judge: Transcending Empiricism," *Cornell Law Review*, vol. 77, no. 5 (July 1992): 1124–1177.

110 Ibid., 1124–1177, 1137.

111 Theodore Eisenberg, Neil LaFountain, Brian Ostrom, David Rottman, and Martin T. Wells, "Judges, Juries, and Punitive Damages: An Empirical Study," *Cornell Law Review*, vol. 87, no. 3 (March 2002): 743–782.

112 Theodore Eisenberg, Neil LaFountain, Brian Ostrom, David Rottman, and Martin T. Wells, "Judges, Juries, and Punitive Damages: An Empirical Study," *Cornell Law Review*, vol. 87, no. 3 (March 2002): 743–782, 760, 774.

113 A later study found much the same thing with the interesting twist that judges had higher ratios of punitive to compensatory damages in cases involving bodily injury in comparison to juries. See Theodore Eisenberg, Jeffrey J. Rachlinski, and Martin T. Wells, "Reconciling Experimental

Incoherence with Real-World Coherence in Punitive Damages," *Stanford Law Review*, vol. 54, no. 6 (June 2002): 1239–1271.

114 Theodore Eisenberg, Neil LaFountain, Brian Ostrom, David Rottman, and Martin T. Wells, "Judges, Juries, and Punitive Damages: An Empirical Study," *Cornell Law Review*, vol. 87, no. 3 (March 2002): 743–782, 775–776.

115 Shari S. Diamond and Loretta J. Stalans, "The Myth of Judicial Leniency in Sentencing," *Behavioral Sciences and the Law*, vol. 7, no. 1 (Winter 1989): 73–89.

116 Ibid., 73–89, 86.

117 Specifically, the sentences lay respondents gave were more lenient than those given by judges in two of the four cases. In the two other cases, the sentences handed down by lay respondents were no different from those of Cook County judges and more lenient than those of non-Cook County judges. Shari S. Diamond and Loretta J. Stalans, "The Myth of Judicial Leniency in Sentencing," *Behavioral Sciences and the Law*, vol. 7, no. 1 (Winter 1989): 73–89, 76–80.

118 Harry Kalven, Jr. and Hans Zeisel, *The American Jury* (Boston, MA: Little, Brown, and Company, 1966).

119 Theodore Eisenberg, Paula L. Hannaford-Agor, Valerie P. Hans, Nicole L. Waters, and G. Thomas Munsterman, "Judge-Jury Agreement in Criminal Cases: A Partial Replication of Kalven and Zeisel's *The American Jury*," *Journal of Empirical Legal Studies*, vol. 2, no. 1 (March 2005): 171–206.

120 A complete description of the data collection protocols can be found in Paula L. Hannaford-Agor, Valerie P. Hans, Nicole L. Mott, and G. Thomas Munsterman, *Are Hung Juries a Problem?* (Williamsburg, VA: National Center for State Courts, 2003).

121 Theodore Eisenberg, Paula L. Hannaford-Agor, Valerie P. Hans, Nicole L. Waters, and G. Thomas Munsterman, "Judge-Jury Agreement in Criminal Cases: A Partial Replication of Kalven and Zeisel's *The American Jury*," *Journal of Empirical Legal Studies*, vol. 2, no. 1 (March 2005): 171–206, 181, Table 1.

122 Theodore Eisenberg, Paula L. Hannaford-Agor, Valerie P. Hans, Nicole L. Waters, and G. Thomas Munsterman, "Judge-Jury Agreement in Criminal Cases: A Partial Replication of Kalven and Zeisel's *The American Jury*," *Journal of Empirical Legal Studies*, vol. 2, no. 1 (March 2005): 171–206, 186, Table 4.

123 Gregory E. Mize, Paula Hannaford-Agor, and Nicole L. Waters, *The State-of-the-States Survey of Jury Improvement Efforts: Executive Summary* (Williamsburg, VA: National Center for State Courts, 2007): 5.

124 Brian C. Kalt, "The Exclusion of Felons from Jury Service," *American University Law Review*, vol. 53, no. 1 (October 2003): 65–189.

125 *Witherspoon v. Illinois*, 391 U.S. 510 (1968).

126 Recently, communications and political science professor John Gastil and his colleagues have argued that juries, in addition to being important for the judicial system, also have salutary effects on the civic engagement and political participation of citizens. See John Gastil, E. Pierre Deess, Philip J. Weiser, and Cindy Simmons, *The Jury and Democracy: How Jury Deliberation Promotes Civic Engagement and Political Participation* (New York, NY: Oxford University Press, 2010).

127 Wikihow, "How to Get Out of Jury Duty," last accessed September 23, 2014 (http://www.wikihow.com/Get-Out-of-Jury-Duty).

128 The median number of hours expended for *voir dire* in state courts is 6 though that central tendency masks a good deal of variation. For example, Connecticut averages 10 hours of *voir dire* for felony cases and 16 for civil cases while states like South Carolina typically take no more than 30 minutes to empanel a jury. The median number in federal courts is 7 hours. See Gregory E. Mize, Paula Hannaford-Agor, and Nicole L. Waters, *The State-of-the-States Survey of Jury Improvement Efforts: Executive Summary* (Williamsburg, VA: National Center for State Courts, 2007): 6.

129 Steve Chapman, "Why Don't We Protect the Privacy of Jurors? The Case for Making Jury Duty Anonymous," *Reason.com*, August 14, 2008 (http://reason.com/archives/2008/08/14/why-dont-we-protect-the-privac). For another example of a colorful description of jury duty, see Bryan Butler, "Jury Duty Is Hell," *Philadelphia Magazine*, August 29, 2014.

130 Some states pay a flat rate per day while others use a graduated rate system, paying jurors who serve a minimum number of days a higher rate. For example, Massachusetts pays jurors $50 a

day after the third day of jury service. Connecticut requires employers to pay their employees who are called for jury duty their regular wages and salaries for the first 5 days. After the fifth day, Connecticut pays $50 per day. See Paula L. Hannaford-Agor and Nicole L. Waters, "National Jury Improvement Efforts," *Examining the Work of the State Courts*, vol. 15, no. 1 (February 2008): 1–8.

131 Administrative Office of the U.S. Courts, "Juror Qualifications," *Jury Service*, last accessed September 23, 2014 (http://www.uscourts.gov/FederalCourts/JuryService.aspx).

132 "Madonna Excused from Jury Service After Two Hours," *BBC.com*, July 8, 2014 (http://www.bbc.com/news/entertainment-arts-28207560). Celebrity jurists are more than a titillating distraction. Tom Hanks, a well-known actor with a string of awards and an extensive filmography, was selected to serve on a jury in a domestic violence case in 2013. A member of the prosecuting attorney's office approached Hanks outside of the courtroom to thank him for his service, which led to the defense attorney in the case asking for a mistrial due to prosecutorial misconduct. Ultimately, the prosecution and the defense settled on a reduced charge (disturbing the peace) with a $150 fine. "Tom Hanks Jury Duty Ends after Misconduct Claim," *BBC.com*, September 12, 2013 (http://www.bbc.com/news/entertainment-arts-24061922).

133 David M. Sams, Tess M.S. Neal, and Stanley L. Brodsky, "Avoiding Jury Duty: Psychological and Legal Perspectives," *Jury Expert*, vol. 25, no. 1: 4–8, 5.

134 "What Would You Do to Get Out of Jury Duty?" *ABC News*, July 12, 2007 (http://abcnews.go.com/GMA/story?id=3369440).

135 David M. Sams, Tess M.S. Neal, and Stanley L. Brodsky, "Avoiding Jury Duty: Psychological and Legal Perspectives," *Jury Expert*, vol. 25, no. 1: 4–8, 4.

136 H.L. Mencken, *A Little Book in C Major* (New York, NY: John Lane, 1916): 39.

137 Susan E. Jones, "Judge Versus Attorney-Conducted Voir Dire: An Empirical Investigation of Juror Candor," *Law and Human Behavior*, vol. 11, no. 2 (June 1987): 131–146. See, also, David Suggs and Bruce D. Sales, "Juror Self-Disclosure in the Voir Dire: A Social Science Analysis," *Indiana Law Journal*, vol. 56, no. 2 (1981): 245–271.

138 Brian J. McKeen and Phllip B. Toutant, "The Case for Attorney-Conducted Voir Dire," *Michigan Bar Journal*, vol. 90, no. 11 (November 2011): 30–33.

139 Stephanie Clifford, "TV Habits? Medical History? Tests for Jury Duty Get Personal," *New York Times*, August 20, 2014.

140 Lauren A. Rousseau, "Privacy and Jury Selection: Does the Constitution Protect Prospective Jurors from Personally Intrusive Voir Dire Questions?" *Rutgers Journal of Law & Urban Policy*, vol. 3, no. 2 (2006): 287–320, 288.

141 See, for example, Paula L. Hannaford, "Making the Case for Juror Privacy: A New Framework for Court Policies and Procedures," *Judicature*, vol. 85, no. 1 (July-August 2001): 18–25. See, also, Michael R. Glover, "Right to Privacy of Prospective Jurors During Voir Dire," *California Law Review*, vol. 70, no. 3 (May 1982): 708–723.

142 Andrew Ross Sorkin, "Juror No. 4 Says No O.K. Sign and No Guilty Vote," *New York Times*, April 7, 2004.

143 "Maryland, Virginia Mull Anonymous Juries," *Washington Times*, July 26, 2009.

144 See, for example, "Secret Justice: Anonymous Juries," Reporters Committee for Freedom of the Press, Fall 2000 (http://www.rcfp.org/rcfp/orders/docs/SJANONJURIES.pdf). See, also, Christopher Keleher, "The Repercussions of Anonymous Juries," *University of San Francisco Law Review*, vol. 4 (Winter 2010): 531–570.

145 Eriq Gardner, "Teller Learns Why It's Not So Easy to Sue a Magician for Stealing a Trick," *Hollywood Reporter.com*, February 26, 2013 (http://www.hollywoodreporter.com/thr-esq/teller-learns-why-not-easy-424577),

146 See, for example, Jeffrey T. Frederick, *Mastering Voir Dire and Jury Selection: Gain an Edge in Questioning and Selecting Your Jury*, Third Edition (Chicago, IL: American Bar Association, 2012).

147 U.S. Constitution, Amend. VI.

148 Mary R. Rose and Shari Seidman Diamond, "Judging Bias: Juror Confidence and Judicial Rulings on Challenges for Cause," *Law & Society Review*, vol. 42, no. 3 (September 2008): 513–550.

149 Ibid., 539.

150 Peremptory challenges originated with Roman law and became embedded in English common law. Though peremptory challenges have since been abolished by Parliament, they remain alive and well (though often controversial) in the American judicial system. See, for example, Patricia Henley, "Improving the Jury System: Peremptory Challenges," Public Law Research Institute, Hastings College of the Law, University of California (http://gov.uchastings.edu/public-law/docs/plri/juryper.pdf). The presence of peremptory challenges in the U.S. and their absence in England is the basis for the "joke among lawyers about the difference between jury trials in England and the United States: in England, the trial starts once the jury selection ends; in America, the trial is already over." Daniel Goleman, "Study Finds Jurors Often Hear Evidence with Closed Minds," *New York Times*, November 29, 1994.

151 See Patricia Henley, "Improving the Jury System: Peremptory Challenges," Public Law Research Institute, Hastings College of the Law, University of California (http://gov.uchastings.edu/public-law/docs/plri/juryper.pdf).

152 Recent efforts to reduce the number of peremptory challenges in California include a push to limit the number of such challenges to five for offenses punishable by imprisonment for 1 year or less. See Kathleen Shambaugh, "Reducing Peremptory Challenges in California," Institute for Court Management, Fellows Program, May 2014 (http://www.ncsc.org/~/media/Files/PDF/Education%20and%20Careers/CEDP%20Papers/2014/Reducing%20Peremptory%20Challenges%20in%20California.ashx): 28–35.

153 Wisconsin Statutes, Ch. 972, §972.03.

154 Wisconsin Statutes, Ch. 805, §805.08.

155 Fed. R. Crim. P. 24(b)

156 28 U.S. Code §1870.

157 Edward J. Larson and Jack Marshall, eds, *The Essential Words and Writings of Clarence Darrow* (New York, NY: Random House, 2007): 78–79.

158 Tricia Bishop, "Jury Selection Confounded by Stereotypes as Lawyers' Bias Assumptions Prove Faulty," *Baltimore Sun*, June 15, 2009.

159 *Batson v. Kentucky*, 476 U.S. 79 (1986).

160 *J.E.B. v. Alabama*, 511 U.S. 127 (1994).

161 *Hernandez v. New York*, 500 U.S. 352 (1991).

162 Though *Batson* held that the discriminatory use of peremptory challenges was unconstitutional in the context of criminal cases, the Court held similarly with regard to civil cases in *Edmonson v. Leesville Concrete*, 500 U.S. 614 (1991).

163 *Batson v. Kentucky*, 476 U.S. 79 (1986).

164 To be clear, Batson was victorious in the sense that the Supreme Court agreed with his argument that peremptory challenges cannot be used in a discriminatory fashion and still be consistent with the Sixth and Fourteenth Amendments. The reversal of his conviction would have led to a new trial, however, so Batson chose to plead guilty to burglary and was given a 5-year prison sentence. See Kay Stewart, " 'Good' Reversal Followed 'Unfair' Trial," *Courier-Journal.com*, November 6, 2005 (http://www.courier-journal.com/apps/pbcs.dll/article?AID=/20051106/NEWS01/511060406&).

165 380 U.S. 202 (1965).

166 Nancy S. Marder, "Justice Stevens, the Peremptory Challenge, and the Jury," *Fordham Law Review*, vol. 74, no. 4 (March 2006): 1683–1729, 1685.

167 This is evidenced in the 2002 sale of DecisionQuest, the largest jury consulting firm, for $31 million. See Richard Seltzer, "Scientific Jury Selection: Does It Work?" *Journal of Applied Social Psychology*, vol. 36, no. 10 (October 2006): 2417–2435, 2417–2418.

168 Franklin Strier and Donna Shestowsky, "Profiling the Profilers: A Study of the Trial Consulting Profession, Its Impact on Trial Justice and What, If Anything, To Do About It," *Wisconsin Law Review*, vol. 1999, no. 3 (1999): 441–499.

169 Audrey Cleary, "Scientific Jury Selection: History, Practice, and Controversy," *Concept*, vol. 28 (2005): 1–17, 1.

170 Caroline B. Crocker and Margaret Bull Kovera, "Systematic Jury Selection," in *Handbook of Trial Consulting*, Richard L. Wiener and Brian H. Bornstein, eds (New York, NY: Springer, 2011): 14.

171   Franklin Strier and Donna Shestowsky, "Profiling the Profilers: A Study of the Trial Consulting Profession, Its Impact on Trial Justice and What, If Anything, To Do About It," *Wisconsin Law Review*, vol. 1999, no. 3 (1999): 441–499, 443.

172   Joel Warner, "Runaway Juror: Can I Use Science to Get Out of Jury Duty?" *Slate*, February 22, 2012.

173   In the book, the suit is initiated because of a death by lung cancer, not by shooting, and the suit is brought against a tobacco company, not a gun manufacturer. See Elvis Mitchell, "*Runaway Jury*: Courtroom Confrontation with Lots of Star Power," *New York Times*, October 17, 2003.

174   William O'Rourke, *The Harrisburg 7 and the New Catholic Left*, 40th Anniversary Edition (Notre Dame, IN: University of Notre Dame Press, 2012).

175   Caroline B. Crocker and Margaret Bull Kovera, "Systematic Jury Selection," in *Handbook of Trial Consulting*, Richard L. Wiener and Brian H. Bornstein, eds. (New York, NY: Springer, 2011): 15–16.

176   According to the National Jury Project's webpage (http://www.njp.com/), "NJP Litigation Consulting offers **valuable insight and strategic thinking** to improve our clients' persuasive abilities. We thoroughly **examine, evaluate, and de-construct and reconstruct** each case to deliver valuable insights on the fact finder's perspective" [emphasis in the original].

177   Saul M. Kassin and Lawrence S. Wrightsman, *The American Jury on Trial: Psychological Perspectives* (Washington, DC: Hemisphere, 1988): 57–58.

178   Richard L. Wiener and Brian H. Bornstein, "Introduction: Trial Consulting from a Psychological Perspective," in *Handbook of Trial Consulting*, Richard L. Wiener and Brian H. Bornstein, eds. (New York, NY: Springer, 2011): 1.

179   Shari Seidman Diamond, "Scientific Jury Selection: What Social Scientists Know and Do Not Know," *Judicature*, vol. 73, no. 4 (December-January 1990): 178–183.

180   Caroline B. Crocker and Margaret Bull Kovera, "Systematic Jury Selection," in *Handbook of Trial Consulting*, Richard L. Wiener and Brian H. Bornstein, eds (New York, NY: Springer, 2011): 24.

181   Franklin Strier, "Whither Trial Consulting? Issues and Projections," *Law and Human Behavior*, vol. 23, no. 1 (February 1999): 93–115.

182   See, e.g., Warren Richey, "O.J. Would Get 'Mock' Acquittal," *SunSentinel*, September 2, 1994.

183   Arizona Republic, "Simpson is 'Not Guilty' in Mock Trial Reportedly Monitored by Prosecution," *Baltimore Sun*, September 2, 1994.

184   Ibid.

185   Jim Newton, "Simpson Not Guilty: Drama Ends 474 Days After Arrest," *Los Angeles Times*, October 4, 1995.

186   Donald E. Vinson, "The Shadow Jury: An Experiment in Litigation Science," *ABA Journal*, vol. 68 (October 1982): 1243–1246.

187   Ibid., 1243–1246, 1243.

188   "Durst Used 'Shadow Jury'," *Texas City Sun*, November 15, 2003.

189   Richard Seltzer, "Scientific Jury Selection: Does It Work?" *Journal of Applied Social Psychology*, vol. 36, no. 10 (October 2006): 2417–2435, 2430–2432.

190   See, for example, Richard Seltzer, Mark A. Venuti, and Grace M. Lopes, "Juror Honesty During the Voir Dire," *Journal of Criminal Justice*, vol. 19, no. 5 (September-October 1991): 451–462.

191   Lori Van Wallendael and Brian Cutler, "Limitations to Empirical Approaches to Jury Selection," *Journal of Forensic Psychology Practice*, vol. 4, no. 2 (October 2008): 79–86.

192   Richard Seltzer, "Scientific Jury Selection: Does It Work?" *Journal of Applied Social Psychology*, vol. 36, no. 10 (October 2006): 2417–2435.

193   Ibid.

194   Franklin Strier and Donna Shestowsky, "Profiling the Profilers: A Study of the Trial Consulting Profession, Its Impact on Trial Justice and What, If Anything, To Do About It," *Wisconsin Law Review*, vol. 1999, no. 3 (1999): 441–499.

195   Maureen E. Lane, "Twelve Carefully Selected Not So Angry Men: Are Jury Consultants Destroying the American Legal System?" *Suffolk University Law Review*, vol. 32 (1999): 463–480.

196   Irwin A. Horowitz, "Juror Selection: A Comparison of Two Methods in Several Criminal Cases," *Journal of Applied Social Psychology*, vol. 10, no. 1 (February 1980): 86–99.

197 James A. Johnson, "Persuasion in an Opening Statement: Generating Interest in a Convincing Manner," *Michigan Bar Journal*, vol. 90, no. 1 (January 2011): 42–45.

198 Roger Haydock and John Sonsteng, *Trial: Theories, Tactics, Techniques* (St. Paul, MN: West, 1991): 294.

199 James W. McElhaney, "Leading Questions," *ABA Journal*, vo. 75, no. 10 (October 1989): 104–108.

200 Charles J. Faruki, "Cross-Examination that Hurts the Witness, Not You," *Litigation*, vol. 33, no. 3 (Spring 2007): 38–42.

201 Kenneth P. Nolan, "Closing Argument," *Litigation*, vol. 20, no. 4 (Summer 1994): 32–34, 70–71, 32.

202 Roger Haydock and John Sonsteng, *Trial: Theories, Tactics, Techniques* (St. Paul, MN: West, 1991): 606.

203 Linda L. Listrom, "Crafting a Closing Argument," *Litigation*, vol. 33, no. 3 (Spring 2007): 19–25, 19.

204 Sara G. Gordon, "What Jurors Want to Know: Motivating Juror Cognition to Increase Legal Knowledge & Improve Decision-Making," unpublished manuscript (Las Vegas, NV: William S. Boyd School of Law, 2014): 1–39, 6.

205 See Walter W. Steele, Jr., and Elizabeth Thornburg, "Jury Instructions: A Persistent Failure to Communicate," *North Carolina Law Review*, vol. 67 (November 1988): 77–119.

206 David U. Strawn and Raymond W. Buchanan, "Jury Confusion—A Threat to Justice," *Judicature*, vol. 59, no. 10 (May 1976): 478–483.

207 Ibid.

208 Some states invest the trial judge with the authority to select as he sees fit; e.g., Arizona, Maine. Andrew Horwitz, "Mixed Signals and Subtle Cues: Jury Independence and Judicial Appointment of the Jury Foreperson" *Catholic University Law Review*, vol. 54 (Spring 2005): 829–878.

209 Reid Hastie, Steven D. Penrod, and Nancy Pennington, *Inside the Jury* (Clark, NJ: Lawbook Exchange, 2013).

210 Dennis J. Devine, Jennifer Buddenbaum, Stephanie Houp, Dennis P. Stolle, and Nathan Studebaker, "Deliberation Quality: A Preliminary Examination in Criminal Juries," *Journal of Empirical Legal Studies*, vol. 4, no. 2 (July 2007): 273–303.

211 Lora M. Levett, Erin M. Danielsen, Margaret Bull Kovera, and Brian L. Cutler, "The Psychology of Jury and Juror Decision Making," in *Psychology and Law: An Empirical Perspective*, Neil Brewer and Kipling D. Williams, eds (New York, NY: Guilford Press, 2007): 367.

212 James H. Davis, Tatsuya Kameda, Craig Parks, Mark Stasson, and Suzi Zimmerman, "Some Social Mechanics of Group Decision Making: The Distribution of Opinion, Polling Sequence, and Implications for Consensus," *Journal of Personality and Social Psychology*, vol. 57, no. 6 (December 1989): 1000–1012.

213 Irwin A. Horowitz and Thomas E. Willging, "Changing Views of Jury Power: The Nullification Debate, 1787–1988," *Law and Human Behavior*, vol. 15, no. 2 (April 1991): 165–182, 169.

214 Harry Kalven, Jr. and Hans Zeisel, *The American Jury* (Boston, MA: Little, Brown, and Company, 1966): 292.

215 The 1957 classic was remade as a television movie of the same name in 1997. The remake included accomplished and storied actors such as Ossie Davis, George C. Scott, Jack Lemmon, and Hume Cronyn. It also starred former *Who's the Boss* actor Tony Danza and James Gandolfini 2 years before he started his iconic role as Tony Soprano on HBO's *The Sopranos*.

216 *The Wire: Took*, HBO (February 17, 2008).

217 473 F.3d 1113 (DC Cir. 1972).

218 473 F.3d 1113, 1136–1137 (DC Cir. 1972).

219 473 F.3d 1113, 1143 (DC Cir. 1972).

220 Irwin A. Horowitz, "The Effect of Jury Nullification Instructions on Verdicts and Jury Functioning in Criminal Trials," *Law and Human Behavior*, vol. 9, no. 1 (March 1985): 25–36.

221 Ibid.

222 Kristen L. Sommer, Irwin A. Horowitz and Martin J. Bourgeois, "When Juries Fail to Comply with the Law: Biased Evidence Processing in Individual and Group Decision Making," *Personality and Social Psychology Bulletin*, vol. 27, no. 3 (March 2001): 309–320.

9

APPEALS

"Even an attorney of moderate talent can postpone doomsday year after year, for the system of appeals that pervades American jurisprudence amounts to a legalistic wheel of fortune, a game of chance, somewhat fixed in the favor of the criminal, that the participants play interminably."

—Truman Capote, American Author and Playwright[1]

"[The] court of appeals is where policy is made. . . . I know this is on tape and I should never say that because we don't make law, I know. I know."

—Sonia Sotomayor, Judge of the U.S. Court of Appeals for the Second Circuit[2]

Over a roughly 2-week period in late August and early September of 2012, the following three stories appeared in the news. Andrew Shirvell, a former Michigan assistant attorney general who was fired for conducting a hate campaign against a gay university student, was ordered by a jury to pay $4.5 million to the victim.[3] Tyrone Nash, a high school teacher in Oklahoma City, was charged with second-degree rape for having sex with an underage student, though documents filed in the case indicated the sex was consensual.[4] Dr. James Sherley, a scientist who opposes federal funding for human embryonic stem cell research, lost his court bid for a decision to halt the practice.[5] What did each of these litigants have in common? Each one swore that he would take his case "all the way to the Supreme Court!" Shirvell even claimed that his would be a "landmark" First Amendment case.

The news is regularly awash with this sentiment. It is not a claim that is unique to Shirvell, Nash, and Sherley. Even actor Wesley Snipes was quoted as saying he wanted to take his fight against federal tax evasion charges all the way to the Supreme Court.[6] In America, the notion of a "right to appeal" is as firmly ingrained in the culture as baseball, hot dogs, and apple pie. While those who utter this phrase are usually lower court losers who seek fairness, justice, and a chance to win at a higher court, the reality is that most cases are never appealed beyond the initial trial court decision.[7] Further, those litigants who appeal often do so simply to delay implementation of the lower court decision, "with the well founded hope of wearing out the opposing side."[8] In addition, the U.S. Supreme Court—so often invoked by frustrated losers—takes such a paltry number of cases each term that the odds of any one appeal being accepted for review are abysmally small. For example, there were 8,952 cases petitioned to the justices during the 2011 term but a mere 79 cases were granted full review, with an additional 137 disposed of without full review.[9] This means that the notion that a losing litigant will have his day in the Supreme Court is a myth rather than a reality for all but the most fortunate of litigants.

There is, however, more to an appeal than simply winning and losing an individual case. Viewed from the perspective of the government, appeals provide people with a chance to air their grievances in an orderly way—as opposed to resorting to violence, rebellion, or revolution. In this sense, the appellate process helps to legitimize and insulate the government from attack.[10] More generally, it serves to satisfy the desire for litigants to have a voice in the legal process.[11] Yet perhaps the most important function of the appeals process—and one that is at odds with another pervasive myth about the courts as merely interpreting but not making the law—is that it provides a venue to make public policy. Put simply, a key function of appellate courts is to engage in the broader policy-making process with executives, legislatures, and the people.[12] Students may learn in civics classes that legislatures legislate the law, chief executives execute the law, and courts interpret the law but, in reality, each of these actors (including the courts) is engaged in law making.

MYTH AND REALITY IN THE APPELLATE PROCESS

MYTH	REALITY
Appellate courts operate much like trial courts in that both are concerned with ascertaining the facts of the case.	Appellate courts review lower court cases for errors in law and procedure (not errors in fact).
Everyone is entitled to take his or her case all the way to the Supreme Court.	The U.S. Supreme Court chooses which cases it will hear.
The disposition of an appeal is important only to the direct litigants in a case.	The disposition of an appeal is often important to third parties, prompting them to attempt to influence the court via *amicus curiae* briefs.
Oral arguments are merely the verbalization of the written arguments already submitted in the legal briefs.	Oral arguments are used by judges to gather additional information beyond the written arguments, and to signal to the other judges the issues that are important to them.
Most losing litigants appeal their cases.	Very few cases are appealed.
Losing litigants appeal only because they want to win.	Losing litigants appeal because they want justice, fairness, and a procedure through which they feel they can have their voice heard.
All losing litigants have an equal chance of winning on appeal.	Losers in civil cases have a far better chance of winning on appeal than do criminal defendants.
Appeals are important because they correct trial errors and provide venues for losers to become winners.	Appeals are important because they give judges opportunities to make public policy that can have a wide impact on society.
Appellate court judges make decisions on the basis of the law and nothing else.	The decision-making calculus of appellate court judges is complex and is structured by a variety of factors, including the attitudes and values of the judges themselves and the institutional features of the courts on which they sit.

How is a case appealed? What are the obstacles that a litigant wishing to appeal an adverse trial court decision might face? How do appellate courts engage in the policy-making process? How do appellate court judges make decisions? In this chapter, we examine the stages of the appellate process, from the initiation of an appeal through its disposition. We discuss common myths about the accessibility of the appellate courts for the average person and identify hurdles litigants must surmount if they wish to appeal a case. We also explain how and why appellate courts engage in making public policy, and include a discussion of the role of organized interests in that context. In short, appealing a trial court decision is a complicated process and the time, money, and legal expertise necessary for successfully pursuing an appeal can be daunting. Further, appellate courts do more than merely review a lower court ruling for errors in process or procedure. Rather, they engage in policy making through the pattern of decisions they issue and the legal rules they articulate when resolving disputes.

THE APPELLATE PROCESS

The prototypical court that comes to mind for most people is undoubtedly a trial court, featuring a judge and jury listening to attorneys for both sides making impassioned arguments. As we have noted before, trial courts are the courts with which people are most familiar, in part, because they are the courts that provide dramatic fodder for compelling television programs and films. For example, the long-running dramatic series *Law & Order* (1990–2010) featured the determined prosecution of wrong doers by District Attorney Jack McCoy—played by Sam Waterston—and his team of assistant district attorneys. The comedic movie *My Cousin Vinny* (1992) starred Joe Pesci as a brash attorney who passed the bar exam on his sixth attempt but nonetheless still successfully defended his clients against murder charges.

POP CULTURE

AMISTAD

The film *Amistad* (1997) portrays the plight of a group of Africans who are kidnapped in Sierra Leone, illegally sold into slavery, and transported across the Atlantic Ocean on a Spanish ship. Off the coast of Cuba, the Africans take over the ship and direct their captors to sail them back to Africa. Instead, the ship sails north and is taken into custody by the U.S. government off the coast of Long Island, New York. The Africans seek their freedom in American courts. They win their case in the federal district (trial) court. Yet during a jubilant celebration over their victory, their attorney—played by Matthew McConaughey—explains to one of the Africans—played by Djimon Hounsou—that the case is not over: "Our president, our big, big man, has appealed the decision to our Supreme Court." Hounsou replies: "You said there would be a judgment, and we would go free." McConaughey answers: "No, no. What I said is that we won it at the state level, we then go on."

In attempting to secure the services of former President John Quincy Adams—played by Sir Anthony Hopkins—to represent the Africans as their attorney before the U.S. Supreme Court, McConaughey notes that their chances of prevailing on appeal are slim as "seven of nine of these Supreme Court justices are themselves Southern slave owners." Adams agrees to take the case and meets with Hounsou to explain who he is and why the case is before the Supreme Court. After Adams's impassioned argument before the nine justices, Justice Joseph Story—played by real-life Supreme Court Justice Harry Blackmun—delivered the 7–1 opinion upholding the lower court ruling and freeing the Africans.

While the film provides an accurate portrayal of how trial court decisions can be appealed to higher courts—often to the dismay of the winning party—there are a number of inaccuracies in this portrayal that stray from the reality of jurisdiction and the appellate process. Two, in particular, stand out. First, McConaughey's assertion that they won at the "state level" is somewhat misleading. While federal district courts are necessarily located within state boundaries—as this one was in Connecticut—they should not be confused with state courts that have jurisdiction over state law. The U.S. District Court for the District of Connecticut is a federal court that handles all trials for federal matters that occur within the boundaries of that state. It does not handle state matters concerning Connecticut state law. A second inaccuracy in the film involves the appellate process. McConaughey explains that the case has been appealed by the president to the Supreme Court. In reality, the case was first appealed to the U.S. Circuit Court for the Connecticut District—a precursor to today's intermediate federal appellate court for that region of the country: the U.S. Court of Appeals for the Second Circuit. Though not depicted in the film, the Africans won again at the intermediate appellate level and that decision was appealed to the U.S. Supreme Court where the Africans again prevailed. Of course, Hollywood often takes shortcuts in movies in order to move the story along. Yet it is important to understand that federal district court decisions are appealed to the courts of appeals first before they are appealed to the Supreme Court.

The entertainment industry has found it much harder to find sufficient dramatic or comedic content in the appellate process to warrant the production of television shows or movies that take appellate courts as their subject matter. There are exceptions, of course, such as the movie *Amistad* (1997), which centered on the fate of enslaved Africans bound for Cuba who seized control of the ship and, thereby, ignited an international legal battle that was ultimately resolved in the U.S. Supreme Court. But the actual amount of screen time in *Amistad* devoted to the processes and procedures of appellate courts pales in comparison to that devoted to the processes and procedures of trial courts in shows like *Law & Order*. Further, while successful courtroom dramas set in trial courts are common, successful courtroom dramas set in appellate courts are not. For example, *Law & Order* ran for an astonishing two decades, making it the longest running American crime drama. An earlier trial court TV show, *Perry Mason,* which starred Raymond Burr, ran for an impressive 11 years from 1957 to 1966. Compare this to two 2002 television shows about the U.S. Supreme Court—CBS's *First Monday* starring Joe Mantegna and ABC's *The Court* starring Sally Field. The former aired all of 13 episodes while a mere three episodes of the latter were aired. The point is that trials (and not appeals) are how most people picture courts. As a result, the distinctions between trial and appellate courts are at best blurred for most people. The reality, however, is that appellate courts differ substantially from trial courts.

As was discussed in Chapter Eight, trial courts determine what occurred in a conflict; that is, the facts of the case. For example, did the owner of an apartment building remove the snow from the entrance to the building? Or, was the defendant found with the weapon linked to the crime scene? In contrast, appellate courts generally accept the trial courts' determination of the facts and are concerned instead with procedure and law. That is, appellate courts are concerned with whether the trial proceedings followed the correct procedure or whether a law is constitutional. For example, were the jury instructions in a tort case consistent with the rules of civil procedure? Or, does a police department's stop-and-frisk policy violate the Fourth Amendment's protection against unreasonable searches and seizures?

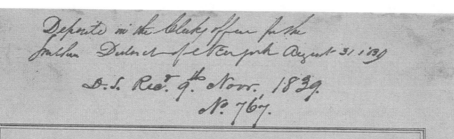

JOSEPH CINQUEZ.

The brave Congolese Chief, who prefers death to Slavery, and who now lies in Jail in Irons at New Haven Conn. awaiting his trial for daring for freedom.

SPEECH TO HIS COMRADE SLAVES AFTER MURDERING THE CAPTAIN &C. AND GETTING POSSESSION OF THE VESSEL AND CARGO

"Brothers, we have done that which we purposed, our hands are now clean, for we have Striven to regain the precious heritage we received from our fathers. We have only to persevere. Where the Sun rises there is our home, our brethren, our fathers. Do not seek to defeat my orders, if so I shall sacrifice any one who would endanger the rest, when at home we will kill the Old Man, the young one shall be saved. he is kind and gave you bread, we must not kill those who give us water.

Brothers, I am resolved that it is better to die than be a white mans slave, and I will not complain if by dying I save you.

Let us be careful what we eat that we may not be sick. The deed is done and I need say no more."

Image 9.1 Amistad
This 1839 lithograph depicts Joseph Cinquez, the leader of a revolt among African slaves aboard the Spanish ship "Amistad" en route to Cuba in June 1839. The slaves seized control of the ship but were soon recaptured and charged with murder and piracy. This portrait was done while Cinquez (or "Cinque") awaited trial in New Haven, Connecticut. John Quincy Adams represented the Africans before the Supreme Court, and thanks to his eloquence, they were set free and allowed to return to Africa. The portrait is sympathetic and informal. The text quotes Cinquez's sober and moving speech to his comrades on board ship after the mutiny. He said, "Brothers, we have done that which we purposed, our hands are now clean for we have Striven to regain the precious heritage we received from our fathers. . . . I am resolved it is better to die than to be a white man's slave . . ." Prints and Photographs Division, Library of Congress, Washington, D.C.

POP CULTURE

Reversal of Fortune

In general, feature films that involve the criminal justice system end with a climactic trial and a verdict of innocence or guilt. In *Reversal of Fortune* (1999), however, we see the trial and verdict at the start of the movie while the bulk of the film is devoted to preparing for an appeal. Millionaire Claus von Bulow—played by Jeremy Irons—is convicted in a Rhode Island trial court of twice attempting to murder his even richer wife Sunny—played by Glenn Close. It is her voice we hear as she lays in a hospital bed in a permanent vegetative state: "You are about to see how Claus von Bulow sought to reverse or escape from that jury's verdict."

Claus hires Harvard Law Professor Alan Dershowitz (who wrote the true-story book on which the film was based and who is portrayed by actor Ron Silver). We quickly learn that Dershowitz is involved in an appeal for two African Americans convicted for a murder Dershowitz insists they did not commit. Dershowitz is obviously an attorney who represents underdogs and looks for challenges—particularly high profile ones. He agrees to take the case and sets out to recruit current and former students to help him with the appeal. He tells one of them: "I only have forty-five days to file." When Claus visits the Dershowitz home to find law students cooking in the kitchen, playing table tennis in the study, and passed out in chairs, Dershowitz informs him: "Thirty-eight days to write 100 pages—only way to get it done." We soon learn that Der-

Reversal of Fortune
Credit: Dick Loek/Toronto Star via Getty Images

showitz's nearly single-minded focus on Claus's case had left him no time to help his African American clients.

One of Dershowitz's students does some research into the Rhode Island Supreme Court. Dershowitz says: "We are not going to win this case on a technicality." His student reports: "I've read every case in the last seven years where the Rhode Island Supreme Court reversed. They don't like to make new law. They don't like to discuss broad legal issues. When they do reverse, the grounds are technical but the reason seems to be they suspect a convicted defendant may be innocent." Dershowitz looks at Claus and replies: "True or not, we have to convince the judges that you are innocent."

When another student informs Dershowitz that there is a Fourth Amendment argument about an illegal search that they can use, Dershowitz is visibly displeased and retorts: "It's a classic technicality. It's a guilty man's argument!" The student protests that the search destroyed evidence but Dershowitz informs her that he knows the law is on their side but that they need more than that in order to make the best appeal possible. Later, the Dershowitz student who is working on the Rhode Island Supreme Court's past decisions informs him of a key precedent for their appeal: "In a case based on circumstantial theory, the case falls apart if any part of the theory is weak." Dershowitz replies: "If there's a weak link in the chain, you throw the whole chain out?" He instructs the student to "find as many alternative theories as possible. There's only seven days left."

When Dershowitz informs his students that they are not going to base their appeal on a technicality but instead explicitly on Claus's innocence, his students protest that innocence or guilt is only determined by trial courts and that appeals are based only on procedure and law. One says: "That's not proper. An appeal has to be based in judicial error." Dershowitz replies: "It is. The judge should have thrown out the case." A student responds: "How can you say there wasn't sufficient evidence when a jury convicted him?" Dershowitz says: "If the rules don't work you change them." Another student says: "The state supreme court shouldn't even look at an appeal based on new evidence." Dershowitz holds fast and implores the troops: "We've got four days left. What we do now is gonna decide this thing. Do you wanna win or not?"

At the Rhode Island Supreme Court, we see the five judges take the bench and Dershowitz begin his oral argument. He explains: "You may not like Claus von Bulow. You may think he is guilty of something but I am here to tell you he is innocent. Our new evidence will clearly indicate . . . " He is immediately interrupted by one of the judges: "You know there isn't a single case that allows you to introduce new evidence on appeal." Dershowitz cites the judge's own precedent and is allowed to continue his remarks: "Get on with it counselor." Dershowtiz continues and ultimately concludes: "I hope will you have the courage to free an innocent man and remedy a grave injustice." Opposing counsel argues that the judges should not allow the introduction of new evidence: "Introduction of new evidence on appeal violates every principle of jurisprudence, every statute, every precedent, every rule of ethics. I am not going to stand before you and argue Mr. von Bulow's guilt. However, I have no choice but to address Mr. Dershowitz's arguments one by one."

When the decision is announced some time later, Dershowitz's students inform him of the good news: "Five-zip. We murdered them!" Dershowitz asks: "Grounds?" The students reply that the judges said that the new evidence proved that some trial court testimony that was not allowed should have been heard by the jury "and that silly, silly guilty man's argument: search and seizure." Dershowitz asks: "Federal or state?" The students answer: "Both. That's important. If it's [a] federal [case] they could appeal it in the U.S. Supreme Court. But because it's Rhode Island they can't. We win!" Dershowitz cautions them not to get too excited as the state may retry Claus. When Dershowitz meets with Claus, he is invited to dinner as Claus assumes they will now be friends. But Dershowitz knows that even though they won the appeal by demonstrating that the prosecution's case was weak, they did not necessarily prove Claus' innocence. Dershowitz tells him: "Legally, this is an important victory. Morally, you're on your own." Ultimately, the state did retry Claus and he was acquitted. By the time the film was released, it ended with the coda that Claus was still married to Sunny, who remained in a coma. After the film's release, the family wrangled over Sunny's estate. Claus agreed to divorce Sunny, gave up all claims to her fortune, and left the country. Sunny remained in a coma until her death from a heart attack in 2008.

One consequence of the fact that appellate courts do not "retry" cases is that, if the government loses a criminal case because it failed to prove that the accused was guilty, the government may not ask an appellate court to review the *facts* and issue a guilty verdict.[13] Appellate courts also *look* very different than trial courts. Instead of a single judge presiding, three or more judges sit together—either in panels or **en banc,** which means all judges of the court—to consider legal arguments made by attorneys. The judges hear no new testimony and consider no new evidence. Unlike in a trial, there are neither witnesses nor juries in an appeal. Instead, the focus in an appeal is on the record of the lower court proceedings and the associated appellate documents.

Though there is certainly variation between and among appellate courts—between state and federal appellate courts as well as among state appellate courts—there are elements of the appellate process that are common across most jurisdictions. Once a trial court has adjudicated a case and has issued its verdict or ruling, a litigant unhappy with that outcome has a specified length of time in which to file a **notice of appeal** with the trial court that originally decided the case. The notice of appeal is the formal, legal announcement by the losing litigant that she is challenging the lower court ruling. The litigant appealing the decision is referred to as the **appellant** or, less commonly, as the **plaintiff in error**. How long the appellant has to file the notice of appeal varies by jurisdiction.[14] For example, a litigant appealing an Illinois trial court decision has 30 days from the date of final judgment to file the notice of appeal. However, a litigant appealing a Missouri trial court decision has only 10 days to do so, except in special cases such as those involving the termination of parental rights or juvenile matters.

Typically, the court sends a copy of the notice of appeal to the other litigant (i.e., the litigant who did not initiate the appeal, otherwise known as the **appellee** or **respondent**). In almost every case, the appellant bears the costs associated with the preparation and transmittal of the trial transcript and associated materials (e.g., court exhibits) to the appellate court.[15] There are a small number of exceptions. For example, South Carolina has no fees levied by the court because the appellant rather than the court is responsible for preparing the record on appeal. In Alabama, the appellant is responsible for the costs; however, fees in criminal cases are only assessed if the conviction is affirmed on appeal and the appellant is not indigent.

Some appellate courts—such as the U.S. courts of appeals and intermediate appellate courts in the states—have **mandatory jurisdiction**, meaning that they must decide cases appealed to them from lower courts. Other courts—such as the U.S. Supreme Court and typically (but not always) the highest court in each state—have **discretionary jurisdiction**, meaning that they can choose which cases they wish to review from among the cases appealed to them. Whether courts have mandatory or discretionary jurisdiction is most often determined by legislative statute. For example, Congress passed the Judges Bill of 1925 relieving the U.S. Supreme Court of much of its mandatory jurisdiction.[16] In the several decades before this law was enacted, the Court regularly heard 200 to 300 cases each term but, in subsequent years, the justices have decided 150 or fewer cases on average.[17] In other words, the myth that everyone is entitled to take his or her case to the Supreme Court is at odds with the statutory reality that it is the Court that will decide whether any individual case appealed to it will be heard or not.

The jurisdiction of the U.S. courts of appeals is likewise determined by Congress and is also governed by legislative statute.[18] Whereas the Supreme Court's jurisdiction is discretionary, the courts of appeals' jurisdiction is almost entirely mandatory. When it comes to state appellate courts, courts of last resort in states that have intermediate appellate courts usually have dockets that are largely (but not exclusively) discretionary, while courts of last resort in states that do not have intermediate appellate courts typically have dockets that are largely mandatory. This makes sense because the commonly understood right to an appeal is presumably handled by the intermediate appellate court, thereby freeing up the court of last resort to select cases for adjudication that have broader legal, political, social, or economic implications, as is the case for the U.S. Supreme Court. As a point of comparison, more than 82 percent of the cases handled by state intermediate appellate courts fall under mandatory jurisdiction compared with only 17 percent of the cases handled by state courts of last resort.[19]

When the appellate court in question has a discretionary rather than a mandatory docket, the first hurdle for an appellant is convincing the court that it should, in fact, accept the case for review. This means that the appellant must file a request for a hearing, which can take different forms depending upon the appellate court. For example, in the U.S. Supreme Court and some state courts, this request is made through a petition for a **writ of *certiorari*.**[20] In some appellate courts (including the U.S. Supreme Court), it takes only a minority of the justices to agree to grant a request for a hearing. In most states, however, a majority of the judges must agree for such a request to be granted.[21] When an appeal is denied, the appellate court makes no ruling on the substance of the case and the lower court ruling stands as is; it is not, however, the equivalent of the appellate court affirming the lower court ruling. The lower court ruling remains standing and has full force and effect, but it has not been given the *imprimatur* of the highest court for that jurisdiction (i.e., U.S. Supreme Court or state supreme court).

Whether an appellate court is required to review a case because it has mandatory jurisdiction or that court has elected to do so under its discretionary jurisdiction, once the case is on a court's decision **docket**—the set of cases awaiting action—the main task of the lawyers representing the litigants in the case is the preparation of the legal briefs. Though some of the specifics vary, depending upon the jurisdiction, a litigant's brief usually begins with a statement of the reasons for the appeal. A brief also lists the relevant facts and provides the legal basis (including reference to the appropriate legal authorities such as statutes and legal precedents) for reversing or modifying the trial court decision.[22]

Legal briefs may also contain other information that the attorneys think is relevant to the case. For example, several years before he became a Supreme Court justice, then-attorney Louis Brandeis submitted a famous brief in the case of *Muller v. Oregon* (1908)[23] that was almost entirely based on medical, psychological, and sociological evidence in support of his argument on behalf of the state to uphold the law being challenged.[24] Indeed, the brief that Brandeis submitted was almost entirely devoted to that type of information and thin, at best, on law and citations to precedential cases. Though this brief was not the first to include such arguments,[25] it was unique in its almost singular focus on that kind of argument and, hence, this type of brief has become known as the **Brandeis brief**. Its technique of supplementing legal argument with broader information has now become standard practice in contemporary appellate litigation.[26]

When we think of a court, no doubt, we think of the primary objective as being the resolution of the case at hand, a resolution of the dispute between the parties on either side of a case. Given that the dispute is between those parties, we might assume that the only briefs that are relevant for the resolution of the dispute are those of the direct litigants in the case. The reality, however, is that the disposition of a given appellate case may have ramifications that extend beyond the direct litigants—and, in fact, if the case

Image 9.3 Louis
Brandeis
*Attorney Louis Brandeis's
legal briefs emphasized
medical, psychological,
and sociological evidence
to support his legal
positions in appellate
cases. His approach
became so well known
and influential that the
term "Brandeis Brief"
was subsequently used to
describe a legal brief that
stressed non-legal facts.*
George Grantham Bain
Collection, Prints and
Photographs Division,
Library of Congress,
Washington, D.C.

is being heard by an appellate court with discretionary jurisdiction, it is virtually certain that the case does have such broader ramification. Accordingly, in addition to the litigant briefs, there may also be briefs submitted by third parties to the case. These third-party briefs are called ***amicus curiae* briefs**, or *amicus* briefs for short. The literal translation of *amicus curiae* is "friend of the court." Such briefs were originally filed by third parties with no stake in the outcome of a case, but whose expertise regarding the issues involved would be of value for a court.[27] There is no doubt that now, however, *amicus* briefs are intended to be tools of advocacy whose purpose is to persuade a court to rule in favor of the litigant supported by the group.

In one recent example, Judicial Watch, a conservative organization with the stated mission of promoting transparency and accountability in government, filed an *amicus* brief in the Pennsylvania Supreme Court case of *Applewhite v. Pennsylvania*.[28] Judicial Watch's brief was filed to buttress the position of the Pennsylvania legislators who initiated and supported a state voter ID law. The primary argument made in the brief was that the voter ID law was intended to ensure the integrity of the electoral process (not disenfranchise voters) and was well within the parameters of legislative authority under the state constitution.[29]

Another recent example is the *amicus curiae* brief filed by the American Civil Liberties Union and ACLU of Virginia in *Bland v. Roberts*, a case heard in the U.S. Court of Appeals for the Fourth Circuit.[30] *Bland* involved a question of whether "liking" something on Facebook constitutes a form of speech protected by the First Amendment. Sheriff B.J.

Roberts fired several employees of the Sheriff's Department in Hampton, Virginia, for having "liked" and posted comments on the Facebook page of Roberts's opponent in the previous election. The *amici* argued that such activity is protected both as pure and symbolic speech, and that internet speech should enjoy the same protection under the First Amendment as more traditional forms of speech.[31]

In these illustrative examples, rather than serving as neutral providers of expertise and information, both Judicial Watch and the American Civil Liberties Union (in conjunction with the ACLU of Virginia) were clearly using their *amicus* briefs to advocate for particular litigants to prevail in their respective cases. Hence, the myth that an appeal's significance is limited to its importance to the direct litigants is in contrast with the reality that an appeal—or more accurately, the disposition of an appeal—often matters enough for interested third parties that they, too, weigh in via *amicus* briefs, hoping to influence the appellate court to rule the way they would prefer.

Whether *amicus* briefs are allowed depends, like so much else in the appellate process, on the particular court. The rules for filing an *amicus* brief in the federal courts are not especially oncrous.[32] Potential *amici* are directed by Supreme Court Rule 37 and the Federal Rules of Appellate Procedure (FRAP) to secure the permission of both direct parties in the case to file an *amicus* brief. If that permission is not forthcoming, however, a potential *amicus* can seek the permission of the court in question to file. Generally speaking, federal courts have been generous in granting that permission, though some federal judges have expressed reservations about how useful *amicus* briefs are.[33] As we will discuss in greater detail in Chapter Ten, it is rare for a U.S. Supreme Court case *not* to include an *amicus* brief (with upwards of 90 percent of cases having at least one *amicus* brief); it is a much less common phenomenon in the U.S. courts of appeals (with less than 10 percent of cases having at least one *amicus* brief).[34]

In terms of *amici* in state appellate courts, virtually all state courts of last resort and most intermediate appellate courts have provisions for the submission of *amici*; however, the restrictiveness of the rules for their participation varies considerably.[35] For example, permission of the court is an absolute requirement in some states but neither the permission of the direct parties nor the permission of the court is required in others. In some jurisdictions, the appellate court can actually invite *amici* to file a brief. According to one recent study, California, Georgia, Oklahoma, and Texas have the most restrictive rules governing the filing of *amicus* briefs, while Kansas, Hawaii, Nebraska, and Wyoming have the least restrictive rules.[36] In terms of how common *amicus* participation in state appellate courts is, the states vary considerably on that dimension as well. Political scientists Paul Brace and Kelly Butler, for example, found that a third of all states had *amicus* participation in less than 5 percent of their cases, while in another five states (California, Michigan, New Jersey, Oklahoma, and Oregon) more than a quarter of all cases included *amicus* participation.[37]

The case may go no further than this stage of the process for two primary reasons. First, the litigants may decide to settle the case. As at the trial stage, at the appellate stage settlement may become attractive to the litigants as the legal expenses continue to mount. Litigants might also come to prefer settlement to shorten the timeframe for resolving the dispute, both as a means of reducing legal costs and for its own sake given the stress ongoing litigation induces. The appeal of settlement might loom larger, too, as each side gains more information about the strengths and weaknesses of one another's arguments and the predictability of a settlement trumps waiting for a final disposition from the appellate court. In extreme cases, the appellant may simply decide to withdraw the appeal. Some appellate courts are actively engaged in encouraging parties to settle. For example, the Michigan Court of Appeals Pre-Argument Settlement Program uses mediators to facilitate settlements in general civil matters (e.g., labor relations, medical malpractice) and domestic relations matters (e.g., child custody, asset division for divorce).[38] The Federal Rules of Appellate Procedure also encourage settlement: "The court may direct the attorneys—and, when appropriate, the parties—to participate in one or more conferences to address any matter that may aid in disposing of the proceedings, including simplifying the issues and discussing settlement."[39]

Second, the appellate court may choose to dismiss the case. There are two types of dismissal: **dismissal with prejudice** and **dismissal without prejudice**. Dismissal with prejudice means that the court terminates the appeal and bars the appellant from appealing the same case in the future. This is a drastic remedy and is generally reserved for the most egregious cases of an appellant's obstruction of (or noncompliance with) the appellate process; for example, delay intended to prejudice the appellee's case. Dismissal without prejudice means that the court terminates the appeal but the appellant may refile the appeal. This is typically as a result of procedural errors that do not significantly affect the rights of the appellant. Dismissal without prejudice is tantamount to the appeal never having commenced at all. Dismissal without prejudice is more common in civil than in criminal appeals because of constitutional safeguards for criminal defendants (e.g., the Double Jeopardy Clause of the Fifth Amendment).

Assuming that the case is neither settled nor dismissed, the appellate court may be called upon next to rule on a variety of motions brought by the litigants. For example, a litigant may make a motion to be released from prison pending the outcome of her criminal appeal. Or, a litigant may make a motion requesting an extension for the submission of supplemental documents that have been requested. After any such motions have been handled, the next stage of the appellate process is **oral argument**, though not all appellate cases involve oral argument. Some cases are disposed of based solely on the briefs filed by the attorneys. For example, during the 2011 term of the U.S. Supreme Court, the justices heard oral arguments in 79 cases but reviewed and decided another 137 cases without oral argument.[40] For the 12-month period ending September 20, 2012, the U.S. courts of appeals collectively disposed of 7,115 cases after oral argument and an additional 27,980 cases after the submission of briefs.[41]

One myth is that oral argument is merely an opportunity for the attorneys representing the litigants to verbally present the arguments they made in their written briefs. It is true that attorneys try to convince the judges of the soundness of their legal arguments during oral argument. But the reality is that oral argument functions as more than that. The questions that the judges ask at oral argument not only help them make up their own minds but also raise issues that they want the other judges to consider.[42] Judges might even speak more often than attorneys in appellate proceedings! In this sense, appellate judges engage in a kind of dialogue through the intermediaries of attorneys.[43] What is communicated through this dialogue between and among the judges can later play a key role in shaping the voting coalitions and, ultimately, the content of the written opinion.[44] Further, it is routine for appellate attorneys to be repeatedly interrupted by judges asking questions. As a result, attorneys prepare for oral argument not by practicing a set speech (e.g., the oral recitation of the arguments appearing in the written briefs) but, instead, by developing answers to the potential questions that judges may ask. This includes questions about the current case, past cases that might be relevant, and hypothetical situations that are similar to the current case but also differ in important ways.

The Practitioner's Guide to the U.S. Court of Appeals for the Fifth Circuit's very practical advice for oral argument includes such pragmatic suggestions as: emphasize "the case's strongest point and the opponent's weaknesses," "try to relax, speak clearly and slowly," and avoid making personal attacks.[45] Justice Samuel Alito, who sat on the U.S. Court of Appeals for the Third Circuit for 16 years before being appointed to the Supreme Court, offered this less formal advice: "It's important to have a feel for the particular tribunal before which you are to appeal," to familiarize yourself with the judges' 'zone of persuasion,' and be flexible enough to adapt to the "signals and vibes you get as to what's working during argument."[46]

Ultimately, the judges go behind closed doors to vote on the case and write opinions deciding the appeal, with a majority vote of the judges determining the outcome. In the U.S. Supreme Court, for example, the justices meet in a private conference—which Justice Frankfurter referred to as "the workshop of the living constitution"[47]—to discuss the cases on which they are adjudicating and to take a preliminary vote as to their dispositions. How opinions are assigned varies across appellate courts. In the U.S. Supreme Court, the most senior justice in the majority vote coalition assigns the opinion. The Chief Justice is defined as the most senior justice so, in practice, this means that the Chief Justice assigns the opinion if he voted with the majority; when the Chief Justice does not vote with the majority, the justice with the longest service on the Court who did vote in the majority makes the assignment.

In the U.S. courts of appeals, the most senior judge on the panel usually makes the assignment, though there are some exceptions. For example, in the U.S. Court of Appeals for the Fourth Circuit, "opinion assignments are made by the Chief Judge on the basis of recommendations from the presiding judge of each panel on which the Chief Judge did not sit."[48] Majority opinion assignment is determined in a variety of ways across state courts of last resort.[49] In some states (e.g., Arkansas, California, Massachusetts, Wisconsin) the chief justice makes the majority opinion assignment. In other states (e.g., Illinois, Maine, Rhode Island, Texas) opinions are assigned on a rotating basis. In yet others, the opinions are assigned on a random basis (e.g., Iowa, Louisiana, New York, Ohio).

Depending on the appellate court, opinion writers may have to undertake multiple revisions in order to secure the signatures of at least a majority of the court.[50] If an opinion writer cannot garner the support of a majority of the court, then the opinion he authors is, by definition, no longer a majority opinion. Majority opinions are not, however, the only opinions that may be associated with the disposition of a given case. Judges on these courts have the prerogative to write separate opinions, if they so desire. A judge may write a **concurring opinion** if she agrees with the outcome (i.e., who wins and who loses) embedded in the majority opinion but does so for reasons that differ from those laid out in the majority opinion or, alternatively, if she agrees with the reasons laid out in the majority opinion but wishes to make a further point or offer what she sees as a necessary clarification. A concurrence that agrees with the majority outcome but for different reasons is a **special concurrence**, while a concurrence that agrees with the majority outcome and for the same reasons is a **regular concurrence**. A judge who disagrees with the majority opinion as to the outcome of the case can choose to write a **dissenting opinion**, which indicates why he disagrees with the majority opinion.

HOW DO WE KNOW?

Do Elected Judges Dissent Strategically?

Political scientist Melinda Gann Hall argues that elected judges, under certain conditions, vote strategically to minimize electoral opposition.[51] Specifically, she expects those justices in elected supreme courts who have preferences contrary to those of their constituents and are in the minority not to distinguish themselves from the rest of the court by dissenting in a case that is salient to the public. "[I]n other words, minority justices should be inclined to join the majority on visible issues, even when their values conflict with their constituencies and the majority on the court."[52] However, she expects only those justices who are fearful of the electorate to disregard their personal preferences. Thus, she expects those in district-based elections, competitive races, and approaching the end of a term to be responsive to their constituents. She also expects justices who have had representational experience to be more responsive to the electorate than those justices who have only served in the judiciary.

Hall gathered data on the characteristics of the justices and the decisions handed down in four state courts of last resort: the Texas Court of Criminal Appeals, the North Carolina Supreme Court, the Louisiana Supreme Court, and the Kentucky Supreme Court. Additionally, she collected voting data on all criminal cases decided during a full term in recent natural courts in order to determine which members of each court were in the ideological minority. A vote in favor of overturning a defendant's sentence or conviction was considered a liberal vote and a vote upholding a defendant's conviction or sentence was classified as a conservative vote. Ten justices were categorized as liberal and thus "likely to find themselves in the difficult position of being incompatible not only with their court majorities but also with their constituencies on criminal issues."[53] Given that public opinion polls conducted in Texas, North Carolina, Louisiana, and Kentucky reveal that the majority of the public favors the death penalty, the author posits that

> [j]ustices who vote liberally in death penalty cases by overturning convictions or sentences are acting inconsistently with the preferences of their constituencies, thereby opening themselves to criticism from angry voters and the possibility of being removed from office through successful challenges of rival candidates. And . . . those justices in the minority who dissent from conservative decisions of the court are placing themselves in particular jeopardy.[54]

Hall then collected information on all non-unanimous death penalty cases decided conservatively in North Carolina, Louisiana, and Kentucky in 1983 through 1988 and in Texas in 1983 through 1986. The dependent variable is dichotomous, with a dissenting vote from a conservative majority court decision coded 0 and a vote with the conservative majority coded 1. Table 9.B1 presents the descriptions for each variable. Table 9.B2 presents the regression results.

TABLE 9.B1
Variable Descriptions

VARIABLE			DESCRIPTION
CAREER	=	1	If vote was cast by a justice with previous representational experience
	=	0	Otherwise
DISTRICT	=	1	If vote was cast by a justice elected from a single-member district
	=	0	Otherwise
FIRSTTERM	=	1	If vote was cast by a justice serving a first term
	=	0	Otherwise
LASTTWO	=	1	If vote was cast by a justice in the last 2 years of a term
	=	0	Otherwise
MAJVOTE	=	1	If vote is with the majority
	=	0	Otherwise
MARGIN	=		Percentage of the vote won in the preceding election by the justice casting the judicial vote

TABLE 9.B2
Probit Estimation of an Electoral Model of Judicial Voting Behavior

VARIABLE	B	STD. ERROR	T
MARGIN	−0.0165	0.0093	−1.7768**
DISTRICT	1.3592	0.2586	5.2571***
LASTTWO	0.5629	0.2962	1.9004**
CAREER	0.3375	0.2632	1.2822*
FIRSTTERM	−0.6301	0.2989	−2.1082**

Constant = .0219
Mean of the dependent variable = 30.3
Percent categorized correctly = 78.2
Reduction in error = 28 percent
Approximate Chi-Square = 32.77 ($p < .001$)
Estimated R^2 = .26
N = 175
*Significant at .10, one-tailed test; **significant at .05, one-tailed test; and ***significant at .0005, one-tailed test.

"As hypothesized, voting with the majority in conservative death penalty cases is associated with a district-based electoral system, obtaining a smaller percentage of the vote in the election preceding the decision, being in the last two years of a term, having prior representational experience, and having participated in judicial reelection campaigns."[55] This leads Hall to conclude that state supreme court justices assume a representational posture under some restricted circumstances.

While there has been much effort devoted to explaining the patterns of separate opinion writing observed in the U.S. Supreme Court—which we will discuss in greater detail in Chapter Ten—there is also a body of scholarship (albeit a smaller one) that takes separate opinion writing in the lower appellate courts as its explanatory focus. With regard to state courts of last resort, most of the scholarly attention has been paid to understanding patterns of dissenting behavior. One consistent finding has been that dissenting behavior across state courts of last resort is by no means rare but it is also not the norm.[56] Several scholars—most notably political scientists Melinda Hall and Paul Brace—have argued that dissenting behavior by judges on state courts of last resort is governed by judges' strategic calculations. For example, there is systematic evidence that indicates judges who are elected are attentive to the preferences of the electorate and, as a consequence are much less likely to dissent from the majority in controversial cases, lest they make themselves stand out and more vulnerable to attack come (re)election time (see How Do We Know? on p. 342–343).[57] Analyses of dissent in state courts of last resort also demonstrate that state supreme courts with more discretionary dockets have greater levels of dissent (presumably because the kinds of cases those courts are selecting are the kinds of cases for which there is no obvious answer), and that those with higher workloads have lower levels of dissent (presumably because workload pressures limit the time available to judges to craft dissents).[58]

At least some scholars who have investigated separate opinions in the U.S. courts of appeals have likewise found that workload pressures decrease the incidence of dissents (and concurrences).[59] Other factors that help to structure separate opinion writing on the courts of appeals include the presence of *amicus curiae* briefs and whether the court of appeals decision is reversing the lower court ruling. In each case, both concurrence and dissent are more likely. Political scientist Virginia Hettinger and her colleagues argued that the presence of *amici* makes separate opinions more likely because the rarity of *amici* in courts of appeals cases means they are good indicators of a case's salience, and salient cases are the kind of cases that might prompt a judge to take the time and energy to write a separate opinion.[60] As to lower court reversal, the fact that the court of appeals decision is reversing a lower court decision suggests that there is ambiguity about the resolution "because it represents a situation in which presumably reasonable federal judges [first the trial court judge and then the panel of appellate court judges], considering the same case, have come to different conclusions as to its appropriate resolution."[61]

Analysis of separate opinion writing (dissent, in particular) in the courts of appeals has also found that some characteristics of individual judges are influential in understanding when separate opinions are more likely. For example, scholars have found that chief judges and new judges (so-called "freshman judges") are both less likely to dissent from the majority. They argue that chief judges are less likely to dissent because their institutional role as head of a court makes them more "concerned that separate opinions have the potential to fray collegial relations within the circuit."[62] As for freshman judges, the fact that they are less likely to dissent has been attributed to their "unfamiliarity with the work of a circuit court judge and deference to senior colleagues."[63]

OBSTACLES TO APPEAL

The fact that there is, at least theoretically, an opportunity for every litigant to have not only one but two chances to be heard—at trial and on appeal—comports nicely with our normative ideas of justice and our cherished image of each individual being equal under the law. Not only does a litigant enjoy the right to have his dispute decided by an impartial arbiter (the trial court judge), she also enjoys the right to have the decision of that impartial arbiter reviewed by another set of impartial arbiters (the panel of appellate court judges). The reality of the appeals process, however, is at odds with this myth because there are two significant obstacles that militate against pursuing an appeal: the cost of an appeal and the likelihood of prevailing on appeal.

First, most litigants are discouraged from appealing because they must expend considerable additional financial resources beyond what they have already paid for their trial. Attorney fees, in particular, can add up quickly, especially if an attorney is billing on an hourly rate rather than on a contingency basis (or the less common flat rate). However, there are also any number of other costs that can drain an appellant's resources before the appeal has really gotten under way, including the previously discussed filing fees and fees for the preparation of the transcript.

To illustrate, in the U.S. Court of Appeals for the Tenth Circuit, the fee for docketing an appeal is $450.[64] There is also a fee of $26 for every search of the court records and certification of the search results; $9 for the certification of any document; $0.50 per page for reproducing any record or paper; $26 for the reproduction of proceedings; $71 for the reproduction of the record in any appeal in which the requirement of an appendix has been dispensed with by any court of appeals; $5 for each microfiche or microfilm copy of any court record; and $45 for the retrieval of a record from a Federal Records Center, National Archives, or other storage location not at the site of the court.

In addition, litigants are usually responsible for paying the fees to have their attorneys admitted for practice before the appellate court, if their attorneys have not already been admitted before that court. The cost for that in the Tenth Circuit is $200 for each attorney ($150 for the national fee plus $50 for new Tenth Circuit bar memberships). Of course, the litigant is responsible for the costs the attorney incurs in preparing the documents necessary for the appeal. Document preparation can be quite costly, especially in light of the detailed requirements regarding the number of copies, paper color, font size, line spacing, pagination, and paper weight for all primary (e.g., briefs) and ancillary documents (e.g., appendices).

Finally, the appeal bond is one expense that losing defendants must take into account when deciding whether or not to appeal. The defendant who files his notice of appeal within the prescribed period of time must post a **supersedeas bond**, commonly known as an **appeal bond**, to stay or suspend the plaintiff's collection of any amount awarded during appellate review.[65] This bond stays the plaintiff's immediate collection of the judgment, but it also guarantees the plaintiff's ability to collect if the appellate court ultimately affirms her damages verdict because the amount of the bond generally is the amount of judgment (plus interest and costs).[66] In the federal system, the district court has discretion to set a lower bond or to forgo requiring one at all, provided the defendant shows "good cause"—such as liquidity, burden, etc.—for doing so.[67] In some state jurisdictions, however, lower courts have no discretion to reduce the amount of the bond.[68]

For some defendants, providing an appeal bond can be devastating. For example, in *Texaco Inc. v. Pennzoil*,[69] Pennzoil won a $10.5 billion verdict against Texaco.[70] The Texas appeal-bond rule required that Texaco post the entire amount of the judgment, plus interest, to stay the execution of the judgment. Texaco attempted to avoid the appeal-bond requirement; however, it was unsuccessful and Texaco ended up filing for bankruptcy. Because of the automatic stay provisions of the Bankruptcy Code, the bankruptcy filing stayed the execution of the judgment and led to a settlement. Since 2000, 39 states have amended their appeal-bond laws by lowering the bond requirements or otherwise making the securing of an appeal bond less onerous for defendants.[71] For example, in Wyoming, a defendant cannot be required to pay more than $25 million to stay execution of the judgment pending appeal, and businesses with 50 or fewer employees cannot be required to pay more than $2 million.[72] Thus, by making it financially less onerous to appeal, the number of appeals may increase.

Second, the odds of winning on an appeal are very slim. For appellate courts with a discretionary docket, the likelihood that any given request for an appeal is granted is quite low. For example, the U.S. Supreme Court receives upwards of 8,000 petitions seeking review each term but decides less than 200.[73] Perhaps the most common reason given for declining an appeal is because the issues in the case are **fact-bound**, meaning that the appeal lacks significant procedural issues or legal questions of the kind that courts of last resort are charged with reviewing. That is, the disposition of the appeal is tied to the very specific circumstances of the case and, as a consequence, it is not a good vehicle for the articulation of broad legal policies. Appellate courts with mandatory dockets are, by definition, obligated to accept all appeals regardless of their merits. As a consequence, their dockets are disproportionately filled with cases that were correctly decided in the lower court, which is not good news for appellants. Thus, it should be no surprise to find that appellate courts with mandatory dockets affirm the overwhelming majority of their cases. In short, appellants are not likely to be successful in persuading appellate courts with discretionary dockets to accept their appeal and appellants are not likely to be successful in winning on the merits in appellate courts with mandatory dockets. However, research does suggest that litigation resources affect who wins on appeal (see How Do We Know? Do the "Haves" Come Out Ahead on Appeal?).

HOW DO WE KNOW?

Do the "Haves" Come Out Ahead on Appeal?

In "Who Wins on Appeal? Upperdogs and Underdogs in the United States Courts of Appeals," political scientists Songer and Sheehan focus on the litigation resources of the parties who appeal to the United States Courts of Appeals to determine if parties with greater resources have a higher rate of success.[74] They coded the nature of the appellant and respondent, the issue, the party of the judges on each panel, the outcome, and the opinion status (published or unpublished) of all cases during the year 1986 in the Fourth, Seventh, and Eleventh circuits (4,281 cases total).

Appellant and respondent were categorized as follows: individual litigants, businesses, state and local governments, the United States government, or other. They assume that individuals have fewer resources than either businesses or government and that governments and businesses may have the same resources, but that government agencies are more likely to be repeat players and thus they will be more likely to win. They then further classified the appellant and respondent into big business (railroads, banks, manufacturing companies, insurance companies, airlines, and oil companies) or other business and individuals and underdog individuals (poor and racial minorities), and used a 7-point scale with the federal government = 7, state government = 6, local government = 5, big business = 4, other business = 3, individuals = 2, and underdog individuals = 1. They then computed a measure of strength of litigants for each case, which equaled appellant minus respondent. Thus, they expected a positive relationship between litigation strength and the rate of appellant success. The dependent variable in the model is the success of the appellant, coded 1 if the appellant won, 0 otherwise.

Tables 9.B3 and 9.B4 present the logit estimates for published decisions and unpublished decisions.

TABLE 9.B3
Logit Estimates for Appellant Success in Published Decisions

INDEPENDENT VARIABLE	MLE	SE	MLS/SE
Intercept	−0.815	0.342	−2.38
Appellant	0.223	0.047	4.74***
Respondent	−0.081	0.041	−1.98*
Economic	−0.217	0.203	−1.07
Criminal	−0.619	0.210	−2.96**
Civil liberty	−0.456	0.248	−1.84
Diversity	0.207	0.280	0.74
Party effect	0.432	0.139	3.11***
Region	−0.488	0.150	−3.25***

Note: Dependent variable = appellant success, mean = 0.297, model chi-square = 108.24, with $df = 8$, $p < .001$, −2 LLR = 1,300.01.
$N = 1,157$
Proportion predicted correctly = 71.7 percent
Reduction in error = 4.9 percent
*significant at .05; **significant at .01; ***significant at .001.

TABLE 9.B4

Logit Estimates for Appellant Success in Unpublished Decisions

INDEPENDENT VARIABLE	MLE	SE	MLS/SE
Intercept	-2.954	0.344	-8.59
Appellant	0.414	0.064	6.47***
Respondent	-0.034	0.064	-0.69
Economic	-0.187	0.194	-0.96
Criminal	-1.498	0.204	-7.34***
Civil liberty	-0.711	0.275	-2.59**
Diversity	-0.651	0.645	-1.01
Party effect	0.797	0.159	5.05***
Region	-0.312	0.256	-1.21

Note: Dependent variable = appellant success, mean = .097, model chi-square = 153.95, with $df = 8$, $p < .001$, -2 LLR = 1,245.61.
$N = 2,201$
Proportion predicted correctly = 90.3 percent
Reduction in error = 0
*significant at .05; **significant at .01; ***significant at .001.

Even after controlling for the effects of issue, party, and region, the nature of the litigants is still statistically significant, meaning that as the strength of the litigant increases, the litigant is more likely to win. "This suggests that the nature of the litigants has an effect on the probability of appellant success in both published and unpublished decisions that is independent of the nature of the issue in the case, regional influences, and the policy preferences of the judges."[75]

Table 9.B5 presents the estimated probabilities for appellant success for the different types of appellants.

TABLE 9.B5

Estimated Probabilities for Appellant Success for Different Types of Appellants in Published and Unpublished Decisions

INDEX	APPELLANT CATEGORY	PUBLISHED DECISIONS SUCCESS RATE*	UNPUBLISHED DECISIONS SUCCESS RATE*
1	Underdog individuals	.237	.363
2	Other individuals	.343	.597
3	Other business	.468	.794
4	Big business	.593	.908
5	Local government	.708	.962
6	State government	.803	.985
7	U.S. government	.872	.994

*Predicted success with values of all other independent variables in the logit model set at their mean values.

Thus, the authors concluded that the "haves" do come out ahead in the courts of appeals, and arguably this is because of their superior litigation resources.

Yet losing litigants still appeal. Why? The obvious reason is that losers want to win. As Judge Richard Posner put it: "[E]veryone prefers winning to losing and winning big to winning small."[76] Indeed, that premise has informed the debate over how best to manage the ever-increasing number of appeals, including proposals to further increase the costs of appeals and slow down the appellate process to dissuade litigants from appealing unless the stakes are very high.[77]

But the answer is more complex than that. Political scientist Scott Barclay suggests that the key to understanding the decision to appeal is appreciating the fact that individuals who appeal are primarily concerned with being treated fairly. Based on interviews with litigants in civil cases, Barclay argues that litigants value fair treatment more than whether they win or lose: " [I]ndividuals are less interested in winning their cases than we have been traditionally led to believe. Instead . . . litigants are motivated primarily by the desire to be treated fairly."[78] For litigants, it is the process that matters more than the outcome. Perceived bias at the trial level—and perceived fairness at the appellate level—prompts losers to appeal. This may explain why, despite the obstacles facing losing litigants, appellate courts have remained steadily busy over the last decade.

APPELLATE COURT WORKLOADS AND OUTCOMES

As is true with regard to trial cases, the vast majority of appellate cases in the United States are adjudicated in the state courts. Since the 1980s, state appellate courts have been handling over 200,000 cases year.[79] Specifically, there were 273,000 appellate cases for 2009, a slight decrease of 6 percent since 2000.[80] Interestingly, the caseload decline was 14 percent at the intermediate appellate court level and only 2 percent for courts of last resort. The decline is even more interesting when one considers that state trial court civil caseloads have increased 10 percent over the same time period.[81] It would appear that the obstacles to appeal have only gotten more difficult to overcome!

Of course individual states have widely different appellate caseloads, which is usually attributable to differences in their populations. For example, Wyoming had only 265 appellate cases in 2009 compared with 33,300 in California. As reported in Table 9.1, when controlling for population, Louisiana has the highest level of appeals (22.9 appeals per 10,000 residents), followed by Florida, Pennsylvania, Oregon, and Ohio. On the other end of the spectrum are North Carolina, Rhode Island, Connecticut, Idaho, and South Dakota with less than 5 appeals per 10,000 residents. Given that there were 106 million cases in state trial courts in 2009, and only one quarter of 1 percent of them reached the appellate level, it is plain that appeals are extremely rare when considering the total volume of trial court decisions. Even if one excludes the large number of cases processed in courts of limited jurisdiction (involving relatively minor matters such as traffic offenses, misdemeanor criminal matters, and small claims), appealed cases still amount to less than 1 percent of the most serious matters.[82] Plainly, the notion that most losing litigants appeal their cases is a myth, not a reality.

In terms of winners and losers, research demonstrates that the vast majority of state trial court losers who appeal lose yet again in the appellate court: more than two-thirds of civil appeals and more than three-fourths of criminal appeals result in the lower court ruling being affirmed.[83] That is, appellants (the lower court losers) are much less likely to prevail than appellees (the lower court winners). But, contrary to the myth that all lower court losers are created equal, the reality is that some lower court losers are advantaged relative to others. According to a study conducted by law professors Theodore Eisenberg and Michael Heise, defendants who lose in civil trials prevail on appeal 42 percent of

TABLE 9.1

Five Highest and Five Lowest Incoming Appeals per Capita States, 2009

STATE	NUMBER OF INCOMING APPEALS	POPULATION (10,000s)	INCOMING APPEALS PER 10,000 RESIDENTS
Highest			
Louisiana	10,275	449	22.9
Florida	28,648	1,853	15.5
Pennsylvania	15,843	1,260	12.6
Oregon	4,520	383	11.8
Ohio	13,081	1,154	11.3
Lowest			
South Dakota	391	81	4.8
Idaho	706	155	4.6
Connecticut	1,416	352	4.0
Rhode Island	366	105	3.5
North Carolina	3,185	938	3.4

Note: Mississippi was not included in the rankings because incoming appeals for 2009 were not reported by the State of Mississippi to the National Center for State Courts.

Sources: Robert C. LaFountain, Richard Y. Schauffler, Shauna M. Strickland, Sarah A. Gibson, and Ashley N. Mason, *Examining the Work of State Courts: An Analysis of 2009 State Court Caseloads* (Williamsburg, VA: National Center for State Courts, 2011): 40; United States, *Statistical Abstract of the United States*, 2010 (Washington, DC: GPO, 2010), Table 12.

the time as compared to a 22 percent appellate success rate for plaintiffs.[84] So, while it is true that both an appellant who was the defendant at trial and an appellant who was the plaintiff at trial are likely to lose on appeal, the former's chances at prevailing are much better than the latter's. Eisenberg and Heise's analysis suggests that this difference is due to appellate judges' perception that trial-level adjudicators are biased in favor of plaintiffs. This may also explain why jury trial verdicts are reversed 34 percent of the time compared with only 28 percent for judge trials.[85]

The type of case also matters for understanding winners and losers in state appellate courts. Defendants win the most on appeal in cases involving professional malpractice (75 percent), assault, slander, and libel (73 percent), and employment contract disputes (62 percent). In comparison, the best chance that losing plaintiffs have of winning on appeal comes in cases involving employment contracts (39 percent) and product liability (38 percent).[86] Though recent and reliable data on criminal appeals in the states is difficult to come by,[87] it is clear that the likelihood of reversal on appeal is even smaller in criminal appeals than in civil appeals. For example, one study of criminal appeals in California found a reversal rate of less than 5 percent.[88] In another study of criminal appeals in Louisiana, the author reported that only 15 percent of cases were either reversed or remanded.[89]

At the federal level, the number of appeals cases has changed dramatically in the past 6 decades. In 1955, there were less than 5,000 cases in the U.S. courts of appeals, while today there are more than 50,000.[90] Despite this dramatic shift from the mid-1950s to the mid-2000s, in the very recent past the U.S. courts of appeals have experienced a slight decline in the number of cases filed, as can be seen in Figure 9.1. This mirrors the slight decline experienced in state appellate courts. Table 9.2 provides an overview of how the courts of appeals have fared with regard to their caseload over the last decade in relation to the trial courts. During the same period that the U.S. courts of appeals experienced a more than 4

FIGURE 9.1

Number of Cases Filed in the U.S. Courts of Appeals, 1993–2012

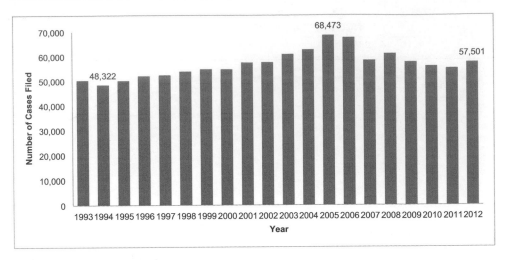

Source: Administrative Office of the United States Courts, *Annual Report of the Director: Judicial Business of the United States Courts* (Washington, DC: GPO, various years).

TABLE 9.2

Change in the Number of Cases Filed Across Lower Federal Courts, 2002–2011

	2002	2007	2010	2011	PERCENT CHANGE SINCE 2002
Courts of Appeals	57,555	58,410	55,992	55,126	–4.2
District Courts—Criminal	88,354	89,306	100,366	102,931	+16.5
District Courts—Civil	274,841	257,507	282,895	289,252	+5.2
Bankruptcy Courts	1,547,669	801,269	1,596,355	1,467,221	–5.2

Note: Cases involving post-conviction supervision and pretrial services have been excluded, as have cases from the U.S. Court of Appeals for the Federal Circuit.

Source: Administrative Office of the United States Courts, *Annual Report of the Director: Judicial Business of the United States Courts* (Washington, DC: GPO, 2011).

percent *decrease* in the number of cases filed (2002–2011), there was a more than 16 percent *increase* in criminal appeals and a more than 5 percent *increase* in civil appeals filed in the U.S. district courts. As is the case in state courts, there are more trial court cases filed at the same time that there are fewer appellate court cases filed in the federal judiciary.

Figure 9.2 provides insight into the origination of appeals in the U.S. courts of appeals. As Figure 9.2 makes clear, the vast majority of cases appealed to the U.S. courts of appeals come from the U.S. district courts (more than four-fifths of the over 53,000 appeals filed in 2012), with a much smaller proportion coming from federal administrative agencies and bankruptcy proceedings. As Figure 9.3 shows, the largest proportion of appeals originating in the U.S. district courts are civil prisoner petitions, followed by criminal appeals, and private civil appeals. Civil prisoner petitions most often allege civil rights violations (e.g., related to the conditions of imprisonment) or seek a writ of *habeas corpus* (i.e., challenging the legality of their imprisonment and requesting an order to be released).

FIGURE 9.2

Number and Sources of Appeals for the U.S. Courts of Appeals, 2012

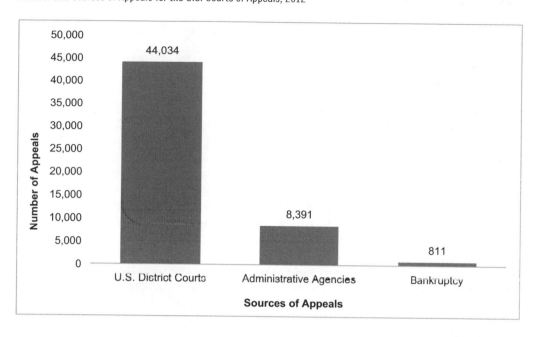

Source: Administrative Office of the United States Courts, *Annual Report of the Director: Judicial Business of the United States Courts* (Washington, DC: GPO, 2012): Table 2.

FIGURE 9.3

Types of Appeals from the U.S. District Courts to the U.S. Courts of Appeals, 2012

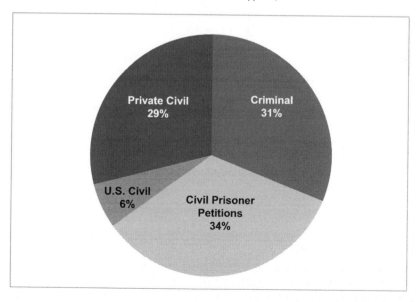

Source: Administrative Office of the United States Courts, *Annual Report of the Director: Judicial Business of the United States Courts* (Washington, DC: GPO, 2012): Table 2.

Concerns over the seemingly ever-increasing rate of such petitions and the resulting workload pressures on the courts have spurred legislative efforts to curtail them. The Prison Litigation Reform Act (PLRA) of 1996 and the Antiterrorism and Effective Death Penalty Act (AEDPA) also of 1996 were targeted at reducing civil rights petitions by state and federal prison inmates and *habeas corpus* petitions filed by state prison inmates, respectively.[91] Despite such legislation, however, these kinds of petitions still comprise a significant proportion of the docket of the U.S. courts of appeals.

Of the criminal appeals, virtually all were appeals brought by defendants who lost at trial, with a very small number of government and cross appeals. Three out of five were sentencing appeals while another two out of five were appeals of conviction only.[92] The remainder of criminal appeals consists primarily of so-called **Anders** briefs. In *Anders v. California*, the U.S. Supreme Court determined that, when a court-appointed attorney files a motion to withdraw from a criminal appeal because she believes the grounds for appeal are frivolous, that motion must be accompanied by a brief that outlines the case and the potential grounds for appeal.[93] The Court further determined that the appellate court is obligated to independently review the case before the motion is granted. If it is granted, then the defendant must be accorded the opportunity to be represented by a different attorney or represent himself *pro se*. After civil prisoner petitions and criminal appeals, private civil appeals (e.g., tort cases) constitute the next largest proportion of cases on the U.S. courts of appeals docket of those that originated in the U.S. district courts, with a much smaller number of cases involving the U.S. government as a litigant.[94]

Overall, appeals from administrative agencies—mostly from the Board of Immigration Appeals, but also from the Environmental Protection Agency and the National Labor Relations Board—constituted 11 percent of the total cases filed in the courts of appeals in 2012.[95] Original proceedings took up 7 percent of the total docket while bankruptcy appeals were only 1 percent. In terms of change over time, cases originating in the courts of appeals showed the only real increase (5.3 percent) while criminal (−4.7 percent) and administrative agency (−3.4 percent) appeals decreased. Why the decline? Appeals related to non-marijuana drugs decreased as fewer prisoners sought shorter sentences for crack cocaine offenses and fewer appeals came from the Board of Immigration Appeals.

TABLE 9.3
Overall Sentencing Disposition Rates for Federal Sentencing Appeals, 2011

	NUMBER	PERCENT
Affirmed	4,360	74.2
Dismissed	752	12.8
Reversed	479	8.2
Affirmed in Part/Reversed in Part[a]	185	3.2
Remanded Only[b]	99	1.7
Total	5,875	100

Source: U.S. Sentencing Commission, 2011 Annual Report (http://www.ussc.gov/Research_and_Statistics/Annual_Reports_and_Sourcebooks/2011/ar11toc.htm): 41.
[a] Of the 185 sentencing appeals affirmed in part/reversed in part, the appellate courts remanded 162 (87.6 percent) to the district courts for further action.
[b] Sentencing appeals remanded to the lower courts without vacating the original sentence.

In terms of outcomes, research shows that at the federal level—as is true at the state level—the vast majority of appealed cases simply uphold the lower court decision, and it is even more difficult to win on appeal at the federal level than it is in the states.[96] Table 9.3 shows the overall disposition rates for federal sentencing appeals. For the vast majority of cases the trial court's sentence remained in place. Only 8 percent of federal criminal sentences are overturned on appeal. This is not surprising given that criminal defendants encounter fewer obstacles to appeal than do civil litigants, primarily because criminal defendants do not have to pay for their appeal so there is little reason *not* to appeal. Also consistent with state-level findings, the type of litigant matters for success in reversing a trial outcome. Federal civil defendants who appeal after losing their trial prevail 33 percent of the time as compared to a 12 percent success rate on appeal for civil plaintiffs.[97] Research suggests that the success rate for defendants on appeal results from appellate judges' misperceptions that both trial judges and juries are pro-plaintiff.[98] This is particularly true of juries and may explain why federal jury verdicts are more likely to be reversed on appeal than are verdicts rendered by judges.[99]

For federal criminal cases, while defendants regularly lose on appeal, when the federal government appeals a criminal sentence—which only happened 53 times in 2011—it wins 77 percent of the time.[100] In terms of offender characteristics, the demographic profile of those who appeal differs from the demographic profile of all those who are originally sentenced. In 2011, federal defendants were 50 percent Hispanic, 26 percent white, and 20 percent African American. Yet of those who appealed their sentences, 41 percent were African American, 31 percent Hispanic, and 25 percent white.[101] Applying what we know about why individuals appeal, we can conclude that African Americans are more likely than other racial groups to feel that their trials and sentences were unjust, unfair, and biased.

JUDICIAL POLICY MAKING

In theory, an appeal is designed to catch legal errors that may occur in trials.[102] Although appellate courts catch some errors, correcting trial mistakes is not what makes them important, except, of course, for the immediate litigants in a case! Instead, appealed cases create opportunities for appellate courts to make broader policies. In short, contrary to the myth of the judiciary as the mere interpreter of law, appellate courts are forums to make and remake the law. Consider the Supreme Court's decision in *Brown v. Board of Education*.[103] Kansas state law mandated racial segregation in public schooling.[104] In *Brown*, the justices unanimously ruled that separate educational facilities are inherently unequal and, therefore, in violation of the Fourteenth Amendment's Equal Protection Clause. The *Brown* decision effectively changed education policy in the United States. No longer were state and local governments legally permitted to enact and enforce laws that segregated students on the basis of race.[105]

State appellate courts, too, participate in policy making. For example, though the U.S. Supreme Court declined to find that education was a fundamental right under the federal constitution—and, hence, declined to find that disparities in school funding within a state give rise to a federal constitutional issue[106]—numerous state courts of last resort have engaged in school-funding policy making.[107] They have done so through the interpretation of their own state constitutions and statutes. In the process, they have single-handedly instituted significant reforms in school financing. As political scientists Robert Howard and Amy Steigerwalt observe, "state legislatures were not acting, nor was the federal court system offering any relief. The courts, by utilizing their state constitutions, were able to move state educational finance policy and help minimize the level

Image 9.4 Colored
School
*Appellate courts pro-
vide opportunities for
judicial policy mak-
ing: changing the law
through litigation. Ra-
cially segregated public
schools such as this "colored school" in Antho-
ston, Henderson County,
Kentucky (photographed
in 1919) were declared
unconstitutional by the
U.S. Supreme Court
in* Brown v. Board
of Education *(1954).*
Prints and Photographs
Division, Library of
Congress, Washington,
D.C.

of inequality in educational opportunity for children."[108] The myth is that courts do not engage in policy making but the reality is that they very much are engaged in that process.

When it comes to policy making in general, it is hardly a novel or shocking claim to say that interest groups attempt to influence the policy-making process and that they expend considerable resources to do so. Citizens see interest group influence as ubiquitous in the policy-making process and bemoan the seemingly unfettered access lobbyists have to policymakers. But the policymakers who typically come to mind are legislators having private meetings in their congressional offices or presidential candidates mingling with lobbyists at expensive and exclusive fundraising events, not judges. However, because appellate courts can and do make policy through their resolution of cases, interest groups—from across the ideological spectrum—expend considerable resources not only in the legislative and executive arenas but in the judicial arena as well. The myth may be of a judiciary being above the fray of the competing interests that buffet the "political" branches, but the reality is that interest groups see the courts as targets of opportunity for the pursuit of their goals as well.[109] There are four primary ways in which organized interests can influence the judicial policy-making process. They can identify potential litigants, file legal briefs in court, publicize issues in the broader political environment, and (sometimes) win cases that change the law and lay the groundwork for future policy development in the larger political environment.[110] We discuss each of these in turn.

First, interest groups identify potential litigants to initiate litigation in order to challenge a law. A group can bring suit on its own behalf, of course, but only if it can demonstrate that it has **standing** to do so. This requires the group to demonstrate that it is directly injured, something that is often difficult to do and which makes the identification of litigants who already do have standing usually more appealing.[111] For example, the NAACP, first under the leadership of Charles Hamilton Houston and later his protégé,

Image 9.5 NAACP
Litigants
*Interest groups attempt
to influence the policy-
making process through
litigation which begins
by identifying ideal
plaintiffs to bring legal
challenges. This 1964
photograph shows the
plaintiffs selected by the
NAACP in their success-
ful litigation strategy
against racial segrega-
tion in public schools:
Linda Brown Smith,
Ethel Louise Belton
Brown, Harry Briggs,
Jr., and Spottswood
Bolling, Jr.* New York
World-Telegram and
the Sun Newspaper
Photograph Collection,
Prints and Photographs
Division, Library of
Congress, Washington,
D.C.

Thurgood Marshall, routinely worked with local organizations to identify ideal plaintiffs
to bring legal challenges to racial segregation laws.[112] Robert A. Levy, a fellow at the Cato
Institute (a libertarian think tank), sought to replicate Marshall's approach.[113] Using his
fortune from a financial investment software company that he founded and later sold,
Levy self-financed a campaign to have the U.S. Supreme Court declare an individual right
to own a gun (rather than merely a right to own a gun in connection with a well-regulated
militia) under the Second Amendment to the Constitution. Levy partnered with Clark
M. Neily of the Institute for Justice (a libertarian public interest law firm) to find the best
plaintiffs they could to begin their litigation strategy. They scoured Washington, D.C.,
to identify the most diverse set of people who had a legitimate and appealing reason for
having a gun at home for self-defense that they could find. Levy explained the process:

> We wanted gender diversity. We wanted racial diversity, economic diversity, age di-
> versity. No Looney Tunes. You know, you don't want the guy who just signed up for
> the militia. And no criminal records. You want law-abiding citizens. We called all
> our contacts in the legal community. We looked at the newspapers: Who was writ-
> ing on the subject? Who was sending letters to the editor about gun laws? Friends
> lead you to other friends, and you just keep talking and talking to people, until
> finally you have your clients.[114]

Ultimately, Levy put together a group of six litigants: two African Americans, four whites; three women, three men; from their 20s to their 60s.

Dick Heller was one of the six and it was his last name that became part of the seminal Supreme Court case of *District of Columbia v. Heller*.[115] As Justice Antonin Scalia described Heller in the opening of the majority opinion finding in Heller's (and Levy's) favor, "Respondent Dick Heller is a D.C. special police officer authorized to carry a handgun while on duty at the Thurgood Marshall Judiciary Building. He applied for a registration certificate for a handgun that he wished to keep at home, but the District refused."[116] Heller was indeed an appealing litigant to press for Second Amendment rights and, ultimately, the Court majority found in his favor.[117] Justice Scalia concluded:

> [W]e hold that the District's ban on handgun possession in the home violates the Second Amendment, as does its prohibition against rendering any lawful firearm in the home operable for the purpose of immediate self-defense. Assuming that Heller is not disqualified from the exercise of Second Amendment rights, the District must permit him to register his handgun and must issue him a license to carry it in the home.[118]

In short, Levy and the Cato Institute were not direct parties to the case but played the crucial role in identifying an appealing direct party whose case could advance their goals.[119]

In addition to identifying litigants (and as discussed earlier in this chapter), interest groups submit *amicus curiae* in existing cases to try to influence judicial decisions.[120] One prominent example is the U.S. Supreme Court case of *Grutter v. Bollinger*, in which a then-record number of *amici* were filed (over 100).[121] *Amicus* briefs were filed in this case by more than 75 companies that wanted the Court to sustain affirmative action in higher education—including 3M, American Airlines, Boeing, Coca Cola, Dow Chemical, Nike, Pepsi, and Xerox—as well as by former military leaders and members of the Pennsylvania legislature. In her majority opinion, Justice Sandra Day O'Connor cited those briefs and, indeed, sustained affirmative action in higher education as permissible in order to prepare students to work and live in diverse environments. The Court revisited affirmative action a decade later in *Fisher v. University of Texas*.[122] This time, the justices received 92 *amicus* briefs in that case, 73 of them in favor of the policy.[123] During the 2011 term of the Court, at least one *amicus* brief was filed in 95 percent of the cases and the dispute over the Affordable Care Act (commonly referred to as "Obamacare") drew a record-breaking 136 briefs from interested parties.[124]

An additional means by which interest groups influence the judicial decision-making process is by publicizing the cases they litigate and, therefore, the broader issues with which they are concerned. For example, political scientist Michael McCann documented how litigation surrounding equal pay for men and women raised the public's awareness of the issue, which in turn helped activists mobilize working women for the larger movement.[125] McCann drew from 28 case studies of pay equity struggles, which were selected on the basis of several dimensions—including whether the issue was being disputed at the state or local level and how extensively advocates used litigation. He surveyed and conducted in-depth interviews with an extensive set of pay equity advocates and undertook rigorous content analysis of newspaper coverage of political fights over pay equity. Based on the evidence he amassed, McCann argued that, even if litigants lost in court, the very act of litigating transformed the larger movement's discourse. It did so by providing an understanding of legal rights (and how those rights can be constrained by

Image 9.6 Gay Rights Demonstration
Gay rights demonstration on 34th Street, at the 1976 Democratic National Convention, New York City. Research shows that organized interests, such as the gay rights movement, can achieve success in changing public policy through litigation—win or lose—by laying the groundwork for victories in the larger political environment outside of the courts. U.S. News & World Report Magazine Photograph Collection, Prints and Photographs Division, Library of Congress, Washington, D.C.

law), and a legal language that could be used in further developing (and publicizing) that understanding. More broadly, when interest groups litigate, they surely wish to succeed; however, success is not limited to securing a win in the immediate case but, rather, may include grabbing the public's attention and mobilizing supporters.

Finally, and closely related to publicizing an issue or cause, organized interests can have success in changing policy by laying the groundwork for victories in the larger political environment outside of the courts.[126] For example, political scientist Thomas Keck demonstrated that litigation strategies in the Lesbian, Gay, Bisexual, Transgender (LGBT) movement not only led to early court victories in Hawaii, Vermont, and Massachusetts, but also electoral victories in dozens of states and localities.[127] Keck found that ambitious litigation—whether successful or not—can clear space for legislative progress in its wake: judges can "provide political cover for legislators to declare their support for a policy that they previously considered too great a political liability."[128] Along similar lines, political scientist Daniel Pinello, writing specifically about the Massachusetts Supreme Judicial Court decision that found that same-sex couples possessed the right to marry under Massachusetts law,[129] had this to say:

> *Goodridge* [the decision in question] brought about enormous social change. . . . [T]he Massachusetts [high court] . . . achieved singular success in expanding the ambit of who receives the benefits of getting married in America, in inspiring political elites elsewhere in the country to follow suit, and in mobilizing grass-roots supporters to entrench their legal victory politically.[130]

Thus, interest groups often can and do see litigation as a means to secure victory not only inside, but outside of the court as well.

MODELS OF JUDICIAL BEHAVIOR ON APPELLATE COURTS

Thus far, we have discussed the mechanics of the appellate process, including the various stages of that process and the obstacles to appeal that can arise. Along the way, we have demonstrated that several myths about appellate courts are at odds with empirical reality. Next, we discuss the dominant models of judicial decision making—the legal model, the attitudinal model, and the strategic model—and consider some of the social science evidence related to each.

Perhaps the most prominent myth about appellate courts is that the judges on those courts rely on the law and only the law in adjudicating the appeals before them. The classic **legal model** suggests that there is some logical form of reasoning internal to law.[131] Its proponents argue that the decisions of judges are substantially influenced by legal considerations. In other words, "judges want only to interpret the law as well as possible"[132] and "legal analysis . . . can and should be free from contaminating political or ideological elements."[133] Although there is some debate regarding how to define the legal model, the use of reasoned judgment based on text and precedent remain key parts of legal decision making.[134]

Until the twentieth century, most lawyers and scholars believed that judging was a mechanistic enterprise in which judges applied the law and rendered decisions without recourse to their own ideological or policy preferences. In the 1920s, however, a group of so-called **legal realists**—including such legal notables as U.S. Supreme Court Justice Oliver Wendell Holmes and Judge Jerome Frank of the U.S. Court of Appeals for the Second Circuit—began to argue that judicial discretion was actually quite broad and that, particularly at the appellate level, it was not common for the law to inexorably lead to one particular result. Rather, the law was often compatible with more than one outcome.[135] The legal realists, in other words, were increasingly finding the myth of judging as a value-free activity at odds with the reality they observed.

The contemporary successors of the legal realists are scholars who advocate for what is known as the **attitudinal model**. Political scientists Jeffrey Segal and Harold Spaeth, the two most prominent advocates of the attitudinal model, describe this model as follows:

> This [attitudinal] model holds that the Supreme Court justices decide disputes in light of the facts of the case vis-à-vis the ideological attitudes and values of the justices. Simply put, Rehnquist votes the way he does because he is extremely conservative, Marshall voted the way he did because he was extremely liberal.[136]

This simple but powerful model of decision making has a remarkable body of evidence that supports it, at least with regard to decision making on the U.S. Supreme Court.[137] As Segal and Spaeth (as well as others) have emphasized, the robust power of the attitudinal model for understanding Supreme Court decision making is a function of the fact that the institutional design of the Court makes it uniquely amenable to the influence of the attitudes and preferences of the justices on the choices they make.[138] In particular, the justices control their own docket and the cases they choose to hear are exactly the kinds of cases in which we would expect judicial preferences to matter. Further, members of the Court are at the pinnacle of their careers and it is unlikely they aspire to higher office (i.e., they have no cause to curb the expression of their preferences for fear of offending those who might be responsible for appointing them to a higher position). Likewise, they enjoy lifetime tenure (i.e., they have no cause to curb the expression of their preferences for fear of offending those who might be responsible for reappointing them to the Court). Finally, the constitutional decisions of the Supreme Court are not subject to review by a higher court.[139]

We will have much more to say about decision making on the U.S. Supreme Court in the next chapter. For now, however, note that neither the U.S. courts of appeals nor the state courts of last resort enjoy quite the same institutional latitude as the Supreme Court. This does not mean that the attitudes and preferences of the judges populating those lower appellate court benches do not matter for the decisions rendered by those courts. In fact, there is compelling evidence that attitudes and preferences manifest a very meaningful effect on the decisions of both U.S. courts of appeals judges and state courts of last resort judges.

For example, political scientists Donald Songer and Susan Haire examined the votes of courts of appeals judges in obscenity cases from 1957 to 1990 and, using the party of the president who appointed a judge as an indicator of that judge's ideology, found that judicial attitudes played an important role in structuring the votes cast in favor of (or opposed to) a lower court decision upholding a restriction on material purported to be obscene.[140] More recently, political scientists Erin Kaheny, Susan Haire, and Sara Benesh analyzed a sample of votes cast by courts of appeals judges across the full range of issues considered by the courts from 1968 to 1998.[141] Relying on a sophisticated measure of judicial preferences based on the preferences of the presidents who nominated the judges (as moderated by the preferences of key senators in the confirmation process),[142] Kaheny and her colleagues found that liberal judges were likely to vote more liberally and, conversely, conservative judges were more likely to vote conservatively, even though how predictably they do so is not necessarily constant over their careers.

Similarly, in the case of state courts of last resort, studies demonstrating the powerful influence of judges' preferences on the choices they make are plentiful. For example, political scientists Sara Benesh and Wendy Martinek examined a sample of votes rendered by judges on state courts of last resort in criminal cases dealing with the challenge to a confession as in violation of the constitutional protection against self-incrimination embedded in the Fifth and Sixth Amendments to the Constitution.[143] Controlling for a host of other factors likely to influence decision making in these kinds of cases, Benesh and Martinek found that the preferences of the judges made a difference as to whether a judge cast a vote in favor of excluding a challenged confession (what would be considered a liberal vote) or against excluding a challenged confession (what would be considered a conservative vote).

A very recent study by political scientists Benjamin Kassow, Donald Songer, and Michael Fix is another example of the empirical evidence in support of the premise that the attitudes of state supreme court judges matter for their behavior.[144] Rather than focusing on the vote choice of individual judges, Kassow and his coauthors examined state supreme court decisions made between 1994 and 2006 that treated a U.S. Supreme Court precedent set in the 1993 and 1994 terms of the Court. Key among their findings was that

a liberal court is more likely to positively treat [a] precedent [from the U.S. Supreme Court] when such a positive treatment will lead to a liberal outcome. And similarly a conservative court is more likely to positively treat [a] precedent [from the U.S. Supreme Court] when such a positive treatment will lead to a conservative outcome.[145]

In short, the preferences of state supreme court judges matter for what they do, in terms of their vote choices and beyond.

The final model of judicial decision making we consider is the **strategic model**. The strategic account, like the attitudinal model, begins with the premise that judges wish to see their personal policy preferences enacted into law. However, unlike attitudinalists, proponents of the strategic model do not believe that judges, even Supreme Court justices, are unconstrained actors. "Rather, [they] are strategic actors who realize their ability to achieve their goals depends on a consideration of the preference of other actors, the choices they expect others to make, and the institutional context in which they act."[146]

In fact, the context within which the lower appellate courts operate suggests that the expression of preferences is likely to be tempered in those courts as compared to their expression in the U.S. Supreme Court. The courts of appeals, for example, occupy an explicitly subordinate position in the federal judicial hierarchy. They are expected to be faithful in the application of Supreme Court precedents and their decisions are subject to review by that court. Indeed, numerous scholars have found that the courts of appeals are sensitive to the dictates of the Supreme Court. For example, Professors Songer and Haire, in their analysis of obscenity decision making on the courts of appeals mentioned above, found that those key factors that identified the Supreme Court's obscenity jurisprudence as important for disposing of obscenity cases mattered as well for courts of appeals decision making.[147] Similar findings were reported by Songer and his colleagues with regard to search-and-seizure cases,[148] Benesh with regard to confession cases,[149] and Luse and her collaborators with regard to cases implicating the Establishment Clause of the First Amendment.[150] Collectively, this empirical evidence suggests that the law (as embodied in Supreme Court precedent) matters for the courts of appeals.

There is another feature of the federal courts of appeals that has been demonstrated to structure the choices circuit judges make. Unlike in the Supreme Court, where all the justices sit together to hear cases (that is, sit *en banc*), in the courts of appeals the vast majority of the cases are heard by panels of three judges. The judges on these panels typically sit together to hear 2 weeks of cases and then rotate on to other three-judge panels to hear a different set of cases. There is a sizable set of social science scholarship devoted to so-called panel effects.

Law professors Frank Cross and Emerson Tiller, for example, used the standard of administrative review the Supreme Court established in *Chevron U.S.A. Inc. v. Natural Resources Defense Council, Inc.*[151] to evaluate whether differences in the partisanship of different members of a three-judge panel made a difference for whether the panel was faithful in its application of the *Chevron* standard.[152] *Chevron* directed lower courts to be largely deferential to federal administrative agency interpretations of statutes. Cross and Tiller reviewed all decisions of the U.S. Court of Appeals for the D.C. Circuit between 1991 and 1995 that cited *Chevron* to determine whether they were deferential (as *Chevron* would require) or not. They then analyzed those decisions on the basis of the partisan composition of the judges and concluded that the presence of even a single Democrat on a panel (who would presumably favor obedience to *Chevron* given Democratic tolerance of government regulation) led to a moderating effect on the Republicans on the panel (who would presumably prefer a less deferential standard for the review of agency decisions given Republican hostility to government regulation). Stated differently, Cross and Tiller found that, at least in some instances, an ideologically mixed panel produces different decisions than an ideologically homogeneous panel.

Another example is the research conducted by political scientist Christina Boyd and her colleagues in which they examined decision making on the courts of appeals in a range

Image 9.7 Laurence Silberman
Research shows that "designated" judges who serve on the courts of appeals—including retired judges—behave differently than regular courts of appeals judges. Judge Laurence Silberman (photographed in 2001 with President George W. Bush) was appointed to the U.S. Court of Appeals for the D.C. Circuit by President Ronald Reagan in 1985. He "retired" with "senior status" in 2000 and continued to serve on that court. National Archives and Records Administration.

of issue areas. They found that, in sex discrimination cases, the presence of a woman on a panel enhanced the likelihood of male judges voting in favor of the litigant making a sex discrimination claim.[153] Similar findings with regard to gender were reported by political scientists Sean Farhang and Gregory Wawro, who, interestingly, found no such effects when it comes to the presence of a racial minority on a panel.[154]

Another feature of the courts of appeals that is markedly different than the Supreme Court has to do with "substitute" judges. Three-judge panels on the courts of appeals can (and often do) include court of appeals judges on senior status[155] and district court judges temporarily serving as a court of appeals judge.[156] For example, in the 12-month period ending September 30, 2012, 192 active and 110 senior district court judges served as designated district court judges.[157] Those 302 district court judges provided almost 4,000 case participations for that period.[158] Scholars who have examined the behavior of these **designated judges** (as well as the behavior of those on the panels on which they serve) have uncovered evidence of some interesting dynamics. For example, such judges are much more likely to join the majority opinion than register a dissent.[159] Further, designated judges are less likely to author majority opinions[160] and, when they do write the majority opinion for the panel, the decision is less likely to reverse the lower court.[161] In a recent analysis of a sample of courts of appeals decisions from 1970 to 1996, political scientist Paul Collins, Jr., and his collaborator found that designated district court judges are much more susceptible to the influence of their panel mates than are regular court of appeals judges.[162] In other words, panel effects are more pronounced for designated district court judges than they are for others serving on three-judge panels in the courts of appeals.

Yet one more feature of decision making on the courts of appeals that has potential ramifications for how judges on those courts make decisions is the fact that any given three-judge-panel decision is subject to review by the entire set of judges in that particular circuit. *En banc* review of a panel decision by the full circuit is not common. As Micheal Giles and his colleagues reported, a mere 94 out of almost 27,000 cases decided by the courts of appeals in 1999 were decided *en banc*.[163] But the incidence of *en banc* review rehearing is not random; in other words, there are patterns about when an *en banc* in the courts of appeals is more likely. For example, in other work, Giles and his collaborators Thomas Walker and Christopher Zorn find that *en banc* review is more likely when there is more legal uncertainty or ambiguity surrounding the case; for example, when there are disagreements between or within circuits about the appropriate legal rule, or the case involves a novel issue for which the court is making the first statement of circuit law.[164]

In terms of the behavior of the judges on a three-judge panel, the fact that the panel decision is subject to review not only by the U.S. Supreme Court but by the court of appeals of which it is a part sitting *en banc*, affords at the least the possibility that the judges on the panel will be sensitive to how their decisions might be viewed by the circuit (in the same way that they are sensitive to how their decisions might be viewed by the Supreme Court). The evidence on this point is decidedly mixed,[165] but the broader point is that court of appeals judges are situated in a very different decision-making environment than are justices of the Supreme Court and that different environment has implications for how they go about making their decisions.

So, too, are the judges who occupy positions on state courts of last resort affected by their environment. In one important sense, state courts of last resort are very much like the U.S. Supreme Court. Just as the U.S. Supreme Court is the final arbiter as to the meaning of the U.S. Constitution and the interpretation of federal statutes (unless that interpretation is overruled by Congress), state courts of last resort are the final arbiters as to the meaning of their respective state constitutions and the interpretation of their respective state statutes (unless that interpretation is overruled by the state legislature). The catch is, however, that when state laws or state constitutional provisions conflict with federal laws or state constitutional provisions then the state court of last resort does not have the final word; the U.S. Supreme Court does.

Political scientists Scott Comparato and Scott McClurg have demonstrated that state supreme courts are actually sensitive to the precedents set by the nation's highest court.[166] They examined a sample of search-and-seizure cases decided by state courts of last resort that cited search-and-seizure decisions issued by the U.S. Supreme Court between its 1983 and 1993 terms. What they found was that Supreme Court precedents do influence the behavior of state supreme courts; they pay attention to the factors that the Supreme Court has identified as important and modify their decisions accordingly. Thus, this finding supports the legal model.

Arguably, however, the most important difference between state supreme courts and the U.S. Supreme Court has to do with tenure and how their members are selected and/ or retained in office. The lifetime tenure of Supreme Court justices is not something that is enjoyed by any but an exceedingly small minority of state supreme court judges. Only the judges of the Rhode Island Supreme Court possess lifetime tenure, though the judges of the Massachusetts Supreme Judicial Court and the New Hampshire Supreme Court are permitted to serve until age 70.[167] Moreover, as discussed in detail in Chapter Five, most individuals serving on state courts of last resort are initially selected via popular election or (if initially appointed by the governor, legislature, or some combination thereof) retained in office via a retention election. This suggests that state court of last resort judges—at least those interested in remaining on the bench—might be sensitive

Image 9.8 Supreme Court of California *Artist Ben Shahn's 1932 painting depicts Chief Justice William H. Waste and the six associate justices of the California Supreme Court. After the Governor makes an appointment to the Court, the new justice is subject to a retention vote at the next general election and thereafter at 12-year intervals.* Hirshhorn Museum and Sculpture Garden, Smithsonian Institution, Washington, DC, Gift of Joseph H. Hirshhorn, 1966.

to the preferences of the electorate or, in the case of judges retained via gubernatorial or legislative action, the preferences of state political elites.

We addressed this influence on the behavior of state supreme court judges earlier in our discussion of separate opinion writing, noting that the evidence indicates that judges are less likely to dissent in, for example, cases in which the death penalty is being upheld. The logic is that such dissents might incur the displeasure of electorates who are leery of those construed as "soft on crime." There is certainly evidence to suggest that elected judges do have reason to be concerned with how their decisions will affect their prospects for remaining in office.

A particularly well-known example is that of Rose Elizabeth Bird, who was appointed to the California Supreme Court in 1977. She was the first woman on that court and only the second woman to serve as a chief justice, but Bird and two of her colleagues on the California Supreme Court (Cruz Reynoso and Joseph Grodin) found themselves the target of an effort to oust them from the court.[168] All three were subject to retention elections in the 1986 election cycle and all three failed to win their retention elections, largely because of their well-publicized opposition to the death penalty on the bench. There is a large body of research that systematically evaluates the relationship between judicial selection/retention and behavior, and virtually all of that scholarship demonstrates that elected judges do alter their behavior depending on the preferences of their electorate.[169]

Appellate court judges are human beings and, as such, judicial decision making is subject to the same forces as decision making in other contexts. This includes the fact that their values, preferences, and ideologies matter for the decisions they make. Those preferences may not be dispositive in the sense of determining each and every decision but they certainly enter into the decision-making calculus. Differences between and among appellate courts with regard to such things as the tenure and selection of their members and their position in the judicial hierarchy shape decision making on those courts, including the translation of preferences into case votes and opinion content. Further, the fact that appellate court judges decide cases in groups rather than alone means that they are at least sometimes sensitive to the roles and identities of their colleagues on the bench and that sensitivity, too, can shape behavior. Hence, the myth that appellate court judging is simply a matter of comparing a case to the relevant precedents, and that regardless of who is doing the judging the outcome will be the same, is belied by the reality evident in the actual behavior of appellate court judges.

CONCLUSION

The myths and misperceptions surrounding appellate courts are many. Much of the confusion stems from the fact that they are different from trial courts in both structure and substance. Instead of a single presiding judge, witnesses, and juries working to establish facts, appellate courts contain multiple judges who question attorneys about law and procedure. Losing litigants appeal not only because they want to win but because they want justice, fairness, and a procedure through which they feel they can have their voice heard. In general, the vast majority of appeals ultimately uphold the original trial court's decision. But for those that are overturned, losers in civil cases have a far better chance of winning on appeal than do criminal defendants.

Appeals are important—not because they correct trial errors and not because they provide venues for losers to become winners—but because they give judges opportunities to make public policy that can have a wide impact on society. In fact, third parties often attempt to influence appellate courts via *amicus curiae* briefs. In this sense, appellate courts should be viewed as policy-making institutions, similar to legislatures.

Finally, although the myth is that appellate court judges make decisions on the basis of the law and nothing else, the reality is that the decision-making calculus of appellate court judges is complex and is structured by a variety of factors, including the attitudes and values of the judges themselves and the institutional features of the courts on which they sit.

Suggested Readings

Scott Barclay. *An Appealing Act: Why People Appeal in Civil Cases* (Chicago, IL: Northwestern University Press, 1999). This volume examines the reasons that individuals choose to appeal in civil cases when they have been unsuccessful in the trial court, concluding that, while winning is nice, most people are driven by a desire to have a fair hearing.

Frank B. Cross. *Decision Making in the U.S. Courts of Appeals* (Stanford, CA: Stanford University Press, 2007). This book undertakes a systematic analysis of the decision making of U.S. courts of appeals and finds that the judges of these courts are influenced not only by ideology but also by legal considerations and, further, that they are largely unaffected by the other branches of government.

Sheldon Goldman and Charles Lamb, eds. *Judicial Conflict and Consensus: Behavioral Studies of American Appellate Courts* (Lexington, KY: University Press of Kentucky, 1986). This book is a a classic collection of original essays by various authors on different facets of the conflict and consensus among appellate court judges.

Laura Langer. *Judicial Review in State Supreme Courts* (Albany, NY: State University of New York Press, 2002). Langer offers an examination of the behavior of judges on state courts of last resort with particular attention paid to when and how the other branches of state government might influence the choices of those judges and their policy-making powers.

Richard A. Posner. *The Federal Courts: Challenge and Reform* (Cambridge, MA: Harvard University Press, 1985). Offering, first, a history of the federal courts and a description of the contemporary institution, this text by a U.S. court of appeals judge goes on to draw from the author's experience, economic theory, and legal analysis to inform a proposal for comprehensive reform of the federal judiciary.

Endnotes

1   Truman Capote, *In Cold Blood* (New York, NY: Random House, 1966): 381.

2   Quoted in Charlie Savage, "A Judge's View of Judging Is on the Record," *New York Times*, May 14, 2009.

3   Steve Williams, "Andrew Shirvell Ordered to Pay Gay Student $4.5 Million," *Care2.com*, August 17, 2012 (http://www.care2.com/causes/andrew-shirvell-ordered-to-pay-gay-student-4–5million.html).

4   Russell Mills, "Attorney Fights to Lower Age of Consent for Student Sex with School Employees," *KRMG.com*, September 6, 2012 (http://www.krmg.com/news/news/local/attorney-fights-lower-age-consent-student-teacher-/nR39K/).

5   Maggie Fox, "Court Rules Controversial Stem Cell Research is Legal," *NBCNews.com*, August 24, 2012 (http://vitals.nbcnews.com/_news/2012/08/24/13458821-court-rules-controversial-stem-cell-research-is-legal).

6   TMZ Staff, "Snipes' Appeal— Let Me Out to Fight in Supreme Court," December 17, 2010 (http://www.tmz.com/2010/12/17/wesley-snipes-tax-evasion-federal-prison-appeal-denied-united-states-supreme-court-united-states-court-of-appeals/).

7   See, for example, Theodore Eisenberg, "Appeals Rates and Outcomes in Tried and Nontried Cases: Further Exploration of Anti-Plaintiff Appellate Outcomes," *Journal of Empirical Legal Studies*, vol. 1, no. 3 (November 2004): 569–688.

8   Grant Foreman, "The Law's Delays," *Michigan Law Review*, vol. 13, no. 2 (December 1914): 100–112, 102.

9   Administrative Office of the U.S. Courts, "Judicial Business of the U.S. Courts," Table A-1 (http://www.uscourts.gov/Statistics/JudicialBusiness/2012/statistical-tables-us-supreme-court.aspx).

10 Martin Shapiro, "Appeal," *Law & Society Review*, vol. 14, no. 3 (Spring 1980): 629–662. See, also, Harlon Leigh Dalton, "Taking the Right to Appeal (More or Less) Seriously," *Yale Law Journal*, vol. 95, no. 1 (November 1985): 62–107.

11 Some scholars have argued that, in fact, this desire to have a voice motivates litigants to appeal even when they expect that the appellate court will not find in their favor. Scott Barclay, *An Appealing Act: Why People Appeal in Civil Cases* (Chicago, IL: Northwestern University Press, 1999).

12 Robert A. Dahl, "Decision-Making in a Democracy: The Supreme Court as a National Policy-Maker," *Journal of Public Law*, vol. 6 (1957): 279–295.

13 This also reflects the double jeopardy protection embedded in the Fifth Amendment: "[N]or shall any person be subject for the same offence to be twice put in jeopardy of life and limb." The Double Jeopardy Clause does not, however, prevent a defendant from being charged, tried, and convicted by two different governmental entities if the act in question separately violates the laws of those different governmental entities. So, for example, the four Los Angeles police officers who were tried and acquitted in state court for the infamous beating of Rodney King were subsequently tried (and two of them convicted) in federal court of federal civil rights violations without a violation of the Double Jeopardy Clause occurring; Akhil Reed Amar and Jonathan L. Marcus, "Double Jeopardy Law after Rodney King," *Columbia Law Review*, vol. 95, no. 1 (January 1995): 1–59.

14 Carol R. Flango and David B. Rottman, *Appellate Court Procedures* (Williamsburg, VA: National Center for State Courts, 1998): Table 2.1.

15 Ibid., Table 2.2.

16 43 Stat. 936 (1925).

17 Jonathan Sternberg, "Deciding Not to Decide: The Judiciary Act of 1925 and the Discretionary Court," *Journal of Supreme Court History*, vol. 33, no. 1 (March 2008): 1–16.

18 28 U.S.C. Part IV §§ 1291–1296. See, also, Thomas E. Baker, *A Primer on the Jurisdiction of the U.S. Courts of Appeals*, Second Edition (Washington, DC: Federal Judicial Center, 2009).

19 Robert C. LaFountain, Richard Y. Schauffler, Shauna M. Strickland, Sarah A. Gibson, and Ashley N. Mason, *Examining the Work of State Courts: An Analysis of 2009 State Court Caseloads* (Williamsburg, VA: National Center for State Courts, 2011): 41.

20 See, e.g., H.W. Perry, Jr., *Deciding to Decide: Agenda Setting in the United States Supreme Court* (Cambridge, MA: Harvard University Press, 1991).

21   Carol R. Flango and David B. Rottman, *Appellate Court Procedures* (Williamsburg, VA: National Center for State Courts, 1998): Table 3.3.

22   Advice on the preparation of persuasive briefs abounds. See, e.g., Bryan A. Garner, *The Winning Brief: 100 Tips for Persuasive Briefing in Trial and Appellate Courts*, Second Edition (New York, NY: Oxford University Press, 2004); Ross Guberman, *Point Made: How to Write Like the Nation's Top Advocates* (New York, NY: Oxford University Press, 2011); Jim McElhaney, "Style Matters: Write Briefs as If They Could Win Your Case—Because They Can," *ABA Journal*, vol. 94, no. 6 (June 2008): 28–29.

23   208 U.S. 412 (1908).

24   Curt Muller challenged an Oregon labor law that limited the number of hours a female wage earner could work to no more than 10 hours per day. The brief prepared by Brandeis included arguments focused on the physiological effects of long working hours on women, particularly the consequences for reproductive roles and maternal functions.

25   Noga Morag-Levine, "Facts, Formalism, and the Brandeis Brief: The Origins of a Myth," *University of Illinois Law Review*, vol. 2013, no. 1 (February 2013): 59–102.

26   The original Brandeis brief can be accessed on the Louis D. Brandeis School of Law's website (http://www.law.louisville.edu/library/collections/brandeis/node/235).

27   Samuel Krislov, "The Amicus Curiae Brief: From Friendship to Advocacy," *Yale Law Journal*, vol. 72, no. 4 (March 1963): 694–721.

28   54 A.3d 1 (2012).

29   The law was declared unconstitutional and a permanent injunction prohibiting the enforcement of the law by a Pennsylvania trial court on January 17, 2014.

30   12–1671, U.S. Court of Appeals for the Fourth Circuit (Richmond).

31   The court ultimately concluded that a Facebook "like" was protected speech.

32   Paul M. Collins, Jr., *Friends of the Supreme Court: Interest Groups and Judicial Decision Making* (New York, NY: Oxford University Press, 2008): 41–43; Paul M. Collins, Jr., and Wendy L. Martinek, "Who Participates as Amici Curiae in the U.S. Courts of Appeals?" *Judicature*, vol. 94, no. 3 (November-December 2010): 128–136, 129–130.

33   See, for example, Judge Richard Posner's statement regarding amici in *Voices for Choices v. Illinois Bell Telephone Company*, 339 F.3d 542 at 545 (7th Cir. 2003).

34   Paul M. Collins, Jr., *Friends of the Supreme Court: Interest Groups and Judicial Decision Making* (New York, NY: Oxford University Press, 2008): 47–49; Wendy L. Martinek, "Amici Curiae in the U.S. Courts of Appeals," *American Politics Research*, vol. 34, no. 6 (November 2006): 803–824, 808.

35   Sarah F. Corbally, Donald C. Bross, and Victor E. Flango, "Filing of Amicus Curiae Briefs in State Courts of Last Resort, 1960–2000," *Justice System Journal*, vol. 25, no. 1 (2004): 39–56.

36   Ibid.

37   Paul Brace and Kelly S. Butler, "New Perspectives for the Comparative Study of the Judiciary: The State Supreme Court Project," *Justice System Journal*, vol. 22, no. 3 (2001): 243–262, 253. See, also, Sarah F. Corbally, Donald C. Bross, and Victor E. Flango, "Filing of Amicus Curiae Briefs in State Courts of Last Resort, 1960–2000," *Justice System Journal*, vol. 25, no. 1 (2004): 39–56: 46, and Scott A. Comparato, *Amici Curiae and Strategic Behavior in State Supreme Courts* (Westport, CT: Praeger, 2003): 71–73.

38   Jeremy L. Fetty, "Pre-Argument Settlement at the Michigan Court of Appeals: A Secret Too Well Kept," *Journal of Appellate Practice and Process*, vol. 7, no. 2 (Fall 2005): 317–333.

39   *Federal Rules of Appellate Procedure* (Rule 33), December 1, 1998.

40   Administrative Office of the U.S. Courts, "Judicial Business of the United States Courts," *2012 Annual Report of the Director* (http://www.uscourts.gov/Statistics/JudicialBusiness/2012.aspx): Table A-1.

41   Administrative Office of the U.S. Courts, "Judicial Business of the United States Courts," *2012 Annual Report of the Director* (http://www.uscourts.gov/Statistics/JudicialBusiness/2012.aspx): Table B-1.

42 Stephen L. Wasby, Anthony A. D'Amato, and Rosemary Metrailer, "The Functions of Oral Argument in the U.S. Supreme Court," *Quarterly Journal of Speech*, vol. 62, no. 4 (December 1976): 410–422: 418. See, also, Timothy R. Johnson, *Oral Arguments and Decision Making on the United States Supreme Court* (Albany, NY: State University of New York Press, 2004).

43 Lee Epstein, William M. Landes, and Richard A. Posner, "Inferring the Winning Party in the Supreme Court from the Pattern of Questioning at Oral Argument," *Journal of Legal Studies*, vol. 39, no. 2 (June 2010): 433–467.

44 Ryan C. Black, Timothy R. Johnson, and Justin Wedeking, *Oral Arguments and Coalition Formation on the U.S. Supreme Court: A Deliberate Dialogue* (Ann Arbor, MI: University of Michigan Press, 2012).

45 United States Court of Appeals for the Fifth Circuit, *Practitioner's Guide to the U.S. Court of Appeals for the Fifth Circuit*, June 2013 (http://www.ca5.uscourts.gov/).

46 "Justice Alito at RWU Law, Pt. 1," *Roger Williams University Law Newsroom*, September 14, 2012 (http://law.rwu.edu/story/justice-alito-rwu-law-pt-1).

47 Felix Frankfurter, *The Commerce Clause Under Marshall, Taney, and Waite* (Chapel Hill, NC: University of North Carolina Press, 1937): 9. Though they are attended only by the justices themselves, some of the justices' conference notes have provided glimpses into the nature of those conference proceedings. See, e.g., Del Dickson, ed., *The Supreme Court in Conference (1940–1985): The Private Discussions Behind Nearly 300 Supreme Court Decisions* (New York, NY: Oxford University Press, 2001).

48 U.S. Court of Appeals for the Fourth Circuit, *Internal Operating Procedures* (I.O.P.-36.1), June 1, 2013.

49 Carol R. Flango and David B. Rottman, *Appellate Court Procedures* (Williamsburg, VA: National Center for State Courts, 1998): Table 3.7. See, also, Melinda Gann Hall, "Opinion Assignment Procedures and Conference Practices in State Supreme Courts," *Judicature*, vol. 73, no. 3 (December-January 1989–1990): 209–214.

50 Like conference deliberations, those rounds of revision take place outside of the public eye. However, the papers of judges and justices often include the multiple iterations of draft opinions that preceded a final opinion and some scholars have used that material to shed light on this "private" aspect of appellate court decision making. See, e.g., Forrest Maltzman, James F. Spriggs, II, and Paul J. Wahlbeck, *Crafting Law on the Supreme Court: The Collegial Game* (New York, NY: Cambridge University Press, 2000).

51 Melinda Gann Hall, "Electoral Politics and Strategic Voting in State Supreme Courts," *Journal of Politics*, vol. 54, no. 2 (May 1992): 427–446.

52 Ibid., 427–446, 431.

53 Ibid., 427–446, 435.

54 Ibid., 427–446, 436.

55 Ibid., 427–446, 438.

56 For example, Eisenberg and Miller report a dissent rate of 26.7 percent across state courts of last resort for cases in which the courts exercised discretionary jurisdiction and of 18.8 percent for mandatory jurisdiction cases. Theodore Eisenberg and Geoffrey P. Miller, "Reversal, Dissent, and Variability in State Supreme Courts: The Centrality of Jurisdictional Source," *Boston University Law Review*, vol. 89, no. 5 (December 2009): 1451–1504, 1583–1484.

57 Melinda Gann Hall, "Electoral Politics and Strategic Voting in State Supreme Courts," *Journal of Politics*, vol. 54, no. 2 (May 1992): 427–446; Melinda Gann Hall and Paul Brace, "Toward an Integrated Model of Judicial Behavior," *American Politics Quarterly*, vol. 20, no. 2 (April 1992): 147–168; Melinda Gann Hall and Paul Brace, "State Supreme Courts and Their Environments: Avenues to General Theories of Judicial Choice," in *Supreme Court Decision-Making: New Institutionalist Approaches*, eds, Cornell W. Clayton and Howard Gillman (Chicago, IL: University of Chicago Press, 1999).

58 Melinda Gann Hall, "Docket Control as an Influence on Judicial Voting," *Justice System Journal*, vol. 10, no. 2 (Summer 1985); Henry R. Glick and George W. Pruet, Jr., "Dissent in State Supreme Courts: Patterns and Correlates of Conflict," in *Judicial Conflict and Consensus: Behavioral*

Studies of American Appellate Courts, eds, Sheldon Goldman and Charles Lamb (Lexington, KY: University Press of Kentucky, 1986); Theodore Eisenberg and Geoffrey P. Miller, "Reversal, Dissent, and Variability in State Supreme Courts: The Centrality of Jurisdictional Source," *Boston University Law Review*, vol. 89, no. 5 (December 2009): 1451–1504, 1583–1484.

59 Donald R. Songer, "Consensual and Nonconsensual Decisions in Unanimous Opinions of the United States Courts of Appeals," *American Journal of Political Science*, vol. 26, no. 2 (May 1982): 225–239. But see Virginia A. Hettinger, Stefanie A. Lindquist, and Wendy L. Martinek, *Judging on a Collegial Court* (Charlottesville, VA: University of Virginia Press, 2006): 63.

60 Virginia A. Hettinger, Stefanie A. Lindquist, and Wendy L. Martinek, *Judging on a Collegial Court* (Charlottesville, VA: University of Virginia Press, 2006): 58.

61 Ibid., 59. See, also, Virginia A. Hettinger, Stefanie A. Lindquist, and Wendy L. Martinek, "The Role and Impact of Chief Judges on the United States Courts of Appeals," *Justice System Journal*, vol. 24, no. 1 (2003): 91–117.

62 Virginia A. Hettinger, Stefanie A. Lindquist, and Wendy L. Martinek, *Judging on a Collegial Court* (Charlottesville, VA: University of Virginia Press, 2006): 59.

63 Ibid., 55.

64 United States Court of Appeals for the Tenth Circuit, "Fee Schedule" (http://www.ca10.uscourts.gov/clerk/index.php?id=fees).

65 Federal Rule of Civil Procedure 62.

66 Richard G. Stuman and Sean P. Costello, "The Appeal Bond—What It Is, How It Works, and Why It Needs to Be Factored Into Your Litigation Strategy," Jones Day (March 2008): 24–31 (http://www.jonesday.com/files/Publication/983c1326–51c1–4ebc-9e6e-001ef4268418/Presentation/PublicationAttachment/daa0a1a0-c224–4cde-a744–64d80a235d12/Spring_2008_The_Appeal_Bond.pdf).

67 *N. Ind. Pub. Serv. Co. v. Carbon County Coal Co.*, 799 F.2d 265 (7th Circuit 1986).

68 Doug Rendleman, "A Cap on the Defendant's Appeal Bond?: Punitive Damages Tort Reform," *Akron Law Review*, vol. 39, no. 4 (2006): 1089–1170, 1100–1101.

69 *Texaco, Inc. v. Pennzoil Co.*, 729 S.W.2d 768 (Tex. App. 1987), *cert. denied*, 485 U.S. 994 (1988).

70 Doug Rendleman, "A Cap on the Defendant's Appeal Bond?: Punitive Damages Tort Reform," *Akron Law Review*, vol. 39, no. 4 (2006): 1089–1170.

71 Richard G. Stuman and Sean P. Costello, "The Appeal Bond—What It Is, How It Works, and Why It Needs to Be Factored Into Your Litigation Strategy," Jones Day (March 2008): 24–31 (http://www.jonesday.com/files/Publication/983c1326–51c1–4ebc-9e6e-001ef4268418/Presentation/PublicationAttachment/daa0a1a0-c224–4cde-a744–64d80a235d12/Spring_2008_The_Appeal_Bond.pdf).

72 Ibid.

73 Administrative Office of the U.S. Courts, "Judicial Business of the U.S. Courts," *2012 Annual Report of the Director*, Table A-1 (http://www.uscourts.gov/Statistics/JudicialBusiness/2012/statistical-tables-us-supreme-court.aspx).

74 Donald R. Songer and Reginald S. Sheehan, "Who Wins on Appeal? Upperdogs and Underdogs in the United States Courts of Appeals," *American Journal of Political Science*, vol. 36, no.1 (February 1992): 235–258.

75 Ibid., 235–258, 252.

76 Richard A. Posner, *The Federal Courts: Challenge and Reform* (Cambridge, MA: Harvard University Press, 1985): 8.

77 Ibid., 6, 10–11.

78 Scott Barclay, *An Appealing Act: Why People Appeal in Civil Cases* (Evanston, IL: Northwestern University Press, 1999): 3. See, also, Scott Barclay, "Posner's Economic Model and the Decision to Appeal," *Justice System Journal*, vol. 19, no. 1 (1997): 77–99.

79 Richard A. Posner, "Demand and Supply Trends in Federal and State Courts Over the Last Half Century," *Journal of Appellate Practice and Process*, vol. 8, no. 1 (2006): 133–140.

80 Robert C. LaFountain, Richard Y. Schauffler, Shauna M. Strickland, Sarah A. Gibson, and Ashley N. Mason, *Examining the Work of State Courts: An Analysis of 2009 State Court Caseloads* (National Center for State Courts, 2011): 40.

81 Ibid., 2.

82 Theodore Eisenberg and Michael Heise, "Plaintiphobia in State Courts? An Empirical Study of State Court Trials on Appeal," *Journal of Legal Studies*, vol. 38, no. 1 (January 2009): 121–155, 150.

83 Ibid., 121–155; Joy A. Chapper and Roger A. Hanson, *Understanding Reversible Error in Criminal Appeals* (Williamsburg, VA: National Center for State Courts, 1989).

84 Theodore Eisenberg and Michael Heise, "Plaintiphobia in State Courts? An Empirical Study of State Court Trials on Appeal," *Journal of Legal Studies*, vol. 38, no. 1 (January 2009): 121–155, 130.

85 Ibid.

86 U.S. Department of Justice, Office of Justice Programs, Bureau of Justice Statistics, *Supplemental Survey of Civil Appeals, 2001* (Ann Arbor, MI: Inter-University Consortium for Political and Social Research) (computer file No. 4539, 2006).

87 The Bureau of Justice Statistics recently funded a project to examine criminal appeals in state intermediate courts and courts of last resort, including key characteristics of the cases appealed and their disposition by the appellate courts. Though that project, which will examine state criminal appeals for 2010, is in-progress, no data is yet available.

88 Thomas Y. Davies, "Affirmed: A Study of Criminal Appeals and Decision-Making Norms in a California Court of Appeal," *Law and Social Inquiry*, vol. 7, no. 3 (July 1982): 543–648.

89 David W. Neubauer, "Published Opinions versus Summary Affirmations: Criminal Appeals in Louisiana," *Justice System Journal*, vol. 10, no. 2 (Summer 1985): 173–192.

90 Richard A. Posner, "Demand and Supply Trends in Federal and State Courts Over the Last Half Century," *Journal of Appellate Practice and Process*, vol. 8, no. 1 (2006): 133–140.

91 Though several provisions of the PLRA have been challenged in the courts (including in the U.S. Supreme Court), it remains in effect; Barbara Belbot, "Report on the Prison Litigation Reform Act: What Have the Courts Decided So Far?" *Prison Journal*, vol. 84, no. 3 (September 2004): 290–316. Provisions of the AEDPA have also been challenged but remain in effect, stirring significant controversy and generating passionate opposition. See, for example, Larry Yackle, "Prisoner Rights and Habeas Corpus: Assessing the Impact of the 1996 Reforms," *Federal Sentencing Reporter*, vol. 24, no. 4 (April 2012): 330–334.

92 U.S. Sentencing Commission, *2012 Annual Report* (http://www.ussc.gov/Research_and_Statistics/Annual_Reports_and_Sourcebooks/index.cfm): 49.

93 386 U.S. 738 (1967).

94 Recall that cases involving the U.S. government as a litigant fall under the original jurisdiction of the U.S. district courts.

95 Administrative Office of the U.S. Courts, "Judicial Business of the United States Courts," *2012 Annual Report of the Director* (http://www.uscourts.gov/Statistics/JudicialBusiness/2012/us-courts-of-appeals.aspx).

96 Kevin M. Clermont and Theodore Eisenberg, "Plaintiphobia in the Appellate Courts: Civil Rights Really Do Differ From Negotiable Instruments," *University of Illinois Law Review*, vol. 2002, no. 4 (2002): 947–977.

97 Ibid.

98 Ibid.

99 Kevin M. Clermont and Theodore Eisenberg, "Trial by Jury or Judge: Transcending Empiricism," *Cornell Law Review*, vol. 87, no. 3 (2001): 125–164.

100 U.S. Sentencing Commission, *2011 Annual Report* (http://www.ussc.gov/Data_and_Statistics/Annual_Reports_and_Sourcebooks/2011/ar11toc.htm): Table 56A.

101 U.S. Sentencing Commission, *2011 Annual Report* (http://www.ussc.gov/Data_and_Statistics/Annual_Reports_and_Sourcebooks/2011/ar11toc.htm): Table 60.

102 See Steven Shavell, "The Appeals Process as a Means of Error Correction," *Journal of Legal Studies*, vol. 24, no. 2 (June 1995): 379–426.

103 347 U.S. 483 (1954).

104 For an accessible account of *Brown* that places it in its historical and cultural context, see Robert J. Cottrol, Raymond Diamond, and Leland B. Ware, *Brown v. Board of Education: Caste, Culture, and the Constitution* (Lawrence, KS: University Press of Kansas, 2003).

105   For a discussion of the difficulty in implementing *Brown*, see Michael J. Klarman, *From Jim Crow to Civil Rights: The Supreme Court and the Struggle for Racial Equality* (New York, NY: Oxford University Press, 2004); Gerald N. Rosenberg, *The Hollow Hope: Can Courts Bring About Social Change?* (Chicago, IL: University of Chicago Press, 1991).

106   *San Antonio Independent School District v. Rodriguez*, 411 U.S. 1 (1971).

107   See Robert M. Howard and Amy Steigerwalt, *Judging Law and Policy: Courts and Policymaking in the American Political System* (New York, NY: Routledge, 2012): Chapter 7.

108   Ibid., 139.

109   Paul M. Collins, Jr., "Interest Groups in the Judicial Arena," in *New Directions in Interest Group Politics*, ed. Matt Grossmann (New York, NY: Routledge, 2013).

110   Of course, interest groups can also attempt to influence judicial policy making by attempting to influence who becomes a judge in the first place. So, for example, interest groups are active in lobbying senators in support of or opposition to nominees to the federal bench. See, e.g., Lauren Cohen Bell, *Warring Factions: Interest Groups, Money, and the New Politics of Senate Confirmation* (Columbus, OH: Ohio State University Press, 2002); Nancy Scherer, *Scoring Points: Politicians, Activists, and the Lower Federal Court Appointment Process* (Palo Alto, CA: Stanford University Press, 2005). They also engage in electioneering activities directed at the selection of the candidates likely to be favorable to those groups' goals in states where some or all of the judges are elected to office. See, e.g., Anthony Champagne, "Interest Groups and Judicial Elections," *Loyola of Los Angeles Law Review*, vol. 34, no. 4 (June 2001): 1391–1409; Michael E. Solimine and Rafael Gely, "Federal and State Judicial Selection in an Interest Group Perspective," *Missouri Law Review*, vol. 74, no. 3 (Summer 2009): 531–554.

111   Difficult does not mean impossible, as the National Federation of Independent Business (NFIB) demonstrated recently in *National Federation of Independent Business v. Sebelius*, 183 L. Ed. 2d 450 (2012). The NFIB, a trade association representing small businesses, was found to have standing to challenge the constitutionality of the Patient Protection and Affordable Care Act (often referred to as Obamacare).

112   Mark V. Tushnet, *The NAACP's Legal Strategy against Segregated Education, 1925–1950* (Chapel Hill, NC: University of North Carolina Press, 1987); Richard Kluger, *Simple Justice* (New York: Vintage, 1977). See also Jack Greenberg, *Crusaders in the Courts: Legal Battles of the Civil Rights Movement* (Northport, NY: Twelve Tables Press, 2004); Mark V. Tushnet, *Making Civil Rights Law: Thurgood Marshall and the Supreme Court, 1936–1961* (New York, NY: Oxford University Press, 1994).

113   Adam Liptak, "Carefully Plotted Course Propels Gun Case to Top," *New York Times*, December 3, 2007.

114   Paul Duggan, "Lawyer Who Wiped Out D.C. Ban Says It's About Liberties, Not Guns," *Washington Post*, March 18, 2007.

115   554 U.S. 570 (2008).

116   554 U.S. 570, 575 (2008).

117   The other five litigants were ultimately found not to meet the requirements for standing.

118   554 U.S. 570, 635 (2008).

119   Interest groups can also serve as sponsors of litigation by facilitating a class action lawsuit. A class action lawsuit is one in which hundreds, perhaps thousands, of individuals who have the same grievance have their claims joined into one suit.

120   Conceptually related to (but still distinct from) participation as an *amicus curiae* is participation as an intervenor. Being granted intervenor status generally requires that a group demonstrate that its interests are in jeopardy and that the group's interests are sufficiently different from those of the direct litigants in the case that the group cannot rely on the direct litigants to represent its interests. See, e.g., Matthew I. Hall, "Standing of Intervenor-Defendants in Public Law Litigation," *Fordham Law Review*, vol. 80, no. 4 (March 2012): 1539–1584.

121   539 U.S. 306 (2003).

122   570 U.S. ___ (2013).

123   Both the federal trial court and the court of appeals found in favor of the University and upheld the legality of its admissions policy. The Supreme Court accepted the case for review but did

not directly revisit the question of whether race was a permissible factor to be considered in admissions decisions. Rather, the Court vacated the lower court decisions and remanded the case for further consideration by the lower court. The Court indicated it was doing so because the lower court had not used the strict scrutiny standard articulated in *Grutter v. Bollinger*—and, before *Grutter*, in *Regents of the University of California v. Bakke*, 438 U.S. 265 (1978).

124 Robert Barnes, "Supreme Court Receives Outpouring of Conflicting Views on Affirmative Action," *Washington Post*, October 7, 2012.

125 Michael W. McCann, *Rights at Work: Pay Equity Reform and the Politics of Legal Mobilization* (Chicago, IL: University of Chicago Press, 1994).

126 For an alternative perspective, see Michael J. Klarman, *From Jim Crow to Civil Rights: The Supreme Court and the Struggle for Racial Equality* (New York, NY: Oxford University Press, 2004).

127 Thomas M. Keck, "Beyond Backlash: Assessing the Impact of Judicial Decisions on LGBT Rights," *Law & Society Review*, vol. 43, no. 1 (March 2009): 151–185.

128 Ibid., 151–185, 159.

129 *Goodridge v. Dept. of Public Health*, 798 U.S.2d 491 (Mass. 2003).

130 Daniel Pinello, *America's Struggle for Same-Sex Marriage* (New York, NY: Cambridge University Press, 2006): 192–193.

131 Frank B. Cross, "Political Science and the New Legal Realism: A Case of Unfortunate Interdisciplinary Ignorance," *Northwestern University Law Review*, vol. 92 (1997): 251–327.

132 Lawrence Baum, *Judges and Their Audiences: A Perspective on Judicial Behavior* (Princeton, NJ: Princeton University Press, 2006): 6.

133 Anthony T. Kronman, *The Lost Lawyer: Failing Ideals of the Legal Profession* (Cambridge, MA: Harvard University Press, 1993): 250.

134 Frank B. Cross, "Political Science and the New Legal Realism: A Case of Unfortunate Interdisciplinary Ignorance," *Northwestern University Law Review*, vol. 92, no. 1 (1997): 251–327.

135 William W. Fisher III, Morton J. Horwitz, and Thomas A. Reed, *American Legal Realism* (New York, NY: Oxford University Press, 1993).

136 Jeffrey A. Segal and Harold J. Spaeth, *The Supreme Court and the Attitudinal Model Revisited* (New York, NY: Cambridge University Press, 2002): 86.

137 A representative set of examples includes Jeffrey A. Segal and Albert D. Cover, "Ideological Values and the Votes of U.S. Supreme Court Justices," *American Political Science Review*, vol. 83, no. 2 (June 1989): 557–565; Harold J. Spaeth and Jeffrey A. Segal, *Majority Rule or Minority Will: Adherence to Precedent on the U.S. Supreme Court* (New York, NY: Cambridge University Press, 1999); Forrest Maltzman, James F. Spriggs III, and Paul J. Wahlbeck, *Crafting Law on the Supreme Court: The Collegial Game* (New York, NY: Cambridge University Press, 2000); and Thomas G. Hansford and James F. Spriggs, *The Politics of Precedent on the U.S. Supreme Court* (Princeton, NY: Princeton University Press, 2006).

138 Jeffrey A. Segal and Harold J. Spaeth, *The Supreme Court and the Attitudinal Model Revisited* (New York, NY: Cambridge University Press, 2002): 92–96.

139 Congress can reverse the Supreme Court's interpretation of statutes; however, no actor (other than a later Court) can reverse the Supreme Court's interpretation of the Constitution. That has not stopped Congress from trying, such as when it tried to overrule the Court's decision protecting flag burning as speech under the Free Speech Clause of the First Amendment in *Texas v. Johnson*, 491 U.S. 397 (1989). Congress passed the Flag Protection Act but that law was invalidated by the Court in *United States v. Eichman*, 496 U.S. 310 (1990).

140 Donald R. Songer and Susan Haire, "Integrating Alternative Approaches to the Study of Judicial Voting: Obscenity Cases in the U.S. Courts of Appeals," *American Journal of Political Science*, vol. 36, no. 4 (November 1992): 963–982.

141 Erin B. Kaheny, Susan Brodie Haire, and Sara C. Benesh, "Change over Tenure: Voting, Variance, and Decision Making on the U.S. Courts of Appeals," *American Journal of Political Science*, vol. 52, no. 3 (July 2008): 490–503.

142 Micheal W. Giles, Virginia A. Hettinger, and Todd Peppers, "Measuring the Preferences of Federal Judges: Alternatives to Party of the Appointing President" (Atlanta, GA: Emory University, 2002).

143 Sara C. Benesh and Wendy L. Martinek, "State Supreme Court Decision Making in Confession Cases," *Justice System Journal*, vol. 23, no. 1 (2002): 109–133.

144 Benjamin Kasso, Donald R. Songer, and Michael P. Fix, "The Influence of Precedent on State Supreme Courts," *Political Research Quarterly*, vol. 65, no. 2 (June 2012): 372–384.

145 Ibid., 372–384, 379.

146 Lee Epstein and Jack Knight, *The Choices Justices Make* (Washington, DC: CQ Press, 1998): 10.

147 Donald R. Songer and Susan Haire, "Integrating Alternative Approaches to the Study of Judicial Voting: Obscenity Cases in the U.S. Courts of Appeals," *American Journal of Political Science*, vol. 36, no. 4 (November 1992): 963–982.

148 Donald R. Songer, Jeffrey A. Segal, and Charles M. Cameron, "The Hierarchy of Justice: Testing a Principal-Agent Model of Supreme Court-Circuit Court Interactions," *American Journal of Political Science*, vol. 38, no. 3 (August 1994): 673–696.

149 Sara C. Benesh, *The U.S. Courts of Appeals and the Law of Confession: Perspectives on the Hierarchy of Justice* (New York, NY: LFB Scholarly, 2002).

150 Jennifer K. Luse, Geoffrey McGovern, Wendy L. Martinek, and Sara C. Benesh, " 'Such Inferior Courts . . . ' Compliance by Circuits with Jurisprudential Regimes," *American Politics Research*, vol. 37, no. 1 (January 2009): 75–106.

151 467 U.S. 837 (1984).

152 Frank B. Cross and Emerson H. Tiller, "Judicial Partisanship and Obedience to Legal Doctrine: Whistleblowing on the Federal Courts of Appeals," *Yale Law Journal*, vol. 107, no. 7 (May 1998): 2155–2176.

153 Christina L. Boyd, Lee Epstein, and Andrew D. Martin, "Untangling the Causal Effects of Sex on Judging," *American Journal of Political Science*, vol. 54, no. 2 (April 2010): 389–411.

154 Sean Farhang and Gregory Wawro, "Institutional Dynamics on the U.S. Courts of Appeals: Minority Representation under Panel Decision Making," *Journal of Law, Economics, & Organization*, vol. 20, no. 2 (October 2004): 299–330.

155 Court of appeals judges who are 65 years or older and have 15 years of experience have the option of taking senior status. With each additional year in age, a judge has the option of taking senior status with 1 less year of service. So, for example, a judge who is 67 years of age and has 13 years of service has that option. Senior judges continue to receive their full salaries but generally hear a reduced caseload.

156 Wendy L. Martinek, "The U.S. Courts of Appeals: Appellate Workhorses of the Federal Judiciary," in *Exploring Judicial Politics*, ed. Mark C. Miller (New York, NY: Oxford University Press, 2009): 128–130.

157 Administrative Office of the U.S. Courts, "Judicial Business of the U.S. Courts," Table V-2 (http://www.uscourts.gov/uscourts/Statistics/JudicialBusiness/2012/appendices/V02Sep12.pdf).

158 A case participation is the participation of one judge in one case. So, for example, each three-judge panel yields three case participations (one for each of the three judges on the panel).

159 James J. Brudney and Corey Ditslear, "Designated Diffidence: District Court Judges on the Courts of Appeals," *Law and Society Review*, vol. 35, no. 3 (2001): 565–606; Virginia A. Hettinger, Stefanie A. Lindquist, and Wendy L. Martinek, *Judging on a Collegial Court* (Charlottesville, VA: University of Virginia Press, 2006): 66–67.

160 James J. Brudney and Corey Ditslear, "Designated Diffidence: District Court Judges on the Courts of Appeals," *Law and Society Review*, vol. 35, no. 3 (2001): 565–606.

161 Virginia A. Hettinger, Stefanie A. Lindquist, and Wendy L. Martinek, "The Role and Impact of Chief Judges on the United States Courts of Appeals," *Justice System Journal*, vol. 24, no. 1 (2003): 91–117.

162 Paul M. Collins Jr. and Wendy L. Martinek, "The Small Group Context: Designated District Court Judges in the U.S. Courts of Appeals," *Journal of Empirical Legal Studies*, vol. 8, no. 1, (March 2011): 177–205.

163 Micheal W. Giles, Virginia Hettinger, Christopher Zorn, and Todd C. Peppers, "The Etiology of the Occurrence of En Banc Review in the U.S. Court of Appeals," *American Journal of Political Science*, vol. 51, no. 3 (July 2007): 449–463, 450.

164 Micheal W. Giles, Thomas G. Walker, and Christopher Zorn, "Setting a Judicial Agenda: The Decision to Grant En Banc Review in the U.S. Courts of Appeals," *Journal of Politics*, vol. 68, no. 4 (November 2006): 852–866.

165 Compare, for example, Steven R. Van Winkle, "Dissent as a Signal: Evidence from the U.S. Courts of Appeals," paper presented at the Annual Meeting of the American Political Science Association (Washington, DC: American Political Science Association, 1997) and Virginia A. Hettinger, Stefanie A. Lindquist, and Wendy L. Martinek, "Comparing Attitudinal and Strategic Accounts of Dissenting Behavior on the U.S. Courts of Appeals," *American Journal of Political Science*, vol. 48, no. 1 (January 2004): 123–137.

166 Scott A. Comparato and Scott D. McClurg, "A Neo-Institutional Explanation of State Supreme Court Responses in Search and Seizure Cases," *American Politics Research*, vol. 35, no. 5 (September 2007): 726–754.

167 Council of State Governments, *Book of the States* (Lexington, KY: Council of State Governments, 2013): Table 5.1.

168 Preble Stolz, *Judging Judges: The Investigation of Rose Bird and the California Supreme Court* (New York, NY: Free Press, 1981).

169 See, for example, Paul R. Brace and Melinda Gann Hall, "The Interplay of Preferences, Case Facts, Context, and Rules in the Politics of Judicial Choice," *Journal of Politics*, vol. 59, no. 4 (November 1997): 1206–1231; Laura Langer, *Judicial Review in State Supreme Courts* (Albany, NY: State University of New York Press, 2002).

10

THE U.S. SUPREME COURT

"Ideology matters."

—Charles Schumer, Democratic Senator from New York[1]

"[P]robably thirty to forty percent of our decisions are unanimous . . . the five-fours account for maybe twenty, twenty-five percent, and it isn't always the same five or the same four."

—Stephen A. Breyer, Associate Justice of the U.S. Supreme Court[2]

Are the justices of the U.S. Supreme Court neutral arbiters of the law or ideologically driven politicians in black robes? Consider the following cases—both decided in 2012. In *Florence v. Board of Chosen Freeholders*, the justices deliberated over whether correctional officers could strip-search prisoners, regardless of the reason for the arrest.[3] Albert Florence was taken into custody when the car in which he was riding (driven by his wife) was stopped for a traffic offense and a computer error listed Mr. Florence as having an outstanding warrant. He was held in two different jails over the course of 6 days, enduring strip searches (in which he was required to lift his genitals) at both jails. The justices voted 5-4 against Mr. Florence's claim that his Fourth and Fourteenth Amendment rights were violated. Perhaps not surprisingly, the five-justice majority was composed of conservative justices appointed by Republican presidents, while the four-justice minority was composed of liberal justices appointed by Democratic presidents. In the same term, in the case of *U.S. v. Jones*, the justices considered the appeal of nightclub owner and convicted drug trafficker Antoine Jones, who claimed that the GPS device police attached to his car (and that tracked his whereabouts 24-7 for four weeks) represented a violation of the Fourth Amendment.[4] The same justices who split along party lines in *Florence v. Board of Chosen Freeholders* found unanimously in *U.S. v. Jones* that the police may not secretly install a GPS device on a vehicle to monitor its movements. How can the same justices who divide on party lines in one case reach a unanimous decision in another?

In the previous chapter, we laid bare the myth of appellate judging as a value-free activity, demonstrating that the preferences of appellate court jurists and certain features of appellate courts also matter for understanding the choices the judges on those courts make. As we noted in that chapter, the unique features of the U.S. Supreme Court (including the lifetime tenure the justices enjoy and the position of the Court at the top of the judicial hierarchy), make it an especially hospitable environment for the reliance on preferences in the judicial decision-making calculus. High profile cases such as *Bush v. Gore*,[5] which decided a presidential election seemingly on ideological grounds, contribute to the image of a Supreme Court whose decisions are governed entirely by the attitudes of the justices and unconstrained by the law. For example, a 2012 poll conducted

by the *New York Times* and CBS News found that three-quarters of respondents felt that
the justices decide cases at least sometimes on their own personal or political views.[6]
But the view of the Court as purely ideological, deciding cases based on political predispositions with little concern for the law itself is also a myth. The reality is much more
nuanced than the justices as unconstrained ideologues or the justices as neutral arbiters;
Supreme Court justices are neither. As *Florence v. Board of Chosen Freeholders* and
U.S. v. Jones illustrate, in some cases the justices agree on what the law requires while in
others they do not. In the former, the justices are able to reach agreement more easily.
In the latter, there is room for reasonable legal professionals to disagree on points of law.
Indeed, those disagreements can manifest themselves based on the ideological cleav-
ages in Court. In short, the justices are unlike politicians in that they are trained in and
beholden to legal norms and conventions. But in those instances in which the law is less
cut-and-dried and more subject to interpretation, the justices can disagree in the same
way that legislators or presidential candidates can over public policy.

   In addition to the question of why justices make the decisions they do, we discuss the
myths and reality of how cases move through the U.S. Supreme Court. We consider the perspectives of the justices themselves, from the agenda-setting stage (where the Court chooses
which cases to hear) through the coalition-formation stage (where the votes of the justices
can change and opinions are drafted). We close this chapter with a brief discussion of some
of the controversies surrounding the Court, including debates over whether cameras should
be allowed in the courtroom and the advisability of the lifetime tenure the justices enjoy.
Ultimately, while it is important to understand that the U.S. Supreme Court is an appellate
court—like those discussed in the previous chapter—it is also distinct from lower appellate
courts because of its unique nature and function as the highest court in the land.

MYTH AND REALITY IN THE U.S. SUPREME COURT

MYTH	REALITY
Justices are objective decision makers who vote strictly in accordance with the law.	Justices have differing attitudes that can lead them to different conclusions when the law is ambiguous or unclear.
Justices are partisan actors who vote based on their ideological predispositions.	Justices are legal professionals trained in law who act in good faith to reach the correct legal result.
The Court is bitterly divided along partisan lines and routinely issues 5-4 decisions.	The Court reaches complete agreement in one-third of the cases it hears and is highly consensual two-thirds of the time.
Justices personally review every petition filed at the Court.	The justices' clerks review petitions and write memos for the justices to review.
Amicus curiae briefs serve to reiterate the arguments contained in the briefs of the direct litigants in a case.	The arguments included in *amicus curiae* briefs overlap with those included in the briefs of the direct litigants in a case; however, substantial minorities of *amicus* briefs present new or novel information.
During oral argument, justices listen quietly while the attorneys make their case.	During oral argument, justices question attorneys, communicating as much with their fellow justices as with the attorneys through the questions asked.
Justices write opinions resolving disputes.	Justices vote on cases and provide the intellectual framework for (and subsequently edit) opinions drafted by clerks.
Unlike the political branches, the Court is not influenced by public opinion.	The Court's decisions generally reflect broad trends in public opinion on most issues.
Supreme Court justices serve for life and either die in office or retire due to old age.	Supreme Court justices have generous retirement benefits and time their departures to coincide with like-minded presidents.

JUDICIAL DECISION MAKING

Research on the decisions of Supreme Court justices shows that they are generally divided along ideological lines.[7] There are currently five **conservatives**: Chief Justice John Roberts and Justices Anthony Kennedy, Antonin Scalia, Clarence Thomas, and Samuel Alito. The Court also has four **liberals**: Justices Ruth Bader Ginsburg, Stephen Breyer, Sonia Sotomayor, and Elena Kagan. Researchers have classified the justices as liberal or conservative based on their votes in the cases that reach the Court. For example, conservative justices favor the state in criminal cases, while liberal justices favor the criminally accused or convicted. Generally speaking, liberal justices also favor congressional authority in economic matters (while conservative justices do not) and the expansion of civil rights for minorities (while conservative

Image 10.2 The Roberts
Court
*The justices of the U.S.
Supreme Court, 2010.
Top row from left: Sonia
Sotomayor, Stephen
Breyer, Samuel Alito,
and Elena Kagan. Bot-
tom row from left: Clar-
ence Thomas, Antonin
Scalia, Chief Justice John
Roberts, Anthony Ken-
nedy, and Ruth Bader
Ginsburg.* Tim Sloan/
AFP/Getty Images.

justices are less inclined to do so). Conservative justices are more protective of gun
rights than are their liberal counterparts, while liberal justices are generally more
protective of speech by unpopular speakers than are their conservative counterparts. Liberal justices favor strict separation between church and state whereas conservative justices are more accommodating to religion in the public sphere. These
are fairly straightforward distinctions and generally align with common understandings of liberal-conservative ideology outside of the judicial context. But not all
issues fall neatly into a conservative-liberal framework. For example, separation-of-
powers questions involving the president's ability to wage war under the auspices of
his role as commander in chief under Article II of the Constitution, with or without an
official declaration of war by Congress pursuant to Article I of the Constitution, have
been difficult to categorize in this way.[8] Still, critics such as Senator Charles Schumer
(D-NY) have argued that the confirmation process should be tougher and focus on
the partisan predispositions of Supreme Court nominees. His call to arms: "Ideology
matters."[9]

Despite the ideological division on the Court, the justices routinely reach high levels of agreement. Figure 10.1 shows that between one-third and one-half of the cases
decided by the Supreme Court each term are unanimous. If highly consensual cases
(those with only one dissent) are included, the percentage climbs to as high as two-
thirds.[10] These numbers suggest that ideology may not be determinant in most cases.
Instead, it may be that the law determines the correct legal answer. Perhaps this should
not be surprising. Unlike members of Congress, the justices do not wear a party affiliation on their sleeves and are supposed to be honest brokers of the law. Justice Sotomayor
described the Supreme Court as follows: "The branch that the public looks at and says,
ah there is an objective viewpoint, there are people who are not a part of a party, who

FIGURE 10.1

Consensus on the U.S. Supreme Court, 1953–2004

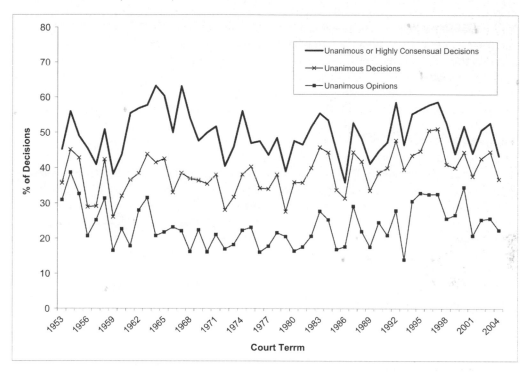

The justices of the U.S. Supreme Court routinely reach high levels of agreement with between one-third and one-half of the cases each term decided unanimously. The rate climbs to two-third for highly consensual decisions—cases with only a single dissent.

Source: Pamela C. Corley, Amy Steigerwalt, and Artemus Ward, *The Puzzle of Unanimity: Consensus on the United States Supreme Court* (Stanford, CA: Stanford University Press, 2013) p. 3.

are not part of an executive branch agenda. They are there to look at this objectively in a neutral way and help us come to a resolution about whatever dispute there may be in an objective way. It's a real testimony to our founding fathers that they created our branch in this way."[11]

Still, justices do disagree and that disagreement tends to fall on ideological lines. This does not mean that the Court is "political" in the way that a legislature is, but it does mean that disagreements in the law can often be explained by ideology (despite some emphatic protestations of the justices to the contrary). Justice Scalia said that it "enrages" him when people refer to the Court as "politicized": "I couldn't care less who the president was. [Judges] vote th[e] way [they do] because that's who they are, they were selected because of who they are, so why should it be surprising."[12] Similarly, Justice Kagan commented: "There is not a single member of this Court, at a single time, who has made a decision, who has cast a vote, based on 'do I like this president, do I not like this president . . . will this help the Democrats, will this help the Republicans?' It is just not the way any member of the Court thinks."[13] Still, she said, "There are certain substantive matters that we divide on because we approach Constitutional decision-making in a different sort of way, because we bring different methodologies to the table, because we have different views about governing precedents and how broad or narrow those precedents are."[14]

LAW CLERKS: SORCERERS' APPRENTICES

It is impossible to accurately discuss the work of the Court without including the vital role of **law clerks**. Here, we provide a primer on what Supreme Court law clerks do, the purpose of which is to provide some background that will be useful as we subsequently discuss the work of the Court. Congress has provided funds to allow each justice to hire four law clerks. Because of his extra administrative duties, the Chief Justice is allowed five—though Chief Justice Roberts has only chosen to hire four. Each retired justice is allowed a single clerk.[15] The clerks assist the justices with their work, a practice started by Justice Horace Gray in the late nineteenth century.[16] The clerks are recent graduates from top law schools. While most of the clerks attended Harvard, Yale, Chicago, Columbia, Stanford, Virginia, and Michigan, many other law schools regularly place clerks with the justices.[17] They are typically male and white,[18] which has, not surprisingly, periodically generated a good deal of criticism of the justices' hiring practices with regard to clerks and concomitant calls for reforms in the clerk selection process.[19] Prior to joining the Court, clerks typically spend one year clerking for a judge on the U.S. courts of appeals, where they gain invaluable experience, and are recommended by so-called "feeder judges" who routinely place their clerks at the Supreme Court.[20] For example, during the 15 years he served on the federal bench, J. Michael Luttig had more than 40 of his law clerks go on to clerk at the U.S. Supreme Court.[21] By far, the circuit that has contributed the most in terms of its clerks moving up to serve on the Supreme Court is the United States Court of Appeals for the District of Columbia.[22] Each justice chooses his or her own clerks, though some delegate the task to trusted confidants.[23] Justice Sotomayor explained what she looks for in potential clerks: "I want smart people but I want people who are good people too. They have to be kind and caring and really smart."[24]

Image 10.3 Overworked Supreme Court
Justice Horace Gray (standing, top, middle) was the first justice to hire a law clerk to assist him with the work of the Court. Prints and Photographs Division, Library of Congress, Washington, D.C.

Image 10.4 Justice Douglas and His Staff *Newly appointed Justice William O. Douglas confers with his secretary Edith Waters and law clerk David Ginsberg, 1939.* Harris & Ewing Collection, Prints and Photographs Division, Library of Congress, Washington, D.C.

Once at the Court, clerks spend one year working on the cases petitioned to the Court as well as the cases the justices accept for review. They read petitions, briefs, and lower court opinions, as well as draft memos and other documents to aid their justices in the decision-making process.[25] Following their year at the Court, Supreme Court clerks are highly sought after and choose to work in private practice, the government, and academia—often commanding salaries far greater than those of the justices for whom they clerked.[26] The role of clerks on the Court has changed over time and they have taken on an increasing amount of responsibility. Retired Justice John Paul Stevens, who clerked for Justice Wiley Rutledge in 1945, had this to say about the changing role of the clerks:

> The clerks have a much larger role in all of the work that goes on. I did very little work on Justice Rutledge's opinions. He wrote them all out in longhand ahead of time and did very little work on comments on other Justices' opinions. We only got one copy of a draft in the chambers, and he would read it, and somebody would send it back and join it—whereas now we all will send at least two copies of a draft opinion around to everyone else because every Justice likes to have his law clerk study the case too before he joins the opinion and see if there are any suggestions that might be helpful to the case. And the clerks now play a much larger role in the entire decisional process than they did when I was a clerk.[27]

As political scientists Artemus Ward and David Weiden detail, the first clerks were as much law students as legal assistants, but changes the Court has wrought in its standard operating procedures (motivated by its increasing workload) mean that contemporary clerks play a role in virtually every aspect of the Court's processing of cases.[28]

This gives rise to the question of whether clerks influence the decisions the justices make or, alternatively, whether clerks merely carry out the orders that their justices give them? For their part, the justices have been adamant that the clerks do not wield power (though the justices acknowledge that the clerks do enrich the work they do). Justice Kagan remarked: "I know the clerks improve my work [but] they are by no means junior varsity judges."[29] Justice Stevens said: "I learn from my clerks, to tell you the truth. I'll write something; they'll sometimes rewrite a paragraph, and gee, that sounds a lot better. And I learn a great deal. It's a constant learning process, yes."[30] Systematic research shows that, while clerks may not be making the decisions for their justices, they can be influential in terms of the recommendations they make and the opinions they draft.[31] Clerks are ever-present through each stage of the decision-making process and, as we detail below, are central to the Court's work.

SUPREME COURT DECISON-MAKING PROCESS

Decision making on the Court begins with the choices the justices make with regard to the cases they will hear. The justices engage in **agenda setting** by choosing the cases that they will formally decide from among the thousands of petitions they receive each year. Subsequently, they read the briefs the attorneys (and *amicus curiae*) submit arguing as to how the case should be resolved. They take the bench to hear **oral argument**, with attorneys making arguments to and answering questions from the justices. The justices then meet in private **conference** to vote on the case outcome. **Opinions** are assigned, written, and circulated. The justices bargain over the details of these opinions and they form their final **coalitions** before the decision is announced. We discuss each of these steps in the process below.

Deciding to Decide: Agenda Setting

The Court largely *chooses* which cases it wants to formally decide.[32] Of course, because the Court can only choose among those appeals that litigants ask it to review, it is very different from Congress or the presidency: unlike legislators and executives, the justices must wait for issues to come to them. As we noted in Chapters Four and Nine, nearly all of the cases that are petitioned to the Court come in the form of a petition for a **writ of *certiorari*.**[33] The word "*certiorari*" is Latin for "make certain." Hence, a petition for *certiorari*—commonly referred to as a "cert petition"—is a request from a litigant to the Supreme Court to make certain that the lower court decision was correct. If the justices decide they wish to hear a case, then they issue a writ of *certiorari*, which directs the lower court to send up the record. While the justices must wait for cases to come to them, the number of petitions has exploded over time, as Figure 10.2 demonstrates. This suggests that, if the Court really wishes to adjudicate on a particular issue, it is likely to be able to find a case among the thousands petitioned to it that can be used for that purpose. Of the 8,000 or more cases appealed to the Supreme Court every year, only 80 or so are decided with full written opinions after oral argument.[34]

How do nine justices examine nearly 200 petitions each week? The reality is that they do not. The justices employ their clerks to prepare brief memos on each case, which aid them in identifying the cases for which cert should be granted. Justice Stevens explained:

FIGURE 10.2

Number of Cases Filed in the U.S. Supreme Court, 1882–2012

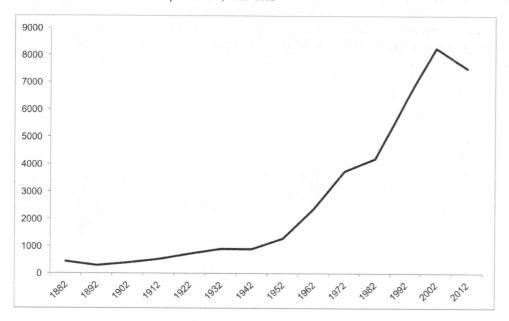

The number of cases filed in the U.S. Supreme Court has exploded over time. In 2012, the justices and their clerks were asked to consider 7,509 petitions.

Source: Adapted from Lee Epstein, Jeffrey A. Segal, Harold J. Spaeth, and Thomas G. Walker, *The Supreme Court Compendium: Data, Decisions & Developments* (Washington, D.C.: Congressional Quarterly Press, 2006) p. 72–75.

We have to be honest that a lot of the cert petitions we do not actually read. I think we all use clerks to give us an awful lot of help in processing cert petitions. I tend to read the cert petition before I vote to grant, but unless one of my clerks has identified it as a potential grant, I usually will not read the original papers myself.[35]

Because each justice employs four law clerks, there are currently 36 people who shoulder the primary responsibility for reviewing the cert petitions the Court receives. The last justice to personally review cert petitions was Justice William Brennan who retired in 1990.[36]

Over time, the justices have sought internal mechanisms to make the review of cert petitions (an onerous task given the volume) relatively manageable. The primary vehicle the Court employs for this purpose is the **cert pool**, which was implemented commencing with the 1972 term of the Court.[37] The plan was that the justices who chose to participate would pool their clerks to divide up the petitions equally so that each clerk had an equal number to review. Instead of the duplication of effort involved in having one clerk for each of the nine justices review the same petition, a single pool clerk would now serve as the only reviewer for all justices participating in the pool.

At first only a handful of justices joined the pool, while the other justices continued to do their own internal-chambers review of each petition. But subsequently, more and more justices joined until there was only one justice who operated on his own; that is, outside the pool. For many years that was Justice Stevens, whose clerks had to divide up all of the petitions among themselves. Following Stevens's retirement, Justice Alito chose to operate

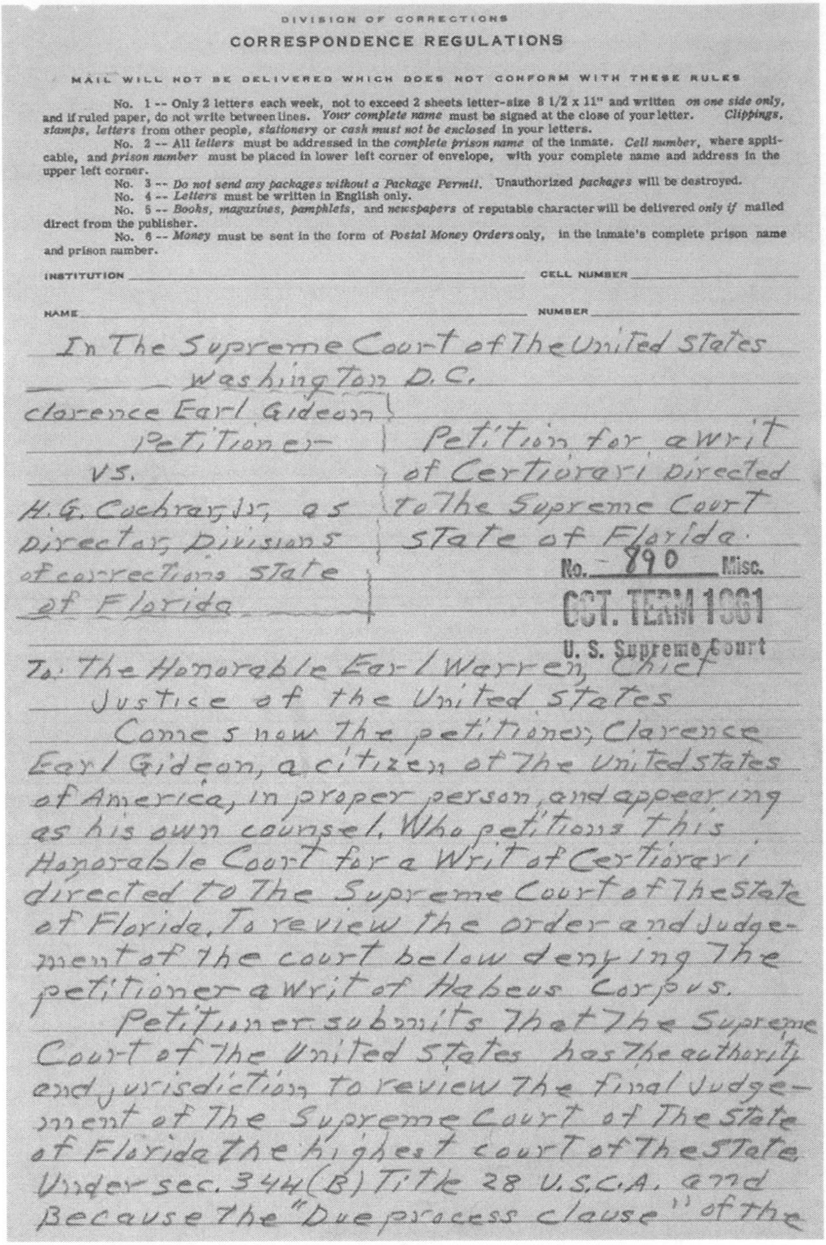

DIVISION OF CORRECTIONS

CORRESPONDENCE REGULATIONS

MAIL WILL NOT BE DELIVERED WHICH DOES NOT CONFORM WITH THESE RULES

No. 1 -- Only 2 letters each week, not to exceed 2 sheets letter-size 8 1/2 x 11" and written *on one side only*, and if ruled paper, do not write between lines. *Your complete name* must be signed at the close of your letter. *Clippings, stamps, letters* from other people, *stationery* or *cash must not be enclosed* in your letters.

No. 2 -- All *letters* must be addressed in the *complete prison name* of the inmate. *Cell number*, where applicable, and *prison number* must be placed in lower left corner of envelope, with your complete name and address in the upper left corner.

No. 3 -- *Do not send any packages without a Package Permit.* Unauthorized *packages* will be destroyed.

No. 4 -- *Letters* must be written in English only.

No. 5 -- *Books, magazines, pamphlets,* and *newspapers* of reputable character will be delivered *only if* mailed direct from the publisher.

No. 6 -- *Money* must be sent in the form of *Postal Money Orders* only, in the inmate's complete prison name and prison number.

INSTITUTION ______ CELL NUMBER ______

NAME ______ NUMBER ______

In The Supreme Court of The United States
Washington D.C.

clarence Earl Gideon
Petitioner
VS.
H.G. Cochran, Jr., as
Director, Divisions
of corrections State
of Florida

Petition for a writ
of Certiorari Directed
to The Supreme Court
State of Florida.

No. 890 Misc.
OCT. TERM 1961
U. S. Supreme Court

To: The Honorable Earl Warren, Chief
Justice of the United States

Comes now the petitioner, Clarence Earl Gideon, a citizen of The United states of America, in proper person, and appearing as his own counsel. Who petitions this Honorable Court for a Writ of Certiorari directed to The Supreme Court of The State of Florida, To review the order and Judgement of the court below denying The petitioner a writ of Habeus Corpus.

Petitioner submits That The Supreme Court of The United States has The authority and jurisdiction to review The final Judgement of The Supreme Court of The State of Florida The highest court of The State Under sec. 344(B) Title 28 U.S.C.A. and Because The "Due process clause" of The

Image 10.5 Gideon's Cert Petition
The first page of Clarence Earl Gideon's handwritten cert petition to the Supreme Court. The justices granted his case and issued the landmark decision Gideon v. Wainwright *(1963) ruling that individuals accused of serious crimes who cannot afford an attorney must be provided one by the state.* National Archives, Washington, D.C.

outside the pool.[38] The justices generally like the fact that there is at least one justice's chambers operating on its own outside of the cert pool. The result is a check of sorts on the cert pool in that at least one clerk from at least two different chambers will examine a given petition. Excluding Justice Alito's clerks, there are 32 clerks in the pool (and sometimes more if the clerks for retired justices participate). As a result, each pool clerk reviews and writes a memo on roughly six cases each week. Justice Alito, like Justice Stevens before him, does not require his clerks to write memos on all of the petitions. If he did, each of his four clerks would be writing nearly 50 memos each week! Instead, they only prepare memos for cases that they believe are important enough to merit discussion by the justices in conference.

Image 10.6 Pool Memo Recommending Grant *In this pool memo, the clerk notes a circuit split and recommends that justices vote to grant the case.* Harry A. Blackmun Papers, Manuscript Division, Library of Congress, Washington, D.C.

PRELIMINARY MEMORANDUM

May 20, 1994 Conference
List 1, Sheet 2 (Page 2)

No. 93-1543-CFX

Christine McKENNON   Cert to CA6 (Kenney, Ryan, Brown [sr])

v.

NASHVILLE BANNER   Federal/Civil   Timely
PUBLISHING CO.

  1. *Summary*: Petr presents the same question as *Milligan-Jensen* v. *Michigan Technological University*, 92–1214 (which was granted and then dismissed when the parties settled) — does evidence of employee misconduct acquired in the course of litigation bar recovery by the employee for discriminatory discharge? There is a circuit split, and though resp attempts to argue that petr would lose under any standard, this seems incorrect. The Court has already decided that the issue is certworthy. GRANT, or CVSG w/v/t GRANT.

HOW DO WE KNOW?

Agenda Setting in the U.S. Supreme Court

Because so few cases ever make it to appellate courts, let alone an appellate court of last resort, the natural question is: why do some cases get picked for review while others do not? Political scientists Ryan Black and Ryan Owens sought to find out the extent to which ideology, law, and other factors influence Supreme Court justices' votes during the agenda-setting stage where they make decisions as to which petitions to grant a full review on the merits.[39] Black and Owens took a random sample of 358 paid,[40] non-death penalty petitions coming from federal courts of appeals that made the Supreme Court's **discuss list** during the 1986–1993 terms. The discuss list is the set of cases (selected from all those petitioned to the Court) that the justices actually discuss in conference. For each justice in each case in their sample, Black and Owens determined whether the justice voted in favor of or in opposition to granting cert by examining the papers of Justice Harry A. Blackmun. In particular, they examined the docket sheets Justice Blackmun used to record the votes of his colleagues on both *certiorari* and the merits.[41]

Black and Owens next ascertained whether the justice was ideologically closer to the predicted policy location of the final vote on the merits of the case or, alternatively, closer to the status quo policy. All things being equal, presumably a justice would be *more likely* to vote in favor of granting *certiorari* if doing so would likely result in a decision on the merits *more* in line with his own preferences and, conversely, be *less likely* to vote in favor of granting *certiorari* if doing so would likely result in a decision on the merits *less* in line with his own preferences. The predicted policy location of the final vote on the merits was determined on the basis of the ideological position of median Supreme Court justice for the term in question. The status quo was determined on the basis of the ideological position of the median judge on the lower court whose decision was being challenged. The ideology of the justices and the lower court judges was measured using Judicial Common Space scores, which place each jurist on a common ideological scale ranging from negative (liberal) to positive (conservative) as derived from their votes on past cases.[42]

The other key explanatory (that is, independent) variables Black and Owens considered were: (1) whether the law clerk noted a conflict in the lower courts; (2) the number of *amicus* briefs filed both supporting and opposing the granting of cert;[43] and (3) whether the lower court struck down a federal law. In each case, the researchers hypothesized that the effect on the likelihood of casting a vote in favor of *certiorari* would be positive. That is, they expected that conflict in the lower courts would enhance the likelihood of a justice casting a vote in favor of granting cert, as would a greater number of *amicus curiae* briefs filed at the cert stage and if the lower court decision being challenged struck down a federal law.

In terms of the empirical evidence, first, the authors confirmed that conflict is crucial in *certiorari* decisions. The predicted probability that a justice casts a policy-based vote to deny *certiorari* decreases from 0.89 in the absence of legal conflict to 0.83 in the presence of weak conflict (determined on the basis of whether the clerk noted that the petitioner alleged a conflict but the clerk discounted it) and plummets to 0.61 in the presence of strong legal conflict (determined on the basis of whether the clerk noted that the conflict alleged by the petitioner is real). The authors concluded: "Simply put, justices who otherwise would have cast policy-based deny votes because they prefer the status quo to the expected outcome on the merits instead are increasingly compelled by the presence of conflict and norms of legal clarity to grant review."[44] Next, with regard to *amicus* participation, an increase in the number of briefs slightly decreases the likelihood of justices casting a policy-based vote to deny *certiorari* from a probability of 0.89 with no *amicus* briefs filed to a probability of 0.87 when one brief is present. Finally, Black and Owens found that the predicted probability of a justice casting a policy-based vote to deny *certiorari* drops precipitously from 0.89 to 0.56 when the lower court has struck down a federal law.

The authors concluded that, while policy goals substantially influence justices' agenda-setting behavior, law and legal norms are also influential. Justices grant review when they believe that the policy outcome of the final decision on the merits will be better for them ideologically than would be the status quo. Conversely, they deny review when they support the status quo policy. Yet the justices do not simply vote their policy preferences at the agenda-setting stage. Legal considerations such as lower court conflict and whether a lower court has exercised judicial review to strike down a federal law are anything but trivial in their effects. Justices who may otherwise vote to deny review on policy grounds may well vote to grant review based on legal norms.

Which petitions are meritorious? The clerks and the justices look for cues: shortcuts that signal that a case is "worthy" of consideration.[45] The most important cue is when there is conflict among courts. Conflict between or among two or more courts of appeals is known as a **circuit split**, but there can also be conflicts between and among state supreme courts as well. When two or more lower courts have reached different conclusions on the same question, the Supreme Court views its role as that of national arbiter—adjudicating between and among different conclusions reached by different courts and, thereby, providing clarity in the law. Another important cue is interest group participation: organized interests file ***amicus* briefs** to persuade the Court to hear a case. The justices and clerks view *amicus* participation as a signal that the case is important to a wide range of parties.[46] A third cue is when the U.S. government is a party to the dispute. The justices and their clerks pay more attention to cases involving the federal government, particularly those in which the government is the petitioner. The Court recognizes that the Office of the **Solicitor General**—the U.S. government's attorney before the Court—is staffed with highly skilled lawyers with the functional equivalent of unlimited resources. Thus, when the Solicitor General thinks a case is important enough to ask the justices to decide it, the Court pays close attention.[47]

Ideology is yet another cue. The justices and clerks look for cases where lower court decisions conflict with the prevailing ideology on the current Supreme Court. In other words, clerks and justices are thinking about the Court's ultimate vote on the merits when they consider whether a petition challenging a lower court decision should be granted or not.[48] Justices who are likely to vote to overturn the lower court result at the merits stage are more likely to grant cert to the case than those who prefer the status quo. Thus, ideology is an important cue in the agenda-setting process. Finally, the law matters: cases in which the Court has an opportunity to make a national pronouncement on an important question of law are often seen by the justices and their clerks as "cert worthy." Not surprisingly, when two or more cues exist in the same case, the chances are greatest that the Court will take the case.

Some justices have their clerks "mark up" the pool memo with their own views and recommendations. Justice Blackmun, in particular, was suspicious of ideological bias and asked his clerks to mark up the pool memo with information about the pool clerk who

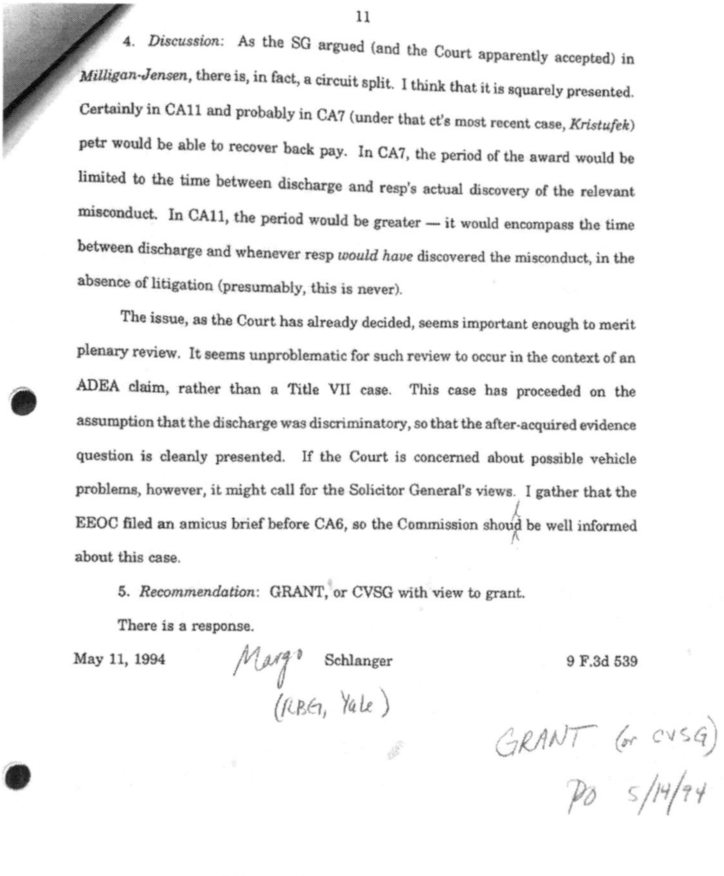

11

4. *Discussion*: As the SG argued (and the Court apparently accepted) in *Milligan-Jensen*, there is, in fact, a circuit split. I think that it is squarely presented. Certainly in CA11 and probably in CA7 (under that ct's most recent case, *Kristufek*) petr would be able to recover back pay. In CA7, the period of the award would be limited to the time between discharge and resp's actual discovery of the relevant misconduct. In CA11, the period would be greater — it would encompass the time between discharge and whenever resp *would have* discovered the misconduct, in the absence of litigation (presumably, this is never).

The issue, as the Court has already decided, seems important enough to merit plenary review. It seems unproblematic for such review to occur in the context of an ADEA claim, rather than a Title VII case. This case has proceeded on the assumption that the discharge was discriminatory, so that the after-acquired evidence question is cleanly presented. If the Court is concerned about possible vehicle problems, however, it might call for the Solicitor General's views. I gather that the EEOC filed an amicus brief before CA6, so the Commission should be well informed about this case.

5. *Recommendation*: GRANT, or CVSG with view to grant.

There is a response.

May 11, 1994   *Margo* Schlanger   9 F.3d 539
                      (RBG, Yale)

GRANT (or CVSG)
PO 5/14/94

Image 10.7 A Marked Up Pool Memo
A clerk for Justice Harry Blackmun marks up the pool memo to note that it was written by "Margo" Schlanger, a clerk who works for Justice Ruth Bader Ginsburg and who attended Yale Law School. Harry A. Blackmun Paper, Manuscript Division, Library of Congress, Washington, D.C.

Image 10.8 Discuss List
*Former Chief Justice
William H. Rehnquist
[WHR] lists cases for
discussion by all of the
members of the Court
in private conference.*
Harry A. Blackmun
Papers, Manuscript
Division, Library of
Congress, Washington,
D.C.

Supreme Court of the United States
Washington, D. C. 20543

CHAMBERS OF
THE CHIEF JUSTICE

May 31, 1994

DISCUSS LIST NO. 1
(For the June 3, 1994 Conference)

93-1612) - NationsBank of NC v. Variable Ann. Life Ins., p. 1 - WHR
93-1613) - Ludwig v. Variable Annuity Life Ins., p. 1 - WHR

93-1615 - IL Dept. of the Lottery v. Marchiando, p. 1 - WHR

93-8050 - Barber v. North Carolina, p. 5 - WHR

93-8109 - Hughes v. Texas, p. 5 - WHR

93-8207 - Espinosa v. Florida, p. 5 - WHR

93-8501 - Gibbs v. North Carolina, p. 6 - WHR

93-8636 - George v. Murray, p. 6 - WHR

93-8707 - Mason v. Ohio, p. 7 - WHR

93-8770 - Gorby v. Florida, p. 8 - WHR

Laverne Frayer
Laverne Frayer
Conference Secretary

drafted the memo: the clerk's first name, the justice for whom he currently clerked, the lower court judge for whom he last clerked, and the law school the clerk attended. One former Blackmun clerk observed:

> In our day, HAB [Harry A. Blackmun] would mark up the pool memos with strange hieroglyphs—indicating some secret coded commentary about the court or specific judges who authored the opinions below, and sometimes—we theorized—on the author of the pool memo from another Chambers, as in "this law clerk is not to be trusted on this sort of issue."[49]

Blackmun's clerks themselves also evidenced concern about bias in the pool memos,[50] though political scientist and law professor H.W. Perry drew the conclusion from his interviews that most memos were not ideologically biased.[51] Regardless of whether the memos evidence ideological bias or not, other (unintentional) bias (such as downplaying factors important to some justices) can potentially creep in. Thus, in-chambers mark-ups of pool memos can serve as an important check against partiality in pool memos.

Given the thousands of cert petitions the Court receives, if the justices were to formally vote on whether or not to grant *certiorari* on each and every one individually, they would have little time for anything else. Commencing in the 1930s, the justices relied on a **dead list** to keep conference discussions manageable. Before conference, the chief justice would circulate a list of cases that were considered lacking in merit and, therefore, would not be discussed at conference. This might seem to have bestowed an awesome gate-keeping power on the chief justice; however, it was not much of a power in that any justice could remove a case from the dead list and, thereby, include it in the pool of petitions discussed in conference.[52] Over time, the dead list has evolved into what is now the **discuss list**. Currently, instead of putting together a list of cases that will *not* be discussed, the chief justice puts together a list of cases that *will be* discussed. As was the case with the dead list, other justices are free to add cases to this **discuss list**. Cases not listed by any justice are automatically denied *certiorari*. The vast majority of pool memos recommend that cases be denied, making it relatively easy to draw up the discuss list. Former Ginsburg clerk Jay Wexler said: "I didn't recommend that the Court grant a single one of the 250 or so petitions I worked on."[53]

Critics suggest that the clerks are reluctant to recommend grants out of a fear that they might be ostracized for being wrong, particularly if the Court initially grants the petition but later dismisses it as "improvidently granted." Wexler explained that when this happens "the clerk at fault will feel like a total jackass, and everyone will look funny at the clerk and say things behind the clerk's back like 'that clerk is bad' or 'that clerk sucks.' . . . This is, as you might imagine, the clerk's worst nightmare . . . ."[54] Yet both the clerks and the justices know that the vast majority of cert petitions will not be worthy of review. Justice Kennedy explained: "We've read a lot of other cert petitions, and we

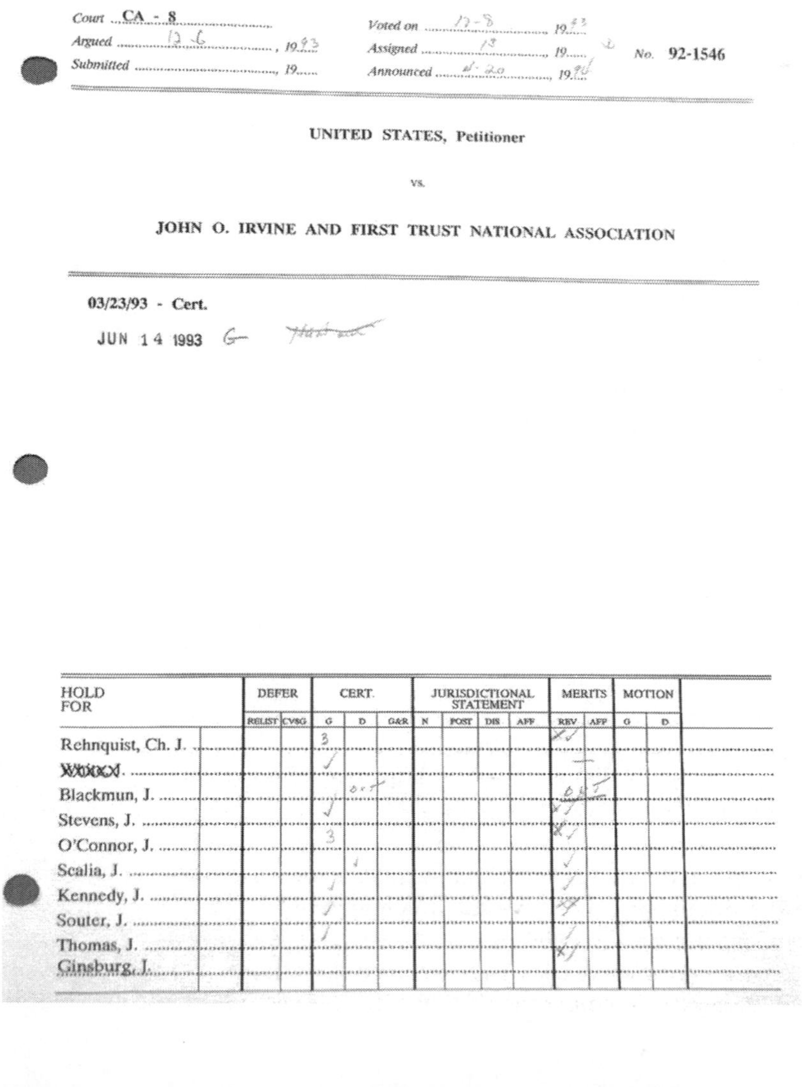

Court CA - 8 | Voted on 12-8, 1993
Argued 12-6, 1993 | Assigned 12, 19....
Submitted ...., 19.... | Announced 1-20, 1994
No. 92-1546

UNITED STATES, Petitioner

vs.

JOHN O. IRVINE AND FIRST TRUST NATIONAL ASSOCIATION

03/23/93 - Cert.
JUN 14 1993 G

HOLD FOR		DEFER RELIST	DEFER CVSG	CERT. G	CERT. D	CERT. G&R	JURISDICTIONAL STATEMENT N	POST	DIS	AFF	MERITS REV	MERITS AFF	MOTION G	MOTION D
Rehnquist, Ch. J.				3							✓			
~~White~~				✓								—		
Blackmun, J.					out						out			
Stevens, J.				✓							✓			
O'Connor, J.				3							✓			
Scalia, J.					✓						✓			
Kennedy, J.				✓							✓			
Souter, J.				✓							✓			
Thomas, J.				✓							✓			
Ginsburg, J.											✓			

Image 10.9 Docket Sheet *Justice Harry Blackmun's record of the vote in this case shows that Chief Justice William Rehnquist and Justice Sandra Day O'Connor voted to "join 3" meaning that if three others want to grant the case, they would also agree to grant it.* Harry A. Blackmun Papers, Manuscript Division, Library of Congress, Washington, D.C.

know about this issue. And we're walking through familiar terrain. And if there isn't something urgent about the case that is expressed to us at the outset, we know that we're not going to do it."[55]

By tradition, cert is granted if at least four of the justices decide a case deserves to be reviewed—the so-called **rule of four**. This "rule" is not an official rule but, rather, a virtually ironclad norm by which the justices abide. When Congress was considering legislation that would ultimately become the Judiciary Act of 1925, Justice Willis Van Devanter explained the operation of the rule, which was virtually unknown outside of the Court at that time, in part of his testimony before Congress.[56] Sometimes, a justice will also vote to **join 3,** meaning that if three other justices wish to grant certiorari to a case, the justice will also agree to grant it.[57] Essentially, a justice voting to join 3 is saying that he did not initially see the case in question as cert worthy but is willing to suspend judgment if three of his colleagues do think it is cert worthy. The docket sheet that appears in Image 10.9 is an example of Chief Justice Rehnquist and Justice O'Connor voting to join 3.

As Figure 10.3 shows, in recent years the justices have dramatically decreased the number of cases for which they grant review. Criticisms and lamentations about this trend have been bountiful. For example, some conservatives have expressed concern that their opportunities to make policy gains have shrunk as the Court's docket has shrunk.[58] More broadly, observers worry that the Court's limited docket means that important issues of national significance are simply not being decided promptly

FIGURE 10.3

The Supreme Court's Shrinking Docket, 1981–2012

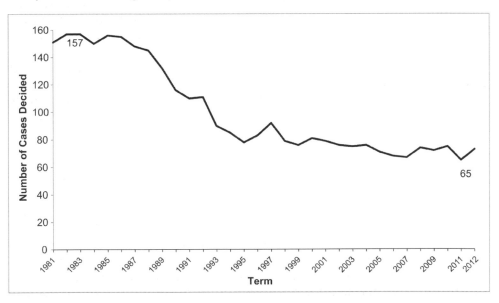

The U.S. Supreme Court's docket is essentially discretionary meaning that the justices choose which cases they want to hear. The number of cases the justices have decided each term has steadily decreased in recent years.

Note: Data reflects the number of cases disposed of each term by signed or per curiam opinion after oral argument.

Source: Adapted from Lee Epstein, Jeffrey A. Segal, Harold J. Spaeth, and Thomas G. Walker, *The Supreme Court Compendium: Data, Decisions & Developments* (Washington, D.C.: Congressional Quarterly Press, 2006) p. 80–81.

enough.[59] A closely related criticism is that the shrunken docket means that "[t]he Justices seldom engage in the process of developing the law through a succession of cases in the common-law tradition. Rather, Court decisions tend to be singular events, largely unconnected to other cases on the docket and even more detached from the work of lower courts."[60] A smaller docket also leaves open the possibility of "capture" by special interests; i.e., the exercise of undue influence by particular groups on the Court. Law professor Richard Lazarus, for example, has demonstrated that the **Supreme Court bar** (a specialized and elite group of attorneys) is particularly efficacious in persuading the Court to accept cases for review that members of the bar wish to be heard.[61] While that may be a wonderful thing for the litigants represented by members of the Supreme Court bar, it may not be so wonderful in terms of its overall effect on the Court's *certiorari* process.

Why has the size of the Court's docket taken a nosedive? Justice Kagan acknowledged that, while "all of us in the abstract would say we should take more cases," the Court is taking half as many cases as it did when she clerked for Justice Thurgood Marshall in 1987.[62] She could not offer an explanation for this trend but hastened to add that she did not believe that important cases were being overlooked. Whether cert-worthy cases are being missed or not, however, the question remains as to why the decline has occurred. One possible culprit is the cert pool. Justice Blackmun was originally of the mind that the cert pool would prompt those preparing pool memos to recommend granting cert more often. "Contrary to Blackmun's concern, [however,] pool clerks did not overzealously recommend grants. Instead the opposite occurred. As the number of justices and clerks joining the pool and reviewing pool memos increased, clerks became more cautious."[63] Further, as Justice Stevens explained it, "You stick your neck out as a clerk when you recommend to grant a case. The risk-averse thing to do is to recommend not to take a case. I think it accounts for the lessening of the docket."[64] Kenneth Starr, a former member of the U.S. Court of Appeals for the District of Columbia who clerked for Chief Justice Warren Burger, has also argued that the cert pool has artificially (and detrimentally) depressed the number of cases granted cert.[65] In typically colorful language, Starr characterized the clerks as follows: "The prevailing spirit among the twenty-five-year old legal savants, whose life experience is necessarily limited in scope, is to seek out and destroy undeserving petitions. The prevailing ethos is that no harm can flow from 'just saying no.'"[66]

Less anecdotally, political scientist and law professor David R. Stras reported evidence that is consistent with the argument that the cert pool is the cause of the decline in the Court's plenary docket. His systematic analysis of the recommendation contained in cert pool memos compared to the ultimate *certiorari* decision by the Court revealed that the level of agreement between the pool and the Court has increased over time, as would be expected as more justices join the pool.[67] Others—including political scientist David O'Brien,[68] and law professors Arthur Hellman,[69] and Margaret and Richard Cordray[70]— offered an alternative explanation for the decline in the Court's docket. In particular, they suggested that the decrease is a function of changes in the Court's membership. Justices who have joined the Court in the past few decades have simply held the view that they can provide the doctrinal guidance necessary with fewer cases. Very recent research by Ryan Owens, a political scientist, and David Simon, a Fellow of the Project on Law and Mind Sciences at Harvard University, demonstrated that the Court's shrinking docket is due to both ideological and contextual factors.[71] Specifically, they showed that the Court's membership changes have led to increasing ideological polarization. When coupled with congressional elimination of the last vestiges of mandatory appeals in 1988, the justices have had more discretion in choosing which cases to hear and have, concomitantly, been more reluctant to grant review.

May It Please the Court: Briefs and Oral Argument

Once the justices have opted to grant *certiorari* and hear a case, the Court directs the parties to prepare **legal briefs**. As we discussed in Chapter Nine, the legal briefs articulate the legal questions to be addressed in a case and lay out the arguments of the appellant and appellee as to how each believes those questions should be answered by the Court. Rule 24 of the *Rules of the Supreme Court of the United States* specifies that only the questions included in the brief will be considered by the Court. " [H]owever, the Court may consider a plain error not among the questions presented but evident from the record and otherwise within its jurisdiction to decide."[72] Scholars have debated about the extent to which the Court hews closely to Rule 24, with some arguing that the justices can and do engage in issue creation by addressing issues not included in the briefs,[73] and others hotly contesting this claim.[74] However, even the strongest evidence in favor of issue creation by the Court makes plain that it is an exception and not the norm.[75] In short, for all intents and purposes, the litigants' briefs are the primary vehicles by which a case is framed for the Court. As Justice Kagan observed:

> The briefs are your avenue into really important, really challenging legal issues, and that's what makes reading briefs fun. And occasionally, very occasionally, you'll read a brief that is just a masterwork of brief-writing, and you'll just enjoy it for that reason alone. But for the most part reading briefs is interesting because the cases are fascinating, and the legal considerations are fascinating. And the briefs are your way—you know, another way—of trying to figure them out and make sense of them. . . . The most important thing in a brief is clarity. If there's one thing about brief-writing you could reform, it's confusing briefs—briefs where you're working too hard to try to figure out what the point is and to figure out how the argument goes. There are two really important things about brief-writing. One is you have to know your best arguments. Second, you have to say those arguments clearly. Sometimes it's frustrating, because you'll be reading a brief and there will be good arguments there, but it's just so hard to get them out of this brief. You have to do so much work by yourself or with clerks to do that. It's a disservice to the real arguments that are there.[76]

Chief Justice Roberts echoed Kagan's comments: "The quality of briefs varies greatly. We get some excellent briefs; we get a lot of very, very good briefs. And there are some where the first thing you can tell in many of them is that the lawyer really hasn't spent a lot of time on it, to be honest with you."[77]

Justice Breyer described his job (and, by extension, the job of his colleagues on the bench) as one of essentially reading: "Most of what we do is in this enormous stack of briefs. Most of what we do is in memos, briefs, reading."[78] However, the briefs the justices (and their clerks) read are not limited to those of the litigants. In recent terms of the Court, each case is almost guaranteed to have at least one *amicus curiae* brief associated with it, and these briefs are another vehicle by which a case is framed for the Court. As political scientist Paul Collins, Jr., documents, *amicus* briefs were present in a third or less of all Supreme Court cases decided on the merits until the late 1950s but the percentage has steadily climbed such that upwards of 90 percent of cases decided on the merits now have *amicus* briefs attached to them.[79] Cases that deal with some areas of the law are more likely to attract *amicus* briefs than others—specifically, cases involving civil rights, economics, and federalism are particularly attractive for *amici*—but "for all issue areas, amicus participation has been on the upswing . . ."[80] One myth is that *amicus curiae* briefs do not provide original information to the Court; that is, information not contained in the litigants' briefs. Based on a systematic examination of every opinion issued in orally argued cases in the Court's 1992 term (and their associated *amicus curiae* briefs), political scientists James Spriggs and Paul Wahlbeck found reality a bit at odds with that myth. While it is true that the *amicus* briefs they evaluated often reiterated arguments contained in the appellant or appellee's briefs, a substantial minority of the *amicus* briefs provided wholly unique arguments not present in a litigant brief (26.2 percent of the briefs supporting the appellant, 24.2 percent of the briefs supporting the appellee).[81]

After the justices receive the legal briefs, they work with their clerks to prepare for oral argument. Former Justice Ginsburg clerk Jay Wexler explained:

> All the justices use their clerks differently for this purpose. Most require their clerks to prepare "bench memos," papers that range anywhere from three to 50 pages long, which summarize the parties' arguments and offer the clerk's own analysis of the relevant legal issues. Some justices discuss the cases intensely with their clerks; Justice Ginsburg tended to do relatively little of that.[82]

Image 10.10 Supreme Court Bench
U.S. Supreme Court Chamber. Carol M. Highsmith Archive, Prints and Photographs Division, Library of Congress, Washington, D.C.

While Justice Stevens did not have his clerks prepare bench memos, he did spend considerable time listening to his clerks:

> I always talk to my law clerks. I don't have them write bench memos, but I always
> review the cases and my thinking about the case both before argument and after
> argument. I ask them to come in, and we sit down and talk about what happened at
> the argument. Then I'll talk to them again before and after a conference. I have a lot
> of conversation with my clerks to get their reaction to a case.[83]

Given that the justices have all the information in a case submitted to them in writing, some have questioned whether oral argument matters: "To say that oral argument
is important seems unremarkable. In truth, however, this statement may be accurate in
only a few close cases."[84] Indeed, some of the justices themselves (e.g., Justice Clarence
Thomas) have downplayed the role of oral argument.[85] But other justices disagree.[86] Justice Sotomayor, for example, described how seeing a litigant in court can make a difference: "When you're in your office reading the briefs you understand the voices that
they're giving you, but when you see their faces it just reinforces that importance in a way
nothing else can."[87] Early in the Court's history, oral argument was virtually unlimited.
Daniel Webster's impassioned arguments on behalf of Dartmouth College in *Dartmouth
College v. Woodward*[88] went on for some 4 hours![89] But, as the Court's caseload increased,
the justices began to feel the pinch of unlimited oral argument and, thus, began to impose
restrictions.[90] For example, in 1849 the Court changed its rules to limit each counsel to no
more than 2 hours, unless the Court explicitly granted permission to exceed that limit.
The Court revised its rules again in 1925 to limit oral argument to no more than 1 hour
per side, and revised them yet again in 1970 to decrease it to 30 minutes per side, except
under special circumstances.

The special circumstances that the Court has found to warrant extending the amount
of time allotted for oral argument have arisen only very occasionally. Not surprisingly,
these cases involve highly complex and high profile matters. For example, the Court
allowed 90 minutes of oral argument in *Bush v. Gore*,[91] which determined the outcome
of the 2000 presidential election, and 4 hours in *McConnell v. Federal Elections Commission*,[92] which adjudicated the constitutionality of the Bipartisan Campaign Reform
Act of 2002 (often referred to as the McCain-Feingold Act).[93] For the vast majority
of cases, however, 30 minutes per side is the reality.[94] Justice Kennedy explained his
frustration with the limited time that he is able to devote to a case in oral argument:
"We have very difficult cases. The amount of time we give is so short that it is cruel.
My colleague Justice Breyer and I wish we had more than 30 minutes per side."[95] Justice Stevens commented on what he expected from attorneys at oral argument: "Be
well prepared, of course. Be intellectually honest; don't try and conceal problems that
the judges are going to find anyway. And do the best you can to explain why your side
should win."[96]

Despite its name, oral argument is not a process in which attorneys deliver prepared remarks and the justices listen intently, silently contemplating the arguments
being made. That myth is clearly at odds with the reality of oral argument, in which the
attorneys attempt to make their most persuasive arguments but are constantly interrupted by a barrage of questions posed by the justices. In fact, there is so much questioning that the current Court has the reputation of having "a hot bench"—one where

the justices ask (perhaps) too many questions. As Judge J. Harvie Wilkinson of the U.S. Court of Appeals for the Fourth Circuit observed, "The Supreme Court bench seems to me to get hotter and hotter and hotter."[97] In discussing the "hot bench," Chief Justice Roberts noted:

> First of all, there are excuses for it. We don't talk about [the disposition on the merits of] cases before the argument. When we get out on the bench, it's really the first time we start to get some clues about what our colleagues think. So we often are using questions to bring out points that we think our colleagues ought to know about. . . . It is too much, and I do think we need to address it a little bit. I do think the lawyers feel cheated sometimes. It's nice for us to get a good feel for where everyone else is, but it also would be nice for them to have a chance to present their argument.[98]

Oral argument as a dialogue between and among the justices (as much as or more so than between the attorneys and the justices) is particularly well illustrated in *Danforth v.*

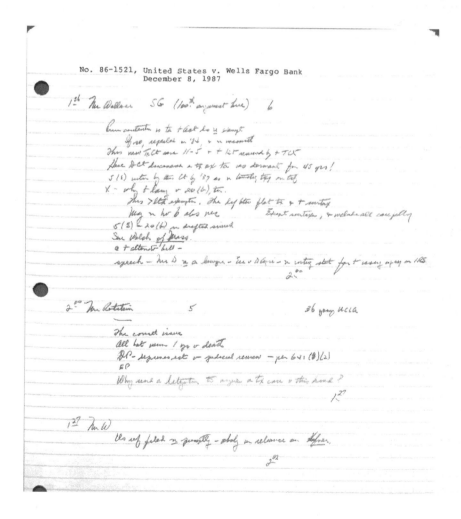

Image 10.11 Oral Argument Notes *Justice Harry Blackmun's oral argument notes provide a grade for each attorney. Deputy Solicitor General Lawrence G. Wallace gets a "6" on a 10-point scale while his opponent, a "young" "36"-year-old from "UCLA" Law School scores a "5".* Harry A. Blackmun Papers, Manuscript Division, Library of Congress, Washington, D.C.

Minnesota, a case dealing with how to interpret and apply retroactive rules in criminal proceedings.[99]

> The exchange began with a long hypothetical posed by Breyer (including a discussion of metaphysics and the retroactivity of law). Diamond [the attorney arguing on behalf of the state of Minnesota] started to respond to this hypothetical question, but Breyer spoke over him and Scalia interrupted Breyer to give his own thoughts about retroactivity and metaphysics. From there, Stevens responded to Scalia, and Breyer sought to clarify his position before Diamond spoke two additional (albeit meaningless) words—"Your Honor." Finally, a sympathetic Chief Justice John Roberts drew chuckles from the gallery when he told Diamond, "I think you're handling these questions very well." Ruth Bader Ginsburg immediately followed the laughter and made it clear the justices were not at all concerned with Diamond's view on this point: "That was not a question addressed to you, Mr. Diamond."[100]

Justice Kennedy has observed that sometimes lawyers are not prepared for oral argument as a conversation between and among the justices: "I think they could understand the dynamic a little bit better. They could understand that when I'm asking a question, I'm sometimes trying to convince my own colleagues, and so they could answer not just me but answer based on what they think the whole Court needs to know to decide the case."[101]

Ample scholarly evidence makes clear that oral argument matters.[102] As is the case in traffic court and student grade disputes, high quality arguments are more likely to prevail than poor quality arguments in oral argument before the Supreme Court. Accordingly, in recent years an elite group of attorneys have come to specialize in Supreme Court oral argument. This Supreme Court bar (the same bar that, as noted earlier in this chapter, is thought by some to exercise undue influence on the Court's *certiorari* decisions) is largely composed of attorneys who formerly worked in the Solicitor General's office or clerked at the Supreme Court. Justice Kagan explained: "They understand what the exercise is about and are extremely good at it. It means we are actually getting answers to our questions."[103] Still, on occasion, a poor argument can win if the justices are either predisposed to ruling that way or persuasive arguments can be marshaled from within the Court by justices or clerks *after* oral argument. Justice Stevens said:

> I can remember a case when I was a law clerk that I think was argued by an attorney general of one of the states. It was a tax case in which I remember all the law clerks in advance of the argument thought there's no way in the world that this guy could win—and particularly when he made his argument, that there's nothing to it. And he was so bad that the clerks decided they'd better try and research the problem and figure out what arguments might be made on that side of the case, and they came up with arguments he totally omitted, and he won the case. But that doesn't happen very often.[104]

In short, quality oral argument is neither a necessary nor sufficient condition for securing a successful outcome in the Court but the odds of prevailing are much greater with high quality rather than low quality oral argument.[105]

HOW DO WE KNOW?

Does Oral Argument Influence Supreme Court Justices?

Political scientists Timothy Johnson, Paul Wahlbeck, and James Spriggs analyzed the evaluations made by Justice Harry Blackmun of the attorneys who participated in oral argument.[106] Blackmun's notes included substantive comments about each attorney's arguments and a grade for their presentation. Specifically, the authors analyzed the grades Justice Blackmun assigned to attorneys during oral arguments in a random sample of 539 cases decided between 1970 and 1994.

First, they examined whether his grades actually measured the quality of oral arguments. Accordingly, the authors considered what factors influenced Blackmun's grades, including his ideology. They found that attorneys with more prior litigating experience and attorneys from the U.S. government, especially those from the Solicitor General's office, received higher grades from Blackmun. When the Solicitor General argued before the Court, his grade was 2.3 points higher on a 100-point scale than those attorneys who were located outside of Washington. Additionally, they found that attorneys who attended elite law schools and Washington insiders earned higher grades. Finally, they examined whether those attorneys who presented arguments compatible with Justice Blackmun's ideological preferences received higher grades and found that his evaluations were not greatly influenced by his own ideological leanings. Although that independent variable was statistically significant in a positive direction, meaning that Blackmun was more likely to give an ideologically compatible argument a higher grade, they found that a 1 unit increase in ideological compatibility only resulted in a .32-point change in Blackmun's evaluation of the attorney. The authors concluded "that our measure of oral argument quality is not appreciably tainted by Justice Blackmun's ideology; thus, it may appropriately be used to explain the other justices' final votes on the merits."

Next, they examined whether high quality arguments affect the justices' votes on the merits of the case. Specifically, they examined whether each justice, excluding Blackmun, voted to reverse the lower court decision. They coded votes to reverse as 1 and votes to affirm as 0. Even when controlling for a justice's ideology and other factors affecting Court outcomes, they found that the oral-argument grade correlates highly with a justice's final vote on the merits. Specifically, when all the independent variables are held at their means, there is a 59.2 percent chance that a justice will vote to reverse. However, when the oral-argument grade is 1 standard deviation above the mean—meaning that the attorney offered a higher quality argument—the probability increases to 64.7 percent. When the appellant's attorney is manifestly better than the appellee's attorney, there is a 77.9 percent chance that a justice will vote for the petitioner, whereas this likelihood decreases to 38.6 percent when the appellee's attorney is clearly better. Thus, the authors demonstrated that justices are more likely to vote for the litigant whose attorney provided higher quality oral advocacy (as measured by Justice Blackmun) even after controlling for ideological considerations, meaning that oral arguments do enter into Supreme Court decision making.

Oral argument affords the justices the opportunity to signal their position on a case (through their questions, comments, and observations), and it is an opportunity they avail themselves of frequently. Justice Alito noted that each term he arrives at the first oral argument "filled with hope that this will finally be the term when all of my colleagues see the light of day"—a hope that "begins to fade five or ten minutes into the first case."[107] As a result of this foreshadowing, journalists attend (and routinely report on) oral argument in an attempt to divine how the justices might ultimately vote on a case. For example, on the first day of the 2013 term, the *Washington*

Post reported on two orally argued cases: "On Monday, the justices seemed unsure about a case. . . . The justices asked tough questions of both sides, and it was hard to predict the outcome of the case. . . . In a second case heard Monday, the justices seemed frustrated. . . . Several justices wondered whether they should try to decide the issue or send it back for more work in lower courts."[108] Research shows that when the justices pay more attention to one side during oral arguments, that side is much more likely to lose its case.[109] One study examined the transcripts of oral arguments of all cases from 1979 to 1995 and found that when the justices ask an equal number of questions to the petitioner and respondent, there is a .64 probability of reversal.[110] When the Court asks 50 more questions of the petitioner, this probability goes down to .39. When the Court asks 50 more questions of the respondent, this probability goes up to .85. Additionally, research shows that when the Court directs more hostile questions toward a particular side's attorney, the Court is less likely to rule in favor of that side.[111] Of course no one (including sometimes the justices themselves) knows for sure how the justices will vote on a case until the final decision is announced many months later.

POP CULTURE

Gideon's Trumpet

In the made-for-TV film *Gideon's Trumpet,*[112] we meet Clarence Earl Gideon, an elderly man (played by Henry Fonda) who is accused of breaking and entering to commit petty larceny; in particular, he is accused of robbing a small-town pool hall late one night after it closed. At his trial, Gideon requests that an attorney be appointed to defend him, as he has no money to secure the services of a lawyer himself. The judge informs Gideon that, under state law, counsel can only be appointed for cases that involve crimes that carry the death penalty. Gideon attempts to provide his own defense at trial but he is unsuccessful in doing so and is convicted by the jury. In prison, Gideon studies the law and hand-writes a petition to the U.S. Supreme Court asking the justices to review his case.

At the Court, the Chief Justice (played by John Houseman) meets with his law clerks. One eager clerk brings Gideon's petition to the chief's attention. The chief explains that under the Court's 20-year-old precedent—*Betts v. Brady*[113]—Gideon is not entitled to counsel. The chief comments to the clerk: "He's asking us to change our minds? Well, we seem to do that every twenty years or so." The chief then tells the clerk to draft a memorandum for the other justices. In conference, the chief brings the case up for discussion and says that the question is whether it is time to overturn *Betts v. Brady*. The justices discuss the matter and five justices vote to grant the request for *certiorari*.

The Court appoints counsel for Gideon: prominent Washington lawyer Abe Fortas—played by Jose Ferrer—who would later be appointed to the Court by President Lyndon Johnson.[114] Fortas is personally moved by the case and tells his associates: "What I'd like to say to the Court is: 'Let's not talk; let's go down there and watch one of these fellows try to defend themselves.'" At oral argument, Fortas begins his argument but speaks for less than a minute before he is interrupted by a question from one of the justices, a member of the majority in *Betts* and a skeptic about overruling that precedent. Fortas continues to answer questions from the justices, including those who wonder what the implications would be should they decide to rule in Gideon's favor. The attorney for the state speaks next and is vigorously questioned by a number of justices who are apparently ready to overturn *Betts*.

After the case is decided, Gideon receives a phone call from Fortas, who informs him that he won in a unanimous verdict. However, Gideon is dismayed to find out that he must stand trial again. Gideon believes that the Double Jeopardy Clause of the Fifth Amendment prohibits a retrial. When he meets with his new lawyers from the American Civil Liberties Union they explain to him that double jeopardy protections do not apply to prisoners who win on appeal. Back in the Florida trial court, Gideon convinces the judge to appoint a local attorney to represent him. While the motion to dismiss the case on double jeopardy grounds is unsuccessful, Gideon's new attorney wins the trial through jury selection, poking holes in eyewitness testimony, and ultimately creating reasonable doubt in the minds of the jurors.

While the film is primarily about Gideon's pursuit of justice—and that of his fellow inmates who also were not provided counsel—it is also about the judicial process and specifically about how cases move from trial to appellate courts and back again. The film is also one of the few that highlights what takes place inside the Court, including vis-à-vis the role of law clerks, the private conference of the justices, and oral argument.

Voting, Opinion Assignment, and Opinion Writing

Once oral arguments have concluded, the justices must then determine how to dispose of the case. As they did when determining which petitions they wished to review in the *certiorari* process, the justices now meet in conference to discuss how they wish to decide (on the merits) the cases they have heard (or are disposing of on the briefs without oral argument). The justices are the only ones present at the conference and, usually, the chief justice begins by stating the facts of the case as well as his vote. Votes proceed in order of seniority with the most junior justice speaking and voting last.[115] There is an informal rule that no justice speaks twice until each justice has spoken at least once,[116] and the discussion of most cases ends after each justice has had his or her initial say (i.e., usually each justice speaks but once on any given case). But on occasion there is further discussion. Justice Kagan explained:

> Certainly that's true if you have a fractured Court and then people will try very hard to try to keep talking until some kind of majority emerges. But in other cases too there will be times when people will want to respond to things that another justice has said or want to say "that strikes me as right or wrong or a good understanding or a bad understanding." People will want to debate a little bit often. People will want to raise questions about what each other has said. So sometimes the conversation after the initial go-round can be fairly extensive. And then other times it's like "We've all said what we've said and that about resolves the matter."[117]

Justice Breyer has observed that all of the justices are actively involved in the process: "The key to that conference is people are saying what they really think. They're not trying to create an impression. And everybody writes down what everybody else says and there is some discussion and it works because we all respect each other as individuals."[118]

The most junior justice is tasked to serve as the official note-taker—though each of the justices takes his or her own notes and keeps track of the voting—and doorkeeper in case anyone knocks or the justices need something to be brought to them. After her first two years performing this duty, Justice Kagan remarked: "I myself think it's some kind of hazing ritual."[119] Because she votes last, Kagan explained, she is unable to say anything at conference to influence her colleagues before they vote. Instead, she uses oral argument as the venue to raise issues and make sure her colleagues are aware of how she is thinking about a case: "I do use argument as a way to, not always but sometimes, as a way to sort of float some ideas in hopes that some or one or many of my colleagues hear them."[120]

A day or two after conference, opinions are assigned by the chief justice if he is in the majority vote coalition. If the chief did not vote in the majority, then the opinion is assigned by the most senior associate justice in the majority. Image 10.14, on p. 402, in an example of an opinion assignment list. Who writes the opinion is important because, if five or more justices agree with the content of that opinion, then that **majority opinion** is the law of the land. Yet the majority opinion author cannot simply write whatever he or she wishes. Instead, the majority opinion is supposed to reflect the collective view of the majority. If the majority opinion does not reflect the majority's views, the other justices in the majority will suggest changes once the opinion is circulated. Thus, majority opinion authors take care to draft an opinion that will gain as many adherents as possible and require as few changes as possible upon circulation to the other justices.

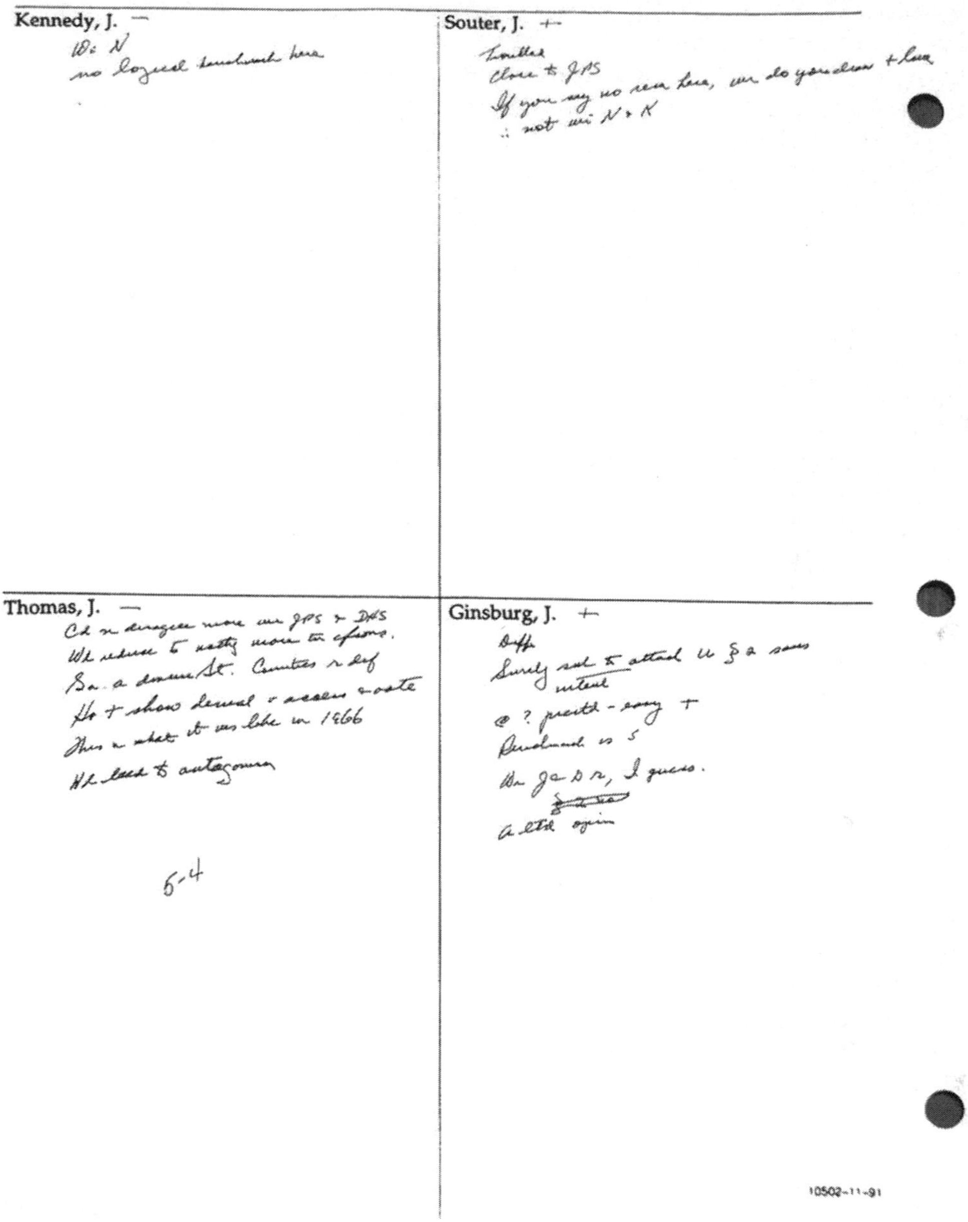
Kennedy, J.
Souter, J.
Thomas, J.
Ginsburg, J.
10502-11-91

Image 10.13
Conference Notes
Justice Harry Blackmun's conference notes show that Justice David Souter said he was "troubled," "close to" the position of Justice "J[ohn] P[aul] S[tevens]," and not with Justices "N[ino Scalia] & [Anthony] K[ennedy]."
Harry A. Blackmun Papers, Manuscript Division, Library of Congress, Washington, D.C.

In making opinion assignments, the chief justice is at least partially concerned with distributing the workload evenly and attempts to make sure that each of his colleagues are assigned an equal number of majority opinions each term.[121] This contributes to the efficiency with which the Court processes its workload. Similarly, taking into account the expertise of the justices when making opinion assignments can have salutary effects on the efficiency of the Court.[122] Indeed, some justices become expert in a particular area of

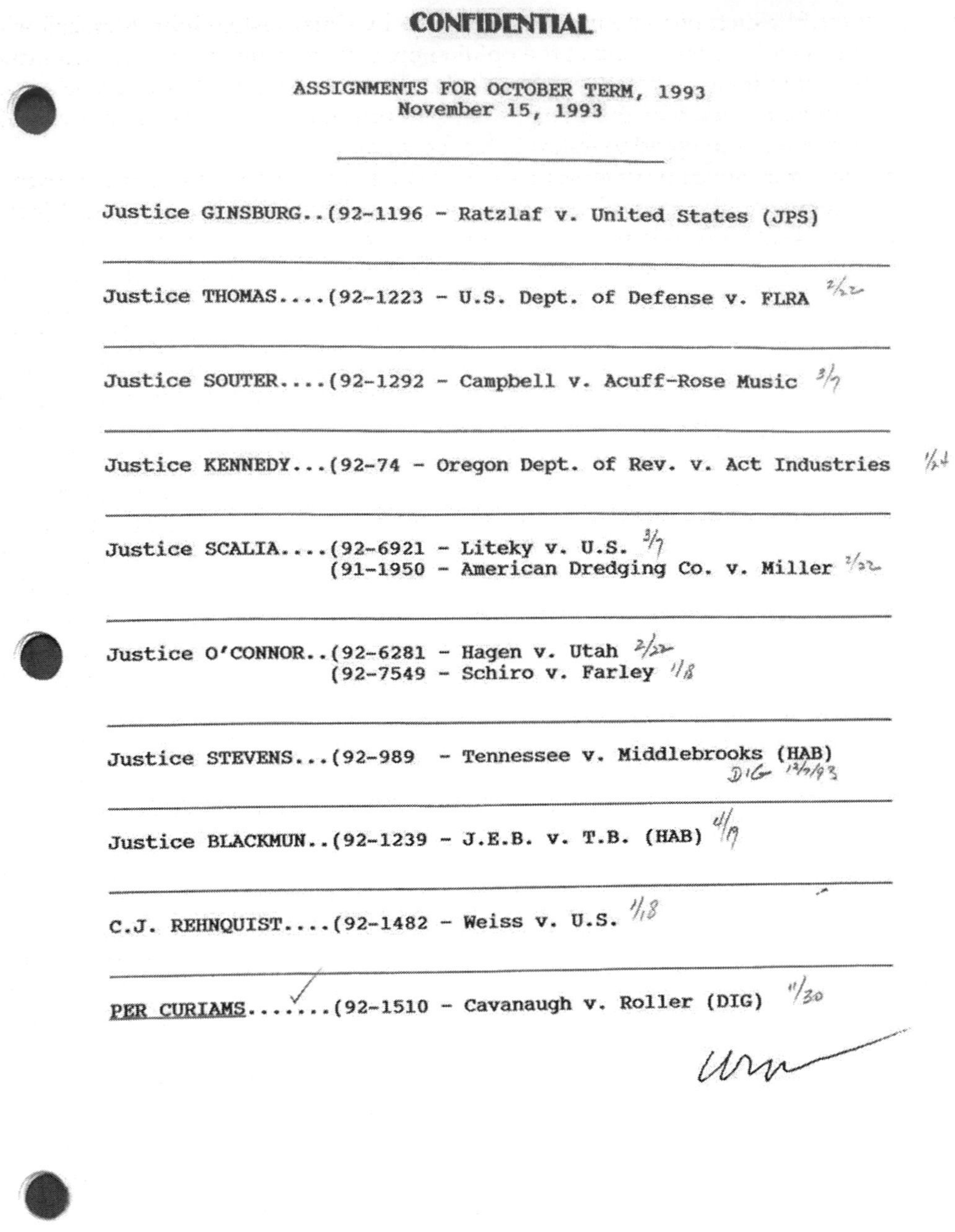

Image 10.14
Assignment Sheet
Chief Justice Rehnquist circulated this Assignment Sheet showing that Justice Stevens assigned one opinion to Justice Ginsburg while Justice Blackmun assigned one to himself and one to Justice Stevens. Harry A. Blackmun Papers, Manuscript Division, Library of Congress, Washington, D.C.

CONFIDENTIAL

ASSIGNMENTS FOR OCTOBER TERM, 1993
November 15, 1993

Justice GINSBURG..(92-1196 - Ratzlaf v. United States (JPS)

Justice THOMAS....(92-1223 - U.S. Dept. of Defense v. FLRA   2/22

Justice SOUTER....(92-1292 - Campbell v. Acuff-Rose Music   3/7

Justice KENNEDY...(92-74 - Oregon Dept. of Rev. v. Act Industries   1/24

Justice SCALIA....(92-6921 - Liteky v. U.S.   3/7
                  (91-1950 - American Dredging Co. v. Miller   2/22

Justice O'CONNOR..(92-6281 - Hagen v. Utah   2/22
                  (92-7549 - Schiro v. Farley   1/8

Justice STEVENS...(92-989   - Tennessee v. Middlebrooks (HAB)
                            DIG 12/7/93

Justice BLACKMUN..(92-1239 - J.E.B. v. T.B. (HAB)   4/19

C.J. REHNQUIST....(92-1482 - Weiss v. U.S.   4/8

PER CURIAMS.......(92-1510 - Cavanaugh v. Roller (DIG)   11/30

the law and routinely get the opinion assignment in those cases.[123] For example, Justice Sandra Day O'Connor was assigned majority opinions in a number of affirmative action cases and Justice Kennedy has written majority opinions in a number of landmark gay rights cases.

Chiefs often assign important, groundbreaking cases to themselves. One reason is to lend the decision an air of legitimacy as the chief justice is often seen as the Court's leader. Another reason is that chiefs—like all justices—want to make their mark on the Courts on which they serve and be thought of as "great justices" by the public, press, and practitioners.[124] Much of this impetus was begun by Chief Justice John Marshall who, in the Court's early years, changed the opinion process from one in which each justice issued his own opinion in every case—*seriatim* (Latin for "in series")—to a single institutional opinion delivered by the chief justice.[125] In this sense, every chief that has served since Marshall has attempted to follow in his footsteps.

There is also evidence to suggest that chief justices are strategic in their approach to opinion assignment. For example, anecdotal accounts have suggested that Chief Justice Burger—who, as chief, would normally have cast his vote first in conference—chose to pass in order to see which way his colleagues were leaning, and then cast a vote that ensured that he was in the majority vote coalition (and, hence, in control of the opinion assignment).[126] Political scientists Timothy Johnson, James Spriggs, and Paul Wahlbeck provide more systematic evidence on this point. Using the conference notes taken by Justice Louis Powell during his time on the Court, Johnson and his collaborators demonstrated that both chief justices and senior associate justices (who, recall, are those with assignment power when the chief is not in the majority coalition) were more likely to pass when they had uncertainty about the votes the other justices will cast.[127] Recent work by political scientists, Kaitlyn Sill, Joseph Ura, and Stacia Haynie goes further and links the decision to pass in the initial conference vote to the subsequent assigning decision.[128] What they find in their analysis of the behavior of Chief Justice Burger is that he assigned opinions to justices who were further from the ideological composition of the Court's majority when he passed in the initial conference vote than when he had not passed: "The chief justice's ability to pass in a conference vote and preserve the option of strategically joining a majority coalition to control the opinion assignment process provides some opportunity to moderate the behavior of majorities that might form at the ideological extremes of the Court."[129]

In closely divided cases, opinions are sometimes assigned to justices who are perceived to have moderate, narrow, or wavering positions—so-called "swing votes." The conventional wisdom is that assigning the opinion to the least ideologically extreme justice in the majority coalition will allow that justice to write an opinion to his or her satisfaction, thereby keeping that justice from defecting to the minority and potentially transforming the minority into the majority. In contrast, a more ideologically extreme justice may write a majority opinion that could cause a swing justice to change his or her vote. In addition, a chief justice may choose to assign an opinion to a moderate member of the majority vote coalition because it could result in an opinion that entices some dissenters to join the majority fold. The evidence as to the efficaciousness of this strategy, however, has been called into question by several scholars. For example, political scientists Saul Brenner and Harold Spaeth found that moderate justices are no more likely to maintain the original majority coalition than are the more extreme members of the majority coalition.[130] In other work, Brenner and Spaeth (along with their colleague Timothy Hagle) provided evidence that suggests that dissenters are not more likely to join a majority opinion written by a moderate justice than a majority opinion written by a less moderate justice.[131]

So, in the end, are chief justices more concerned about advancing policy goals or furthering administrative efficiency? Scholars Forrest Maltzman and Paul Wahlbeck offer persuasive evidence that chiefs pursue policy goals when they can but that they remain attentive to institutional constraints.[132] They examined the initial opinion assignment sheets found in the papers of Chief Justice Earl Warren, Justice William Brennan, and Justice Thurgood Marshall, using them to determine the assignments made by Chief Justices Warren, Burger, and Rehnquist for an almost 40-year span (1953–1990). Taking into account both ideological factors (e.g., the ideological proximity of the chief justice and the opinion writer) and non-ideological factors (e.g., equity, expertise, efficiency), Maltzman and Wahlbeck found that, all things being equal, chiefs were more likely to assign

Image 10.15
Draft Opinion
*Justice Harry Black-
mun's hand-written
corrections to his
clerk-written draft
of a death penalty
case where Blackmun
decided, "I no longer
shall tinker with the
machinery of death."*
Harry A. Blackmun
Papers, Manuscript
Division, Library of
Congress, Washington,
D.C.

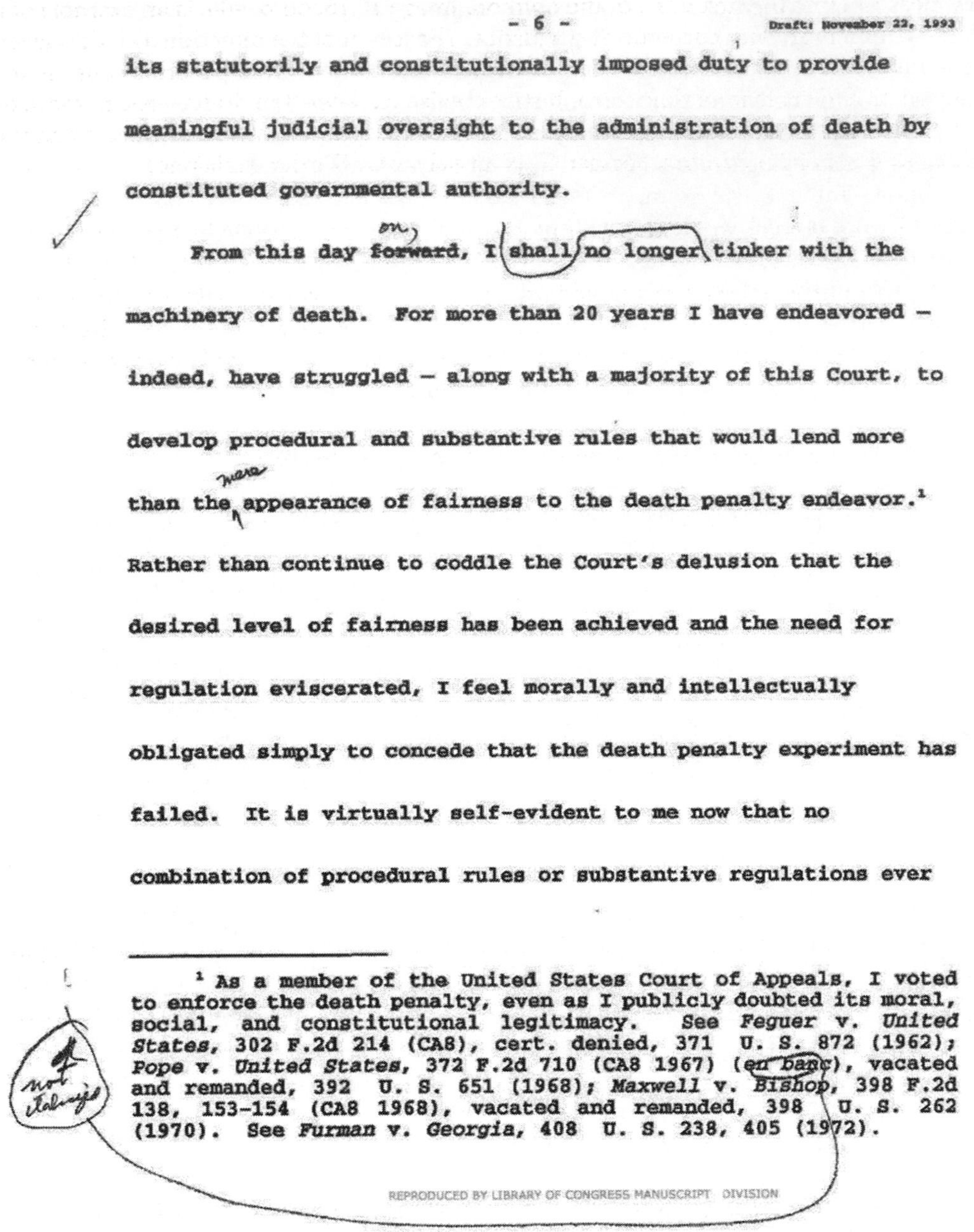

- 6 -   Draft: November 22, 1993

its statutorily and constitutionally imposed duty to provide

meaningful judicial oversight to the administration of death by

constituted governmental authority.

From this day ~~forward~~, I shall no longer tinker with the

machinery of death. For more than 20 years I have endeavored —

indeed, have struggled — along with a majority of this Court, to

develop procedural and substantive rules that would lend more

than the appearance of fairness to the death penalty endeavor.[1]

Rather than continue to coddle the Court's delusion that the

desired level of fairness has been achieved and the need for

regulation eviscerated, I feel morally and intellectually

obligated simply to concede that the death penalty experiment has

failed. It is virtually self-evident to me now that no

combination of procedural rules or substantive regulations ever

---

[1] As a member of the United States Court of Appeals, I voted
to enforce the death penalty, even as I publicly doubted its moral,
social, and constitutional legitimacy. See *Feguer* v. *United
States*, 302 F.2d 214 (CA8), cert. denied, 371 U. S. 872 (1962);
Pope v. *United States*, 372 F.2d 710 (CA8 1967) (en banc), vacated
and remanded, 392 U. S. 651 (1968); *Maxwell* v. *Bishop*, 398 F.2d
138, 153-154 (CA8 1968), vacated and remanded, 398 U. S. 262
(1970). See *Furman* v. *Georgia*, 408 U. S. 238, 405 (1972).

opinions to ideological allies but that the pursuit of organizational needs constituted an
independent motivation (that is, unconditioned by ideological goals). Their empirical
results lead them to conclude: "Far from single-mindedly seeking ideological gains, the
chief justice pursues multiple goals through his power of assignment. . ."[133]

The myth is of a learned justice laboring alone, pouring over legal tomes and treatises
before crafting a well-honed legal opinion that is so masterful that its "truth" is obvious
to all that behold it. The reality is quite a bit messier. Once the opinion assignment has
been determined, the justice to whom the opinion is assigned most often directs his or her

law clerk to write the first draft of the opinion. Image 10.15, on p. 404, is an example of a clerk-written draft with correction by a justice. The extent of the direction a clerk is given depends on the individual justice. Some provide minimal input while others lay out the key arguments and cases in outline form. Justices revise clerk-written drafts—again, more or less depending on both the individual justice's level of engagement in the process and the clerk's skill at opinion writing. Former Ginsburg clerk Jay Wexler explained:

> The clerks usually write a first draft of the opinions that their justice has been assigned to write. Some people find this shocking, but it really is not that big a deal. At least in Justice Ginsburg's chambers, the boss would give us a detailed outline to work from and then, once we turned in our drafts, totally rewrite them. The best you could really hope for as a clerk is to get a little pet phrase or goofy word or other quirky something-or-other into the final opinion.[134]

Justice Kennedy described the process in his chambers as follows:

> Right when I hear the opinion's assigned, I'll write out what I think should be the key portions, but then I obviously have to discuss the cases and so forth. I tell my clerk what I want written, but I can't read what the clerk writes until I've read my own. Because the clerk spends a long time on it, and if you're on a scale of 1 to 10, he'll be at level 8. And if I haven't written anything, I'm still at level 1. And I won't know the false starts that the clerk made, or the blind alley, whatever the metaphor is, until I've gone down the blind alley or made the false start myself. There are certain things that you think immediately will be the way to decide the case, but that doesn't work. But you have to almost try them yourself before you understand that. So it's very hard to read someone else's writing unless you've written something on it before. Then you know why this suggestion is being made.[135]

Justice Kagan explained that after she receives a clerk-written draft, she displays it on her computer screen alongside a blank document in which she composes a fresh opinion, using the clerk draft to orient her in terms of structure and order and to see what does and does not substantively work: "I write all my own opinions. For me it's really important that an opinion sounds like me. I am quite sure that I have had clerks who are better purer writers than I am but it's not the way I write. For me, I don't think through a problem until I write through a problem."[136] What does a Kagan opinion sound like? Law professor Laura Krugman Ray explained Kagan's style like this:

> Whether she is writing for the Court, concurring, or dissenting, Kagan's style is remarkably conversational. She employs a range of rhetorical strategies to speak directly to the reader, suggesting that her enterprise is less indoctrination than a more congenial mode of persuasion. Leavening her legal prose with colloquial diction, she engages the reader in something approaching an informational, if one-sided, chat.[137]

It has become increasingly rare for justices to write their own opinions with little or no clerk input prior to drafting. John Paul Stevens explained why he endeavored to write his own opinions during his tenure from 1975 to 2010: "I think a judge learns more about a case if he has to put his thoughts down on paper. It helps you think through a case, and when you write it out yourself, you often learn things about the case that you hadn't realized. It's part of the learning process and decisional process that I think is really quite important."[138] In short, Stevens saw the act of writing an opinion as an important part of arriving at the most appropriate resolution of the case.[139] Early in the history of the Supreme Court law clerk, clerks might occasionally be given the job of writing an opinion draft; however, that was "largely an exercise in learning the law and not for use by their justice."[140] One humorous (yet poignant) example was recounted by John Knox, a former clerk for Justice James McReynolds. Upon presenting his justice with an opinion he drafted (in fact the only one he ever drafted for the Justice), Knox observed that Justice McReynolds "quietly reached across the desk and silently, almost gently let my opinion slide downward into his wastebasket."[141] Over time, the justices have relied on the clerks more and more in the opinion-writing process. While they originally were most likely to employ a **retention model** (in which a justice drafts her own opinion and calls on the clerks for editing, adding citations and footnotes, and the like), they are now more likely to employ a **delegation model** (in which a clerk drafts the first draft of an opinion and the justice then revises that draft).[142]

Critics suggest that opinions have gotten longer—and therefore more convoluted—over time because the clerks have taken on the primary responsibility for drafting the opinions.[143] Justice Stevens agreed:

> When a judge writes out an opinion, he can explain what his thinking is and do it in so many words, and that's the end of it, whereas the capable, scholarly law clerks tend to feel they really have to prove everything. And so they will often be much more thorough in their research and their consideration of all the arguments than the judge who just sort of thinks he maybe has to tell the world what motivated his particular actions, so I really think that's part of it.[144]

Whether long or short, when the justice is satisfied with the result, the opinion draft is circulated to the other justices via written memoranda. While their law clerks regularly use e-mail to communicate with one another, the justices prefer to do things the traditional way. Justice Kagan noted: "We communicate by written message. A messenger walks around the corner to deliver them."[145] With the opinion drafted and circulated, the process of forming a coalition behind the opinion begins in earnest.

Join Me: Coalition Formation

After the majority opinion author circulates a draft, the clerks from the other chambers review it and, if necessary, suggest changes and make recommendations to their respective justices. The goal is to achieve as much consensus as possible and, contrary to popular myth, the reality is that the justices reach unanimity about one-third of the time and reach a high-level of agreement more often than not.[146] Justice Kagan commented: "We agree more than people know and more than we're given credit for. Many of our opinions are unanimous and if they're not unanimous they're 8-1 or 7-2."[147] As political scientist Lee Epstein, law professor William Landes, and Judge Richard Posner of the United States Court of Appeals for the Seventh Circuit report, high levels of unanimity do not mean that the ideology of the justices does not come into play.[148] But it is nonetheless remarkable that the justices are so often in agreement. That agreement often requires a good deal of negotiation and compromise between and among the justices.[149]

After reviewing the draft majority opinion, the clerks and justices write memoranda that are sent to the opinion author. These memos may be as simple as two words:

"Join me," meaning that a justice agrees entirely with the draft opinion and requests no changes, so he should be "joined" to the opinion as written. Alternatively, the memos may suggest numerous changes (both big and small) and detail the rationale behind those suggested changes. Depending on the justice, those memos may contain a "mixture of appeals, threats, and offers to compromise."[150] In the majority opinion author's chambers, the clerk who originally drafted the opinion reviews these memos and makes recommendations to her justice about what should (or should not) be changed and why. Justice Alito commented: "What you *want* is a memo saying, 'Perfect! Don't change a word!' What you *get* is, 'if you take this or that [part of the opinion] out, I'll sign.' "[151] Chief Justice Roberts said: "You have to remember this is a collegial enterprise, and when you're judging authorship, you have to appreciate that compromises are made to get a Court. Somebody says, 'Put in this language' to get a vote. It may not be the language I would have chosen, but I'll do it if I need the vote."[152]

This process of forming a majority coalition that is entirely satisfied with the majority opinion (or at least satisfied sufficiently to sign off on the opinion) can take months to complete. Image 10.16, on p. 408, is an example of how Justice Blackmun kept track of the memos and opinions in each case. Throughout the process, the clerks mine the **clerk network** during lunchtime, in the hallways, and on the basketball court (the highest court of the land[153]) to glean information to share with their justice on the positions of the other justices and what changes might be needed to secure a majority.[154] In this sense, the clerks act as informal ambassadors during the negotiating and bargaining process, while justices rarely if ever bargain face-to-face or over the phone (though that does happen on occasion). The empirical evidence on point demonstrates that bargaining over the content of the majority opinion is structured, in part, by the ideological distance between the individual justices and the draft opinion.[155] That is, each justice is interested in negotiating to get the final content of the opinion as close as possible to his preferred position. However, the justices are not naïve in their responses to majority opinion drafts. Rather, they are cognizant of the fact that the justice writing the majority opinion must accommodate not just one, but at least four justices (plus himself) to ensure the opinion is, in fact, the majority opinion.[156]

Indeed, justices who are wholly unsatisfied (or only partially satisfied) with the reasoning and/or result of the majority opinion may write their own separate opinions to lodge a concurring or dissenting view.[157] A justice authoring a **concurring opinion** (or joining one authored by another justice) may see it as necessary because, while there is agreement over the outcome of the case, the majority opinion author may be unwilling (or perhaps unable) to accommodate everything the justice sought in the bargaining process that produced the majority opinion. Concurring opinions may also further illuminate and reinforce a point made by the majority opinion or take the form of a "counter-dissent" defending the majority opinion against charges made by dissenting justices.[158] As noted in Chapter Nine, a concurrence that agrees with both the outcome and the reasoning for that outcome as articulated in the majority opinion is referred to as a **regular concurrence**, while a concurrence that agrees with the outcome but not the reasoning for that outcome as articulated in the majority opinion is referred to as a **special concurrence**. Any justice in the majority coalition may issue a concurring opinion in any case and for any reason he may desire. Unlike the majority opinion author, a concurring justice is not obligated to bargain over the contents of a concurring opinion or accommodate the requests of those wishing to join that concurrence, unless she wishes to do so.

No. 92-1168, Harris v. Forklift Systems

Assigned: 10/18/93   Announced: 11/9/94

RBG joins & writes conc. 10/22/93   Circulated: 10/21/93
chief joins, 10/25/93 (with comments)
JPS joins 10/25/93   Recirculated: 10/25/93
CT joins 10/26/93   10/28/93
DHS joins + agrees w/HAB - 10/26/93
HAB joins, 10/27/93
AMK joins, 10/28/93

SOC to HAB & DHS hopes change ok - 10/27, DHS still on bd. 10/27; soc to nmr re "and" & "or"; HAB has sugg. 10/22; SOC responds to HAB - 10/25; HAB to SOC - 10/26

Concurrences:	Circulated:
RBG	10/22/93
RBG	10/26/93
RBG	10/27/93
AS (w/ cover note)	10/28/93
RBG	10/29/03

Dissents:	Circulated:

Justices who disagree with the majority both in terms of outcome *and* reasoning may write **dissenting opinions**. The senior justice in the minority may write the main dissent in a case or assign it to another justice in the minority coalition.[159] But, like concurring opinions, any justice in the minority coalition may write a dissent if he or she chooses. Justice Kagan explained how writing a dissent differs from the enterprise of writing a majority opinion: "When you're writing the dissent, even when you expect some other justices to join the dissent, there's an expectation that you can be more yourself. Sometimes I feel that when I sit down at my computer and I'm writing the dissent and you just have this feeling like 'now I'm being myself' in a way that maybe you're not when you're writing for the Court."[160] Justice Scalia, too, finds writing a dissent something quite different:

> To be able to write an opinion solely for oneself, without the need to accommo-date, to any degree whatever, the more-or-less differing views of one's colleagues; to address precisely the points of law that one considers important and *no others*; to express precisely the degree of quibble, or foreboding, or disbelief, or indignation that one believes the majority's disposition should engender—that is indeed an unparalleled pleasure.[161]

While dissents do not have the force of law, justices who dissent hope to influence the future direction of the law. Justice Scalia explained how his oftentimes caustic dissents are written for the next generation of lawyers—current law students: "My tone is some-times sharp. But I think sharpness is sometimes needed to demonstrate how much of a departure I believe the thing [that is, the majority opinion] is. Especially in my dissents. Who do you think I write my dissents for? . . . [Law students] will read dissents that are breezy and have some thrust to them. That's who I write for."[162]

On occasion, a justice will change his mind and switch his initial conference vote during the coalition formation stage. Scholars refer to this as **voting fluidity**.[163] Some-times this occurs because a justice feels that the dissent has made the better argument. Justice Alito explained: "It's not a change of position by the opinion-writing judge, but it's a change of position by others on the Court. When you read the majority opinion and you read the dissent, and you say, 'Well, the dissent actually seems to be correct', and then a vote can change. That does happen."[164] He further noted that the majority becomes the minority about once each term because of these switches.[165] Justice Breyer said that, while the justices can be persuaded to change their minds, it becomes less likely as the case progresses through the Court:

> I'm holding myself open to being persuaded and if I come out of that oral argument and I change my mind, as I do on occasion sometimes, more often than people think, I don't think, oh how stupid I was. I think how great. You see I'm holding myself open. I want to be persuaded, so persuade me. And then we go into the conference. You see it's becoming narrower and narrower. By the time that conference is finished, I say it's tentative but it isn't really so tentative. And by the time people write drafts of opinions and circulate them we change sometimes, once a year, twice a year . . .[166]

Justice Ginsburg described her perspective as follows: "It ain't over 'til it's over. People change their minds about what they thought. So it isn't at all something extraordinary, and that's how it should work. We're in the process of trying to persuade each other and then the public."[167]

Even more rare than changing a vote after having read a majority opinion is a change of vote *while* writing a majority opinion. When asked how often this happens, Justice Stevens said: "Not very often, but once in a while it does happen. Once every couple of years at the most."[168] Justice Scalia remarked that he has switched his votes: "I have not only done that, I have changed my mind after having been assigned to write the majority opinion. I've written the opinion the other way, it just wouldn't write. There is nothing wrong with that."[169] But when it happens in landmark cases there is an unusual amount of scrutiny and press coverage on the switch. For example, in *National Federation of Independent*

Business v. Sebelius[170] reporter Jan Crawford reported that Chief Justice Roberts initially voted with his four conservative colleagues to strike down the Affordable Care Act—popularly known as "Obamacare"—but changed his mind after he and his clerks began working on the majority opinion and upheld the law.[171]

After the process of opinion drafting (and redrafting as part of the bargaining and negotiation process) concludes, the final opinion that secures the support of at least five justices is the majority opinion and the official opinion of the Court. There are some instances in which no one opinion secures a majority of votes from among the justices. For example, six justices may agree as to the appropriate outcome in a case but only four of those six agree as to the rationale. In this case, the opinion agreed to by those four justices is the opinion of the Court but it is a **plurality opinion**, rather than a majority opinion. A plurality opinion is one that received the support of more justices than any other opinion, though not the support of the majority of the justices. Such opinions "represent extreme dissensus."[172] Plurality opinions are certainly not the modal category of opinion but they do occur in a nontrivial number of the Court's cases. For example, the justices issued plurality opinions 12 percent of the time in 2005.[173] What makes plurality opinions vexing for lower courts trying to discern the dictates of their judicial superior and lawyers trying to provide sound guidance to their clients is that they leave ambiguous what the actual rule of law is.[174] The very existence of plurality opinions belies the myth of Supreme Court judging as simple a matter of laying the relevant law side-by-side with the dispute at hand, thereby arriving at the obviously "correct" decision. But the content of those plurality opinions (and of the regular concurrences, special concurrences, and dissents that accompany them) suggests that the justices care about finding a legally sound basis for the decisions they render.

Whether the opinion of the Court is a majority opinion or a plurality opinion, that opinion represents "the law" as determined by the Supreme Court. While it is true that the opinion of the Court determines who wins and who loses in the instant case, the true import of the opinion lies in the legal precedent set by it. It is that precedent upon which lawyers rely in advising their clients. It is that precedent that is binding on lower courts. It is that precedent that means that the Supreme Court is a full-fledged participant in law making in the United States.

SUPREME COURT ISSUES

In *Federalist No. 78,* Alexander Hamilton explained that the Supreme Court is a relatively powerless institution compared with Congress (which has the power of the purse) and the presidency (which has the power of the sword). Instead, the Court must rely on its legitimacy in the eyes of the public. But how does the Court cultivate an air of legitimacy? To be sure, the decisions the justices make are grounded in law,[175] even though other factors contribute to the choices they make. Unlike elected officials, Supreme Court justices must produce the reasons for their decisions in writing and justify their positions in terms of the law. Thus, the process of written decision making based on law helps to legitimize the Court. But beyond process, the Court carefully cultivates a public image that protects and enhances its legitimacy. The justices meet in a marble structure modeled on the classical architecture of ancient Greece and Rome. They sit behind a raised bench looking down on litigants and the public. They wear black robes on the bench, at presidential inaugurations, and when attending joint sessions of Congress.[176] Indeed the justices refrain from clapping in a partisan fashion in the way that members of Congress

Image 10.17
Alexander Hamilton
*Alexander Hamilton,
author of* Federalist
No. 78. Prints and
Photographs Division,
Library of Congress,
Washington, D.C.

do when the president speaks for or against certain policies.[177] In short, the justices want to appear neutral, above politics and partisanship.

Legitimacy, Anonymity, and Cameras in the Court

Perhaps one factor that contributes to the Court's legitimacy is its anonymity. As a general matter, the justices are relatively unknown to the citizenry. Seventy-seven percent of Americans can name two of Snow White's seven dwarfs but only 24 percent can name two Supreme Court justices.[178] In a 2006 survey of the public, the two most cited justices were Clarence Thomas—not surprising given his sensational confirmation hearing—and Antonin Scalia, who was named far less often than Thomas. Justice Alito quipped: "I was just glad that people don't think Grumpy, Dopey, and Sleepy are justices on the Court!"[179] A 2012 poll was even bleaker, with two-thirds of Americans unable to name a single justice. Those who could named Chief Justice Roberts (20 percent) followed by Justices Thomas and Scalia (16 percent each).[180]

Perhaps the major reason for the justices' anonymity is due to their own rule prohibiting cameras in the Court. For years, journalists and members of Congress have pressed the Court to allow cameras to photograph, record, and broadcast what takes place inside the Supreme Court chamber.[181] C-SPAN even created an entire network—C-SPAN 3—that would be exclusively devoted to carrying the Court's proceedings live.[182] Yet the justices have kept the ban in place. Justice Scalia explained: "I am against

it because I do not believe, as the proponents of television in the court assert, that the purpose of televising our hearings would be to educate the American people. . . . What most of the American people would see would be 30-second, 15-second takeouts from our arguments. . . . I am sure it will mis-educate the American people."[183] Justice Alito echoed Scalia's concerns: "We're a very old-fashioned institution [and cameras would] change the structure of the arguments."[184] He noted that news shows and campaign advertisements would inevitably take comments out of context, which could not only prove misleading to viewers but could have a chilling effect on the attorneys or justices who know they are being filmed. Justice Kagan agrees: "I have a few worries, including that people might play to the camera. Sometimes you see that when you watch congressional hearings."[185]

Despite the ban on cameras, the justices do record the audio at oral arguments, which has been done since 1955. While oral arguments are not broadcast live, the justices make the recording and transcript available soon thereafter. Justice O'Connor remarked: "Remember that every word that is said in that courtroom is transcribed and available that same night, and if anybody wants to see and read what was said, there it is in black and white. It's not that there is a lack of ability to know what's going on."[186] In major cases, C-SPAN plays the recordings on television and includes photographs of the justices and attorneys when they are speaking. Furthermore, the transcripts and recordings are made available online,[187] and the Oyez Project located at Chicago-Kent College of Law maintains an impressive digital historical archive of oral arguments (as well as a host of other materials related to the Supreme Court's cases).[188]

Controversial Decisions and Public Opinion

Some of the most controversial issues in America have been decided by 5-4 votes on the Supreme Court: a presidential election,[189] affirmative action,[190] school prayer,[191] and abortion,[192] to name a few. Sometimes the Court reflects the broad preferences of the American people (as with the right to abortion where a consistent majority of Americans support access to that procedure), and sometimes it does not (as in the case of school prayer where a consistent majority of Americans disagree with forbidding state-sponsored prayer and Bible reading in public school). As Justice Alito explained, the justices are adamant that following public opinion is "exactly what we're *not* supposed to do."[193] Yet research shows that, with some exception, the Court is generally reflective of broader public sentiment.[194] This should not be too surprising given that the justices are appointed by popularly elected presidents and confirmed by popularly elected senators. Still, the justices have lifetime appointments and serve for many decades and there have been periods where an aging Court has seemed out of step with the changing times, as happened during the New Deal when President Franklin Roosevelt attempted to pack the Court with younger justices who were more favorable to his policies.[195]

Public approval for the Court has declined in recent years. Once considered far more trustworthy than Congress or the presidency, the Court has reached record lows in recent public opinion surveys. For example, according to surveys conducted by the *New York Times*, the Court has declined from an approval high of 66 percent in the 1980s, to 50 percent in 2000, and most recently 44 percent in 2012.[196] The newspaper suggested

Image 10.19
Fireside Chat on
Court Packing Plan
President Franklin Delano Roosevelt delivers his fireside chat on his plan to "pack" the U.S. Supreme Court, 1937.
Harris &
Ewing Collection,
Prints and Photographs
Division, Library of
Congress, Washington,
D.C.

that the decline "could reflect a sense that the court is more political, after the ideologically divided 5-to-4 decisions in *Bush v. Gore*, which determined the 2000 presidential election, and *Citizens United v. FEC*, the 2010 decision allowing unlimited campaign spending by corporations and unions."[197] Retired Justice Sandra Day O'Connor was aware of the decline:

> In the past, when the public is asked about the three branches of government, the Court has generally had—the judicial branch has had—the highest respect among the three. And now it's about the same for all and it's all down. So that's a great disappointment to me to see. I'm sorry. There's been some suggestion that the trend down began with the *Bush v. Gore* decision. That could be something that triggered public reexamination.[198]

Scholarly research suggests that O'Connor may be correct. Public approval or disapproval for individual decisions and other short-term events can have an effect on the subsequent long-term evaluation of the Court as in institution.[199] The public may have a certain level of trust in the Court—perhaps because the Court is perceived as above politics and the protector of order and democracy—but if the justices hand down individual decisions with which the public disagrees, strike down an unusually high number of popularly enacted laws, or are criticized by opinion leaders, that trust can be eroded over time.[200] In this sense, public support for the Court is a dynamic process by which public approval for the Court is conditioned on the cases they decide and the reaction by influential elites. The perfect storm of public disapproval would come from a highly politicized confirmation process that portrays justices as little more than politicians in robes, an activist Court that takes on and strikes down popularly enacted laws, and elected officials—including presidents and senators—regularly criticizing the justices. It remains to be seen if that perfect storm has arrived.

Life Tenure

In Chapter Five, we discussed the process of selecting judges, including the appointment of Supreme Court justices. But before an appointment can be made, a vacancy must occur. Justices have life tenure, though many Court observers think that there should be term limits. A recent poll revealed that only 30 percent of the American people believe that life tenure is a "good thing" while 60 percent said it was a "bad thing."[201] Though some have suggested that life tenure could be changed by a simple act of Congress, most agree that it would require a constitutional amendment. Proponents of term limits argue that the justices will be less likely to overstay their usefulness and be more responsive to the current preferences of the American people. Asked in 2012 whether he was in favor of term limits for Supreme Court justices, Justice Scalia—then age 76 and beginning his 26th year on the Court—said that he did not think so: "I'm the oldest one there, I'm not drooling yet."[202] Justice Oliver Wendell Holmes, Jr., is the oldest justice ever to serve, retiring at age 90 in 1932.[203]

The only formal way to force a justice from office is through the impeachment and removal process as specified in the Constitution.[204] No justice has ever been removed from office. Justice Samuel Chase was impeached by the House in 1804 but escaped conviction in the Senate,[205] thereby establishing an informal precedent that federal judges, including Supreme Court justices, should not be removed because of partisan disagreement.[206] Instead, members of Congress have based their impeachment and removal

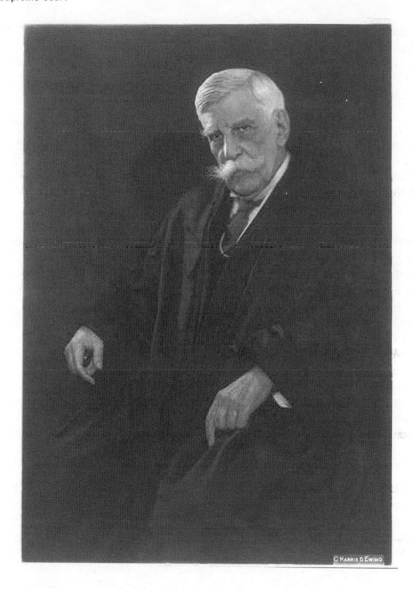

Image 10.20
Oliver Wendell
Holmes, Jr.
*Justice Oliver Wendell
Holmes, Jr., ca. 1930.*
Prints and Photo-
graphs Division,
Library of Congress,
Washington, D.C.

decisions on legal or ethical misconduct for the few federal judges who have been subject to the process.

Short of removal or death, all federal judges may retire with their full salary and may continue to serve on lower federal courts as specified in the "Rule of 80"—any combination of age (past 65) and years of service on the federal bench that totals 80 makes a federal judge eligible for retirement. When Supreme Court justices retire they routinely cite age and other nonpolitical concerns when leaving the bench. When Justice Thurgood Marshall was asked why he was departing he famously said, "I'm old!" Justice Sandra Day O'Connor cited concerns for her husband's failing health and her desire to care for him in his final years.[207] Yet the notion that the departure decisions of the justices are not political is a myth. Research demonstrates that justices time their departures to coincide with presidents likely to appoint like-minded successors.[208] Scalia has admitted this is his case:

"Of course I would not like to be replaced by someone who immediately sets about undoing everything that I've tried to do for 25 years, 26 years. Sure, I mean, I shouldn't have to tell you that. Unless you think I'm a fool."[209] When it was suggested at the start of the 2013 term that she retire before the end of Democratic President Barack Obama's second term, then 80-year-old liberal Justice Ginsburg admitted that she felt no sense of urgency to step down because she felt confident about who would win the 2016 election: "I think it's going to be another Democratic president."[210] Given that, on average, presidents get to make two appointments during a 4-year term, the stakes of presidential elections for the future direction of the Supreme Court are high.

CONCLUSION

The Supreme Court generally takes care to protect its legitimacy in the eyes of policy-makers and the public. Research shows that the decisions the justices make are the product of both law and attitudes. The decisional process includes agenda setting, oral argument, opinion writing, and coalition formation and the justices work closely with their law clerks at each stage. Justices vote on cases and provide the intellectual framework for and subsequently edit the opinions that are issued under their names. Clerks screen the petitions, make recommendations on which cases the Court should take, draft opinions, and act as informal ambassadors during the process of coalition formation.

There are number of controversial issues surrounding the Court. While many would like the Court's proceedings to be televised, the justices are reluctant to allow cameras in the courtroom. Recent controversial decisions have been unpopular with certain segments of the American people and some have suggested that these decisions are responsible for a general decline in the Court's approval rating. The justices have life tenure and time their departures to maximize the chances of being replaced by like-minded successors. While there have been calls to place term limits on the justices, most experts agree that it would take a constitutional amendment to change the current system. In all, the myth that the Court is solely a legal body divorced from politics has been dispelled by research that shows the Court to be both a legal and a political institution.

Suggested Readings

Ryan C. Black, Timothy R. Johnson, and Justin Wedeking. *Oral Arguments and Coalition Formation on the U.S. Supreme Court* (Ann Arbor, MI: University of Michigan Press, 2012). Relying on a comprehensive analysis of oral argument transcripts from the U.S. Supreme Court, as well as the notes taken by Justices Powell and Blackmun during oral arguments, this volume examines oral argument as a vehicle for information gathering to permit the justices to form opinion coalitions to dispose of the cases on its docket.

Forrest Maltzman, James F. Spriggs, II, and Paul J. Wahlbeck. *Crafting Law on the Supreme Court: The Collegial Game* (New York, NY: Cambridge University Press, 2000). Examining the papers of the justices, particularly internal memos circulated among the justices, the authors present an analysis of the bargaining and accommodation in which the justices engage in the process of opinion writing.

David M. O'Brien *Storm Center: The Supreme Court in American Politics*, Ninth Edition (New York, NY: W.W. Norton, 2011). This book offers an engaging narrative of the many facets of the Court—including the *certiorari* process, the role of law clerks, and opinion writing—demonstrating that it represents a nexus of law, politics, and personality from which the Court's precedents arise.

H. W. Perry. *Deciding to Decide: Agenda Setting in the United States Supreme Court* (Cambridge, MA: Harvard University Press, 1991). Based in part on interviews with key actors, including unprecedented interviews with some of the justices themselves, this text offers unique insights into the Court and develops a richly detailed account of how the justices act in the processing of their cases.

Jeffrey A. Segal and Harold J. Spaeth. *The Supreme Court and the Attitudinal Model Revisited* (New York, NY: Cambridge University Press, 2002). With the use of a comprehensive database of cases decided by the Court, these scholars offer a systematic evaluation of the evidence in support of a purely legal model of decision making versus the evidence in support of an attitudinal model of decision making, finding the evidence to be weak or nonexistent for the former and quite strong for the latter.

Artemus Ward and David L. Weiden. *Sorcerers' Apprentices: 100 Years of Law Clerks at the United States Supreme Court* (New York, NY: New York University Press, 2006). Using a multi-method approach that includes archival research, interviews, and surveys, these researchers provide a historical account of the development of the law clerk role at the Court as well as a rigorous evaluation of the influence of clerks on both the *certiorari* and decision-on-the-merits stages of the Court's work.

Endnotes

1   Quoted in Carrie Budoff Brown, "Schumer to Fight New Bush High Court Picks," *Politico*, July 27, 2007 (http://www.politico.com/news/stories/0707/5146.html).

2   Quoted in Pamela C. Corley, Amy Steigerwalt, and Artemus Ward, *The Puzzle of Unanimity: Consensus on the U.S. Supreme Court* (Stanford, CA: Stanford University Press, 2013): 2.

3   566 U.S. ____ (2012).

4   565 U.S. ____ (2012).

5   531 U.S. 98 (2000).

6   Adam Liptak, "Approval Rating for Justices Hits Just 44% in New Poll," *New York Times*, June 7, 2012.

7   Jeffrey A. Segal and Harold J. Spaeth, *The Supreme Court and the Attitudinal Model Revisited* (New York. NY: Cambridge University Press, 2002).

8   More broadly, scholars such as Benjamin Lauderdale and Tom Clark have argued that the preferences of the justices vary over both time and issue; Benjamin E. Lauderdale and Tom S. Clark, "The Supreme Court's Many Median Justices," *American Political Science Review*, vol. 106, no. 4 (November 2012): 847–866.

9   Carrie Budoff Brown, "Schumer to Fight New Bush High Court Picks," *Politico.com*, July 27, 2007 (http://www.politico.com/news/stories/0707/5146.html).

10 Pamela C. Corley, Amy Steigerwalt, and Artemus Ward, *The Puzzle of Unanimity: Consensus on the U.S. Supreme Court* (Stanford, CA: Stanford University Press, 2013).

11 Susan Swain, "Interview with Justice Sonia Sotomayor," C-SPAN, September 16, 2009 (http://supremecourt.c-span.org/assets/pdf/SSotomayor.pdf).

12 Associated Press, "Scalia in NYC: 'Politicized Court' Criticism 'Enrages' Me," WNBC-TV – NBC New York, September 17, 2012 (http://www.nbcnewyork.com/news/local/Antonin-Scalia-Supreme-Court-Politicized-Comments-New-York-Book-Event-170119636.html).

13 Katie Vloet, "Justice Kagan Highlights South Hall Dedication Weekend," *MLaw Newsroom*, September 8, 2012 (http://www.law.umich.edu/newsandinfo/features/Pages/kagan_SHdedication.aspx).

14 Ibid.

15 Robert Barnes, "Justice Stevens Hires Just One Clerk for 2010 Term," *Washington Post*, September 3, 2009.

16 Todd C. Peppers and Artemus Ward, "Introduction" in *In Chambers: Stories of Supreme Court Law Clerks and Their Justices*, eds, Todd C. Peppers and Artemus Ward (Charlottesville, VA: University of Virginia Press, 2012).

17 Artemus Ward and David L. Weiden, *Sorcerers' Apprentices: 100 Years of Law Clerks at the United States Supreme Court* (New York, NY: New York University Press, 2006): 72.

18 Ibid., 92, 97.

19 See, for example, Christopher R. Benson, "A Renewed Call for Diversity Among Supreme Court Clerks: How a Diverse Body of Clerks Can Aid the High Court as an Institution," *Harvard Black-Letter Law Journal*, vol. 23 (Spring 2007): 23–54. See, also, Artemus Ward and David L. Weiden, *Sorcerers' Apprentices: 100 Years of Law Clerks at the United States Supreme Court* (New York, NY: New York University Press, 2006): 87–98.

20 Corey Ditslear and Lawrence Baum, "Selection of Law Clerks and Polarization in the U.S. Supreme Court," *Journal of Politics*, vol. 63, no. 3 (August 2001): 869–885. See, also, Artemus Ward and David L. Weiden, *Sorcerers' Apprentices: 100 Years of Law Clerks at the United States Supreme Court* (New York, NY: New York University Press, 2006): 76–85.

21 Adam Litpak, "A Sign of the Court's Polarization: Choice of Clerks," *New York Times*, September 6, 2010.

22 Artemus Ward and David L. Weiden, *Sorcerers' Apprentices: 100 Years of Law Clerks at the United States Supreme Court* (New York, NY: New York University Press, 2006): 81.

23 For example, Justice William Brennan delegated the selection of his clerks in the 1960s to Paul Freund, a Harvard Law School professor; Todd C. Peppers, *Courtiers of the Marble Palace: The Rise and Influence of the Supreme Court Law Clerk* (Stanford, CA: Stanford University Press, 2006): 156.

24 Susan Swain, "Interview with Justice Sonia Sotomayor," C-SPAN, September 16, 2009 (http://supremecourt.c-span.org/assets/pdf/SSotomayor.pdf).

25 Todd C. Peppers, *Courtiers of the Marble Palace: The Rise and Influence of the Supreme Court Law Clerk* (Stanford, CA: Stanford University Press, 2006). See, also, Todd C. Peppers and Artemus Ward, "Introduction" in *In Chambers: Stories of Supreme Court Law Clerks and Their Justices*, eds Todd C. Peppers and Artemus Ward (Charlottesville, VA: University of Virginia Press, 2012).

26 While the justices make just over $200,000 per year, their former clerks can command comparable or larger salaries at major law firms as well as signing bonuses that reach $300,000 or more. See, for example, Marisa M. Kashino, "Hiring Supreme Court Clerks: The $500,000 Gamble," *Washingtonian.com*, August 1, 2013 (http://www.washingtonian.com/blogs/capitalcomment/scotus-watch/hiring-supreme-court-clerks-the-500000-gamble.php). See, also, David Lat, "The New Going Rate for Supreme Court Clerk Bonuses," *Above the Law*, September 13, 2012 (http://abovethelaw.com/2012/09/the-new-going-rate-for-supreme-court-clerk-bonuses/).

27 Bryan A. Garner, "Justice John Paul Stevens," *The Scribes Journal of Legal Writing* (2010): 41–50, 42 (http://legaltimes.typepad.com/files/garner-transcripts-1.pdf).

28 Artemus Ward and David L. Weiden, *Sorcerers' Apprentices: 100 Years of Law Clerks at the United States Supreme Court* (New York, NY: New York University Press, 2006).

29 Larry O'Dell, "Justice Kagan Describes Workings of Court to Students," *Brooklyn Daily Eagle*, September 20, 2012 (http://50.56.227.138/articles/justice-kagan-describes-workings-court-students).

30 Bryan A. Garner, "Justice John Paul Stevens," *The Scribes Journal of Legal Writing* (2010): 41–50, 50 (http://legaltimes.typepad.com/files/garner-transcripts-1.pdf).

31 Artemus Ward and David L. Weiden, *Sorcerers' Apprentices: 100 Years of Law Clerks at the United States Supreme Court* (New York, NY: New York University Press, 2006); Todd C. Peppers and Christopher Zorn, "Law Clerk Influence on Supreme Court Decision Making: An Empirical Assessment," *DePaul Law Review*, vol. 51 (Fall 2008): 51–78.

32 H.W. Perry, *Deciding to Decide: Agenda Setting in the United States Supreme Court* (Cambridge, MA: Harvard University Press, 1994).

33 The Court does receive some petitions for extraordinary writs (e.g., a writ of *habeas corpus*) and occasional certification cases, in which a court of appeals seeks the Court's guidance as to a question or proposition of law necessary for the proper decision in a pending case. As discussed in Chapter Four, the Court also has original jurisdiction in cases involving ambassadors and disputes between states. *New Jersey v. New York* (523 U.S. 767, 1998), which involved a dispute over ownership of a portion of Ellis Island, is one such example. However, petitions for extraordinary writs, certified questions, and original-jurisdiction cases comprise a miniscule number of the total cases on the Court's docket.

34 Administrative Office of the U.S. Courts, "Judicial Business of the U.S. Courts," Table A-1 (http://www.uscourts.gov/Statistics/JudicialBusiness/2012/statistical-tables-us-supreme-court.aspx).

35 Bryan A. Garner, "Justice John Paul Stevens," *The Scribes Journal of Legal Writing* (2010): 41–50, 45 (http://legaltimes.typepad.com/files/garner-transcripts-1.pdf).

36 Bernard Schwartz, *Decision: How the Supreme Court Decides Cases* (New York, NY: Oxford University Press, 1996): 50.

37 Credit for initiating the cert pool is generally given to Justice Louis F. Powell, though Chief Justice Earl Warren claimed the original idea was his; Barbara Palmer, "The 'Bermuda Triangle?' The Cert Pool and Its Influence Over the Supreme Court's Agenda," *Constitutional Commentary*, vol. 18, no. 1 (Spring 2001): 105–120, 107.

38 Adam Litpak, "A Second Justice Opts Out of a Longtime Custom: The 'Cert. Pool,'" *New York Times*, September 25, 2008.

39 Ryan C. Black and Ryan J. Owens, "Agenda Setting in the Supreme Court: The Collision of Policy and Jurisprudence," *Journal of Politics*, vol. 71, no. 3 (July 2009): 1062–1075.

40 Petitions to the Court come as either paid or unpaid petitions. Unpaid petitions are those filed *in forma pauperis* ("in the manner of a pauper"). The rules of the Court regarding *in forma pauperis*

petitions permit indigent litigants to file without meeting the same exacting standards as are applicable to paid petitions. See Wendy L. Watson, "The U.S. Supreme Court's In Forma Pauperis Docket: A Descriptive Analysis," *Justice System Journal*, vol. 27, no 1 (2006): 47–60. See, also, Cristina Lane, "Pay Up or Shut Up: The Supreme Court's Prospective Denial of In Forma Pauperis Petitions," *Northwestern University Law Review*, vol. 98, no. 1 (October 2003): 335–366, 338–345.

41 Political scientists Lee Epstein, Jeffrey A. Segal, and Harold J. Spaeth have created a freely accessible digital archive of Justice Blackmun's papers; Lee Epstein, Jeffrey A. Segal, and Harold J. Spaeth, *The Digital Archive of the Papers of Justice Harry A. Blackmun* (2007) (http://epstein.wustl.edu/blackmun.php). Scholars have profitably mined those papers for a variety of purposes but they are also fascinating (and fun!) to browse for anyone with an interest in the Court.

42 Lee Epstein, Andrew D. Martin, Jeffrey A. Segal, and Chad Westerland, "The Judicial Common Space," *Journal of Law, Economics, & Organization*, vol. 23, no. 2 (June 2007): 303–325.

43 Those *amici* submitting briefs at the *certiorari* stage arguing against the granting of cert obviously are hopeful the Court will not grant cert. However, whether an *amicus* files a cert brief in favor of or in opposition to the granting of cert, the more briefs that are filed, the stronger the signal that "the legal implications [of the case] are broad and important;" Ryan C. Black and Ryan J. Owens, "Agenda Setting in the Supreme Court: The Collision of Policy and Jurisprudence," *Journal of Politics*, vol. 71, no. 3 (July 2009): 1070. See, also, Gregory A. Caldeira and John R. Wright, "Organized Interests and Agenda Setting in the U.S. Supreme Court," *American Political Science Review*, vol. 82, no. 4 (December 1988): 1109–1127.

44 Ryan C. Black and Ryan J. Owens, "Agenda Setting in the Supreme Court: The Collision of Policy and Jurisprudence," *Journal of Politics*, vol. 71, no. 3 (July 2009): 1062–1075, 1070.

45 A classic articulation of cue theory is Joseph Tanenhaus, Marvin Schick, Matthew Muraskin, and Daniel Rosen, "The Supreme Court's Certiorari Jurisdiction: Cue Theory," in *Judicial Decision Making*, ed., Glendon Schubert (New York, NY: Free Press, 1963).

46 Ryan C. Black and Ryan J. Owens, "Agenda Setting in the Supreme Court: The Collision of Policy and Jurisprudence," *Journal of Politics*, vol. 71, no. 3 (July 2009): 1062–1075, 1070.

47 Ryan C. Black and Ryan J. Owens, "Solicitor General Influence and Agenda Setting on the U.S. Supreme Court," *Political Research Quarterly*, vol. 64, no. 4 (December 2011): 765–778.

48 H.W. Perry, Jr., *Deciding to Decide: Agenda Setting in the United States Supreme Court* (Cambridge, MA: Harvard University Press): 198–212. See, also, Ryan C. Black and Ryan J. Owens, "Agenda Setting in the Supreme Court: The Collision of Policy and Jurisprudence," *Journal of Politics*, vol. 71, no. 3 (July 2009): 1062–1075.

49 Clare Cushman, *Courtwatchers: Eyewitness Accounts in Supreme Court History* (Lanham, MD: Rowman & Littlefield, 2011): 191.

50 Amanda Bryan, "Principled Agents or Legal Rasputins? Influence, Ideology, and the Cert. Pool on the U.S. Supreme Court," paper presented at the annual meeting of the Southern Political Science Association, New Orleans, LA, January 12–14, 2012.

51 H.W. Perry, Jr., *Deciding to Decide: Agenda Setting in the United States Supreme Court* (Cambridge, MA: Harvard University Press, 1994): 56.

52 See Gregory A. Caldeira and John R. Wright, "The Discuss List: Agenda Building in the Supreme Court," *Law & Society Review*, vol. 24, no. 3 (1990): 807–836, 809–803.

53 Jay Wexler, "I Made Clarence Thomas Laugh," *Salon.com*, August 18, 2012. (http://www.salon.com/2012/08/18/i_made_clarence_thomas_laugh/).

54 Ibid.

55 Bryan A. Garner, "Justice Anthony M. Kennedy," *The Scribes Journal of Legal Writing* (2010): 89–98, 97 (http://legaltimes.typepad.com/files/garner-transcripts-1.pdf).

56 Richard L. Revesz and Pamela S. Karlan, "Nonmajority Rules and the Supreme Court," *University of Pennsylvania Law Review*, vol. 136, no. 4 (April 1988): 1067–1133, 1069–1073.

57 Though this practice is little studied and there is no definitive evidence as to when it took root, the "join three" practice most likely began under Chief Justice Warren Burger; David M. O'Brien, "Join-3 Votes, the Rule of Four, the Cert. Pool, and the Supreme Court's shrinking plenary docket," *Journal of Law & Politics*, vol. 13, no. 4 (Fall 1997): 779–808, 784.

58 Richard Wolf, "Shrinking High Court Docket Bedevils Conservatives," *USA Today*, December 16, 2013.

59 Frederick Schauer, "Is It Important to Be Important?: Evaluating the Supreme Court's Case-Selection Process," *Yale Law Journal Online*, vol. 119 (2009): 77–86.

60 Arthur D. Hellman, "The Shrunken Docket of the Rehnquist Court," *Supreme Court Review*, vol. 1996 (1996): 403–438, 433.

61 Richard J. Lazarus, "Docket Capture at the High Court," *Yale Law Journal Online*, vol. 119 (2009): 89–97.

62 "Conversation with Supreme Court Justice Elena Kagan," C-SPAN, September 20, 2012 (http://www.c-span.org/video/?308291-1/conversation-supreme-court-justice-elena-kagan).

63 Artemus Ward and David L. Weiden, *Sorcerers' Apprentices: 100 Years of Law Clerks at the United States Supreme Court* (New York, NY: New York University Press, 2006): 143.

64 Tony Mauro, "Justices Give Key Role to Novice Lawyers," *USA Today*, June 5, 1998.

65 Kenneth W. Starr, "The Supreme Court and Its Shrinking Docket: The Ghost of William Howard Taft," *Minnesota Law Review*, vol. 90, no. 5 (2006): 1363–1385.

66 Ibid., 1363–1385, 1376.

67 David R. Stras, "The Supreme Court's Gatekeepers: The Role of Law Clerks in the Certiorari Process," *Texas Law Review*, vol. 85, no. 4 (March 2007): 947–997.

68 David M. O'Brien, "The Rehnquist Court's Shrinking Plenary Docket," *Judicature*, vol. 81 (September-October 1997): 58–65.

69 Arthur D. Hellman, "The Shrunken Docket of the Rehnquist Court," *The Supreme Court Review*, vol. 1996 (1996): 403–438.

70 Margaret Meriwether Cordray and Richard Cordray, "The Supreme Court's Plenary Docket," *Washington & Lee Law Review*, vol. 58 (Summer 2001): 737–794.

71 Ryan J. Owens and David A. Simon, "Explaining the Supreme Court's Shrinking Docket" *William & Mary Law Review*, vol. 53, no. 4 (March 2012): 1219–1285.

72 United States Supreme Court, *Rules of the Supreme Court of the United States*, April 19, 2013 (http://www.supremecourt.gov/ctrules/2013RulesoftheCourt.pdf): 28.

73 Kevin T. McGuire and Barbara Palmer, "Issue Fluidity on the Supreme Court," *American Political Science Review*, vol. 89, no. 3 (September 1995): 691–702.

74 Lee Epstein, Jeffrey A. Segal, and Timothy Johnson. 1996. "The Claim of Issue Creation on the U.S. Supreme Court," *American Political Science Review*, vol. 90, no. 4 (December 1996): 845–852.

75 Disfavoring the treatment of issues not clearly raised in the record before the Court is known as the *sua sponte* ("of one's own accord") doctrine.

76 Bryan A. Garner, "Full Transcript of Bryan A. Garner's Interview with Elena Kagan," *ABA Journal*, September 1, 2012 (http://www.abajournal.com/magazine/article/full_transcript_of_bryan_a._garners_interview_with_elena_kagan).

77 Bryan A. Garner, "Chief Justice John G. Roberts, Jr.," *The Scribes Journal of Legal Writing* (2010): 5–40 (http://legaltimes.typepad.com/files/garner-transcripts-1.pdf).

78 Larry King, "Supreme Court Justice Stephen Breyer Interview," *CNN Larry King Live*, November 23, 2005 (http://transcripts.cnn.com/TRANSCRIPTS/0511/23/lkl.01.html).

79 Paul M. Collins, Jr., *Friends of the Supreme Court: Interest Groups and Judicial Decision Making* (New York, NY: Oxford University Press, 2008): 47. See, also, Joseph D. Kearney and Thomas W. Merrill, "The Influence of Amicus Curiae Briefs on the Supreme Court," *University of Pennsylvania Law Review*, vol. 148, no. 3 (January 2000): 743–855.

80 Paul M. Collins, Jr., *Friends of the Supreme Court: Interest Groups and Judicial Decision Making* (New York, NY: Oxford University Press, 2008): 47.

81 James F. Spriggs, II and Paul J. Wahlbeck, "Amicus Curiae and the Role of Information at the Supreme Court," *Political Research Quarterly*, vol. 50, no. 2 (June 1997): 365–386, 371.

82 Jay Wexler, "I Made Clarence Thomas Laugh," *Salon.com*, August 18, 2012. (http://www.salon.com/2012/08/18/i_made_clarence_thomas_laugh/).

83 Bryan A. Garner, "Justice John Paul Stevens," *The Scribes Journal of Legal Writing* (2010): 41–50, 47 (http://legaltimes.typepad.com/files/garner-transcripts-1.pdf).

84 Michael Duvall, "When Is Oral Argument Important? A Judicial Clerk's View of the Debate," *Journal of Appellate Practice and Process*, vol. 9, no. 1 (Spring 2007): 121–131.

85 Tony Mauro, "Courtside: When Planets Collide," *Legal Times*, March 29, 2004.

86 Timothy R. Johnson, *Oral Arguments and Decision Making on the United States Supreme Court* (Albany, NY: State University of New York Press, 2004): 15–17.

87 Susan Swain, "Interview with Justice Sonia Sotomayor," C-SPAN, September 16, 2009 (http://supremecourt.c-span.org/assets/pdf/SSotomayor.pdf).

88 17 U.S. 518 (1819).

89 David M. O'Brien, *Storm Center: The Supreme Court in American Politics*, Fifth Edition (New York, NY: W.W. Norton, 2000): 257.

90 Matt Morrison, "U.S. Supreme Court Oral Arguments," Cornell University Law Library (http://www.lawschool.cornell.edu/library/whatwedo/researchguides/supreme-court-oral.cfm).

91 531 U.S. 98 (2000).

92 540 U.S. 93 (2003).

93 The oral argument in *McConnell v. FEC* is also unique in that it occurred during the justices' summer recess, something that had not happened since the case of *U.S. v. Nixon* (481 U.S. 683, 1974), in which the Court required President Nixon to turn over tapes he had secretly made of Oval Office conversations.

94 The Court's rules do allow for participation in oral argument by *amici* but it requires consent of the party on whose behalf the *amicus* wishes to argue or, absent that consent, permission from the Court, which "will be granted only in the most extraordinary circumstances," United States Supreme Court, *Rules of the Supreme Court of the United States*, April 19, 2013 (http://www.supremecourt.gov/ctrules/2013RulesoftheCourt.pdf): 36.

95 Bryan A. Garner, "Justice Anthony M. Kennedy," *The Scribes Journal of Legal Writing* (2010): 89–98, 95 (http://legaltimes.typepad.com/files/garner-transcripts-1.pdf).

96 Bryan A. Garner, "Justice John Paul Stevens," *The Scribes Journal of Legal Writing* (2010): 41–50, 48 (http://legaltimes.typepad.com/files/garner-transcripts-1.pdf).

97 Adam Liptak, "A Most Inquisitive Court? No Argument There," *New York Times*, October 7, 2013.

98 Adam Liptak, "Inquisitive Justices? No Argument There," *New York Times*, October 7, 2013.

99 552 U.S. 264 (2008).

100 Ryan C. Black, Timothy R. Johnson, and Justin Wedeking, *Oral Arguments and Coalition Formation on the U.S. Supreme Court: A Deliberate Dialogue* (Ann Arbor, MI: University of Michigan Press, 2012): 17–18.

101 Bryan A. Garner, "Justice Anthony M. Kennedy," *The Scribes Journal of Legal Writing* (2010): 89–98, 95 (http://legaltimes.typepad.com/files/garner-transcripts-1.pdf).

102 Timothy R. Johnson, *Oral Arguments and Decision Making on the United States Supreme Court* (Albany, NY: SUNY Press, 2004). See, also, Timothy R. Johnson, Paul J. Wahlbeck, and James F. Spriggs, "The Influence of Oral Arguments on the U.S. Supreme Court," *American Political Science Review*, vol. 100, no. 1 (February 2006): 99–113.

103 Janet Miller, "Supreme Court Justice Elena Kagan Tells U-M Crowd about Serious and Not-So-Serious Workings of the High Court," *AnnArbor.com*, September 7, 2012 (http://www.annarbor.com/news/supreme-court-justice-elena-kagan-discusses-the-serious-and-not-so-serious-workings-of-the-high-cour/#.UF8_ho2PU1M).

104 Bryan A. Garner, "Justice John Paul Stevens," *The Scribes Journal of Legal Writing* (2010): 41–50, 49 (http://legaltimes.typepad.com/files/garner-transcripts-1.pdf).

105 Timothy R. Johnson, Paul J. Wahlbeck, and James F. Spriggs, "The Influence of Oral Arguments on the U.S. Supreme Court," *American Political Science Review*, vol. 100, no. 1 (February 2006): 99–113.

106 Ibid.

107 "Justice Alito at RWU Law, Pt.1," *Roger Williams University Law Newsroom*, September 14, 2012 (http://law.rwu.edu/story/justice-alito-rwu-law-pt-1).

108 Robert Barnes, "Supreme Court Returns to Work, Hears R. Allen Stanford's Ponzi Scheme," *Washington Post*, October 7, 2013.

109 John G. Roberts, "Oral Advocacy and the Re-emergence of a Supreme Court Bar," *Journal of Supreme Court History*, vol. 30 (2005): 68; Sarah Levien Shullman, "The Illusion of Devil's Advocacy: How the Justices of the Supreme Court Foreshadow Their Decisions During Oral Argument," *Journal of Appellate Practice and Process*, vol. 6 (2004): 271–293; Timothy R. Johnson, Ryan C. Black, Jerry Goldman, and Sarah A. Truel, "Inquiring Minds Want to Know: Do Justices Tip Their Hands with Questions at Oral Argument in the U.S. Supreme Court?" *Washington University Journal of Law & Policy*, vol. 29 (2009): 241–261.

110 Timothy R. Johnson, Ryan C. Black, Jerry Goldman, and Sarah A. Truel, "Inquiring Minds Want to Know: Do Justices Tip Their Hands with Questions at Oral Argument in the U.S. Supreme Court?" *Washington University Journal of Law & Policy*, vol. 29 (2009): 241–261.

111 Black, Ryan C., Sarah A. Treul, Timothy R. Johnson, and Jerry Goldman, "Emotions, Oral Arguments, and Supreme Court Decision Making." *Journal of Politics*, vol. 73, no. 2 (April 2011): 572–581.

112 The 1980 movie was based on a book of the same name: Anthony Lewis, *Gideon's Trumpet* (New York, NY: Random House, 1964).

113 316 U.S. 455 (1942).

114 Fortas served on the Court for only a scant 4 years. His elevation to chief justice failed in the Senate due to some questionable payments he received from private sources. Another scandal came to the fore when it was revealed that Fortas had entered into an arrangement with a foundation established by a Wall Street financier to receive $20,000 per year for life. The implication was of a *quid pro quo* in which Fortas would help the financier avoid criminal charges or, in the event of a conviction on such charges, secure a presidential pardon; Laura Kalman, *Abe Fortas: A Biography* (New Haven, CT: Yale University Press, 1992).

115 Larry O'Dell, "Justice Kagan Describes Workings of Court to Students," *Brooklyn Daily Eagle*, September 20, 2012 (http://50.56.227.138/articles/justice-kagan-describes-workings-court-students).

116 David Lat, "Justice Breyer at the New Yorker Festival: Some Highlights (Part 2)," *Above the Law*, October 12, 2006 (http://abovethelaw.com/2006/10/justice-breyer-at-the-new-yorker-festival-some-highlights-part-2/).

117 "Conversation with Supreme Court Justice Elena Kagan," C-SPAN, September 20, 2012 (http://www.c-span.org/video/?308291-1/conversation-supreme-court-justice-elena-kagan).

118 Larry King, "Supreme Court Justice Stephen Breyer Interview," *CNN Larry King Live*, November 23, 2005 (http://transcripts.cnn.com/TRANSCRIPTS/0511/23/lkl.01.html).

119 Larry O'Dell, "Justice Kagan Describes Workings of Court to Students," *Brooklyn Daily Eagle*, September 20, 2012 (http://50.56.227.138/articles/justice-kagan-describes-workings-court-students).

120 "Conversation with Supreme Court Justice Elena Kagan," C-SPAN, September 20, 2012. (http://www.c-span.org/video/?308291-1/conversation-supreme-court-justice-elena-kagan).

121 Sara C. Benesh, Reginald S. Sheehan, and Harold J. Spaeth, "Equity in Supreme Court Opinion Assignment," *Jurimetrics*, vol. 39, no. 4 (Summer 1999): 377–389.

122 Saul Brenner, "Issue Specialization as a Variable in Opinion Assignment on the U.S. Supreme Court," *Journal of Politics*, vol. 46, no. 4 (November 1984): 1217–1225.

123 Saul Brenner and Harold J. Spaeth, "Issue Specialization in Majority Opinion Assignment on the Burger Court," *Western Political Quarterly*, vol. 39, no. 3 (September 1986): 520–527.

124 Lawrence Baum, *Judges and Their Audiences: A Perspective on Judicial Behavior* (Princeton, NJ: Princeton University Press, 2006).

125 Henry J. Abraham, *The Judicial Process: An Introductory Analysis of the Courts of the United States, England, and France*, Sixth Edition (New York, NY: Oxford University Press, 1993): 199. See, also, M. Todd Henderson, "From Seriatim to Consensus and Back Again: A Theory of Dissent," *Supreme Court Review*, vol. 2007, no. 1 (2007): 283–344, 303–311.

126 Evan Thomas, "Law: Inside the High Court," *Time*, November 5, 1979. See, also, Bob Woodward and Scott Armstrong, *The Brethren: Inside the Supreme Court* (New York, NY: Avon Press, 1979).

127 Timothy R. Johnson, James F. Spriggs, II, and Paul J. Wahlbeck, "Passing and Strategic Voting on the U.S. Supreme Court," *Law & Society Review*, vol. 39, no. 2 (June 2005): 349–377.

128 Kaitlyn L. Sill, Joseph Daniel Ura, and Stacia L. Haynie, "Strategic Passing and Opinion Assignment on the Burger Court," *Justice System Journal*, vol. 31, no. 2 (2010): 164–179.

129 Ibid., 164–179, 176.

130 Saul Brenner and Harold J. Spaeth, "Majority Opinion Assignments and the Maintenance of the Original Coalition on the Warren Court," *American Journal of Political Science*, vol. 32, no. 1 (February 1988): 72–81.

131 Saul Brenner, Timothy Hagle, and Harold J. Spaeth, "Increasing the Size of the Minimum Winning Original Coalitions on the Warren Court," *Polity*, vol. 23, no. 2 (Winter 1990): 309–318.

132 Forrest Maltzman and Paul J. Wahlbeck, "A Conditional Model of Opinion Assignment on the Supreme Court," *Political Research Quarterly*, vol. 57, no. 4 (December 2004): 551–563.

133 Ibid., 551–563, 561.

134 Jay Wexler, "I Made Clarence Thomas Laugh," *Salon.com*, August 18, 2012 (http://www.salon.com/2012/08/18/i_made_clarence_thomas_laugh/).

135 Bryan A. Garner, "Justice Anthony M. Kennedy," *The Scribes Journal of Legal Writing* (2010): 89–98, 96 (http://legaltimes.typepad.com/files/garner-transcripts-1.pdf).

136 "Conversation with Supreme Court Justice Elena Kagan," C-SPAN, September 20, 2012 (http://www.c-span.org/video/?308291-1/conversation-supreme-court-justice-elena-kagan).

137 Laura Krugman Ray, "Doctrinal Conversation: Justice Kagan's Supreme Court Opinions," *Indiana Law Journal Supplement*, vol. 89 (2012): 1–11, 2.

138 Bryan A. Garner, "Justice John Paul Stevens," *The Scribes Journal of Legal Writing* (2010): 41–50, 42 (http://legaltimes.typepad.com/files/garner-transcripts-1.pdf).

139 Interestingly, the notion of learning through the writing process is not limited to opinion writing on the Supreme Court. It is a learning strategy that has strong support in the education community. Indeed, the National Commission on Writing noted, "writing is not simply a way for students to demonstrate what they know. It is a way to help them understand what they know. At its best, writing is learning"; National Commission on Writing, *Writing and School Reform*, (May 2006): 51 (http://www.nwp.org/cs/public/print/resource/2542). In other words, students wishing to do well in school would do well to emulate Justice Stevens!

140 Artemus Ward and David L. Weiden, *Sorcerers' Apprentices: 100 Years of Law Clerks at the United States Supreme Court* (New York, NY: New York University Press, 2006): 203.

141 Dennis J. Hutchinson and David J. Garrow (eds), *The Forgotten Memoir of John Knox: The Life of a Supreme Court Clerk in FDR's Washington* (Chicago, IL: University of Chicago Press, 2002).

142 Artemus Ward and David L. Weiden, *Sorcerers' Apprentices: 100 Years of Law Clerks at the United States Supreme Court* (New York, NY: New York University Press, 2006): 212–224.

143 See, for example, Richard A. Posner, *The Federal Courts: Challenge and Reform* (Cambridge, MA: Harvard University Press, 1996): 146.

144 Bryan A. Garner, "Justice John Paul Stevens," *The Scribes Journal of Legal Writing* (2010): 41–50, 42–3 (http://legaltimes.typepad.com/files/garner-transcripts-1.pdf).

145 Janet Miller, "Supreme Court Justice Elena Kagan Tells U-M Crowd about Serious and Not-So-Serious workings of the High Court," *AnnArbor.com*, September 7, 2012 (http://www.annarbor.com/news/supreme-court-justice-elena-kagan-discusses-the-serious-and-not-so-serious-workings-of-the-high-cour/#.UF8_ho2PU1M).

146 Pamela C. Corley, Amy Steigerwalt, and Artemus Ward, *The Puzzle of Unanimity: Consensus on the U.S. Supreme Court* (Stanford, CA: Stanford University Press, 2013).

147 "Conversation with Supreme Court Justice Elena Kagan," C-SPAN, September 20, 2012 (http://www.c-span.org/video/?308291-1/conversation-supreme-court-justice-elena-kagan).

148 Lee Epstein, William M. Landes, and Richard A. Posner, "Are Even Unanimous Decisions in the United States Supreme Court Ideological?" *Northwestern University Law Review*, vol. 106, no. 2 (2012): 699–713.

149 Forrest Maltzman, James F. Spriggs, II, and Paul J. Wahlbeck, *Crafting Law on the Supreme Court: The Collegial Game* (New York, NY: Cambridge University Press, 2000).

150 Walter Murphy, *Elements of Judicial Strategy* (Chicago, IL: University of Chicago Press, 1964): 42.

151 "Justice Alito at RWU Law, Pt.1," *Roger Williams University Law Newsroom*, September 14, 2012 (http://law.rwu.edu/story/justice-alito-rwu-law-pt-1).

152 Bryan A. Garner, "Chief Justice John G. Roberts, Jr.," *The Scribes Journal of Legal Writing* (2010): 5–40 (http://legaltimes.typepad.com/files/garner-transcripts-1.pdf).

153 The basketball court is located on the top floor of the Supreme Court building; Gina Holland, "Legal Eagles Tip Off in 'Highest Court in the Land,' " *Los Angeles Times*, September 8, 2002.

154 Artemus Ward and David L. Weiden, *Sorcerers' Apprentices: 100 Years of Law Clerks at the United States Supreme Court* (New York, NY: New York University Press, 2006): 159–170.

155 Forrest Maltzman, James F. Spriggs, II, and Paul J. Wahlbeck, *Crafting Law on the Supreme Court: The Collegial Game* (New York, NY: Cambridge University Press, 2000).

156 James F. Spriggs, II, Forrest Maltzman, and Paul J. Wahlbeck, "Bargaining on the U.S. Supreme Court: Justices' Responses to Majority Opinion Drafts," *Journal of Politics*, vol. 61, no. 2 (May 1999): 485–506.

157 See Pamela C. Corley, *Concurring Opinion Writing on the U.S. Supreme Court* (Albany, NY: SUNY Press, 2010).

158 Gerald T. Dunne, "Justices Hugo Black and Robert Jackson: The Great Feud," *St. Louis University Law Journal*, vol. 19, no. 2 (1975): 465–487.

159 Beverly Blair Cook, "Justice Brennan and the Institutionalization of Dissent Assignment," *Judicature*, vol. 79, no. 1 (July-August 1995): 17–23

160 "Conversation with Supreme Court Justice Elena Kagan," C-SPAN, September 20, 2012 (http://www.c-span.org/video/?308291-1/conversation-supreme-court-justice-elena-kagan).

161 Antonin Scalia, "The Dissenting Opinion," *Journal of Supreme Court History*, vol. 19 (1994): 33–44, 42.

162 Jennifer Senior, "In Conversation: Antonin Scalia," *New York Magazine*, October 6, 2013.

163 J. Woodford Howard, Jr., "On the Fluidity of Judicial Choice," *American Political Science Review*, vol. 62, no. 1 (March 1968): 43–56. See, also, Timothy M. Hagle and Harold J. Spaeth, "Voting Fluidity and the Attitudinal Model of Supreme Court Decision Making," *Western Political Quarterly*, vol. 44, no. 1 (March 1991): 119–128.

164 Michelle R. Smith, "Alito Says Supreme Court Misunderstood by Media," *Deseret News*, September 14, 2012 (http://www.deseretnews.com/article/765604212/Alito-says-Supreme-Court-misunderstood-by-media.html).

165 A recent analysis of justices' initial conference votes and final votes on the merits reports that "defection from the majority" happens about 7.5 percent of the time; Jeffrey R. Lax and Kelly T. Rader, "Bargaining Power in the Supreme Court," Typescript (New York, NY: Columbia University, 2011).

166 Larry King, "Supreme Court Justice Stephen Breyer Interview," *CNN Larry King Live*, November 23, 2005 (http://transcripts.cnn.com/TRANSCRIPTS/0511/23/lkl.01.html).

167 Joan Biskupic, "Exclusive: Justice Ginsburg Shrugs Off Injury," *Reuters*, August 8, 2012 (http://www.reuters.com/article/2012/08/09/us-usa-court-ginsburg-idUSBRE87801920120809).

168 Bryan A. Garner, "Justice John Paul Stevens," *The Scribes Journal of Legal Writing* (2010): 41–50, 42 (http://legaltimes.typepad.com/files/garner-transcripts-1.pdf).

169 Chris Wallace, "Justice Antonin Scalia on Issues Facing SCOTUS and the Country," *Fox News Sunday*, July 29, 2012 (http://www.foxnews.com/on-air/fox-news-sunday/2012/07/29/justice-antonin-scalia-issues-facing-scotus-and-country).

170 567 U.S. ____ (2012).

171 Jan Crawford, "Roberts Switched Views to Uphold Health Care Law," *CBSNews.com*, July 2, 2012 (http://www.cbsnews.com/8301-3460_162-57464549/roberts-switched-views-to-uphold-health-care-law/).

172 Pamela C. Corley, Udi Sommer, Amy Steigerwalt, and Artemus Ward, "Extreme Dissensus: Explaining Plurality Decisions on the United States Supreme Court," *Justice System Journal*, vol. 31, no. 2 (2010): 1–21.

173 Ibid., 1–21, 2.

174 Though the Court attempted to provide guidance for the interpretation of plurality opinions in *Marks v. United States* (430 U.S. 188, 1977)—indicating that the controlling holding in the event of a plurality should be considered to be the position agreed to by those who concurred as to the outcome on the narrowest grounds—that guidance has not been particularly useful since the Court itself applies the *Marks* rules only inconsistently; Adam S. Hochschild, "The Modern Problem of Supreme Court Plurality Decision: Interpretation in Historical Perspective," *Journal of Law & Policy*, vol. 4 (2000): 261–287.

175 Jack Knight and Lee Epstein, "The Norm of *Stare Decisis*," *American Journal of Political Science*, vol. 40, no. 4 (November 1996): 1018–1035.

176 James L. Gibson, Milton Lodge, and Benjamin Woodson, "Legitimacy, Losing, but Accepting: A Test of Positivity Theory and the Effects of Judicial Symbols," typescript (St. Louis, MO: Washington University in St. Louis, 2014). See also, Barbara A. Perry, "The Israeli and United States Supreme Courts: A Comparative Reflection on Their Symbols, Images, and Functions," *Review of Politics*, vol. 63, no. 2 (Spring 2001): 317–339.

177 That does not mean that a justice might not let something a president says during a State of the Union address get the better of him. During the State of the Union address in January 2010, President Obama criticized the Court for overturning two of it precedents with regard to campaign finance. Justice Alito shook his head and mouthed the words "not true," something that attracted a firestorm of criticism (some directed at the President for taking the justices to task as they sat in front of him at the State of the Union, some directed at Justice Alito for giving in to the impulse to respond). See, for example, Terry Moran, "State of the Union: The Slam, the Scowl and the Separation of Powers," ABC News, January 28, 2010 (http://abcnews.go.com/Politics/State_of_the_Union/state-of-the-union-president-obama-justice-alito-political-theater/story?id=9688639).

178 "New National Poll Finds: More Americans Know Snow White's Dwarfs Than Supreme Court Judges, Homer Simpson Than Homer's Odyssey, and Harry Potter Than Tony Blair," *Business Wire*, August 14, 2006 (http://www.businesswire.com/news/home/20060814005496/en/National-Poll-Finds-Americans-Snow-Whites-Dwarfs).

179 "Justice Alito at RWU Law, Pt.1," *Roger Williams University Law Newsroom*, September 14, 2012 (http://law.rwu.edu/story/justice-alito-rwu-law-pt-1).

180 Andrew Cohen, "Better Know a Justice! A Supreme Court Cheat Sheet," *The Atlantic*, August 21, 2012.

181 See, for example, Gene Policinski, "Making the Case for Cameras in the Supreme Court," First Amendment Center, April 2, 2013 (http://www.firstamendmentcenter.org/making-the-case-for-cameras-in-the-supreme-court); Adam Liptak, "Bucking a Trend, Supreme Court Justices Reject Video Coverage," *New York Times*, February 18, 2013.

182 C-SPAN nonetheless maintains an informational webpage (http://supremecourt.c-span.org/Default.aspx) that includes a variety of material, including a virtual tour of the Supreme Court building, clips from the justices, and historical information about the Court.

183 Tal Kopan, "Scalia: Cameras in Supreme Court would 'Mis-Educate' Americans," *Politico.com*, July 26, 2012 (http://www.politico.com/blogs/under-the-radar/2012/07/scalia-cameras-in-supreme-court-would-miseducate-americans-130246.html).

184 "Justice Alito at RWU Law, Pt.1," *Roger Williams University Law Newsroom*, September 14, 2012 (http://law.rwu.edu/story/justice-alito-rwu-law-pt-1).

185 Janet Miller, "Supreme Court Justice Elena Kagan Tells U-M Crowd about Serious and Not-So-Serious workings of the High Court," *AnnArbor.com*, September 7, 2012 (http://www.annarbor.com/news/supreme-court-justice-elena-kagan-discusses-the-serious-and-not-so-serious-workings-of-the-high-cour/#.UF8_ho2PU1M).

186 Julie Percha, "Sandra Day O'Connor: 'Unfortunate' Attacks on Chief Justice Roberts Underscore Need for Civics Education," *ABCNews.com*, July 25, 2012 (http://abcnews.go.com/blogs/politics/2012/07/sandra-day-oconnor-unfortunate-attacks-on-chief-justice-roberts-underscore-need-for-civics-education/).

187 A description of what is available on the Court's website (as well as links to that material) can be found by navigating to http://www.supremecourt.gov/oral_arguments/availabilityoforalargumenttranscripts.aspx.

188 The Oyez Project is housed at www.oyez.org.

189 *Bush v. Gore*, 531 U.S. 98 (2000).

190 *Grutter v. Bollinger*, 539 U.S. 306 (2003).

191 *Lee v. Weisman*, 505 U.S. 577 (1992).

192 *Stenberg v. Carhart*, 530 U.S. 914 (2000).

193 "Justice Alito at RWU Law, Pt.1," *Roger Williams University Law Newsroom*, September 14, 2012 (http://law.rwu.edu/story/justice-alito-rwu-law-pt-1).

194 The classic study of this question is Robert A. Dahl's, "Decision-Making in a Democracy: The Supreme Court as a National Policy-Maker," *Journal of Public Law*, vol. 6, no. 2 (1957): 279–295. For a recent review of the research in this area see Lee Epstein and Andrew Martin, "Does Public Opinion Influence the Supreme Court? Possibly Yes (But We're Not Sure Why)," *Pennsylvania Journal of Constitutional Law*, vol. 13, no. 2 (December 2010): 263–281.

195 See Jeff Shesol, *Supreme Power: Franklin Roosevelt vs. the Supreme Court* (New York, NY: W.W. Norton, 2010).

196 Another poll by the Pew Research Center for People & the Press showed the Court with an approval rating of 52 percent in 2012—the lowest score for the justices since the Pew Center began its poll in 1985; "Supreme Court Favorability Reaches New Low," Pew Research Center, May 1, 2012 (http://www.people-press.org/2012/05/01/supreme-court-favorability-reaches-new-low/). A Gallup poll taken in 2012 found the Court's approval rating to be 46 percent, unchanged since Gallup's last poll in September 2011; Simon Ammon, "New Supreme Court Polling," *National Review*, July 18, 2012.

197 Adam Liptak, "Approval Rating for Justices Hits Just 44% in New Poll," *New York Times*, June 7, 2012.

198 Lindsey Boerma, "Sandra Day O'Connor Defends Roberts on Health Care Ruling," *CBSNews.com*, August 5, 2012 (http://www.cbsnews.com/8301-3460_162-57481926/sandra-day-oconnor-defends-roberts-on-health-care-ruling/); Dave Jamieson, "Sandra Day O'Connor Says Public Disapproval of Roberts Court 'A Great Disappointment,' " *Huffingtonpost.com*, August 5, 2012 (http://www.huffingtonpost.com/2012/08/05/sandra-day-oconnor-supreme-court_n_1744056.html).

199 Valerie J. Hoekstra, *Public Reaction to Supreme Court Decisions* (New York, NY: Cambridge University Press, 2003).

200 See, for example, Gregory A. Caldeira and James L. Gibson, "The Etiology of Public Support for the Supreme Court," *American Journal of Political Science*, vol. 36, no. 3 (August 1992): 635–664; Gregory A. Caldeira, "Neither the Purse Nor the Sword: The Dynamics of Public Confidence in the United States Supreme Court," *American Political Science Review* vol. 80, no. 4 (December 1986): 1209–1226; James L. Gibson, Gregory A. Caldeira, and Lester Kenyatta Spence, "Measuring Attitudes toward the United States Supreme Court," *American Journal of Political Science*, vol. 47, no. 2 (April 2003): 354–367; James L. Gibson and Gregory A. Caldeira, *Citizens, Courts, and Confirmations: Positivity Theory and the Judgments of the American People* (Princeton, NJ: Princeton University Press, 2009).

201 Adam Liptak, "Approval Rating for Justices Hits Just 44% in New Poll," *New York Times*, June 7, 2012.

202 Associated Press, "Scalia in NYC: 'Politicized Court' Criticism 'Enrages' Me," WNBC-TV – NBC New York, September 17, 2012 (http://www.nbcnewyork.com/news/local/Antonin-Scalia-Supreme-Court-Politicized-Comments-New-York-Book-Event-170119636.html).

203 Artemus Ward, *Deciding to Leave: The Politics of Retirement from the United States Supreme Court* (Albany, NY: State University of New York Press, 2003): 121–124.

204 Specifically, Article I of the Constitution authorizes the House of Representatives to determine if formal charges for crimes committed in office should be brought forth against a civil officer of the government. If the House votes in favor of articles of impeachment, the Senate then serves as the trial body to determine if the individual should be convicted on any of the articles of impeachment. In this sense, the House's role is comparable to that of a district attorney or grand jury while the Senate's role is comparable to that of a trial court judge or jury. A simple majority vote in the House is sufficient to impeach but conviction in the Senate requires a super majority vote of two-thirds.

205   The efforts to impeach and convict Justice Chase were politically motivated.

206   William H. Rehnquist, *Grand Inquest: The Historic Impeachments of Justices Samuel Chase and President Andrew Johnson* (New York, NY: William Morrow, 1992).

207   Richard W. Stevenson and Linda Greenhouse, "O'Connor, First Woman on High Court, Resigns After 24 Years," *New York Times*, July 1, 2005.

208   Artemus Ward, *Deciding to Leave: The Politics of Retirement from the United States Supreme Court* (Albany, NY: SUNY Press, 2003).

209   "Justice Antonin Scalia on Issues Facing SCOTUS and the Country," *Fox News Sunday*, July 29, 2012 (http://www.foxnews.com/on-air/fox-news-sunday/2012/07/29/justice-antonin-scalia-issues-facing-scotus-and-country).

210   Robert Barnes, "The Question Facing Ruth Bader Ginsburg: Stay or Go?" *Washington Post Magazine*, October 4, 2013.

IMPLEMENTATION AND IMPACT

"The judiciary . . . has no influence over either the sword or the purse. . . . It may truly be said to have neither FORCE nor WILL but merely judgment; and must ultimately depend upon the aid of the executive arm even for the efficacy of its judgments."

—Alexander Hamilton, Founding Father and Secretary of the Treasury[1]

"The decision of the Supreme Court has fell still born, and they find that it cannot coerce Georgia to yield to its mandate."

—Andrew Jackson, Seventh President of the United States[2]

Christian Chapman of Charlotte, North Carolina is a preacher—a self-described traveling evangelist. On Thursday, September 1, 2011, he held forth before a rapt audience about how Jesus Christ had saved him from drugs. He exhorted them to commit their own lives to Christ, saying, "[A] relationship with Jesus is what you need more than anything else."[3] After Chapman concluded his remarks, rapper B-SHOC (a.k.a., Bryan Edmonds) took the stage and, with a light show and music playing in the background, B-SHOC shouted the Lord's praise and he, too, encouraged members of the audience to pledge themselves to Christ. Many of the audience members did just that. But this was not an Evangelical tent revival meeting like that depicted in HBO's *True Detective*, where the tough police detectives played by Matthew McConaughey and Woody Harrelson engaged in an existential discussion of religion while positioned at the back of a raucous tent revival presided over by a charismatic preacher. It was not at a prayer meeting, at vacation Bible school, or even in a church. Rather, this event took place in a South Carolina public school gymnasium before an assembly of middle school students during school hours. School principal Larry Stinson organized the event and, indeed, the principal routinely opened school programs with prayer and often invited Christian speakers. Chapman explained the purpose for his presence in the public schools: "I definitely think that we should try to get our relationship with Christ back into the schools. Jesus represents everything we want our students to live by."[4] It is likely that none of this would have come to light outside of the local community had B-SHOC not posted a video on YouTube including the following statement: "324 kids at this school have made a decision for Jesus Christ. I don't know if it gets any better than that. We are in a public school and we did a show for the sixth grade, the seventh grade, and then the eighth grade."[5] But he did post the video and, perhaps not surprisingly, a threatened lawsuit soon loomed large.

Half a century after the Supreme Court declared school prayer and officially sanctioned Bible reading in schools unconstitutional in *Engel v. Vitale*[6] and *Abington School District v. Schempp*,[7] events such as the one described above regularly occur throughout the nation. They are especially common in the rural South. For example, in a high school ar Pensacola, Florida, teachers explained the Bible as fact to students and a teacher aching with the aid of a bullhorn regularly greeted students as they arrived on campus h morning.[8] In another example, at schools in Sumner County, Tennessee, teachers uently led students in prayer and proselytized to students during both classes and acurricular activities.[9] Further, members of Gideons International[10] had been per- ed to distribute Bibles to students in those schools, with some teachers encouraging students to accept the Bibles and put their names in them. Yet one more example comes from Baltimore, Maryland, where the principal for a combined elementary and middle school held prayer services to help students prepare for tests. Fliers advertising the prayer event praised it as a way "to come together, as one, in prayer and ask God to bless our school to pass the MSA [the Maryland School Assessments, a set of standardized tests]."[11] In each case, the Constitution—as spelled out by the Supreme Court—was being ignored and it took litigation or the threat of litigation by the American Civil Liberties Union (ACLU) and other watchdog groups, such as Americans United for Separation of Church and State (AU)[12] and the Freedom From Religion Foundation (FFRF),[13] to end the practices.

The idea that courts are powerful institutions whose pronouncements are always followed is a myth. It is a powerful myth but a myth nonetheless. The American public certainly thinks of judicial rulings as definitive and authoritative, as evidenced by the fact that there is no paucity of disputes brought to the courts, which we discussed in detail in Chapter Four. However, as Alexander Hamilton explained in *Federalist No. 78*, courts have no formal power and must depend on others to see their policies carried out. Who are those "others" upon whom the courts, including the Supreme Court, are dependent for putting their decisions into force and effect? A reasonable assumption might

Image 11.1 Gideons Bibles
This 1913 photograph shows 5,000 Gideons Bibles ready for distribution to Washington, D.C., hotels. Is there a constitutional difference between distributing Bibles to hotels as opposed to distributing them to students at public schools? Harris & Ewing Collection, Prints and Photographs Division, Library of Congress, Washington, D.C.

be the president. However, (in)famous assertions—such as President Andrew Jackson's purported statement, "[Chief Justice] John Marshall has made his decision now let him enforce it"—suggest that presidents might not always be inclined to do so.[14] What about Congress? Well, the evidence suggests that Congress, like the president, may not be so keen on always faithfully abiding by the dictates of the Court if Congress is not partial to those dictates. For example, Congress has continued to rely on something called a legislative veto[15] despite the fact that the Supreme Court found in *INS v. Chadha*[16] that the legislative veto subverted the legislative process as outlined in the Constitution.[17] Lower courts, too, have demonstrated themselves to be inconsistently faithful implementers of Supreme Court rulings,[18] as have implementers such as the police[19] and frontline bureaucrats.[20] Further, "[t]hough there is a Supreme Court police force, the mission of that force is to protect the justices, the Court, and visitors to the Court, not to compel other actors to follow the will of the Court."[21] This means that the reality is that the judicial process does not end with a formal judicial decision or resolution of the conflict at hand. Instead, courts necessarily rely on other actors for the implementation of their decisions.

Judicial implementation is the process by which a court's decision is put into practice and enforced, ultimately affecting the behavior of others. For example, lower courts are expected to apply the rules established by higher courts, executives are expected to enforce judicial decisions, and, ultimately, the public is expected to comply with the rule of law in order for the system to function effectively. If executive officers, legislative

MYTH AND REALITY IN JUDICIAL IMPLEMENTATION AND IMPACT

MYTH	REALITY
Courts are powerful institutions whose pronouncements are always followed.	Courts are relatively weak institutions that rely on the power of other governmental actors to enforce their decisions and on individuals to follow their pronouncements.
The judicial process ends with a formal judicial decision or resolution of the conflict at hand.	Judicial decisions are part of an ongoing process of resolving conflicts in society.
Brown v. Board of Education ended racial segregation in America.	*Brown v. Board of Education* helped bolster the civil rights movement's push to end segregation and racial discrimination.
Lower courts comply with and follow the decisions of higher courts.	Lower courts may not comply with the decisions of higher courts because of unclear language, new and complex situations, perceptions of shifts in higher court preferences, and simple disagreement.
The public is largely unaware of court decisions.	The public is largely aware of court decisions.
Court decisions have a positive effect on public opinion with public support shifting toward a court decision after it is handed down.	Court decisions polarize public opinion between groups that were already on one side or the other of the issue, unless the issue is relatively personally less salient.

actors, and lower courts (not to mention everyday people) are not affected by high court rulings, then the rule of law is little more than an academic exercise. Scholars have vigorously debated whether courts have any such meaningful influence,[22] with some going so far as to suggest that decisions on controversial issues can even spur a backlash to the detriment of the goal the courts sought to achieve.[23] In this concluding chapter we discuss the various facets involved in implementing court decisions and the impact of courts generally on public opinion.

EXECUTIVE AND LEGISLATIVE RESPONSE

In the Supreme Court case of *Worcester v. Georgia*, Chief Justice John Marshall declared that Native Americans had a right to federal protection against enforcement of unconstitutional state laws.[24] President Jackson (not a fan of the Supreme Court[25] or of Native Americans[26]) was not pleased, to say the least. While he may never have uttered the words, "John Marshall has made his decision, now let him enforce it," Jackson did say, "The decision of the Supreme Court [in *Worcester v. Georgia*] has fell still born, and they [i.e., the members of the Court] find that it cannot coerce Georgia to yield to its mandate."[27] This quote is illustrative of the general point that, without willing executives to enforce judicial decisions, courts are powerless. Indeed, Jackson and Congress blatantly opposed the Court's developing support for the rights of Native Americans by ignoring treaties, seizing Native American land, and forcing them to march from their ancestral homelands on the Trail of Tears to what was then considered distant, foreign lands in what is today Oklahoma.[28] The result was a genocide in which thousands of Native Americans died of exposure, disease, and starvation.[29]

As legal scholar Jeffrey Yates notes, "The relationship between the president and the United States Supreme Court is indeed an enigmatic one."[30] Presidents and other executive officials are supposed to ensure that court rulings are implemented. Nonetheless, chief executives can order executive officials (such as law enforcement, attorneys general, and secretaries of defense) to ignore judicial decisions. Executives may be resistant to complying with judicial rulings because they sincerely disagree with the wisdom of the policies that courts pronounce. But they may also be resistant to doing so when they feel that their own policy-making prerogatives are threatened by judicial action.[31]

Further, virtually all executive officials, including the president, lack the job security enjoyed by many judges. This may lead them to react to pressure from organized interests or their broader constituencies, pressure that is at odds with the dictates of the courts. This can be particularly acute at the state and local level where state officials may oppose court decisions on matters of local significance, as exemplified by the resistance of the executives of southern states to the U.S. Supreme Court's decision in *Brown v. Board of Education*.[32]

The consequences of noncompliance (or outright disobedience) on the part of presidents are potentially much more far-reaching than what it means for any given case. As presidential scholars Terry Moe and William Howell observe,

There is no higher executive authority than the president, so no other executive is going to come riding to the Court's rescue to force the president into action. The president, moreover, is in charge of the entire federal executive branch and thus has a major say in how all the Court's decisions are enforced at that level. Thus, the

Court has a double problem. If it decides against the president on an issue that the president cares about, he may evade compliance. And if it decides against the president on lots of issues . . . the president could well become anti-Court in his general enforcement responsibilities throughout the executive branch. . . . [33]

In short, courts have a delicate balance to strike if they are to be able to secure the assistance of executive officials for the implementation of their decisions without alienating those same officials with rulings that curtail executive power and authority beyond their tolerance levels.

When it comes to congressional response to judicial decisions, Congress has significant power and responsibility with regard to both **statutory decisions** and **constitutional decisions**. A statutory decision is one in which a court is interpreting and applying a statute. A constitutional decision is one in which a court is interpreting and applying the Constitution. When a federal court interprets a statute, Congress may negate that interpretation simply by enacting new legislation. For example, in *Grove City College v. Bell*,[34] the Supreme Court ruled that only the specific parts of a college that received federal aid were subject to Title IX of the Education Amendments rather than the entire college. In doing this, the decision in *Grove City* limited the reach of federal civil rights protection. But 4 years later, Congress responded by passing the Civil Rights Restoration Act,[35] which rejected the Supreme Court's interpretation of Title IX and made it clear that an entire college is subject to federal civil rights protections when any program or activity of that college receives federal assistance.[36] While not a commonplace event, but one that does occur with at least some regularity, the Court itself (or a member of the Court writing in concurrence or dissent) will invite Congress to overturn its statutory interpretation by including language that either encourages those on the losing side to pursue action in Congress or draws attention to congressional authority to take such action. For example,

Image 11.2 George Wallace Blocks Integration
This June 11, 1963, photograph shows Governor George Wallace defiantly standing in the doorway of a University of Alabama building in an attempt to block racial integration. Deputy U.S. Attorney General Nicholas Katzenbach confronted him and, with the aid of federal marshals and the Alabama National Guard, forced Wallace to step aside and allow two African American students—Vivian Malone and James Hood—to enter. Would Alabama officials have complied with court-ordered integration if the executive branch of the federal government had not intervened? U.S. News & World Report Magazine Photograph Collection, Prints and Photographs Division, Library of Congress, Washington, D.C.

political scientists Lori Hausegger and Lawrence Baum found that there were more than two dozen invitations to Congress from the Court to override its statutory interpretation (plus three additional invitations to do so embedded in concurrences and 12 embedded in dissents) during the 1986 through 1990 terms of the Court.[37]

Given the Court's preeminent role as the authoritative interpreter of the Constitution, overruling the Court's constitutional decisions is much more difficult. Difficult does not, however, mean impossible. Congress may express disagreement with a constitutional decision made by the Court by amending the Constitution, revising the legislation, or repealing the old legislation and replacing it with new legislation that (presumably) does not have the same constitutional defect as the original.[38] When the Supreme Court (or any court) reviews legislation to determine whether it squares with the Constitution, the Court is said to be engaging in judicial review (whether the legislation is upheld or struck down on the basis of that review).[39] Political scientist J. Mitchell Pickerill collected data on Supreme Court decisions that engaged in judicial review and resulted in the invalidation of federal legislation. He then tracked what happened to the legislation after the Court decision from 1953 to 1997.[40] During that period of time, the Court struck down 74 separate federal statutory provisions. Subsequently, Congress amended the Constitution once, when Congress passed (and the states ratified) the Twenty-Sixth Amendment[41] lowering the national voting age to 18 in the wake of a Supreme Court decision striking down a congressional statute that attempted to do the same.[42] In addition, Congress amended statutes in response to judicial review more than two dozen times, and repealed legislation to replace it with new legislation eight times. In all, the Court responded to judicial invalidation of federal legislation 48 percent of the time. Pickerill's findings underscore the reality that judicial decisions are not always the end of the story in terms of resolving a conflict.

Further, consider the illustrative example of *United States v. Lopez*, in which the Supreme Court struck down the Gun-Free School Zones Act of 1995.[43] That federal statute banned guns within 1,000 feet of a school; however, the Court held that the statute exceeded congressional authority under the Constitution's Commerce Clause. The Commerce Clause, which appears in Article I of the Constitution, reads, in part, Congress shall have power "[t]o regulate Commerce with foreign Nations, and among the several States, and with the Indian Tribes."[44] It was authority from the Commerce Clause to regulate interstate commerce that Congress invoked in passing the Gun-Free School Zones Act. In the Court's view, however, it was too big a stretch to interpret the possession of a gun in a local school zone as an economic activity that might substantially affect interstate commerce to reasonably see it as falling under congressional Commerce Clause authority. In response to the constitutional invalidation of the statute, Congress amended it to require the federal government to demonstrate that the firearm had either moved in interstate commerce or otherwise affected interstate commerce. The *Lopez* decision and subsequent legislative action represent a dialogue about the issue of guns and schools through legislation and judicial decisions. It serves as another illustration of the reality of Court decisions as part of an ongoing process for resolving policy conflicts and a further repudiation of the myth of Court decisions as always being the definitive and final word.

Congress may also express disagreement with a federal court by protecting rights that the courts ruled were not protected. In *Goldman v. Weinberger*,[45] for example, the Supreme Court upheld an Air Force regulation that prohibited an observant Jew from wearing a yarmulke. A yarmulke, also known as a *kippah* or *kippa*, is a cap worn by Jewish men (and, less frequently, women) during prayer according to Jewish law. Some interpretations of Jewish law also prescribe the use of the yarmulke to cover the head at all times.

S. Simcha Goldman faced a quandary with regard to his yarmulke. As an Orthodox Jew and ordained rabbi, he could not simultaneously abide by the Air Force's prohibition against wearing his yarmulke while on duty and in uniform and the strictures of his faith that required him to wear a head covering at all times to honor God. Though Goldman successfully threaded this needle at first by staying close to his duty station (a health clinic) and wearing his regulation service cap over his yarmulke when outdoors, eventually a complaint was lodged against Goldman and disciplinary action ensued. Goldman, in turn, was prompted to seek legal redress. When the case found its way to the Supreme Court, the Court focused on the distinction between the free exercise of religion in the context of military service as opposed to the free exercise of religion in civilian society. Importantly, the Court did not bar the wearing of religious apparel; rather, it found that the Constitution simply did not provide an absolute right to do so. This gave Congress room to act and, indeed, Congress subsequently did take action allowing service members to express their faith by wearing religious apparel. The takeaway point is that courts—even the U.S. Supreme Court—do not necessarily have final say on the meaning of federal statutes or, at times, even the Constitution. The reality is much more nuanced than the myth.

COURTS AND SOCIAL CHANGE: HOLLOW HOPE OR POLITICAL MOBILIZER?

One perennial concern of legal scholars and political observers is whether courts, acting alone, can generate meaningful social change.[46] Famously, in *The Hollow Hope*, political scientist and law professor Gerald Rosenberg examined the decision in *Brown v. Board of Education*[47] and asked whether that decision made a real contribution to society.[48] He argued that courts are the least able of any of the branches of government to produce change because they lack the necessary tools to do so. They are the "least dangerous branch" because they lack budgetary or coercive power. As a consequence, Rosenberg argued, court decisions furthering the interests of the disadvantaged will only be implemented when the other branches of government are willing to do so. Specifically, he examined *Brown* in the context of two types of influence: the **judicial path of influence** and the **extra-judicial path of influence**.[49]

The judicial path of influence is determined by examining the direct outcome of the judicial decision; the question is whether a court-mandated change actually came to pass. Rosenberg argued that, nearly a decade after *Brown*, virtually nothing had changed for African American students living in the 11 states that required race-based school segregation by law. Rosenberg argued that there was no change because there was no political pressure to implement the decision and a great deal of pressure to resist it. On the executive level, there was little support for desegregation until the presidency of Lyndon Johnson. President Eisenhower refused to support *Brown*[50] and President John F. Kennedy did not make civil rights a top priority.[51] Local politicians were passing a variety of pro-segregation laws and there was also resistance from the American public.[52] According to Rosenberg, public resistance, supported by local political action, can almost always effectively defeat court-ordered civil rights, thereby blocking any judicial path of influence.

The extra-judicial path of influence acknowledges that court decisions may produce social reform by inspiring individuals to act or persuading them to examine and change their opinions. Did *Brown* lead to change through this path? Rosenberg considered several possibilities.[53] The first hypothesis Rosenberg examined was that *Brown* gave civil rights prominence, putting it on the political agenda. However, Rosenberg counted press stories over time and found that there was no evidence that press coverage of civil rights issues changed after *Brown*. The second hypothesis Rosenberg examined was that *Brown* influenced both the president and Congress to act. To assess this possibility, Rosenberg investigated whether members of Congress and the president mentioned *Brown* as a reason for introducing and supporting civil rights legislation; what he found is that *Brown* was hardly mentioned at all. The third hypothesis Rosenberg considered was that *Brown* favorably influenced white Americans in general about civil rights and that they, in turn, pressured politicians. Rosenberg argued that, in order for *Brown* to have "pricked the conscience" of white Americans, people must be aware of the Court and what it does. He examined polls charting reaction to *Brown* by Southerners over time and found that these polls showed very little support for desegregation and, in fact, lessening support throughout the 1950s. Finally, Rosenberg examined the hypothesis that *Brown* influenced African Americans to act in favor of civil rights, which then influenced white political elites either directly or indirectly. However, Rosenberg found no difference in the number of civil rights demonstrations after *Brown* as would be expected if this were the case. Specifically, while there was a considerable increase in 1956, the number of civil rights demonstrations subsequently dropped and did not increase again until the 1960s—6 or more years after the *Brown* decision.

Image 11.3 President Johnson Go to Selma Now!
This March 15, 1965, photograph shows southern African American protesters urging President Lyndon Johnson to go to Selma, Alabama—site of the Selma to Montgomery marches where 600 civil rights demonstrators were brutally beaten by Alabama state troopers one week earlier in what was known as "Bloody Sunday." Did Supreme Court decisions such as Brown v. Board of Education *(1954) inspire and embolden the civil rights movement of the 1960s?* New York World-Telegram and the Sun Newspaper Photograph Collection, Prints and Photographs Division, Library of Congress, Washington, D.C.

Schools in the South were finally desegregated, but only 18 years after *Brown* and only because of action taken by Congress and the executive branch. Specifically, Title VII of the Civil Rights Act of 1964 permitted federal funds to be cut off from programs in which racial discrimination was practiced.[54] Further, the Elementary and Secondary Education Act of 1965 provided substantial federal funds to poor Southern schools.[55] But, Rosenberg maintained that those changes were not a result of Court action but, rather, of action on the part of others. Though Rosenberg's treatment of the subject was both broad and deep, a number of scholars challenged his conclusions.[56] For example, political scientist Michael McCann argued that the executive branch and the legislative branch are not solitary organs of change either. "It is certainly true that courts are limited in their capacities to deal with complex social problems. But what institution is not highly limited . . .?"[57] In other words, it is unreasonable to expect courts to single-handedly effect change and to believe that they are not necessarily any less able to do so than the other branches of government.

Additionally, McCann noted that Rosenberg presumed that change started at the top with the Supreme Court decision and then trickled down to other actors. This is a **court-centered model of legal change**, and the standard for ascertaining effective change with such a model is direct compliance with (or action that is inspired by) courts.[58] McCann argued, however, that a **de-centered model of legal change** is a more accurate way to think about law and courts. This model places primary emphasis on non-judicial actors involved in a social struggle.[59] McCann argued that non-judicial actors should be the center of analysis, as they are the real agents for change and not mere reactors to judicial commands.[60] According to this line of reasoning, indirect effects matter more, not because people are inspired and change how they feel morally, but because people can see what is realistic and understand what resources they can exploit to advance their cause. Accordingly, McCann argued that the initial focus of impact should be on organized African Americans and whites in the South and, in this regard, the evidence shows that *Brown* had a significant impact on the NAACP and middle-class, southern African Americans. Specifically, the NAACP mobilized African Americans into action.

POP CULTURE

Lee Daniels's *The Butler*

The 2013 film *The Butler* follows the life of an African American butler by the name of Cecil Gaines (played by Academy Award–winning actor Forest Whitaker) who works at the White House during the civil rights movement. Early in the film, a young Cecil Gaines is seen serving a group of white men in the Excelsior Hotel in Washington, D.C., in 1954. One of the men says: "Best decision that court ever made was to slow this whole mess down. Nigger boys in school with white girls?! Who ever heard of such a thing? Next thing you know they'd be fornicatin'. Gentlemen, this could start another Civil War." Noticing the African American butler serving him, the man asks Gaines: "What do you think about niggers going to school with white children?" The butler replies: "To be honest with you, Mr. Jenkins, I tend to not be too concerned with American or European politics." Jenkins continues: "Nor should you . . . they're all criminals. Earl Warren should be shot and hanged. That dumb son-of-a-bitch is trying to integrate our schools. I think Judge Warren is going to find that quite a challenge."

Subsequently hired to work at the White House, Gaines is in the Oval Office when President Dwight Eisenhower (played by another Academy Award–winning actor, Robin Williams), Attorney General Herbert Brownell, and Chief of Staff Sherman Adams discuss the role of the executive branch in enforcing the Supreme Court's decision in

Brown v. Board of Education in the face of recalcitrant state actors such as Arkansas Governor Orval Faubus.[61] Adams asks: "Send federal troops to Little Rock?" Brownell responds: "If it comes to it, yes." Eisenhower weighs in: "I can't see any situation where I'd send troops to the South. Ever. It would cause another Civil War." Brownell explains: "Sir, if the Federal government doesn't enforce Brown, then who will? The South must comply with the law." Eisenhower replies: "It's just going to take some time to adjust, that's all." Brownell continues: "I understand, Mr. President, but if Faubus continues to block the negro children then what do we do? We must enforce the Constitution." Adams sides with Eisenhower: "Give Faubus more time. With a little persuading, he'll back down. We just want to move slowly."

Throughout the film Gaines and his elder son, Louis Gaines (played by British-born actor David Oyelowo), argue and clash over civil rights and the pace of change. Louis becomes increasingly radicalized through sit-ins at the whites-only section of a Woolworth's lunch counter, ultimately joining the Black Panther Party.[62] In one exchange, after being arrested and sentenced to jail for a lunch counter sit-in, Louis explains: "Something special's going on here, Dad." Gaines replies: "What's so special about a colored man in jail?" His son answers: "I'm trying to change the way negroes are perceived—" Gaines interrupts him: "You're breaking the law. That judge just sentenced you to 30 days in the County Work House. You're fixin' to get killed." His son is adamant: "If I can't sit at any lunch counter I want then I might as well be dead. We're fighting for our rights. We're going to change the nation's consciousness toward the American negro."

The film is an important illustration of how legal and social change occurs—not by judicial pronouncement but by public awareness, social movements, and the involvement of other actors in society. In this sense, *The Butler* is very much a film about the judicial process even though it is not directly about the Supreme Court's decision in *Brown* or about law and courts specifically. Court decisions like *Brown* do not end the process of legal, political, and social change but are part of an ongoing dialogue among political actors and the American people.

LOWER COURT COMPLIANCE

An important aspect of the rule of law is the notion that lower court judges will comply with, follow, and implement the decisions of higher courts. ***Stare decisis*** (translated from Latin as "to stand by things decided") is the legal principle that requires lower courts to abide by the dictates of the U.S. Supreme Court and it is considered critical for stability in the law.[63] Hence, if the Supreme Court hands down a decision interpreting the Constitution, federal appellate and district courts, as well as state and local courts, are (in principle) bound (by *stare decisis*) to implement the legal rule or standard articulated in that decision in future cases. Although lower courts are generally compliant with Supreme Court decisions, it is a myth that lower courts always follow the decisions of higher courts. Consider the case of *Taylor v. Louisiana* (1975).[64] Billy Taylor was indicted, tried, and convicted for aggravated kidnapping.[65] He used a butcher knife to force his way into a car in which a woman, her daughter, and her grandson were driving. Taylor then forced the woman to drive to a deserted area where he raped her. His trial was before an all-male jury, which was not surprising given that women were not automatically entered into the *venire* (i.e., the set of prospective jurors, also known as the jury pool) in Louisiana at that time. The terms of the state constitution excluded women from jury service unless they took the necessary steps to submit special paperwork to affirmatively opt into the *venire*. Though it seemed doubtful that women would have been more sympathetic to the defendant, Taylor's defense attorney, Bill King, made the argument that it did not matter. The fact that the jury did not represent a fair cross-section of the community should be sufficient to throw out Taylor's conviction and the sentence that had been imposed.[66]

As it happened, the Court was persuaded that state laws that automatically excluded women from jury pools were unconstitutional.[67] Though that seems like a straightforward ruling on its face, what exactly does that precedent require or allow? If women were now automatically included in jury pools, could they simply opt out of a jury pool by virtue of their sex? After all, the Court made clear that it was not in the business of telling states the exact details of how they were to construct their jury pools:

> Our holding does not augur or authorize the fashioning of detailed jury-selection codes by federal courts. The fair-cross-section principle must have much leeway in application. The States remain free to prescribe relevant qualifications for their jurors and to provide reasonable exemptions so long as it may be fairly said that the jury lists or panels are representative of the community.[68]

Explicitly mindful of the precedent set in *Taylor*, the Missouri Supreme Court stated that, while excluding women in the absence of action on their part to opt into the jury pool was unmistakably unconstitutional, permitting women to be excused upon request (as was permitted, for example, for persons over the age of 65, members of the clergy, and doctors of medicine) did not suffer from the same constitutional defect.[69] Yet in *Duren v. Missouri*[70] the U.S. Supreme Court reversed the state court decision precisely because it found it to be inconsistent with *Taylor*.

Taylor and *Duren* illustrate that lower court compliance is not necessarily automatic. The question, then, is why lower courts might choose to be noncompliant with the dictates of their ostensible judicial superiors. First, the language in judicial opinions may not be clear. With rare exception, "ambiguity will work against effective implementation

Image 11.4 First Woman Jury
This 1911 photo shows the first all-woman jury in California who acquitted the editor of the Watts News of printing indecent language. Women could be automatically excluded from juries unless they affirmatively opted in until the U.S. Supreme Court's decision in Taylor v. Louisiana *(1975). Yet, in a subsequent case, a state supreme court allowed women to opt out of juries simply because of their gender. Did the lower court fail to comply with* Taylor? George Grantham Bain Collection, Prints and Photographs Division, Library of Congress, Washington, D.C.

[of superior court decisions by subordinate courts] in two ways: by leaving loyal judges uncertain as to their superior's intent and by providing leeway which recalcitrant judges may use to evade obedience to a directive."[71] Such ambiguity or vagueness could result from poor writing, but more often than not, it is due to the compromises that necessarily take place among judges on collegial courts.[72] Additionally, it is not uncommon for the U.S. Supreme Court to remand a case back to a lower court with instructions that the case be handled by further "proceedings not inconsistent with this opinion." Therefore, unclear or vague language may not only allow but also actually require the exercise of lower court discretion. Recently, scholars Jeffrey Staton and Georg Vanberg argued that vagueness also permits courts to shield anticipated noncompliance on the part of other branches of government from the broader audience of the public as a means to avoid the erosion of public confidence.[73] Regardless of the underlying reason for a precedent's vagueness or ambiguity, lower court judges may find themselves unwittingly noncompliant because they lack clarity as to what the precedent requires.

Second, even when the actual language in an opinion is unambiguous and precise (rather than vague), opinions with different levels of support on the Court (as indicated by the vote split) can generate different levels of compliance. Though some early research failed to find support for the idea that precedents set with larger majorities were more likely to enjoy greater compliance than those with smaller majorities,[74] later work has found compelling evidence that unanimity (or the lack thereof) does, indeed, structure lower courts' compliance behavior. For example, judicial scholars Benjamin Kassow, Donald Songer, and Michael Fix have found state high courts to provide more favorable treatments to Supreme Court precedents that were set with greater vote margins as compared to those with smaller vote margins.[75] In addition, two other judicial scholars, Sara Benesh and Malia Reddick, considered how quickly federal courts of appeals complied when the Supreme Court overruled existing precedent, and key among their findings was the fact that unanimity increased the likelihood of compliance.[76] More recently, political scientist Pamela C. Corley analyzed how the courts of appeals respond to Supreme Court **plurality opinions** (that is, opinions that have received the most, but not a majority, of the votes on the Court) as compared to **majority opinions** (that is, opinions that have received a majority of the votes on the Court).[77] Her key finding was that the lower courts are less likely to follow plurality opinions than they are to follow majority opinions:

> Plurality opinions . . . create precedential uncertainty because lower courts not only have to find the rationale of each opinion but must decide *which* opinion's ratio-nale governs. In addition, plurality decisions may not be perceived [to be] as au-thoritative as majority decisions . . . [P]lurality decisions lead to lower compliance, resulting in the erosion of the Court's credibility and authority as a source of legal leadership and, ultimately, the influence of the Court being diminished.[78]

In short, the less support for a precedent on the Court when it is set then the less compli-ant lower courts are likely to be, much to the detriment of the Court.

Third, lower court judges may sense that a change in higher court doctrine is on the cusp of occurring and, therefore, they may feel stuck between the Scylla of violating the norm of *stare decisis* (by following what they perceive to be the current position of the Court) and the Charybdis of risking being overturned (by abiding by the existing precedent).[79] Thus, the lower court may choose to be noncompliant because it anticipates that the Court is poised to overrule the precedent in question, what scholars Malia Reddick and Sara Benesh characterize as being prescient.[80] Lower courts might take into consideration the preferences of the Supreme Court that is sitting at the time the lower court interprets the precedent (relative to the preferences of the Supreme Court that handed down the precedent) and decide that disobedience to the precedent will not be punished.[81] In fact, research conducted by a team of social scientists shows that increasing ideological distance between the median member of the Supreme Court decision coalition that handed down the precedent and the median member of the contemporary Supreme Court significantly reduces compliance with precedents on the part of federal courts of appeals panels.[82] Other research demonstrates that courts of appeals panels are similarly constrained by the anticipated response of the circuit *en banc* (that is, when all judges on a circuit sit to review a decision made by a three-judge circuit panel),[83] and that district court judges are sensitive to the anticipated responses of the supervising circuit.[84]

Finally, lower court judges may simply disagree with a higher court ruling. While lower court judges are technically supposed to follow the precedents handed down by higher courts in accordance with the principle of *stare decisis*, lower court judges are not merely appendages of their superior courts. Rather, they, like superior court judges, have policy preferences and are influenced by those preferences in the decisions they render, which we previously discussed in Chapter Nine. This includes the decisions of lower court judges and courts vis-à-vis compliance with the dictates of superior courts. Along these lines, political scientists Pamela C. Corley and Justin Wedeking showed that as the difference in ideology between the Supreme Court and a deciding federal court of appeals panel increases, the likelihood that lower courts will comply with the precedent decreases.[85] Lower court judges undoubtedly take seriously their obligations to be faithful to the principle of *stare decisis*, but they are human beings (not legal automatons) and they may (at least on occasion) shirk their obligations as agents of superior court principals when their own preferences conflict with those principals.[86]

The very nature of the structure of the judicial system—organized as a hierarchy of courts as discussed in detail in Chapter Four—implies that lower courts are to be obedient to higher courts. The value of that obedience is multifold: "Adherence on the part of lower court judges to the dictates of the Supreme Court fosters uniformity in terms of the meaning and scope of the Constitution, contributes to stability in the legal system, and provides a framework on which both public officials and citizens can rely when making decisions."[87] But, as is the case with regard to presidents and Congress, there is no ready mechanism at the disposal of superior courts (even the U.S. Supreme Court) to force inferior courts to obey. Just as the Supreme Court police cannot march over to the Capitol or the White House to compel those actors to comply with Supreme Court rulings, neither can they or will they march over to lower federal and state court buildings to oblige judges on those lower courts to comply. The myth may be that lower courts automatically and faithfully comply with the decisions of their judicial superiors, but the reality is that they may not for any number of reasons.

INFLUENCE ON THE PUBLIC

Very few individuals have direct experience as a participant in Supreme Court litigation[88] and the conventional wisdom has been that the public knows little to nothing about the courts, including the Supreme Court.[89] In truth, however, a significant body of research demonstrates that the public actually is aware of Supreme Court decisions, though the level of awareness is subject to ebbs and flows.[90] The public is particularly aware of decisions handed down later in the Court's term.[91] This is likely due to the fact that the Court issues the most controversial decisions at the end of the term, though there is evidence to suggest that the marginal impact of the issuance of a decision on awareness of decisions is actually greater for lower salience cases than it is for higher salience cases.[92] Furthermore, awareness is greater in local communities that are affected directly by the decision.[93] Of course public awareness is conditioned by media coverage and research shows that cases involving civil rights and liberties receive more coverage than those involving economic matters.[94] Though public awareness is admittedly greater for other political developments such as presidential events, the myth of an unaware public when it comes to judicial decisions clashes with the reality of a public that is at least moderately aware.[95]

Given that the public is aware of court decisions, what effect do those decisions have? Can courts positively influence public opinion? According to **legitimation effects (or positive response) theory**, courts (the U.S. Supreme Court, in particular) act to legitimate certain policies. In other words, after the Court hands down a decision, public opinion shifts towards the Court's opinion. Indeed, scholars have found modest increases in public support for the positions taken by the Court.[96] One example is an experimental study conducted by political scientists James Gibson, Gregory Caldeira, and Lester Spence.[97] The research team surveyed a random sample of the American mass public, providing each interviewee with a vignette (i.e., a short story) about a group of Florida citizens demanding that a government panel take custody of presidential ballots in dispute, with varying sets of additional information provided for different groups of study participants. The empirical results from aggregating the responses of the different groups of participants demonstrated that citizens are slightly more willing to accept the policy choice of the Court than that of Congress (though the difference is not enormous) and, further, that the perceived legitimacy of an institution makes a difference as to how willing individuals are to acquiesce to the decisions of that institution. Judicial scholar Robert Hume used an experimental survey design to evaluate whether state courts could also serve to legitimate public policies.[98] He found that state courts can build public support but that the level of judicial independence conditions a state court's capacity to do so. Specifically, judges in states in which judicial selection is via partisan or nonpartisan elections, which diminish judges' independence, are hampered in their capacity to confer legitimacy on public policies.

HOW DO WE KNOW?

What Impact Does the Supreme Court Have on Public Opinion?

In order to assess what impact the Supreme Court has on public opinion, political scientists Valerie Hoekstra and Jeffrey Segal designed a study examining the effect of a Supreme Court decision, *Lamb's Chapel v. Center Moriches* (1993), on public opinion in the local community in which the case originated (Center Moriches, New York) and in the surrounding region (Suffolk County).[99] At issue in the case was whether religious groups could be denied access to public facilities to which secular community groups were granted access. In particular, Lamb's Chapel (a Christian church) sought permission to show a six-part film series of family lectures given by influential evangelical leader James Dobson on school property after school hours. The school district refused to grant permission because the film was church related and the school district did not want to violate the Establishment Clause, which prohibits the government from making any law "respecting an establishment of religion." When the case made its way to the Supreme Court it came down on the side of the church. The reasoning undergirding the decision in favor of the church was two-fold. First, prohibiting religious groups from using school property but allowing other (nonreligious) groups to have access represented viewpoint discrimination in violation of the Free Speech

Clause of the First Amendment. Second, because the films would be shown outside of school hours and would be open to the general public, permitting the church to use school premises would not have constituted a violation of the Establishment Clause of the First Amendment as the school board had argued.

Hoekstra and Segal were interested in understanding if the decision in *Lamb's Chapel* affected public opinion on the matter being contested (i.e., use of public school property by religious groups during non-school hours). Broadly speaking, scholars theorized that the public is willing to accept what is essentially an undemocratic institution (the Court) due to a perception of the Court as the sole legitimate interpreter and protector of the Constitution. Thus, the Court has a legitimation effect. As a consequence, the expectation is that, when the Court speaks on an issue, the public changes its attitudes about the issue. However, Hoekstra and Segal argued that there are two conditions that must be met for the Court to be persuasive in this way. First, people must be aware of the decision. Also, people must not have thought too much about the issue before the Court's decision; i.e., the case is not personally salient. In the abstract, personal salience should be greatest for the direct parties to a case. The degree to which an issue is personally salient affects the amount of time an individual thinks about an issue, how much information that individual is likely to seek out, how susceptible the individual will be to being persuaded by opposing arguments, and, ultimately, how strongly and consistently the individual feels about the issue. If something is far removed from an individual's life, the less incentive or motivation there is to actively gather information and arrive at a strongly held opinion. To illustrate:

	PERSONAL SALIENCY	
AWARENESS	High	Low
High	Resistant to Persuasion	Susceptible to Persuasion
Low	Not Exposed to Message	Not Exposed to Message

For the typical Supreme Court decision, personal saliency is extremely low for most individuals. With regard to the *Lamb's Chapel* case, however, Hoekstra and Segal expected that the Supreme Court decision would be highly salient for people in Center Moriches (those most directly affected) and less salient to people in Suffolk County, although people in both communities would be more likely to have heard about the decision than those outside of those communities. Thus, the authors expected greater attitude change (i.e., susceptible to persuasion) due to the Supreme Court's decision for those in the surrounding communities (Suffolk County people) than for those directly affected by the decision (Center Moriches people).

During the months of March, April, and May of 1993, the research team interviewed a sample of Long Island residents: a random sample of Center Moriches residents and another random sample of Suffolk County residents. They contacted the same people during the two-week period after the Court handed down the decision in *Lamb's Chapel*. What they found, first, was that 84.6 percent of the Center Moriches sample and 84.7 percent of the Suffolk County sample correctly identified how the Court had ruled in the case. In other words, the first condition necessary for persuasion (awareness of the Court's decision) was met.

They next examined opinion change based on the Court's ruling in *Lamb's Chapel*. To do so, they examined support for church use of school facilities before and after the ruling. Respondents' level of support was measured on a scale from 1 (indicating "very strongly agree") to 7 (indicating "very strongly disagree"). The distribution of support the research team reported is as follows:

	CENTER MORICHES	**SUFFOLK COUNTY**
Support Before Ruling	2.68	3.20
Support After Ruling	2.58	2.45
	No statistically significant change	Statistically significant change

Note: Cell entries are means

Though there was a change in support among Center Moriches residents (a change corresponding to the direction of the Court's ruling), the change was quite small and was not statistically significant. In contrast, the change among Suffolk County residents (also a change corresponding to the direction of the Court's ruling) was statistically significant.

Recognizing that there might well be other factors beyond locale that shape or influence opinion change, Hoekstra and Segal then estimated a multivariate statistical model to take into account the following potential influences: ideology, level of education, evaluation of the Supreme Court, level of attention to the news media, and strength of the initial opinion regarding a church's right of access to the school facility. The research team examined the effect of each of these variables on whether a participant in the study was or was not persuaded by the Court. They did so using a logit model, which is suitable for situations in which the dependent variable is dichotomous (i.e., there are two possible outcomes or conditions). As the table of results (partially reproduced as Table 11B.1) reports, only two variables—town of residence and strength of initial opinion—were statistically significant (i.e., demonstrated an effect on change in opinion):

TABLE 11.B1
Logit Analysis of Change in Opinion Regarding Church Use of School

	ESTIMATED COEFFICIENT	STANDARD ERROR	t VALUE
Town of Residence*	−1.41	0.52	2.72
Ideology	0.16	0.13	1.30
Evaluation of Supreme Ct.	0.16	0.13	1.19
Education	−0.17	0.22	0.76
Attention to News Media	0.03	0.05	0.66
Strength of Initial Opinion*	−1.80	0.41	4.35
Intercept	2.40	1.54	1.55
Log Likelihood	−55.864		
Percent Correctly Predicted	73.0 percent		
Reduction in Prediction Error	31.0 percent		
Number of Observations	110		

Dependent Variable: Opinion Change (1 = positive change, 0 = no change/negative change).
Strength of initial opinion: 3 = "very strongly agree/disagree," 2 = "strongly agree/disagree," and 1 = "not so strongly agree/disagree."

To translate these statistical estimates into something more substantively meaningful, the authors used them to calculate predicted probabilities for various conditions, as reported in Table 11B.2.

TABLE 11.B2
Predicted Probability of Changing Opinion in Direction of Court's Ruling

	STRENGTH OF INITIAL OPINION		
	STRONG	MODERATE	WEAK
Center Moriches	0.04	0.20	0.61
Suffolk County	0.15	0.51	0.86

As the strength that an individual held his initial opinion decreased (from strong to moderate to weak), the probability that individual would be persuaded by the Court's decision increased substantially. For participants hailing from Center Moriches (the immediately affected area), the probability of changing opinion in the direction of the Court's ruling was a mere 0.04 for those whose initial opinions were strongly held, to 0.61 for those whose initial opinions were only weakly held. The changes in the probability of changing opinion were more pronounced for those hailing from Suffolk County (the surrounding area): the likelihood of changing opinion in the direction of the Court's ruling was a 0.15 for those whose initial opinions were strongly held to a whopping 0.86 for those whose initial opinions were only weakly held.

As they originally hypothesized, Hoekstra and Segal found that the more immediate the situation was to an individual's personal life, the less likely that individual was to defer to the judgment of (that is, be persuaded by) the Supreme Court. Even though the outcome of the decision had much more bearing on those individuals in the immediate community than those residing in the surrounding county, residents of the local community presumably spent more time thinking about the case and/or discussing the case with other people, thereby crystallizing their opinion before the Court had the opportunity to change their minds. Thus, the Supreme Court can influence public opinion when the public has high levels of information about the decision and when the decision is relatively less salient.

Political scientists Charles Franklin and Lianne Kosaki challenged the positive response theory, offering a **structural response (or polarization) theory** as an alternative.[100] According to this theory, public opinion changes its structure (but not necessarily its aggregate level of support for a policy) as a result of a Supreme Court decision. Specifically, after the Court hands down a decision, there will be a polarization of attitudes between groups that were already on one side or the other of the issue in question. In their study, Franklin and Kosaki examined public response to *Roe v. Wade*.[101] What they found was that those who favored greater access to discretionary abortions before *Roe* became even more supportive after the Supreme Court decision, and those who opposed access to discretionary abortions before *Roe* became even more opposed after the Supreme Court decision. In other words, rather than changing public opinion about abortion per se, *Roe* polarized public opinion on the issue. Interestingly, political scientists Timothy Johnson and Andrew Martin found evidence that this polarization effect is conditional: "At times the public will react (when an issue is initially brought to the forefront of political discourse by a landmark Court decision), but at others it will not (when the Court rules on an issue again)."[102]

Two key empirical findings about the courts and public opinion are, first, that the public is generally aware of judicial decisions and, second, that judicial decisions influence public opinion, not necessarily by changing aggregate support for a given policy but by changing the structure of support for that policy. The evidence does not support the myth that the public is (blissfully or otherwise) ignorant of Court decisions. The conventional wisdom that judicial opinions can serve to legitimate policies supported by the Court, while generally speaking is true, in fact is more nuanced in that the Court can influence public opinion when the public has high levels of information about the decision and when the decision is relatively less salient. Otherwise, the effect of Court opinions is more pronounced in terms of structure than in moving public opinion closer to the direction of the Court's decision.

CONCLUSION

As the school prayer example at the start of this chapter demonstrates, longstanding decisions by courts—including the U.S. Supreme Court—are ignored and violated every day by individuals and institutions throughout the nation. The myth that courts are powerful institutions is undermined by the reality of the implementation process. Executive officials may fail to enforce court rulings because they disagree with the decision or see the decision as a threat to their own ability to make policy. Legislative actors can respond to unfavorable court decisions by amending the Constitution or existing legislation, or even by passing new legislation. Although lower courts are generally compliant with higher courts, they do not always follow the decisions of higher courts. Finally, although the public is aware of court cases, judicial decisions tend to polarize, rather than change, existing public opinion on issues unless the issue is relatively less salient. In all, courts are not the final word but are instead engaged in an ongoing dialogue with other political actors and the American people.

Suggested Readings

Sara C. Benesh. *The U.S. Court of Appeals and the Law of Confession: Perspectives on the Hierarchy of Justice* (New York, NY: LFB Scholarly, 2002). The author theorizes that the relationship between the U.S. courts of appeals and the Supreme Court is a modified principal-agent relationship and evaluates that theory with the use of multiple methodologies to measure the impact of legal, attitudinal, strategic, and institutional influences on appellate court decision making.

Bradley C. Canon and Charles A. Johnson. *Judicial Policies: Implementation and Impact*, Second Edition (Washington, DC: Congressional Quarterly Press, 1998). This book assesses the implementation, impact, and consequences of judicial rulings through the systematic exploration of the effects of judicial decisions on the people who carry them out, and on the individuals and organizations who feel their impact.

Matthew E. K. Hall. *The Nature of Supreme Court Power* (New York, NY: Cambridge University Press, 2011). This book examines the nature of Supreme Court power by identifying conditions under which the Court is successful at altering the behavior of state and private actors, using a set of longitudinal analyses to find that the Court is most successful when implementation relies on lower courts and less successful when implementation relies on non-court entities.

Valerie J. Hoekstra. *Public Reaction to Supreme Court Decisions* (New York, NY: Cambridge University Press, 2003). Using original survey data and extensive analysis of media coverage, the author teases out how people's opinions of the Supreme Court are affected by its decisions, finding that media coverage and knowledge have meaningful effects on how decisions are viewed by the public.

Michael J. Klarman. *From Jim Crow to Civil Rights: The Supreme Court and the Struggle for Racial Equality* (New York, NY: Oxford University Press, 2006). This book analyzes the consequences of Supreme Court decisions on race—paying particular attention to the effects of the civil rights movement and demographic changes that impacted Court rulings—and considers litigation as a form of civil rights protest and education.

Michael W. McCann. *Rights at Work: Pay Equity Reform and the Politics of Legal Mobilization* (Chicago, IL: University of Chicago Press, 1994). In this book, the author explains how wage-discrimination battles have raised public legal consciousness and helped reform activists mobilize working women in the pay equity movement.

Gerald N. Rosenberg, *The Hollow Hope: Can Courts Bring About Social Change?* Second Edition (Chicago, IL: University of Chicago Press, 2008). This volume presents a sweeping analysis of key Supreme Court decisions in an effort to understand whether courts can activate political and social reform, which the author asserts is difficult to impossible to do.

Endnotes

1 Alexander Hamilton, "Federalist No. 78," in *The Federalist Papers*, Clinton Rossiter, ed. (New York, NY: New American Library, 1961).

2 Quoted in Richard P. Longaker, "Andrew Jackson and the Judiciary," *Political Science Quarterly*, vol. 71, no. 3 (September 1956): 341–364, 349.

3 Erik Eckholm, "Battling Anew Over the Place of Religion in Public Schools," *New York Times*, December 27, 2011.

4 Ibid.

5 Daniel Bullard-Bates, "A SHOC-king Disregard for the Constitution," Blog of Rights, ACLU.com, September 26, 2011 (https://www.aclu.org/blog/religion-belief/shoc-king-disregard-constitution).

6 370 U.S. 421 (1962).

7 374 U.S. 203 (1963).

8 Erik Eckholm, "Battling Anew Over the Place of Religion in Public Schools," *New York Times*, December 27, 2011.

9 Sonya Thompson, "ACLU Threatens Lawsuit Against Board of Education," *Portland Leader*, April 28, 2011.

10 According to Gideons International's webpage (http://www.gideons.org/?HP=USA&sc_lang=en), it is "an Association of Christian business and professional men and their wives dedicated to telling people about Jesus through sharing personally and providing Bibles and New Testaments." Founded in 1899, it originated as a group of Christian travelers (e.g., businessmen who traveled frequently for their jobs) and became most well known for its Bible Project directed at placing a Bible in every hotel room.

11 Erica L. Green, "Prayer Service at City School Called Improper," *Baltimore Sun*, March 13, 2011.

12 AU was founded in 1947 as Protestants and Other Americans United for Separation of Church and State in response to pending congressional proposals that would have extended government aid to religious schools. The AU webpage (https://www.au.org/) includes the following mission statement: "Americans United for Separation of Church and State is a nonpartisan educational organization dedicated to preserving the constitutional principle of church-state separation as the only way to ensure religious freedom for all Americans."

13 FFRF was founded in 1976 by Anne Nicol Gaylor and her daughter, Annie Laurie Gaylor, in Madison, Wisconsin. The latter is currently the organization's co-president (along with her husband, Dan Barker, who is a former Pentecostal minister). The FFRF webpage (http://ffrf.org/) notes, "The purposes of the Freedom From Religion Foundation, Inc., as stated in its bylaws, are to promote the constitutional principle of separation of state and church, and to educate the public on matters relating to nontheism."

14 Despite this quote's frequent attribution to President Jackson, it is doubtful he ever actually said it. See Paul F. Boller, Jr. and John George, *They Never Said It: A Book of Fake Quotes, Misquotes, and Misleading Attributions* (New York, NY: Oxford University Press, 1989): 53.

15 With a legislative veto, Congress delegates the authority to undertake some action to the president but does so in such a way that Congress can invalidate that action without having to pass new legislation (e.g., with a resolution in one or the other or both of the chambers of Congress). This is in contrast with the constitutionally prescribed path of legislation, which requires passage of legislation (in identical form) in both chambers of Congress and that such legislation be presented to the president for action before it can be considered law.

16 462 U.S. 919 (1983).

17 See, for example, the analysis offered in Louis Fisher, "The Legislative Veto: Invalidated, It Survives," *Law and Contemporary Problems*, vol. 56, no. 4 (Autumn 1993): 273–292.

18 See, for example, Sara C. Benesh, *The U.S. Court of Appeals and the Law of Confession: Perspectives on the Hierarchy of Justice* (New York, NY: LFB Scholarly, 2002).

19 See, for example, Neal A. Milner, "Supreme Court Effectiveness and the Police Organization," *Law and Contemporary Problems*, vol. 36, no. 4 (Autumn 1971): 467–487.

20 See, for example, James F. Spriggs II, "Explaining Federal Bureaucratic Compliance with Supreme Court Opinions," *Political Research Quarterly*, vol. 50, no. 3 (September 1997): 567–593.

21 Sara C. Benesh and Wendy L. Martinek, "Lower Court Compliance with Precedent," In *New Directions in Judicial Politics*, ed. Kevin T. McGuire (New York, NY: Routledge, 2012): 259.

22 See, for example, Gerald N. Rosenberg, *The Hollow Hope: Can Courts Bring About Social Change?* Second Edition (Chicago, IL: University of Chicago Press, 2008) and Matthew Hall, *The Nature of Supreme Court Power* (New York, NY: Cambridge University Press, 2011).

23 See, for example, Michael J. Klarman, *From Jim Crow to Civil Rights: The Supreme Court and the Struggle for Racial Equality* (New York, NY: Oxford University Press, 2004). But, see, Thomas M. Keck, "Beyond Backlash: Assessing the Impact of Judicial Decisions on LGBT Rights," *Law & Society Review*, vol. 43, no. 1 (March 2009): 151–186.

24 31 U.S. 5251 (1832).

25 Richard P. Longaker, "Andrew Jackson and the Judiciary," *Political Science Quarterly*, vol. 71, no. 3 (September 1956): 341–364.

26 Brian Hicks, "The Cherokees v. Andrew Jackson," *Smithsonian Magazine*, March 2011.

27 Quoted in Richard P. Longaker, "Andrew Jackson and the Judiciary," *Political Science Quarterly*, vol. 71, no. 3 (September 1956): 341–364, 349.

28 Matthew L. Sundquist, "*Worcester v. Georgia*: A Breakdown in the Separation of Powers," *American Indian Law Review*, vol. 35, no. 1 (2010-2011): 239–255.

29 Theda Perdue and Michael Green, *The Cherokee Nation and the Trail of Tears* (New York, NY: Penguin Books, 2008).

30 Jeff Yates, *Popular Justice: Presidential Prestige and Executive Success in the Supreme Court* (Albany, NY: State University of New York Press, 2002).

31 Forrest Maltzman, "The Politicized Judiciary: A Threat to Executive Power," In *Presidential Leadership: The Vortex of Power*, eds Bert A. Rockman and Richard W. Waterman (New York, NY: Oxford University Press, 2007).

32 347 U.S. 483 (1954). See J.W. Peltason, *58 Lonely Men: Southern Federal Judges and School Desegregation* (Champaign, IL: University of Illinois Press, 1971).

33 Terry M. Moe and William G. Howell, "Unilateral Action and Presidential Power: A Theory," *Presidential Studies Quarterly*, vol. 29, no. 4 (December 1999): 850–873, 868.

34 465 U.S. 555 (1984).

35 100 P.L. 259, 102 Stat. 28.

36 Stephen C. Halpern, *On the Limits of the Law: The Ironic Legacy of Title VI of the 1964 Civil Rights Act* (Baltimore, MD: Johns Hopkins University Press, 1995): 199–206.

37 Lori Hausegger and Lawrence Baum, "Inviting Congressional Action: A Study of Supreme Court Motivations in Statutory Interpretation," *American Journal of Political Science*, vol. 43, no. 1 (January 1999): 162–185, 166.

38 J. Mitchell Pickerill, "The Supreme Court and Congress: What Happens in Congress after the Court Strikes Down Legislation?" *Insights on Law & Society*, vol. 7, no. 1 (Fall 2006): 10–28, 27.

39 The Court famously asserted its prerogative to engage in judicial review in *Marbury v. Madison*, 5 U.S. 137 (1803), in which the Court invalidated a portion of the Judiciary Act of 1789. Interestingly, however, that is not the first time that the Court exercised judicial review. Rather, the first time the Court did so was in *Hylton v. United States*, 3 U.S. 171 (1796), in which the Court found that a federal carriage tax did not violate the Constitution. *Hylton* is useful in making clear that judicial review occurs not only when a court reviews and invalidates a law as being unconstitutional but also when a court reviews and upholds a law as being constitutional.

40 J. Mitchell Pickerill, "The Supreme Court and Congress: What Happens in Congress after the Court Strikes Down Legislation?" *Insights on Law & Society*, vol. 7, no. 1 (Fall 2006): 10–28, 27.

41 The Constitution provides two pathways for its amendment. An amendment may be proposed by Congress with a vote of two-thirds of the membership in each chamber. Alternatively, an amendment may be proposed by a constitutional convention called for by a vote of two-thirds of state legislatures. In either case, a proposed amendment must be ratified by either a three-fourths majority of state legislatures or special conventions called in three-fourths of the states. No amendments to the Constitution have been proposed by constitutional convention. Only one amendment has relied on the state convention approach for ratification (the Twenty-First Amendment, which repealed prohibition).

42 *Oregon v. Mitchell*, 400 U.S. 112 (1970).

43 514 U.S. 549 (1995).

44 U.S. Const. Art. I, § 8, cl. 3.

45 475 U.S. 502 (1986).

46 See, for example, Stuart Scheingold, *The Politics of Rights* (New Haven, CT: Yale University Press, 1974); Donald L. Horowitz, *The Courts and Social Policy* (Washington, DC: Brookings Institution, 1977); Joel Handler, *Social Movements and the Legal System* (New York, NY: Academic Press, 1978); and Matthew Hall, *The Nature of Supreme Court Power* (New York, NY: Cambridge University Press, 2011).

47 347 U.S. 483 (1954).

48 Gerald N. Rosenberg, *The Hollow Hope: Can Courts Bring About Social Change?* Second Edition (Chicago, IL: University of Chicago Press, 2008): 39–156.

49 In addition to civil rights, Rosenberg also considered abortion, women's rights, the environment, reapportionment, and criminal law in *The Hollow Hope*.

50 Gerald N. Rosenberg, *The Hollow Hope: Can Courts Bring About Social Change?* Second Edition (Chicago, IL: University of Chicago Press, 2008): 75–76.

51 Ibid., 76–78.

52 See, for example, Brian J. Daugherity and Charles C. Bolton, eds, *With All Deliberate Speed: Implementing Brown v. Board of Education* (Fayetteville, AR: University of Arkansas Press, 2008).

53 Gerald N. Rosenberg, *The Hollow Hope: Can Courts Bring About Social Change?* Second Edition (Chicago, IL: University of Chicago Press, 2008): 107–156.

54 Frank Brown, "The First Serious Implementation of Brown: The 1964 Civil Rights Act and Beyond," *Journal of Negro Education*, vol. 73, no. 3 (Summer 2004): 182–190.

55 Carl F. Kaestle and Marshall S. Smith, "The Federal Role in Elementary and Secondary Education, 1940-1980," *Harvard Educational Review*, vol. 53, no. 4 (Winter 1982): 384–408, 402-405.

56 A representative sample of those critics include the following: Neal Devins, "Judicial Matters," *California Law Review*, vol. 80, no. 4 (July 1992): 1027–1069; Malcolm M. Feeley, "Hollow Hopes, Flypaper, and Metaphors," *Law & Social Inquiry*, vol. 17, no. 4 (Autumn 1992): 745–760; Michael W. McCann, "Reform Litigation on Trial," *Law & Social Inquiry*, vol. 17, no. 4 (Autumn 1992): 715–743; Bradley C. Cannon, "The Supreme Court and Policy Reform: The Hollow Hope Revisited," in *Leveraging the Law: Using the Courts to Achieve Social Change*, ed. David A. Schultz (New York, NY: Peter Lang, 1998); Roy B. Flemming, John Bohte, and B. Dan Wood, "One Voice Among Many: The Supreme Court's Influence on Attentiveness to Issues in the United States, 1947-92," *American Journal of Political Science*, vol. 41, no. 4 (October 1997): 1224–1250.

57 Michael W. McCann, "Reform Litigation on Trial," *Law & Social Inquiry*, vol. 17, no. 4 (Autumn 1992): 715–743, 727.

58 Ibid., 715–743, 731.

59 Ibid., 715–743, 735–737.

60 Other scholarship in this same vein includes Frances Kahn Zemans, "Legal Mobilization: The Neglected Role of the Law in the Political System," *American Political Science Review*, vol. 77, no. 3 (September 1983): 690–703; Marc Galanter, "The Radiating Effects of Courts," in *Empirical Theories about Courts*, Keith Boyum and Lynn Mather, eds (New York, NY: Longman, 1983); and John Brigham, *The Cult of the Court* (Philadelphia, PA: Temple University Press, 1991).

61 Faubus was the governor who ordered the Arkansas National Guard to prevent African American students from attending Little Rock Central High School. Interestingly, there is some evidence to suggest that the governor's defiance was less about a steadfast attachment to segregation than it was about maneuvering for political advantage in the state, and that Faubus was initially a racial liberal as judged by the standards of the times. See, for example, Reed Roy, *Faubus: The Life and Times of an American Prodigal* (Fayetteville, AR: Arkansas University Press, 1999).

62 Huey P. Newton founded the Black Panther Party in 1966. The Party's original focus was on monitoring and challenging police brutality but subsequently branched out into community programs, including community health clinics and free breakfast programs for children. It was characterized

by J. Edgar Hoover, Director of the Federal Bureau of Investigation at the time, as "the greatest threat to [the] internal security of the county;" "Hoover and the F.B.I.," *A Huey P. Newton Story*, NPR.org, last accessed September 28, 2014 (http://www.pbs.org/hueypnewton/people/people_hoover.html).

63　Hon. Edward D. Re, "Stare Decisis," paper presented at a Seminar for Federal Appellate Judges, Federal Judicial Center, May 13–16, 1975 (http://www.fjc.gov/public/pdf.nsf/lookup/staredec.pdf/$file/staredec.pdf).

64　419 U.S. 522 (1975).

65　Cindy Chang, "Point of View: A Woman's Place Is in the Jury Box," *Times-Picayune*, June 15, 2009.

66　The original sentence imposed at trial was the death penalty. However, the Louisiana Supreme Court had set that sentence aside with instructions to impose life imprisonment before the case made its way to the U.S. Supreme Court.

67　Taylor was retried, found guilty, and given a lengthy sentence of imprisonment at hard labor.

68　419 U.S. 522, 537-538 (1975).

69　*State v. Duren*, 556 S.W. 2d 11 (Mo. 1977).

70　439 U.S. 357 (1979).

71　Lawrence Baum, "The Implementation of Judicial Decisions: An Organizational Analysis," *American Politics Quarterly*, vol. 4, no. 1, (January 1976): 86–114, 92.

72　See, for example, Sidney Ulmer, "Earl Warren and the *Brown* Decision," *Journal of Politics*, vol. 33, no. 3, (August 1971): 689–702.

73　Jeffrey K. Staton and Georg Vanberg, "The Value of Vagueness: Delegation, Defiance, and Judicial Opinions," *American Journal of Political Science*, vol. 52, no. 3 (July 2008): 504–519.

74　Charles A. Johnson, "Lower Court Reactions to Supreme Court Decisions: A Quantitative Examination," *American Journal of Political Science*, vol. 23, no. 4 (November 1979): 792–804.

75　Benjamin Kassow, Donald R. Songer, and Michael P. Fix, "The Influence of Precedent on State Supreme Courts," *Political Research Quarterly*, vol. 65, no. 2 (June 2012): 372–384.

76　Sara C. Benesh and Malia Reddick, "Overruled: An Event History Analysis of Lower Court Reaction to Supreme Court Alternation of Precedent," *Journal of Politics*, vol. 64, no. 2 (May 2002): 534–550, 546.

77　Pamela C. Corley, "Uncertain Precedent: Circuit Court Responses to Supreme Court Plurality Opinions," *American Politics Research*, vol. 37, no. 1 (January 2009): 30–49. See, also, Pamela C. Corley, *Concurring Opinion Writing on the U.S. Supreme Court* (Albany, NY: State University of New York Press, 2011): Chapter 4.

78　Pamela C. Corley, "Uncertain Precedent: Circuit Court Responses to Supreme Court Plurality Opinions," *American Politics Research*, vol. 37, no. 1 (January 2009): 30–49, 44.

79　In Greek mythology, Scylla was a six-headed monster while Charybdis was a deadly whirlpool. They were located opposite one another, making safe navigation for Odysseus (and others) difficult at best. The less colorful, blander modern interpretation: between a rock and a hard place.

80　Malia Reddick and Sara C. Benesh, "Norm Violation by the Lower Courts in the Treatment of Supreme Court Precedent: A Research Framework," *Justice System Journal*, vol. 21, no. 2 (2000): 117–142.

81　David E. Klein, *Making Law in the United States Courts of Appeals* (New York, NY: Cambridge University Press, 2002); John Gruhl, "Anticipatory Compliance with Supreme Court Rulings," *Polity*, vol. 14, no. 2 (Winter 1981): 294–313.

82　Chad Westerland, Jeffrey A. Segal, Lee Epstein, Charles Cameron, and Scott Comparato, "Strategic Defiance and Compliance in the U.S. Court of Appeals," *American Journal of Political Science*, vol. 54, no. 4 (October 2010): 891–905.

83　Rachael K. Hinkle, "Strategic Anticipation of *En Banc* Review in the U.S. Courts of Appeals," Typescript, University of Buffalo, last accessed September 29, 2014 (http://rachaelkhinkle.com/research.html).

84　Kirk A. Randazzo, "Strategic Anticipation and the Hierarchy of Justice in U.S. District Courts," *American Politics Research*, vol. 36, no. 5 (September 2008): 669–693.

85 Pamela C. Corley and Justin Wedeking, "The (Dis)Advantage of Certainty: The Importance of Certainty in Language," *Law & Society Review*, vol. 48, no. 1 (March 2014): 35–62.

86 More generally with regard to shirking by lower courts, see Sara C. Benesh, *The U.S. Court of Appeals and the Law of Confession: Perspectives on the Hierarchy of Justice* (New York, NY: LFB Scholarly, 2002) and Sara C. Benesh and Wendy L. Martinek, "Lower Court Compliance with Precedent," in *New Directions in Judicial Politics*, ed. Kevin T. McGuire (New York, NY: Routledge, 2012).

87 Jennifer K. Luse, Geoffrey McGovern, Wendy L. Martinek, and Sara C. Benesh, " 'Such Inferior Courts . . .': Compliance by Circuits with Jurisprudential Regimes," *American Politics Research*, vol. 37, no. 1 (January 2009): 75–106.

88 Even those who are named parties to a suit being heard before the Supreme Court are not likely to be present in the courtroom, contrary to court procedure as depicted in *First Monday*, a dramatic series about a fictionalized version of the Court airing on CBS from January to June of 2002. One episode included a scene in which a transsexual seeking asylum in the United States is not only present when the Court hears oral argument but questioned directly by the justices, something that would not happen in real life. See Hal Erickson, *Encyclopedia of Television Law Shows: Factual and Fictional Series about Judges, Lawyers and the Courtroom*, 1948–2008 (Jefferson, NC: McFarland, 2009): 106.

89 Richard Morin, "Wapner v. Rehnquist: No Contest: TV Judge Vastly Outpolls Justices in Test of Public Recognition," *Washington Post*, June 23, 1989.

90 See, for example, Charles H. Franklin and Liane C. Kosaki, "Media, Knowledge, and Public Evaluations of the Supreme Court," in *Contemplating Courts*, ed. Lee Epstein (Washington, DC: Congressional Quarterly Press, 1995); Herbert M. Kritzer, "The Impact of Bush v. Gore on Public Perceptions and Knowledge of the Supreme Court," *Judicature*, vol. 85, no. 1 (July-August 2001): 32–38; Valerie J. Hoekstra, *Public Reaction to Supreme Court Decisions* (New York, NY: Cambridge University Press, 2003); and James L. Gibson and Gregory A. Caldeira, "Knowing the Supreme Court? A Reconsideration of Public Ignorance of the High Court," *Journal of Politics*, vol. 71, no. 2 (April 2009): 429–441.

91 Charles H. Franklin, Liane C. Kosaki, and Herbert M. Kritzer, "The Salience of Supreme Court Decisions," paper presented at the annual meeting of the American Political Science Association, Washington, DC, September 2–5, 1993.

92 Kevin M. Scott and Kyle L. Saunders, "Supreme Court Influence and the Awareness of Court Decisions," paper presented at the annual meeting of the American Political Science Association, Philadelphia, PA, August 31–September 3, 2006.

93 See, for example, Valerie J. Hoekstra and Jeffrey A. Segal, "The Shepherding of Local Public Opinion: The Supreme Court and *Lamb's Chapel*," *Journal of Politics*, vol. 58, no. 4 (November 1996): 1079–1102. See also Valerie J. Hoekstra, *Public Reaction to Supreme Court Decisions* (New York, NY: Cambridge University Press, 2003).

94 See, for example, Rorie Spill and Zoe Oxley, "Philosopher Kings or Political Actors? How the Media Portray the Supreme Court," *Judicature*, vol. 87, no. 1 (July-August 2003): 22–29 (2003). See also Eliot E. Slotnick and Jennifer A. Segal, *Television News and the Supreme Court: All the News That's Fit to Air?* (New York, NY: Cambridge University Press, 1998).

95 Charles H. Franklin, Liane C. Kosaki, and Herbert M. Kritzer, "The Salience of Supreme Court Decisions," paper presented at the annual meeting of the American Political Science Association, Washington, D.C., September 2–5, 1993.

96 Thomas R. Marshall, "Public Opinion, Representation, and the Modern Supreme Court," *American Politics Quarterly*, vol. 16, no. 3 (July 1988): 296–316; Charles A. Johnson and Bradley C. Canon, *Judicial Policies: Implementation and Impact* (Washington, DC: Congressional Quarterly Press, 1984).

97 James L. Gibson, Gregory A. Caldeira, and Lester Kenyatta Spence, "Why Do People Accept Public Policies They Oppose? Testing Legitimacy Theory with a Survey-Based Experiment," *Political Research Quarterly*, vol. 58, no. 2 (June 2005): 187–201.

98   Robert J. Hume, "State Courts and Policy Legitimation: An Experimental Study of the Ability of State Courts to Change Opinion," *Publius*, vol. 42, no. 2 (Spring 2012): 211–233.

99   Valerie J. Hoekstra and Jeffrey A. Segal, "The Shepherding of Local Public Opinion: The Supreme Court and *Lamb's Chapel*," *Journal of Politics*, vol. 58, no. 4 (November 1996): 1079–1102.

100 Charles Franklin and Lianne C. Kosaki, "Republican Schoolmaster: The U.S. Supreme Court, Public Opinion, and Abortion," *American Political Science Review*, vol. 83, no. 3 (September 1989): 751–771.

101 410 U.S. 113 (1973).

102 Timothy R. Johnson and Andrew D. Martin, "The Public's Conditional Response to Supreme Court Decisions," *American Political Science Review*, vol. 92, no. 2 (June 1998): 299–309.

Index

Page numbers in *italics* represent *tables*; page numbers in **bold** represent **figures**; page numbers followed by 'n' refer to notes

Neily, C.M. 355
New Deal 62, 120, 413
New Hampshire Supreme Court 362
New Hampshire v. Louisiana (1883) 112
New Jersey v. New York (1998) 121
New York Civil Liberties Union (NYCLU) 243
New York Times 44, 130, 293, 376, 413–14
news media 237, 444
newspaper advertising 140
Nixon, R. 141, 145, 155
Nolan, K.P. 312
nominating commission 167–70, 173
nominations 145, 153, 158–9, 162; appellate court
    160–1, **160**; courts of appeals 146; district
    court 159; executive 162; federal 146–50, 159;
    female 160–1; ideology 156–9; judicial 143–52,
    159–61; lower court 146, 154–6, 159; politics
    156; presidential 143–50, 155–6, 160–1;
    qualifications 156–9; racial minority 160–1;
    Senate 145–6, 155, 160, 177; Supreme Court
    145–6, 150, 153–9, 378
noncompliance 432
nonpartisan elections 163–8, *169*, 174–6, 442
norms 244; legal 266, 376, 386; organizational
    258; professional 198
North Carolina Hospital Association (NCHA)
    291
North Carolina Supreme Court 342
*Northern Pipeline Construction Co. v. Marathon
    Pipe Line Co.* (1962) 123
notice of appeal 335
nuclear option 155–6
nullification: instruction 317; jury 283, 314–17

Obama, B. 14, 105, 120, 145–6, 149–50, 153, 161
Obamacare 153–4, 218, 356, 410
O'Brien, D. 391
obscenity cases 359–60
O'Connor, S.D. (Associate Justice of Supreme
    Court) 139, 153, 176, 356, 389–90, 402, 412–15
offenses 256; criminal 251, 256, 288, 298; drug
    248–9, *250*, 254, 265; petty 288; property 249,
    250; traffic 243–6, 375
Office of Economic Opportunity (OEO) 88
Office of Tribal Justice (OTJ) 79
one-shotters 206–9, 223; and repeat players
    206–9
opening statements 205, 257, 283, 311–13
operationalization 13
opinion assignment 341, 399–406
opinion writing 343–4, 363, 399–406, 417
opinions 344, 382, 404–8, 414, 444–5; change of
    444–5, *444*; concurring 341, 407; dissenting

341, 408; draft 404–7, 410, 417; judicial 439,
    445; majority 341, 361, 400–3, 406–10, 440;
    plurality 410, 440; public 342, 413–14, 442–6;
    written 382
oral argument 119, 340–1, 382, 399–400, 412,
    417; and briefs 392–9; influence on Supreme
    Court justices 397
oral depositions 204
Organ, J. 81
original jurisdiction 12, 108, 121
Owens, R.: and Black, R. 385–6; and Simon, D.
    391
Oyez Project 412, 427n

Paper Chase, The (1973) 23–4, 37–8
parole: life without 247, 260–1
partisan agenda 150, 177
partisan elections 150, 163–8, *169*, 173–7, 442
partisanship 154, 360, 411
partnerships 75–6, 84
party affiliation 14, 174–5, 378
patent law 69, 94, 127
patent lawsuits 103–5
patent litigation 103
patent reform 105
path of influence 435
Pelican Brief, The (1993) 148–9
penalties 9, 239, 314, 318; citizenship 261;
    reduced 262; regulatory 288; statutory 288
Penn, W. 285
Pennsylvania Supreme Court 338
People for the American Way (PFAW) 158
perception problem 33
peremptory challenge 303–7, 318
Perry, H.W. 388
Perry Mason (CBS) 4, 332
Perry Mason Syndrome 2–4
personal agenda 150
personal injury 116, 127, 194, 208, 221
personal jurisdiction 103, 126, 203
personal law 68–9, 94
personal property 191
personal service 204
Peterson, D. 297
Peterson, S. 302
petitions 122, 345, 352, 382–9, 398–9, 417; cert
    382–4, 388–90; civil rights 352; merit 385–8,
    392, 397; prisoner 216, 350–2
Pickerill, J.M. 434
Pineapple Express (2008) 204
Pinello, D. 357
plaintiffs 108–9, 202–6, 213–15, 218–20, 297–8,
    311–14, 317–18; business 206; civil 353; in